www.wadsworth.com

wadsworth.com is the World Wide Web site for Wadsworth and is your direct source to dozens of online resources.

At wadsworth.com you can find out about supplements, demonstration software, and student resources. You can also send email to many of our authors and preview new publications and exciting new technologies.

wadsworth.com
Changing the way the world learns®

Understanding Crime

Theory and Practice

Second Edition

L. THOMAS WINFREE
New Mexico State University, Las Cruces

HOWARD ABADINSKY

THOMSON
™
WADSWORTH

Australia • Canada • Mexico • Singapore • Spain • United Kingdom • United States

THOMSON
WADSWORTH

Executive Editor: *Sabra Horne*
Editorial Assistant: *Paul Massicotte*
Technology Project Manager: *Susan Devanna*
Marketing Manager: *Dory Schaeffer*
Marketing Assistant: *Neena Chandra*
Advertising Project Manager: *Stacey Purviance*
Project Manager, Editorial Production: *Belinda Krohmer*
Print/Media Buyer: *Judy Inouye*

Permissions Editor: *Joohee Lee*
Production Service: *Vicki Moran, Publishing Support Services*
Copy Editor: *Tom Briggs*
Cover Designer: *Yvo Riezebos*
Cover Printer: Transcontinental—Louiseville
Compositor: Thompson Type
Printer: Transcontinental—Louiseville

For more information about our products,
contact us at:
Thomson Learning Academic Resource Center
1-800-423-0563
For permission to use material from this text,
contact us by:
Phone: 1-800-730-2214
Fax: 1-800-730-2215
Web: http://www.thomsonrights.com

Library of Congress Control Number: 2002114085

ISBN 0-534-55748-1

Wadsworth/Thomson Learning
10 Davis Drive
Belmont, CA 94002-3098
USA

Asia
Thomson Learning
5 Shenton Way #01-01
UIC Building
Singapore 068808

Australia
Nelson Thomson Learning
102 Dodds Street
South Melbourne, Victoria 3205
Australia

Canada
Nelson Thomson Learning
1120 Birchmount Road
Toronto, Ontario M1K 5G4
Canada

Europe/Middle East/Africa
Thomson Learning
High Holborn House
50/51 Bedford Row
London WC1R 4LR
United Kingdom

Latin America
Thomson Learning
Seneca, 53
Colonia Polanco
11560 Mexico D.F.
Mexico

Spain
Paraninfo Thomson Learning
Calle/Magallanes, 25
28015 Madrid, Spain

In memory of my father, Latham Thomas Winfree, Sr., who, though he lost his sight to retinitis pigmentosa, never lost his vision. Thank you.

LTW

CONTENTS

❋

PREFACE

TO THE STUDENT

Theory is a daunting subject in any academic discipline. Crime theories are no less challenging, but they should at least be interesting. This book represents our attempt to compress what are often complex and bewildering crime theories into a consumable format. The frustrations and satisfactions associated with teaching this subject led us to prepare this book. We hope that you receive some positive benefits from our experiences as you learn about crime theories.

For at least 200 years, students of crime—we call them criminologists today—have wondered about the causes of crime and the reasons behind fluctuations in crime rates. Some of the answers provided in the eighteenth century or earlier may sound strange, and even laughable, to people living in the twenty-first century. Others might strike a responsive chord, even with the passage of hundreds of years. Still others may sound, and are, racist when viewed through the lens of time. Even more critically, theories that have elicited the wrath of some criminologists and the support of others were penned not 200 years ago, or 100 years ago, or even 50 years ago, but late in the twentieth century. All are important, as they provide the context for how contemporary society views crime and criminals, and how formal agencies of social control—the police, courts, and corrections—have responded and continue to respond to both.

We approached these theories, and the theorists behind them, in the following fashion: In the first chapter we provide the tools you will need to develop a greater appreciation for crime theories and theorists. For example, we describe the structure of theory, including the building blocks of theories—their basic assumptions and assertions. Other topics include the goals and challenges for theories; the relationships between human nature, government, and public policy; the nature of crime and laws; and the origins of crime theories. The first chapter also outlines the organization of this text. A careful review of this chapter will enhance your understanding of crime theories.

The next eight chapters provide a systematic review of 22 perspectives on crime and specific crime theories. We present the following information for each of the 22 clusters of theories or specific theories: (1) an overview of its development, assumptions, and causal arguments; (2) an assessment of tests of these arguments; and (3) a discussion of the implications for public policy and criminal justice practices. Each cluster, or learning module, begins with a series of questions and observations to get you thinking about the relevance of the theories to everyday life. You may find it useful to reflect on these bulleted items before and after you read the associated module. You may also find it instructive to compare questions between modules within a chapter to understand the points of divergence and convergence for each cluster's assertions and assumptions.

The final chapter explores the future of crime theories. We approach this task by seeking answers to a series of questions. The questions (and the answers we provide) are intended to be a starting point for your own examination of the future of crime theorizing.

The study of crime theories is all about connectivity, as no contemporary theorist is totally oblivious to the contributions of other theorists. Indeed, it is possible that your professor will present the modules contained in this text in a sequence different from ours. That is not a problem; rather, it is a matter of emphasis and reflects as much about your professor's exposure to crime theory as it does about this book.

We hope that you derive some enjoyment from the chapters ahead. Theory is important, and it can be interesting. Open your mind and cast out preconceptions about theory, and you will find that understanding crime is a far more agreeable endeavor.

TO THE INSTRUCTOR

We began this effort at making sense of crime theories for reasons similar to those that may be motivating you: We were tired of talking about abstract ideas that most students thought were irrelevant to them or to contemporary life. Our first effort was earnest but somewhat flawed. However, what we did well in the first edition, and continue to do in this one, is link crime theories to criminal justice policies and practices. This edition contains even stronger conceptual grounding for the use of theory to inform criminal justice policy makers and practitioners in Chapter 1, an emphasis that continues through each chapter, including the final one on speculations about the future of crime theory.

Several important features are repeated periodically in this text. Knowing what they are and what to expect from them will make for a far more enjoyable teaching experience.

- *"Comments and Criticisms" Boxes.* Many theories contained in this book have generated deep and abiding controversies about, for example, their value to the study of crime or the assumptions they make about human beings, our systems of laws and their administration, and society at large. In these boxes we highlight specific concerns that critics have expressed about the theories.

- *Figures.* At times a picture really is worth a thousand words, especially when dealing with theory. We have tried to represent faithfully numerous theories in graphic form. Such images are necessarily simplistic and may not reflect the complexities of some theories. Our intent is to provide a graphic representation of the theory's main ideas and causal premises. These images are meant to be pedagogical, or teaching, devices.

- *Theory Summary Tables.* At the conclusion of each chapter, we provide tabular summaries for each theory, along with brief statements about the major figures, central assumptions, causal arguments, strengths, and weaknesses of each.

These summaries are no substitute for reading the entire chapter, but they should serve to remind students of the critical differences between the theories explored in each chapter.

- *Key Terms.* In the body of each chapter, we boldface a number of terms and provide definitions for each. At the end of each chapter, after the summaries, we provide a list of these terms. Mastering the chapter's content includes having a working understanding of these terms and their application to crime theories.

- *Critical Review Questions.* Following the summary of each chapter is a series of study questions. These are not requests to regurgitate information covered in the chapter. Instead, they encourage students to think critically and analytically about what they have read. The questions both challenge students and represent enjoyable learning exercises. If your students apply themselves to these questions, they will master each chapter's content.

- *In Their Own Words Boxes.* In many instances no one expresses an idea or responds to a criticism better than the originator of the idea. In these boxes we include the specific remarks of theorists. These are more than random observations on the issues being discussed or simple citations. They will motivate readers to think about terms, concepts, ideas, and theories in different ways; to question the development of a given theory; and to understand the context in which it was developed. In fact, at times we raise the issue with the specific intent to "put a stick in the hornet's nest." These remarks often tell a great deal about the evolution of the specific theory and the controversies in the study of crime and criminals.

In preparing this edition, we edited and reorganized every chapter, updating research findings and expanding (or in rare instances contracting) each theory's policy and practical implications. In the process *Understanding Crime* increased from 6 chapters and an epilogue to 10 chapters. This edition also has several new features, including the following:

- A module on the structure of theory, including the assumptions and assertions of theories as their building blocks, the goals of theory, and the challenges of theory testing and theory building (Chapter 1)

- An overview of the rationale for this text (Chapter 1)

- A module that reviews informal deterrence and related processes, especially Braithwaite's reintegrative shaming and restorative justice (Chapter 2)

- A module on developmental theories from a largely psychological perspective, including Moffitt's pathways hypothesis and Loeber and Le Blanc's developmental criminology (Chapter 5)

- The inclusion of left realism and peacemaking criminology in the module on Marxism and crime (Chapter 9)

- The inclusion of Tittle's control balance theory and Sampson and Laub's sociological life-course criminology as new exemplars of integrated theory (Chapter 10)

ACKNOWLEDGMENTS

As with every book ever written, people other than the author, or in this case the authors, played some role—major or minor—in its preparation. We would like to thank the folks at Wadsworth, but especially our executive editor Sabra Horne.

Several groups of reviewers and general readers must be acknowledged. First, we must thank several "generations" of students who put up with our efforts to make sense of crime theories in the classroom and who as a group pushed us not only to provide the key components of the various theories but also to clarify their practical and policy implications. Second, we thank those who reviewed our manuscript for this edition and provided valuable suggestions: Eric J. Fritsel, University of North Texas; James J. Nolan, III, West Virginia University; J. Gayle Mericle, Western Illinois University; John Myers, Rowan University; Matt Robinson, Appalachian State University; and Steve Stack, Wayne State University. A third group of reviewers provided us with "expert" comments as individuals who used the first edition or otherwise reviewed both the old and new versions of this book. They include Christine S. Sellers, University of South Florida; Mike Norris, Capital University; Ken Mentor, New Mexico State University; and Gene Starbuck, Mesa State College.

Two other individuals also contributed to this work. Margery Cassidy read and commented on every chapter in the first edition. Her death in 1998 deprived us of our most helpful critic, and we have tried to honor her spirit with this edition. Angelita Talavera, an undergraduate criminal justice student at New Mexico State University, read the entire book and checked all references and key terms.

We owe a considerable debt to the collective input of all of these reviewers, commentators, and colleagues; this edition is better for their critical reading of our collaborative work. Any mistakes, however, remain those of the authors.

Tom Winfree
Howard Abadinsky

1

Theory and
the Study of Crime

CHAPTER OVERVIEW

LEARNING OBJECTIVES

- Appreciate how theorizing as a process both differs from and resembles other forms of human inquiry, and how theories must be held to higher standards than other musings about human behavior.
- Explore the various parts of theories—how they fit together and how they yield insights into crime and criminals.
- Assess the linkages between theorizing about and researching crime, and the role of ethics and government in these important processes.
- Learn the roles played by philosophical perspectives on the nature of crime and criminals in shaping both crime theories and crime control policies.
- Review the organization of the text and its approach to the subject matter.

INTRODUCTION

"Three strikes and you're out" has become a popular "get-tough-on-crime" metaphor—life without parole for a third felony conviction. As a crime control policy it raises important questions, not the least of which has to do with cost. Besides the spiraling costs associated with maintaining a prison system for millions of offenders with an average age in the mid-30s, we risk turning some prisons into high-security (and thus expensive) nursing homes for tens of thousands of elderly offenders. Yet some policy makers believe that imprisonment serves as a deterrent to crime, thereby offsetting the high costs. They suggest that second-time felony offenders or others who contemplate crime, and who risk life in prison or one more strike, might reconsider their actions.

A **deterrence**-based crime control policy assumes that humans possess free will and make carefully considered, rational choices. According to this line of thinking, all people choose between good and evil, between law-abiding and law-violating behavior. For most of us crime may not be a seriously considered alternative, owing to internalized rules and values. For the rest the prospect of punishment should shift the balance toward law-abiding behavior. After all, what rational person, facing the loss of personal freedom, would choose to risk something so highly valued? But if the basic assumptions are wrong and crime represents irrational behavior, escalating penalties will do little to deter crime. Moreover, if criminals do not believe that they will be detected and convicted, even the threat of capital punishment has little deterrent value.

If crime is related to the debilitating effects of poverty—prisons are filled with poor persons—a "three strikes" policy may be inappropriate. Perhaps criminal behavior is inherited or results from the improper child-rearing practices of ill-equipped parents. What are the policy implications of these additional ideas? How do they fit with the assumptions of rationality and free will? Is there a Democrat or Republican, or a liberal or conservative, theory explaining the causes of crime and offering meaningful policy responses? Where can we turn for insights into seemingly unfathomable acts of terror perpetrated upon communities in the name of religion or political ideology? Perhaps crime simply represents the behavior of evil persons. Can evil be subjected to deterrence? If not, would "one strike and you're out" be a more effective public policy?

This book is about crime theories—also called criminological theories—and their infusion into criminal justice policies and practices. We begin with the structure of theories.

THE STRUCTURE OF THEORIES

What is a theory? This question has many answers. In the interest of parsimony, we offer the following: A **theory** is a highly organized statement of the basic assumptions and logically interrelated assertions about the phenomenon or class of phenomena under study, which attempt to describe, predict, explain, and control the subject matter.

Theories are often abstract and complex. By "abstract" we mean that they consist of statements that generally are dissociated from any material objects, specific circumstances, facts, or observations. Abstractness is both a curse and a blessing. On the one hand, abstractness tends to confuse the uninitiated, especially newcomers to **criminology,** the scientific study of crime and criminals. Detractors describe theories as lacking concreteness, which they often do. In fact, statements that purport to tell us about crime generally may not *directly* assist those who are responsible for reducing crime. Indeed, theorists sometimes fail to concern themselves with the practical applications of their abstract statements about crimes and criminals.

On the other hand, criminologists tend to see theoretical abstractness as more of a blessing than a curse because the assertions in theories must go beyond the immediate time and place. A theory about some phenomenon in Indiana should also apply in Maine, and it should apply in both places today, last year, in the last century, and the next one. The extent to which a theory is tied to a particular set of events or people may help us understand what is happening here and now, but this same concreteness limits the theory's ability to provide the same types of insights for other places, times, and peoples. This comparison—concreteness versus abstractness—helps explain why most information obtained from the media or other individualistic, unsystematic observations yields few insights applicable beyond a specific set of circumstances.

Assumptions and Assertions:
The Building Blocks of Theories

The complexity of theories lies in their assumptions and assertions. What does a given theory assume about human beings and, by extension, human behavior? For example, some theories are rooted in the assumption that people have the ability to choose freely alternative life paths, that they have **free will.** Alternatively, other theories assume that forces beyond people's control largely shape individual and social behavior. This position is often described as **determinism,** with the specific underlying force signifying the form of determinism. For example, if a theorist proposes biological forces such as brain functioning or mental illness as the "culprit" in some phenomenon, then the theory has its roots in biological determinism. It is important to note that a theory's assumptions are beyond testing; that is, they constitute the theory's core belief system. Assumptions are taken as given and are either accepted or rejected, but they are not generally subject to testing or to modification.

Once the assumptions are stated, understood, and accepted, the next task is to consider the assertions. Theoretical assertions, or the relationships they imply, must be testable. If the assertions are incapable of being evaluated in the "real world" in which we live, then we are talking not about theory but rather about something akin to **ideology** or **theology,** strongly held beliefs that are not subject to testing or, in some cases, critical review of any sort. Many theorists refer to their assertions as **propositions,** generalized statements about relationships, usually between two or more things. Verifiable propositions, ones that receive consistent and strong support when tested, are called **laws;** other propositions, ones still subject to study or for which the body of research is less compelling, are called **hypotheses.** For example, economic forces such as poverty or unemployment may be viewed as leading to crime within the specific segments of society that evidence these characteristics. The economic force is the cause, and crime is the effect; without the former the latter would not exist. Such a general relational statement about two facts is a hypothesis, and this specific one represents an economic theory of crime.

Strategies for the Scientific Enterprise

Any explanation of crime that aspires to the level of theory requires an application of the scientific enterprise, whose principles include a series of processes and products. Figure 1.1 summarizes the scientific enterprise in terms of four such processes and four associated products (see also Wallace 1971). First, theory is either the starting point for **deductive research** (i.e., theory-testing studies) or the ending point for **inductive research** (i.e., theory-building studies). Deductive researchers base their work on past theorizing that leads to research questions or testable hypotheses. Inductive researchers allow the data to "speak for themselves," providing findings that may emerge as theory.

Whether criminologists follow inductive or deductive logic, they are guided by a **research design,** which answers questions like these: Why are we doing the research? Who or what will we study in our search for answers? What do we want to know about the objects of study? Over what period will we conduct the study? Researchers often adopt a single mode of observation: They collect **qualitative data** (i.e., non-numerical examinations and interpretations of observations intended to reveal the object of study's essence or basic nature) or **quantitative data** (i.e., numerical examinations and manipulations of observations intended to express the object of study in terms of accurate numerical equivalents). Less frequently researchers seek both kinds of information. In any case, they follow literally dozens of steps beginning with the decision to test a particular theory or generate information on a particular topic. A detailed elaboration of the process is beyond the scope of this book. However, because many of these steps are linked to reasons we might question a given study, we will make reference to the relevant ones at the appropriate junctures.

Theory Testing: Deductive Reasoning and the Scientific Enterprise Assume that the task is theory testing (as opposed to theory building). This deduc-

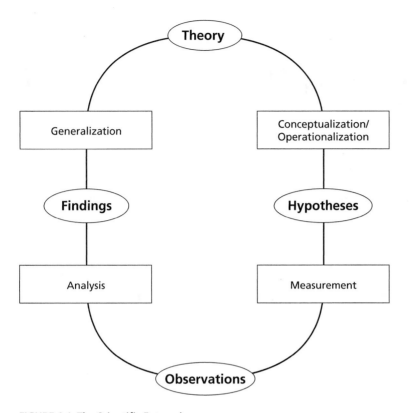

FIGURE 1.1 The Scientific Enterprise

Source: Modified from Wallace (1971).

tive approach begins with specific statements of causation and proceeds down the right side of Figure 1.1. The first stop—what may be referred to as a product—is a hypothesis. To get to this point, criminologists generally follow several processes. Through **conceptualization** they provide reasonably general and logical definitions for each important term contained in the theory. The products of conceptualization, called **concepts,** may have meanings beyond the issue at hand. Consequently, criminologists try to ground them in the subject matter without sacrificing important meaning.

For example, the concept of crime has many meanings, both religious and secular, including evil or undesired behavior. In legal terms crime may be defined as the failure to follow prescriptive or proscriptive rules that have been adopted as part of a community's formal conduct norms, the violation of which results in punishment imposed by designated members of the community. In other words, people commit crime when either they fail to do what the community's rules tell them to do (i.e., failure to follow proscriptive norms) or they do what the rules say is forbidden (i.e., failure to follow prescriptive norms). As a consequence, rule (or law) violators must suffer the consequences of their act or failure to act. As this example suggests, concepts are shorthand expressions for complex ideas.

After defining the concepts and specifying their interrelationships, the criminologist-as-conceptualist specifies the ways in which the concepts can be measured and the linkages actually tested. This stage is sometimes called **opera-tionalization.** Through operationalization criminologists provide the specific steps that allow for the measurement of the theory's key terms.

The operationalization process transforms concepts—a theory's abstract build-ing blocks—into **variables,** things that can be counted, observed, or otherwise measured.[1] In the social sciences data collection efforts are limited to what can be measured by smell, sight, taste, touch, or hearing. Intuition or other so-called senses cannot provide empirical data, the basis for testing theories. Hence, opera-tionalization refers to the steps by which concepts are grounded in the world of sense impressions; that is, described in terms that make them measurable. For ex-ample, crime is not, by itself, measurable using the moral, secular, or legalistic def-initions previously provided. If, however, we ask *how often* a specific act—say, stealing an object worth more than $25 but less than $500—was committed be-tween January 1, 2000, and December 31, 2000, in Dayton, Ohio, then we have provided an operational definition of crime. Granted, this highly restrictive defi-nition does not cover all crimes or legal jurisdictions, but it does qualify as one possible operational definition of the concept of crime.

Hypotheses are another product of operationalization.[2] The theory may pro-vide explicit linkages between concepts called propositions, or it may suggest to the researcher what will happen in comparing two or more variables. Recall the alleged linkages between poverty and crime or between deterrence and crime. In any event, once the concepts are operationally defined and the variables identi-fied, one or more hypotheses result. Hypotheses, then, are statements that assert specific relationships between certain observable facts.

By this stage in the research enterprise, the process of operationalization has yielded one or more variables for each concept. For example, a crime is a law vio-lation, and a robbery is a type of serious crime; however, both are relatively ab-stract concepts. In contrast, the exact number of armed robberies reported to police in East Rutherford, New Jersey, in a specific 12-month period is a concrete variable. Bearing in mind the previous statements about poverty, deterrence, and crime, consider the following scenarios:

- Assume that for one 12-month period the economy of East Rutherford was booming, followed by 12 months of economic bust. The theory predicts that crime, including perhaps armed robbery as an economically-based offense, will increase over the second 12 months. In this example the hypothesis is clear: The sum total of armed robberies in East Rutherford will be higher in the 12 months of economic decline than in the 12 months of economic prosperity.

- Assume that on 1 January New Jersey instituted "enhanced" sentencing for armed robbers: Persons convicted of armed robbery will receive a mandatory 20-year prison sentence. Moreover, the East Rutherford Police Department, which has been plagued in the previous 12 months by a series of unsolved armed robberies, has instituted an Armed Robbery Task Force. Consequently the severity and certainty of punishments for armed robberies has increased dramatically. The hypothesis for this set of variables is the opposite of the previous one: The sum total of armed robberies in East Rutherford will be lower in the second 12-month period of enhanced deterrent effects than in the prior 12 months.

The theory-testing process continues up the left side of Figure 1.1. We explore these processes and products in detail in the section on theory building, but a brief overview is warranted here. The resulting variables and hypotheses can be subjected to measurement, tested, and either accepted or rejected. Should the analysis stage support rejecting the hypotheses, then, by extension, we must reconsider the propositions and concepts as well. In essence, rejecting the research hypotheses calls into question all or part of the theory, or the operationalization of the variables, or both.

Even if the hypotheses are accepted, or at least not rejected, the theory is not taken as factual. Rather, the research is seen as contributing to the body of knowledge related to the theory in question. Eventually, given sufficient corroborating evidence, the theory's propositions may achieve the stature of law, meaning that the stated assertions are no longer theoretical, but are proved. As you might suspect, this level of proof for criminological theories simply does not exist. Does this mean that research efforts are in vain? We think not and suggest that you reserve judgment.

Theory Building: Inductive Reasoning and the Scientific Enterprise Inductive reasoning starts at the bottom left-hand side of Figure 1.1. The goal is to create generalizable findings that may yield systemic and organized assertions from **empirical observations.** Researchers who use this method also make assumptions about human behavior and the best ways to develop theories. Thus, theory is not so much tested as built from the ground up, starting with the data.

Inductive researchers use qualitative and quantitative information. Unlike deductive researchers, who look to pre-existing theory for guidance, these researchers let the observations, no matter how they are collected, paint a picture of the phenomenon under study. **Analysis** is the process by which researchers look for patterns and ways of organizing their observations or data in systematic ways. The products of analysis are the **findings,** which, through a second process called generalization, may yield statements that extend the findings beyond the particular set of circumstances. Theory is the final product of inductive reasoning.

The generalization process is the obverse of operationalization and conceptualization. Here, the researchers essentially take the information gleaned about the object of study (i.e., a specific case) and make broad statements about similar objects (i.e., the general class of similar events or phenomena); they synthesize the observations derived from the data collection and make a general statement called an empirical generalization. An **empirical generalization** is, in essence, an individual proposition about or statement of the relationship between facts revealed by the data; moreover, this statement has the potential to go beyond the present case and so has causal implications for all similar phenomena.

Again, it is crucial to reiterate that Figure 1.1 is only a graphic representation of the ties between theory and research. The right half is representative of activities best described as theory testing; the left side represents theory-building activities.[3] Dividing the figure in half, top to bottom, yields a different perspective on the scientific enterprise. The processes and products in the top half are far more abstract and removed from the world of sense impressions than those in the bottom half: The top half involves theorizing, and the bottom half represents research and analysis.

The Goals of Theory

According to our definition there are at least four separate and equally important goals for crime theories. First, theory *as description* means that the statements embodied in the theory mesh with what we know about crime and criminals. The descriptions must have high levels of accuracy, reliability, and validity. The descriptive questions are framed in a "What is it?" format.

Theory *as explanation* answers a different ("Why is it?") set of questions: Explanation suggests a deeper penetration into the problem of crime, especially compared to simple description. They account for the very being of the things under study, providing the reason or reasons that such phenomena as crimes exist. Any theory—criminological or otherwise—that fails to explain contributes little to the theoretical enterprise.

Theory *as prediction* shifts the emphasis a bit, in that prediction—the act of foretelling or making known beforehand—emphasizes time. In this context prediction involves identifying when something will occur by specifying the conditions conducive to its occurrence. As such, prediction involves the "When is it?" question. Social, behavioral, and physical scientists often express prediction in probabilistic terms, stating the likelihood that, given a set of conditions, some event—in this case crime—will occur. It may have a 10 percent or a 90 percent probability of occurring; however, even physical scientists rarely deal in zero probability or 100 percent probability.

Achieving the final goal, theory *as control,* is sometimes problematic for criminologists, because they may view themselves not as providers of solutions to problems, but rather as value-free observers of the social world. As a consequence they place a premium on pure science—the creation of knowledge for its own sake—at the expense of the pursuit of applied knowledge. This same dilemma was faced several generations ago by the nuclear scientists who provided the theoretical basis for atomic and eventually nuclear weapons but failed to establish policies for their use. Increasingly social, behavioral, and physical scientists who study crime—whether they are sociologists, psychologists, physiologists, or biochemists, are becoming involved not only in the first three goals (i.e., describing, explaining, and predicting crime and criminals) but also in the ways that the resulting knowledge serves to control behavior. The position of those who view theory as a control mechanism is simple: If the theorists who know the most about such issues do not get involved, then persons who know less about the theory's constituent parts and about its strengths and weaknesses will define the policy and practice agenda.

Challenges for Theory Testing and Theory Building

To this point we have summarized some of the logical and practical challenges awaiting anyone who engages in theorizing about physical, behavioral, or social phenomena. Many others remain unexplored and, owing to space considerations, are beyond the scope of this text. We turn next to a review of some of the most important remaining challenges. These concerns—correlation versus causation, tautological traps, and the role played by values in both theorizing and researching—often cause the public, policy makers, and even criminologists to stumble as they search for answers.

Correlation versus Causation When exploring theory, and especially when looking at data for emergent relationships or testing hypotheses, we must avoid confusing causation with correlation. A **correlation** ties two variable measures of events together. To say that two phenomena are correlated means that a change in one is followed by a change in the other. Perhaps the presence or absence of alleged cause A is sufficient to alter effect B. In this case the correlation is expressed as follows: In the presence (or absence) of A, B changes in certain ways. For example, poverty and birthrates are closely correlated, but low income does not *cause* pregnancy. Similarly poverty is correlated with crime, but it does not *explain* crime. That is, most known criminals—with emphasis on the term *known*—are from an economically deprived background, but they represent only a small fraction of the poor, and criminals come from all economic backgrounds. Another variable, perhaps a biological or sociological one, may explain *both* poverty and crime (or the birthrate).

Causation, an equally complex concept, refers to anything that produces an effect. In the language of science, for one event to be viewed as the *cause* of another, it must satisfy three criteria. First, the putative (alleged) cause must precede the effect in time, a requirement referred to as time-order sequencing. The amount of time (e.g., seconds, weeks, months, years, or millennia) is largely irrelevant—except to the person seeking the cause. For example, the child who touches the surface of a hot stove will recoil immediately as the nerve endings send a message to the child's brain. Conversely the consequences of building homes on landfill poisoned by contaminated waste may not be evident for decades until medical researchers observe increased rates of birth defects or cancer.

According to the second criterion, once they establish that the cause indeed precedes the effect in time, researchers must demonstrate the presence of a correlation. If the correlated variables can be counted, the resulting relationship may be expressed in statistical terms and described as strong, weak, or somewhere in between.[4]

The third criterion is the absence of a spurious link between the alleged cause and effect. **Spuriousness** is a quality accorded certain types of relationships. It refers to an observed relationship between two measures (or variables) that is due to the influence of a third measure (or variable). We can make this statement because, when we control for the third variable's influence, the relationship disappears. The third variable is "a rival causal factor" (F. Hagan 1989:32).

The difference between correlation and causation is shown in Figure 1.2. In this case the observed relationship between crime and broken windows serves as an exemplar. That is, as observed by James Q. Wilson and George Kelling (1982), when a single window is broken in, say, an abandoned apartment building, and no one bothers to fix it, soon a few more, then dozens more, and eventually all the windows in the building will be broken. Just as importantly, crime in the neighborhood surrounding the building will increase at a rate that approximates that of the breaking of the windows in the building. This correlation is represented in diagram a in Figure 1.2. You might be tempted to state, however erroneously, that the broken windows caused the crime, as this is what the correlation seems to imply. But this statement represents a spurious interpretation of the facts. Indeed, as Wilson and Kelling (1982) maintained, both the broken windows and the increased crime share a common cause: community malaise. The same sense

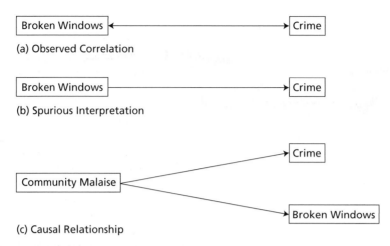

FIGURE 1.2 Correlation versus Causation: The Case of Crime and Broken Windows

of uneasiness and disconnectedness within the neighborhood that caused community members not to fix the windows—or to demand that they be fixed—led to increased crime.

The Tautological Trap A final cautionary note about assumed causal ordering is warranted. That is, in expressing or testing a theory, tautological, or circular, reasoning must be avoided. A **tautology** occurs when the variable being studied is stated as the cause or the explanation. For example, Sigmund Freud's pleasure–pain principle is often given as an example of a tautology: "If one says that a man does what is pleasurable to him and that he does not do what is painful, then *everything* he does is pleasurable by *definition* (Simon 1969:211; emphasis in original). At times the issue of tautological relationships can be tricky. For example, one of the theories we will examine in a later chapter, differential association, argues that the strength of one's patterns of association—prosocial or antisocial—determines behavior, law-abiding or criminal. According to this explanation criminal association leads to criminality, but criminal association is also the result of criminality—"birds of a feather flock together."

Does the use of these variables constitute a tautology? Perhaps, but if it can be shown that criminality did not exist prior to criminal associations, then a possible interpretation is that, due to increased criminality in a community, youths have fewer opportunities to associate with noncriminals. Thus there is a feedback loop between criminality and criminal associations, a condition that is not, strictly speaking, a tautology.

Research, Theory, and Values The theory-as-control goal creates problems. Specifically, in the minds of many researchers, the scientific method also presumes neutrality in the search for "truth." For example, can scientists have values (is a lack of values possible?), and if so, what will be the influence of these values on the types of scientific questions and evidence pursued? Although theory is the basic building block for the advancement of human knowledge, the testing of crime theories is problematic. In the natural sciences, such as chemistry and biology, theories can usually be subjected to rigorous laboratory testing and replication (e.g., testing the effects of certain chemicals on genetically engineered—and nearly identical—laboratory rats). The social or behavioral sciences are concerned with behavior that is peculiarly human, and testing is limited accordingly. We could subject rats to extreme levels of physical stress and then study their reaction to morphine. We would not, however, subject humans to similar levels of stress, expose them to morphine, and then see if they became drug addicts. Social scientists often must study the etiology of drug addiction in a more circuitous manner.

In the search for causal relationships, theories that are too broad or too complex can be difficult to test, and attempts may yield conflicting results. Even theories that either have not been subjected to empirical research or have garnered little support may be promoted by those who decide crime policy. For example, consider the following purported "truth statement": Increasing the number of police officers on patrol will reduce crime. Although a popular policy argument ("Let's put 100,000 more police on the nation's streets"), it has long been challenged by research (Kelling et al. 1974). The policy of providing more police as a way of reducing crime may defy logic: It is reasonable to believe that a person will not commit a crime when a uniformed officer is present; it is illogical to believe that this will deter further criminal behavior or reduce crime when the officer is someplace else on the beat.

According to one view in sociology—called symbolic interactionism—the perception of reality determines the outcome. In other words, if policy makers behave as if a particular theory is correct, then (whatever the objective reality) the theory is real in its consequences. However, research that fails to support a particular theory does not necessarily undermine its validity because the theory may be modified to account for the findings. Too many modifications, however, may result in a theory so broad that its usefulness is reduced, if not eliminated.

Some theories may be too broad to be tested or too limited in their application to explain crime across social classes, cultures, or history. For example, theories that link a lack of legitimate economic opportunity to criminal behavior fail to account for individual differences among those with limited opportunities. Wilson and Richard Herrnstein (1985), in a review of crime theories, restricted their search to crime that was predatory and to criminals who committed serious crimes at high rates, overlooking the fact that much corporate and white-collar crime is predatory as well. In other words, they chose those crimes most likely to be committed by individuals at the bottom of the social scale. Any policy evolving out of their theory, therefore, will be class-specific. The choice of particular crimes—those most likely to be committed by persons in the lower stratum of society, for example—often reflects a bias brought to the research by the researchers (or those funding the research).

Limits of Criminological Knowledge What are the limits to our ability to generate usable crime theories, ones that are applicable to criminal justice policies and practices? The answer depends upon whom you ask, as responses could be arrayed on a continuum from "all theories are useful" to "no theories are useful." But the reality is that many theories emerge with very practical goals in mind. For example, criminologists in Chicago in the early twentieth century viewed that city as having endemic problems that "caused" crime in certain parts of the city, problems that could be changed by vigorous social action. Later generations of criminologists suggested theories to help probation or parole officers by creating conditions of release that minimized exposure to the social forces thought to be at the heart of crime.

As Kurt Lewin (1951) once observed, "There is nothing so practical as a good theory." This statement, however, has not taken broad hold in criminology. During the 1960s and 1970s the links between theory and practice, especially in sociology, were questioned and, in the minds of many academics, devalued. Part of the problem was that some sociologists participated in government-sponsored research intended to disrupt and replace communist–socialist regimes in Central and South America (Horowitz 1967). This trend led to an extended debate about the value-neutrality of the social sciences (see also Weber 1947[1918]).[5] There was also a tendency to devalue theory-guided or theory-driven research in criminal justice in the 1980s and early 1990s. Funding agencies—those state and federal organizations paying for most of the nation's crime control practices—did not see much value in either basic research or theory-driven research in criminal justice, although there are important exceptions to this generalization (see Visher 1994). Such factors may explain the lack of theory-based programming in terms of the interests and preferences of theorists, researchers, and funding agencies, but they do not address the fundamental question: Can theories contribute to crime control policies and practices?

Glen Leavitt (1999) provided a thought-provoking and instructive answer to this latter question. His answer is straightforward: no, not at this time. His reasoning is equally clear. Crime theories are, in his estimation, far too discursive—that is, rambling or digressive in nature (see also Gibbs 1972, 1985). Criminological theorizing, he further observed, increasingly is gaining scientific status, but much of it fails to identify clearly the key assumptions, provides ill-defined concepts and murky propositions, and confuses the assumptions and the assertions. As Leavitt (1999:398) stated, "Similar to judgments about works of art such as paintings and musical compositions, opinions vary markedly among criminologists regarding the merits (or lack thereof) of these theoretical creations."

In Leavitt's opinion, and one we suspect is shared by others in and outside of academic criminology, crime theories are more art than science. Hence, the ability of criminology to serve as a "handmaiden of the criminal justice machinery" is quite limited (Leavitt 1999:398). This is not, in Leavitt's opinion, a bad thing. Any aid that criminology provides to social control agents is "a byproduct of the search for knowledge" (Leavitt 1999:398). He also advocates for more rigorous, formal theories, as opposed to the less rigorous, discursive ones that he claims dominate criminology, but he is not too sanguine about that occurring any time soon.

As you read the chapters that follow, we recommend that you reflect on Leavitt's concerns. We also suggest that you independently assess the value of the various theories discussed. Consider the following question as well: If contemporary theories are too discursive *and* of little practical use to criminal justice practitioners, is it not possible that the call to be useful and practical might motivate theorists and researchers to make theories more formal and rigorous?

HUMAN NATURE, GOVERNMENT, AND PUBLIC POLICY

Two additional elements undergird every theory of crime. First, crime theories can be distinguished by how their supporters conceive of the nature of human behavior. Nearly all theories make assumptions about human nature; these untestable assumptions are, as previously mentioned, essential grounding for crime theory. Prominent in any discussion of human behavior is the nature-versus-nurture controversy. Both sides in the controversy address the same question: What is the dominant force shaping human behavior? Supporters of the **nature** position argue that behavior can be explained primarily by genetic, biological, or other properties inherent in individuals. In short, human behavior is inherited. Conversely, proponents of the **nurture** position look to the social environment for the causal factors; that is, human behavior is largely the product of social interaction.

Whether a theoretician views one set of forces as overriding the other is important. If criminal behavior is part of human nature—and so beyond fixing short of genetic engineering—then that fact suggests rather different perspectives on what society can and should do with law violators. Alternatively, if the source of the problem lies largely within society's mechanisms of socialization—the family, schools, and other social institutions—then different responses may be appropriate. Perhaps an even greater dilemma is reflected in the perspective adopted by many students of crime: Nature and nurture are both important, but in different ways and at different times in people's lives. For example, nature may limit a person's ability to learn within the traditional educational system; however, that same system may play a large role in ostracizing and penalizing underperformers, further limiting their life choices and chances.

Second, crime theories generally assume that society is based on consensus, or pluralism, or conflict (Michalowski 1977). According to the **consensus** viewpoint definitions of right and wrong are not disputed, and law is an expression of this collective agreement, a codification of social norms. Such agreement is necessary for a society to survive—law is functional, a position associated with functionalist sociology. Law serves all people equally, and persons who violate the law represent a unique subgroup. Conservatives think of criminals as deserving punishment or deterrence; liberals see a need to bring them back into conformity. Although supporters of the consensus viewpoint argue for universal conduct norms, most crime theories have focused on the crimes most likely to be committed by young working- or lower-class, males.

According to the **pluralist** view society is made up of diverse groups based on race, ethnicity, gender, geography, economics, and religion. These groups often do not agree on what is right and wrong. Moreover, they may expound different—sometimes competing—interests, values, and goals. Law is the method by which conflict is managed without threatening society's destruction. Moreover, laws and the legal system provide a value-free framework for divergent interests to coexist within a democratic framework. Crime definitions further reflect a coalition of interests.

In the **conflict** view society is made up of many diverse interest groups that are often at odds with one another and, consequently, compete for power and position within society (e.g., farmers, industrialists, and union members; atheists and fundamentalists; liberals and conservatives). The winners get to define "crime." Thus, the definition of crime reflects power relationships in society and serves the interests of those in control. In capitalist societies the owners of the means of production—the wealthy—also maintain the power to define laws and their enforcement.

Government, Policy, and Practice

Among other things, theory refers to explanations, whereas policy is a planned course of action designed to deal with some problem. For crime, policy is typically the responsibility of government. Theory has the potential to support policy; however, conflicting theories can confound policy alternatives. Research that supports or weakens a theory will obviously impact policy. Because crime theory can never be proved in the criminal law sense (i.e., proof beyond reasonable doubt), policy guided by research-grounded theory will always be tentative. Theory-driven policy must pass a myriad of political tests that are part of a democratic system. But what are the alternatives? Policy by public opinion? Policy by "gut feelings"? Policy by the most powerful, for the most powerful?

Some theories do not easily translate into policy response. For example, theories that focus on the family may challenge the sanctity of the family: How do we modify the "cause" without intruding on private interests? Interestingly the federal government is addressing just this problem. During the last few years of the twentieth century and continuing into the present one, the Office of Juvenile Justice and Delinquency Prevention, a U.S. Department of Justice agency, has supported research and programs intended to "strengthen" America's families (Alvarado and Kumpfer 2000; Erickson 2001). Parents are encouraged to seek empowerment through skills training and family therapy (Kumpfer and Tait 2000; Robbins and Szapocnik 2000). These programs derive from decades of research on family-centered sources of crime and delinquency (Alvarado and Kumpfer 2000; see also Huizinga, Loeber, and Thornberry 1995). These programs notwithstanding, attempts to influence families remain controversial.

Reformers find more attractive theories that focus on that which (given the political will) can be altered. Important correlates of crime are seemingly beyond the ability of policy to affect. Consider the influence of age on crime: "Criminal behavior depends as much or more on age than any other demographic characteristic—sex, social status, race, family configuration" (Wilson and Herrnstein 1985:126). The crime-prone ages are roughly 15–25, and it is unusual to find criminals whose illegal behavior began after the age of 25.

Additional obstacles to translating theory into practice exist. Theories often support alternative policies, which means that drawing policy conclusions from theory-guided research can be problematic. Facts do not speak for themselves; they suffer from definitional problems and subjective influences that determine not only what facts are sought but also how they are measured. For whom do the researchers work? The government? Corporations? Foundations? Is an ideology involved in the research effort? Does research drive policy, or are researchers in the employ of entities that have a stake in the outcome? In fact, most research into criminal behavior is sponsored by the government, which, of course, is tied to the prevailing policies of the administration in control of the executive branch, the legislative branch, or both.

These are the four basic positions on the relationship between theory and policy:

1. If crime is the result of individual dynamics that can be changed or modified, then policy may endorse deterring, punishing, or treating the offender.

2. If crime is the result of individual dynamics that are beyond society's ability to change, then policy may endorse warehousing offenders or otherwise removing them from the community.

3. If criminal behavior is the result of modifiable environmental conditions, then policy may be geared to changing that environment, thereby eliminating or altering the forces creating crime.

4. If criminal behavior is the result of environmental conditions that are resistant to change, then policy may follow a path similar to that endorsed in position #2.

Given some of these alternatives and their implications for criminal justice practices, it is not difficult to understand why some criminologists shun the policy aspects of theorizing.

The Case for Considering Theory

The basic questions seem so simple: Why is there crime? Why do we have criminals? We should not lose sight of the fact that theory, whatever the specific manifestation, provides the best insights into the "why?" and "how?" of the phenomenon under investigation. It is in the testing and applying of those ideas that we learn about their "goodness of fit" with reality. Consider the following observations about the possible linkages between crime theory, research, policy, and practice:

- Theories that are essentially untestable are of little use in crime studies, especially if we seek to understand crime, predict its occurrence, and ultimately control it.

- Theories that have no policy implications may likewise be viewed rather negatively by those involved in similar attempts to describe, understand, predict, and control crime. In fact, all theories have some policy implications although, for political, moral, economic, or social reasons, it may be impossible to implement the policies suggested by a given theory.

- Research that is atheoretical (i.e., has no connection to theory)—or perhaps is even antitheoretical—may yield interesting short-term insights into the phenomenon under study. However, unless that phenomenon is static and immutable, the long-term utility of such research and any policy decisions based upon it are limited.

- Policies that are devoid of theoretical underpinnings likewise may have limited utility, as they may meet immediate needs if based on current research but be unable to meet the demands of a changing society.

- Policies that have only tentative ties to practice—especially if the persons proposing the policies have little appreciation of the problems faced by those charged with their implementation—may be doomed to failure.

- Practices that are not subjected to exhaustive research—especially evaluation research—can undermine the authority of their source, whether that is a specific criminal justice agency (e.g., police misuse of firearms or high-speed chases) or society in general (e.g., laws criminalizing the ingestion of a drug that enjoys widespread use in society at large, or laws increasing the sanctions for violent juvenile offenders).

- Practices that are not grounded in formal policy statements have the potential to subject the practitioners to civil and criminal action; that is, we do not expect or desire such people to "make it up as they go along."

Figure 1.3 schematically represents the central ties between crime theory, research, policy, and practice. All four elements address the problem of crime. Each one depends on the adjacent elements for basic inputs; however, the information flow is in both directions (e.g., theory depends on research, and research upon theory). The model also suggests that theory impacts practice only indirectly through research and policy. This indirect linkage may account for the reluctance of some practitioners to be persuaded by theoretical discussions.

In the chapters that follow, we examine both theories and their supporting research, as well as any associated policies and practices. By simultaneously considering all four basic elements, our understanding of crime theory is enhanced. Before we can evaluate the various crime theories, however, we must briefly and critically examine the underpinnings of most contemporary views on the nature of laws and crimes.

THE NATURE OF LAWS AND CRIMES

The term *law* is believed to be derived from the old Norse *log* or *lag,* the former meaning "to lay down or determine" and the latter meaning "to bind people together" (Aubert 1983). Although it is central to the functioning of society, law defies authoritative definition. Even lawyers and judges have no generally agreed-upon definition of law: "For them it is simply what they practice and what courts do" (Loh 1984:23). The German philosopher Emmanuel Kant (1724–1804) faulted lawyers for being unable to agree on a definition of their profession's subject matter. He proceeded to construct his own definition, which found no more universal acceptance than those he criticized (Berman and Greiner 1980).

Origins of Law

Order is essential for society (Hoebel 1974:12), and law can be conceived of as simply a body of rules governing a social order. But social scientists disagree over the point at which law can be said to exist in a society: How is law to be distinguished from social rules and customs, the norms of a society? **Norms** indicate societal expectations of what is right or "normal," of what ought to be (i.e., prescriptive norms); norms may also indicate what is wrong or "abnormal," what ought not to be (i.e., proscriptive norms).

The American sociologist William Graham Sumner (1840–1910) ordered norms in hierarchical fashion. Sumner (1906) saw social control as either informal or formal. Informal social control promotes conformity, said Sumner, not through some rational basis but by nearly automatic adherence, owing to child-

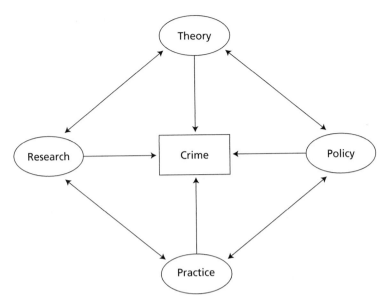

FIGURE 1.3 Ties between Crime Justice Theory, Research, Policy, and Practice

hood socialization. Violators are confronted by their peers, who enact appropriate sanctions or punishments. Yet not all norms are created equal. **Folkways** define what is socially approved or disapproved, but they do not reflect a sense of moral obligation. Their meaning is perhaps best captured by this phrase: Thou *should* or *should not* do something. The penalties that accompany their violation are relatively mild and include ridicule and ostracism. **Mores** (singular, **mos**) are also informal norms, but adherence is far more obligatory: Thou *must* or *must not* do something. Violation of a mos is met with a strong sense of moral indignation; moreover, the penalties that accompany the violation of mores are far more severe, including, in extreme cases, the death penalty. Importantly neither type of social norm is formalized in law, nor is there, generally speaking, a specialized institution within the community for enacting penalties. Rather, imposing the punishment is the duty of all members of the community.

Formalization of folkways and mores generates law. Sumner saw the process of moving from informal to formal social control as taking thousands of years and involving the development of some form of centralized government. Laws have at least two forms. **Customary laws** are perhaps the oldest form; they represent the codification of traditional practices and include definitions of the condemned act or omission, the procedures for determining guilt or innocence, and the punishments for those found guilty. As described by Sumner, customary laws bear a striking resemblance to common law as practiced by the English and others. When systematized and codified, customary laws never break with tradition, but rather reflect the social intent and moral force of the mores and folkways upon which they are based. This was the case when the Twelve Tables were created by the Romans around 450 B.C.E. These codes had their origins in the *mos mariorum,* the oral traditions of the ancient Romans. Formally recorded on twelve bronze tablets in the

Roman Forum, the laws were highly formalistic; they governed all aspects of life and death in Rome—including crimes and punishments—for nearly 2000 years. In contrast, **enacted laws,** although similar to customary laws, are deliberately recorded by an official representative or representatives of the community—they are explicit and carry the weight of the community. Sumner saw enacted law as far more advanced; not only did it no longer rely upon customary law for guidance, but it often contradicted the latter. Indeed, he viewed the intent of enacted law punishments as deterring crime rather than merely serving as retaliation or revenge.

The German sociologist and economist Max Weber (1864–1920) stated that laws are "norms which are directly guaranteed by legal coercion" (1967[1925]:14). Conduct that violates a social norm may be impolite or perhaps eccentric, and it can cause the violator to be shunned by those who are aware of the behavior. Behavior that violates the law, however, draws punishment. Punishment, if it is to be "lawful," must be imposed by persons specifically authorized by society to do so. Thus, law represents the rules of conduct backed by the organized force of the community (Abraham 1975).

Both Sumner and Weber emphasized that law and custom are not the same. The act of creating formal laws "endows certain selected individuals with the privilege–right of applying the sanction of physical coercion" (Hoebel 1974: 276). Former Supreme Court Associate Justice Benjamin Cardozo pointed to the necessity of regular enforcement by courts of law. Law, he said, "is a principle or rule of conduct so established as to justify a prediction with reasonable certainty that it will be enforced by the courts if its authority is challenged" (1924:52). That norms require formal mechanisms for enforcement presupposes that there may be those who do not, or will not, support them in all instances. At the same time, as Weber (1967[1925]) pointed out, custom may be far more determinative of conduct than the existence of legal enforcement machinery.

Contemporary law includes formalized and codified rules stipulated by courts of law and coercively enforced by control agents. Some laws restrict behavior; others compel it; still others (e.g., contract law) facilitate voluntary actions by providing guidelines. Laws create benefits, such as Social Security, and empower bureaucratic entities, such as transportation departments responsible for building and maintaining roads. In short, it is difficult to conceive of any aspects of contemporary life that are not influenced by laws.

In societies ruled by custom, folkways and mores serve as conduct guides and, in so doing, help hold the community together. In other societies, political bodies create, interpret, and enforce laws. Laws are just as important for social control and social cohesion although the mechanisms are far more formalized and result in the creation of institutions to attain the same goals. Modern laws provide alternatives to customs as a means of providing order in the far more complex and diverse societies of contemporary times.

Defining Crime

Crime also has no generally accepted definition. For many people crime is any behavior that is harmful to individuals or groups. This normative definition leaves open the question of what constitutes harm. Moreover, the fate of people who cause the harm is not addressed.

In legal terms crime is any behavior that violates the criminal statutes; it is a wrongful act or omission subject to official punishment. This definition raises several questions of its own:

- Who determines the criminal law?
- What constitutes "a wrong"?
- Can governments commit crimes?

Certainly governments have committed many atrocious acts, including the concentration camps of Nazi Germany, the Gulags of Stalin's Soviet Union, the murderous predations of the Pol Pot regime in Cambodia, and nearly everyone involved in the recent Balkan turmoil. Were the civil rights protesters in the American South during the 1950s and 1960s criminals because they deliberately violated statutes that supported segregation? Were the antiwar protesters of the Vietnam era criminals? Was the well-known traitor to the English crown, George Washington, a criminal? Is Osama bin Laden a garden-variety criminal, a terrorist, a war criminal, a freedom fighter, or a religious warrior?

Determining what is or is not a crime—and who is or is not a criminal—depends on time and place. Jesus was deemed a criminal and executed alongside two common thieves. Many of Jesus' followers met a similar fate. Later generations of Christians defined so-called heretics and non-Christians as criminal and treated them as badly as the Romans had Christianity's founder. From 1920 to 1933 the sale and possession of alcoholic beverages were crimes in the United States, and prior to 1914 heroin and cocaine were legal. The ability to express opinions and write books is protected in the United States by the First Amendment; in other countries such exercises are illegal or fraught with danger. In the early 1990s, for example, an Egyptian author was convicted of the crime of heresy for the content of his book and sentenced to eight years in prison. Around the same time Salman Rushdie, author of *The Satanic Verses,* was tried by Iran in absentia and sentenced to death under Islamic law for apostasy, acts that threaten God's word. In Germany it is a crime to write materials that deny the existence of the Holocaust, the systematic attempt by the Nazis to exterminate all the Jews in Europe. Such activities, however misguided and inaccurate, would be "protected speech" in the United States.

Classifying Crime

Laws provide a formal mechanism for the creation and maintenance of social order in complex societies. They define what is a crime, how to determine whether a crime has been committed, and whether a given person is guilty of the act; ultimately, they also describe the offender's punishment. Making sense of the morass of criminal laws—determining their intent and purpose—is a separate task. Criminologists resort to *typologies* as a means of classifying crime, several of which we have already employed.[6] The level of "evilness" is the basis of one such typology. **Mala in se,** Latin for "evil in itself," refers to crimes that are intrinsically evil, such as murder. Although societies may differ on the details of acts that constitute murder, all prohibit the behavior. This term contrasts with **mala prohibita,** Latin for "wrong because it is prohibited," which refers to activities that have been outlawed not because they are obviously evil, but because they violate certain standards

---

COMMENTS AND CRITICISMS: What Is a Crime? Who Is a Criminal?

Consider these real-life examples of "criminality":

- The judge determined that Karl-robert Kreiten had indeed violated paragraph 91b of the German Criminal Code; he sentenced the defendant to death. Kreiten was subsequently executed. His crime: making derogatory remarks to friends about Hitler's Nazi regime.

- Thirty to forty persons—men, women and children—were herded into a tight circle. One man gave the order, and two others opened fire with automatic weapons. A few children, shielded by their parents, survived the murderous barrage. The man who gave the orders calmly walked over and fired his automatic pistol into each surviving child. Only he would subsequently be tried and convicted of his actions. Lieutenant William Calley, United States Army, served three years for the My Lai "incident" of 18 March 1968.

- The Taliban soldiers herded the three women to the edge of the Tabul soccer stadium, where the women, garbed in the traditional Afghani burqa—a garment that covers the wearer from head to toe and provides limited vision through a veil—were made to kneel on the goal line. They waited in silence as thousands of cheering spectators watched a soldier walk up behind each one, place the barrel of an AK-47 against her head, and fire a single round. Each woman's body was unceremoniously dumped in a pickup truck's bed. The women's crimes? They were found guilty of prostitution, behavior they engaged in only after their "normal" vocations of school teachers, physicians, and civil servants were denied them under the strict gender-control rules of the Taliban.

Sources: Brown (2001); Mueller (1991); Peers (1979).

---

governing behavior. This classification includes insider trading—a violation of accepted business practices—and possession of heroin, a crime since 1914. Neither act, in and of itself, threatens the social fabric; instead, someone, in some place and at some time, decided to declare the acts illegal. Most discussions of this latter typology center on questions of values, rightness or wrongness, and morality.

Law distinguishes noncriminal, or civil, offenses (also called torts) from criminal ones, and criminal law distinguishes **misdemeanors** from **felonies** based upon the legalistic idea that the more serious offender should receive the more serious punishment. Crimes are distinguished from one another in terms of the length of punishment and place of confinement. Misdemeanors can be punished for no more than one year of incarceration in a city or county jail or federal correctional center; felonies are punishable by more than one year in a state or federal prison or correctional institution. Other miscreant acts, deemed very minor, call for the creation of **ordinances,** the violation of which are resolved most often by a fine. Such acts include some traffic offenses and violations of local regulatory rules, such as parking regulations, smoking restrictions, and noise abatement rules.

Some theorists, especially those espousing conflict or critical arguments, push for crime classifications based on social harm. Marshall Clinard and his associates (1979) noted that the criminal law reflects differences in power; burglary prosecutions, for example, routinely invoke more significant penalties than those for white-collar crime. Just one case of corporate law violation may involve millions or even billions of dollar in losses. The injuries caused by defective products, including pharmaceuticals, can involve thousands of persons in a single case. For example, in the electrical price-fixing conspiracy of the early 1960s (see R. A. Smith 1961a,b), losses amounted to more than $2 billion, a sum far greater than the total losses from the 3 million burglaries each year in that era. At the same time, the average loss from a larceny-theft or a burglary is far less, and the persons who commit these offenses may receive sentences of 5–10 years or more. The sole punishment for crimes committed by large corporations often consists of warnings, consent orders, or comparatively small fines. As the title of a book by Jeffrey Reiman (2001) aptly points out, *The Rich Get Richer and the Poor Get Prison*.

ORIGINS OF CRIME THEORIES

The classical, positive, and conflict approaches to crime loom large in the world of criminology, where most theories fall into one or the other camp. Whereas positivism implies a scientific approach, the classical position is best described as legalistic—it provides the basis for the administration of the U.S. system of justice. Conflict stands in opposition to both. An examination of all three demonstrates each one's respective impact on our definitions of crime and justice. These three perspectives on crime have influenced—and continue to influence—mainstream thinking about crimes and criminals, their causes and solutions.

Classical and Neoclassical Theory

Classical theory is an outgrowth of the European Enlightenment of the eighteenth century (sometimes referred to as the "Age of Reason"), whose adherents rejected spiritual and religious explanations of criminal behavior. During this era philosophers such as Charles-Louis de Secondat, Baron de La Brede et de Montesquieu (1689–1755), and François-Marie Arouet Voltaire (1694–1778) spoke out against the French penal code and punishments that were both inhumane and inequitable. Jean-Jacques Rousseau (1712–1778) and Cesare Bonesana, marchese di Beccaria, usually referred to as Cesare Beccaria (1738–1794), argued for a radical new concept of justice. At a time when laws and law enforcement were unjust and disparate, and punishment often brutal, they demanded justice based on equality and punishment that was humane and proportionate to the offense. This landmark doctrine—equality—found a voice in the American Revolution with the declaration that "all men are created equal," and in the French Revolution, during which the National Assembly enacted a "Declaration of the Rights of Man and Citizen" (1789) emphasizing the equality of all citizens. The roots of this legal and political philosophy can be found in the concepts of natural law and contract theory.

Natural Law and Contract Theory **Natural law** dates to the Middle Ages, where it served the interests of the Roman Catholic Church in its dealings with secular powers. In the hands of the Papacy it was an impediment to the growth of nation-states (Aubert 1983). According to church doctrine the source of all natural law was divine, and the church steadfastly refused to acknowledge any law that contradicted its own. Later an emerging middle class used the concept of natural law in an effort to counter the feudal nobility's power and, eventually, the monarch's divine right. Thus, natural law places limits on political power, and in England it was embodied in the common law.

Natural law stresses moral and rational elements in legal reasoning, and, say its proponents, exists whether or not there is a specific enactment by the government. Thus, natural law transcends all formal human constructs, and any law contrary to natural law necessarily flows from the coercive force of the state, and not the voluntary compliance of the governed. As the English legal scholar William Blackstone (1723–1780) observed in *Commentaries on the Laws of England* (1760), any human law contrary to natural law has no validity.

The social contract derives from natural law but expands on it. According to this mythical agreement, when humans abandon the "state of nature" to form a new society, they must surrender certain rights and freedoms. In return, government assumes certain responsibilities for its citizens. The social contract must therefore acknowledge these natural rights, or, as Blackstone observed, it has no validity.

The English philosopher John Locke (1632–1704) expressed natural law concepts in his statements that all men are by nature free, equal, and independent, and that no one can be subjected to the political power of another without his own consent. The U.S. Declaration of Independence incorporated these sentiments: "All men are created equal whose governments are instituted among men, deriving their just powers from the consent of the governed." Whereas Locke (1962[1690]) referred to the natural law rights of "life, liberty, and property," Thomas Jefferson, in the Declaration, enumerated the inalienable rights to "life, liberty, and the pursuit of happiness."

Classical Theory, Crime, and Punishment The classical notion of the social contract stipulates that, all men being created equal, conditions of law are the same for all: "The social contract establishes among the citizens an equality of such character that each binds himself on the same terms as all the others," and thus, Rousseau asserted, "One consents to die—if and when one becomes a murderer oneself—in order not to become a murderer's victim" (1954[1762]:45, 48). In order to be safe from crime, we have all consented to punishment if we resort to crime. This constitutes the greatest good for the greatest number; the social contract is rational and motivated by selfishness (Roshier 1989).

The classical school, standing in opposition to the manner in which law was being enforced at the time, argued that the law should respect neither rank nor station—all men are created equal. This premise was formalized by Beccaria who, in *An Essay on Crimes and Punishments* (1963[1764]: English edition, 1867), stated that laws should be drawn precisely and matched to punishment intended to be applied equally to all classes of men. The law, he argued, should stipulate a particular penalty for each specific crime, and judges should mete out identical sentences for each occurrence of the same offense.

According to the classical position advanced by Beccaria, Jeremy Bentham (1748–1832), and others, punishment is justified because the offender is rational and endowed with free will. Every person has the ability to distinguish and choose between right and wrong, between being law-abiding and criminal. Law-violating behavior is, therefore, a rational choice made by a reasoning person with free will.

The classical school argues that because human beings tend toward hedonism—
that is, they seek pleasure and avoid pain—they must be restrained from unlawful
pleasurable acts by fear of punishment. Crime is "caused" by the inability of laws—
and the punishments they embody—to deter would-be criminals from committing their crimes. Accordingly the purpose of the criminal law is not simply
retribution, but also deterrence.

Classical theory emphasizes the **certainty** of punishment over its **severity** as
the way to deter crime; but the reality of criminal justice is otherwise: Severity is
more easily accomplished than is certainty. As a consequence, the trend in criminal justice today is toward greater punishment (not greater deterrence). These
facts help to explain popular support for the death penalty, whose deterrent value
is questionable. The fusion of two requirements—certainty *and* promptness—
rounds out the classical position. If law is to serve its deterrent purpose, the
would-be violator must fear the consequences of his or her actions. This element
of fear requires certainty; promptness, or **celerity,** which seems to be based on a
primitive form of behaviorism, is necessary to make a more lasting impression—
it serves to connect the deed directly to the punishment.

Neoclassicalism According to the classical position punishment is justified because the offender who violates the social contract is rational, endowed with free
will, and so, responsible for his or her actions. The focus is on laws and the legal
system, not the nature of criminal motivation. In fact, under our system of justice,
an explanation is not a justification unless it reaches the level of a (legal) compul-
sion, at which point the law does not blame the perpetrator—no *mens rea*.

Classicalism provided the basis for a rational legal system that was relatively
easy to administer, except for one annoying problem: Implementing a criminal
code with perfect equality proved elusive. This problem became apparent when
the drafters of the French Code of 1791 attempted to implement Beccaria's reforms. Equality and proportionality proved more difficult in practice than in theory, and the French increasingly added to the discretionary powers of judges,
resulting in a type of neoclassicalism (Roshier 1989).

Neoclassicalism–classicalism maintains the basic belief in free will while
paving the way for the entry of mitigation (and subsequently aggravation) into
criminal justice based on past criminal record, insanity and retardation, and age.
Punishment can be justified only if crime is reasoned behavior. The neoclassicist
revisions created a need for nonlegal experts, including psychiatrists, psychologists, and social workers, in the realm of criminal justice (Taylor, Walton, and
Young 1973:8). These experts determine the presence of mitigation while the
system is able to continue to maintain a belief in free will. Allowing for the possibility of differences between offenders raises the specter that offenders' choices
are limited, the basic premise of positivism.

The U.S. system of jurisprudence—and criminal justice—is steeped in classical philosophy. Contemporary crime theories also contain more than a modicum
of the same basic ideas originally laid down by Beccaria and Bentham more than
200 years ago, including deterrence and opportunity theories (see Chapter 2).
The idea that people are responsible for their own actions—and that society,
through its formal and informal social control mechanisms, can make clear that
lesson—has proved to be quite hardy indeed.

Positivism and Scientific Determinism

The moment we entertain the possibility that criminal behavior may be caused rather than chosen, we move toward a denial of free will and toward determinism. Determinism is sometimes described as "hard" (complete) or "soft" (partial) (Matza 1964); that is, either all or some human social behavior is caused by forces beyond human control. In the nineteenth century determinism merged with positivism to form scientific determinism. According to **positivism,** the scientific approach, which has proved so successful in the study and control of the physical world, has equal validity and promise in the study of humanity and society. Following the precepts of scientific determinism, science can focus on crime and be used to separate out the various deterministic forces—be they biological, economic, psychological, or social in origin—that cause such miscreant behavior.

Origins of Positivism Positivism places great stock in the idea that the only real knowledge of our physical world—natural phenomena—comes from sensory experiences, from our five senses. It relies on the scientific method, "which views all occurrences as the result of certain cause–effect relationships"—natural laws governing physical and social phenomena (Michalowski 1977:28). Positivists search for underlying causes that are applicable universally. With respect to crime, if this search is successful, it will allow for the prediction of criminal behavior and therefore suggests ways of preventing or controlling it. As formulated by the French philosopher Auguste Comte (1798–1857), positivism refers to a method for examining and understanding social behavior. Comte argued that the methods and logical forms of the natural sciences—the scientific method—are applicable to the study of humans as social beings, from whence we get the social sciences. Social phenomena, Comte stated, must be studied and understood by observation, hypothesis, and experimentation in a new discipline he called sociology. Whereas the classical school is based on philosophy and law, the positive school is based on empiricism.

The positivistic approach to the study of crime became known as *criminology,* a discipline whose early efforts are identified with Cesare Lombroso (1835–1909), a Venetian physician. In his *L'uomo delinquente* (*The Criminal Man*), first published in 1876, Lombroso argued that the criminal is an atavist or "primitive throwback" to earlier developmental stages through which noncriminal "man" had already passed (the influence of social Darwinism is obvious). Lombroso's research centered on physiological characteristics believed to be indicative of criminality although his later work (published in 1911) noted the importance of environmental factors in causing crime (see Lombroso 1968). Instead of the classical emphasis on criminal behavior as rational, positivists tend to see it as a symptom of some form of biological, psychological, or social pathology—the criminal as *mad* (not *bad*).

Contemporary Positivism Criminologists who consider crime to be highly relative or a matter of definition are critical of positivism. As opposed to physical entities, subjective factors influence measures of "crime." From this perspective "absolute objectivity becomes an impossible goal: facts do not speak for themselves. 'Facts' are the product of the work of those with the power to define what is to be taken to be 'factual' and of the willingness of those without such power to accept the given definitions" (Taylor, Walton, and Young 1973:26).

Crime statistics, for example, are determined subsequent to the establishment of definitions that lead to categories into which these defined classes fall. Positivism takes society as it is given and, thereby, supports the status quo; avoided is the issue of defining crime—how the definition differs from society to society, and from time to time, for example, with respect to drugs, alcohol, gambling, insider trading, and pollution. Those who hold "definitional views" conceive of crime as a societal construct that has no particular objective referent but is explained by power relationships in a society. Thus, South Africa's most famous criminal—one who spent most of his adult life in prison—eventually became its president. In the United States, to avoid the prospect of a disgraced former president going to prison, his successor pardoned him for all "high crimes and misdemeanors" he might have committed as president.

Positivism is alive and well in the twenty-first century. Included in contemporary positivism—and their progenitors—are biological forms (see Chapter 3), psychological forms (see Chapters 4 and 5), and sociological forms (see Chapters 6 and 7). Although the more recent forms little resemble the version Lombroso proposed, they share at least one commonality: The criminologists espousing positivism continue to believe that science allows them to come to know crime and criminals.

Marxism and Conflict Theory

In the nineteenth century Karl Marx (1818–1883) described industrialized nations as divided societies. According to Marxist theory **capitalists** own the means of production; workers, or the **proletariat,** provide the labor. Power derives from ownership of property and control over the means of production. Capitalists use power to subjugate the workers, guaranteeing consolidation of wealth in their hands. Thus, society is characterized by a class struggle between capitalists and the proletariat. In this struggle, or class war, capitalists mobilize the resources of government and religion to protect their positions of advantage. As capitalism advances, so does the gap between capitalists and workers, with the former gathering wealth at the expense of the latter.

Outside these two classes—owners and workers—is the **lumpenproletariat,** a parasitical group whose predations are based on selfishness and the desire to survive. Their behavior is antithetical to the capitalist order. They and members of the working class defined by capitalists as dangerous or disposable stand the greatest probability of becoming criminals. Over time the **bourgeoisie,** or the middle class, and the **petite bourgeoisie,** or shopkeepers and government officials, evolve between the capitalists and worker classes.

A crucial idea to Marxists is **false consciousness.** This condition exists when workers, and even members of the middle class, "buy into" the idea of a societal consensus on critical social issues like crime and justice. A key aspect of false consciousness is the belief that capitalists care about interests other than their own. Thus, capitalists may promote positive-sounding doctrines such as freedom of the press. Marxists believe that an inevitable revolution will signal the end of capitalism and the beginning of communism. To achieve this end, Marxists must expose the false consciousness and, in so doing, reveal the capitalist system's inequities.

Marxists and Crime Marxists express unique views on crime, distinguishing between three types. Crimes of the proletariat are usually directed at capitalists and so are revolutionary. Crimes of the lumpenproletariat are typically directed against the working class and, to the extent that we can define them as "political," are reactionary. Crimes of the capitalists are the real crime—acts of greed and avarice typically directed against the workers and harmful to the common good (e.g., industrial pollution).

Marxists view crime as capitalism's inevitable by-product. They condemn positivists for studying only the intervening or low-level variables. Positivists, they argue, fail to see the larger social context of crime—the bigger picture in which capitalism leads to a class system of severely differentiated wealth. The resulting social system is one in which the behavior of the weak has a greater chance of being defined as criminal than the actions of the powerful. Wealth and power inequities also cause **alienation** and **demoralization.** The alienated underclass reacts in ways defined by capitalists as deviant. Some abuse alcohol and drugs, while others seek even more destructive escapes from the crushing boot of capitalism. The resulting demoralization generates criminal behavior.

Contemporary Marxism and Conflict Theory Marxists do not "own" the concept of conflict. Many sources of conflict exist, giving rise to many conflict theories. In two subsequent chapters we explore what might be called soft and hard conflict. That is, labeling and conflict theories (see Chapter 8) place great emphasis on the use of power to identify, stigmatize, or otherwise designate certain people as worthy of special attention; the intent is rarely malicious or malevolent, hence the sobriquet of soft conflict. Marxist and feminist theories (see Chapter 9), in contrast, contend that power is used to subjugate a specific population; for Marxists it is the working class, and for feminists it is women (and often working women).

UNDERSTANDING CRIME

This chapter provides the tools to examine with a critical eye a wide range of crime theories. That is, an understanding of crime theories discussed in this text is predicated on knowledge of the elements of theories, the ability to assess them, and awareness of linkages to criminal justice policies and procedures.

Elements of Theories

Theories have many parts. The first section of this chapter explored the role of assumptions and assertions in the structure of theory, as well as the challenges that confront all who offer a crime theory. In subsequent chapters we explore each theory's (1) underlying assumptions, whatever their source; (2) causal arguments, including, where appropriate, propositions and hypotheses; (3) implicit concepts and variables; (4) empirical support for the causal arguments, including quantitative and qualitative forms; and (5) fulfilled, unfulfilled, or ignored goals.

IN THEIR OWN WORDS: Bentham, Lombroso, and Marx

The views of such theoreticians as Jeremy Bentham, Cesare Lombroso, and Karl Marx—representing the classical, positivistic, and conflict orientations, respectively—indicate the diversity of ideas related to crime, criminality, and society, among other things.

- *Bentham on pain and pleasure:* "Nature has placed mankind under the governance of two sovereign masters, *pain* and *pleasure*. It is for them alone to point out what we ought to do, as well as to determine what we shall do. On the one hand the standard of right and wrong, on the other the chain of causes and effects, are fastened to their throne. They govern us in all we do, in all we say, in all we think: every effort we can make to throw off our subjection, will serve to demonstrate and confirm it" (p. 1; emphasis in original).

- *Lombroso on positivism:* "The Modern, or Positive, School of Penal Jurisprudence . . . maintains that the antisocial tendencies of criminals are the result of their physical and psychic organization, which differs essentially from that of normal individuals; and it aims at studying the morphology and various functional phenomena of the criminal with the object of curing, instead of punishing him" (p. 217–218).

- *Marx on the state and the will:* "The more powerful the State, and therefore the more *political* a country is, the less likely it is to seek the basis of *social* ills and to grasp the *general* explanation of them, in the *principle of the State* itself, that is in the *structure of society*, of which the State is active, conscious and official expression. . . . The principle of politics is the will. The more partial, and the more perfected, political thought becomes, the more it believes in the omnipotence of the will, the less able it is to see the *natural* and mental *limitations* on the will, the less capable it is of discovering social evils" (p. 215; emphasis in original).

Sources: Bentham (1948[1789]); Lombroso (1968[1911]); Marx (1956).

Equally important to the theoretical enterprise is the contextualization of theory. That is, we must consider each theory in terms of the time in which it was created or first proposed, and the forms and types of supporting evidence provided. It is also important to consider the role of the government as an advocate, opponent, or neutral party in response to the theory and its implications for social policy. This activity becomes a history lesson at times, as we consider theories that emerged over the last three centuries. Unless we clearly understand the social, historical, and political context out of which a theory emerged, it is not possible to appreciate fully that theory's relevance—past or present—to the study of crime.

The discussion of each theoretical orientation begins with a series of questions related to the theory. We suggest that you review and seriously consider every one of them. They are not rhetorical questions, asked simply as a means of amplifying an obvious point. Embedded within these questions are sample assumptions, propositions (and hypotheses), or concepts (and variables) that provide the gist of each theory. We purposely grounded the questions (and a few statements) in nontheoretical, real-world terms as a means of providing a connection between theory and reality. Spending a few minutes considering these questions will make it easier to understand the elements of the various theories.

Assessing Theories

Theories are intrinsically neither good nor bad. Such value judgments simply do not apply to theories. Yet we often talk about "good theories," as opposed to "bad theories," meaning that a theory (1) is readily understood and makes sense (i.e., has logical merit); (2) stands up well under empirical scrutiny, whether it is qualitatively or quantitatively; and (3) generally achieves some (or all) of the goals of theory (i.e., describes, predicts, explains, or controls the phenomena under study). Having said this, however, you will not find the phrases "this is a good theory" or "this is a bad theory" in this text. The purpose is, rather, to review the evidence and let the theory rise or fall, without specific comment, based on the evidence.

Some theories that make sense, are logically consistent, and have powerful implications for criminal justice practice, such as labeling theory and anomie theory (see Chapter 8), have not faired well when subjected to empirical verification. Does this mean that they are "bad" or weak theories? Hardly. What it may mean is that adequate tests have yet to be constructed or that the operationalization of key concepts is incomplete. As a case in point, consider the fate of social disorganization theory, a macro-sociological explanation (see Chapter 6). Shortly after it was applied to urban blight and crime in the 1920s and 1930s, criminologists abandoned it as suffering from an intrinsic and fatal error: The cause could not be separated from the effect. In the late 1980s, however, this same theory, with a few refinements, better data, and far more sophisticated analytic procedures, enjoyed an explanatory renaissance.

In each of the chapters that follow, we provide two sections on theory assessment. First, after reviewing the assumptions and assertions of each theory, we provide an overall assessment of the evidence. The purpose of this is to summarize the key critical themes, the strengths and shortcomings, and the general tenor of the evolving body of theory-specific research. Second, at the end of each chapter, we provide a table summarizing the following information about every theory in the chapter: its name or names, its major proponents (and critics), its central assumptions, its causal arguments (and key terms), and its strengths and weaknesses.

The process of assessing is often viewed in terms of judging, measuring, or evaluating the worth of something. Here we provide (1) the theory's truth claims—what the theory's proponents say it intends to describe, explain, predict, or control—and (2) the body of evidence supporting those claims. Thus, assessing theories in the present context is more of an ongoing, up-to-date appraisal than a final judgment. This goal is in keeping with the spirit of the theoretical enterprise.

Criminal Justice Policies and Procedures

The discussion of each theory concludes with a section on criminal justice policies and procedures. Certain theories are ripe with implications for the criminal justice system. In some cases laws have been formulated in response to crime theories; in others, legislative responses mimic the theories but have no direct connection. Crime theories also help us understand law enforcement, judicial, and correctional agencies; indeed, the actions, both law-violating and law-abiding, of individuals within these entities sometimes can be understood in terms of crime theory. Some theories have few direct implications for criminal justice policies or

Table 1.1 Organizing Crime Theories

Chapter Number and Title	Theories Explored
2. Deterrence and Opportunity Theories	Formal and informal deterrence; rational choice; routine activities; opportunity
3. Biological and Biochemical Theories	Physiognomy; phrenology; criminal anthropology; body types; genetic factors hypotheses; karotype studies; biochemical imbalance hypotheses
4. Psychological Abnormality Theories	Psychoanalytic theories; deviant personality theory; psychopathy hypothesis
5. Psychological Learning and Developmental Theories	Feeblemindedness; IQ–crime hypothesis; behaviorism; constitutional learning; developmental theories
6. Social Organizational Theories	Social disorganization; anomie and strain; subcultural
7. Social Process Theories	Differential association; social learning; social control; social bond; self-control; control balance
8. Labeling and Conflict Theories	Labeling; culture conflict; group conflict
9. Marxist and Feminist Theories	Instrumental and structural Marxism; left realism and peacemaking criminology; liberal, radical, socialist, and Marxist feminist theory

procedures but allow for a better general understanding of why the system responds as it does to certain threats to the social order.

Organizing Crime Theories

The chapters in this text examine literally dozens of theories. How, you might ask, did we arrive at the organizational schema we employed? In point of fact, there are nearly as many ways of representing theories as there are criminology textbooks. Earlier we observed that modern criminology owes much to three main themes (or paradigms): classicalism, positivism, and conflict. The eight substantive chapters, which explore the various theories, owe much to these distinctions, as we make clear in discussions of modern versions of each one.

Table 1.1 contains a summary of the contents of Chapters 2–9, including the specific theories described and assessed in each chapter. We hope that you enjoy the journey as much as we enjoyed preparing the itinerary.

SUMMARY

You now possess the basic definitions and philosophical orientations we employ in subsequent chapters, along with the organizational structure and rationale for reviewing a wide array of theories, all intended to generate a better understanding of crime. In addition, this chapter contains three important lessons. First, we must not lose sight of the fact that crime theories are developed, tested, and rejected or accepted in a sociopolitical context. Our understanding of a specific crime theory is often enhanced by a knowledge of its implicit, and sometimes explicit, social and political implications. Second, crime theory is inextricably linked to crime research, which is essential either to test or to build theories. Studying theories without reviewing the related research (or data) is, with all due respect to Sherlock Holmes, akin to making bricks without straw. Third, if we are to gain a full sense of the links between crime theory and research, we must also clearly delineate the ties of each to crime policy and "crime fighting" practices. The theories presented in subsequent chapters are valuable solely for the contributions they make to our understanding of human social behavior. However, in the minds of some criminologists and criminal justice practitioners, crime theories should also contribute to the control of crime. In subsequent chapters we return to these lessons and explore how the various crime theories relate to each.

As important as the lessons are, the philosophy that underlies how members of society see crimes and criminals is equally important. Classicalism and positivism are not merely terms generated by ivory-tower academics in the distant past, the musings of individuals long dead. Rather, they continue to shape how society views—and responds to—crime and criminals in the new century.

KEY TERMS

alienation

analysis

bourgeoisie

capitalists

causation

celerity

certainty

concepts

conceptualization

conflict

consensus

correlation

criminology

customary laws

deductive research

demoralization

determinism

deterrence

empirical generalization

empirical observations

enacted laws

false consciousness

felonies

findings

folkways

free will

hypotheses

ideologies

inductive research

laws

lumpenproletariat

mala in se

mala prohibita

misdemeanors

mores

mos

natural law

nature

norms

nurture

operationalization

ordinances

petite bourgeoisie

pluralist

positivism

proletariat

propositions

qualitative data

quantitative data

research design

severity

spuriousness

tautology

theologies

theory

variables

CRITICAL REVIEW QUESTIONS

1. What are the elements that constitute law? How are laws that compel conduct distinguished from laws that facilitate voluntary actions?

2. Why is it so difficult to define crime?

3. What are the elements of a theory?

4. How is correlation distinguished from causation?

5. What is a tautology?

6. Why is theory testing in the natural sciences easier than in the social sciences?

7. How do the consensus, pluralist, and conflict views of society differ?

8. What are the elements that constitute classical theory?

9. Why might it be comforting to believe in theories that explain crime according to qualities inherent in the individual criminal actor?

10. What are the elements comprised in neoclassical theory?

11. What is natural law? How does the concept of natural law limit the government's power?

12. What aspects of classical theory are found in the U.S. system of law and justice?

13. How did the approach of the classical school support the interests of a rising eighteenth-century middle class?

14. How does neoclassicalism differ from classicalism?

15. What is meant by positivism? How does it differ from classicalism?

NOTES

1. Not all variables are created equal. They exist on several different levels. Although the details are unimportant in the present context, they are very important to statisticians. Suffice it to say that some variables, like gender, are nominal in nature and reflect only an observable characteristic. Ordinal variables are ranked and reflect more or less of the item under study. For example, crimes may be ranked from very serious, such as Index Crimes (e.g., murder, manslaughter, rape, robbery, assault, auto theft, and arson), to less serious, such as non-Index Crimes (e.g., literally all other crime reported in the FBI's Uniform Crime Reports). With interval variables the differences between values are equal. For example, an army private in basic training is classified as an E-1 while a three-stripe sergeant is an E-5; the sergeant is four ranks, or intervals, above the private. Finally, ratio-level variables have all of the previous qualities and one more: There is an absolute absence of the variable under study, or a real zero value. Money is a good ratio-level variable. You may have one dollar; your friend, who won the lottery, may have a million dollars; and your sister may have no money.

2. For some philosophers of science and theoreticians, the distinction between a proposition and a hypothesis is as important as how the term *fruit* is different from *apple:* In each case the former is more abstract and generalizable than the latter. For our purposes we will distinguish between them only insofar as a given theorist may provide general propositions for the theory in question or testable hypotheses.

3. The following discussion is taken largely from Wallace (1971) and the use of his "Wheel of Science" by others (Babbie 1975; Hagan 1999).

4. Statisticians employ a variety of measures of association, often related to the type of information being analyzed. For example, we might be interested in knowing how often members of certain groups are arrested (i.e., is gender or race related to arrest rates?); however, the strength of this relationship

would be difficult to estimate because group memberships are nominal-level data and arrest rates are ratio-level data. These statistical requirements and limitations aside, researchers, including those testing and building theories, prefer statistics that range from zero (no association) to 1 (maximum association) with the sign (plus or negative) indicating the direction of the relationship, where appropriate. They summarize these associations using terms like "very strong," "moderately strong," "moderate," "weak" and "very weak," among others.

5. Following the detonations of the atomic bombs in World War II (and perhaps even before these monumental events), physical scientists, including the mathematicians and physicists who worked on the Manhattan Project that created the nation's first nuclear weapons, debated whether they had the moral obligation to question how their work was to be used or whether they should even get involved in such activities in the first place.

6. A typology is a systematic method of classifying information according to clearly specified rules; it allows for the collapsing of information into more manageable and logical clusters or groups.

2

Deterrence and Opportunity Theories

CHAPTER OVERVIEW

LEARNING OBJECTIVES

- Appreciate the ties between classic deterrence theory and modern versions.
- Understand that for some people crime is but one of many choices and, given a particular set of circumstances, a reasoned and reasonable choice.

- Recognize the routine nature of some offending and the role of opportunity in defining its routineness.
- Distinguish between formal and informal deterrence, and speculate about which approach holds more promise for controlling human behavior, including crime.

INTRODUCTION

Nearly every organized religion describes the fate of those who fail to follow the rules laid down by the supreme being or godhead. Ancient laws such as the *lex talionis* not only are prescriptive and proscriptive, telling people what they must and must not do, but also describe the sanctions that befall those who stray from the righteous path. Historical and archeological evidence of such rules—and often graphic accounts of accompanying punishments—suggests a longstanding belief in their power to promote compliance.

As discussed in Chapter 1, Cesare Beccaria, the eighteenth-century Italian social critic, provided one of the first philosophical treatises on the ties between formal sanctions—those flowing from governments and enforced by their social control agents—and compliant behavior. Criminological interest in the deterrent power of formal sanctions diminished 100 years ago as positivists searched for the causes of crime in other venues. Rediscovered in the 1960s, deterrence has become, in one form or another, a mainstay of criminological research, especially that funded by state and federal governments.

Over the last two decades of the twentieth century, criminologists looked at two deterrence-related processes. Many criminologists consider the first perspective, rational choice, to be a restatement of deterrence theory because it suggests that some people have already decided what laws they will break, given a certain set of circumstances and rationalizations. As with deterrence the goal is to make the choice to commit crime as unpleasant in its consequences as possible. A second perspective, routine activities, views crime as a part of life. The supply of criminals and victims is constant. More importantly, we are constantly bombarded with clues about where and when crime is likely to occur—clues available to potential criminals and victims and to social control agents. The central idea is to reduce or eliminate the opportunity to offend.

The deterrent effects of informal sanctions appeal to contemporary criminologists, partly due to rediscovered penal philosophies employed by societies lacking formal justice systems. Laws do not control people. Rather, the most powerful social controls are informal sanctions—including exclusion, derision, humor, humiliation, and shaming—enforced by relatives, friends, and neighbors. Recent conceptualizations also recognize the power of informal processes not only to exclude norm violators but also to reintegrate them into the social group after instances of norm breaking.

The theories in this chapter explore the choices people make. All assume some level of volition or the exercise of free will, and all have deep roots in Western history and culture. These theories explore the mechanisms that shape and influence individual choices either to engage in normative behavior or to violate rules, norms, and laws. We begin with a theory that has proved to have great longevity, formal deterrence theory.

FORMAL DETERRENCE THEORY

- Have you every wondered why people commit illegal acts even when they know the specified punishments, perhaps from prior experience or from knowledge of what happened to friends who committed the same crime?

- Certainty—celerity—severity: Which single element in formal deterrence theory do you think is most instrumental in achieving it goals? Is it as simple as identifying one as most instrumental, or is the issue more complex?

- What about people who know someone who commits a crime and gets away with it? What does this situation have to do with deterrence? Is it a reflection of the failure of deterrence, the failure of the criminal justice system, or something else?

Cesare Beccaria saw the choices between good and evil as simple and straightforward (see Chapter 1). Several assumptions about humankind led him to this conclusion.[1] First, he saw all *men* as possessing free will; that is, they could choose to act or not to act of their own volition.[2] Second, he believed that humans were capable of rational thought; they had the power to weigh alternative courses of action and, depending on which one was most advantageous, select it from among the available choices. Third, he viewed humans as virtual slaves to their own basest desires, as mankind was hedonistic by nature, preferring pleasure to pain. The concept of **hedonism** leads to his fourth and most critical assumption: A system of just punishments, based on the principles of certainty, celerity, and severity, was needed to control people's conduct, cloaking humanity's hedonistic proclivities under a shroud of deterrence.

Classicalism led to a revolution in criminal justice. The injustices of late eighteenth-century European laws and penal practices motivated Beccaria to write his famous tract on crimes and punishments, *Dei delitti e delle pene* (*On Crimes and Punishments*), in 1764. Laws were different for people based on their station in life, and members of the nobility were often exempted from criminal responsibility. But it was the behavior of judges that most enraged Beccaria, and it was for them that he reserved his harshest criticism. Judges of his day frequently gave very different punishments for identical offenses, practicing an extreme form of individualized justice. Moreover, most punishments accorded offenders at the time were harsh by any standards and at times barbaric.

The 26-year-old Beccaria made a series of recommendations for the administration of justice throughout Europe. He believed that legislatures should define the crimes and associated punishments, and that the public should be informed of the crimes and associated punishments, thereby eliminating secret accusations and torture. Punishments should equal the threat of the crime to society—no more, no less—as **proportionality** was essential for deterrence to work. Beccaria saw punishments that exceeded proportionality as tyrannical and evil, and as undermining the purposes of deterrence.[3] With the enactment of just laws, the judge's role would be the determination of guilt or innocence. Given a finding of guilt, the judge would simply consult the law and pronounce the sentence, thereby reducing or, as was Beccaria's hope, eliminating judicial discretion. Finally he proposed that imprisonment replace capital punishment and that living conditions in jails and prisons be made more humane. Beccaria (1963[1764]:99) summarized these ideas as follows: "In order for punishment not to be, in every instance, an act of violence of one or of many against a private citizen, it must be essentially public, prompt, necessary, the least possible given the circumstances, proportionate to the crimes, dictated by laws."

Deterrence is the cornerstone of the contemporary criminal justice system's response to criminals, a philosophy that, but for a few brief experiments with less punitive alternatives, has continued unabated for more than 200 years. Beccaria's book, translated into French and English, impacted even the royal houses of Europe, which rushed to embrace the classical approach to crime and justice. Catherine the Great of Russia requested Beccaria's presence at her court to assist with judicial reforms (Beccaria 1963[1764]), and the French Legal Code of 1791 was based in part on classical philosophy.

Criminologists' interest in deterrence theory waned in the last quarter of the nineteenth century. The influential writings of Charles Darwin, Herbert Spencer, and Cesare Lombroso, whose contributions we explore in the next chapter, led to a positivistic revolution in explanations of human behavior. Criminologists shifted from the study of laws and punishments to the study of criminals, both in society and in its prisons, a locus they largely maintained until the 1960s. For 100 years criminologists took one path, and policy makers followed an entirely different one.

The 1960s brought about many changes in American society, ranging from desegregation to near political anarchy. In those tumultuous times two social scientists shifted criminologists' attention back to deterrence theory. In 1968, Jack Gibbs published "Crime, Punishment, and Deterrence," in which he attempted to test the deterrence hypothesis. This was the beginning of **perceptual deterrence** studies. Also in 1968 economist and 1992 Nobel Prize winner Gary S. Becker published "Crime and Punishment: An Economic Approach," a work that generated great interest in a perspective called **cost–benefit analysis.** With the publication of these two works, deterrence theory was once more on the agenda of criminologists. One irony in this rediscovery of deterrence is that positivistic criminologists began applying the scientific method in an attempt to reveal punishments' deterrent effects.

Defining Deterrence

Beccaria's ideas about deterrence were simple and straightforward. Beginning in the 1960s a series of works reviewing past deterrence research and suggesting new avenues of exploration provided new insights into the mechanisms of deterrence (Gibbs 1975; Zimring and Hawkins 1973). For example, **general deterrence** reflects the idea that persons watching, hearing about, or otherwise becoming aware of a sanctioning process will view the outcomes as too costly and not engage in the punished conduct. This idea is reflected in the saying "There but for the grace of God go I." In "olden times," when punishments were carried out in public and most offenses resulted in either corporal punishment or the death penalty (or in some cases both), being present was thought to have an ameliorative impact on potential offenders, including those who had committed previous offenses but had

IN THEIR OWN WORDS: Bentham on Moral Calculus

Jeremy Bentham's *An Introduction to the Principles of Morals and Legislation* helped spread the classical ideas. Bentham and Beccaria were utilitarians, meaning they held that the rightness or wrongness of an act is determined by the goodness or badness of its consequences. Bentham wrote the following about calculating good and evil:

> Sum up all the values of all the *pleasures* on the one side, and those of all the *pains* on the other. The balance, if it be on the side of pleasure will give the *good* tendency of the act upon the whole, with respect to the interests of that *individual* person; if on the side of pain, the *bad* tendency of it upon the whole.
>
> Take an account of the *number* of persons whose interests appear to be concerned; and repeat the above process with respect to each. *Sum up* the numbers expressive of the de-

gree of good tendency, which the act has, with respect to each individual, in regard to whom the tendency of it is *good* upon the whole: do this again with respect to each individual, in regard to whom the tendency of it is *bad* upon the whole. Take the *balance;* which, if on the side of *pleasure,* will give the general *good tendency* of the act, with respect to the total number or community of individuals concerned; if on the side of *pain,* the general *evil tendency,* with respect to the same community.

A generation later, the English philosopher Herbert Spencer, famous for his phrase "survival of the fittest," developed a form of utilitarian ethics based on evolutionary change (see Chapter 3).

Source: Bentham (1948[1789]:32; emphasis in original).

not been caught and those contemplating them. In fact, public executions often included the accused person's recitation of the sins that had led them to the gallows (or other place of execution). They were often assisted in this task by a minister, preacher, or priest who facilitated the confession.

Specific (or **individual**) **deterrence,** the second major form, is intended chiefly for persons who have been caught, convicted, and punished. The intent of imprisonment or, prior to the mid-twentieth century, corporal punishment, was to encourage offenders to change their life paths to noncriminal ones. Otherwise, they would suffer increasingly harsh sanctioning at the hands of the court for their misdeeds.

Social scientists added two other concepts to the mix: absolute and restrictive deterrence. **Absolute deterrence** suggests that, once individuals come to see either the error of their ways or the potential losses they face, they will refrain from all crime, great or small, related or unrelated to the specific offenses contemplated. Just as importantly, those who have never been caught in a criminal act, as well as those who have been caught and punished, may exhibit the effects of absolute deterrence. For example, suppose a young man spends 10 years, from age 18 to 28, in federal prison for dealing crack. At the time of his mandatory release, thanks to the federal prison industries program, he knows how to build furniture. He subsequently secures a good-paying job and leaves behind his life as a drug dealer. Meanwhile, a 16-year-old friend back in the neighborhood, who was also contemplating a career as a drug dealer, hears about the 10-year sentence and decides to return to high school, where he gets his degree, and then goes on to college. The same day his old friend is released from federal prison, the wannabe drug dealer assumes a position as a criminal justice professor at the local community college. In both cases absolute deterrence is at work.

The second concept is **restrictive deterrence,** whereby offenders may refrain from the act that previously landed them in trouble or that threatens trouble, but modify their criminal conduct rather than abandon it. For example, suppose our hypothetical 18-year-old drug dealer decides, upon release from prison, to stop selling crack, because the police are targeting that particular drug, and embarks on a new career as a medical marijuana wholesaler. He has not entirely given up his life of crime, but he has modified it as a result of being punished, in an attempt to reduce his risks to more manageable levels. Meanwhile our hypothetical 16-year-old wannabe drug dealer pursues his education, but when he joins the faculty at the community college, he starts wholesaling "sex drugs" to the selected nonstudent dealers, who then saturate a neighboring college campus with the drug. Again, behavioral adjustments are chosen over abandonment.

Another modification to the deterrence model was offered by Mark Stafford and Mark Warr (1993); Figure 2.1 depicts this model. Stafford and Warr observed that previous conceptualizations were flawed, in that they failed to take into account people who "got away" with crime. That is, each time someone escapes notice or punishment, what is the implication in terms of that law's ability to deter? Warr and Stafford suggested several possible answers. First, people who commit crimes and escape apprehension (or conviction), thereby having personal experience with attempts to deter them, may view this as license to commit more crimes. Second, individuals who know of others who similarly escaped paying for their crimes may be disposed to engage in crime because they see no downside to criminal activity. Third, individuals with personal or vicarious experience with a sanctioning process that was more effective and efficient should be deterred.

Deterrence conceptualizing in the 1960s and 1970s benefited from the collective work of Jack Gibbs, Richard Hawkins, Franklin Zimring, and Stafford and Warr, among others (cf. Geerken and Gove 1975; Meier and Johnson 1977; Nagin 1978; Silberman 1976; Tittle and Rowe 1974). They demonstrated that, if there was a deterrent effect to sanctioning, it was not the simple process envisioned by Beccaria. The power of simple messages from formal sanctioning authorities is largely a myth. As Raymond Paternoster and Ronet Bachman (2001:16) observed about the complex processes at work whenever sanctions are threatened or applied, "It is not difficult to see that the deterrence message may get mixed because often our personal and vicarious experiences are at odds." Present-day deterrence conceptualizing, then, little resembles the moral calculus of Bentham or Beccaria. Whether the world has become more complex or they were simply optimistic about the power of a fair and just state to deter crime is beyond testing. Contemporary researchers have added to the debate, one that is far from resolved.

Assessing Formal Deterrence

Recent deterrence studies have focused on punishments' certainty and severity effects (Blumstein, Cohen, and Nagin 1978; Gibbs 1975; Tittle 1969). Researchers have evaluated the links between what people think about the certainty and

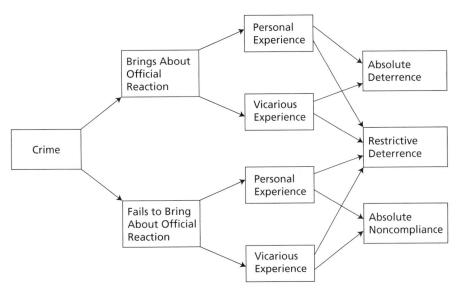

FIGURE 2.1 Complexities of Perceptual Deterrence

severity of punishments and their subsequent self-reported criminal behavior and deviance (Paternoster 1987; Waldo and Chiricos 1972). However, in his review of perceptual deterrence studies, Paternoster (1987) found that the theory did not fit the data, largely because of poor research designs. The operationalizations of punishments' certainty or severity effects were inadequate.

Julie Horney and Ineke Marshall (1992), in a study of the experiential interpretation of sanctions by a sample of prison inmates, addressed this last issue. High involvement in crime should lead to perceptions of low certainty of punishment only in situations in which the offenders go unpunished for their criminal acts. The researchers found that, consistent with deterrence theory, active offenders, or those who reported any involvement in a given crime, formulated their perceptions of punishment probabilities based on their past experiences with legal sanctions.

As a rule perceptual deterrence studies yield mixed results. Perceptions of severity of punishment tend to be unrelated to offending, whereas perceptions of certainty do exhibit such a relationship. But how this happens, and why severity and certainty function differently, is unclear.

Sociologists also have examined the actual application of sanctions and subsequent objective criminality measures (Gibbs 1975). Although some researchers have found that capital punishment has a general deterrent effect on homicide rates, contradictory evidence is equally impressive (cf. Bailey and Peterson 1989; Stack 1987). Deterrence arguments have also been applied to "lesser" offenses, including drunk driving, but again the findings are inconclusive (cf. Ross, 1982; Votey 1984). As with perceptual deterrence, objective punishment studies tend to support a certainty effect, but not a severity one (Liska and Messner 1999:98).

Several thematic questions reappear in assessments of deterrence, including these:

- *Is it a theory or a hypothesis?* Deterrence is often called a hypothesis, meaning that it is a testable idea but lacks fully developed theoretical arguments—mainly propositions—about its putative operation and effects (Tittle and Rowe 1974). As Matthew Silberman (1976:442) noted, classical deterrence employs strongly stated arguments steeped in untested assumptions about human nature and philosophical treatises on the use of punishments to secure normative conduct. This is hardly the level of conceptual thinking that leads to empirical verification.

- *Whether theory or hypothesis, can deterrence stand on its own, or must it be tied to other theories?* Modern tests of deterrence include variables never envisioned by Beccaria or Bentham, including opportunity structures discussed later in this chapter. Deterrence theory is often integrated with other ideas about human beings, such as Chapter 3's genetic arguments, Chapter 4's notions of psychopathic personality disorders, and Chapter 5's IQ–crime links. That is, owing to various biological or psychological anomalies, certain people are undeterred by penal sanctions. Larry Sherman and associates (1992), in an attempt to explain the variable deterrent effects of arresting spousal abusers (see Chapter 10), joined deterrence and labeling theory (see Chapter 8) to control theory (see Chapter 7). Theory integrations such as these reinforce the observation that deterrence is a hypothesis with limited utility to explain behavioral choices.

- *Is the theory's conceptual base too narrow?* Classic deterrence theory addressed compliance flowing from formal sanctions. This narrow view of human behavior is perhaps the theory's biggest weakness. As Bob Roshier (1989:16; emphasis in original) argued, "In general, the classical perspective contains a peculiarly narrow view of what it actually is that controls human behavior. . . . There was no consideration at all given to the possibility of disincentives operating in the informal social context, and a total neglect of social and economic *incentives* of all kinds." Robert Meier and Weldon Johnson (1977) examined legal *and* extralegal production of conformity. However, their test included social support mechanisms that accounted for more conformity than the legal factors, an observation that reinforces previous concerns about the utility of the deterrence hypothesis alone.

- *What does deterrence tell us about irrational behavior?* If deterrence theory can explain choices made by reasoning people and is predicated on the assumption that they must be rational, then all crime that is irrational or senseless is beyond the theory's scope. What about spontaneous crimes or accidental crimes? At the core of this question is the idea of moral or rational calculus. That is, for any number of reasons, not everyone possesses the same skills in risk assessment or in reasoning ability. Just as senseless and spontaneous behavior is beyond the theory's scope, so is the conduct of the mentally challenged or mentally ill.

Deterrence research continues in spite of lackluster support (Nagin 1998). For example, punishment's certainty may exhibit a correlation with the frequency of criminal behavior, but that correlation is relatively low (D'Alessio and Stolzenberg 1998). Punishment's severity has even less support. Several researchers suggest that, although the death penalty may serve as a deterrent for some types of homicide, executions may actually cause the homicide rate to rise. They report increased stranger homicides following executions, suggesting that the exercise of capital punishment may incite murders (cf. Bailey 1998; Cochran, Chamlin, and Seth 1994). The **deterrence/brutalization thesis** is interesting given Beccaria's opposition to the death penalty.

Formal Deterrence, Public Policy, and Criminal Justice Practices

The deterrence model has dominated U.S. criminal justice policies for most of the nation's history. From the time of the nation's founding to World War II, deterrence defined criminal justice policies and practices. From 1945 to 1975, however, various jurisdictions experimented with rehabilitation and treatment models, which differed considerably from the deterrence approach. According to these philosophies and practices, humans are malleable and redeemable. Psychology and social psychology provide the theoretical and practical rationale for most treatment modalities, ideas explored in later chapters. But by the mid-1970s faith in rehabilitation was shaken (cf. Cullen and Gilbert 1982; Farabee 2002; Lipton, Martinson, and Wilks 1975; Martinson 1974, 1979), and, as importantly, new, far more punitive philosophical positions on offenders emerged, including just deserts and retributive justice (Fogel 1975; van den Haag 1975; von Hirsch 1976).[4] Law violators deserved harsh punishments, irrespective of whether those punishments deterred them or others. Society demanded and deserved the sanctioning of those who posed threats to the safety and security of its citizens.

Deterrence coexisted with rehabilitation and continued to provide a legitimate rationale for punishment in the 1980s and 1990s and into the new century. Merged with an old idea, *lex talionis* or just deserts, deterrence resumed its age-old position at the pinnacle of penal philosophies: Deter criminals, and if you cannot deter them, then give them the punishment they deserve. The idea that fear of punishment and respect for the law deter most people is popular with the public, politicians, and other policy makers. Deterrence, then, provides the primary justification for the nation's "get tough" crime policy, initiated in the mid-1970s and continuing to the present (Hagan 1995).

Police Practices Many police practices have roots in deterrence theory (Gay, Schell, and Schack 1977). Consider, for example, the practice of placing police cars, sometimes with lights flashing, in high-visibility locations on highways as a way of slowing traffic. The intent is not to catch speeders, but to remind them about the certainty of apprehension. The same goal is evident when police public information officers inform local radio and television stations about DUI checkpoints or random stops on local streets and highways. The public policy of funding more police and placing them on the streets (e.g., "100,000 more police") is also intended both to increase the actual certainty of arrest and to raise perceptions of certainty.

From cruising by local parks, recreational centers, and school grounds to stopping and questioning "suspicious persons," nearly all police patrol practices serve a deterrent function. Other police investigative and intervention practices, including arresting the aggressor in misdemeanor domestic violence cases, are also based on deterrence theory (Sherman and Berk 1984a,b). In summary many police activities—and many police officers—are heavily invested in the assumptions and operating principles of deterrence theory.

Judicial Practices In rendering their decisions, judges and juries provide both the public and the accused with lessons about what is right and wrong, and about what happens to those who violate the law. Thus the judiciary functions much as Beccaria hoped it would—as an open and unfettered disseminator of information about crime and punishment. Since the mid-1980s the courts have increasingly resembled Beccaria's "ideal courts" in another way: a diminished ability to exercise sentencing discretion.

For most of the twentieth century, two types of sentences dominated in U.S. courts. The first, **indeterminate sentencing,** derived from the positivistic belief that people could change, an idea fully captured by the **medical model:** Crime is an illness, and what is needed is the right treatment to cure the offender (Abadinsky and Winfree 1992:441). With indeterminate sentences an underlying assumption was that the correctional system was best situated to assess when the offender was sufficiently changed. Thus the department of corrections, prison system, or parole board determined the actual time served by offenders. An alternative was **determinate sentencing,** which has three main forms: (1) narrow discretion, whereby all felonies of a certain type result in the same sentence; (2) wide discretion, whereby judges can sentence an offender to a specific term within a relatively wide range of possibilities, (e.g., 5–10 years); and (3) presumptive sentencing, whereby a narrow sentence range is provided for a given crime, from which the judge may not deviate unless there are aggravating circumstances (i.e., compelling reasons to increase the sentence) or mitigating circumstance (i.e., compelling reasons to reduce the sentence).

Since the 1970s mandatory sentencing has further decreased judicial discretion. **Mandatory sentencing** defines punishments for certain crimes (usually violent and drug offenses), meaning convicted offenders may not be placed on probation and must serve a specific sentence prior to release on parole, if parole is an option. By the late 1990s "three-strikes" sentencing laws (see Chapter 1) had been adopted by 24 states and the federal government, and were being considered by every other jurisdiction in the United States, earning the strategy the label of "politicized crime control policy" (Benekos and Merlo 1995). The net result is that courts in the United States at the start of the twenty-first century closely resemble Beccaria's eighteenth-century vision of the ideal court.

Correctional Practices One could argue that the entire correctional system serves at least a specific deterrent function, if not a general deterrent one. Two well-known practices owe their existence to deterrence theory. The first have been called "scared straight" programs, the practice of exposing young, and presumably impressionable, adolescents to the "horrors" of crime, usually by putting them in a room with prison inmates. One of the first systematic programs of this nature operated at New Jersey's Rahway Prison and was the subject of a 1978 documentary film, *Scared Straight,* and an evaluation. The film gave the impression that the program was highly successful. However, evaluators of New Jersey's Juvenile Awareness Program found two things: (1) Most participants were low-risk, middle-class children, and (2) those youths who participated in the program later committed four times the number of offenses as members of a control group who had no exposure to prison inmates (Finckenauer 1982). Programs in other states similar to that at Rahway Prison also failed to show a deterrent effect (Jensen and Rojek 1998).

Boot camp or **shock incarceration** is a second popular program heavily indebted to deterrence theory for its theoretical underpinnings. Boot camp is often a sentence accorded first-time felony offenders, who are sent to a special prison and subjected to three to six months of military-style basic training. In some jurisdictions educational, vocational, and treatment programs supplement basic training. Following successful participation in the program, "graduates" return to the community under some form of enhanced supervision. The actual mechanisms vary across the nation; some jurisdictions use probation (i.e., conditional release from the sentencing court, which is part of the judicial branch), and others prefer parole (i.e., conditional release from the correctional system, which is part of the executive branch). In practice the conditional release often translates into intensive supervision, with several contacts per month between the probationer/parolee and the supervising agent.

Do boot camps deter youthful offenders? The evidence suggests that they do not (cf. MacKenzie 1993; MacKenzie, Gover, Armstrong, and Mitchell 2001; MacKenzie, Shaw, and Gowdy 1993; Peters, Thomas, and Zamberlan 1997). Youthful participants may exhibit some prosocial attitudes and orientations as a result of participating, but it does not appear that boot camps achieve their primary goal: deterring future offending.

RATIONAL CHOICE THEORY

- Juan cannot find a job. His wife is pregnant and has special dietary needs. They have tried to get help from local and state social service agencies, but as newcomers to the city, they have experienced difficulty obtaining the needed documentation. Juan's command of English is poor, and he cannot read or write in any language, so he often simply leaves the social services office in embarrassment. Upon entering a grocery store, he puts what his family needs in a basket and runs out the door with it. What might Juan have been thinking before he committed this crime?

- Much crime appears spontaneous, committed without prior thought or preparation. These crimes are often predatory in nature, with offenders taking advantage of someone weaker or otherwise ill-prepared to fend them off. Do you believe that criminals give the idea of committing a crime much thought prior to actually doing so?

Economists, who view crime as they do any decision that has associated costs and benefits, provide another perspective. If someone analyzes the costs and benefits associated with purchasing any household item, goes the logic, then he or she will perform similar cost–benefit analyses prior to committing crime (Becker 1968; Sullivan 1973). For example, Isaac Ehrlich (1975) applied cost–benefit analysis to the death penalty. His conclusion: Executing one person saves seven to eight other lives (Ehrlich 1975); however, flaws in Ehrlich's data largely discredit this finding (Forst 1983; Klein, Forst and Filatov 1978). Critics point to the Ehrlich study as an example of manipulating data to prove a specific point (Klein et al. 1978).

For his part Gary Becker provided the groundwork for a new crime theory by suggesting that decisions to commit crimes involve the same decision-making processes as in buying, for example, a car. Even absent all needed information about possible outcomes (e.g., the roadworthiness of the car or its repair history), people make decisions based on an **expected utility principle.** They glean information about cars (or crimes), store it in memory, and use it to analyze a given decision (e.g., buy the car or commit an illegal act). The rationality they employ may be imperfect, but it is framed by the information they possess, recall, and act upon in a given situation at a given time. They may make imperfect decisions (e.g., buy a bad car or get caught committing a crime), say economists, but it is the best decision at the time.

Criminology has seen a rebirth in classical deterrence themes since the late 1970s, couched—thanks to Becker's simple and elegant suggestion that criminologists consider "the economist's usual analysis of choice" (1968:170) and Ehrlich's cost–benefit analysis of the death penalty—in the language of economics. These new-generation deterrence theories, called the **Neuve Classical School** by Raymond Paternoster and Ronet Bachman (2001:19), were manifested in two primary forms: rational choice theory and routine activities theory.

Fundamentals of Choice and Choice Structuring

In *The Reasoning Criminal* Derek Cornish and Ronald Clarke (1986:1) observed (1) that offenders seek to benefit themselves by their criminal behavior; (2) that this involves the making of decisions and choices, however rudimentary these processes might be; and (3) that these processes exhibit a measure of *rationality,* albeit constrained by limits of times and ability and the availability of relevant information. Apparently Cornish and Clark accepted the economists' idea of cost–benefit and the classical/deterrence theorists' idea of free will, forming rational choice theory. This theory is a restatement of Becker's expected utility principle, framed in terms of a crime decision process. There are also psychological forces at work in the exercise of these rational choices. Indeed, Cornish and Clarke included such background factors as intelligence, temperament, and cognitive style in their explanatory schema.

Given Cornish and Clarke's emphasis on criminal acts as sources of possible rewards or punishments, you might think that this is a theory of property crime only. But nothing could be further from the intent of rational choice theory. Even violent crimes with no apparent motivation are, claim the proponents, explained by this theory. That is, even crime that appears purely impulsive has rational elements. For example, graffiti artists enjoy not only the act of creating their art but also the dangers associated with it (e.g., possible contact with law enforcement, rival gang members, and other graffiti artists, or the possibility of falling off of a highway overpass onto a busy highway) and the notoriety that follows a successful act of vandalism. Nonutilitarian violence, for its part, appears to be rewarding to those who engage in such acts, perhaps due to the complete domination of the victims and the senseless (and unpredictable) nature of the act itself.

The theory *is* crime-specific, meaning that different crimes provide different offenders with varying means of meeting their respective needs. Extending this thesis to its logical conclusion, offenders actually choose specific crimes based on their own personal characteristics, needs, and skills (e.g., previous experience and learning, background, and generalized needs) and offense characteristics (e.g., proximity to a victim and likelihood and severity of punishment).

Choice Structuring In the process of **choice structuring,** individuals assess their own skills and needs in light of a specific crime's characteristics. Cornish and Clark asserted that each crime has a unique choice-structuring process associated with it. Even the crime of burglary is not a single generic crime, they claimed, as "it may be necessary to divide burglary simply into its residential and commercial forms" (Cornish and Clarke 1986:2). It may also be necessary to distinguish between burglary committed in middle-class suburbs, in public housing, and in wealthy residential enclaves. Having followed a choice-structuring process for one type of burglary does not lead automatically and inevitably to the choice to commit another type of burglary. Empirical studies suggest that the kinds of individuals committing these different forms of residential burglary, as well as their motivations and their methods, differ considerably. Figure 2.2 contains a graphic representation of this model of the choice-structuring process. The first step is the involvement decision.

Involvement Decisions The **involvement decision** is a multistage evaluation process that ends with the decision to get involved in crime. In this step a person's social, familial, demographic, and psychological background constitute the interpretive context for crime involvement decisions. That is, these background factors, along with various experiences (e.g., direct or vicarious criminal behavior, contact with police, and conscience and moral attitudes), provide the individual with the means to evaluate legitimate and illegitimate solutions for achieving generalized needs felt by everyone (e.g., money, sex, friendship, status, and excitement).

The evaluation of solutions includes an appreciation for (1) the amount of work involved (i.e., too much or just the right amount), (2) the amount and immediacy of the reward (i.e., too little reward too far in the future versus the right amount immediately), (3) the likelihood and severity of punishment (an element easily recognized from classical deterrence theory), and (4) moral costs (i.e., values tied to one's upbringing, especially family factors). Once the individual evaluates a particular illegitimate solution as acceptable, a readiness to commit the crime is said to exist. Crimes occur when individuals with such readiness or a pre-existing involvement decision react illegitimately to chance events, such as an easy opportunity, a need for cash, persuasive friends, drunkenness, or quarrelsome demeanor, among others.

Event Decisions The **event decision** is made immediately before the commission of a crime but after the involvement decision. This decision is based on information about the criminal act being considered. This step occurs quickly and without much contemplation on the offender's part. For the offender this is a rational response to chance events, a decision that is based on pre-existing inclinations and a readiness to engage in illegitimate acts.

Opportunity is an important event decision element. Without the opportunity to engage in a crime, the involvement decision is, in sports parlance, all windup and no pitch. Cornish and Clarke did not see crime, even economic crime, as well planned and carefully executed. The rationality associated with

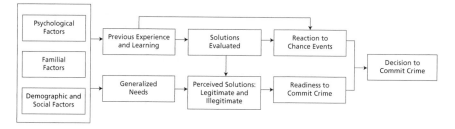

FIGURE 2.2   Cornish and Clarke's Rational Choice Theory

crime goes into the decision to get involved in crime. Certain factors—including previous punishments—constrain choices, moving the individual away from a decision to get involved in crime. After the initial decision has been made to commit a particular crime, however, the person moves quickly to its commission, given the right set of circumstances.

Assessing Rational Choice Theory

Rational choice theory is itself the source of definitional problems. First, some theorists and researchers view rational choice as an extension of the deterrence model (Akers 1990). Howard Grasmick and Robert Bursik (1990:439–42) suggested that individuals take into account three kinds of potential costs in the rational choice process: (1) state-imposed physical and material deprivation (i.e., fines and incarceration), (2) self-imposed shame, and (3) socially imposed embarrassment. Their variant of rational choice theory extends the deterrence model by including both legal and nonlegal costs associated with criminal behavior; the latter are not dependent upon imposition of the former. In their study of tax cheating, drunk driving, and petty theft, Grasmick and Bursik found support for the idea that shame has "a strong deterrent effect" but that embarrassment does not. However, their measures of rational choice were simplistic, lacking the actual multistage process described by Cornish and Clarke.

Some scholars maintain that rational choice theory traces its roots more closely to economic theory (i.e., expected utility) than to behaviorism (see Chapter 5). The economist's utilitarian view of choice is the basis of a test by Irving Piliavin and associates of deterrence and rational choice models. They summarized the model using variables such as the actor's expected utility from a contemplated activity, the likelihood of being punished for the activity, the anticipated return (material or psychological) from the activity, and the anticipated penalty if punished for the activity. "According to this statement, if for a given person, the expected utility of an illegal (legal) act is greater than the expected utility of other alternatives, the person will engage in the illegal (legal) act" (Piliavin, Gartner, Thornton, and Matsueda 1986:102).

Piliavin and his associates found support for the opportunity and reward elements of the rational choice model but failed to find support for the risk component, which included personal and formal risks. Indeed, the deterrence elements were the weakest, with choice proving to be stronger. In spite of positive findings about rational choice theory, they worried that it oversimplifies the cognitive process behind criminality: "Persons' evaluations or imputed meanings of sanctions are important in determining their behavior. These evaluations or meanings may be *conditioned* by elements within the immediate situation confronting the individual" (Piliavin et al. 1986:115; emphasis added).

A third group links rational choice and deterrence with numerous sociological and psychological variables (cf. Bachman, Paternoster, and Ward 1992; Paternoster 1989a,b). Paternoster (1989a) tested a deterrence/rational choice model of delinquent offending that, in many respects, reflected the thinking of Piliavin and his associates. Indeed, he described his model as incorporating deterrence into "a more general rational choice model of offending" (Paternoster 1989a:305). To accomplish this task, Paternoster employed a series of variables, such as attachment to family members and peer involvement in delinquency, that some critics felt were more closely linked to social learning and social bonding (see Chapter 7) than to either deterrence or rational choice theories (Akers 1994:60).

Paternoster found little support for the integration of deterrence effects and perceived risk "into a more general rational choice model of offending" (Paternoster 1989a:305). He did find support for the certainty of punishment as it pertained to the onset of delinquency (see also Paternoster 1989b). As Ronald Akers observed, "Paternoster's findings that these variables are related to delinquent behavior, therefore, tell us little about the empirical validity of rational choice theory. However, it does tell us about the validity of social learning and social bonding theories" (Akers 1994:60; see also Akers 1990:674).

About the only thing the rational choice supporters and detractors agreed upon was that, in this context, *rational* did not mean "careful thinking and sensible decisions by someone's standard" (Felson 1993:1497). Rather, rational choice proponents argued that offenders may think, but not necessarily with great care, preferring to engage in "illegal decision analysis" (Felson 1993:1497). Often offenders engage in behavior that can only be described as "irrational" (Tunnell 1990). Akers (1990:663) further noted that even Cornish and Clarke "assert a very minimal assumption of rationality, which does not seem to differ very much from the level of rationality assumed in most criminological theories." In short, there is very little agreement in the literature as to exactly what constitutes an adequate test of rational choice theory. Simply including a number of reward and sanction models does not necessarily capture the full intent of either the rational decision-making process or the economists' idea that actors behave in ways that maximize their own expected utility (Akers 1990, 1994; Heineke 1988).

Choices, Public Policy, and Criminal Justice Practices

Rational choice theory adds critical dimensions to the basic deterrence theme. First, knowledge of the possible legal and social costs is essential, just as Beccaria maintained more than 200 years ago. This translates to greater emphasis on legal education in primary and secondary schools. Second, the theory spells out the processes by which choices are made to get involved in crime and then to engage in specific crimes. In these ways rational choice theory expands our understanding of how deterrence works or does not work for some individuals.

However, one policy on the prevention of sexual offending, especially acquaintance rape, has ties to rational choice and deterrence. First, there must be "an appeal to morality by educating males that unwanted sexual intercourse under any condition is an act of violence and a morally deplorable offense," followed by the employment of the threat and imposition of formal punishment (Bachman, Paternoster, and Ward 1992:367). This strategy is based on the idea that, "in the absence of moral inhibitions, would-be offenders may still be effectively deterred by the threat of formal punishments" (Bachman, Paternoster, and Ward 1992:268).

ROUTINE ACTIVITIES/OPPORTUNITY THEORY

- Willy Sutton, a famous bank robber, was once asked why he robbed banks. Willy's reply: "That's where the money is!" What does this suggest to you about crime?

- Are there places in your city you know to avoid? Or, to the contrary, are they "dangerous places" and that is part of their attraction? (If you answered yes to the second question, you should enjoy the next chapter. You are probably a risk taker or thrill seeker, and theories about impulsivity may interest you more.) If you cannot answer this question, talk with a local police officer or sheriff's deputy. Ask them, "Are there physical addresses in your jurisdiction that you know are always going to have more than one call for service on any given night?" You are now a criminologist.

- From the 1960s through the 1980s, by some accounts, the crime rate increased dramatically. How would you react if criminologists suggested that forces such as technology, demographic trends, and women entering the workforce were partly to blame?

Routine Activities Theory

In the late 1970s criminologists began to pull several disparate theoretical ideas and empirical findings together under a conceptual umbrella that has been called both opportunity theory and routine activities theory. Armed with the findings of victimization surveys and motivated by a general interest in understanding better the fate of crime victims, Lawrence Cohen and Marcus Felson (1979) first proposed routine activities theory. They expressed the belief that both criminal motivation and the supply of potential offenders are constants: There is a never-ending supply of individuals who are ready, willing, and able to engage in **predatory crime,** that is, violent crimes against persons and crimes of theft in which the victim is present. The statistical summaries of criminal victimizations, however, showed that crime was not evenly distributed throughout society. Indeed, Cohen and Felson assumed that predatory crime depends upon the *coincidence* of (1) a **motivated offender** (e.g., someone who feels the need for cash, items with immediate liquidity, or other items of value such as clothing or cars), (2) a **suitable target** (e.g., a well-heeled pedestrian in the wrong part of town, a rental car in search of the interstate, or a house with valuable goods), and (3) the absence of a **capable guardian** (e.g., no homeowner present, no police, or a lone traveler).

Cohen and his associates (1981) later stipulated that target suitability has four dimensions:

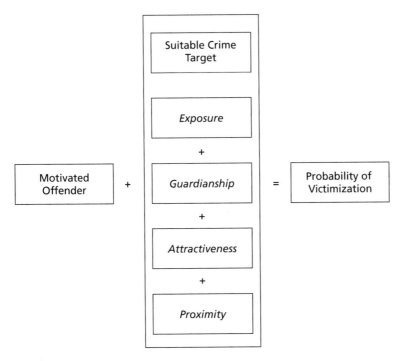

FIGURE 2.3 Routine Activities Theory

1. **Exposure:** the visibility and physical accessibility of the target
2. **Guardianship:** the ability (and presence) of persons or objects to prevent crime from occurring
3. **Attractiveness:** the material or symbolic value of persons or property
4. **Proximity:** the physical distance between potential targets and populations of potential offenders

Figure 2.3 graphically depicts routine activities theory.

Cohen and Felson's theory offers an explanation for why crime rates increased between 1960 and the early 1980s, and what the future is likely to hold. With respect to the former, they observed that in the post–World War II era increasing numbers of women entered the workforce, taking their children to day care and leaving their homes unguarded. Furthermore, the number of people living in single-household dwellings located in impersonal suburban neighborhoods increased. Traditional neighborhoods declined, and there was a further erosion of guardianship. Basic demographics impacted the number of motivated offenders available. During the period from 1960 to 1980, the "baby boom generation," the large group of post–World War II babies, experienced a "coming of criminal age" (Felson and Cohen 1980:396–99). There was, as a result, a surplus of motivated offenders. Finally the increased opportunity to commit predatory crimes substantially reduced the ability of the criminal justice system, the community, and the family to respond effectively to the increased threat. That is, the certainty, celerity, and value of the rewards of crime are vastly greater than the certainty, celerity, and severity of any punishments (Cohen and Felson 1979:606).

Judged by Cohen and Felson's theory, traditional law-and-order policies to reduce predatory crime may be doomed to failure. Those features of modern life that improve the quality of life—such as better transportation, more electronic durable goods, and greater opportunities for recreational activities outside the home—may increase the opportunity for predatory crime, result in lower guardianship, and increase the pool of suitable targets.

The implications for crime reduction, wrote Cohen and Felson (1979:606), are clear: "Indeed the opportunity for predatory crime appears to be enmeshed in the opportunity structure for legitimate activities to such an extent that it might be very difficult to root out substantial amounts of crime without modifying much of our way of life." They also disdained the idea that crime is related to the breakdown in the social structure of large cities: "Rather than assuming predatory crime is simply an indicator of social breakdown, one might take it as a byproduct of freedom and prosperity as they manifest themselves in the routine activities of everyday life" (Cohen and Felson 1979:606).

Assessing Routine Activities/Opportunity Theory

Routine activities theory has proved to be a most popular theory for testing. One recent trend is to apply qualitative research designs. For example, Leslie Kennedy and Stephen W. Baron (1993) used the case study approach and unstructured field interviews to study delinquent street groups. However, they reported that the routine activities model alone is insufficient to explain escalating street crimes committed by these youths. Rather, the authors suggested that routine activities theory should be integrated with rational choice and subcultural theories (see Chapter 6). "Behavior is sometimes guided by choice, sometimes influenced by cultural norms and processes, and at other times by routine activities" (Kennedy and Baron 1993:108-9). Escalation of violence is related not only to motivated offenders, suitable victims, and low guardianship but also to subcultural definitions of what is acceptable and tolerable within these interactions (Kennedy and Baron 1993:108). The entry of youths into a criminal subculture "influenced their routine activities, exposing them to situations where the chances of victimizations are increased, but their decision to engage in violence appeared to be made on the basis of rational choice: Respond or be beaten" (Kennedy and Baron 1993:109).

Another trend is to use the theory to explain previously observed phenomena. For example, Dennis Roncek and Pamela Maier (1991) extended routine activities theory to the examination of so-called **hot spots.** Hot spots are well known to local police and patrons alike. Bars, taverns, and cocktail lounges known to "attract" unseemly and troublesome customers are hot spot prototypes; many fights, brawls, and even murders occur there as well (Roncek 1981; Roncek and Bell 1981; Roncek and Pravatiner 1989; see also Sherman, Gartin, and Bueger 1989). Analyzing residential blocks, Roncek and Maier found links between crime and the presence of taverns and lounges. After eliminating the potentially confounding effects of being located in high-crime environments, they reported that crime of every type was significantly higher on residential blocks with taverns or lounges than on others. "Across all blocks, the number of taverns-lounges was associated with a higher probability of having crime in areas that were safe as well as a higher level of crime on blocks that already had crime" (Roncek and Maier 1992:747). They reaffirmed the importance of dangerous places in understanding crime rates, an emphasis that Felson (1987) added to routine activities theory.

A third use of the theory provides insights into macro-level trends and crime-related issues (cf. Jackson 1984; Stack 1995). For example, Steven Messner and Judith Blau (1987) examined the variability in leisure-time activities and crime rates in the nation's largest Standard Metropolitan Statistical Areas (SMSAs). They predicted that household-bound leisure activities would be negatively related to crime rates because people would primarily stay at home and out of harm's way. They also predicted that the aggregate volume of nonhousehold leisure activities would be positively related to crime rates, given the increased opportunity for victimizations provided by engaging in leisure activities in the community. Their findings strongly supported these hypotheses.

Several central issues related to the testing of routine activities theory reappear in the literature, including these:

- *Is this a crime theory or a victimization theory?* This is not a trivial point. As first stated, the theory explored why crimes occur, where they are likely to occur, and who is likely to engage in them. Some victimologists—researchers who study crime victims—have linked routine activities concepts to activity-specific risks of property and personal crime victimizations (Miethe, Stafford, and Long 1987), gender-specific risks for victimization (Mustaine 1997), college student lifestyles (Mustaine and Tewksbury 1998), and community disorganization (Moriarty and Williams 1996). The results provide modest-to-high support for elements of routine activities theory, usually opportunity. Although there is nothing in the theory that restricts tests to the explanation of criminal motivation and behavior, its use as a victimology theory is an important shift in emphasis. For his part Felson (2000:16) was clear about the theory's intent: "The routine activities approach . . . places the crime incident at the center of inquiry. Crime is a physical act, and we must not forget it."

- *Are the indicators of opportunity measuring what we want them to measure?* Terance Miethe and associates (1991) observed that the indicators of criminal opportunity theory are the same ones used in other theories of crime. For example, a household activity ratio that involves the number of female labor force participants with a husband present and those with a husband absent, divided by the total number of households, reflects social disorganization theory (see Chapter 6) and opportunity theory. This ratio exhibits a linkage to burglary, but given the prior status of disorganization theory, it is unclear what opportunity theory adds to our understanding of burglary.

- *Where are the offender motivation studies?* This question is a corollary of the first one. Wayne Osgood and his associates (1996) reported that participation in routine activities—including the presence of peers, absence of authority figures, and lack of time-delimited structure in their lives—accounted for much of their youth sample's involvement in deviant behavior. Few other tests of routine activities hypotheses include measures of offender motivations (Bryant and Miller 1997).

- *Where are tests of all the central elements of routine activities?* Tests rarely include more than one of the theory's central elements. Richard Bennett (1991), for example, explored target suitability, proximity to a pool of motivated offenders, and guardianship, using a sample of 52 nations over a 25-year period. He found that the routine activities model is crime-specific and does a better job of explaining property crime than personal crime. Just as importantly, various elements of the theory played different roles depending on the crime type. Guardianship played no role in explaining personal crimes, but it was important in the study of violent crimes. Moreover, given the study's cross-national nature, his finding that routine activities worked best in certain types of social structures (e.g., ones with attractive and accessible targets, proximity, and low guardianship) is significant. Bennett's work demonstrates the importance of considering as many elements of routine activities as possible (see also Anderson and Bennett 1996). A piecemeal approach to the testing of routine activities may lead to a false sense that the theory has been tested when, in fact, only limited hypotheses drawn from it have been subjected to empirical verification.

- *What is the role of formal guardians?* Formal guardians played central roles in early statements of the theory. The absence of suitable guardians was problematic, but the absence of the police could signal other community-level problems as well. In later works Felson (1994, 1998) tended to devalue formal guardians, preferring to emphasize the informal guardianship that occurs when people interact as a part of everyday life. Sociologists have long accentuated informal social control, even if Felson failed to acknowledge it (Akers 2000:32).

Routine Activities, Opportunity, Public Policy, and Criminal Justice Practices

According to Felson (1994, 1998) routine activities theory provides broad-ranging policy implications for structuring our communities and our lives. He described his contribution to criminological theory as "a very versatile theory of crime" (2001:43). Some level of victimization is inevitable, as the supply of victims and perpetrators is a constant. Where and when those crimes take place, however, is within the control of citizens at large, especially through collective guardianship and control of exposure. Police anticrime efforts, too, have explicit links to such practices as hot spot analysis. Indeed, many of the ideas developed by Felson have been incorporated into ecological approaches to crime control (see Chapter 7). The centrality of routine activities to combatting crime is clear to Felson, a fact he made clear in his definitive work on the subject, *Crime and Everyday Life* (1998).

INFORMAL DETERRENCE AND RELATED PROCESSES

- Have you taken a cultural anthropology class or otherwise read about violations of folkways and mores among social groups without formal justice systems? What forces kept people in their place, following the group's rules?

- As you were growing up, when did you first become aware of rules other than those of your family? In many cases the first such external rules come from schools or similar institutions. Which concerned you more—your parents' rules or those of the school? Given the possibility of being caught, whose wrath did you fear more—that of your parents or that of the principal?

- In your early teenage years, as you learned the "rules of the road" for such activities as parties, dating, and cruising, which system of rules—that of your friends, that of the formal laws, or some other system—had the greatest influence on your conduct? What was the force behind those rules?

A war philosophy underlies most modern criminal justice practices. The personnel staffing the nation's police and correctional agencies typically wear uniforms, employ military insignias and ranks, use paramilitary training tactics, and view criminals as "the enemy." At times they use weapons of war, including armored personnel carriers, and resort to military tactics, especially in crowd control. The language of warfare permeates efforts to curb crime and redirect criminals. For example, politicians, bureaucrats, and others responsible for implementing anticrime programs may describe crime as threatening the peace, safety, and security of the nation and its citizenry. Legislators and policy makers often describe new anticrime strategies as wars, as in the War on Crime and the War on Drugs (Inciardi 1992; Liska and Messner 1999:104–6). Beginning in the 1990s drug czars directed antidrug efforts from high-tech headquarters that rivaled those of the Department of Defense. In 2001 the director of the newly created Office of Homeland Security coordinated federal law enforcement, military units, and other intelligence-gathering agencies assigned to fight terrorism in the United States. In the aftermath of the September 11 attacks, state governments also created their own homeland security agencies, mimicking the federal initiatives. Not all of the targets of antiterrorism efforts are foreign-born enemies. The War on Terrorism is both a policing effort and a military one, further blurring the distinctions between civilian law enforcement and military participation in keeping the peace and protecting the public.[5]

There are many problems associated with applying the language of war to crime-fighting efforts, a term that is itself grounded in war terminology. Democracies have great difficulty using paramilitary units and tactics against their own citizens, and when they do, some groups inevitably compare them to totalitarian regimes. The enemy usually is drawn from the same population as those being protected. That is, most criminals are citizens of the nation that seeks to destroy them, or at least to reduce the threat they pose. In essence, by employing the language of war against criminals, a nation effectively has declared war against itself.

The language of war is also exclusionary. In order for society to declare war against an enemy, members of that group—in this case criminals—must be identified as outsiders. This practice has at least two consequences. First, it is far easier to violate the rights of those considered outsiders by choice, people who should not enjoy the same constitutional protections as law-abiding citizens. Second, once they are identified as outsiders—as enemies of the state—reintegration of criminals into society becomes a very difficult task.[6]

The peace model provides an alternative to the war model. Peace is the antithesis of war. The goal is to restore justice and civility in areas impacted by war or to maintain the peace, however fragile. The language of peace is far more conciliatory, harmonious, integrative, and stabilizing than that of war. Moreover, peacemakers may be viewed as idealists, a description often extended to peacemakers who study crime. Their use of the peace model led to two contemporary perspectives on crime and justice. Peacemaking criminology, along with left-realist criminology, is the twenty-first-century heir to Marxist criminology (see Chapter 9). Reintegrative shaming, along with restorative justice, represents a second conceptual product of the peace paradigm.

Crime, Shaming, and Social Disapproval

Shame is a very old idea. References to the behavior-shaping role of shame—an internal emotional response to embarrassing actions, ideas, words, or thoughts that, when made public, threaten to diminish a person's value or standing in the family or community—are found in nearly all religious and cultural traditions. Charles Darwin (1872) described the biological and social origins of shame. In fact, he saw perceptions of a negative assessment of oneself—with blushing as an external marker—as the cause of shame. Darwin believed that "shame is *the* social emotion, arising as it does out of the monitoring of one's own action by viewing one's self from the standpoint of others" (Scheff 1988:398; emphasis in original). Other early twentieth-century sociologists and psychologists explored the capacity of shame to control behavior (Cooley 1922; MacDougall 1908). African and Asian cultures continue to use shame as a means of maintaining social control over a host of behaviors (Braithwaite 1989).

More recently Kirk Williams and Richard Hawkins (1986) broadened the deterrence concept of costs by suggesting that legal sanctions alone, including fines and incarceration, do not deter crime. People respond to other direct and indirect costs as well, including fear, loss of respect, and loss of employment. Thomas Scheff (1988), in exploring the social and psychological aspects of shame as a mechanism of social control, suggested that human beings receive deference and feelings of pride for conformity to exterior norms, and are punished for nonconformity by a lack of deference and shame.

John Braithwaite (1989) has provided the most elaborate theoretical grounding for shame's role in maintaining social control in contemporary society. He noted that **shaming** involves "all social processes of expressing disapproval which have the intention or the effect of invoking remorse in the person being shamed and/or condemnation by others who become aware of the shaming" (1989:100). Shaming is stigmatizing (or disintegrative) if it blames offenders and denies them reentry into the community. Shaming processes are reintegrative if they first establish the deed's wrongfulness (as opposed to the person's evilness) and then provide an equally public and ritualistic means to restore the offender to the community or group. The key to **reintegrative shaming** is the ritualistic reinforcement of the person's status within the group. The last step in reintegrative shaming is gestural forgiveness, which must be extended ceremonially to the shamed person. This step is absent from **disintegrative shaming,** as are affective contacts between the person(s) doing the shaming and the one being shamed. Figure 2.4 depicts graphically the consequences to society of reintegrative shaming versus stigmatization.

Shaming, whether integrative or disintegrative, should not be viewed as a minor sanctioning process. Some of the rituals of both types, which can involve

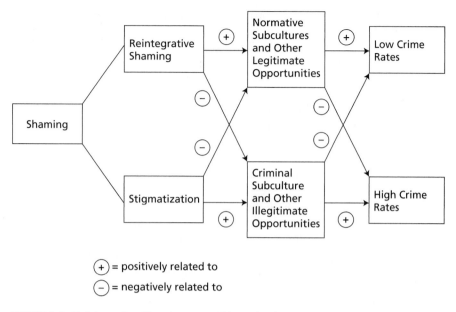

FIGURE 2.4 Reintegrative Shaming versus Stigmatization

Source: Braithwaite (1989).

painful and lengthy processes, are virtually indistinguishable from one another. The actual rituals are not important; rather, it is the goals of the rituals, and the processes by which they occur, that merit close inspection.

Braithwaite described two sets of processes, one operating at the societal (macro) level and the other at the individual (micro) level, that underlie shaming. Braithwaite's vision of contemporary societies suggests that urban communities with high levels of mobility typically exhibit low interdependency among residents. These communities lack, in Braithwaite's terms, **communitarianism,** as the citizenry is not "densely enmeshed in interdependencies that have the special qualities of mutuality and trust" (1989:100).

Communitarian communities view dependency as a positive social force and further emphasize the need for "mutuality of obligation in interdependency (to be both dependent and dependable)," a condition Braithwaite associated with the Japanese (1989:104) and certain Afghan tribes (2000:282). Low-communitarianism communities widely practice shaming that is stigmatizing or disintegrative. The result is that groups of stigmatized individuals form mutually reinforcing criminal subcultures, groups that provide the learning environments for criminal and other illegitimate activities.[7] The low levels of communitarianism, and the growth of criminal subcultures, further erode the existing communitarianism, exacerbating the crime problem.

Communities high in communitarianism typically practice reintegrative shaming. Public shaming is important for effective social control, and public ceremonies help promote a shared understanding of acts defined as criminal or immoral. However, the moralizing and shaming should be accomplished informally within the offender's social network. Heavy reliance on the public forum invites disintegrative shaming because at this level there may be less interdependency (i.e., attachment to parents, schools, and neighbors) and lower communitarianism.

At the individual (micro) level disintegrative shaming has the most negative impact on individuals who already possess little connectivity to conventionality—young, unmarried, unemployed males with low educational and occupational aspirations. Such individuals lack the interdependencies that serve (1) to negate stigmatizing shame and (2) to foster reintegration. Disintegrative shaming further weakens their already attenuated ties to conventionality. Absent effective social controls, the objects of disintegrative shaming join subcultures that endorse antisocial, criminal values. Thus, in Braithwaite's view, disintegrative shaming, owing to its stigmatizing power, results in continued, and perhaps even increased, crime.

Again at the micro-level, with reintegrative shaming, given its heavy reliance on and involvement of prosocial community forces, criminal subcultures appear less attractive to potential offenders. As Braithwaite (1989:1) warned, "Shaming is the most potent weapon of social control unless it shades into stigmatization. Formal criminal punishment is an ineffective weapon of social control partly because it is a degradation ceremony with maximum prospects for stigmatization." The individual who enjoys multiple interdependencies is most susceptible to reintegrative shaming. The result is lower offending.

Assessing Informal Deterrence Theories

Tests of reintegrative shaming typically take one of two paths, one of which explores its macro-level claims. Mitchell Chamlin and John Cochran (1997) tied social altruism levels to crime rates in a sample of several hundred U.S. cities.[8] **Social altruism** is a community's willingness to "share scarce resources to the aid and comfort of their members, distinct from the beneficence of the state" (1997:204). Chamlin and Cochran hypothesized that crime would vary inversely with altruism levels, a prediction consistent with communitarianism. This linkage was present for both property and personal crimes, leading them to speculate that "communities that effectively teach their members to respect and engage in behaviors that promote the welfare of others enjoy relatively lower rates of crime" (Chamlin and Cochran 1997:221).

A second, more common approach is to explore reintegrative theory's micro-level hypotheses. Three examples—one looking at reintegrative court practices, another involving parents' use of reintegration and shaming, and a third focusing on governmental inspectors—provide insights into these processes. For example, Terance Miethe and his associates (2000) compared recidivism outcomes for two samples of felony drug offenders. One group participated in a drug court that operated on principles with philosophical roots in reintegrative shaming. As Miethe and associates (2000:529) observed, "Deviance is both certified and decertified in a public forum; the defendant has multiple contacts with the judge that should lead to greater interdependencies, and the treatment approach (through family counseling and comprehensive therapy) is designed to maintain the social embeddedness of the offender." The other group, matched to the first in all significant ways, received normal processing through the criminal justice system. The researchers also conducted field observations of drug court sessions.

The results were not what reintegrative shaming theory predicted. Miethe and associates offered an explanation based on their observations of drug court proceedings. They found that (1) the court directed shaming at *both* the offense and the offender, (2) the offender was not embraced and offered opportunities in the community, and (3) shaming was not, as a general rule, practiced by someone closely related to or highly respected by the law violator. In short, the problem may not have been with the theory, but with the way it was operationalized and practiced in court.

Carter Hay (2001b) investigated the extent to which the reintegrative shaming practices of parents explained the projected deviance of their children. The study focused on parental reintegrative practices and shaming. Parent–child interdependency was, as predicted by the theory, strongly related to parents' use of reintegrative practices and, to a lesser degree, their use of shaming. However, the research generated more questions than answers about the influence of shaming. For example, Hay reported that the data supported the idea that reintegrative sanctioning of children leads to high parent–child interdependency, rather than the reverse relationship as predicted by the theory. Also, the negative effects of shaming on offending were not dependent on the level of reintegration—again, a finding not supportive of reintegrative shaming. Hay proposed that stigmatization may be important but that the moralizing effects of shaming may be overstated, with something else the source of harmful stigmatization (Hay 2001b:148).

Toni Makkai and John Braithwaite (1994) provided insights into what occurs when rule enforcers act differentially toward the same type of problems. They explored methods of rule enforcement used by Australian nursing home inspection teams and reported on the results achieved by three different approaches to compliance. Teams using a restorative justice approach noted a significant increase in compliance by homes following the inspection; homes visited by teams using a stigmatizing approach had a corresponding drop in compliance; compliance at nursing homes visited by tolerant or understanding teams fell in between the two extremes. Reintegrative shaming worked even better when there was interdependency between the nursing home and the inspection team, a finding that further supports Braithwaite's theory.

Comments and concerns about reintegrative shaming fall into several categories:

- *Does Braithwaite's work represent an explanatory theory or a normative theory?* An explanatory theory consists of propositions about how a particular theorist views the world. Braithwaite (2000:294) saw a normative theory as a similarly ordered set of propositions about how a theorist thinks the world ought to be. Braithwaite cited Bentham as one who proposed unifying an explanatory theory (deterrence) and a normative theory (utilitarianism), and noted that unification of this type is a rarity. Braithwaite's theory is such a unification. He argued that behavior should be shamed only when "doing so will increase freedom as non-domination." Braithwaite's non-nomination or republication conception of freedom looked for the minimum level of state punishment necessary to keep the promise of security (see, e.g., Braithwaite and Pettit 1990). To punish only because people "deserve" it is, under this model of freedom, immoral, in that it increases the amount of oppression in the world. Because Braithwaite closely links his explanatory and normative theories, some criminologists and policy makers find this duality problematic.[9]

- *Is this a new theory or a new way of looking at old theories?* Braithwaite argued that disintegrative shaming establishes fertile ground for other social forces to act upon individuals, leading to crime. Hence, it is difficult to describe reintegrative shaming as a totally new theory. When you read about, for example, subcultural theories (in Chapter 6), control and learning theories (in Chapter 7), or labeling theory (in Chapter 8), you might want to return to this chapter and review Braithwaite's idea.

- *Is this solely a theory about predatory crime?* A central reintegrative shaming assumption is that the consensus surrounding a rule-breaking act generates the shame: no consensus, little shame. Thus the theory's scope is limited to explaining predatory offenses against persons and property (Hay 2001b:135).

- *Can effective tests of the macro-level constructs be conducted?* Barriers to tests of reintegrative shaming theory's macro-level constructs are significant (Braithwaite 1989:120–21; Hay 1998:424). Large-scale surveys of shaming across communities, cultures, or societies would be prohibitively expensive. Just as importantly, measures of the levels of reintegrative shaming do not currently exist.[10] In the absence of tests that involve the fully explicated theory, Braithwaite's theory about the role of shame in producing or reducing crime remains interesting but unsubstantiated.

Reintegrative shaming, or ideas related to the basic principles described by Braithwaite, is embedded in much criminological theorizing. Larry Sherman (1993) has argued that sanctions based on reintegrative principles promote deterrence and that stigmatizing sanctions elicit defiance in those who are punished. Other theories, including developmental theories (see Chapter 5), labeling and conflict theories (see Chapter 8), and life-course criminology (see Chapter 10), acknowledge Braithwaite's macro- and micro-forces. In the final analysis it is not the explanatory theory that bothers many of the theory's critics, but Braithwaite's normative theory.

Informal Deterrence, Public Policy, and Criminal Justice Practices

Reintegrative shaming provides at least part of the theoretical basis for **restorative justice** (RJ), an idea that is also very old. The notion that rule violators can be brought back into the community fold, healing the rifts that their misbehavior caused, has roots in long-standing Western and non-Western cultural traditions (Braithwaite 1999). Ancient Arabs, Greeks, Romans, and Germanic peoples practiced restorative or healing rituals. Buddhists, Hindus, Taoists, and Confucianists all recognize the importance of restoring community harmony and balance after a wrongful or disruptive act. The aboriginal peoples of many countries have long practiced peacemaking and reintegration, and their practices have given rise to "newly discovered" ideals of restorative justice (Winfree 2002).

From a policy standpoint the world has embraced restorative justice. Programs based on its principles are found in the current criminal justice systems of such politically diverse nations as Austria, Australia, Belgium, Canada, the Czech Republic, Germany, Great Britain, and New Zealand, to name a few. In 1999 the Committee on Ministers for the Council of Europe adopted the language and principles of restorative justice for penal matters. As early as 1997 the United Nations considered the need for basic principles to guide member states in the adoption of RJ operating principles and programs, and in 2001 the United Nations adopted these principles. Whether the model receives even broader acceptance remains to be seen. In any case many existing criminal justice practices view crime from an RJ perspective.

Law Enforcement Practices Braithwaite (1997) observed that the police are crucial gatekeepers in restorative justice. He stressed that police, like offenders, must be brought into the process; police should be essentialized and not stigmatized. Indeed, the police in several nations participate formally in restorative justice programs. For example, in the Navajo Nation members of the tribal police force who view themselves as traditionalists are far more likely than modernists to make recommendations for peacemaking courts, a form of restorative justice based on Navajo religious principles (Gould 1999). Police officers in New Zealand play pivotal roles in **family group conferencing,** a program that brings all parties together to begin healing the wounds caused by criminal events. An accused juvenile offender cannot be sentenced without the recommendation of the family group conference, in which a youth service officer reads the charges and participates in the decision-making process (Goenner 2000). Similar programs are being used in Australia, in several U.S. states (e.g., Minnesota, Montana, and Vermont), and in several Canadian provinces (Bazemore and Umbreit 2001:5). Preliminary results from those programs that involve the police directly in RJ goal attainment are promising (McCold and Wachtel 1998; Sherman, Strang, Barnes, et al. 1998). However, officers who are willing to participate in RJ programs may be undervalued by others within their departments (Winfree 2002).

Judicial Practices Victim–offender mediation (VOM) programs provide a safe environment in which victims can confront offenders. These voluntary programs allow the victim to begin the healing process. Offenders learn about the crime's impact on their victims and, ideally, take responsibility for their actions. Recommendations are made by judges, probation officers, victim advocates, prosecutors, and law enforcement officials. Just as critically, they provide an opportunity for both parties to develop a plan that addresses the harm done by the crime that is agreeable to all. More than 300 VOM programs operate in the United States and Canada, and another 700 in Europe (Bazemore and Umbreit 2001:2). Victims report that, although restitution is important, the most significant aspect of VOM programs is that they enable the victim to talk about the impact of the crime, meet the offender, and learn the offender's circumstances (Coates and Gehm 1989; Umbreit 1994).

Circle sentencing—sometimes called peacemaking circles—has its roots in the customs of North American aboriginal peoples. The practice is used in several Canadian provinces and in Minnesota (Pranis 1997). Circle sentencing involves five steps: (1) a request by the offender to participate in the process, (2) a healing circle for the victim, (3) a healing circle for the offender, (4) a sentencing circle to establish a consensus on an effective sentencing plan for the offender, and (5) follow-up circles to monitor the offender's progress. Participants in the circles include the "keeper" of the circle (i.e., a respected community member skilled in peacemaking), the offender and the offender's support group, members of local police and correctional agencies, a judge, the prosecutor and defense attorneys, the victim and the victim's support group, and community leaders. The goals include promoting healing among all parties, empowering all participants, and addressing the underlying causes of the crime.

Correctional Practices RJ-based corrections programs operate in many U.S. states, including Minnesota, Vermont, Texas, and Oregon (Kurki 1999). To date, however, no state has incorporated RJ principles into statewide services.

Not all correctional practitioners view RJ programs in the same way, even those who support it in principle. Some see it as a better way to do what they have been doing all along; others see an entirely new paradigm for corrections (M. Smith 2001:2). Some supporters who advocate merging RJ principles into corrections worry that it will be relegated to minor forms of misbehavior and trivialized as a correctional philosophy and practice. Finally not everyone embraces restorative justice. Although there can be no denying the progressive ideals of restorative justice—and, for that matter, reintegrative shaming—the risk is very real that it will be corrupted to serve nonprogressive goals and thus do more harm than good (Leverant, Cullen, Fulton, and Wozniak 1999). Moreover, the research to date fails to support the idea that RJ-based programs will reduce recidivism. Perhaps these concerns and problems reflect Braithwaite's warning that without his normative theory reintegrative shaming—and any programs derived from it—may be corrupted. (See Table 2.1 for an overview of deterrence and opportunity theories.)

SUMMARY

Life is a series of choices, or so would claim the theorists in this chapter. This emphasis on choosing between alternatives has proved to be a powerful and enduring idea, based on equally powerful and seductive assumptions about human behavior. Even in the absence of definitive proof, deterrence theory remains a powerful icon in crime theory. The new incarnations of deterrence, extensions into rationality and opportunity, have extended the theory's life into the twenty-first century. However, even lacking these new conceptualizations and attendant research findings, the political appeal of deterrence arguments likely accounts for most of its popularity with policy makers and the public at large.

Deterrence theory demonstrates by the sanctioning process what happens to those who break the law. It says little about their fates after being sanctioned, except to note that they had better learn their lessons. Informal sanctioning, but especially reintegrative shaming, acknowledges that most offenders do indeed return to the community. The question becomes, What do we want them to be like when they return? They may return as outcasts, a consequence of disintegrative shaming. The alternative is to bring them back into the community fold through a process not unlike that which shamed them, and engage in forgiveness. Clearly reintegrative shaming, with roots in the peace model—as opposed to the war model that guides most criminal justice system responses to crime—is an acquired taste. It remains to be seen whether this approach to deterring criminals will prove as popular as classic deterrence and its more recent incarnations.

Table 2.1 Theories of Deterrence and Opportunity

Theory	Major Figures	Central Assumptions	Causal Arguments (Key Terms)	Strengths	Weaknesses
Formal deterrence	Beccaria, Bentham, Gibbs, Tittle, Becker	Humans are rational beings, endowed with free will and capable of making informed choices between good and evil; humans are also hedonistic beings, seeking out pleasure over pain.	Hedonistic tendencies threaten the social order unless the penalties for crimes are certain, swift, and appropriately severe—elements modified by some theorists.	Seems intuitively correct, as most people abide by the law—especially when there is widespread public support—because they fear the punishments; a familiar theory, as the criminal justice system is largely built upon its philosophical premises.	Hypotheses generated by the theory proved hard to test, largely due to operationalization difficulties.
Rational choice	Cornish, Clarke	Crime is, for many offenders, a reasonable alternative to other less palatable and possibly more costly outcomes.	Offenders' choice structuring lays the foundation for the kind of crime (involvement decision) they are willing to commit, followed by the event decision at the time of the crime.	Provides a logical decision-making context to deterrence ideas; explains how some crime occurs so quickly when the opportunity presents itself to potential offenders.	May be little more than deterrence theory cast in econometric terms (costs versus benefits), ones that sound suspiciously like the words of Bentham.
Routine activities/opportunity	Felson, Cohen	Criminal motivation and the supply of potential offenders are constants; the supply of potential victims varies and determines the level of crime in a given community or geographic area.	Predatory crime depends upon the timely convergence of the following: (1) a motivated offender, (2) a suitable target (high exposure, low guardianship, high attractiveness, and close physical proximity), and (3) absence of a capable guardian.	Provides an explanation for increased crime rates from the 1960s to the 1980s; also provides a theoretical base for observations about "hot spots"; embedded in in theory is the concept of opportunity, which implies prevention strategies; allows for integration with other theories, including rational choice.	Primarily addresses only predatory crime, leaving out a great deal of the breadth and depth of crime.
Informal deterrence and related processes	Braithwaite	The best and most effective way to secure rule compliance is to use informal social groups; people care more about what their relatives and friends think of their actions than a judge or jury.	Reintegrative shaming leads to contact with legitimate subcultures and other prosocial contacts, and low crime; disintegrative shaming leads to contact with illegitimate subcultures, other antisocial contacts, and high crime.	See Formal deterrence; Reflects the idea that what is feared is not a formal sanction alone, but also the loss of respect and the shame that follow being caught; most social rituals may be inclusionary, such as restorative justice practices.	Is seen as extralegal by many deterrence hardliners; however, some nations have included principles related to informal deterrence at the point of decisions about diversion, sentencing, and prison release.

KEY TERMS

absolute deterrence

attractiveness

boot camp

capable guardian

choice structuring

circle sentencing

communitarianism

cost–benefit analysis

determinate sentencing

deterrence/brutalization thesis

disintegrative shaming

event decision

expected utility principle

exposure

family group conferencing

general deterrence

guardianship

hedonism

hot spots

indeterminate sentencing

individual deterrence

involvement decision

mandatory sentencing

medical model

motivated offender

Neuve Classical School

perceptual deterrence

predatory crime

proportionality

proximity

reintegrative shaming

restorative justice

restrictive deterrence

shaming

shock incarceration

social altruism

specific (individual) deterrence

suitable target

victim–offender mediation

CRITICAL REVIEW QUESTIONS

1. How do you feel about Beccaria's eighteenth-century recommendations for sentencing reform?

2. Which of Beccaria's ideas might explain problems with mandatory sentencing?

3. Why do you think that the classical position has had such a powerful influence on U.S. jurisprudence and penal philosophy?

4. What kind of research would convince you that the death penalty either deters crime or creates a brutalization effect that invites acts of violence?

5. What do you see as the greatest flaw in deterrence research? Why do you think researchers failed to demonstrate clearly the power of formal sanctions to deter crime?

6. Are people calculating machines, constantly engaging in cost–benefit analysis? Do you engage in this process when you consider what classes to take (e.g., X amount of work for Y credit and Z knowledge equals too much work for too little gain)? Do you think people who cheat on tests (or on other people) do econometric analysis?

7. If you broke the law, whom would you be more concerned about finding out—your family or the police?

8. How might rational choice theory expand our understanding of the relationship between routine activities and predatory crime?

9. What are your impressions of informal deterrence? Can formal and informal deterrence work together? What might make them compatible or incompatible?

10. How important is the peace paradigm to an understanding of restorative justice?

11. What are the strengths (or weaknesses) inherent in restorative justice that most impressed you? What made them stick out in your mind?

12. Which deterrence-related criminal justice practices—no matter the form of deterrence—strike you as most likely to be successful? Which ones are likely, in your opinion, to fail? Support your answers with insights gleaned from this chapter.

NOTES

1. The following derives from Martin, Mutchnick, and Austin (1990) and Monachesi (1955).

2. The use of gender-specific pronouns in discussions of classical theory is consistent with the philosophy, in that females were not viewed as having the same rationality as men. French neoclassical law largely exempted females from the legal expectations accorded males.

3. For this reason Beccaria opposed the death penalty, as the state essentially declared war on the individual, an unfair struggle given the resources of the state.

4. Fogel, von Hirsch, and others supporting the use of sanctions for their own sake—as just deserts—are sometimes called neoclassicalists (Einstadter and Henry 1995:46).

5. In the late 1990s elite Marine Corp units operated on the nation's southern border as ancillaries in the War on Drugs. These actions required a loosening of the 100-year-old Posse Comitatus Act, which prohibits the use of military troops in domestic police activities. They were officially withdrawn after the accidental death of a civilian.

6. These themes are important to another theoretical perspective, labeling theory (see Chapter 8).

7. See Chapter 6 for more on the role of subcultures in promoting criminal conduct.

8. Owing to missing information, Chamlin and Cochran examined personal crime in 273 cities and property crime in 279 cities. These samples represented roughly 70 percent of all U.S. cities that reported at least $1 million in contributions to their United Way campaigns.

9. Braithwaite (2000:295) viewed deterrence theory as dangerous; moreover, reintegrative shaming without an accompanying normative theory, such as republican political theory, could be nearly as dangerous.

10. Recall that Chamlin and Cochran looked at altruism, which at best reflects communitarianism, and not the presence of reintegrative shaming.

3

Biological and Biochemical Theories

CHAPTER OVERVIEW

Origins of Biological Explanations

Evil Spirits, Demons, and Crime

Nature and Crime

Social Darwinism

Criminal Anthropology

Criminals and Body Types

Assessing Primitive Biological Theories

Primitive Biological Explanations, Public Policy, and Criminal Justice Practices

Genetics and Crime

Genetic Factor Studies

Karyotype Studies

The Human Genome Mapping Project and the Future of "Crime Genetics"

Assessing Genetic Explanations

Genetics, Public Policy, and Criminal Justice Practices

Biochemistry and Crime

Substance Abuse

Serotonin, Monoamine Oxidase, and Criminal Behavior

Other Biochemical and Neurological Explanations

Assessing Biochemical Explanations

Biochemistry, Public Policy, and Criminal Justice Practices

LEARNING OBJECTIVES

- Place the biological theories of crimes and criminals in their appropriate historical and social context, and thereby appreciate the nature of the early biological quest for the "born criminal."

- Recognize the extent and nature of modern genetic theories of crime, particularly the way these theories attempt to answer the criticisms leveled against earlier primitive biological markers of crime.

- Speculate on the potential for advances in biochemistry to confirm biology's role in crime.

- Appreciate the extent to which chemicals of all sorts—whether introduced into the human body or naturally present—shape human actions.

INTRODUCTION

Throughout the twentieth century American society turned to science and technology for answers to a wide range of problems, from wars against international aggressors to wars against other "enemies," including disease, drugs, and crime. Science has provided answers to some, but not all, of these problems. The failure of science and technology to eradicate drug abuse and crime serves as reminders of their limitations.

Two sciences, in particular, have long interested criminologists. Biology and chemistry provide systematic knowledge of nature and the physical world. Biology addresses, among other things, the physiology, origins, and development of animal and plant life; chemistry deals with the composition and properties of substances, and with the reactions by which such substances are created or converted into others. Criminologists have also shown an interest in biochemistry, the branch of chemistry that deals with plants and animals and their life processes, especially their susceptibility to natural and artificial chemical compounds. Chemicals such as alcohol, heroin, and cocaine have well-documented ties to criminal conduct. We know that humans must manufacture certain chemicals to maintain normal physical, psychological, and social states—that is, homeostasis. Too much or too little of these chemicals is bad for the host organism. The physical environment also can contain many toxic substances, chemicals linked by scientific research to crime and other forms of antisocial behavior.

Before biologists and chemists turned to the study of crime, other equally deterministic explanations dominated penal philosophy and practices. Some were the forerunners of the most primitive scientific theories about crime. Their central themes, including the assumptions they make about human behavior and the causal forces they blame, have existed for millennia.

ORIGINS OF BIOLOGICAL EXPLANATIONS

- Have you ever crossed the street to avoid a dangerous-looking person, because the person's physical appearance intimidated you?

- After reading a newspaper article or watching a television report on a particularly heinous crime, have you thought that the perpetrator was not human?

- Have you ever thought that evil—real evil—is the source of many of society's ills, including crime?

- After passing a homeless shelter, have you ever wondered why anyone subsidizes people who fail to help themselves?

In previous millennia, community elders, religious leaders, and others with special insights into human nature saw something within offenders as the cause of their behavior. These primitive explanations of crime focused on the evildoer. At that time no laws governed behavior because no formal, organized governments existed, and rule-violating behavior was thought to be caused by evil spirits, demons, and devils. Such theories were deterministic, individualistic, and prescientific.

Evil Spirits, Demons, and Crime

Humans have long blamed evil forces for troubling events. Graeme Newman (1978:130) summarized the issue: "Myth is part of culture, and as such has shaped human response to crime for thousands of years." Early humans believed that supernatural powers caused life's harsh conditions and the natural disasters that added to its unpredictability, a concern that evolved into spiritualistic explanations: Where gods reign, demons exist as well.

Not all attempts to rid the community of a demon or evil spirit were grounded in a concern for the afflicted. Punishments based on spiritualistic explanations are especially instructive in this regard. **Apotropaic punishments,** or actions intended to ward off evil spirits, were common. Practitioners believed that **corporal punishment,** in which they subjected the evildoer's body—the demon's host—to excruciating pain, drove out the demon. Similarly, **capital punishment,** which ended with death, was directed as much at the demon as the human. In the Middle Ages hanging, in particular, was thought to protect society from the demonic powers of the condemned (Newman 1978:37). On the way to the gallows, the offender was not allowed to have direct contact with the earth. Once hanged, the body often was left to rot on the rope, and return naturally and harmlessly to the earth.

Throughout history societies around the world have executed unknown numbers of people, perhaps millions, accused of demonic possession.[1] Punishment often followed canonical (religious) or secular (civil) trials. Many scholars believe that such demonological explanations reached fever pitch in medieval times. According to the criminologist George Vold (1979:5), the Middle Ages saw "a fusion of the intellectual conceptions of demonism and the political and social organization of feudalism. The Inquisition reflected the resulting theocracy—it was a period of witch-hunting."

Unlike the involuntary demonic possession of the Middle Ages, the Renaissance era's witchcraft involved the exercise of free will. Witches, as persons who made pacts with the devil, freely gave up the faith. As Elliott Currie (1968:8) observed about this brand of witchcraft and its control, "On the Continent, they usually prosecuted witchcraft as a form of heresy, and in England as a felony whose essence was primarily mental." Apotropaic punishments continued with the emergence of Protestantism in the sixteenth-century Reformation (Sharpe 1997). Perhaps the most famous episodes in the American colonies occurred at Salem and other locations in New England (Erickson 1966).[2]

Nature and Crime

The ancient Phoenicians, Greeks, and Romans developed **naturalistic explanations** of the world as they understood it. Unlike spiritualists naturalists sought causal arguments from the physical and material world. Thus, the Greek writer Hippocrates (c. 460–370 B.C.E.) based his conclusions on objective observation and deduction. The philosopher Democritus (c. 460–370 B.C.E.) created an atomic theory, holding that all living things were composed of tiny indivisible particles, called atoms, and that their constant motion explained the creation of the universe. He accomplished this feat without an electron microscope or an orbiting satellite telescope. What he did have, like Hippocrates, was a great mind, and keen powers of observation and deduction.

Naturalists like Hippocrates and Democritus sought to understand the "nature of things." Later naturalists, living in far different times, adapted this philosophy, honed it, and made it science. Even in times dominated by demonology, naturalistic explanations gained popularity. In the era of naturalistic explanations, however, it was an easy deduction that a person's exterior, which naturalists could observe, corresponded to an unobservable inner self. This idea of external manifestations of social tendencies came to maturation in the disciplines of physiognomy and phrenology.

Physiognomy: Crime and the Human Face Physiognomists make judgments about individuals' mental qualities, character, and personality based on their external physical characteristics, especially facial features. J. Baptista della Porte (1535–1615) founded human **physiognomy.** Della Porte, like many early positivists, studied criminals' cadavers. He concluded that specific characteristics, including small ears and bushy eyebrows, indicated certain criminal types. Being a determinist, della Porte held out little hope for changing offenders. Criminals were victims of their physical features, and no amount of moral persuasion could alter that fact.

In 1775 the Swiss theologian Johan Caspar Lavater (1741–1801) published a four-volume work titled *Physiognomic Fragments,* in which he classified persons according to certain physical qualities called **fragments.** For example, shifty-eyed, beardless men with weak chins were untrustworthy. Lavater's main contribution to criminology was to generate interest in "the best organized and logically more impressive view that has come to be known as phrenology" (Vold 1989:53).

Phrenology: Curing Criminal Tendencies The followers of **phrenology** looked at the skull's shape and protuberances, with the latter supposedly suggesting latent or manifest criminality. According to phrenologists persons with these characteristics were now, may once have been, or were likely to become, criminals. Franz Joseph Gall (1758–1828), an Austrian anatomist, described his study of the human skull as **cranioscopy.** Gall visited prisons and insane asylums, physically examining inmates' skulls for bumps, lumps, and other abnormalities. He then codified and systematized his observations, publishing a series of works on the physiology and function of the human brain. But his greatest contribution may have been his student John Gasper Spurzheim (1776–1832), who emphasized the skull's shape and any facial imperfections. In refining his master's work he became phrenology's greatest proponent. Late in his career, traveling to England and America, he outlined phrenology's three basic assumptions:

1. The skull's exterior conforms to its interior shape.
2. The brain consists of "faculties"—Gall and Spurzheim differed on how many.
3. Each faculty relates to a specific area of the brain, and each bump is an indicator of a specific "organ" of the faculty.

Unlike the immutable human condition predicted by della Porte, phrenologists held that they could change a person with well-developed propensities toward crime. Adults and children, diagnosed through phrenological screening, could be diverted from the path to criminality by a regimen of moral exercise and "right living." In the United States in the last quarter of the nineteenth century, phrenologists such as Charles Caldwell (1772–1853) traveled the nation, much like itinerant medicine men. They spoke to the crowds about the connections between crime and the brain, held readings, and provided treatment plans for the "afflicted" (Schaefer 1969; Vold 1989).

Today criminologists reject physiognomy and phrenology as unscientific. In the opinions of some scientists, however, physiognomists and phrenologists were looking in the right place: "Despite its shaky scientific foundations, phrenology is enjoying a measure of respect from those who study the brain today. . . . Of course, today scientists look at changes in neurochemistry and synaptic connections rather than 'brain organs,' but the principle is the same" (Morse 1997:24, 28).

Social Darwinism

Charles Darwin's (1809–1882) *The Descent of Man* (1871) included the idea that **natural selection** shaped humanity. Specifically nature eliminated a species' weaker members or, given an uncorrectable flaw, an entire species. The English philosopher Herbert Spencer (1820–1903) advanced Darwin's thesis by placing natural selection in a social context. Spencer (1961) believed that perpetuating artificially society's weakest members through public welfare or private charity did them—and society—a disservice. Such actions threatened all of society by allowing the weak to reproduce. **Social Darwinism** alleviated the concerns of the wealthy about helping the suffering of the poor. After all, the suffering of the poor was the inevitable price of the struggle for existence and the advancement of the stronger stock, a struggle destined to end in the "survival of the fittest," a term coined by Spencer, and the elimination of the unfit (Andreski 1971:26).

Darwin and Spencer wrote about human evolution and its effect on society. Criminal anthropology, initiated by Cesare Lombroso in 1876, used evolution to explain the "criminal man."

Criminal Anthropology

Cesare Lombroso (1835–1909), a Venetian physician, was a military doctor early in his professional life, treating and studying soldiers. Later he studied thousands of

---

IN THEIR OWN WORDS: Spencer on Survival of the Fittest

The move toward using science to explain criminality owes much to the work of Charles Darwin. Darwin wrote about the idea that the forces of natural selection shaped humanity, which became the credo for social Darwinism. The English philosopher Herbert Spencer used Darwin's thesis in a social context, condemning the emerging practice of **social engineering.**

- *On the relationship between sociology and biology:* "There can be no rational apprehension for the truths of Sociology until there has been reached a rational apprehension of the truths of Biology" (p. 334).
- *On the dangers of engaging in programs for the poor:* "If the unworthy are helped to increase, by shielding them from that mortality which their unworthiness would naturally entail, the effect is to produce, generation after generation, a greater unworthiness" (p. 344).
- *On the goals of social Darwinism:* "Fostering the good-for-nothing at the expense of the good, is an extreme cruelty. It is a deliberate storing-up of miseries for future generations. There is no greater curse to posterity than that of bequeathing them an increasing population of imbeciles and idlers and criminals" (p. 344).

Source: Spencer (1961).

---

convicts, using **anthropometry,** a branch of anthropology that uses body measurements to determine differences in races and individuals. In 1876, pulling together his diverse findings on diseases of the nervous system, the brains of criminals, and their anthropometrical measurements, Lombroso published *L'uomo delinquente* (*The Criminal Man*). Perhaps influenced by the work of Darwin and other evolutionists, Lombroso concluded that criminal behavior was the result of arrested evolution. Lombroso called this state **atavism,** from the Latin word for "ancestor."

According to Lombroso, atavistic man had peculiar physical characteristics, which he called **stigmata.** He included the following among dozens of stigmata: facial asymmetry; an enormous jaw; prominent cheekbones; large ears; fleshy, swollen, and protruding lips; abnormal dentition; a receding or excessively long chin, or a short and flat one, as in apes; excessive arm length; and more than the normal complement of fingers, toes, or nipples. He also included a series of predatory habits, including a craving for evil for its own sake and a desire not only to kill but to mutilate victims. Lombroso stressed that these were not the *causes* of crime, but were simply the signs of atavism.

Facing mounting criticism, Lombroso modified his position by including environmental factors in later editions of *L'uomo delinquente.* He concluded that, given access to money and the ability to steal, even the wealthy are tempted to commit crimes. They avoid discovery or prosecution, he observed, by exercising influence. Gina Lombroso-Ferrero, his daughter, included many of these modifications in her English-language version, *Criminal Man* (1979[1911]). Although no longer ascribing all criminality to atavism, Cesare Lombroso argued that atavists pose the most serious threat to society.

The English Convict: Goring's Refutation of the "Born Criminal" The shortcomings of Lombroso's "research" became obvious even in his own time.

Charles Goring (1870–1919) examined 3000 convicted offenders and a comparison group of unconvicted Englishmen, a 12-year effort; he presented his findings in *The English Convict: A Statistical Study* (1972[1913]). Goring was looking for statistical correlations between the objective measures of physical and mental anomalies and known crime. Not only was he unable to distinguish offenders from nonoffenders based on the anomalies, he also failed to find significant differences between types of offenders, as predicted by Lombroso (e.g., comparing burglars to forgers or murderers).

Goring's criminals were shorter in stature and lower in body weight than members of his comparison group, differences he attributed to hereditary inferiority, the "real" source of criminality. As for the "born criminal," Goring (1972[1913]:173; emphasis in original) observed, "Our results nowhere confirm the evidence [of the born criminal], nor justify the allegations of criminal anthropologists. They challenge their evidence at almost every point. . . . Our inevitable conclusion must be that *there is no such thing as a physical criminal type.*"

The American Criminal: Hooton's Rejoinder In spite of Goring's critique, others attempted to build on the basic premise of a physical criminal type—most notably, Earnest Albert Hooton (1887–1954). A Harvard physical anthropologist, Hooton published *The American Criminal: An Anthropological Study* in 1939. For years he and colleagues at other universities collected body measurements from 17,000 individuals, roughly 14,000 of whom were prison inmates. His control group was a cross-section of college students, police officers, and firemen.

Hooton performed many meticulous comparisons between the inmates and the control group. Among his conclusions were the following:

- For more than half of the anthropometric measurements, significant differences existed between criminals and civilians.

- Tattooing was more common among criminals than among civilians.

- Low, sloping foreheads; long, thin necks; and sloping shoulders—all were similarly excessive among criminals in comparison to civilians.

- Physical inferiority was important given its association with mental inferiority.

Hooton also analyzed body types as they related to crime type. For example, he concluded that tall, thin men were more likely to be murderers and robbers, and that tall, heavy men were more likely to be killers and to commit fraud and forgery as well. What Hooton failed to note was that over half his prison subjects were repeat offenders, and many had previously committed different offenses (Vold 1979:63). Hooton (1939:309) nonetheless concluded:

> Criminals are organically inferior. Crime is the resultant of the impact of environment upon low grade human organisms. It follows that the elimination of crime can be effected only by the extirpation of the physically, mentally, and morally unfit; or by their complete segregation in a socially aseptic environment.

Hooton saw the differences between his sample of white male prisoners and his far smaller and no more representative control group as signs of criminal degeneracy, an inherited trait. This process is a classic illustration of circular reasoning: "Use criminality to discover inferiority, then turn around and use inferiority to explain or account for criminality" (Vold and Bernard 1986:57; see also Gould 1981).

Criminal Anthropology in the United States Criminal anthropology was past its peak in the United States by 1911, the year an English-language version of Lombroso's work was published. Between 1893 and 1909 a group of U.S. anthropologists essentially took Lombroso's work and "Americanized" it (Rafter, 1992). Their central assumption was clearly Lombrosian in nature, but tempered by the moralistic, Victorian–Edwardian times in which they lived: "The body must mirror moral capacity" (Rafter 1992:535). They integrated Lombroso's ideas of atavism with generation theory, arguing that socially problematic groups inherited their tendency toward various forms of devolution. Moreover, poverty, mental illness, and crime were symptoms of the underlying organic malaise found in these degenerate groups.

Criminology's origins in criminal anthropology account for three contemporary problems. First, criminal anthropologists kept their discipline's boundaries extremely fluid, "making it a field in which specialists from other areas flowed" (Rafter 1992:542). If these cross-disciplinary forays have strengthened criminology, the lack of disciplinary boundaries found in other sciences has been a source of weakness. Second, criminology is an immature science that lacks a central, generally agreed-upon method of study. This weakness derives from the fact that criminal anthropologists were unable to define the nature and practice of their science. Again, although current criminology is flexible and fertile, the study of crime is also fraught with antipositivism and methodological shortcomings. Lastly critics have identified some criminal anthropologists in the United States with eugenicists. **Eugenics** is the practice of ridding the human species of unfit biological stock, largely through sterilization, life sentences in prison, or death. Contemporary tensions between those who seek knowledge about crime for its own sake and those who would use it for control purposes stem largely from this early debate. Figure 3.1 summarizes Lombrosian-style explanations of crime.

Criminals and Body Types

During the 1930s and 1940s, the physician William Sheldon (1898–1977) employed **embryonics** to explain the criminal man. An embryo, he noted, is like a tube with three layers of tissue, each becoming a different bodily function or part. The endoderm yields the digestive tract; the mesoderm gives bone and muscle; and the ectoderm provides the nervous system. One element can dominate, yielding a specific body type, or **somatotype,** and an accompanying temperament.

Sheldon measured the body types of 200 young males housed in a small residential rehabilitation home for boys and 200 male college students. Based on comparisons between these known juvenile delinquents and the noncriminal students, Sheldon (1949) found a correlation between body type and criminality. In his study the delinquents were more **mesomorphic** (i.e., having muscular bodies and aggressive tendencies) and less **ectomorphic** (i.e., having fragile, skinny bodies, small faces, and introversive tendencies) than the noncriminal comparison group. However, some students were mesomorphs, and some delinquents were ectomorphs.

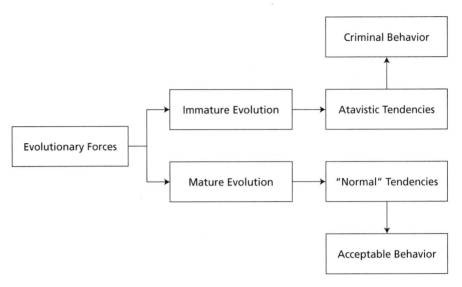

FIGURE 3.1 Lombrosian Explanations of Crime

Eleanor and Sheldon Glueck supported the connection between mesomorphy and delinquency. Assessing the body types of 500 delinquents and 500 "proven nondelinquents," they identified more than half of the delinquents as mesomorphs, as compared to fewer than a third of the nondelinquents (Glueck and Glueck 1956:9). They found that mesomorphs had personality traits "particularly suitable to the commission of acts of aggression . . . with a relative freedom from such inhibitions to antisocial adventures as feelings of inadequacy, emotional instability, and the like" (Glueck and Glueck 1956:226). They also reported that several sociocultural factors, all related to the home, were associated with mesomorphic delinquency.

The Gluecks were not true biological determinists, but rather viewed biological features as setting "the context for social forces" (Laub and Sampson 1991:1423). That is, body types cannot motivate criminal behavior, but they may be a factor in determining the direction of any set of behaviors, including crimes. **Endomorphs,** whose bodies tended to be soft and round, were rarities within the population of known delinquents. Sheldon (1949) associated each body type with a tendency toward a specific temperament. For example, endomorphs tended to seek comfort and love luxury; mesomorphs were dynamic and assertive and tended to behave aggressively; ectomorphs tended to be introverts, sensitive to noise and other distractions. Temperament and body type combined to form a person's propensity for delinquency. Figure 3.2 summarizes theories of body type and crime-proneness.

Assessing Primitive Biological Theories

The major weakness of the primitive biological explanations is also, paradoxically, an enduring strength: There is virtually no way to test them. True believers accept as an article of faith the alleged causal factors. Even the pseudoscientific phrenologists admitted that their entire discussion of the "physiological organs of the mind" was hypothetical. They could construct no meaningful tests (Vold and Bernard 1986), and if you cannot prove something, you cannot disprove it either.

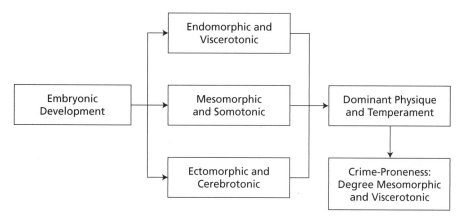

FIGURE 3.2 Body Types and Crime-Proneness

Few contemporary criminologists give the ideas of physiognomists or phrenologists serious consideration. They generally credit the latter at least for focusing attention on the human brain, an organ central to contemporary psychological and sociopsychological theories. The popular appeal of these "theories" to some segments of contemporary society is undeniable—many people, including police and correctional workers, believe that they know a criminal when they see one. But the obverse position also seems to have some merit. That is, what about offenders who do not fit the expected pattern? What if, like serial killer Ted Bundy, the criminal looks like the harmless next-door neighbor? Offender **profiling** is a contemporary extension of the use of physical appearance to determine criminal tendencies.

Criminal anthropologists applied the best science of their day, but this does not mean that critics were silent on the matter of science. Goring failed in his attempt to find a link between Lombroso's stigmata and crime. For his part Lombroso maintained that some stigmata defied measurement and that only "trained observers" could detect them (Vold and Bernard 1986). Goring may have been all too eager to disprove Lombroso (Driver 1972:440). Although Goring demeaned Lombroso's data, the samples used in *The English Convict* would hardly satisfy contemporary survey research standards. And Hooton used a method similar to Goring's. Thus, the generalizability of both sets of findings—Goring's and Hooton's—is suspect.

Body typing was not without its critics. Edwin Sutherland (1951) reanalyzed Sheldon's calculations, classifying each youth in the case histories according to offense seriousness and consistency of delinquency involvement. He argued that Sheldon's methods for doing these tasks were questionable, that the selective manner in which Sheldon included cases for examination called into question the entire study. Sutherland concluded that Sheldon had failed to show any real differences between the physical appearances of offenders and nonoffenders.

Sutherland was also critical of the Gluecks' research. However, his criticisms may have had ideological roots, given that he viewed their work as representing a dangerous trend in criminological research. Sutherland had no interest in the biology of crime and demeaned the work of those who suggested even the possibility of biological factors, a characterization that circumscribed the Gluecks' work (Laub and Sampson 1991:1422).

The use of subjective body measurements to identify crime potentialities seems odd because the human body is subject to many external forces. Moreover, Sheldon's study focused exclusively on boys, a shortcoming corrected by the Gluecks. Nonetheless, the mutability of the human form and its susceptibility to environmental forces make body typing a dubious proposition at best.

Primitive Biological Explanations, Public Policy, and Criminal Justice Practices

Darwin, in *The Descent of Man,* described humanity as shaped by natural selection. He also emphasized a hierarchy among human societies, an idea that lent support to the rampant racism of the nineteenth century. Various strains of social Darwinism relegated all efforts for physical, mental, or social improvement as predestined to fail. By logical extension this led to the conclusion that the destruction of the physically, mentally, and socially weak would serve to improve the human species. Indeed, natural selection justified both slavery and imperialism (Degler 1991).

Judicial and Political Practices Policy flowing from these observations focused on eugenics (i.e., controlled breeding). In many states intermarriage between races was forbidden; in others officials ensured control over reproduction of inferior stock through sterilization, with Indiana enacting the first law authorizing sterilization in 1907. By 1915 thirteen states had such laws, and by 1930 thirty states permitted the sterilization of certain criminal offenders and so-called mental defectives in public institutions (Degler 1991). The U.S. Supreme Court upheld these laws in a 1927 decision. Oliver Wendell Holmes, one of the nation's most respected jurists, plainly declared his support for Virginia's sterilization law in the 1927 case of *Buck v. Bell.* Carrie Buck was the daughter of a "mental defective" and the mother of a daughter adjudged feebleminded at age 7 months. Referring to Carrie, Justice Holmes remarked, "We have seen more than once that the public welfare may call upon the best citizens for their lives. It would be strange if it could not call upon those who already sap the strength of the state for these lesser sacrifices. . . . *Three generations of imbeciles is enough*" (emphasis added). In 1932 Vivian Buck, Carrie's "imbecile child," died of an intestinal disorder, but not before she completed the second grade and her teachers judged her to be "very bright." They also sterilized Carrie's sister Doris. She did not discover the truth of her "surgical procedure" until 1980, when a newspaper article revealed that Virginia had sterilized some 7500 people between 1924 and 1972. The article mentioned the two Buck sisters by name (Locurto 1991; see also Gould 1981).

The view that criminals derive from poor biological stock supports eugenics, a policy that denies the fact of crime. Being a runaway slave in the pre–Civil War United States meant being a criminal, in much the same way that a Jew in Nazi Germany held criminal status. Defining behavior as criminal, then, is a legal act, not a scientific one. Consequently eugenics is more social prejudice than objective science (Gould 1981).

Law Enforcement Practices Whether we can discern a biological basis of crime, current police practices sometimes reflect such arguments. Police often use body typing and general criminal anthropology, if informally, in their work. For example, the arresting officers described Rodney King at his 1993 civil rights trial as "a monster" largely due to his physique and alleged drug use. He was, in the terminology of the street, "buffed-out." Police may learn from experience to look for physical characteristics that mark a person as a threat. These markers could include well-developed physiques (mesomorphic somatotype); "shifty" eyes (a physiognomic fragment); and twisted, upturned, or flattened noses (atavistic anomalies). Just as with the primitive biological researchers, the employment of these markers by police is very much a hit-and-miss proposition. Informal discussions with police, however, reveal that physical markers continue to set off alarms. Singling out persons for stops because they fit a physical profile not only may violate suspects' civil rights, but also places the officers at legal risk (Del Carmen and Walker 1991; see also Kappeler and Del Carmen 1990).

GENETICS AND CRIME

- Do you question whether crime is *either* a nature *or* a nurture matter, or perhaps both?

- With all the talk recently about genetics and human behavior, is it possible that crime is genetically determined, that a crime gene exists?

- Do you believe that genes play a role in determining human social behavior? In this context does genetic theorizing represent a modern-day search for the "criminal man," not dissimilar to the ones conducted by Lombroso, Hooton, and others?

- What kind of evidence would convince you of crime's genetic origins?

Genetics is the study of heredity. The science emerged in 1900 when researchers rediscovered Gregor Mendel's (1822–1884) work on inherited characteristics or traits. Mendel viewed every trait as potentially transmittable within a species. He believed that both parents, as hereditary units, contributed some of their respective traits to their offspring through reproductive cells called gametes. In the field of genetics, two key terms are *chromosomes* and *genes.*

Chromosomes are high-density genetic storage devices, the carriers of human hereditary characteristics that reside in all of the body's cell nuclei. Males have an X and a Y chromosome in each cell; females have two X chromosomes. An ordinary body cell contains 23 pairs of chromosomes to which genes are assigned. **Genes** are chromosome segments—humans have about 70,000 genes—that are the means by which living organisms transmit inheritable characteristics to the next generation of their species. Genes consist of **deoxyribonucleic acid (DNA)** and array themselves along the length of each human chromosome.

One way to visualize gene segments is to think of a spiral staircase with two intertwining rails, described by geneticists as the double helix (Watson 1990). One rail contains subunits called **nucleotides,** and the opposing rail has a mirror image of subunits, arrayed in chemically bonded groups that form traits or **alleles.** The human organism has more than 3 billion nucleotides. Scientists believe that about 300,000 of these DNA bases form human genes. Hence, every human cell, except for red blood cells, contains an exact copy of that individual's DNA. We refer to the sum of these DNA genes as the **human genome**—instructions, written at the molecular level, for constructing an entire human being.

The science of genetics is at the core of two types of criminological studies. The first type looks at inheritable genetic factors. These studies, which began prior to the 1953 discovery of DNA, may seem primitive by today's standards. The second type of study looks at the arrangement of sex chromosomes inherited from one's mother and father, the so-called X and Y **sex chromosomes.** Collectively they form the genetics of criminology.

Genetic Factor Studies

Genetic factor crime studies take one of two main forms. The first is the **twin study.** Twins exist in two genetic versions: (1) identical or **monozygotic twins,** which evolve from a single fertilized ovum or egg and share the same genetic material, and which resemble each other in every possible genetic comparison, and (2) fraternal or **dizygotic twins,** which evolve from two separate eggs, fertilized by different spermatocytes, and which have less genetic material in common. Twin studies assume that, if the criminal activities of identical twins are more similar than those of fraternal twins, then hereditary factors are the cause.

The **adoption study** is the second main form. Twin studies rarely take into account the interaction of genetics and the home environment. Studying the criminality of adopted children separated at an early age from their biological parents can overcome this weakness. Researchers compare the crime and delinquency rates of these children with those of both their biological *and* their adoptive parents. When the adopted children's behavior more closely resembles that of their biological parents, supporters point to this as evidence of a genetic predisposition.[3]

Twin Studies Concordance, the key measurement in twin studies, is the degree to which twins share some behavior or condition—in this case criminal behavior. Germany's Johannes Lange published the first criminological twin study in his 1929 book *Crime as Destiny.* Of monozygotic twins 75 percent were concordant pairs on subsequent criminality, but only 12 percent of the dizygotic twins were also concordant.

Curt Bartol (1991:36) summarized the findings from 12 twin studies published between 1929 and 1977, studies that examined 339 identical twin pairs and 426 fraternal twin pairs. Patricia Brennan and her associates (1995:69) also reported on eight twin studies, three from Germany and one each from Holland, the United States, Finland, England, and Japan. These latter eight studies, published between 1929 and 1979, examined a total of 138 pairs of monozygotic twins and 145 dizygotic twins, and included many mentioned by Bartol (1991). Brennan and her associates identified crime concordance levels for monozygotic twins ranging from 50 to 100 percent, with most between 60 and 70 percent. Crime concordance levels for fraternal twins were much lower, ranging from zero to 60 percent, with most between 10 and 15 percent. Indeed, the overall average was 52 percent for monozygotic twins and 21 percent for dizygotic twins (see Raines 1993:79).

The twin studies have several important shortcomings. For one thing, those reporting very high concordance for identical twins involved as few as two to four sets of twins. The three studies with the largest numbers of identical twin pairs, between 28 and 37 sets, exhibited concordance levels between 61 and 68 percent. The highest level of concordance (54 percent) for dizygotic twins was in the same study that reported only an average concordance level among the monozygotic twins (66 percent). Few medical researchers would accept so few cases as definitive. Moreover, the chief outcome variables—crime, delinquency, or some other indicator of misconduct—rely on the timely intercession of the criminal justice system or a judgment by a researcher. These facts make the conclusions of the twin studies highly suspect.

When a major Norwegian study failed to show a significant difference between the criminality of identical and fraternal twins, Karl Christiansen (1977:82), who studied Danish twins, was troubled. He suggested that perhaps "some special conditions exist in Norway that would dampen the expression of genetic factors." Given the high level of cultural and racial homogeneity found in the Scandinavian countries of Denmark, Finland, Norway, and Sweden, this is a remarkable statement. The same qualification could be expressed about nearly all genetic studies because the largest and most sophisticated have, in the main, taken place in Scandinavian countries. These findings beg an important question: What is being measured? Is it, perhaps, the impact of nationality or geographic boundaries on genetics?

Adoption Studies The adoption studies yielded the same general findings: Adopted children whose natural parents have criminal records are much more likely to be convicted of a crime than when the natural parents have no criminal records (Hollin 1989). Barry Hutchings and Sarnoff Mednick (1977) compared adopted children who had a criminal biological father and a noncriminal adoptive father with those who had a noncriminal biological father and a criminal adoptive father. The former were twice as likely as the latter to become criminals themselves.

In a far larger study Mednick and his associates (1984, 1987) found support for the genetic transmission of crime traits. However, the type of crime committed by biological parents was not related to their child's specific crime. If the police had arrested either biological parent, the child of that union, whatever gender, was much more likely to have a criminal record.

Proponents of a gene–crime link believed that adoption studies would control for environmental effects, particularly those that made the findings of twin studies suspect. The evidence is generally consistent with the heritable factors thesis. However, researchers have been unable to rule out the interactive effects of the biological parents' social status and such factors as prenatal alcoholism (Cadoret, Troughton, and O'Gorman 1987; Duyme 1990; Van Dusen, Mednick, Gabrielli, and Hutchings 1983). That is, child-rearing patterns in different social classes and communities compound the problems rather than eliminate them. According to Lee Ellis and Anthony Walsh (2000:439), "Adoption studies indicate that genetic and environmental factors interact to affect criminal/antisocial behavior."

Karyotype Studies

Karyotype studies allow scientists to learn the number and type of chromosomes in individuals. In 1965 scientists resurrected Lombroso in *Nature,* the respected British scientific journal. P. A. Jacobs and associates (1965) pointed to a genetic abnormality as a possible key to some criminal behavior. They based this claim on the fact that sex chromosomes determine gender: An XX pairing is a female, and an XY is a male. Using karyotyping the researchers observed that a chromosomal abnormality occurs when the fertilized ovum receives an extra Y chromosome. They speculated that the extra Y chromosome created an XYY pattern (Jacobs 1965:1351), which is extremely rare (Hoffman 1977:447). The **XYY male** is usually over six feet tall, exhibits low mental functioning, suffers from acute acne, and is often clumsy (Clark, Tefler, Baker, and Rosen 1970; Hoffman 1977; Horgan 1993; Hunter 1977).

Criminologists focus on XYY males for two main reasons. First, as reported in the *Nature* article, the XYY pattern occurred 5 to 10 times more often among prison inmates than predicted by chance alone (Jacobs, Bruton, McCrille, Brittain, and McClemont 1965; see also Ellis and Walsh 2000:440). Researchers subsequently found high proportions among a population of mental hospital patients (Price, Strong, Whatmore, and McClemont 1966). However, it is possible that the observed overrepresentation of XYY males in certain environments is due to non-scientific explanations associated with the XYY males' physical appearance and intellect. That is, because XYY males are often tall, unattractive, and fearsome-looking, they may be more likely to come to the attention of the police; moreover, their lower-than-average intelligence may mean that they are less able than others to participate in their own defense (Hunter 1966; Sarbin and Miller 1970). The XYY karyotype may also be class-biased, given that the appearance of this anomaly is linked to lower-class living conditions (Kessler and Moos 1970). Social class, and not genetic makeup, may account for their higher-than-expected showing: Most inmates are members of the lower class. Finally marginal mental functioning may be yet another cause of their alleged overrepresentation (Hunter 1966).

Second, allegedly XYY males are more aggressive than XY males (Jacobs et al. 1965). Contributing to the interest in a hyper-violent male was the highly publicized trial of mass murderer Richard Speck, who used the "fact" that he was an XYY male as part of his defense. By the late 1970s, however, the scientific consensus was that the hyper-violent XYY male was a myth. Indeed, such individuals, when compared to genetically normal males, tend to exhibit higher levels of passivity (Sarbin and Miller 1970). Only for so-called sex crimes do XYY males appear more often than we would expect by chance alone (Reiss and Roth 1993). The definition of sex crimes, however, is broad and not limited to violent sex crimes. As H. A. Wilkin and associates (1977:187) observed about such men, "No evidence has been found that men with either of these chromosome complements [XY or XYY] are especially aggressive. Because such men do not appear to contribute to society's problem with aggressive crimes, their identification would not serve to ameliorate this problem."

The Human Genome Mapping Project and the Future of "Crime Genetics"

James Watson and Francis Crick discovered DNA in 1953. However, mapping the human genome was an elusive goal until the invention of machines called automatic genetic sequencers in the 1990s. More than 1000 scientists and technicians at 16 laboratories in six countries completed the **Human Genome Map-**

ping Project (**HGMP**) at a cost of $250 million. It took the scientists four years to map the first billion markers, four months to move to 2 billion, and 12 weeks to finish the task ("Decoding the human body" 2000:52; Friend 2000:1).

Scientists have mapped dozens of diseases and genetic defects, all with a hereditary basis. For example, birth defects associated with dietary problems or poisoning, like fetal alcohol syndrome, may have no location on the human genome. However, genetic markers may show who is most at risk for developing problems as a result of environmental factors. Few markers exist for social behavior, except for some forms of mental retardation. The discovery of other behavioral markers, particularly concerning depression and neurological conditions that may reflect heritable predispositions, awaits further scientific advances (McInerney 1999).

Genetic engineering, a term used to describe a wide range of biogenetic techniques, holds considerable promise. Once scientists locate the genes for specific diseases and genetic defects, other researchers can develop treatments to counteract them. In one scenario healthy or corrected genes will replace bad or defective ones, perhaps even before birth. However, it may be the middle of this century before the medical sciences can fully exploit the information provided by the HGMP.

What does the human genome map mean for criminology? Ellis and Walsh asked if the HGMP has led to identification of a crime gene. Their answer: "No. In this sense, there is still no proof that criminal/antisocial behavior is genetically influenced. However, scientists have not yet located any specific genes for height either. Yet, there is no reason to doubt that height is genetically influenced" (Ellis and Walsh 2000:436). They pointed out that height may be the result of several genes, and not one "height gene," and the same could be true of crime.

Genetic scientists "have solid leads on genes for different temperaments, body builds, stature, and cognitive abilities" ("Decoding the human body," 2000:55). Whether they discover crime genes remains highly speculative.[4] Figure 3.3 summarizes the genetic explanations of crime.

Assessing Genetic Explanations

As with any crime theory, the true test lies in the demonstrated links between what theorists believe and what researchers discover. Genetics–crime assessments generally take two forms. First, as happened with XYY theory, critics may challenge the basic premise upon which proponents base the theory. That is, does the addition of an extra Y chromosome really suggest a "supermale"? Skeptics argue that the extra Y chromosome does not predict criminality, but at best predicts the likelihood of apprehension. An excessively tall, awkward, acne-scarred man with a low IQ who commits a crime has a greater chance of being arrested and convicted than someone smarter, more agile, and less physically distinctive (Hunter 1966; Kessler and Moos 1970; Witkin et al. 1977). Because only 3 percent of the prison population fits the XYY pattern (Jacobs et al. 1965), the theory, even if correct, explains very little criminality. Lastly the research on XYY individuals suggests that they are usually passive and *underrepresented* in the noninstitutionalized criminal population (Sarbin and Miller 1970). Perhaps labeling theory, and not biology, better explains XYY as a correlate of prison placement (see Chapter 8).

Second, the genetic researchers' methods receive special attention. According to David Rowe (1990) genetics cannot explain criminal behavior in a single person;

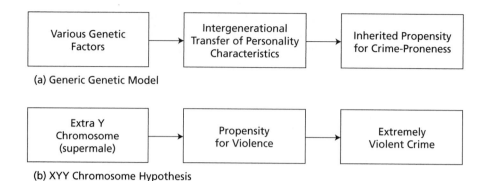

(a) Generic Genetic Model

(b) XYY Chromosome Hypothesis

FIGURE 3.3 Genetic Explanations of Crime

rather, genetic explanations provide reasons some *groups* are more prone to certain types of behavior, including antisocial behavior. Rowe and Wayne Osgood (1984) found significant links between genetic factors and the self-reported criminality of twin pairs. Rowe (1990) concluded that neither family nor other environmental factors serve as suitable causal factors in explaining adult crime or delinquency. Genetics may predispose children toward antisocial behavior, with their heredity accounting for one-third to two-thirds of the explanation (Rowe 1983, 1990; Rowe and Gulley 1992). Diana Fishbein (1990:45) was critical of the research methods sociobiologists used, especially in twin studies: "No definitive conclusions can be drawn from twin studies of aggressive behavior because no consistent pattern of genetic influences emerges."

The general criticisms of crime gene research, then, fit into these clusters:

- *Sampling issues.* The samples in twin and adoption studies are, as a rule, small. When researchers employ larger samples, the differences are less significant. Mednick and associates (1984, 1987) overcame this deficiency in a study of 14,427 Danish adoptees (but see "measurement problems" below); however, few researchers achieve this sample size, especially with twin studies.

- *Alternate explanations issues.* Studies of the potential links between genetics and crime rarely employ sophisticated statistical controls or use sufficiently matched control groups. Environmental variables, from social class and family to contaminated living conditions, are strong candidates to explain the findings attributed to genetics.

- *Measurement problems.* Michael Gottfredson and Travis Hirschi (1990:60), after calculating the correlation in Mednick's adoption study, concluded that "the magnitude of the 'genetic effect' as determined by adoption studies is near zero."

- *Overstated cases.* **Biocriminologists** cite statistically significant differences as proof that heredity determines behavior. However, the fact that two groups exhibit a statistical difference on a given characteristic is not proof of causation. One study of Danish identical and fraternal twins that considered social factors estimated the effects of heredity as very modest and, in one case, nearly zero (Carey 1992).

The greatest genetic variability exists at the individual level, not the racial level (Cavalli-Sforza 2000). In contrast to the tiny number of genes that determine a person's skin color, traits such as intelligence are likely shaped by perhaps tens of thousands of genes (Angier 2000). These facts hardly bolster the credibility of crime gene arguments.

Genetics, Public Policy, and Criminal Justice Practices

Public policies derived from modern genetics are as controversial as earlier variants. The ethical and philosophical arguments against "biomedical" crime factors are widely recognized (Brennan, Mednick, and Volavka 1995:65–66). First, as noted previously, biological explanations have ties to nineteenth-century social Darwinism and to twentieth-century Nazi ideology and practice, such as Josef Mengele's horrific experiments on twins at Auschwitz.[5] The racist legacy of genetics lingers. Second, some critics decry a genetics–behavior link because it eliminates free will and criminal responsibility—in legal parlance, *mens rea*. Third, the **nature-*versus*-nurture** argument "created an 'either/or' context of research on crime causation" (Brennan, Mednick, and Volavka 1995:66). A **nature-*plus*-nurture** model allows for the effects of free will.

Patricia Brennan and her associates (1995) identified several policy implications with regard to genetics and crime. They pointed to the finding that we can predict antisocial behavior from the interaction of perinatal factors (those occurring during a child's delivery) and unstable family environments. Providing prenatal health care to mothers and early hospitalization should help to reduce perinatal problems. According to Brennan and associates (1995:88–89), "The focus of this program would be to change the biological factor in potentially adverse social conditions. . . . Children who have suffered from perinatal complications should be targeted for parent-training interventions or school enrichment programs that would help to ameliorate the effects of their biological defects."

Law Enforcement Practices Recent explosions in genetic knowledge have led to changes in DNA-related police practices. The 1994 Crime Act established the FBI's Combined DNA Index System (CODIS), a national DNA database. The logic behind CODIS is threefold. First, convicted and released offenders may think twice about committing another offense if their DNA is in a database. Second, these databases should make the identification and conviction of repeat offenders far easier if the suspects leave blood or other biological specimens at the crime scene. Third, DNA evidence can exonerate suspects, something that happens in at least one-quarter to one-fifth of the cases (National Research Council 1996).

In 1996 nearly half of all state prosecutors' offices used DNA evidence. Most cases involved rape and murder/manslaughter (DeFrances and Steadman 1998:6). By 1997 the nation's DNA labs had analyzed 287,000 convicted-offender samples, adding about 50,000 samples a year (Steadman 2000:1). All states currently require DNA sample collection, primarily from convicted sex offenders. Some also collect samples from persons convicted of assault, robbery, carjacking, home invasion, stalking, and endangering children (Steadman 2000:1). As of 2001 the nation's publicly operated forensic crime labs reported backlogs totaling over

16,000 suspects and 265,000 convicted offenders (Steadman 2002:1). The FBI formally unveiled CODIS in late 1998, but as of 2000, the database included data from less than half the states.

The standard DNA-typing procedure, the RFLP-VNTR[6] method, is fine in laboratory and clinical settings but less practical in the field. RFLP-VNTR requires many clean specimens, an unlikely occurrence at most crime scenes, especially if a robbery or violent crime has taken place. A new method, called PCR-STR,[7] overcomes the RFLP-VNTR's forensic limitations (Hammond and Caskey 1997). The PCR-STR method produces "reliable results with degraded specimens, is quick, and can be automated to permit the creation of a vastly improved database of DNA profiles of convicted offenders" (Hammond and Caskey 1997:1).[8]

DNA lineups are a potential investigative tool. Investigators may use voluntary **DNA dragnets,** a technique first applied in a 1986 English homicide case (Mays, Fields, and Thompson 1994). In a DNA dragnet law enforcement officers and technicians move through an area where they believe a suspect lives or works, gathering voluntary samples from a defined group of suspects. Angus Dodson (2000) proposed compulsory sampling *absent probable cause.* DNA lineups enable police and grand juries to test small groups of individuals based on the "reasonable suspicion" standard. Support for this method is provided by existing federal jurisprudence on evidence seizure for identification purposes absent probable cause and Fourth Amendment case law for seizing both bodily fluids and tissues (Dodson 2000). The key is to create an operational framework with sufficient civil rights protections.

Judicial Practices Genetically identifiable biological matter may be the single most damaging form of physical evidence available to crime scene investigators. Three judicial aspects of DNA evidence support this claim. First, the O. J. Simpson case aside, DNA evidence has a dramatic impact at trial, where challenges to it are rarely successful. Second, prosecutors may employ DNA evidence to blunt possible charges of racism or questionable cross-racial eyewitness testimony (Purcell, Winfree, and Mays 1994). Witnesses can be biased or make mistakes; science is, correctly or not, viewed as neutral. Finally the use of DNA evidence to establish the innocence of convicted felons has increased since the mid-1990s (Connors, Lundregan, Miller, and McEwen 1996). The implementation of PCR techniques, which use highly degraded samples, has helped exonerate many convicted felons. By the late 1990s more than 75 convicted felons had been released based on DNA evidence (Reno 1999).

Genetics-related affirmative defenses meet with judicial skepticism, as Richard Speck's case highlights. The State of Illinois tried and convicted Speck in 1967 for the murder of eight Chicago nurses. His lawyer incorrectly claimed that Speck was an XYY male. Speck and others who have attempted to blame their criminal deeds on their chromosomal structure have been unsuccessful. The plea "I am a victim of my genes" has fallen on deaf judicial ears.

BIOCHEMISTRY AND CRIME

- How do you respond to the claim that alcoholism and other forms of drug abuse are diseases meriting treatment, not punishment?

- Even if you are willing to view these forms of behavior as addictions and medical problems, can you understand why some people resist this idea?

- Alcohol and controlled substances are only a few of the many chemicals in the environment. Do you think that exposure to other chemicals also has the potential to alter human behavior?

Humans depend on a wide array of chemicals—their actions, interactions, and reactions—to accomplish all bodily functions. For example, the autonomic nervous system (ANS) governs digestion, respiration, and heartbeat, and **neurochemicals** enable these processes to work. The central nervous system (CNS) consists of the brain and spinal column. Other neural stimuli are necessary to operate the smooth muscle groups, which requires cooperation between the ANS and the CNS. A delicate balance of neurochemicals maintains the information flow between the ANS and the CNS, keeping humans alive and functioning.

The human brain is at great risk from biochemical imbalances, particularly as related to antisocial behavior. The brain, weighing just three pounds and containing 10 billion neurons, performs two basic functions: (1) It integrates and processes information, and (2) it serves as a storage and retrieval system for information. The ANS and CNS, but especially the brain, are similar to a very sensitive computer system. Change the current, alter the direction of that current or somehow misdirect the incoming messages, and unpleasant consequences will result.

Substance Abuse

Understanding substance abuse—and perhaps even controlling it—is important because substance-involved criminals account for the majority of those arrested (U.S. Department of Justice 1994, 1999). Moreover, once they are caught, convicted, and incarcerated, these individuals pose unique jail and prison management problems (Mays and Winfree 2002; see also U.S. Department of Justice 1999, 2000). Alcohol use and criminality are positively correlated both nationally and cross culturally for property crime, violent offenses, and delinquency; the same is true for self-reported offenses (Ellis and Walsh 2000:234–35).

Any understanding of substance abuse begins with an examination of the central nervous system's operation and the significance of neurotransmitters. CNS cells, or neurons, come in many sizes and shapes, and form chains of specialized and excitable cells. They differ from other body cells in that they can conduct information in the form of electrical impulses. The body's 100 billion neurons send signals or impulses as information in the form of electrical energy.

Neurotransmitters carry CNS information; they inhibit or enhance the release of ions, electrical charges, and communication between neurons when these electrical impulses activate a sufficient number of synapses. They are fast-acting neurochemicals. For example, if you touch a sharp object with your finger, chemicals allow your brain to quickly define the incident. They accomplish this feat by passing an electrochemical signal or message between millions of nerve cells that finally arrives at your brain. A key part of your brain then interprets this signal as an unpleasant event. The CNS contains roughly 100 neurotransmitters. Some, such as dopamine, epinephrine, and norepinephrine, excite or speed up the "firing" of ions between neurons; others, such as endorphins, slow down this "firing."

The body uses these chemicals to trigger anger or to regulate the operation of different organs. Each neurotransmitter has a receptor site—proteins located on the surfaces of the neurons—designed to receive it, and the ensuing reaction may stimulate or inhibit a specific bodily function.

Dopamine (DA), one of many neurotransmitters found in the CNS, has received special attention from psychopharmacologists because of its apparent dual roles in the regulation of (1) mood and affect, and (2) motivation and reward processes. Researchers have found that the reinforcing effects of psychoactive drugs in humans are associated with increases in brain DA (Volkow et al. 1999). Although the brain contains several DA systems, the mesolimbic DA system appears to be the most important for motivational processes. Some addictive drugs produce their potent effects on behavior by enhancing mesolimbic DA activity. Scientists speculate that some forms of clinical depression may result from unusually low DA levels.

Repeated use of psychomotor stimulants like cocaine and depressants like heroin can deplete the mesolimbic DA system, causing normal rewards to lose motivational significance. As a result the mesolimbic DA system becomes even more sensitive to pharmacological substances (Addiction Research Unit/SUNY at Buffalo 1998).

Abstinence from drugs such as cocaine and morphine after repeated administration may decrease DA levels in the brain system, which may, in turn, be related to the intense cravings associated with withdrawal in drug-dependent humans. The subjective experience of craving is related to relapse into drug-taking behavior following abstinence and so is an important factor in drug addiction.

Stimulants may compensate for a deficiency in the neurotransmitters dopamine, serotonin, and norepinephrine—chemicals that determine a person's mood. Cocaine or amphetamine users, according to this theory, are attempting to stave off the apathy and depression caused by a chemical deficiency (Khantzian 1985), drug use being homoeostatic. Chronic cocaine users, in self-administering doses throughout the day, are counteracting DA deficiency (Gold, Washton, and Dackis 1985:133). In extroverted persons with high levels of DA, even small doses of cocaine are intensely rewarding, exposing them to higher risk of dependence (Goleman 1990).

During the 1970s scientists discovered morphinelike neurotransmitters within the brain, along with CNS-specific receptor sites programmed to receive these compounds. These **endorphins** (short for "endogenous morphine") relieve pain when they reach receptor sites in the spinal cord and brain. Although these sites receive naturally occurring neurotransmitters, or endorphins, they are receptive to external ones, such as heroin, as well.

Endorphins also enable people to deal with psychological stress by curbing autonomic overreactions and promoting a sense of calm. They slow respiration, reduce blood pressure, and lower the level of motor activity. A "deficiency in an endorphin system that ordinarily would support feelings of pleasure and reinforcement might lead to feelings of inadequacy and sadness" (Levinthal 1988:149). Persons at risk for opiate addiction may suffer from an endorphin deficiency. Their predisposition to heroin addiction could be a biological response to a genetically acquired deficiency, or it could represent a temporary or permanent impairment of the body's ability to produce endorphins. This finding helps account for the puzzling individual variability in the addictive power of opiates.

If an endorphin deficiency exists, however, the question remains about what precipitating circumstances might lead to such a deficiency. Among the possible causal forces are the environment, genetics, or both (Levinthal 1988).

The National Institute on Drug Abuse (1998) sponsored research revealing that an individual's genetic makeup is a major factor in drug abuse vulnerability. The researchers found that, although family and social environmental factors determine whether an individual will begin using drugs, progression from use to dependence is largely due to genetic factors, particularly for males. In addition, the genetic influence for heroin addiction surpasses that of any other drug (Zickler 1999). Thus, even though drug abuse is the result of a complex interplay of environmental, social, psychological, and biochemical factors, genetics plays an important role in individual vulnerability to drug use—the more severe the abuse, the greater the role of genetic factors (Comings 1995).

Although genes are important in the control of behavior, they do not directly cause a person to become a drug user. Some researchers also suggest that genes produce a predisposition to respond in a specific way to a given drug: "Thus, genes are not the sole determinant of alcoholism or drug dependence, but their presence (or absence) may increase the likelihood that a person will become alcoholic or drug dependent" (Pickens and Svikis 1988:2).

Serotonin, Monoamine Oxidase, and Criminal Behavior

Two other neurochemicals have ties to criminal behavior. **Serotonin** is a stimulating neurotransmitter sometimes connected to violence. Persons with low serotonin levels are more inclined toward aggression and violence than those with normal amounts. We do not know how serotonin influences behavior—whether it has a direct impact or lessens impulse control. In any event, because of this link, serotonin levels are a rough predictor of criminal behavior. Although the correlation between serotonin and crime is clear, it is unclear whether the environment influences serotonin levels. It is also possible that serotonin levels (and other biological factors) have roots in social conditions, such as extreme poverty and accompanying malnutrition.

Monoamine oxidase (**MAO**) is a neurologically active enzyme linked to criminality since the 1970s (Ellis 1991). MAO seems to play a role in brain functioning (Roth, Breakefield, and Castiglione 1976). The enzyme, found throughout the human body, apparently helps regulate key neurotransmitters. MAO, in two forms, works on serotonin, norepinephrine, and dopamine, which, in turn, influence behavior. No one knows what the exact nature of MAO activity in the brain is or how it influences human behavior. Biologists have only studied what they call "peripheral MAO," or MAO outside the nervous system. This is the form of MAO—found in red blood cells—measured by scientists who study human behavior, including crime. Just as importantly, biocriminologists believe that genes influence MAO in the bloodstream. Although MAO may be important to criminologists, scientists do not agree on how genetics influence MAO levels or if this is even important to criminal justice (Ellis 1991:230–31). In any case an MAO deficiency is associated with borderline retardation. Furthermore, low-MAO persons exhibit a tendency toward aggressive outbursts, often in response to anger, fear, or frustration. Finally several studies report relationships between MAO deficiency and abnormally aggressive behavior in males (Brunner et al. 1994).

MAO, Misconduct, and Crime Lee Ellis (1991) provided an exhaustive review of this biochemical marker. Some individuals have elevated MAO levels, causing a state of depression. Similarly, easily bored persons may suffer from MAO overload, a condition that could induce risk taking (e.g., contact sports, mountain climbing, or skydiving) or lawbreaking. At the other end of the spectrum, Ellis observed (1991) that low MAO activity is an apparent precursor for psychopathology, illegal drug use, and criminality. However, in most studies of inappropriate behavior, "the associations tend to be modest" (Ellis 1991:234). Ellis's behavioral correlates include "defiance of authority," "impulsiveness and monotony avoidance and job instability," "childhood hyperactivity," "poor academic performance," "sensation seeking," "recreational drug use in general, but especially tendencies for excessive use of alcohol," and "preference of active social life (or extraversion)." He concluded that "low platelet MAO is a biological marker for criminality itself, *albeit one of modest strength*" (Ellis 1991:235; emphasis added). He also noted, as further support of his contention, that, consistent with current statistics on crime:

- Males have lower MAO levels than females, and also have much higher arrest rates.

- MAO levels are much lower during the second and third decades of life, which official and self-report statistics on crime show to be the most crime-prone years.

- African Americans have lower MAO activity than whites but have higher arrest and conviction rates.

Three points limit the generalizability of Ellis's assertions. First, MAO levels in the brain remain unknown. Second, researchers have observed at best a modest correlation between platelet MAO and crime, but not a causal relationship. Third, even if adding MAO might reduce criminality, society must balance any alleged benefits against its long-term effects on humans in general and on the group most affected—African American males—in particular.

Other Biochemical and Neurological Explanations

The potential list of biochemical and neurological influences on criminality is extensive (Ellis and Walsh 2000). Among the many existing explanations three specific types yield interesting insights into biology-based criminality, as well as having policy and practical implications. The first type involves the ingestion of alien chemical substances other than psychoactive drugs. The ingestion process may be environmental, or it may result from purposive acts such as eating or drinking. The ingested chemical either is nontoxic in low doses but toxic in higher doses or is toxic at any level. In either case the underlying premise is that toxicity may negatively influence behavior.

Another biochemical hypothesis involves abnormal levels of hormones. When something interferes with the production, movement, or absorption of hormones, physiological and behavioral alterations often result. Could hormonal changes, researchers have speculated, cause antisocial behavior?

Finally the work of Franz Joseph Gall inspired criminologists to explore brain functioning. Gall's phrenology fell into disfavor, but modern abnormal psychology (see Chapter 4) and neurological crime theories evolved from his pioneering work. Some of these explanations focus on chemicals and the brain. However, the ones we examine in this chapter involve defects in brain functioning with organic origins—that is, changes in the brain's structure.

Foods, Toxins, and Crime Criminals and delinquents often exhibit vitamin deficiencies, poor eating habits, and low blood-sugar levels, all conditions—particularly low blood sugar or hypoglycemia—related to hyperactivity and aggression (Hippchen 1978, 1982; see also Shah and Roth 1974). The exact causal links to crime are unclear. One case exemplifies the confusion about these ties. In 1982, in San Francisco, former city supervisor Dan White, the assassin of Mayor George Moscone and Supervisor Harvey Milk, blamed the murders on his consumption of too many Hostess Twinkies. White did not deny that he committed the crimes, but argued that something intervened to eliminate the necessary *mens rea* component of criminal responsibility. The media-dubbed **Twinkies defense** resulted in a finding of guilty on lesser charges. In the wake of this trial, the idea of a chemically based defense gained popularity. Other courts, however, have shown less inclination to accept this as a legitimate mitigating factor or an affirmative defense. In any event the questionable methodology of most hypoglycemia studies casts doubt on the central argument that low blood sugar, caused in part by an excess sugar intake, is associated with violence (Kanarek 1994).

Heavy metals, including lead, mercury, and cadmium, are environmental toxins. Biochemists have long recognized the toxicity of these metals even in small doses, and they are pandemic in our environment, largely in lead-based paints and industrial waste. Speculations about their possible ties to antisocial behavior are of recent origin. For example, a postmortem laboratory analysis of an alleged mass murderer's hair revealed significantly elevated lead and cadmium levels. After eliminating other possible medical explanations, the researcher concluded that heavy-metal poisoning may have affected the accused's inhibitory mechanisms (Hall 1989).

The **neurotoxicity hypothesis** (**NH**), especially as applied to lead toxicity (Denno 1993; Masters 1997), holds that "chemical imbalances in heavy metals and other toxins may contribute significantly to anti-social behavior by disrupting the normal functioning of a person's brain chemistry" (Crawford 2000:6). NH proponents view lead, manganese, and cadmium as likely candidates. Pulling together several biological hypotheses, they suggest that genetic makeup and psychoactive chemicals, especially alcohol, along with heavy-metal poisoning, can interact to cause antisocial behavior.

This thesis may contain a class bias. Members of the lower class are at greatest risk from the primary environmental lead sources: lead-based paints and lead plumbing. Scientists believe that manganese lowers the levels of serotonin, norepinephrine, and dopamine (Masters, 1997; Masters, Hone, and Doshi 1998). Individuals with diets low in calcium and other essential vitamins are especially vulnerable to manganese uptake and neurotransmitter depletion. Such dietary deficiencies are quite common in African American and Hispanic American infants (Masters, Hone, and Doshi 1997:158).

Hormonal Influences and Crime Another biochemical explanation of criminality focuses on abnormal hormone levels. **Hormones** are also chemical messengers secreted by the endocrine system, a series of ductless glands in the body that include the pituitary and thyroid glands, pancreas, kidneys, ovaries, and testes. They move through the bloodstream or pass slowly through cell walls to various parts of the body, where they regulate cell metabolism—speeding up, maintaining, or slowing cell activity. Hormones are secondary chemical messengers and are generally slow-acting.

In 1850 scientists observed the physiological and psychological effects of the **endocrine system**'s hormones (Vold and Bernard 1986:98). The importance of hormonal balance—and imbalance—for human behavior was observed early in the twentieth century. Louis Berman (1938) later suggested that institutionalized offenders in New York State had glandular problems at a rate two to three times greater than that of a control group. However, a series of studies conducted in New Jersey on incarcerated and "normal" juveniles found no such differences (Moltich 1937).

The **PMS defense** is an extension of the hormonal imbalance theme. Premenstrual syndrome is a little-understood medical condition that afflicts some women around the onset of their menses, perhaps leading to irrational, bizarre, or aggressive behavior. Katherine Dalton (1964) viewed natural chemicals in women suffering from PMS as the cause of their aberrant, law-violating behavior. The menstrual cycle creates large fluctuations in female biochemistry (Fishbein 1992). In the early stages of menstruation, women experience a depletion of female hormones (ovulation marks the highest level), and reduced levels of estrogen are associated with aggressiveness. Doctors give many women who suffer from the symptoms of PMS progesterone and estrogen therapy. Considerable research is needed to determine if PMS, alone or in concert with environmental factors, actually "causes" criminal behavior. This research could then inform the separate legal issue of whether society should excuse persons so afflicted from criminal responsibility for their acts (Horney 1978).

Research scientists have also linked testosterone, an essentially male hormone, to inappropriate conduct in teenagers and adults, ranging from excessive aggressiveness to violent behavior (Dabbs, Frady, Carr, and Beach 1986; Kreuz and Rose 1972; Olweus, Maattson, Schalling, and Low 1980; Udry 1990). This linkage is especially appealing because a high testosterone level signifies a "supermale." However, the testosterone–deviance link remains more of a statistical association than a single variable statement of cause and effect; testosterone's role in producing antisocial behavior is not clear (Booth and Osgood 1993:95). Rather than ruling out social explanations, Alan Booth and D. Wayne Osgood (1993) suggested that a combination of biological and social explanations is helpful. They envision a balanced-influence model in which testosterone contributes indirectly to crime. Specifically the hormone affects temperament, interpersonal relationships, and even performance of important social roles, which relate to criminal and other antisocial behavior.

Neurological Crime Theories Neurophysiology looks at both the central nervous system (CNS) and the autonomic nervous system (ANS) in seeking explanations of criminality. Biocriminologists, using neurophysiology, trace much criminality to events in early childhood. Injuries to the brain—what doctors call brain insults—can lead to defective brain functioning. Intrusive agents such as gunshots and knives, brain and spinal-column injuries, and even fevers brought on by infectious diseases qualify as brain insult. Brain lesions and tumors, whether malignant or nonmalignant, are also candidates in the search for neurological origins of crime. People with these types of injuries or disorders—especially to the cerebral cortex—exhibit, among other things, psychotic episodes, depression, homicidal urges, massive personality alterations, and even hallucinations (Ellis and Walsh 2000; Yeudall 1977).

CNS disorders, such as **learning disabilities, attention deficit disorder (ADD)**, and **hyperactivity,** although not by themselves criminogenic, are statistically linked to antisocial behavior. For example, some researchers maintain that learning-disabled children violate the law at the same rate as the non–learning disabled (Murray 1976). Others, however, report that the learning disabled exhibit high official delinquency and crime rates (Buikhuisen 1987; Holzman 1979); they studied the same condition but reached different conclusions.

Behaviors related to brain dysfunctions include aggressiveness, dyslexia, and other "abruptly appearing, maladaptive behavior that interrupts the life style and life flow of an individual" (Siegel 1992:162). ADD and childhood brain dysfunctions amplify the problem. ADD-related behaviors include lack of attention to details and tasks, outbursts of impulsivity and instances of "acting without thinking," and hyperactivity (e.g., the classic fidgety child who shows excessive motor activity even during sleep). This disorder manifests itself in poor school performance, stubbornness, and an unwillingness to obey authority figures. About 3 percent of the nation's children suffer from ADD, mostly boys. Both ADD and brain dysfunctions may be related to growing up in dysfunctional families although the causal ordering is elusive (Moffitt and Silva 1988). Early diagnosis and treatment may lower the risk for antisocial and criminal behavior. Figure 3.4 summarizes biolochemical explanations of crime.

Assessing Biochemical Explanations

The idea that chemical imbalances cause behavioral changes in human beings is very appealing. We know that severe brain damage will impact behavior (Mednick, Brennan, and Kandel 1988). There are documented cases of otherwise normal persons receiving an injury to the brain, followed quickly by obvious changes in aggressiveness, demeanor, personal attitudes, mental functioning, and conduct. However, in view of the volume of crimes committed in the nation annually, brain trauma no doubt accounts for only a small portion. Even the observation that a specific mass murderer suffered from a brain tumor may be of little help except to understand that single case. Nor can we be sure that a tumor was the cause of any murderous behavior—most people who suffer from this affliction do not climb to a high spot and gun people down. Conversely a predisposition to alcoholism or other forms of addiction may show strong ties to criminality, but we must carefully review any conclusions. Crime is a *correlate* of addiction, and there also may be a *biological predisposition* to addiction. But a predisposition to addiction does not *cause* crime—or even addiction—as many addicts commit no crimes and many criminals are not addicts.

In fact, for most drug-abusing criminals, criminality preceded addiction (Abadinsky 2001). Alcohol may also be a crime's immediate precursor, the proximate cause. That is, alcohol lowers individuals' inhibitions and hinders their

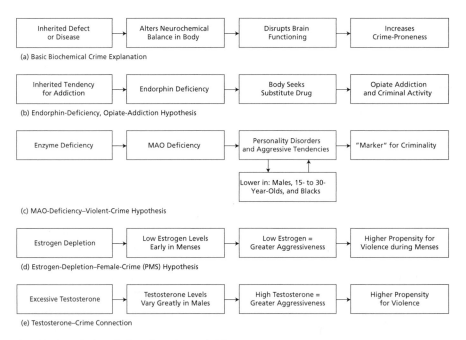

FIGURE 3.4 Biochemical Explanations of Crime

judgment, which facilitates the commission of a crime and, often, the subsequent arrest. Drunk driving is the cause of about 16,000 deaths annually; more than 60 percent of homicides involve alcohol use by both offender and victim; and about 65 percent of aggressive sexual acts against women involve alcohol use by the offender. Research has suggested that the pharmacological effects of alcohol can cause aggression in some persons, and alcohol is a factor in nearly 50 percent of murders, suicides, and accidental deaths, and a factor in nearly 40 percent of violent crimes in the United States (Chermak and Taylor 1995; Greenfield 1998).

What is the causal link? Did alcohol provide "liquid courage" for an act that was already being planned? We know that alcohol consumption can lead to the loss of inhibitions, but what distinguishes the "life of the party" from a felonious assaulter? Alcohol can also impair the processing of information, thereby causing a misinterpretation of events or the behavior of others, resulting, for example, in assault or aggressive sexual behavior (e.g., date rape). Although we may not want to make too much of the intoxication levels of arrestees, these observations do not diminish the importance of biochemical susceptibility to alcoholism or other drug addiction. Susceptibility by itself does not tell us why some people who drink to excess commit crimes and others do not. But it does suggest treatment modalities to eliminate the proximate cause of both the crime and the arrest.

Ideas like the neurotoxicity hypothesis may eventually explain some criminal behavior. For example, in comparing U.S. counties with no reported release of lead or manganese to counties with toxic releases, one researcher found that the former had violent crime rates below the national average and that the latter's rates were four times greater than the national average (Masters 1997:32). Although interesting, this study drew individual-level inferences from group-level data—most persons exposed to high levels of toxins did not commit violent crimes.

Biochemistry is the business of physical scientists. Problems emerge when criminologists tie biochemistry to crime, which is, after all, human social behavior. Major criticisms of the biochemistry of crime follow familiar patterns:

- *Methodological issues.* Many biochemistry–crime studies suffer from methodological shortcomings. Only carefully controlled and replicated clinical studies will eliminate this concern. Of course, designing a controlled experiment in which the level of heavy metals is manipulated and analyzed may pose unsurmountable ethical and practical challenges (Crawford 2000). The samples used in these studies are often unrepresentative, and generalizing to the population at large is nearly impossible. Biocriminologists also employ contestable criminality indicators, especially official crime records, or vague surrogate measures such as "antisocial behavior."

- *Causal ordering problems.* Researchers may also confuse cause with effect—for example, the alleged PMS–female crime link, whereby irregular menstruation brings on psychological and physical stressors associated with aggression (Dalton 1961, 1964). Perhaps the psychological and physical stresses associated with aggression bring on irregular menstruation (Horney 1978).

- *Overstated cases.* Hormone–crime studies yield inconsistent and unremarkable results. At best testosterone–crime ties are negligible; they also have nonchemical explanations (Booth and Osgood 1984). One study did find higher testosterone levels among violent offenders—including rapists and armed robbers—than among nonviolent offenders or nonoffenders; however, testosterone levels for *all* subjects were within normal ranges (Rubin 1987). Drugs have lowered testosterone levels and offending rates for some sex offenders, but the drugs do not affect their nonsexual violence (Rubin 1987). Generally criminologists reject the endocrine system secretion thesis as lacking theoretical foundations and, when applied to crime, unsupported by the evidence (Hurwitz and Christiansen 1983; Wolfgang and Ferracuti 1967).

Biochemistry, Public Policy, and Criminal Justice Practices

If humans are basically chemistry experiments, holding persons accountable for their behavior—known in law as *mens rea*—is illogical (although incapacitation would be logical.) Critics of this deterministic position reject the notion that humans are not responsible for their actions, that they do not have free will. The centrist position is that behavior is the result of nature plus nurture, but the role of volition remains ambiguous. Society and the legal system have walked a fine line between these positions, generally favoring free will over "the devil (or genes or chemistry or diet) made me do it." Thus, although the medical community recognizes alcoholism as an addictive state, society does not legally excuse individuals who commit crimes while intoxicated. It may, however, mitigate their punishment, resulting in a shorter prison or jail term, probation, or other creative sanction.

Public policy on biochemically induced crimes generally boils down to a single issue: If actions beyond the control of the alleged perpetrator induced the physical state, then the act lacks the element of criminal responsibility. For example, accidental exposure to chemicals may poison the accused and induce paranoia or other aberrant thought processes, leading the judge or jury to find the defendant not guilty. Similarly someone could have forced the accused to take a drug or administered it without his or her knowledge and consent, in which case the same outcome is likely: The accused is not guilty. In this way the legal community recognizes that some physical states are nonvolitional. However, most chemical inducement arguments are, at best, reasons for the mitigation of punishment, not its nullification. The neurotoxicity hypothesis may challenge these practices, especially on questions of criminal responsibility (Crawford 2000).

There is also the self-medication issue—some neurological theories describe the drug abuser as a person whose body is malfunctioning with respect to the production of crucial neurotransmitters, making drug use a form of self-medication (Abadinsky 2001). If the drug is alcohol or a legally prescribed substance, the victim of this physical disability is not labeled a criminal. If the substance is illegal, however, the results often are quite different. Policy considerations to deal with this anomaly center on the controversial legalization/decriminalization debate.

Judicial Practices The implications for biochemical issues and judicial decision making are unclear. Trial courts usually hold drug addicts or abusers, including those using alcohol, accountable for their acts. However, convicted offenders may receive more lenient sentences than sober offenders. Drunk drivers are one exception to this observation. Given citizen groups such as MADD (Mothers Against Drunk Driving) and "get tough" state laws, the trial courts are less forgiving and the mandatory penalties far stiffer (Walker 1994:108–16). Yet even here the trend may be toward forms of treatment, as DWI-drug courts and programs intended to offer first-time drunk drivers a combined second chance and treatment gain in popularity (Breckenridge, Winfree, Maupin, and Clason 2000; Taxman and Piquero 1997).

Any biological explanations of crime will meet with limited acceptance in court, especially those intended to exculpate the offender. Society bases the law, as C. Ray Jeffery and his associates (1991) pointed out, largely on the concept of free will. We more closely relate its philosophical base to classicism than to empiricism or science: "As long as the law rejects science and remains committed to concepts of punishment, revenge and the mind rather than concepts of prevention, treatment and brain defects, the crime problem will remain exactly where it is today" (Jeffery, Myers, and Wollan 1991:6). The widespread use of biogenic defenses or even mitigating circumstances is unlikely. Instead, a piecemeal and occasional use of certain affirmative defenses is the more likely course.

Correctional Practices The strong association between crime and alcohol and other drugs has been the focus of much research since the 1980s. For example, in 1987 the National Institute of Justice established the Drug Use Forecasting program to measure drug use among arrested persons. In 1998 nearly one-half of all arrestees in DUF-reporting cities were under the influence of one or more drugs at the time of arrest (U.S. Department of Justice 1999). Other studies have revealed links between drugs, crime, and criminals (Brounstein, Hatry, Altschuler, and Blair 1990; Brownstein and Goldstein 1990; Fagan 1989; Fagan and Chin 1991; Mays, Fields, and Thompson 1989), especially violent crimes committed by users of crack (McBride and Swartz 1990).

In spite of this body of research, drug treatment programs have received low priority in recent times (Abadinsky 2001; Inciardi 1992). This is not to say that drug treatment programs for criminals do not exist. As early as 1972 the federal government sponsored the TASC (Treatment Alternative to Street Crime) program, which diverted substance-abusing offenders from the court system to community treatment. Later the federal government expanded this program to include persons on probation and parole. "TASC identifies, assesses, and refers appropriate drug- and/or alcohol-dependent offenders accused or convicted of nonviolent crimes to community-based substance abuse treatment, as an alternative to or supplement to existing criminal justice sanctions and procedures" (Cook and Weinman 1988:99). (See Table 3.1 for an overview of primitive biological, genetic, and biochemical explanations of crime.)

SUMMARY

Contemporary biocriminology clearly is not the same biological theorizing of 100 or even 50 years ago. Yet serious methodological and logical problems remain, and biocriminologists face daunting tasks. Ethical issues must be resolved, in terms of both the types of research they may conduct and the ends to which the resulting knowledge is put. The lessons of nineteenth-century social Darwinism and twentieth-century fascism are too important to neglect.

Genetic and biochemical research forces us to rethink many old ideas about crime. First, the concept of race is present in this research, both as an empirical finding and as an ethical concern. Genetic evidence is persuasive that no race gene exists, that race is a sociological and political idea (Begley 1995; Cavalli-Sforza et al. 1994; Wheeler 1995). However, the high offending rates of African American males seem tied to their lower MAO activity. Besides questions about the viability of race as a unique genetic condition, at least two other problems exist. First, the MAO being measured is not brain MAO, so we can only speculate about its impact on thought processes, judgment, and decision making. Second, the neurotoxicity hypothesis offers an equally credible explanation. African American and Hispanic American children have different heavy-metal risk factors in their respective environments, especially compared to Caucasian children. Exposure to the heavy metals clearly alters the levels of MAO and important neurotransmitters. That the supporting research to date is weak does not diminish the potential social and legal impact of the hypothesis.

Biocriminologists are prone to overstate the importance or significance of their studies. The findings sections of their research reports may contain negligible or minimal effects, but the conclusions drawn from those findings often overstate the results (Akers 2000; Gottfredson and Hirschi 1990). Just as importantly, the findings are often inconsistent and contradictory. For example, do the twin studies support the genetic transmission thesis? Was the concordance observed in the early twin studies inflated or deflated? Both outcomes are possible. The findings from the early studies, when techniques for distinguishing monozygotic from dizygotic twins were in their infancy, support the inflation argument.

Gender was both present and missing in this chapter. That is, geneticists focus on the process of determining sex, but modern genetics yields virtually no insight into female criminality. For example, the twin studies virtually ignored females. In two twin studies that did have female twin pairs, a genetic influence was present for males

TABLE 3.1 Primitive Biological, Genetic, and Biochemical Explanations of Crime

Theory	Major Figures	Central Assumptions	Causal Arguments (Key Terms)	Strengths	Weaknesses
Physiognomy	della Porte, Lavater	Human behavioral characteristics have external physical manifestations, especially related to facial characteristics.	Facial features (*facial fragments*) reveal inner criminal tendencies.	Represents an advancement over demonological theories; eliminates society's responsibility.	Lacks scientific foundation; is untestable by traditional means; was used to criminalize people simply due to the way they looked.
Phrenology	Gall, Spurzheim, Caldwell	See Physiognomy.	The skull's external surface conforms to key brain areas; bumps and dips reveal amoral and criminogenic tendencies (*higher* and *lower propensities*).	Allows for change: Lower-propensity people could, by a mental or moral exercises, overcome natural evil tendencies.	See Physiognomy.
Social Darwinism	Spencer	Natural selection is the best method of determining who should survive and who should die; the state should not interfere with the laws of nature.	Only the fittest should survive; all others, including those who drain society's valuable resources, should perish (*natural selection*).	Tends to reinforce existing prejudices and racial or ethnic stereotypes; also, allowed those against social engineering and governmental interference.	See Strengths.
Criminal anthropology	Lombroso, Hooton	Biological characteristics determine men's and women's ultimate destinies.	Criminals are born, a throwback to more primitive life forms (*atavism, born criminal*).	Provides simple answers to hard questions; brands people with unusual characteristics as evil.	Uses measurements that are subjective and prone to mismeasurement; test samples also highly suspect.
Criminal body types	Sheldon, the Gluecks	The adult body derives from embryonic tissues developed during gestation.	Criminals more *mesomorphic* than the general population.	Explains why criminals are physically tougher than victims.	See Criminal anthropology; uses highly subjective body-type placement.
Genetic explanations	Brennan, Rowe, Hutchings, Mednick, Hunter, Lee, Walsh	Criminal tendencies may be passed from one generation to the next through genetic mechanisms, including, but not limited to, DNA.	Some people, given genetic predispositions, are more likely to succumb to crime than those without such genes.	In twin studies reveals odd anomalies; in adoption studies reveals that people born of criminal parents, but reared apart, continue parents' crime patterns; some criminal tendencies may be inherited.	Employs suspect research methods; too few XYY men to explain much crime; may be based on a poor understanding of genetics.
Biochemical explanations	Levinthal, Ellis, Hippchen, Berman, Dalton	Humans are cauldrons of biological chemicals, many of which are susceptible to external influences and internal disturbances or imbalances.	Disturbances or imbalances in electrochemistry and biochemistry (e.g., *hormones* and *neurotransmitters*) may cause socially unacceptable behavior or even criminal conduct.	Provides logical explanations; the scientific community seems to support many of these arguments; provides answers to irrational criminal conduct.	Has the same problems as noted for genetic research; alternative explanations abound; even if a biochemical basis is found, is society willing to view them as nonvolitional medical conditions?

but not for females (Rushton 1996; Stevenson and Graham 1988). These findings led Lee Ellis and Anthony Walsh (2000:437) to speculate that "female delinquency may not be genetically influenced." This speculation seems similar to Karl Christiansen's (1977) claim that Norwegians are genetically different from Danes.

Gender received more attention in the biochemistry section, with its focus on endocrine system secretions. For example, the so-called PMS defense views some women as prisoners of their hormones. Besides the questionable causal ordering in this hormonal-imbalance hypothesis, the research supports neither it nor, for the most part, the equally suspect hormonal explanation for testosterone-derived violence. Given the tremendous differentials in official offending rates for males and females, this failure to offer more insights is a major shortcoming. Because gender is determined by chromosomes, this shortcoming may signify that the gender–crime connection has no biological basis.

Physical and social environment may be very important to our understanding of crime, or at least the conditions under which crime is most likely to occur. For example, the XYY chromosome pattern has social class and environmental origins. The copresence of heavy metals and crime still depends on residential segregation and other social factors. Even twin and adoption studies were unable to rule out the social environment as a major force in shaping the propensity to commit crimes. Just how much is nature and how much is nurture remains in dispute. Clearly both forces play a role in the etiology of crime.

In spite of important scientific advances, the influence of genetics and biochemistry on human social behavior remains largely speculative. Biogeneticists may rewrite the book on biology–crime links in the next decade or less. New research in biocriminology may alter criminological thinking about nature versus nurture. The trend is toward a view of biologically induced human susceptibility to criminality. The current consensus favors this nature-plus-nurture perspective, one in which biology determines individual susceptibility to other crime-causing forces (Fishbein 1990; see also Plomin 1989).

KEY TERMS

adoption study

alleles

apotropaic punishments

anthropometry

atavism

attention deficit disorder (ADD)

biocriminologists

capital punishment

chromosomes

concordance

corporal punishment

cranioscopy

deoxyribonucleic acid (DNA)

dizygotic twins

DNA dragnet

DNA line-up

dopamine (DA)

ectomorphic

embryonics

endocrine system

endomorphic

endorphins

eugenics

fragments

genes

hormones

human genome

Human Genome Mapping Project (HGMP)

hyperactivity

karyotype studies

learning disabilities

mesomorphic/
mesomorphy

monoamine oxidase
(MAO)

monozygotic twins

natural selection

naturalistic explanations

nature plus nurture

nature versus nurture

neurochemicals

neurophysiology

neurotoxicity hypothesis
(NH)

neurotransmitters

nucleotides

phrenology

physiognomy

PMS defense

profiling

serotonin

sex chromosomes

social Darwinism

somatotype

stigmata

twin study

Twinkies defense

XYY males

CRITICAL REVIEW QUESTIONS

1. Do you think that physiognomy and phrenology are laughable?

2. What do you make of Lombroso's shift to environmental influences late in his career? What would he have made of Hooton's attempts to find the "criminal man"?

3. What were Sheldon's findings? How did the Gluecks expand on these findings?

4. Describe the basic ideas behind the genetics–crime linkage. Are any ethical issues involved here?

5. Summarize the strengths and weaknesses of genetic theories of crime. Which one is most damaging to the arguments? Which one is most supportive?

6. Can you see a way that twin or adoption studies could be made more definitive in the search for a genetic basis of crime? In preparing your answer, you might want to consider the most damaging weakness and the strongest point for each perspective.

7. What does XYY research suggest about the physical characteristics of persons with this chromosomal structure? Why are the alternative explanations persuasive?

8. Which general criticism of genetic theories of crime did you find most

persuasive? Which one was least persuasive? Explain your answers.

9. Are you optimistic or pessimistic about the future of genetic theories of crime? Explain your answer. What role does the Human Genome Mapping Project play in your answer?

10. Describe the basic ideas behind the biochemistry–crime linkage. Do the biochemical arguments have practical implications for criminal justice? What are they?

11. Given the nature and extent of drug and alcohol abuse by criminals, how important is it that we understand the brain chemistry associated with these behaviors?

12. Which do you think plays a larger role in helping us understand criminal behavior, neurotransmitters or hormones? Explain your answer.

13. What light does the neurotoxicity hypothesis shed on Ellis's statements about MAO and race? In spite of the fact that biochemistry plays a role in its causal arguments, does the hypothesis change the locus of that search? Explain your answers to both questions.

14. Which of the policies reviewed in this chapter do you think poses the greatest threat to democratic ideals?

Which one holds the greatest promise for reducing crime?

15. Few biological theories attempt to explain female criminality, beyond suggesting that female criminals seem more like men than like women. What does this suggest to you?

NOTES

1. The precise number of persons executed for witchcraft is unknown. In some parts of Europe, exact figures were kept because the supposed witch's possessions reverted to the Crown, went to the accuser, or were shared by both parties (Currie 1968). Some people claim that as many as 9 million so-called witches were put to death in Europe alone from the Dark Ages to the Reformation, but more credible estimates put the number at about 90,000 (Sharpe 1997).

2. Erickson (1966) argued that the Salem witch trials were less about the devil than about politics. According to Hoffer (1997) they were motivated by true believers who feared the devil's power.

3. A confounding factor is that adoption agencies, particularly with a surplus of potential adoptive parents, engage in a matching process to find homes similar to the biological homes.

4. Web information about the HGMP is available at (1) www.mhgri.nih.gov, (2) www.celera.com, and (3) www.ncbi.nim.nih.gov/genome/seq.

5. Mengele, the so-called Angel of Death, was inspired by the German twin studies.

6. Stands for *Restricted Fragment Length Polymorphism*—*Variable Number of Tandem Repeats*.

7. Stands for *Polymerase Chain Reaction*, a technique used to replicate DNA, and *Short Tandem Repeat*, or the appearance on a DNA strand of a repeated sequence of alleles.

8. Scientists developed two PCR methods. PRC-Nuclear DNA may be used for a wide variety of samples that are quite small, perhaps with only 50 or 100 cells. This is the method of choice for degraded biological materials. PCR-Mitochondrial DNA is used for samples not suitable for the other methods, including bones, teeth, and hair shafts.

4

Psychological Abnormality Theories

CHAPTER OVERVIEW

Psychoanalytic Theories

Psychosexual Development and Crime

Psychoanalysis

Assessing Psychoanalytic Theories

Psychoanalysis, Public Policy, and Criminal Justice Practices

Deviant Personalities and Psychopathologies

Personality and Crime

Psychopathy, Sociopathy, and Crime

Assessing Personality Theory and the Psychopathy Hypothesis

Personality, Public Policy, and Criminal Justice Practices

LEARNING OBJECTIVES

- Appreciate the distinctions between psychology and psychiatry, and the importance of those distinctions for criminology and criminal justice.
- Recognize the psychoanalytic origins of human internal conflicts.
- Understand the unique role played by psychometric testing, both for diagnosing and classifying offenders and for selecting and promoting criminal justice personnel.
- Comprehend the strengths and weaknesses of *psychopathy,* a term rich in visual imagery but poor in definitional preciseness.

INTRODUCTION

In Greek and Roman mythology, Psyche, a beautiful wood nymph elevated to the status of an immortal, was the personification of the soul. The Greek word *psyche* means "soul." Two distinct forms of scientific inquiry and practice have addressed questions of the human mind or, as defined by the ancient Greeks and Romans, the human soul. **Psychology** examines individual human and animal behavior; it is concerned chiefly with the mind and mental processes—feelings, desires, motivations, and the like. Psychology is both an area of scientific study and an academic behavioral science, although some clinical psychologists engage in the treatment of mental disorders. Practitioners often have the terminal research degree, or doctor of philosophy (Ph.D.), and considerable practical experience dealing with mentally troubled or disoriented patients. Some states, however, license clinical psychologists with lower levels of education. **Psychiatry**—literally "healing the soul"—is the branch of medicine primarily concerned with the study and treatment of mental disorders, including **psychoses,** or very serious personality disorders, and **neuroses,** or milder personality disorders. Psychiatrists possess the medical doctor degree (M.D.), and many states also license practitioners, such as psychiatric social workers, who possess a master's degree in social work. In summary, psychology is dedicated to both normal and abnormal behavior, whereas psychiatry, as a branch of medicine, employs the disease model and deals principally with abnormal behavior.

Few psychogenic theories, or behavioral explanations of the mind's functioning, evolved as crime explanations. Crime is a *legal* term, and not a *medical* one. Accordingly psychologists and psychiatrists seek explanations of individual human behavior, not criminal behavior. Like biogenic crime explanations, psychogenic theories focus on individual differences. Psychogenic theories are also deterministic, which means that the causal factors associated with criminal behavior are beyond individuals' control or manipulation. As Gresham Sykes and Francis Cullen (1992:324; emphasis added) noted about the development of early twentieth-century psychological theories, "Crime, it was said, was a bursting forth of instinctive impulses, and the criminal was acting out what most civilized men and women had learned to restrain. *The criminal was regarded as abnormal, but the abnormality was now centered in the mind.*"

Two ideas dominated psychological thinking about crime through the first half of the twentieth century. The explanatory roots of the first lie deep in psychoanalytic theory. Psychoanalysis, a part of contemporary popular culture, often provokes strong mental images. Psychoanalytic theories suspend the notion of free will; crime becomes far more deterministic and far less volitional than in many other theories examined in this text. The reason is simple: The motivation to commit the crime is unknown to the offender, residing as it does in the unconscious. Therefore, before we consider whether psychoanalytic theory holds any promise of explaining criminality, we must review the theory itself.

The second major psychological explanation reviewed in this chapter became a significant analytical tool during the second half of the twentieth century. Personality is central to deviant personality theory, with its associated inventories, and to the psychopathy hypothesis. They, like psychoanalysis, have also entered the lexicon of popular culture.

Conventional psychiatry, particularly early in its history, was unconcerned with criminality, except with regard to the issue of **insanity.** Hearkening back to English common law, the medical profession that specialized in diseases and defects of the mind established the definition of sanity and legal competence. In fact, medical terms were quite often used to define the legal notion of insanity, including the landmark McNaghten case of 1843 (Simon 1967), whose modern equivalent is the Durham Rule (*Durham v. United States,* 1954). This rule includes the phrase "the accused is not criminally responsible if his unlawful act was the product of mental disease or mental defect." Psychogenic theory moved into the realm of criminality in the early twentieth century, just as psychoanalytic theory was gaining prominence.

PSYCHOANALYTIC THEORIES

- What do you think when you hear the term *psychoanalysis?* Would you be surprised to learn that some practitioners of psychoanalysis believe that dysfunctional sexual development is a factor in crime?

- Have you ever heard the quip directed at someone who says something very revealing about his or her personality: "Oops, your Freudian slip is showing"? The implication that the person unconsciously meant to be revealing, so the revelation, however accidental it may appear, was intentional.

Psychoanalysis, the common element in these questions, is a method of treatment based on the work of Sigmund Freud (1856–1939). Over the years both theory and method have undergone change, although Freud's basic exposition of unconscious phenomena in human behavior remains unchanged. He viewed the unconscious as "essentially dynamic and capable of profoundly affecting conscious ideational or emotional life without the individual's being aware of this influence" (Healy, Bronner, and Bowers 1930:24). Furthermore, people are not aware of this determination of their behavior. In stark contrast to classical theorists, psychoanalysts believe that reason does not rule human behavior (Cloninger 1993).

Freud postulated unconscious processes, which, although not directly observable, he inferred from actual case studies. He divided unconscious mental phenomena into three groups:

1. The **conscious**—those phenomena about which we are currently aware

2. The **preconscious**—thoughts and memories, just below the surface, that we can easily call into conscious awareness

3. The **unconscious**—repressed memories and attendant emotions that we can pull to the conscious level only with much effort

According to Freud the unconscious serves as a repository for painful memories and the highly charged emotions associated with them. We accumulate these repressed memories and emotions as we pass through life on our way to adulthood or **psychosexual maturity.** The stages of psychosexual development are, like much else in the world of psychoanalysis, repressed and, therefore, unconscious. Yet they serve as a guiding force of conscious behavior. Moreover, they are a source of anxiety and guilt, the basis for psychoneurosis and psychosis. Some people, then, are victims of breakdowns in their psychosexual development.

Psychosexual Development and Crime

Most psychoanalysts identify five stages of **psychosexual development:**

1. The **oral stage** (birth to 18 months). The mouth, lips, and tongue are the predominant organs of pleasure for the infant. In the normal infant the source of pleasure becomes associated with the touch and warmth of the parent who gratifies oral needs. Infants enter the world as asocial beings, not greatly dissimilar to criminals: unsocialized and without self-control.

2. The **anal stage** (age 1–3 years). The anus becomes the primary source of sexual interest and gratification. Children of this age closely connect pleasure to the retention and expulsion of feces, to the bodily process involved and the feces themselves. During this stage the partially socialized child acts out destructive urges, breaking toys or even harming living organisms, such as insects or small animals. Disruptions in this stage may yield a great deal of psychopathology in the adult, including violent behavior and sociopathological personality disorders, topics covered in this chapter's second section.

3. The **genital stage** (age 3–5 years). The genitals provide the main sexual interest and in "normal" persons continue to do so afterwards. During this stage, the child experiences **Oedipus** (in boys) and **Electra** (in girls) **wishes,** or fantasies about the opposite-sex parent. The path to normal psychosexual maturity involves relinquishing paternal or maternal attachment and overcoming the sadness that follows.

4. The **latent stage** (age 5 to adolescence). The child experiences a lessening of interest in sexual organs. Nonsexual, expanded relationships with same-sex and same-age playmates become paramount.

5. The **adolescence/adulthood stage** (age 13 to death). Genital interest and awareness reawakens. Late adolescents and young adults repress the incestuous wish, and mature sexuality replaces it.

Note that the stages overlap, the transition from one to another is gradual, and the time spans are approximate. In addition, each stage is left behind but never completely abandoned. Some amount of **cathexis,** or psychic energy, remains linked to earlier objects of psychosexual attachment. When the strength of the cathexis is particularly strong, it is expressed as a **fixation.** For example, rather than transferring affection to another adult of the opposite sex in the adolescent–adult stage, the child may stay fixated on the opposite-sex parent. Psychoanalysts refer to the state when a person reverts to a previous mode of gratification as regression. We can see this type of behavior in young children who revert to thumb sucking or have elimination "accidents" when a sibling is born.

Psychic Development While a child is passing through the first three stages, his or her mind concomitantly undergoes the development of three psychic phenomena:

1. **Id.** The id consists of impulses or instincts that have parallels in classical theory. The id impulses define humans as hedonistic. This mass of powerful drives seeks immediate discharge or gratification, with no restraints.

2. **Ego.** The ego is the great mediator. Infants modify their id drives through contact with the world around them and through parental training. Psychoanalysts call this stage **ego development.** Infants can obtain maximum gratification with a minimum of difficulty from the restrictions in their environment. For example, the ego controls an id drive (desire) to harm sibling rivals by providing an awareness of the consequences of such action—the punishment that may result. Without the ego to act as a restraining influence, the id would destroy the person through its blind striving to gratify instincts with complete disregard for others. A person may remain at the ego level of development if he or she experiences disturbance in psychosexual development: "The child remains asocial or behaves as if he has become social without having made actual adjustments to the demands of society" (Aichhorn 1973[1925]:4). Feelings of rage and aggression associated with the anal stage lurk in the background, awaiting an opportunity to erupt.

3. **Superego.** During normal development the child integrates outer (social) discipline and self-imposes it. As personal control gains the upper hand over instinctual impulses, the child experiences the beginnings of a superego (Smart 1970). Psychoanalysts often view the superego as a conscience-type mechanism, a counterforce to the id. It exercises a criticizing power, a sense of morality over the ego.

Psychoanalysts link the superego to the incestuous feelings of the genital stage. Control development becomes an internal matter, no longer exclusively dependent upon external forces (e.g., parents). A healthy superego is the result of identification with a parent or parents during the genital stage of psychosexual development. Conversely an unhealthy superego can support criminality when the child internalizes the actions of antisocial parents (Smart 1970). The superego may fail to develop sufficiently because of abuse or neglect; in fact, many prison inmates experienced neglect or abuse as children (Mays and Winfree 1998).

Psychic Drives Id drives impel a person (via the ego) to activity leading to a cessation of the tension or excitement caused by the drives. The person seeks discharge, or gratification. For example, the hunger drive will cause activity through which the person hopes to satisfy (gratify) his or her appetite. Psychoanalysts divide these drives into two categories, but elements of each appear with the activation of basic drives. The **primary process** is that which tends toward immediate and direct gratification of the id impulses. The **secondary process** involves the tendency to shift from the original object or method of discharge when something—including the superego—blocks a drive. A shift may also occur when gratification is simply inaccessible by legitimate, acceptable means.

In the Freudian scheme the mind has several defense mechanisms, all initiated by the secondary process, that allow it to adapt to the environment. Included among these mechanisms are these:

- **Denial.** This state exists when an individual refuses to acknowledge a painful reality, resulting in a distortion of reality.

- **Displacement.** In this case an individual expresses unacceptable id impulses through an acceptable outlet. For example, the individual may unconsciously transfer, or displace, a desire to play with feces to playing with mud or clay.

- **Repression.** This is an ego activity that prevents unwanted id impulses, memories, desires, or wish-fulfilling fantasies from entering the conscious-thought level. Psychoanalysts believe that the repression of highly charged material, such as incestuous fantasies, requires the expenditure of considerable psychic energy and results in a permanent conflict between the id and the ego. The delicate balance between the charged material and the opposing expenditure of energy, called **equilibrium,** generally causes great stress. When the means of repression are inadequate to deal with charged material, psychoneurotic or psychotic symptoms develop.

- **Reaction formation.** This mechanism allows an individual to replace so-cially unacceptable behavior with behavior that is socially acceptable. As distinct from displacement, reaction formation involves behavior that is the opposite of that expressed by the original desire or drive. For example, a child who wants to kill a sibling will become very loving and devoted. In adulthood a sadistic impulse can result in a person becoming involved in the care and treatment of highly dependent persons or animals.

- **Projection.** This mechanism allows an individual to attribute her or his own wishes or impulses to others. For example, John may say to Mary, "Fred wants to ask you out on a date," when, in fact, it is John who wants to ask her out. Paranoia is an extreme and dangerous form of projection.

- **Sublimation.** This mechanism is employed by an individual who cannot experience a continuous drive in its primary form. A sadist might overcome the urge to cut people, for example, by substituting acceptable alternatives, such as becoming a surgeon or a butcher.[1]

According to psychoanalysts the unconscious must maintain a delicate balance as people experience the various sociocultural and biological aspects of life. But this balance is easily upset—there's a thin line between normal and neurotic, and between neurotic and psychotic. When repressed impulses begin to overwhelm the psyche and threaten to enter the conscious, external defense mechanisms come into play as neuroses and, in extreme cases, psychoses. These responses take the form of phobias, or unreasonable fears, involving heights, insects, closed spaces, and the like. Employing reaction formation, for example, a person may channel the destructive urges of the anal stage into prosocial activities, such as becoming a veg-etarian. Failing in this, the person may succumb to the threat posed by the re-pressed wishes and desires, and resort to extreme antisocial behavior, such as that of serial killers or rapists.

Crime and the Superego The "psychoanalytic theory of crime causation," noted Gerhard Falk (1966:1), "does not make the usual distinction between be-havior as such and criminal action." This distinction is a legal one; that is, crime is behavior defined by society as illegal (see Chapter 1). From a psychoanalytic per-spective antisocial behavior is a neurotic manifestation whose origins can be traced back to early stages of development: "There is no fundamental difference between the neurotic criminal and all those socially harmless representatives of the group of neurotic characters; the lawbreaker chooses a form of acting out [of] his impulses which is socially harmful or simply illegal" (Alexander and Staub 1956:106).

According to August Aichhorn (1973[1935]:221) the superego takes its form and content from identifications that result from the child's effort to emulate the parent. It reflects not only the parent's love of the child but also the child's fear of the parent's demands. However, Freud (1933:92) stated that "the superego does not attain full strength and development if overcoming of the Oedipus [in males] complex has not been completely successful."

The superego keeps most people from acting on primitive id impulses. Only the ego restrains persons with poorly developed superegos; however, the ego alone cannot exercise adequate control over id impulses. Such a person suffers almost no guilt from engaging in socially harmful behavior. Similarly the person whose superego is destructive cannot distinguish between *thinking* bad and *doing* bad.

Unresolved conflicts between earlier development and id impulses that people have normally repressed or dealt with through reaction formation or sublimation create a severe sense of (unconscious) guilt. They experience this guilt (again at the unconscious level) as a compulsive need for punishment. To alleviate this guilt, the criminal commits acts for which punishment is virtually certain. Delinquents of this type are victims of their own morality (Aichhorn 1973[1935]). For example, employees of the criminal justice system often see cases in which the offenders apparently desired capture, so poorly planned and executed were the crimes.

In summary, psychoanalysts relate criminal behavior to the functioning of the superego, the result of offenders' abnormal relationships with parents (or parental figures) during early childhood. Parental deprivation—through absence, lack of affection, or inconsistent discipline—hinders the proper development of the superego. Deprivation during childhood thus weakens parental influence, and in adulthood the individual is unable to adequately control aggressive, hostile, or antisocial urges. Rigid or punitive parental practices can lead to the creation of a superego that is likewise rigid and punitive, leading the person to seek punishment as a means of alleviating unconscious guilt.

Psychoanalysis

Psychoanalysts treat psychic disorders using **psychoanalysis.** According to Freud psychoanalysis "aims at inducing the patient to give up the repressions that belong to his early life and replace them with reactions of a sort that would correspond better to a psychically mature condition." To accomplish this, the psychoanalyst attempts to get the patient to "recollect certain experiences and the emotions called up by them which he has at the moment forgotten" (Reiff 1963:274). The psychoanalyst ties present symptoms to repressed elements of early life—the primary stages of psychosexual development. The symptoms will disappear when the patient exposes the repressed material under psychoanalytic treatment.

To expose repressed material, psychoanalysts use several techniques, including free association, dream interpretation, and transference. With **free association** the patient verbally expresses ideas as they come to mind. The psychoanalyst then works with the patient to understand why he or she uttered the words or phrases—that is, to learn their true meaning.

Dream interpretation encourages patients to recall and analyze dreams. Freud believed that dreams held the key to the individual's makeup. He also saw a difference between the dream's experienced content and its actual meaning: The former is what the patient was doing or having done to him or her, and the latter is the actual meaning of the dream, which the unconscious mind conceals. It is up to the therapist to help the patient understand the actual, repressed meaning.

With **transference** the patient develops a negative or positive emotional attitude toward the psychoanalyst. This attitude is a reflection or imitation of emotional attitudes that the patient experienced in relationships during his or her psychosexual development. Thus the patient may unconsciously come to view the therapist as a parental figure. By using transference, the therapist re-creates the emotions tied to early psychic development, unlocking repressed material and freeing the patient from his or her burden. As Freud noted, transference "is particularly calculated to favor the production of these (early) emotional conditions" (Reiff 1963:274).

Limitations of Psychoanalysis Generally psychoanalysis is not used to treat delinquents or criminals for several reasons. The first limitation Freud himself acknowledged: Psychoanalysis requires a special attitude toward the analyst, one that may be lacking in delinquents and criminals. Instincts dominate these individuals, which means that the therapist must adapt the method to meet the client's needs (Aichhorn 1973[1925]:vii). Treatment can take many years and, as a "talking therapy," requires a verbal ability beyond that of most criminals. Therapists also may underestimate how hard it is for people to verbalize their experiences, even for otherwise verbal patients (Omer and London 1988). Prison and jail inmates tend not to be all that verbal, especially about what got them into trouble in the first place. However, psychoanalysis does provide a theoretical basis for treating criminals in psychological and social work settings (see, e.g., Abadinsky 2000, 2001).

Freudian, Adlerian, or Jungian: Does Form Matter? Does the psychoanalyst's orientation make a difference? The short answer to this question is, yes, orientation is important. For example, Freudian criminologists view sex as playing a major role in shaping criminals' responses to their environments, just as does the need for apprehension and punishment. Followers of Alfred Adler (1870–1937), an associate of Freud, reject sex, placing the emphasis on feelings of inferiority. In *The Individual Psychology of Alfred Adler* (1963) Adler wrote that this sense of inferiority derived from restrictions on the individual's self-assertion (see also Adler 1927). Adler's work influenced a generation of gang theorists in the 1950s, including Albert K. Cohen, James F. Short, Richard A. Cloward, Lloyd E. Ohlin, and Walter B. Miller, who all depicted the status-seeking delinquents in Adlerian terms (Schaefer 1969:213).

Carl Gustav Jung (1875–1961) also rejected Freud's emphasis on sex. Jung believed that the unconscious, which holds the key to individuals' adjustment to life, consists of the repressed or forgotten parts of their lives. However, he added an element missing from Freud's perspective: the collective unconscious acts and mental patterns shared by all members of the human species. Whereas for Freud and Adler dreams represented a personal reality, Jung believed that inborn mental structures—what he called archetypes—shape dreams and that these archetypes originate in the collective unconscious of the human species. As Jung observed in *Psychological Types* (1921), the harmony achieved between the conscious and unconscious is the key to understanding behavior. Interestingly Jung also wrote a book that reflects back on the moral roots of psychology: *Modern Man in Search of a Soul* (1961[1933]).

Other of Freud's disciples and colleagues formed their own variants on strict psychoanalysis. Karen Horney (1885–1952) placed far greater emphasis on cultural and interpersonal experiences. She believed that feelings of helplessness naturally arise in a hostile world and lead to anxiety. Culture creates the hostility, and some members of society simply deal with it better than others. Otto Rank (1884–1939), a member of Freud's inner circle, argued that the trauma of the birth event, and not a hostile world, gives insight into the crises and conflicts people exprience. Rank assigned the will a central role in conflict resolution: When the will fails, guilt surfaces.

As a rule, then, each variant of psychoanalytic theory has its own view of the origins of the crime problem. Freudians blame psychosexual development, Adlerians address feelings of inferiority, and Jungians look to shared innate structures. The followers of Horney, Rank, and other psychoanalysts, in turn, emphasize different forces. The solution, however, is generally the same: psychoanalysis that will reveal the deep-seated, unconscious cause of the miscreant behavior.

Assessing Psychoanalytic Theories

During the 1930s and 1940s psychoanalytic theory was considered one of the best hopes for understanding the criminal mind (Schaefer 1969:214-6; Vold 1979:133–38). August Aichhorn (1973[1935]), a psychoanalytic psychologist, described delinquents as "wayward youth," children who needed convincing that society cared about them. Kurt R. Eissler, a follower of Freud who expressed sociologically oriented ideas, believed that aggression was an abnormal reaction to society's value system.[2] Franz Alexander and William Healy (1935) provided a carefully documented psychoanalytical account of seven criminals in a work titled *Roots of Crime.* The ages, crimes, and psychological histories of the offenders differed. However, the cause of the criminality was identical in each case: Crime was a necessary substitute for something tied to a repressed and unconscious conflict, deeply felt by each offender.

Healy teamed up with Augusta F. Bronner (1936) in *New Lights on Delinquency and Its Treatment,* a massive empirical study that matched 105 sets of same-sex siblings, one delinquent and the other nondelinquent.[3] Healy and Bronner psychoanalytically assessed each pair. Their principal finding was that 9 out of 10 delinquent youths expressed significant emotional disturbances, compared to roughly 1 out of 10 nondelinquents.

Their study was not without critics. Edwin Sutherland and Donald Cressey (1974:164) based their challenge of Healy and Bronner's findings on three points. First, the researchers had a predisposition to find emotional disturbances, and they knew the identities of group members. Second, even if emotional disturbances were present, Healy and Bronner could not state categorically that they were the *cause* of the delinquency. Finally the researchers did not investigate the alleged emotional disturbance beyond noting its presence.

IN THEIR OWN WORDS: Lindner on Psychoanalysis and Crime

Robert M. Lindner's (1944) *Rebel without a Cause* is perhaps the best-known psychoanalytic work on crime and deviance that employs a fairly strict Freudian methodology. Lindner claimed to have caused a nearly miraculous cure of Harold, a virtually blind prison inmate. He explained that Harold's criminal career was the result of feelings of anxiety, fear, and guilt stemming from having witnessed, at the age of 8 months, his parents having sex. When the inmate realized this fact, claimed Lindner, his eyesight improved, along with his hope for rehabilitation.

- *On crime causation:* "Modern analytic theory predicates criminality and all other activities of an aggressive or debasing order upon the prepotency of the *Death Instinct,* which is believed to exert an influence sufficient to catapult an individual toward self-destruction" (pp. 8–9).

- *On traditional rehabilitative practices:* "We have glimpsed the utter futility, the sheer waste, of confining individuals in barred and turreted zoos for humans without attempting to recover [their] secrets. Harold's case makes a mockery of current penological pretense. It points the finger of ridicule at the sterile corridors of modern prisons . . . in brief, the whole hollow structure of rehabilitation that is based upon expediency, untested hypotheses, [and] unwarranted conclusions from a pseudo-scientific empiricism" (p. 228).

Source: Lindner (1944).

General criticisms of psychoanalytic theory follow a familiar pattern. The first concern is definitional. According to Susan Cloninger (1993) psychoanalytical theories have not clearly specified the operational definitions of their theoretical ideas, making conclusions based on observations scientifically questionable. Scientific testing may not be possible because psychoanalytic theory purports to explain *all* observations, so *no* observation is inconsistent with the theory. For example, consider the so-called students' dilemma: Those who arrive early to class are anxious; those who arrive late are hostile; those who arrive on time are compulsive.

Diagnosis is also extremely subjective, because descriptions of a subject's mental state may reveal more about the training of the psychologist than the condition of the patient. The psychologist's training and orientation determine where he or she looks for the causes of misbehavior. How, then, does a third person—not the psychoanalyst or the patient—address the reliability and validity of the diagnosis?

The third concern is methodological, given the small samples typically used to develop psychogenic theories; few involve more than a dozen or so subjects. How generalizable, critics ask, are these studies? If we study 2 people or 20, can we generalize to the U.S. population at large? Besides misinterpretation and overgeneralization, what about the question of misrepresentation? Subjects are patients and enjoy confidentiality, so verifying that the psychotherapist has given an accurate and faithful account is virtually impossible.

Perhaps the greatest shortcoming of psychoanalytic theories is the **tautological trap.** What psychoanalysts define as antisocial instincts, or repressed urges, or unresolved complexes may be alternative labels for the behaviors they seek to explain. This tautology makes the theory essentially untestable.

Among psychotherapists Freud in particular believed that criminals engage in law-violating activity to get caught. Although this may be true for some very violent criminals, "most offenders do not appear frustrated or guilt ridden by the fact that their 'crimes pay' at least some of the time. In fact, the success of their crimes seems to be a major gratification in their lives" (Wrightsman, Nietzel, and Fortune 1994:100).

In recent years Freud himself has been at the heart of debates about psychoanalysis. He based the theory on case studies of mostly middle-class white women. Freud's medical practice also must be considered in historical context: This was the Victorian era, a time of repressed human sexuality. His theory has all the limitations associated with theories based on a small sample during a particular historical period. Clinical evidence of this type may be inaccurate. We must consider the influence of the analyst, "who may bias the kinds of information reported, subtly encouraging reports that are consistent with psychoanalytic assumptions and discouraging others" (Cloninger 1993:26).

Nevertheless, psychoanalytic theory provides insight into a host of human maladies, and its explanation for such problematic behavior as substance abuse has strong intuitive appeal (Abadinsky 2001). It is also the basis for therapeutic efforts in many treatment disciplines. Figure 4.1 summarizes the psychoanalytic perspective on crime.

Psychoanalysis, Public Policy, and Criminal Justice Practices

The wide variety of psychogenic theories of crime and criminality has led to nearly as many different policies and practices. Psychoanalytic theory stresses unconscious psychic mechanisms—id, ego, superego—directing conscious behavior, including that defined as criminal. This view of criminals, in essence mitigating some level of responsibility and, in legal terms, *mens rea,* has important implications for crime policy and criminal justice system practices.

Psychoanalytic theory is concerned with the early developmental years of a child. Dysfunctional adults, including those whose neurotic behavior is criminal, are the sum of their early childhood experiences. An environment that fails to nurture, or perhaps that is characterized by neglect and abuse, will yield an adult whose behavior is likely to conflict with social norms.

The relationship between child abuse and subsequent criminality is not clear. Cathy Spatz Widom (1989) brought a subculture-of-violence perspective to the study of child abuse. She reported that abused and neglected individuals had higher rates of adult criminality than members of a control group, as well as many more arrests as an adult. In short, Widom found considerable support for the notion of a cycle of violence, with abused and neglected women manifesting their earlier victimizations in far more subtle ways than men: The former suffer from depression and psychiatric hospitalizations, and the latter have greater involvement in violent criminal behavior.

Matthew Zingraff and his associates (1993) saw Widom's work as critical to understanding the cycle of violence. They extended her work, looking at all children with substantiated reports of abuse or neglect. Moreover, Zingraff and associates used a random control group rather than a matched control group, as Widom did.

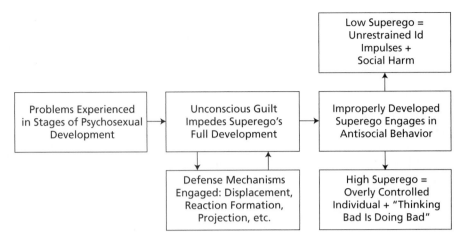

FIGURE 4.1 Psychoanalytic Perspective on Crime

The former allowed for far better estimates of the delinquency among the control group, making the comparisons between the maltreated group and the comparison group far more valid. The researchers reported that the maltreated children differed significantly from the control group only with regard to status offenses. But specific forms of maltreatment did not predict any offense type. Zingraff and associates (1993:196) concluded that "the risk of delinquency for maltreated children claimed by much previous research has been exaggerated." On this latter point, however, other researchers disagree. Research by Barbara Tatem Kelley and her associates (1997) found that "subjects with a history of maltreatment were more likely to engage in serious and violent delinquency, use drugs, perform poorly in school, display symptoms of mental illness and (for girls) become pregnant."

Another, related area of considerable dispute in psychology and psychiatry is "recovered memory." Clinical psychologists describe this as memories long forgotten or suppressed but subsequently recalled; they often link it to very traumatic events, such as rape, incest, and other sex-related or violent crimes, particularly childhood abuse. The debate over recovered memory centers on two questions (Coughlin 1995). First, is it possible to suffer a horrible trauma, repress that memory, and subsequently recall it? Second, is that memory reliable?

At the heart of this controversy is Freud's concept of repression. Repression, like many Freudian ideas, elicits high levels of skepticism from many contemporary psychologists and psychiatrists. For his part Freud largely discounted the stories told him by his female patients about sexual abuse by their fathers, viewing the "memories" as repressed sexual fantasies.

Contemporary memory experts question whether recollections tied to traumatic events can be considered reliable (Coughlin 1995; Monaghan 1992). Consequently they question whether recovered memories are even recollections of true events, the fruit of seeds planted by well-meaning psychotherapists, or simply scrambled messages in the brain. No less an authority on memory than Elizabeth Loftus, writing with Katherine Ketcham (1994), called repressed memory a myth. The debate has led some skeptics—and "victims"—to form the False Memory Syndrome Foundation, an advocacy group for accused parents (Coughlin

1995:A9). As the debate rages, criminal courts continue to hear the testimony of victims who have suddenly and often spontaneously recovered supposedly long-forgotten memories.

Criminal justice policy based on psychoanalytic theory offers treatment services for those manifesting antisocial behavior or found guilty of criminal conduct. However, such services are costly. Ironically illegal drugs may be the users' way of controlling their own antisocial impulses—self-medicating against crime. Many psychoanalysts view the use of depressants—including heroin, alcohol, barbiturates, and tranquilizers—as a means to manage sadistic and masochistic impulses. That is, such individuals take depressants not to obtain pleasure, but to control internal rage. Cocaine and amphetamines, as stimulants, may offer understimulated persons an alternative to antisocial, although exciting, behavior. Such actions, of course, violate our nation's current drug laws (see Abadinsky 2000).

DEVIANT PERSONALITIES AND PSYCHOPATHOLOGIES

- Have you ever taken a personality inventory such as the Minnesota Multiphasic Personality Inventory? If you are headed for a career in criminal justice, the odds are you will encounter such a test at some time.

- The term *psycho* has a negative connotation, often serving as a warning to stay away from a particular person. Can you think of any books or movies with a psychopath as the main villain? Whether you prefer fiction or nonfiction, you have probably encountered examples of the remorseless killer.

- Are you a person who craves excitement, lives on the edge, and challenges yourself physically? If so, we have a theory for you.

Following World War II questions about personality traits became increasingly important in the work world and elsewhere. As a result of management science and generally progressive views on employees in the postwar era, managers turned increasingly to psychometric screening devices. The idea was to identify for employment only those candidates who had the right personality traits for the job (Houston 1995:17–18; Swanson, Territo, and Taylor 1998:101–6). American correctional philosophy and practices were also undergoing a revolution of sorts, with scientific management practices extending to correctional facilities (no longer called prisons) as well. Interestingly not just employees were subjected to screening. The "clients" of that system also were screened for entry into rehabilitative programs and general institutional management (Clear and Cole 1997; Mays and Winfree 1998).

At about the same time another psychological perspective on crime was gaining respectability. Personality theory, along with the twin concepts of psychopathy and sociopathy, seemed to suit the criminal justice system's needs. As with contemporary psychoanalytic theories, proponents of these perspectives did not view them specifically as a means to describe, predict, or explain criminality. Policy makers and practitioners often observed empirical ties between personality theory and crime after the theory had been applied to other purposes, such as employee screening.

Most importantly, personality theory offered psychometric diagnostic instruments that gave uniform, reliable, and quick—and, some would argue, simplistic—answers concerning personality traits.

Personality and Crime

Personality theory is based on the assumption that the key to understanding all behavior lies in the way individuals express their habitual patterns and qualities of behavior. These habitual patterns and qualities are physical or mental, behavioral or attitudinal.

Eysenck's Personality Theory The primary personality theory is Hans Eysenck's criminal personality theory, a mix of behaviorism, biology, and personality theories. A critic of sociological crime theories (Eysenck and Gudjonsson 1989), Eysenck saw crime as an interaction between environmental conditions and inherited nervous system features. Like many other psychobiologists Eysenck (1973:171; see also Eysenck 1977) believed that focusing on the nature-versus-nurture controversy was no way to resolve the crime causation debate. In another divergence Eysenck asked, "Why doesn't everyone commit crime?" To this point psychologists have concerned themselves with a different question: What made this person commit crime?

Eysenck suggested that, although criminal behavior is not an inherited trait, certain inherited characteristics make social expectations more difficult to achieve. In particular, he pointed to the nervous system as providing an explanation for personality differences. Eysenck divided the controlling of behavior into that which is the result of the quality of conditioning and that which is inherited, and so reflects the sensitivity of the **autonomic nervous system** (**ANS**). The ANS regulates involuntary bodily functions (e.g., heart, lungs, and digestion), including ones that have opposite effects. For example, sympathetic functions act or, more correctly, react to mobilize the organism for action, as in the classic "fight or flee" scenario; parasympathetic functions deal with the digestive system and act to conserve bodily resources. The ANS plays an important role in delineating between personality types: the extravert (not used in the more conventional sense) is compatible with or identical to those types discussed in sociopathy in general and arousal theory in particular, topics we address in the next section.

Personality, Eysenck believed, depends on four "higher-order factors," including **ability,** or intelligence (a quality he called **g**), and three temperaments: **extraversion, neuroticism,** and **psychoticism.** Although g is important in understanding crime, Eysenck claimed that the three temperaments are far more critical. Two of these, extraversion and neuroticism, are related; the third, psychoticism, is unique. For Eysenck extraversion reflected basic central nervous system (CNS) functioning. Neuroticism depended on nerve pathways outside the CNS, in particular the ANS. Psychoticism had no specified neural links.

According to Eysenck two personality types exhibit the greatest crime-proneness. The first includes **neurotic extraverts,** or persons who, because of their biology, require high stimulation levels from their environments. Moreover, their sympathetic nervous systems are quick to respond without much counterbalancing from the parasympathetic system. The second type, the **psychotics,** are persons who, due to reasons of unknown physiological origin, are cruel, hostile, insensitive to others, and unemotional, but not necessarily "out of touch with reality." By themselves, however, these personality types do not explain *why* crime occurs.

Eysenck merged his genetically determined personality types with instrumental learning, or behaviorism, to provide a complete answer to his key question about why *everybody* does not commit crime. Instrumental learning occurs in the individual's environment; some action must be engaged in that elicits either a reward or a punishment. About this process Curt Bartol (1991:51) observed:

> Most people . . . do not participate in criminal activity . . . because after a series of trials they have made strong connections between [criminal activity] and aversive consequences. On the other hand, those persons who have not made adequate connections, either because of poor conditionability (e.g., extraverts) or because the opportunity to do so was not presented (socialization), are more likely to display deviant or criminal behavior. According to Eysenck, these people do not anticipate aversive events strongly enough to be deterred; the association has not been sufficiently developed.

Criminal behavior, in Eysenck's model, is thus the product of environmental factors (conditioning/learning habits) and biology (personality type intensifiers).

Psychopathy, Sociopathy, and Crime

In general usage **psychopath** and **sociopath** denote unpredictability, untrustworthiness, and instability.[4] When combined with *criminal,* each term takes on a new meaning: The psychopathic criminal is totally without conscience, capable of unspeakable acts, but showing no external signs of psychoses or neuroses. Paul Tappan (1960:137) described psychopathy as "a condition of psychological abnormality in which there is neither the overt appearance of psychosis nor neurosis, but there is a chronic abnormality of response to the environment." This rather vague definition and description aside, the resulting body of work is often called the **psychopathy hypothesis.**

Samuel Guze (1973:35–36) offered a more concrete definition of *sociopathy,* a term used interchangeably with *psychopathy.* Sociopathy exists "if at least two of the following five manifestations were present in addition to a history of police trouble (other than traffic offenses): a history of excessive fighting . . . school delinquency . . . poor job record . . . a period of wanderlust, or being a runaway. . . . For women, a history of prostitution could be substituted for one of the five manifestations." Clinical definitions—the means by which the disorders are diagnosed—center on behavior (Vold and Bernard 1986:122). Even when objective tests are used, however, the definitions are arbitrary, and personality researchers have little agreement as to their use (Meier 1989).

The definitions of the term *psychopath* are so broad that they can be applied to any criminal (Cleckley 1976:137). Indeed, these characteristics may be shared by many members of Congress, employees of the Internal Revenue Service and Central Intelligence Agency, and university administrators. It would be difficult to find a prison inmate lacking all five of Guze's manifestations. If all inmates are, in fact, sociopaths, it could be costly for taxpayers, given Guze's recommendation that all sociopaths be locked up until they reach middle age (Guze 1976:137).

The nonfiction character portrayed by Joe Pesci in *Goodfellas* exemplifies this type of personality.

Ellis's Arousal Theory Arousal theory represents a major expansion of the ties between psychopathy and crime. As Ellis (1991:37) observed:

> According to arousal theory, persons who are most apt to be reinforced for engaging in criminal behavior (and less likely to learn alternative behavior patterns) have reticular [the brain's information intake system] functioning patterns that quickly habituate to incoming stimuli. Persons with this genetic makeup are most apt to be reinforced for engaging in anti-social behavior and less likely to learn alternative behavior patterns. Subjectively, such persons regard many ordinary environments as "boring" and "unpleasant," and thus should be motivated to seek novel and/or intense sensory stimulation to a degree most people would choose to avoid.

High-arousal persons, Ellis (1990) claimed, (1) exhibit impulsive and hyperactive behavior, (2) are prone to take risks and seek excitement at virtually any cost, (3) are inclined to use psychoactive drugs to modify their mental state when other means of doing so are not viable, (4) prefer chaotic and varied social and sexual experiences, and (5) consider academic tasks boring. In short, high-arousal persons show few qualities or personality characteristics that hold out much hope for prosocial change.

A key difference between arousal theory and garden-variety psychopathy theory is that the former provides a biopsychological explanation for antisocial and asocial conduct, whereas the latter is primarily a diagnosis and treatment in search of a cause. Like Eysenck's personality theory, arousal theory looks to the stimulation levels needed and sought by individuals. Some persons need more stimulation than others, owing to problems with their **reticular activating system (RAS)**, the part of the brain responsible for attentiveness to the surrounding world. Psychopaths, say arousal theorists, may need excessively high levels of stimulation, the kind provided only by behavior that generates pathological excitement and thrill levels.

Interestingly, underaroused psychopaths, whose RAS barely keeps them awake, may be relatively immune to efforts to alter their undesired behavior. It has been theorized that only increased stimulation leads to corrective learning. Indeed, researchers have found that punishment administered in low-arousal contexts, which include prisons and classrooms, have little aversive influence. The psychopath seems unable to benefit from learning and punishing in such environments (Bartol 1991; see also Chesno and Kilmann 1975).

Assessing Personality Theory and
the Psychopathy Hypothesis

The definitional imprecision of psychopathy and sociopathy renders them virtually meaningless for criminology and, by extension, criminal justice. As Sutherland and Cressey (1973:169) observed, "The term 'psychopathic personality' . . . is useless in psychiatric research. It is a diagnosis of convenience arrived at by a process of exclusion. . . . It serves as a scrap basket to which is relegated a group of otherwise unclassified personality disorders and problems."

Research findings on psychopathy are mixed. Early studies of psychopathic characteristics, even among prison inmates, failed to provide a useful basis for distinguishing the least psychopathic from the most psychopathic (Cason 1943, 1946). One prison-based study, which used a nonprison comparison group, found that psychopathy was concentrated among males age 20–29. This finding suggests that what has been described as an unalterable condition decreases after the age of 30 (Cason and Pescor 1946). In the late 1990s and early 2000s, clinical comparative studies of brain activity revealed differences in the brains of persons diagnosed as psychopaths (Raine and Mednick 1997; Raine et al. 2000). For whatever reasons their brains seemed to work differently from nonpsychopaths and other psychologically disordered persons.

A longitudinal study of over 500 patients in a child guidance clinic found that, compared to "normal school children," the clinic juveniles led far more disordered adult lives; 1 in 5 of the patients was diagnosed as sociopathic, compared to 1 in 50 members of the control group (Robins 1966). Whether a personality disorder "caused" the subsequent criminality or whether the intervention of the juvenile courts and guidance clinic assumed a causal role is unclear (Gibbons 1977:175). In an even more recent study, William McCord and José Sanchez (1983), who followed the former residents of a juvenile institution for 25 years, found little evidence to support the notion that those defined as psychopathic were more crime-prone than other delinquents.

The evidence fails to support Eysenck's personality theory, which was created specifically to explain criminality. The fault, however, may not lie with the theory. Research design flaws make the findings of personality theory research highly suspect (Passingham 1972; see also Farrington, Biron, and LeBlanc 1982). In particular, adequate control groups are generally missing. Even the experimental groups employed—in some cases prison inmates—may be incapable of accounting for confounding factors, such as the type of crime committed. Indeed, few "pure type" offenders are found in prison; that is, few offenders are guilty of only one type of criminal activity. In at least one study criminals scored lower than members of the control group on a personality scale derived from Eysenck's work (Bartol and Holanchock 1979).

A key problem with the concept of psychopathy is the lack of consensus in the psychological community as to its definition and prognosis. Moreover, we are unsure of the predictive value of such concepts. Following the deinstitutionalization of nearly 1000 "criminally dangerous" mental patients, less than 3 percent were returned to mental hospitals with a diagnosis as criminally insane (Steadman 1972). In addition to an inability to predict "future dangerousness," circularity is a central concern. That is, the clinical method or test often used to determine the condition has in it the very symptom defined as problematic. Subsequently the diagnostic test (e.g., a personality inventory) is highly correlated with known, self-reported, or even future criminality or delinquency. What may be at work is one of the most reliable truisms in all the behavioral and social sciences: Past behavior is the single best predictor of future behavior for both criminals and Boy Scouts.

Personality theories, like most psychogenic explanations, are prone to tautologies. This is particularly true of the concept of psychopathy, for which the symptoms of the personality disorder are taken as evidence of its existence, and vice versa. This approach has limitations if we are interested in understanding and

---

COMMENTS AND CRITICISMS: Psychopathology: The Debate Continues

Psychologists continue to see value in psychopathology. In a recent **meta-analysis**—an evaluative procedure that allows for the overall assessment of a body of research on a topic and a method employed in later chapters—researchers reviewed the findings of 59 different studies conducted from 1963 to 2000 and reported that several dimensions of psychopathy bear a moderate resemblance to antisocial behavior (ASB). Psychologists Joshua Miller and Donald Lynam defined ASB broadly to include self, parent, and teacher ratings. However, like many psychopathology researchers before them, they also included "personality scales" from personality inventories, including the MMPI Pd scale. Lastly they included studies employing the antisocial personality disorder (APD) diagnoses or criteria. They acknowledge the existence of high intercorrelation between the various measures of ASB. Miller and

Lynam (2001:780) offered the following description of the personality traits of persons with ASB characteristics: "Individuals who commit crimes tend to be hostile, self-centered, spiteful, jealous, and indifferent to others. . . . They tend to lack ambition, motivation, and perseverance, have difficulty controlling their impulses, and hold nontraditional and unconventional values and beliefs."

The commingling of crime and delinquency measures with scale scores and APD diagnoses does little to resolve tautological concerns. The broad concept of ASB confuses the issue because not all antisocial behavior is criminal. Whether, as psychologist Robert Hare suggested, psychopathology is "a clinical construct whose time has come," remains to be seen. Most criminologists need more definitive evidence than that provided by Miller and Lyman.

Sources: Hare (1996); Miller and Lyman (2001).

---

explaining the behavior. In a related vein many psychogenic theories, including arousal theory and Eysenck's personality theory, incorporate biological elements based on little-understood neural processes. The abandonment of a pure nature or pure nurture position can only be viewed as a positive. However, the inclusion of explanations from highly limited studies of the human brain or genetics may be a poor substitute.

Personality, Public Policy, and Criminal Justice Practices

For decades personality inventories—such as the **Minnesota Multiphasic Personality Inventory (MMPI)** and the **California Personality Inventory (CPI)**—and more general psychological tests—such as the **Rorschach Inkblot Test** and the **Thematic Appreciation Test (TAT)**—have plumbed the depths of the human personality. The goal has been to identify "crime personality" markers or characteristics. Those who interpret the tests and inventories point out that certain response patterns suggest specific personality disorders.

Assessment for crime-proneness using the Rorschach and TAT is rare (Siegel 1992). These tests require clinicians trained in the subjective interpretation of test results. More common is the use of checklist personality inventories. Key among these inventories is the MMPI, first used to study crime by R. Starke Hathaway and Elio Monachesi (1953). Their work supported the use of the **psychopathic**

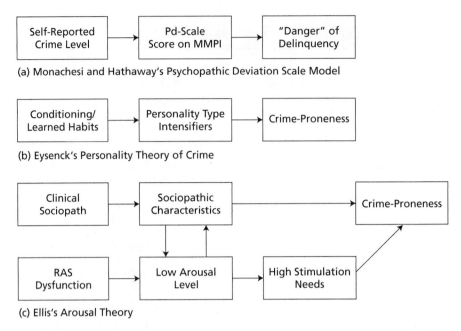

(a) Monachesi and Hathaway's Psychopathic Deviation Scale Model

(b) Eysenck's Personality Theory of Crime

(c) Ellis's Arousal Theory

FIGURE 4.2 Deviant Personalities, Psychopathologies, and Crime

deviation (Pd) scale as a delinquency correlate. Figure 4.2 summarizes the main theoretical approaches to deviant personalities, psychopathologies, and crime.

Some researchers question the MMPI's ability to predict criminality or delinquency. For example, Gordon Waldo and Simon Dinitz (1967), in a review of 94 MMPI-based personality studies published between 1950 and 1965, found that more than 8 in 10 studies reported significant differences between delinquent and nondelinquent youths. Nonetheless, the researchers reported that the evidence about the MMPI's predictive usefulness was inconclusive. A major reason for this conclusion may be that the Pd scale includes self-reported acts of delinquency. In other words, the use of the MMPI to predict delinquency status is a tautology. The MMPI may be inappropriate because any significant differences between the psychology of criminals and noncriminals "are based on tautological arguments" (Tennenbaum 1977:228). That is, criminals are those persons reporting to have engaged in criminal behavior.

Moreover, the MMPI–delinquency linkage is based on official delinquency as the outcome, or dependent, variable. The following scenario suggests itself: The MMPI's Pd scale may tap into those personality characteristics among delinquents—aggressiveness, irresponsibility, lack of maturity—associated with the chances of getting caught and punished by the criminal justice system (Tennenbaum 1977). The scale creates a problem with circular reasoning. Hindelang (1972:81) reported that youths who commit delinquent activities are "impulsive, shrewd, uninhibited, aggressive and pleasure-seeking." When we add a tendency to disregard social mores, the result is an interesting but relatively useless description of delinquents. The purpose of criminological theory is to find out why youths and adults engage in crime. The CPI and MMPI seem to do little more than *describe* characteristics associated with the commission of crime and delinquency.

The creators of the CPI based it less on such negativistic ideas as the "psychopathic deviate," and relied instead on the extent of individual socialization, expression of self-control, and acceptance of responsibility for personal actions. Although not created with this purpose in mind, the CPI is also used to distinguish between offenders and nonoffenders (Gough 1965; Megargee 1972, 1977). Michael Hindelang (1972) found the CPI to be correlated with self-reported delinquency.

The personality-based psychogenic theories offer scant hope for changing behavior. Their focus is more on what we can do *to* offenders than what we can do *for* them or the general population to prevent crime. For example, consider the implications of psychopathy/sociopathy and arousal theories. Beyond identification and separation from the general population, what can we do for individuals who have basic personality flaws that will not respond to any known treatment? Perhaps psychotropic drugs will ameliorate this condition, as they have for other behavioral maladies with organic causes.

As with earlier IQ testing, the attractiveness in psychometric personalty testing may be the appearance of impartiality. These tests are also quick, uniform, and reliable even if their validity remains in question (i.e., we are not sure exactly what is being measured). But when it comes to employment and promotion decisions, they are a policy maker's dream. Commonly and widely used, and generally accepted by the scientific community, such tests are difficult to attack in the courts. Given the tautology implicit in them, and assuming respondent honesty, they are also a cross-check for self-reported deviance and law-violating behavior.

For the clients of the criminal justice system—from the accused to the ex-con—such tests have become a way of life. Again policy makers rely heavily upon psychometric tests, which provide neat, clean, and impartial means of making all sorts of decisions about system clients. Testing removes the specter of discrimination or arbitrary judgment. The tests are used to inform decisions about everything from jail and prison classification, to treatment program access, to release on probation and parole.

The criminal justice system bases many policies and practices on these theories. The fact that there is little associated empirical support or generalizable data does not seem to faze policy makers or implementers.

Law Enforcement Practices Police work has long had strong ties to psychogenic explanations of behavior. First, police departments frequently use personality inventories to screen job applicants and determine the suitability of candidates for promotion.[5] In fact, the MMPI was recommended as an appropriate device by the 1967 Presidential Commission on Law Enforcement, and the 1973 report of the National Advisory Commission on Criminal Justice Standards and Goals reinforced this opinion. The initial purpose of such psychometric tests was to screen in candidates with highly desired qualities and screen out candidates who possessed characteristics deemed less desirable. But the former goal often lost out to the latter (Benner 1986).

Geoffrey Alpert (1993) observed that the same problems that apply to the IQ tests discussed in Chapter 5 affect the MMPI's ability to screen police candidates. According to Alpert (1993:103) "The selection and promotion of police candidates must move beyond political patronage and approach a scientific method. A balance must be reached among screening in, selecting out, and avoiding discriminatory practices. It is to be hoped that the psychological test will be used simply to screen out [unsuitable] candidates" A late-1980s study revealed that half of all major law enforcement agencies use psychological testing; furthermore, of the 72 larger metropolitan law enforcement agencies surveyed, nearly half used the MMPI (Strawbridge and Strawbridge 1990).

If such tests enjoy widespread use, what about deceptions—attempts by candidates to "beat the test"? Researchers have observed such efforts, especially attempts at "faking good" among prison inmates (Gendreau, Irvine, and Knight 1973), general offenders (Wasyliw, Grossman, Haywood, and Cavanaugh 1988), and police recruits (Grossman, Haywood, Orlov, Wasyliw, and Cavanaugh 1990). Recent studies suggest that "faking good" is more difficult if test results are examined for internal consistency. Such attempts are especially difficult when the test interpreter differentiates "healthy defensiveness from the intentional effort to ignore or minimize difficulties" (Borum and Stock 1993:159). Skilled administrators and test interpreters are important. They not only screen in (or out) certain kinds of candidates but also ascertain the veracity of applicants' answers.

The **police personality** concept describes undesired police characteristics, with the chief one, according to Arthur Niederhoffer (1969), being authoritarianism. The term was popularized at the end of World War II to help psychologists understand how the Germans cooperated with Hitler and his goals (Adorno et al. 1985). Authoritarianism refers to a personality type characterized by undemocratic tendencies, **cynicism,** and a readiness to condemn others solely on the basis of race or ethnicity (Adorno, Frenkel-Brunswick, Levinson, and Sanford 1985). The police are said to be more authoritarian than members of the general public. However, it is not clear whether high authoritarians are drawn to police work or whether policing creates high authoritarianism (cf. Lipset 1969; Van Maanen 1973).

Some social psychologists view the police personality as in line with a more general personality syndrome called **dogmatism.** Milton Rokeach (1956:3) described this condition as "(a) a relatively closed cognitive organization of beliefs and disbeliefs about reality, (b) organized around a central set of beliefs about absolute authority which in turn, (c) provide a framework for patterns of intolerance and qualified tolerance toward others." It is unclear whether all aspects of authoritarianism, cynicism, or dogmatism are out of place in the police work world. Police administrators may "evaluate police performance positively when they exhibit skepticism toward a volatile and dangerous public" (Anson, Mann, and Sherman 1986:304).

Law enforcement agencies, including violent-crime task forces and special investigative units, often employ personality theory to develop criminal profiles, especially concerning so-called psychopaths (Egger 1990; Holmes 1990; Ressler, Burgess, and Douglas 1988). The application of these psychogenic theories may be perfectly acceptable and appropriate because profiling is intended to bring together all relevant information on a single subject and identify a pattern of human behavior. A major criticism of personality theory and the psychopathy hypothesis is that they are overly concerned with using past behavior to predict future behavior, something police investigators need to do, especially in the pursuit of serial offenders (e.g., rapists, burglars, and murders). Police investigators are less concerned with determining why a person committed a crime than with developing a list of possible suspects or potential victims.

Table 4.1 Theories of Psychological Abnormalities and Crime

Theory	Major Figures	Central Assumptions	Causal Arguments (Key Terms)	Strengths	Weaknesses
Psychoanalytic	Freud, Healy, Aichhorn	The unconscious self can shape the conscious self in profound ways.	In developmental stages (*oral, anal, genital, latent, adolescent, adult*), imperfect passage may create problems, especially if weak *superego* gives in to hedonistic and antisocial *id* (see *displacement, repression, reaction formation,* and *sublimation*).	Suggests that, by unlocking the unconscious, psychoanalysis may change antisocial criminals; this approach has much commonsense appeal, especially when we view the offender as crazy: "No normal person would commit a crime like that."	Is based on questionable definitions (e.g., repression); studies include few people; theories are largely tautological; therapy is expensive.
Deviant personality	Monachesi, Hathaway, Megargee, Eysenck	The key to normal and abnormal behavior lies in the way we express our valued habitual patterns and qualities in life; psychological tests can reveal these personality markers, including those associated with crime.	Exactly how personality causes crime is missing, except for Eysenck's theory, which views crime-proneness as the product of conditioning/learned habits multiplied by personality type intensifiers (e.g., *neurotic extraverts* and *psychotics*).	Provides a way to determine the risk for criminal behavior (e.g., MMPI's psychopathic deviation scale score); MMPI and similar tests have widespread uses in criminal justice, for both system clients and personnel.	May be tautological: Self-reported delinquency yields a score on the MMPI that indicates danger of delinquency; tests of Eysenck's theory failed to include adequate control groups.
Psychopathy (sociopathy) hypothesis	Guze	Some people are totally without conscience, capable of acting without any concern for others and without any external manifestation of mental illness.	Owing to a lack of conscience, *psychopaths* (*sociopaths*) can commit a wide range of unacceptable acts, from lying with impunity to mutilation murders.	Provides a rationale for social sanitation: Little can be done for psychopaths except to institutionalize them; enjoys popular appeal; "The person who did this must have been psycho!"	Has imprecise definitions; research findings are mixed; the term tends to be used as a classification of the last resort, reinforcing a concern that this is another tautology.
Arousal	Ellis	See psychopathy. (The theory is an extension of psychopathy.)	See psychopathy. Criminals have brains that quickly habituate to incoming stimuli; they are under-aroused psychopaths; arousal theory adds a biopsychological explanation to the psychopathy hypothesis.	Explains why some criminals adjust well to prison and jail life (low stimuli) but cannot adjust to the free world (high stimuli); also explains why they are relatively immune to rehabilitation (i.e., they are barely awake in low-stimuli environments).	Is an interesting idea that has yet to receive a great deal of empirical support; prisons and jails are boring living environments.

Correctional Practices Correctional psychology is a major area of academic study and practice. First, personality inventories, such as the MMPI, are regular features of the intake process for newly arrived prison inmates (Champion 1990:213–15; Hawkins and Alpert 1989:192–94; Snarr and Wolford 1985:229). Such tests allow for the separation of certain inmates from the general population in order to treat their ailments and protect them. Given the limited psychotherapeutic resources of most prisons, this task may be an exercise in futility. It may be possible to place such inmates in a protective custody unit, away from predatory inmates.

The primary function of psychometric-based testing at intake and classification is to measure an inmate's ability to adjust to prison life and determine a suitable security level. The Megargee Inmate Typology (Megargee and Carbonell 1985), based on the MMPI, classifies inmates into 1 of 10 prisoner types and predicts the likelihood that the inmates will violate prison rules or otherwise act aggressively while incarcerated. The ability of this instrument and others to achieve their stated goals has been questioned (see, e.g., Farrington and Tarling 1985; Gottfredson and Gottfredson 1988; Louscher, Hossford, and Moss 1983). Nonetheless, they remain staples of prison classification systems. (See Table 4.1 for an overview of theories of psychological abnormalities and crime.)

SUMMARY

This chapter focused on explanations that look primarily within the individual for the causal answers. Biogenic and psychogenic theories of crime share a common history: They emerged from the naturalistic (positivistic) explanation of crime that replaced earlier spiritualism. However, even the most modern psychological theory has not entirely escaped the idea that residing within the individual is some characteristic, identifiable by modern scientific methods, that can be viewed as causing the undesired behavior. For these reasons psychogenic theories may be classified as individualistic and deterministic.

The theories reviewed in this chapter alert us to several important linkages to theories presented later in this book, and they serve as cautionary reminders of the limitations of theory. Increasingly psychogenic explanations have included an "appreciation" for environmental influences. For example, Eysenck's personality theory, one of the major psychogenic theories, acknowledges the importance of both social and psychological factors. However, contemporary tests of these and related theories have yet to show the predictive efficacy of the combined models. Moreover, this development is viewed with mixed feelings by many in criminology.

Public debate is often quite heated about both psychoanalysis and personality testing. For example, consider that a Smithsonian retrospective of Freud's life was canceled in 1995, only to be reinstated, after criticisms were added, in 1998 ("Criticized Freud show is revised and on"). Nonetheless, the theories contained in this chapter paved the way to new generations of psychogenic theories, ones reviewed in the next chapter.

Psychoanalytic theory and the psychopathy hypothesis may contain tautologies. That is, what the analyst or tester is measuring is the forbidden characteristic, usually crime or delinquency and less often other forms of deviant behavior.

If the predictor or measurement instrument has as an independent variable the thing being predicted, high correlations are inevitable.

Finally Bartollas and Simon Dinitz (1989) provided an insightful analysis of both biological and psychological positivism. They suggested that as the medical profession grew in stature practitioners medicalized certain forms of deviance. By "medicalization" Clemens and Bartollas meant that certain forms of deviant and criminal behavior were no longer viewed as moral problems but rather as medical ones. As a consequence medicine could aid in controlling these "illnesses." Badness became defined as an illness. Eventually the medical model fell out of favor with criminologists, but the search for biological and psychological explanations continues.

KEY TERMS

ability (g)

adolescence/adulthood stage

anal stage

arousal theory

autonomic nervous system (ANS)

California Personality Inventory (CPI)

cathexis

conscious

cynicism

denial

displacement

dogmatism

dream interpretation

ego

ego development

Electra wish

equilibrium

extraversion

fixation

free association

genital stage

id

insanity

latent stage

meta-analysis

Minnesota Multiphasic Personality Inventory (MMPI)

neuroses

neurotic extraverts

neuroticism

Oedipus wish

oral stage

personality theory

police personality

preconscious

primary process

projection

psyche

psychiatry

psychoanalysis

psychology

psychopath/psychopathy

psychopathic deviation scale (Pd scale)

psychopathy hypothesis

psychoses

psychosexual development

psychosexual maturity

psychoticism

psychotics

reaction formation

repression

reticular activating system (RAS)

Rorschach Inkblot Test

secondary process

sociopath/sociopathy

sublimation

superego

tautological trap

Thematic Aptitude Test (TAT)

transference

unconscious

CRITICAL REVIEW QUESTIONS

1. What's the difference between psychology and psychiatry? Why is this distinction important to criminology? Why is it important to criminal justice?

2. According to psychoanalytic theory what is the importance of unconscious phenomena to human behavior? How does the preconscious differ from the unconscious?

3. According to psychoanalytic theory what role does psychosexual development play in creating a criminal?

4. What do you see as critical criticisms of the psychoanalytic approach to crime causation?

5. How are personality disorders believed to be linked to crime?

6. How does Eysenck's personality theory differ from general personality theory?

7. What are the links between psychopathy/sociopathy and crime?

8. What do you see as the most devastating criticism of personality theory and the psychopathy hypothesis?

9. Which of the psychological theories contain general social policy implications that not only would be difficult to implement but might raise serious constitutional issues?

10. What are the policy implications of drug use serving as a form of self-medication for psychologically disturbed individuals?

11. Should the role of psychometric testing in selecting personnel for the criminal justice system be reduced or increased? Why do you feel this way?

12. What is the single most important idea that you learned from this review of psychoanalysis, personality, and psychopathy? Explain your answer.

NOTES

1. Not all surgeons or butchers are sadists engaging in sublimation, but we suspect that you already knew that.

2. Stephen Schaefer (1969:211) observed that, had he lived longer, Freud might have become "one of the greatest sociologists." Schaefer saw in Freud's later writings a declaration for the role of societal factors in human behavior, including aggression. Perhaps this shift had an impact on followers like Eissler.

3. An interesting metaphor emerges from the criminological studies using a psychoanalytic orientation: bringing light to darkness. Eissler's and Healy and Bronner's books both included the word *light* in the title. This metaphor is all the more interesting given the emphasis psychoanalysts place on the darker recesses of the unconscious.

4. Late in the twentieth century, the American Psychiatric Association recommended that the term *antisocial personality disorder* replace the more common term *psychopathy* (Ellis and Walsh 2000:16). Given its widespread and common usage in criminology, especially as compared to sociopathy, we prefer the less cumbersome term *psychopathy*.

5. As with IQ testing (see Chapter 5), the use of psychometric devices, including the MMPI, in the selection process is not limited to police work. It is also found in other criminal justice employment areas, especially entry-level positions in corrections. It is interesting to note, however, that rarely are attorneys or judges, let alone sheriffs and chiefs of police, subjected to these same personality inventories.

5

Psychological Learning and Developmental Theories

CHAPTER OVERVIEW

LEARNING OBJECTIVES

- Appreciate the complex biological, psychological, and sociological interconnections that determine measured intelligence, and the problems created by its use as a predictor of criminality.

- Establish a knowledge base for studying the IQ–crime link, including the role of race.

- Understand the multiple roots of behaviorism and their meaning for contemporary psychological learning theories of crime.

- Gain an appreciation for crime's variable nature as a reflection of human physical, social, and psychological development, including pathways to and from crime.

INTRODUCTION

At about the same time that Cesare Lombroso was writing in Italy about born criminals, psychologists and others in the United States began investigating what was believed to be an inherited mental condition: feeblemindedness. They saw a person's mental capacity as providing behavioral insights, criminal and otherwise, an idea that helped generate popular support for intelligence testing. Early advocates rarely looked for any explanatory factors linking intelligence and crime. What they acted upon was an often reported correlation: the lower the mental functioning, the higher the criminal activity.

By the end of the first quarter of the twentieth century, psychologists had abandoned feeblemindedness, as both a diagnosis and an explanation, even as intelligence testing was finding broader practical applications in U.S. society, including the study of crime and criminals. The persistent IQ–crime correlation continued to intrigue criminologists and eventually formed the basis of several different explanations of criminality. Some of these looked to race as a possible force in determining both IQ and crime, making this argument one of the most controversial in criminology.

Besides intelligence and the psychological abnormalities explored in the previous chapter, what other psychological forces are at work in the creation of criminals? How is it that some forms of behavior continue and others disappear? The early psychologists who explored these questions, first with animals and then with humans, were behaviorists, followers of a branch of psychology that places great emphasis on the objective, measurable investigation of individual actions and reactions. They explored unique psychological learning mechanisms associated with stimuli in the environment and individual responses to them. Recognizing the complex nature of human responses to their environments, cognitive psychologists modified the behaviorist perspective on learning and offered insights into crime and misbehavior that shaped many generations of practitioners in corrections and related fields.

Two psychological theories explore developmental paths that may lead to crime. The first one, far more psychological in focus, addresses why some youths engage in limited misbehavior while others are far more persistent offenders. The second perspective explores within-individual changes in offending over time, including causal factors—many of which are discussed in this chapter—that may explain the distinct stages of offending.

Like psychological abnormality theories the psychogenic theories in this chapter evolved to explain individual divergence from normalcy or general psychological development, not crime. However, the time was often short between their creation and their application to the study of crime and criminals. This certainly was true for intelligence testing.

INTELLIGENCE AND CRIME

- By the time they enter college, most people have taken at least one standardized intelligence test. Have you? Did you benefit from the results?

- Should inmates in jail and prison be denied access to certain kinds of programs or treatments based on their IQ scores?

- Do you believe that intelligence tests provide reasonably accurate measures of a person's native intelligence and, therefore, should be widely used?

These questions center on an idea that gained popularity during the first decade of the twentieth century: Low intelligence, an inherited condition, is a correlate of crime. For the idea to take hold, an "objective" measure of intelligence was needed. In 1905 the French psychologist Alfred Binet (1857–1911), working in collaboration with Theodore Simon, provided this measure as a series of tasks of increasing complexity, from those intended for children through those for adults. Three years later Simon assigned a mental age to groups of tasks. A colleague suggested that he divide mental age by chronological age and multiply the results by 100, and so in 1912 the **IQ** score was created. Smarter people had IQ scores above 100 and duller ones were below that figure.

Herbert Goddard, using a modified Binet-Simon test, studied IQ score distributions in American society. He concluded that as few as 28 percent and as many as 89 percent of the nation's prison inmates had IQ scores of 75 or less (Goddard 1914). The perceived link between weak morals and weak minds gained in popularity during the early decades of the twentieth century (Degler 1991).

By the start of World War II, intelligence testing had gained a strong foothold in American society, and its popularity has carried over into the twenty-first century. The contemporary search for the links between IQ and crime, however, has its roots in the far older studies of feeblemindedness, a term popularized in the nineteenth century.

Feeblemindedness and Early IQ Tests

No one is sure when scholars, researchers, social critics, and popular authors started describing mental degeneracy as hereditary and a force propelling individuals toward a lower type of existence. Nineteenth-century proponents of **feeblemindedness** defined it as a condition of mental deficiency and generally resorted to value-laden terms such as *imbecile, moron,* and *idiot* to describe those so afflicted. Stephen Schaefer (1969) observed that proponents of mental degeneracy supported their assertions with family histories. In this form of research, "the crime and deviance of the members were explained by hereditary mental degeneration, based on a methodologically dubious collection of data" (Schaefer 1969:205). For example, Richard L. Dugdale's study of the Juke family stressed the high incidence of both crime and feeblemindedness. Originally published in 1877 in *The Jukes,* Dugdale's claims were highly speculative and imaginative, based on faulty definitions of both crime and feeblemindedness (Vold 1979:78).

Goddard was the leading proponent of the use of feeblemindedness as legal and social categories, as well as an ironic figure in the IQ–crime debate. Goddard provided two types of support for his thesis. First, in 1912 he published *The Kallikak Family: A Study in the Heredity of Feeble-Mindedness.* In the Dugdale tradition he detailed the crimes and other aberrations of the 976 descendants of Martin Kallikak and two women. During the Revolutionary War Kallikak had an affair with a "feebleminded" girl who bore him an illegitimate son, a pairing that ultimately yielded 480 descendants. After the war he married a Quaker girl from a "good family," a union that led to 496 descendants. In the former family Goddard found 143 feebleminded descendants and dozens of criminal or immoral persons; in the latter, he found only one mental defective and no criminals.

Two years later Goddard published *Feeblemindedness: Its Causes and Consequences,* in which he reported on intelligence tests given to all inmates of the New Jersey Training School for the Feeble Minded. No inmate had a mental age greater than 13. Goddard (1914) deduced that the upper limit for feeblemindedness was a mental age of 12 or an IQ of 75. In *Feeblemindedness* Goddard also reported on many studies linking feeblemindedness and crime. These studies of prison inmates typically found high levels of feeblemindedness, and Goddard believed that they firmly established the IQ–crime connection.

In 1921 Goddard, in writing about a study of wartime draftees, observed a high proportion with IQ scores of 75 or lower, a finding that called into question his operational definition of feeblemindedness. Goddard could not accept that nearly a third of the draftees, and perhaps of Americans were feebleminded. He reckoned that the feebleminded accounted for only 1 percent of the U.S. population (Goddard 1921:173). Faced with these results, he concluded that mental defectives had IQ scores far below 70, a finding that also cast doubt on his IQ–crime link.

Few criminologists or psychologists today take seriously the idea of feeblemindedness. Whatever its failings, however, the concept was the progenitor of contemporary IQ–crime arguments.

Contemporary Explorations of the IQ–Crime Connection

Between the 1920s and the 1960s, criminologists acknowledged the tie between IQ and crime but speculated little about what it meant.[1] For years they relegated the correlation to the category of an invalid and spurious connection (Bartol 1999:39). The IQ–crime connection became controversial in the 1960s when Nobel laureate William Shockley (1967) stated that the difference between the IQ scores of African Americans and European Americans was rooted in genetics.[2] Moreover, he claimed, genetics might explain the variable poverty and crime

---

IN THEIR OWN WORDS: Goddard on Feeblemindedness

H. H. Goddard was in a unique position to assess the utility of feeblemindedness for two reasons. First, he used data drawn from both qualitative and quantitative sources to support feeblemindedness as a precursor for crime and deviance. Second, he lived long enough to see his own benchmark for feeblemindedness crumble under the weight of evidence provided by his own tests. His insights on feeblemindedness's role in causing crime and delinquency are, nonetheless, instructive.

- *On the role of the environment in criminal responsibility:* "Environment will not, of itself, enable all people to escape criminality. The problem goes much deeper than the environment. It is the question of responsibility. Those who are born without sufficient intelligence to know either right from wrong, or those, who if they know it, have not sufficient willpower and judgment to make themselves do the right and flee the wrong, will ever be a fertile source of criminality" (p. 7).

- *On the merger of environment and temperament:* "Whether the feebleminded person actually becomes a criminal depends upon two factors, his temperament and his environment. If he is of a quiet, phlegmatic temperament with thoroughly weakened impulses he may never be impelled to do anything seriously wrong. . . . On the other hand, if he is a nervous, excitable, impulsive person he is almost sure to turn in the direction of criminality. . . . But whatever his temperament, in a bad environment he may still become a criminal" (p. 514).

Source: Goddard (1914).

---

rates observed between the two groups. He urged others to study this problem. He did not have to wait long, as Arthur Jensen had by that time spent several years looking at the race–IQ link.

IQ and Race: Arthur R. Jensen The IQ–crime link received a boost when psychologist Arthur Jensen (1969) published an essay on genetic heritage. Like his mentor Hans Eysenck, Jensen was a differential psychologist—he explored how and why people behaved differently from one another. He divided intelligence into Level I—**associative learning,** the simple retention of input, or rote memorization of simple facts and skills—and Level II—**conceptual learning,** the ability to manipulate and transform information. Jensen believed that IQ tests measured Level II intelligence.

Interested in how culture, development, and genetics influence IQ, Jensen began extensive testing of minority group children in the 1960s. This study led him to two conclusions. First, he believed that 80 percent of intelligence was based on heredity (nature) and the remaining 20 percent on the environment (nurture). Second, he contended that, although all races were equal in terms of Level I intelligence, Level II occurred with significantly higher frequency among whites than blacks, and among Asian Americans somewhat more than whites. Given his first premise, he was led to the conclusion that whites were inherently better able to engage in conceptual learning than blacks, a conclusion viewed by many as racist (Lederberg 1969).

Race, IQ, and Delinquency: Robert Gordon Jensen found a champion in Robert Gordon, who carried the argument to its next level. In an early statement supporting the connection between race, IQ, and delinquency, Gordon (1976) cited Jensen's belief about the dominant role played by genetics in IQ. He also saw striking parallels between IQ scores and delinquency rates in court records and commitment data for juveniles. Gordon, largely without supporting evidence, argued for a connection between IQ and delinquency that was common to both African Americans and Caucasians. Without saying it in so many words, he was laying the groundwork for a race–IQ–delinquency argument.

Gordon later (1987) completed this argument in an attack on the sociological claim that what is being measured is socioeconomic status (SES), and not IQ. He subsequently endorsed a race–IQ–delinquency thesis. After conducting a series of analyses of lifetime delinquency prevalence rates, he reported that IQ is a better predictor of delinquency than SES (Gordon 1987:91). As for the race–IQ–crime connection, Gordon (1987:92) stated that "it is time to consider the black-white IQ difference seriously when confronting the problem of crime in American society." Black-white differences in delinquency rates, he claimed, were best explained by an IQ-based model.

IQ as a Crime Correlate: Travis Hirschi and Michael Hindelang Sociologists have long observed the ties between intelligence test results and crime. Travis Hirschi and Michael Hindelang (1977) reviewed a series of studies on the IQ–crime connection. They reported these conclusions about the research: (1) Low IQ is at least as important as low social class or race in predicting official delinquency, but more important in predicting self-reported offending; (2) within social classes and racial groups, persons with a low IQ are more likely to be delinquent than higher-IQ individuals; and (3) the relationship between IQ and crime is mediated by negative school experiences.

What are the origins of criminologists' biases against IQ? Hirschi and Hindelang pointed to the criminological mainstream that decried criminal anthropology early in the twentieth century. Social forces, and not individual factors, they claimed, should be studied to learn more about criminality. Edwin Sutherland (1931), a major opponent of the mental-inferiority-of-criminals thesis, argued that imprecision in the idea of a normal mental age meant that the concept was of little use in crime studies. (We return to the disciplinary barriers theme in Chapter 10.)

The Bell Curve: Richard Herrnstein and Charles Murray In *The Bell Curve* psychologist Richard Herrnstein and social scientist Charles Murray argued for a clear and consistent link between low intelligence and criminality.[3] Since the 1940s IQ tests have consistently placed the offender population at between 91 and 93, and the general population at about 100. Herrnstein and Murray (1994:235) saw this as an incontrovertible fact:

> Among the most firmly established facts about criminal offenders is that their distribution of IQ scores differs from that of the population at large. . . . The relationship of IQ to criminality is especially pronounced in the small fraction of the population, primarily young men, who constitute the chronic criminals that account for a disproportionate amount of crime.

Herrnstein and Murray (1994:235) acknowledged the possibility that high IQ could provide "some protection against lapsing into criminality for people who otherwise are at risk." In analyzing the National Labor Youth Survey, a longitudinal self-report study of young males, Herrnstein and Murray (1994:235) found that "offenders who have been caught do not score much lower, if at all, than those who are getting away with their crimes."

Intelligence is correlated with socioeconomic status: the lower the SES, the lower the IQ. However, the lower the SES, the more likely the identification as a criminal, a fact that skews the IQ–crime connection. What are we measuring, IQ or SES? "In general, attempts to equalize SES, cultural, or family backgrounds of offenders and nonoffenders reduce, but do not eliminate, the IQ separation between them" (Wilson and Herrnstein 1985:156). Herrnstein and Murray believed that, independent of SES, IQ predicts criminality.

Race is central to Herrnstein and Murray's theorizing, just as it was to Jensen's and Gordon's. According to this argument race is a key precursor of IQ. Hence, certain races, but particularly blacks, genetically fated as a group to lower-than-normal intelligence, also exhibit a similarly higher tendency to commit crimes. Herrnstein and Murray did allow that not all low-cognitive-ability persons commit crime. Moreover, recent crime rate changes cannot be attributed solely to changes in cognition, as other factors place low-cognition persons at greater risk than in the past.

Race-based criminality claims receive much criminological attention (see, e.g., Katz and Chambliss 1991; Scott 1987). Are they modern versions of the racist theories of early criminal anthropologists? Carl Degler (1991) asked if this was simply a matter of creating theories based on constitutional differences (e.g., physiognomic, atavistic, or IQ differences) to justify the differential treatment of lower-class persons or minority-group members. Assessments of the alleged ties between race, IQ, and crime provide answers to some of these questions.

Assessing IQ and Crime Links

Three positions dominate the debate on the IQ–crime connection—yes, no, and maybe. First, many independent studies support the claim that IQ is a significant delinquency predictor. For example, Terrie Moffitt and associates (1981) found a strong relationship between IQ and delinquency in Denmark. Deborah Denno (1985) reported that chronically violent youthful offenders scored lower on verbal and general IQ tests than one-time offenders.

Other studies report no causal link. For example, Scott Menard and Barbara Morse (1984:1374), using a longitudinal research design, concluded that "IQ is not causally related to delinquent behavior. It is one of man's individual characteristics which social institutional patterns of behavior may or may not reward." Their research is not without its critics (Harry and Minor 1985). Nonetheless, Menard and Morse (1985:967) maintained that the IQ–crime correlation is "an artifact of institutional selection of IQ as something to which the institution may respond."

The third position underscores environment–delinquency ties. Although students' IQ test scores predict school achievement, researchers have found no direct link between mental ability and delinquency (Denno 1985). It is possible that delinquents do poorly both in school *and* on IQ tests. The use of IQ scores to predict criminality is limited to those crimes most likely to be committed by persons with limited intelligence, pushing the IQ–crime connection close to a tautology. We could confidently predict that corporate crime, organized crime, or even political and computer crime requires superior intelligence. Does this mean that high IQ predicts criminality?

Questioning IQ Tests: What Is Being Measured? An overriding issue concerns exactly what it is that IQ tests measure. Are they influenced by environmental and cultural factors? If, as we suspect, the corporate offender's IQ differs from the street criminal's, what are the implications? IQ tests predict success in school, but they may be reliable predictors because such measures also predict middle-class status. Middle- and upper-class children tend to score higher on IQ tests than lower-class youths. We might expect that those who are less successful in school (i.e., children with lower IQ) would be more likely candidates for criminal behavior. In addition, education is positively correlated with economic opportunity. Intelligence quotients, argued Charles Locurto (1991), are also very malleable, easily influenced by many social, physical, and environmental forces. Moreover, he suggested the need for a serious reevaluation of IQ centered on a single question: How do we know that IQ is a measure of intelligence?

As Curt Bartol (1991:132) observed, "IQ scores and the concept of intelligence should *not* be confused. The term *IQ* merely refers to a standardized score on a test. Intelligence, on the other hand, is a broad, all-encompassing ability that defies any straightforward or simple definition." Herrnstein and Murray (1994) stated that not only are the races different on IQ but we may also have to treat them differently. They believed that a place exists for everyone in society but that some individuals may be destined, due to their low IQs, to occupy lower positions than others. Not surprisingly academics and the media have attacked this position (Fraser 1995; see also Allman 1994; Cose 1994; Hancock 1994; Mercer 1994; Morganthau 1994).

Unlike skeptics of IQ (Eysenck and Kamin 1981; Gartner, Greer, and Reissman 1974; Locurto 1991), Herrnstein and Murray cited questionable studies of IQ, heredity, and race. More recently a meta-analysis of IQ studies suggested that Jensen was far from the mark with his claim that 80 percent of IQ is due to heredity. Bernie Devlin and associates (1997) observed that perhaps less than 50 percent of IQ is the result of genetics, with the rest determined by the environment, a chief contender being prenatal care. Devlin saw these figures as challenging key contentions of *The Bell Curve.*

Some critics of *The Bell Curve* see the book as fraught with logical and empirical shortcomings (Fraser 1995). For example, most prison inmate samples, such as those discussed by Herrnstein and Murray, have high numbers of members with low intelligence. These are the criminals society has detected, apprehended, and convicted; they are *failed* criminals. Those who avoid detection, arrest, prosecution, or conviction may be smarter. Or they may have chosen crimes with a lower probability of detection or successful prosecution. The ability to postpone gratification, a middle-class value, may also be at work: Successful criminals may plan their activities, and the payoff comes later. Less intelligent criminals may go for the quick money—for immediate gratification—with all its attendant risks. White-collar criminals, in particular, pose problems for this generalization. What about the account executive who falsifies stock sales and collects false bonuses, or the car battery executive who knowingly exposes workers to hazardous conditions rather than engaging in costly and time-consuming safety measures? To ascend to a position in which white-collar crime is a possibility, the would-be criminal must possess at least average intelligence and possibly professional degrees. These qualifications hardly fit the criminal type circumscribed by the IQ–crime argument. In spite of skepticism about the fundamental arguments presented in *The Bell Curve,* many psychologists view it as a faithful representation of fact and good science (Chabris 1998).

Race: A Troubling Concept Some critics see the role given race in the race–IQ–crime hypothesis as scientifically problematic. Over the past 20 years sociologists and anthropologists have repeatedly issued a warning: The term *race,* as used since the days of Swedish taxonomist Carolus Linnaeus in the eighteenth century, currently provides virtually meaningless and unscientific classifications. For example, the American Anthropological Association has proposed a "race-debunking" statement for its members. Recent efforts to classify the races have been dismissed as futile. The old ways of dividing races—by hair texture, skin color, and facial features—are superficial and may be responses to climate and sexual selection. Even previously reliable genetic traits such as antibodies do not provide a basis to classify humans. As Kenneth A. R. Kennedy observed, "In the social sense, race is a reality. In a scientific sense, it is not" (Wheeler 1995:A15). Thus, any theory that uses race as a variable is relying on a social idea, and not a scientific one.

Proponents of the IQ–crime connection, including those who see race as a precursor of IQ, must (1) account for possible testing artifacts, (2) include a less culture-based measure of intelligence, (3) smooth out the effects of early child-rearing patterns, (4) answer critics who question the use of the term *race* as a biological rather than a sociological construct, and, most importantly, (5) tell us exactly what the tests are measuring. Until then it is best to treat the observed ties as an intriguing but spurious correlation. That is, IQ and crime may share a common cause, but high or low intelligence is not the cause of crime. Figure 5.1 summarizes the various IQ–crime hypotheses.

Intelligence, Public Policy, and Criminal Justice Practices

Intelligence testing may be one of the most powerful legally sanctioned instruments of discrimination created in the twentieth century. In a society that seems to live and die by quantitative information, IQ tests fit right into the cultural mainstream. They provide a simple and seemingly objective means to make what is often a difficult decision.

Standardized tests have a dark side: They can disguise racist motives, as many critics of *The Bell Curve* contend (cf. Chabris 1998; Fraser 1995). If, for cultural reasons, minority-group members score poorly on certain standardized IQ tests, using one as an entry requirement creates an insurmountable barrier. Over-reliance on IQ testing may also create a situation in which everybody loses and nobody wins. Those whom IQ tests exclude or misclassify may have career doors closed to them or be denied access to training that would change their lives for the better. Indeed, some prison inmates find themselves ineligible for job-training or other career-related opportunities while incarcerated because they are not intellectually up to the task—at least as determined by IQ tests and other psychometric tests. Employers

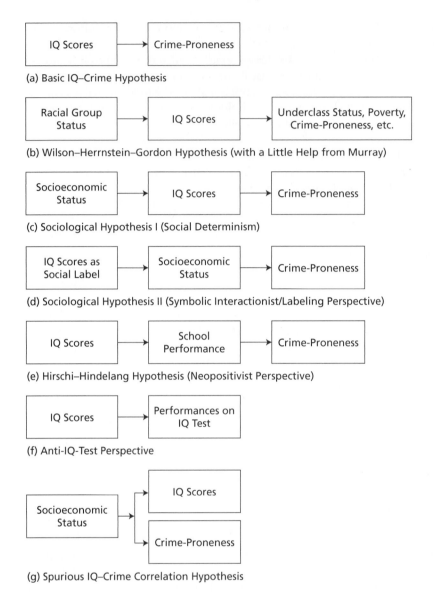

FIGURE 5.1 Various IQ–Crime Hypotheses

may lose potentially valuable employees, and educational programs may lose unique students.

For more than 100 years, the causal links between intelligence and offending have been tenuous at best. Even with the best, most current IQ–crime studies, the conclusions seem to point in all directions at once. A statistical correlation may exist between a person's IQ score and likelihood of offending, but the reasons are unclear. We have posited several interpretations of this correlation. Given the various potential answers, building public policy on an idea that points in so many different directions may be imprudent, lest the result be a form of social Darwinism.

Spencer, and others of his ilk, provided a theoretical underpinning for programs of, at best, benign neglect and, at worst, genocide. Intelligence testing and its alleged links to crime provide some measure of support for similar social programs. From this perspective society may need to resort to neglect or, worse, negative eugenics to weed out the inferior intellectual and genetic material.

Several socially liberal Scandinavian countries, those bastions of socialism and the welfare state, established eugenics programs in the 1930s. Between 1935 and 1976, the Swedish government authorized the sterilization of no fewer than 60,000 Swedish women deemed mental defectives to halt the propagation of their weak genes (Gallagher 1998). About 11,000 Danish women met similar fates, along with 1000 Norwegians (Broberg and Roll-Hansen 1996). In the United States public health officials estimate that perhaps 60,000 women underwent forced sterilization during the 1930s (Reilly 1991; Sofair and Kaldjian 2000). The Nazis also practiced several types of eugenics, ranging from involuntary euthanasia for German citizens to genocide for members of undesired races (Sofair and Kaldjian 2000).

What is needed next, the authors of *The Bell Curve* claimed, are simpler rules and a far simpler criminal justice system, with less "ambiguously administered punishments that give short shrift to personal excuses or social circumstances" (Cullen, Gendreau, Jarjoura, and Wright 1997:401). Francis Cullen and his associates saw such logic as playing into the hands of those who support the **penal harm movement.** Proponents argue that (1) crime causation can be expressed as a simple formulation—low IQ causes crime—meaning that easily understood laws will cure the problem; (2) offenders are unchangeable, so we need expend no valuable resources in a fruitless effort to make them better (recall social Darwinism); and (3) the punishments for law violation must be sufficiently painful to serve as an object lesson for simple-minded offenders. An IQ-based public policy "seeks to lock up stupid people" (Cullen et al. 1997:403), hardly the basis of a good crime control policy, let alone one rooted in solid criminological theory or sound research.

Law Enforcement Practices For more than 85 years, intelligence testing has been an integral part of police officer selection. Stanford University psychologists used IQ evaluations of police applicants in 1916 for the San Jose (California) Police Department. Because the average applicant had an IQ of 84, they recommended that the minimum standard be set at 80 (Wrightsman, Nietzel, and Fortune 1994:116). Officers have challenged the tests as culturally biased and discriminatory, not new arguments in this ongoing controversy. What is interesting is that "many departments . . . cling to tradition and use some form of multiple-choice IQ test for initial screening purposes" (Roberg and Kuykendall 1993:284).

Can we assume that scores on standardized IQ tests distinguish good police candidates from bad ones? Even within this upwardly mobile group, members of racial and ethnic minorities score lower than Caucasians. The reasons are more cultural than biological. Nonetheless, where IQ tests are considered essential measures of candidate suitability, this requirement alone has denied many otherwise suitable recruits access to law enforcement careers.

Judicial Practices Persons with low intelligence are not legally insane; however, they may not recognize that what they did was wrong, or appreciate the quality of the illegal act, or understand why they receive punishment. In fact, trial courts have convicted several individuals with low IQs—below 75—of homicide, sentenced them to die, and ultimately executed them. As a case in point, consider Morris Odell Mason, a retarded African American male with an IQ of 66, who was executed in 1985 for multiple rapes and murders. If the defendants are profoundly retarded, should they be subjected to the full force of the sanctioning process? If they are incapable of distinguishing right from wrong, should the courts sanction them at all? Don't we excuse the very young, those less than 10 years of age, from any criminal or even juvenile justice processing? What if the person is the mental equivalent of a 10-year-old or even a 5-year-old?

Historically trial and appellate courts, including the U.S. Supreme Court, have been unimpressed with these questions. In *Penry v. Lynaugh* (1989), writing for the majority, Associate Justice Sandra Day O'Connor noted, "There is insufficient evidence of a national consensus against executing mentally retarded people convicted of capital offenses for us to conclude that it is categorically prohibited by the Eighth Amendment." In *Penry* the state of Texas convicted the accused of capital murder. At the time of his trial, Penry was found to have the mental age of a 6½-year-old, and socially he was 9 or 10. However, the Supreme Court did find that the trial judge should have instructed the jury that mental retardation can be a mitigating circumstance, and as a consequence Penry's life was spared.

In 2002 the Supreme Court reversed itself, claiming that the missing consensus had been achieved. The case involved a 1996 abduction, armed robbery, and capital murder for which Daryl Renard Atkins was convicted and sentenced to death. At trial a forensic psychologist concluded that Atkins was "mildly retarded," and according to school and court records and to a standard intelligence test, he had an IQ of 59. In a 7–2 decision the Court, led by Justice John Paul Stevens, held that "such punishment is excessive and that the Constitution 'places a substantive restriction on the State's power to take the life' of a mentally retarded offender." (*Atkins v. Virgina* 2002:17). One reason cited by the Court in reversing itself—and the trial court's decision in *Atkins*—was the fact that by 2002 eighteen states and the federal government had enacted laws prohibiting the execution of those with mental retardation, meaning that a total of 33 jurisdictions in the United States had either total bans on executions or substantive restrictions. The methods by which various states will implement *Atkins* remain to be seen.

Sentencing is another area in which the IQ test may influence decision making. IQ tests, along with personality inventories such as the MMPI and the TAT (see Chapter 4), are often used in assessing suitability for probation—that is, in measuring **dangerousness.** Given the attitude of the nation's highest court, the most that low-IQ defendants can hope for is that at sentencing judges may view their affliction as a mitigating circumstance. Judges may choose to ignore it; in fact, given the average IQ of prison inmates, the latter situation seems to occur with regularity. Researchers have estimated that between 2 and 10 percent of the nation's prison population are mentally retarded or developmentally disabled (Davis 2000). Given these estimates, on any given day state and federal prisons in the United States hold between 24,000 and 120,000 mentally retarded inmates (Beck and Karberg 2001:1).[4] And jails may have higher percentages than prisons because they have become a holding area for the nation's mentally impaired citizens (Abadinsky and Winfree 1992:491–94; see also Adler 1986; Guy, Platt, Zwelling, and Bullock 1985; U.S. Government Accounting Office 1980).

These figures may also signify that low IQ results in a higher-than-normal probability of the mentally retarded offender being (1) caught, (2) convicted, and (3) sent to prison. According to Richard Bonnie (1990) few attorneys, judges, or juries recognize the symptoms of "legally significant" mental retardation. Bonnie (1990:421) suggested that "it seems reasonable to assume that a substantial portion (perhaps half) of the defendants with mental retardation are not referred for pretrial competency evaluation."

Correctional Practices As in law enforcement, candidates for entry-level correctional system positions, including correctional officers and other staff in prisons and jails, may have to take IQ tests. Test results also help staff manage inmates. Prison and jail classification schemes, which may include IQ tests, establish new inmates' security levels. These tests also may be used to judge suitability for facility-based treatment or rehabilitation programs, including education, job training, and drug or alcohol treatment. As Clemens Bartollas and John Conrad (1992:525) noted:

> The IQ tests are not truly reliable instruments to administer to men and women who have just arrived in prison, many of them depressed, many of them unskilled at reading, and many quite unmotivated to do their best on the batteries of tests that are impersonally administered to the newly arrived "fish." Still, the results give a rough—very rough—idea of the intellectual capabilities of the new prisoners.

Low-functioning individuals may find that in prison or jail they are again at the mercy of IQ test results, unable to "pass muster" for the few available programs (Bartollas and Conrad 1992; Clear and Cole 1997; Mays and Winfree 2002).

Cullen and associates (1997) identified two areas in which IQ score may have a positive impact. The first involves the **responsivity principle,** under which "services designed to reduce offender recidivism will be enhanced if the style and modes of service are matched to the learning styles and abilities of the offender" (Cullen et al. 1997:403; see also Andrews and Bonta 1994). In this context IQ is but one of a series of personality factors, including anxiety, depression, and mental disorder, that may play important roles in the delivery of treatment. Recall Bartollas and Conrad's observation about IQ tests given in prisons and jails: They are notoriously inaccurate. Nonetheless, the results may be important predictors of the receptivity of a given offender to correctional treatment (Cullen et al. 1997:404).

In addition, Cullen and associates (1997) suggested expanding IQ to include practical intelligence (see also Gould 1981, 1995). For example, we may possess verbal intelligence, linguistic intelligence, mathematical intelligence, and emotional intelligence. **Practical intelligence** is "a person's ability to learn and profit from experience, to monitor effectively one's own and others' feelings and needs, and to solve everyday problems" (Cullen et al. 1997:404; see also Gardner 1983; Sternberg 1985). Practical intelligence may be more amenable to change than conventional IQ. Cullen and associates (1997:405) viewed the inclusion of practical intelligence measures in correctional treatment as a positive way to influence an offender's future: "Positive behavioral change is possible and can be made more likely when treatment interventions take into account people's individual differences including their intellectual competencies."

BEHAVIORISM AND LEARNING THEORY

- As a small child, you sipped a cup containing a hot beverage, one so hot that it scalded your lips. You learned to check similar cups, blowing into them before tasting the contents. What elements of this process have criminological implications?

- You watch a news report about a major forest fire. Apparently inmates from a local prison volunteered to fight the fire even though their volunteerism exposed them to considerable danger. After discounting their community spirit as an attempt to escape (who can escape into a forest fire?), you ask yourself another question: Why can't prison inmates learn to be contributing members of society in other ways?

These questions relate to a branch of psychology called **behaviorism,** whose history parallels that of modern psychology. John B. Watson (1878–1958) first used the term nearly 100 years ago, in 1913, when he penned an article titled "Psychology as the Behaviorist Sees It."[5] He later wrote, "Learning in animals is probably the most important topic in the whole study of behavior" (1914:45). Watson (1930:2) contrasted the subject of "old" psychology—consciousness—with his variant in his final edition of *Behaviorism:* "Behaviorism, on the contrary, holds that the subject matter of human psychology is the behavior of the human being." It was learning, and not instincts, that earned the most praise from Watson. Understanding the means of habit formation was the key, Watson (1914) believed, to controlling human activity.

The Russian psychologist Ivan Petrovich Pavlov (1849–1936) influenced Watson. Pavlov experimented with dogs, the most famous of which was one whom he taught to associate food with bell chimes, so that the dog salivated at the sound of the bell alone. For Watson behavior was merely a physiological response to a given stimulus. The theories discussed in Chapter 4 notwithstanding, Watson saw no place in this process for the conscious or the unconscious, and he spent much of his career debunking what he saw as the psychoanalytic myth, translating psychoanalytic ideas into Pavlovian conditioning (Rilling 2000). It remained for others, but especially the American behavioral psychologist B. F. Skinner (1904–1990), to explain the complex nature of these learning mechanisms, and for still others, including Julian Rotter and Albert Bandura, to tie this perspective to crime.[6]

Operant Conditioning

Behaviorists see all behavior as resulting from learned responses to distinct stimuli. As noted by Skinner, when some aspect of behavior (animal or human) is followed by a certain type of consequence—a reward—it is more likely to recur. The reward is a **positive reinforcer.** However, a reward becomes a positive reinforcer, and punishment becomes a **negative reinforcer,** only when actually influencing behavior in a specified manner. These concepts form the basis for **operant conditioning,** whereby behavior patterns are shaped incrementally by reinforcement.

Disturbed behavior results from learning inappropriate responses—either directly from others (e.g., peers) or due to the failure to discriminate between competing norms, lawful and unlawful, because of inappropriate reinforcement. When conforming behavior is not adequately reinforced, or is perhaps negatively reinforced, an actor can more easily be influenced by competing, albeit antisocial, sources of positive reinforcement. Under controlled conditions, such as when one is conducting an experiment or training animals, the punishment/reinforcement, if it is to be effective, needs to occur as close to the event as possible. Our criminal justice system's effectiveness as a conditioning agent, therefore, may be limited due to the question of timeliness: How long does it take to discover the undesired or desired behavior and either extinguish it or reinforce it?

According to Skinner (1974:63) "Punishment is easily confused with negative reinforcement. The same stimuli are used, and negative reinforcement might be defined as the punishment of not behaving, but punishment is designed to remove behavior from a repertoire, whereas negative reinforcement generates behavior." For example, in the event an offender is fined or put in prison, what is actually occurring is not the presentation of a negative stimulus, but rather the removal of a positive one, a situation that has thus far positively reinforced the aberrant behavior (Skinner 1974:63). Skinner saw those who were punished as still possessing a tendency to behave as before but avoiding punishment by acting in a different manner to escape detection. In other words, punishment is effective in controlling behavior only in the short term, unless the subject can be continually monitored and punished. Effective behavioral changes require reinforcing alternative behavior. Figure 5.2 summarizes the basic behaviorist models.

Behaviorism and Crime

Hans Eysenck, the noted psychologist whose crime theory we examined in Chapter 4, saw the conscience as controlling antisocial behavior. This is not the mechanism that Freud ascribed to the superego, but instead is the result of conditioning, a process that often sounds like an admixture of classical deterrence, atavistic determinism, and modern behaviorism. As Eysenck put it:

> The young child, as he grows up, is required to learn a number of actions which are not, in themselves, pleasant or pleasurable and which in fact go counter to his desires and wishes. . . . In every society there is a long list of prohibitions of acts which are declared to be bad, naughty and immoral, and which, although they are attractive to him and are self-rewarding, he must nevertheless desist from carrying out. . . . In childhood it is possible to administer such punishment at the right moment of time; the child who does something wrong is immediately slapped, told off, sent upstairs, or whatever punishment it may be. . . . [A]fter a number of repetitions of this kind, the act itself would produce the conditioned response. . . . The child acquires, as it were, an "inner policeman" to help in controlling his atavistic impulses and to supplement the ordinary police force which is likely to be much less efficient and much less omnipresent. (quoted in Taylor, Walton, and Young 1973:48–49).

Most conventional crime involves substantial risk and relatively modest external rewards. Therefore, reinforcement for such activity may involve internal rewards through the release of potentially pleasant neurotransmitters such as endorphins and dopamine (Gove and Wilmoth 1990). Eysenck noted the need for timeliness in order for reinforcement to be effective: "An action followed by a

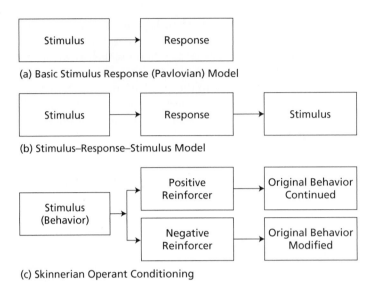

(a) Basic Stimulus Response (Pavlovian) Model

(b) Stimulus–Response–Stimulus Model

(c) Skinnerian Operant Conditioning

FIGURE 5.2 Behaviorist Models

small but immediate gratification, will tend to be repeated, even though it is followed by a large but delayed painful consequence" (quoted in Taylor, Walton, and Young 1973:47).

Behaviorism has several implications for criminology. We explore two such learning theories, beginning with cognitive learning.

Cognitive Learning Theory Human behavior is more complex than the relatively simple responses of lower species, as it is often mediated by beliefs and symbols. The readiness to fight or die for a "cause" or a strongly held belief system, such as those associated with religious symbols, embodies some of the most abstract complexities of human behavior. This recognition has led to **cognitive behavior theory,** which is based on the idea that "human behavior is mediated by unobservables that intervene between a stimulus and a response to that stimulus" (Gold 1980:8). Many mediating constructs are important to a full understanding of emotion and behavior, including beliefs, strategies, attributions, and expectancies. The way a person evaluates a given situation, in light of these mediating constructs, determines the affective and behavioral response (Gold 1980). For example, based on past learning, a twisted cross (swastika) may have different meaning to a Jew (for whom it is a symbol of the Holocaust) than to a member of the Navajo Nation (for whom it is a cosmic religious symbol). As Susan Cloninger (1993:369) observed, to "describe people's overt behavior without paying attention to what people are thinking cannot provide an adequate model of personality. Behaviorism that does not involve extended consideration of cognitive variables risks neglecting much that is human."

Julian Rotter (1954) proposed that a cognition or expectation leads to a certain outcome or consequence. People weigh their actions' possible consequences in terms of recollections about what has happened previously in similar circumstances. The possible rewards—how much value they attach to the outcome—may determine whether people engage in certain behaviors. These "generalized expectancies" are relatively stable in similar situations (Mischel 1976).

Rotter's **expectancy theory** describes how people make decisions about all human action, and not just crime. As for applying the theory to crime, Curt Bartol (1999:120) wrote:

> We would say that when people engage in unlawful conduct, they expect to gain something in the form of power, security, material goods, or living conditions. The violent person, for example, may elect to behave that way in the belief that something will be gained. The serial murderer might believe that God has sent him on a mission to eliminate all "loose" women; the woman who poisons an abusive husband looks for an improvement in her life situation. . . . Usually when people act violently, they do so because that approach has been used successfully in the past (at least they believe it has been successful).

Humans use their cognitive powers to look simultaneously into the past and the future, make decisions about likely outcomes, and act upon them. What happens if they lack the experience to draw conclusions about the future? Bandura provided an answer to this question.

Psychological Modeling Theory Albert Bandura is best known for his Bobo doll experiments. In this experiment children first watched while an adult model attacked a plastic clown doll called Bobo, kicking it and committing other aggressive acts against it. Next the children were placed in a room with attractive toys that they were not allowed to touch until they grew visibly agitated and frustrated. They were then moved to still another room with a Bobo doll and the same toys used by the adult model to attack Bobo. Bandura found that nearly 9 in 10 children imitated the attack on Bobo, and about 4 in 10 reproduced the behavior when placed in a similar physical situation eight months later (Bandura and Huston 1961; Bandura, Ross, and Ross 1963).

Bandura's learning theory blends reinforcement theory with cognitive psychology.[7] He revealed his cognitive roots in the following statement: "By representing foreseeable outcomes symbolically people convert future consequences into motivations of behaviour" (1974:859; see also Bandura 1989). He called the process by which this happens **observational learning** or **modeling,** a process that need not involve direct reinforcement. Instead, humans are capable of learning vicariously through four steps (Bandura 1977:24–28):

1. **Attention.** Learners must perceive what is happening and pay attention to the modeled behavior's important features, including what the model is saying and doing (e.g., if a whack with a hammer follows the statement "bad Bobo must be punished").

2. **Retention.** Learners must encode the information into long-term memory for later retrieval. Memory is a key cognitive element for successful observational learning.

3. **Motor reproduction.** Learners must be capable of reproducing the model's behavior. They must have the basic motor skills and physical attributes to carry out the behavior. If the child cannot pummel the doll, learning aggressive

behavior is not possible; if the child cannot reach the pedals, learning to ride a bike is not possible.

4. **Motivations (reinforcements).** Learners must comprehend and appreciate the positive reinforcements that accrue for the modeled behavior, the first step being to observe the model's reinforcement. Without motivation the behavior is not repeated.

Bandura's research and theorizing largely involved aggression, and the theory is best couched in those terms. For example, the person most likely to learn to be aggressive is the individual who observes much aggressive behavior, is reinforced for acting aggressively, and is the object of aggression. Bandura identified the primary models as family members, members of one's subculture, and symbolic models provided by the mass media.[8] Behavioral diagnosis and treatment, especially for aggression in children, were best undertaken during childhood (Bandura 1977). Treatment involved modeling socially acceptable behavior, following the same four steps.

Behaviorism as an explanation for crime is uncritical of the social order, the legal system, and its enforcement apparatus, instead adopting a consensual view of society. Much of what is done in the name of behaviorism is dependent on one's definition of the situation. As a technique for altering behavior, it is amoral or politically neutral and easily lends itself to misuse. For example, in *The Gulag Archipelago* Alexander Solzhenitsyn (1974) described the prison hospitals maintained in the former Soviet Union and their reliance on modified Pavlovian behaviorist principles as a means of eliminating dissent. Behavior modification has met with varying degrees of success in helping to maintain prison discipline and order in the United States as well (see the discussion to follow).

Assessing Behaviorism

How have behaviorist theories fared in the hands of researchers? Most behaviorist contributions to crime and justice issues have been largely indirect, through other theories such as social learning (see Chapter 7) and rational choice (see Chapter 2). The exception is the work of Bandura (1973), whose theory of aggression includes the influence of symbolic models, particularly the mass media (i.e., television and movies). Research on Bandura's learning model has linked exposure to TV violence with increased aggression in children and adults, although this relationship is clearer for short-term effects and among those who were already aggressive (Freedman 1984, 1986; Freidrich-Cofer and Huston 1986; Pearl, Bouthilet, and Lazar 1982).

Critics of behaviorism, however, have noted the following problems:

- *Failure to consider the role of biology.* Although Bandura (1973) acknowledged that genetic endowment can influence the rate at which learning takes place, biological theorists complain that behaviorists ignore the individual's biological state. What, they asked, are the individual differences in learning given variations in genetics, brain functioning, and learning (Jeffery 1985)? Not everyone, observed critics, is equally prepared to learn. Moreover, two people witnessing the same violent event (e.g., a hanging or a murder) might respond in very different ways.

- *Questions of manipulation and ethics in research.* The Bobo doll experiments have been criticized as manipulative (i.e., the children were teased and became frustrated because they could not touch the toys); moreover, the research may have been unethical in that it trained children to be aggressive (Worthman and Loftus 1992:45).

- *The catharsis effect.* Bandura and other cognitive behaviorists expressed concern about television violence because of the opportunity to model aggressive behavior. But many researchers have reached the opposite conclusion, suggesting that the act of viewing violence may lower aggression (Feshbach and Singer 1971). According to the **catharsis effect** viewing violence allows some people to release aggressive thoughts and feelings by relating to those engaged in violence (Gerbner and Gross 1976, 1980).

Behaviorism, Public Policy, and Criminal Justice Practices

The role of operant conditioning principles—such as negative reinforcers and positive punishers—in criminal justice policy is far from clear. Equally unclear is whether, issues of due process aside, the criminal justice system is capable of responding quickly and consistently enough to accomplish **behavior modification.** Similar problems confounded deterrence theory's system of rewards and punishments (see Chapter 2). Behaviorism adds operant conditioning language to the punishment process. The complex psychosocial nature of reinforcers and punishers suggests why sanctions alone may not deter offenders. Good behavior helps people avoid a visit to the local jail or revocation of parole or probation. Such negative reinforcers are intended to promote continued good behavior. Similarly punishments entail the loss of something valued (e.g., the prospect of a particular job, perhaps in the field of criminal justice, requiring the absence of a felony conviction record) should the undesirable behavior continue or reach a certain level. In short, behaviorism exerts considerable influence on criminal sanctions. The problem is that small, immediate rewards tend to be repeated even though they are followed by large, painful but delayed punishments.

Behaviorism holds the promise of changing behavior. Schools use **token economies,** a form of behavior modification, to teach students the rewards of good behavior. However, most behaviorists place less faith in the capacity of punishers to extinguish behavior than in the capacity of rewards to encourage it. This lesson is often lost on policy makers, who tend to emphasize positive punishers and neglect the other elements of operant conditioning, cognitive learning, or behaviorism generally. Just as importantly, most of these theories emphasize early intervention, especially Bandura's. Modifying adult behavior through behaviorist principles may be a difficult task.

Correctional Practices Behaviorists' constructs play major roles in programs of inmate change and institutional control. Cognitive therapy, a dominant theme in research on learning, memory, personality, and motivation, has long addressed undesired youthful behavior (Bartol 1991:366). One such approach, **reality therapy (RT),** is a form of self-control therapy posited by the correctional psychiatrist William Glasser (1975), who stated that offenders must take responsibility for their own behavior. From this perspective crime is viewed as irrational, rather than the result of a mental disease or disorder.

Many mental problems, Glasser argued, are symptomatic illnesses that have no presently known medical cause. They act as companions for the lonely people who *choose* them from a lifetime of experiences residing in the unconscious. The RT practitioner proposes first substituting the term *irresponsible* for mental health labels (e.g., *neurotic, personality disorder,* or *psychotic*). A "healthy" person is called *responsible*, and the task of the therapist is to help an irresponsible person to become responsible. Glasser (1980:48) saw RT as "based upon the theory that all of us are born with at least two built-in psychological needs: (1) the need to belong and be loved, and (2) the need for gaining self-worth and recognition."

RT is widely accepted and applied in corrections. The therapy flows easily from the need to hold the offender accountable for his or her behavior. Some critics maintain that the RT's value emphasis coincides with correctional workers' traditionally paternalistic and perhaps authoritarian attitudes. As Carl Bersani (1989:188) stated, "Glasser's writings do not provide a systematic methodology for clearly separating the moral standards of the counselor from that of the client."

Although Glasser did not deal with theory, and RT is practice-oriented, its theoretical underpinnings are quite close to those of behavior modification. Instead of manipulating the environment or using tangible reinforcers, the therapist develops a close relationship with the client and uses praise or concern as the positive and negative reinforcers. For this method to be carried out effectively, the practitioner needs to be a genuinely warm and sympathetic person, able to relate to offenders who may have committed very unpleasant acts and whose personalities may leave a great deal to be desired.

Behavior modification is also important to prison administrators. For example, the punishments most often used in prison are (1) loss of privileges (e.g., commissary privileges, use of recreational facilities, and visitations by family and friends), (2) loss of good time (i.e., time off one's sentence due to good behavior in prison), and (3) confinement in punitive segregation (i.e., solitary confinement) (Clear and Cole 1986:362). Two of these punishments are not, strictly speaking, positive punishments, but rather negative punishments that are withdrawn only if bad behavior replaces good behavior. Punitive segregation is clearly a positive punishment.

Some prison programs directly integrate behavior modification principles in unique ways. In a procedure that sounds like it might have been dreamed up by *A Clockwork Orange*'s Anthony Burgess, some inmates have been "deconditioned" from inappropriate behavior via involuntary injections of a vomit-inducing drug. However, this specific treatment—unless (1) it is voluntary, (2) the drug is administered by a physician, and (3) the rule-violating behavior was witnessed by a staff member—has been ruled cruel and unusual punishment (Wexler 1975). Constitutional questions are not germane to token economies, programs in which inmates earn privileges and even experience certain living-arrangement inducements (Wexler 1975). For example, during the 1970s inmates in one multitiered building at Louisiana's Angola State Prison started prison life on a tier with access to only the most basic human needs (i.e., shelter, clothing, food, and security) and with good behavior "graduated" to far more comfortable surroundings.

Corrections involves both extrainstitutional or community-based programs and prisons and jails (Mays and Winfree 2002), and psychogenic theories are no less important in these settings. Behavior modification is used to treat criminals in semisecure residential treatment settings located between the prison environment and the "free" world, as well as those who remain at large, outside the nation's prisons and jails. For example, probation—the conditional release from a judicial authority (court system)—and parole—the conditional release from an executive authority (prison system)—both employ key elements of operant conditioning to control participants (Abadinsky 2002; Mays and Winfree 2002). Such conditions include the following:

- Those offenders who follow the written conditions of their release remain in the community, but violating the rules can mean immediate confinement (negative reinforcer, positive punisher).

- At the beginning of supervised release, clients may have to report in person on a weekly basis. With good behavior, reporting periods become less frequent and may be accomplished by letter or phone (positive reinforcer).

- If the offender is drug-involved, probation/parole supervisors may use routine and random drug testing. Positive outcomes could result in weekends in jail, loss of certain privileges, or confinement for the duration of the original sentence (negative reinforcers, positive punishers).

- The release conditions generally include restrictions on (1) movement, such as leaving the supervision area to take a vacation, visit a friend or relative, or move to a new residence; (2) specific activities that require licensing, such as driving a car, getting married, or going hunting or fishing; (3) rights of assembly, such as getting together with friends who are also convicted felons; and (4) various other behaviors, including but not limited to owning or possessing a firearm and voting. The inclusion of any given conditions constitutes a positive punishment, and their exclusion—or later restoration for good behavior—serves as a positive reinforcer.

Intermediate sanctions may also modify behavior. Offenders under home detention/house arrest stay in their homes except when they are working or shopping for necessities (Ball, Huff, and Lilly 1988). Often these programs are combined with electronic monitoring systems, allowing "community control officers" to oversee offenders with increasingly sophisticated technology. In the absence of electronic monitoring, officers might make unannounced visits to the detainee's home (Flynn 1986). The underlying idea is that the prospect of losing one's freedom and the threat of incarceration will work to control and modify law-violating behavior. Despite the lack of definitive studies about program success, correctional experts are optimistic that both home confinement and electronic monitoring programs will serve the interests of the criminal justice system (McShane and Krause 1993:115–148).

DEVELOPMENTAL THEORIES

- Two adolescent friends begin a spurt of youthful misconduct at age 13. A few years later one stops misbehaving, graduates high school and college, and at age 25 becomes an executive trainee for a *Fortune* 500 company. The other continues on the path they both started at age 13, comes in contact with the police for increasingly serious and violent crimes, and at age 25 receives a third strike—life in prison. Why did they turn out so differently?

- As a child you observe a friend who seems to go through several troubling (and troublesome) stages beginning around age 13. First, she becomes exceedingly stubborn, doing silly things that seem to serve no purpose other than to challenge the authority of her parents and teachers. She starts staying out late, sneaking out in the middle of the night, and eventually running away from home. Can criminological theory explain what is happening?

Criminals only rarely emerge suddenly, without warning, no matter what causal factors are at work. Over the past 20 years this observation has pushed criminologists in different directions. In the early 1980s criminologists debated the issue of criminal propensity versus criminal careers. The impetus was a longitudinal study conducted in Philadelphia by Marvin Wolfgang and his associates (1972), who explored delinquency in a single birth cohort (i.e., all persons sharing the same birth year). They found that 6 percent of the juveniles accounted for 52 percent of all juvenile–police contacts and an astounding 70 percent of all juvenile contacts for felony offenses.

However, criminologists disagreed over the theoretical and practical implications of the Philadelphia cohort study. One group's position was summed up in *Criminal Careers and "Career Criminals,"* a two-volume report authored by Albert Blumstein and his associates (1986). They saw **career criminals** as chronic offenders who engage in a high volume of crime over a long time. A **criminal career** is simply a description of the type, volume, nature, and length of a person's involvement in crime. Some careers are short, and others are long. Career criminal advocates focused on high-frequency offenders and examined the **onset** (beginning) and **desistance** (ending) of their careers, as well as the seriousness and duration of their criminal activity. They challenged the long-held belief that rates of offending rise rapidly in the mid-teens, peak in the late teens or early 20s, and drop steadily throughout the 20s. The contrasting idea embodied in the career criminal concept was that frequency of offending does not change, but rather the pool of offenders dips, owing to death or incarceration. Hence, anyone committing crimes after age 20 was a career criminal and a threat to public safety, which lent support to the idea of selectively incapacitating persons designated as career criminals (see Chapter 1).

Michael Gottfredson and Travis Hirschi (1989) opposed the career criminal thesis, proposing instead the **criminal-propensity thesis**—that some people are simply more prone to commit crime than others. Variations in the amount of offending follow the same age–crime curve for all types of crime-prone individuals. The greatest involvement occurs in the late teens, followed by declining involvement. Thus, the curve's appearance is the same for low-crime-prone persons and high-crime-prone ones. The magnitude—the peak offending level—is what differs. Whatever other forces are at work, claimed Gottfredson and Hirschi, as they mature people outgrow criminality. Attempts to identify career criminals are wasted effort, and more importantly, selective incapacitation simply will not work as a crime reduction technique.

The career criminal/crime propensity controversy eventually evolved into the related debate about the type of data necessary to test theories. Gottfredson and Hirschi (1987) argued that, because the age–crime relationship is invariant (unchanging over time), researchers need only employ cross-sectional studies. Blumstein, Jacqueline Cohen, and David Farrington (1988) argued for longitudinal studies (see also Menard and Elliott 1990). Still others argued that it is not a question of *either* crime propensity *or* criminal careers, of *either* cross-sectional *or* longitudinal studies. Rather, criminology has room for both concepts and both types of information (Nagin and Land 1993).

This debate was healthy for criminology. Gottfredson and Hirschi developed their event-propensity theory, a general theory of crime, or what others call self-control theory (see Chapter 7). Adherents to the career criminal position explored theoretical reasons for the empirical claims of Blumstein and his associates. Out of this latter work came developmental crime theories.

Developmental theories contain psychological principles and concepts, but they are not exclusively psychogenic in their explanations of criminality. They look not only at the process of becoming delinquent or criminal but also at why some offenders quit the crime path early, others quit later, and still others never quit—at least not until it is too late. We begin with the most psychological and move to ones in which psychogenic factors play somewhat lesser roles.

Persistent and Limited Offending

Psychologist Terrie Moffitt (1993a,b), while studying a sample of New Zealanders, observed two crime trajectories or pathways. **Life-course persistent (LCP) offenders** embark on paths that begin at a very early age. At age 4 and younger, LCP offenders engage in "acting out" behavior such as biting and hitting; by age 10 they are shoplifters and truants. Crime seriousness increases with age, so that by their 20s they are engaging in robbery and rape, and by their 30s are committing fraud and child abuse. Moffitt found that many LCP offenders have neurological problems throughout childhood, perhaps even attention deficit disorder (see Chapter 3) and certainly learning difficulties during their school years. As youths they miss out on the acquisition of interpersonal and prosocial skills for two reasons: (1) They are rejected and even avoided by their peers, and (2) their own parents become frustrated with them and often psychologically abandon them (Moffitt 1993a). Living in disorganized homes and violent neighborhoods only exacerbates the LCP offenders' growing tendencies toward antisocial behavior.

LCP offenders are in the minority among delinquents, as a second form accounts for the majority of delinquents. **Adolescent-limited (AL) offenders** begin offending with the start of adolescence and cease causing trouble (desist) around age 18. These offenders differ in several other ways from LCP offenders. First, their developmental histories do not contain the same early and persistent antisocial behavior observed for LCP offenders. Second, AL offenders learn to get along with others, something LCP offenders rarely master. Third, AL offenders do not exhibit the same depth and duration of neurological problems. Fourth, although the frequency of offending for AL offenders may mimic that of LCP offenders, and neither group can be distinguished in terms of most indicators of antisocial and problem behaviors in earlier childhood, this changes during the teenage years. Fifth, AL offenders, more so than LCP offenders, exhibit a tendency to become involved in acts associated with adulthood and in expressions of autonomy from adult control, including vandalism, alcohol and drug offenses, theft, truancy, and running away. Lastly, unlike the LCP offenders, AL offenders in their late teens can abandon their miscreant ways should they interfere with adult-like goals, such as getting a full-time job or going to college.

Moffitt's theory blends neuropsychology and developmental psychology. Her work on different trajectories to delinquency and crime helps explain the unique social control threats posed by a small group of early-onset, long-term offenders. It also explains why most delinquents, as AL offenders, have the developmental histories and skills to explore alternative life pathways.

Developmental Criminology

Rolf Loeber and Marc LeBlanc (1990) coined the term **developmental criminology** to provide a way of looking at criminals that shares three aims:

1. Explore within-individual changes, allowing for comparisons between the subject's offending at different times.

2. Identify those explicative or causal factors that predate behavioral development and, consequently, impact its course, making it possible to clarify not only the possible causes of onset, escalation, de-escalation, and desistance in offending but also individual differences in these factors among offenders.

3. Study important transitions in the life cycle and other factors as they affect offending.

Developmental criminology owes a debt to the propensity/criminal career debate. Loeber and LeBlanc (1990) contended that only by studying and describing within-individual differences in criminal careers can criminologists hope to understand why some youths become more deeply involved than others. Developmental criminologists assume that causal factors "operate at equal strength at any given point along the developmental time line" (Loeber and Stouthamer-Loeber 1996:13).

Loeber and D. F. Hay (1994) described three developmental pathways to offending. The first is an **authority-conflict pathway,** which children begin before age 12, starting with stubborn conduct, moving to defiance, and settling into authority avoidance. Although followers of this pathway are a nuisance, they pose minimal threats to society. A **covert pathway** consists of minor hidden behavior as the first step; however, the misconduct escalates quickly to property damage (e.g., vandalism and arson) and moderate forms of delinquency (e.g., burglary, car theft, and fraud). An **overt pathway** tends to manifest itself as aggression and violence; bullying and annoying behavior are the first step, followed by fighting and, finally, major aggressive acts, including assault and rape.

The identification of a child as an **experimenter** type or a **persister** type is particularly important to developmental criminologists (Loeber, Keenan, and Zhang 1994). Both may start on their respective paths at an early age, but one stops (desists) and the other continues (as in the hypothetical vignette at the beginning of this section). Given developmental criminologists' emphasis on within-individual changes, classification of this type requires more than one assessment over time—hence their penchant for longitudinal research.

Overt and covert aggression pose differential threats to the community (Loeber and Stouthamer-Loeber 1998). *Behaviorally* overt aggressors commit their acts in the open and in direct contact with victims; covert aggressors do not like confrontations, preferring to be sneaky, dishonest, or concealed. In developmental criminology terms, then, violent crimes are examples of overt aggression, whereas property crimes are acts of covert aggression. *Emotionally* anger is more important to overt aggression; covert aggression entails far less emotionality. *Cognitively* people who use overt aggression are hostile and exhibit cognitive deficiencies associated with violence-proneness, qualities missing in people who use covert aggression. *Developmentally* overt aggression generally begins early in life (see Moffitt's life-course persistent offenders), but not all overt aggressors come to their acts early. **Late-onset offenders,** though a minority, must be examined and described like early-onset ones (Loeber and Stouthamer-Loeber 1998).

Loeber and Stouthamer-Loeber have maintained that developmental criminology, with its attendant longitudinal and within-individual analytic procedures, may identify "keystone" behaviors for other, even more problematic ones. "In other words, we should know at what ages or developmental stages certain potential targets for intervention become more stable and less malleable" (Loeber and Loeber-Stouthamer 1996:22).

Assessing Developmental Explanations

Developmental criminology assumed a relatively prominent research position in the last decade of the twentieth century. Not only are the questions posed and the answers provided theoretically important, but, as with the Philadelphia cohort study and the crime propensity/criminal career debate, the results often generate even more questions, including these:

- *Are developmental theories really theories, or are they hypotheses or taxonomies?* Loeber and his associates described their efforts as moving in the direction of a theory. They provided assumptions for developmental theory and many pathways, models, and testable hypotheses; however, clearly stated conceptual linkages are missing. Moffitt, in fact, described her efforts as taxonomical, meaning the focus was on classifying offenders into discrete categories, describing their collective characteristics, and trying to determine the forces responsible for their membership in a given category.

- *Is developmental criminology anything more than a merger and restatement of personality theories, the IQ–crime hypothesis, and various behavioral theories?* Moffitt and others who have looked at neuropsychological risk tended to use test scores and psychological assessments not unlike those explored earlier in this chapter and in Chapter 4 (Simons, Johnson, Conger, and Elder 1998; Tibbetts and Piquero 1999). It is unclear how these conceptual arguments about pathways escape the limitations associated with personality theories, impulsivity hypotheses, and IQ testing.

- *How many developmental paths are there?* Moffitt identified two paths, inferring the possibility of more. Loeber and Loeber-Stouthamer described three pathways. After studying the paths taken by British boys, Daniel Nagin and Kenneth Land (1993) outlined four: (1) Moffitt's adolescence-limited offenders; (2) high-level chronic offenders, basically lifetime-persistent offenders; (3) low-level chronic offenders, individuals who reached a relatively low plateau of offending early on and stayed there after turning 18 (or subdivisions of Moffitt's life-course persistent offenders); and (4) never-convicted offenders. Given the developmental criminologists' methodology, the task of uncovering pathways may be unending or divisible into increasingly smaller pathway groups.

- *Do developmental models/taxonomies/theories/hypotheses fit the data?* The research results are mixed. Studies by developmental criminologists, including a merger of Pittsburgh and Dunedin (New Zealand) youths, support divergent crime pathways (Caspi, Moffitt, Silva, Stouthamer-Loeber, Krueger, and Schmutte 1994; Moffitt, Lynam, and Silva 1994). Stephen Tibbetts and Alex Piquero (1999) tested one of Moffitt's hypotheses—the interaction between increased risk for neuropsychological disorders and disadvantaged childhood environments. They found, consistent with Moffitt, that these factors interact to predict early-onset but not late-onset offending. Tibbetts and Piquero also specified gender-specific models: Males had the interactions, but females did not. Although Moffitt's theory distinguished between early and later initiators of violence, Todd Herrenkohl and his associates (2001) found that youths who initiated violence early *and* late follow similar pathways during adolescence. Rather than more pathways, there may be fewer, or the pathways may be more complex than previously thought, differing for males and females.

Developmental theories serve as a rich source of speculation about the mix of neuropsychological conditions, prenatal and perinatal events, and environments that produce offenders. They are an equally rich source of policies and practices.

Developmental Theories, Public Policy, and Criminal Justice Practices

Developmental theories have important public policy implications. For example, Moffitt's theory of life-course persistent offenders suggests that impulsivity, early neuropsychological problems, and cyclical interactions with parents intensify the childhood misbehavior problems common to most adolescents. The troubles manifest themselves as school-based difficulties, especially as related to impulsivity, and eventually as delinquency and adult crime. Understanding impulsivity alone may assist in changing the lives of many high-risk children. Interrupting any trajectory can potentially lower the probability of criminality.

The theories suggest that prenatal and early interventions by trained medical staff may offset criminality trajectories. This contention would seem to have merit. For example, David Olds and his associates (1998) reported on a 15-year follow-up of prenatal and early-childhood home visitations conducted in upstate New York. The researchers randomly assigned volunteer test subjects to one of four treatment conditions, including some combination of the following: prenatal care, free transportation, sensory and developmental screening services, clinical evaluations and treatment, and nurse visitations in the home (the number of visits before and after birth varied widely). The children were re-examined 15 years later, through self-reports, probation or family court data, and school or teacher report data.

The findings supported the idea that program effects were greatest with regard to early-onset antisocial behavior (in contrast to more common and less serious puberty-related antisocial behavior). Compared to the other groups, adolescents born to women who received nurse visits during pregnancy and postnatally—and who had high risk factors for antisocial behavior (e.g., unmarried mothers and mothers in low-SES households)—reported less incidence of running away; fewer arrests, convictions, and probation violations; fewer lifetime sex partners; and fewer days of having consumed alcohol in the past six months (Olds et al. 1998). Their parents reported that their children had fewer behavioral problems related to the use of alcohol and other drugs.

In the absence of prenatal and early childhood interventions, other interventions hold promise. That is, the timely treatment of early neuropsychological problems or the introduction of special classes in parenting skills with high-risk children may lower the risk for school failure (Greenwood, Model, Rydell, and Chiesa 1996). An experiment in Montreal, Quebec, explored this question by randomly assigning boys (and their volunteer families) identified as disruptive in kindergarten to either an experimental group, where their parents received special training, or a control group (Tremblay et al. 1992). Parents in the experimental group received training based on the Oregon Social Learning Center's program of consistent, nonphysical discipline (Patterson 1982; Patterson, Reid, Jones, and Conger 1975).[9] After two years of training, which included social skills training for the boys, and a total elapsed time of five years, the experimental subjects were less physically aggressive in school, were in age-appropriate regular classrooms, and reported fewer delinquent behaviors. However, there may be limits to the ability of preschool programs to impact positively the lives (and crime pathways) of children with serious medical conditions observed after birth (Pagani, Tremblay, Vitaro, and Parent 1998).

The Office of Juvenile Justice and Delinquency Prevention (OJJDP), part of the National Institute of Justice, launched its Strengthening America's Families Initiative in the mid-1980s and serves as a clearinghouse for family-oriented programs. Even earlier, a project funded by the National Institute of Mental Health evolved into the Nurturing Parenting program. This ongoing family-centered and culture-sensitive parenting initiative targets the cycle of violence with roots in the family. Among the goals are helping parents learn effective parenting and avoid abusive parenting and child-rearing practices (Bavolek 2000). In 1992 Prevent Child Abuse America created Healthy Families America, and by 2001 this organization was serving 420 communities in 39 states, the District of Columbia, and Canada (Erickson 2001:1). Healthy Families America initiates services prenatally or at birth, providing risk factor assessment and treatments.

The National Institute of Justice views the strengthening of America's families as a fundamental principle of its overall Strategy for Serious, Violent and Chronic Juvenile Offenders (Coolbaugh and Hansel 2000). Often the family-strengthening programs make direct or implicit references to Bandura and other behaviorists as providing the theoretical grounding for their programs. In nearly all, the family is central both to the problem and to the solution, with key causal forces described in terms familiar to learning theorists. Many employ a developmental approach to delinquency and drug use prevention and intervention.

The specific role of agents of social control under the umbrella of developmental criminology is unclear. The theory describes pathways beginning as young as age 3 or 4 and recommends early interventions. Hence, there is little that law enforcement or corrections can do to aid in this process. Police removal of youths from abusive families or diversion of the family into one of the family-strengthening programs is one possibility, as the police are often the first respondents in cases of parent–child conflicts. The courts, especially family and juvenile courts, may also play a role in altering a given pathway by ordering participation in one of the programs, although voluntary participation is generally best. Removal of an at-risk child from an abusive family situation is another alternative.

SUMMARY

Psychological forces clearly play important roles in creating and maintaining criminal tendencies, and in changing the criminals as well. This statement may seem self-evident, although demonstrating which forces work, do what, and how has proved to be far more difficult. In the previous chapter abnormal personality development and unresolved lapses in psychosexual development provided answers to key questions about who was likely to offend and why. The theories in this chapter shifted the focus to the specific psychological factors behind how individuals learn to be offenders, lack the proper psychosocial development to adjust to contemporary life, or travel one of many life paths to offending, either permanently or temporarily.

Intelligence testing has proved to be divisive as a crime explanation. Testing is allegedly a mirror or indirect indicator of some inner intellectual quality, although on this point there is much disagreement. Pushing the causal sequence back beyond intelligence has led to theories about an alleged genetic condition known as feeblemindedness and to questions about the role of race as a precursor of intelligence. Although researchers challenge these hypotheses, both in terms of what the tests really measure and how suitable race is as a variable in this IQ–crime equation, IQ testing remains a fixture of American life. Recent efforts to broaden the conceptual and operational definitions of intelligence to include other forms of intelligence suggest that the IQ–crime link will continue to find supporters among criminal justice policy makers in the twenty-first century.

Behaviorism has assumed high visibility within the criminal justice system, especially in terms of correctional practices. The cognitive and modeling theorists suggest specific ways humans make decisions and factors that may influence or disrupt the decision-making processes. However, it is unclear whether some people are more susceptible to the cues and processes than others, and if they are, why this is the case. Nonetheless, the behaviorists' contributions to specific correctional practices are rarely matched by proponents of other theoretical perspectives on crime.

The developmental theorists place considerable emphasis on within-individual changes over time; consequently they strongly endorse longitudinal designs and exhibit equally high support for the career criminal concept. A priority among developmental criminologists is the identification of those pathways and keystone behaviors that most threaten society. Using this knowledge, they argue for interventions that are timed to coincide with high malleability, or susceptibility to change. Thus, developmental criminologists place considerable stock not only in how people become offenders but also in how they naturally desist and, further, in how this knowledge can be used to promote desistance.

The psychological learning and developmental theories contribute much to the study of crime and delinquency. They also suggest that the mechanisms causing crime and delinquency may also be employed to reduce their likelihood and to change offenders. (See Table 5.1 for an overview of psychological learning and developmental theories.)

Table 5.1 Psychological Learning and Developmental Theories

Theory	Major Figures	Central Assumptions	Causal Arguments (Key Terms)	Strengths	Weaknesses
Feeble-mindedness thesis	Dugdale, Goddard	Mental functioning is inherited, and weak minds run in certain families.	Low-functioning individuals (i.e., the *feebleminded*) seek out crime to compensate for an inability to gain money through honest labor.	Explains why whole families seem to turn to crime as vocation.	May have fabricated studies; is an overly simplistic representation of the role of intelligence in daily life.
IQ–crime hypotheses, race–IQ–crime hypothesis	Jensen, Hirschi, Hindelang, Wilson, Herrnstein, Murray, Gordon	IQ tests measure innate intelligence, which is human destiny's major delimiter.	Criminals have lower IQ scores than noncriminals; three crime links exist: (1) IQ predicts criminality; (2) the IQ–crime link is an artifact of other forces such as SES; and (3) IQ affects performance at school, which *is* related to delinquency and, later, crime; some versions see race as a precursor for IQ.	Reports some version of IQ–crime links; gives policy makers something toward which to respond (i.e., IQ score is an overt indicator of innate criminogenic tendencies; enables society to then classify and categorize people by IQ scores).	Is not clear what IQ tests measure (i.e., the validity of IQ tests remains highly questionable); the wide range of different tests makes meaningful comparisons difficult; there are few studies of self-admitted serious offenders with no formal criminal justice system contacts; largely ignores social factors as causes of crime and delinquency.
Behaviorism and learning theories	Pavlov, Watson, Skinner, Rotter, Bandura	All forms of behavior are learned in response to certain stimuli; in order to change behavior, change stimuli.	Children learn, by rewards and punishments, to repeat some behaviors and avoid others (*conditioned response*); an inner policeman controls atavistic leanings.	Appeals to those who hold that punishments and rewards should shape behavior (see also the discussion of deterrence theory in Chapters 1 and 2).	Receives little empirical support outside of animal experiments; human behavior—especially crime—is complex and hard to fit in classic behaviorist models.
Developmental criminology	Moffitt, Loeber, Stouthamer-Loeber, Farrington, Le Blanc	There are multiple pathways to offending, some with neurological origins and others found in adolescent rebellion and development; criminology is best served by studying within-individual differences across time.	*Life-course persistent offenders* begin early, have many neurological problems and few skills; *adolescent-limited offenders* begin later, have fewer behavioral troubles and more social skills, and may return to normal path; *overt* and *covert pathways* lead from predelinquent problems to delinquent acts; age at *onset* differs.	Seems to fit well with observations about highly active serious offenders who account for a disproportionate amount of crime and delinquency; treatment suggestions fit with behavioral ideas about changing people; also explains why most delinquents eventually assume normal path.	Uses measurement of early neuropsychological problems dependent on personality and IQ measurement instruments (see also Chapter 4); status of perspective as a crime theory is questionable; longitudinal data requirement poses an insurmountable barrier to some researchers (i.e., cost and time).

KEY TERMS

adolescent-limited (AL) offenders

associative learning

attention

authority-conflict pathway

behaviorism

behavior modification

career criminals

catharsis effect

cognitive behavior theory

conceptual learning

covert pathway

criminal careers

criminal-propensity thesis

dangerousness

desistance

developmental criminology

expectancy theory

experimenter

feeblemindedness

IQ

late-onset offenders

life-course persistent (LCP) offenders

modeling

motivations

motor reproduction

negative reinforcer

observational learning

onset

operant conditioning

overt pathway

penal harm movement

persister

positive reinforcer

practical intelligence

reality therapy (RT)

reinforcements

responsivity principle

retention

token economies

CRITICAL REVIEW QUESTIONS

1. How might low intelligence, including feeblemindedness, influence criminal behavior? Why is this linkage a poor theoretical explanation?

2. Why is any sample of prison inmates likely to be skewed in favor of the less intelligent? Can you think of a way to link definitively intelligence with crime?

3. Do you believe that we should treat law violators with very low IQs differently from those who fully appreciate the serious nature of their illegal acts? Why or why not?

4. What is the likelihood that some new and improved measure of IQ can influence corrections in a positive fashion?

5. How does behaviorism explain criminal behavior? What criticisms most damage behaviorism's ties to crime and delinquency? How do they do the most damage?

6. How does Rotter's cognitive behavior theory differ from Bandura's learning theory?

7. How do the developmental theories differ from one another?

8. What is the greatest strength of developmental theories? What is their greatest weakness?

9. In your opinion, how did criminology benefit from the crime propensity/criminal career debate?

10. What ties link the first two sections of this chapter to the last one?

11. Which of the policies reviewed in this chapter do you think poses the greatest threat to democratic ideals? Which one holds the greatest promise for reducing crime?

12. You have been asked by your employer, the Division of Youth Services (or the equivalent agency in your state that develops statewide policy for children, youths, and

families), to prepare a proposal to fund early-intervention programs for at-risk families and their children. What do you include as theoretical and empirical support?

NOTES

1. Psychometrics, or mental measurements, is an important and useful tool for mental health professionals and psychologists, who prefer the term *psychometric intelligence* (PI) to IQ. In the interests of clarity and continuity with the literature, we employ the latter term.

2. Shockley received the Nobel Prize in physics for inventing the transistor.

3. Herrnstein (1971) wrote an essay defending Jensen. Herrnstein proposed that intelligence separates the classes and that attempts to ignore it will result in deeper stratification.

4. Mental health treatment and the use of psychotropic drugs are only proxy measures for mental retardation and other psychological disabilities among inmates; however, in 2000, 1 in 8 state prisoners received mental health therapy or counseling, and nearly 1 in 10 received antidepressants, stimulants, sedatives, tranquilizers, or other antipsychotic drugs (Beck and Maruschak 2001:1).

5. Much of the following discussion is based on Rilling (2000).

6. Not all psychologists see behaviorism, especially Watson's version, in a positive light. John Mills (1998) suggested that it is an ideology of science without much vision (see also Mos 1999; Smith 2001). He saw evidence of this shift in the resistance of 1960s neobehaviorism to speculation about the perspective's pragmatism and concern with prediction. For more on these ideas as applied to theory and crime, see either Chapter 1 or Chapter 10.

7. Bandura's contribution is also called social learning theory; however, we reserve the use of this term for Akers' social learning theory.

8. In his collective works Bandura was a frequent critic of the mass media, especially with regard to violence on television and in motion pictures.

9. Gerald Patterson (1982) saw families of delinquency-prone youths as inadvertently reinforcing antisocial behavior and failing to reinforce prosocial behavior.

6

Social Organizational
Theories

CHAPTER OVERVIEW

Crime and Social Ecology

Social Disorganization Theory and Crime

The Legacy of Social Disorganization Theory

Assessing Ecological Theories

Ecology, Public Policy, and Criminal Justice Practices

Crime and Social Structure

Structural Functionalism, Anomie, and Crime

Strain Theory: The Americanization of Anomie

Anomie Theory Rediscovered

Assessing Strain Theory

Social Structure, Public Policy, and Criminal Justice Practices

Crime and Subcultures

Delinquent Subcultures

Subcultural Delinquency

Assessing Subcultural Theories

Subcultures, Public Policy, and Criminal Justice Practices

LEARNING OBJECTIVES

- Explore the social-ecological roots of social disorganization, an outlook on criminality with practical implications.

- Appreciate that society's formal structure—its roles and statuses—provides unique insights into all behavior, including crime and deviance.

- Understand that criminologists propose two distinct ways to understand the crime and delinquency of groups we call subcultures.

- Recognize that in the twentieth century, macro-sociological theories shaped local and national policies, and these ideas still intrigue criminologists and policy makers.

INTRODUCTION

One way to look at crime is to step back and see the "big picture." The three perspectives in this chapter share the big-picture view, a **macro-sociological** orientation in which society and social processes hold the key to understanding criminality. That is, if we wish to understand crime, we must know society's role in shaping its members, only some of whom are criminals. Society is not "blamed" for crime—it is the social cauldron from which crime emerges.

Social ecology, the first such orientation, uses the ecological model as a social prism through which to view a city's crime patterns. In this context sociologists study all of the interrelated social and physical elements of the immediate community in which crime is an endemic problem. Crime is thus a social phenomenon that exists apart from the people who reside in the community and continues long after they are gone. Here researchers examine the conditions of working and playing, living and dying. Crime becomes a feature of the landscape, one related to the other elements of social disorganization present in the community.

Social structure, including the roles and statuses that stabilize social relations, is central to the second group of theories. Structural functionalists believe that every integral element in society is either part of the solution or part of the problem. When social conditions change dramatically, the result is generally bad. Society enters a state, called anomie or normlessness, in which the usual rules governing behavior do not seem to apply. Later structural functionalists applied anomie to individual social behavior and suggested that crime is one possible response when the reality of life is too far from the dream.

Subcultures are at the core of the third orientation, in which two views dominate. In both, subculturalists see crime as the result of behavior by societal subgroups. The delinquent subculture theorists suggest that the misbehavior of subordinate members of society is easily understood in terms of the conflict between the subculture's values and those of the dominant culture. The subcultural delinquency theorists do not limit their scope to subordinates, but rather look at how both subordinates and superordinates take the dominant culture's values and push them to the extreme, creating subterranean values that are both exciting and threatening, and often illegal.

All three perspectives employ a macro-sociological framework for viewing social problems. The macro-sociologists provide broad answers to critical questions about crime and society. However, the policies and practices they suggest generally are useful only at the societal level, and they have little to say about why individuals commit crimes or engage in delinquent acts.

CRIME AND SOCIAL ECOLOGY

- Are you aware of ethnic or racial neighborhoods in your community? Do you see a connection between these areas and crime? When answering the second question, some in society blame racial or ethnic groups whose presence is higher in high-crime areas.

- Have you noticed homes in your community with bars over the windows? Are there residential areas that have guarded entrances, speed bumps, curvy streets, or small green areas instead of large open parks? Each of these anti-crime techniques has its roots in an ecological perspective on crime.

- Have the police in your community adopted a high profile in certain neighborhoods? Although this approach to policing comes from several sources, one in particular exhibits strong ties to the material in this chapter.

Early in the twentieth century, Robert Park proposed a parallel between human society and the plant and animal kingdoms, one that reflects principles of ecology. **Ecology** is the branch of biology that studies the relationships between organisms and their environment. To understand plant or animal life, one must master plant or animal ecology. Similarly, to achieve insights into human life, one must focus on human ecology.

Using the multicultural and racially diverse city of Chicago as a social laboratory, Park and his colleagues at the University of Chicago saw "natural areas" where vastly different types of people lived. For example, Robert Burgess, Park's colleague, divided the city into five **concentric zones,** differentiating each zone according to land use, population types, and other physical, economic, and social characteristics. Burgess referred to the central business district as Zone 1. Surrounding the industrial and business base was Zone II, the zone in transition. Burgess described it as an **interstitial zone,** a slum area with high levels of social deterioration; for most urban immigrants Zone II was their first home. Moving outward, the next area was Zone III, home to the city's working class, where living costs were higher and housing was better. Two characteristics distinguished Zone IV residents from those in Zone III: even higher incomes and smaller families. Arrival in Zone V, also called the commuter's zone, signified economic prosperity and stability.

Eventually the inner-city community ceased to function as an effective social control agent, while the interstitial zone exhibited few characteristics of a neighborhood and had little social cohesion. These inner-city zones had high concentrations of social ills (e.g., crime, poverty, illiteracy, mental illness, and alcoholism). They also had the highest levels of what Park and Burgess called **social disorganization,** which is "any disturbance, disruption, conflict or lack of consensus within a social group or given society which affects established social habits of behavior, social institutions, or social controls so as to make relatively harmonious functioning impossible without some significant intermediate adjustments" (Elliott 1967:280–81).

Social Disorganization Theory and Crime

Clifford Shaw and Henry McKay used social ecology to study the geographic distribution of law-violating behavior in Chicago. They equated social disorganization with weak community controls, which led to geographic areas with high crime and delinquency. They did not view people as inherently deviant or delinquent; rather, the problem was the area. Once a high crime rate became established, no matter who lived in these areas, the rate remained high. It was as if a tradition of deviance was passed along to successive generations of residents. What they found were not high-delinquency *groups,* but rather high-delinquency *areas.*

To prove their claim, Shaw and McKay collected massive amounts of quantitative data on delinquency. They studied court actions, arrest statistics, and commitment rates, which they overlaid on city maps. The Chicago School (as this group was known) complemented these quantitative studies, including *Juvenile Delinquency and Urban Areas* (1942), with first-person accounts of criminal careers, such as *The Jackroller* (1930) and *Brothers in Crime* (1938). This approach, especially the first-person accounts, became a significant part of the Chicago tradition. Autobiographies, or life histories, allowed the juveniles to tell their "own story" as a part of a total case history. The veracity of the life histories was never at issue. As Shaw (1930:3) observed, "Rationalizations, fabrications, prejudices, exaggerations are quite as valuable as objective descriptions, provided, of course, that these reactions be properly identified."

The Chicagoans painted a picture of chronic social disorganization. Whether looking at arrests, commitments, or court processing, they noted that, as the distance from the Chicago Loop—the **zone of transition**—increased, the rates decreased (Shaw and McKay 1942). Shaw reported that the community of the "brothers in crime" was neither unique nor unusual. He described it as "part of the large area of deterioration that surrounds the Loop. . . . Physical deterioration, low rentals, confusion of cultural standards, and a disproportionately large number of school truants, juvenile delinquents, and adult offenders are characteristic of this whole area" (Shaw 1938:357). Figure 6.1 summarizes social disorganization theory.

The Legacy of Social Disorganization Theory

The University of Chicago's social ecologists had several long-lasting effects. First, their efforts generated richly descriptive ideas for later generations of criminologists. Second, an entire approach to crime reduction, called environmental criminology, owes a major intellectual debt to social ecology. Finally, during the 1980s criminologists rediscovered social disorganization theory and placed it in a more contemporary community context.

From One Generation to the Next: The Cultural Transmission Thesis

Three general findings reported by Shaw and McKay set the stage for later **cultural transmission theories.** First, Shaw and McKay (1972:173) described socially disorganized neighborhoods as brimming with attitudes and values conducive to delinquency and crime, particularly organized crime, which provided pathways to adult crime. Second, they observed that one generation passed on their attitudes, values, and crime techniques to the next. Trapped in their neighborhoods, children saw not only the delinquency present in similarly aged youths but also the actions of older offenders. As Shaw and McKay (1972:174) stated, "This contact means that the traditions of delinquency can be and are transmitted down through successive generations of boys, in much the same way

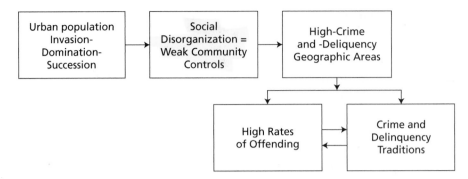

FIGURE 6.1 Shaw and McKay's Social Disorganization Theory

that language and other social forms are transmitted." Finally Shaw and McKay suggested that conflict was inevitable in this mix of cultures that characterized the city of Chicago. The values of the larger, more conventional society may have held little meaning for the youthful residents of these inner-city areas.

Shaw and McKay (1972:172) viewed the community as a source of many conflicting messages: Children should obey laws even if their parents and other adults do not; crime does not pay, but sometimes it does; people should obey the law, unless it runs counter to what their local neighborhood expects of them. How could society expect youths living in these environs to be anything but confused when exposed to such conflicting sets of values? This was the position of the Chicagoans and later generations of cultural transmission theorists.

Environmental Criminology Beginning in the 1960s environmentalists connected crime to land use. For example, Jane Jacobs (1961) theorized about the connection between the use of residential and commercial land. In analyzing the quality of interactions along residential streets, she noted that interaction increased surveillance, which, in turn, increased safety and reduced crime. Land use diversity, especially commercial use close to residential use, was the key to safety and low crime levels. When land was used strictly for commercial purposes, owners essentially abandoned their property for long periods, creating opportunities for crime.

Throughout the 1960s researchers conducted a series of architectural design studies in public housing projects. They looked for a relationship between residential social interaction and levels of self-policing, but their findings were inconclusive (see, e.g., Leudtke and Lystad 1970; Rainwater 1966; Wood 1961). These early studies lacked a conceptual base upon which to build an ecological theory of crime and space.

Oscar Newman (1972) provided key theoretical ideas in *Defensible Space*. The idea of **defensible space** evolved from four factors. First, **territoriality** means that one's home is sacred. Second, **natural surveillance** links an area's physical characteristics to the residents' ability to view what is happening. Third, **image** is the capacity of the physical design to impart a sense of security, for both residents and potential "invaders." Finally **milieu** addresses other features that might influence security, such as the proximity of a park or shopping mall (Newman 1972:50; see also Davidson 1981; Greenberg and Rohe 1984). An area's physical design enhances or inhibits the feelings of control and sense of responsibility that inhabitants experience. Crime becomes a product of the level of the inhabitants' informal social control and a measure of economic deprivation (Newman 1972).

C. Ray Jeffery, in *Crime Prevention through Environment Design* (1971), expressed the idea that a three-part strategy could prevent crime. First, he believed that physical design could make an area more defensible. Second, he emphasized the importance of higher levels of citizen involvement in preventing crime. Finally, he advocated for a more effective criminal justice system. Jeffery saw heightened police effectiveness in detecting and arresting criminals as an essential element, and suggested that more efficient court and correctional systems would buttress the work of the police and complete the punishment cycle. Figure 6.2 summarizes Newman's and Jeffery's models.

Redefined Social Disorganization Theory During the 1980s social disorganization proponents redefined its conceptual base (e.g., Bursik 1986; Esbensen and Huizinga 1990; Fagan, Piper, and Moore 1986; Laub 1983; Stark 1987; Taylor and Covington 1988). For example, Robert Sampson and W. Byron Groves (1989) developed a community-level version. Besides economic status, ethnic heterogeneity, residential mobility, family disruption, and urbanization, they tied community social disorganization to the strength of social network systems in those communities (see, e.g., Berry and Kasarda 1977). These systems include informal controls (e.g., friendship ties), formal controls (e.g., participation in religious or civic groups), and the collective supervision related to troublesome local concerns (e.g., youth groups). Figure 6.3 contains a schematic representation of this theory.

Sampson and Groves (1989) tested their ideas using British crime surveys. They found that communities in Great Britain with few friendship networks, unsupervised teenage groups, and low organizational participation had disproportionately high crime and delinquency rates. According to Sampson and Groves (1989:799), "We have thus demonstrated that social-disorganization theory has vitality and renewed relevance for explaining macro-level variations in crime rates."

Assessing Ecological Theories

Three measurement problems plagued early statements of social disorganization theory. First, later generations of criminologists dismissed it as a tautology. That is, Shaw and McKay's model had few independent measures of social disorganization. If an area was crime-ridden, this alone was evidence of a lack of social controls and social disorganization; socially disorganized areas were crime-ridden. Robert Bursik (1988) wondered, given its natural tautological tendency, how we could measure social disorganization. Social scientists now use a different definition: Social disorganization is "the capacity of a neighborhood to regulate itself through formal and informal processes of social control" (Bursik 1988:527; see also Sampson and Groves 1989).

Second, critics noted the presence of the **ecological fallacy,** which involves making inappropriate *individual*-level inferences from *group*-level data. For example, suppose we find that for 200 communities the extent of participation in civic organizations is related to the level of reported crime. We may commit the ecological fallacy if we state that a given community has a greater likelihood of high

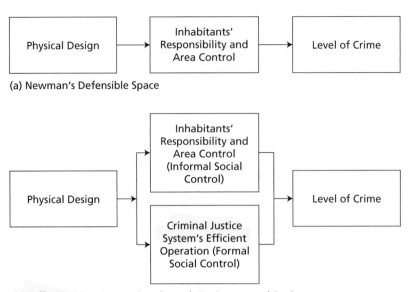

(a) Newman's Defensible Space

(b) Jeffery's Crime Prevention through Environmental Design

FIGURE 6.2 Environmental Criminology

crime because rates of participation in civic organizations are low or that crime can be reduced by increasing that participation. What is true for the group may not be true for the individual.

Third, obtaining, compiling, and analyzing the information needed to test social disorganization theory is a difficult undertaking. The findings from smaller-scale studies, often including only a few neighborhoods, support Shaw and McKay's predictions (Bursik 1988:532). However, questions remain about the validity and reliability of available crime statistics. Even in the 1930s criminologists questioned official statistics (Robison 1936). Criminologists have long argued that reliance on official data is a bad practice because the police and courts may have community-specific biases. We do not know the extent to which neighborhood crime and delinquency rates are artifacts of local decision making. For example, one consequence of placing more police in a neighborhood may be more arrests and, therefore, a higher reported crime rate.

The idea of defensible space also presented researchers with a methodological problem. Early archival studies, which did not include residents' attitudes and behavior, all found that crime co-varied with environmental design. How they measured design—as a general location, a street, or even the neighborhood level—was irrelevant (Bevis and Nuttler 1977; Greenberg, Rohe, and Williams 1982). One study did find "physical, social, and attitudinal (territorial) variables as relevant to crime and fear at the level of the street block" (Taylor, Gottfredson, and Brower 1984). Contrary to what Newman believed, we cannot rely upon physical factors alone to preserve the local order and promote feelings of security. Territoriality provided far greater insights into crime and fear than did defensible space features (Taylor, Gottfredson, and Brower 1984; see also Taylor and Gottfredson 1986).

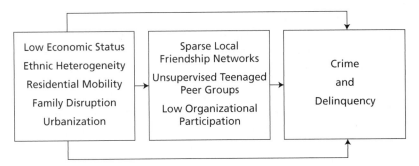

FIGURE 6.3 Causal Model of an Extended Version of Shaw and McKay's Theory of Community Systemic Structure and Rates of Crime and Delinquency

Source: From p. 783 in "Community structure and crime; Testing disorganization theory," by Robert J. Sampson and W. Byron Groves, *American Journal of Sociology,* 94, p. 774–802. Copyright © 1989 the University of Chicago Press. Reprinted by permission of the publisher.

Gerald Suttles (1968) used territoriality to study "defended neighborhoods" as recognized ecological niches in which inhabitants form cohesive groups and seal themselves off through the efforts of delinquent gangs, restrictive covenants, and a forbidding reputation. A reputation for territoriality, and not necessarily the neighborhood's physical qualities, provided effective crime control. In the Italian section of New York's Greenwich Village, for example, "street corner boys" enforced the social order, making the streets safe. Their self-appointed role was backed by the formidable reputation of the neighborhood's organized crime figures (Tricarico 1984).

Macro-Level Studies of Social Disorganization Principles Social disorganization has figured prominently in several innovative studies. For example, Darrell Steffensmeier and Dana Haynie (2000) looked at gender differences in crime rates by applying a structural disadvantage model that included gender-specific poverty measures, income inequality, female-headed households, percentage black, and joblessness as social structural elements of status and class. They examined intercity variations in the 1990 rates for 178 cities.[1] The patterns they found were essentially the same for men and women: the greater the disadvantages, the higher the rates of offending.[2] As Steffensmeier and Haynie (2000:431) concluded, "Clearly, the macrolevel causes of female crime are not fundamentally different from those of male crime."

Social order and disorder have played key roles in other innovative macrosociological studies of crime. Paul Bellair (1997), in exploring serious crime rates in 60 urban neighborhoods, examined the level and type of social interaction found in each neighborhood. Bellair (1997:697) reported that neighbors' getting together once a year or more had the strongest positive impact on burglary, motor vehicle theft, and robbery rates. This finding, he suggested, means that "neighbors may be willing to engage in supervision and guardianship regardless of whether they consider themselves to be close friends with their neighbors" (Bellair 1997:697). The key is knowing the neighbors.

Wayne Welsh and his associates (1999, 2000) investigated disorder in Philadelphia's middle schools. Their study included community-related predictors such as poverty, residential stability, and community crime. The researchers looked for both within-group and between-group differences in violence and its precursors. Welsh and associates (1999:106) concluded that "the thesis 'bad' kids or 'bad' neighborhoods directly import violence into any school is unsupported by our results." They also reported that "the effects of community variables on school disorder were strongly mediated by school stability, illustrating that analyses of institutional processes have much to add to the explanation of school disorder" (Welsh, Stokes and Green 2000:243).

Ruth Peterson and her associates (2000) explored whether local institutions influence crime rates in disadvantaged neighborhoods in Columbus, Ohio. The researchers included such stabilizing factors as libraries, recreational facilities, and retail businesses, and a single destabilizing one, bars; they looked for each in every census tract. They found that only recreational facilities had a stabilizing influence on violent crime rates. They also reported that "the effects of economic deprivation and residential instability on violent crime are independent of the institutional structures explored here." Local institutions may be ameliorative, but they cannot "counter the macro-structural factors that increase economic deprivation and lead to inner-city crime."

Finally, after reexamining Sampson and Groves' data, Bonita Veysey and Steven Messner (1999) failed to find the same level of support for social disorganization theory, particularly the observation that social disorganization is a single construct. Much of what Sampson and Groves reported came from a single piece of information: community perception of unsupervised teens. Veysey and Messner (1999:171) concluded that the support claimed for social disorganization theory was overstated. They nonetheless concurred with Sampson and Groves' final observations about the "vitality and renewed relevance" of social disorganization theory for criminology, particularly its focus on processes that influence macro-level variations in crime. Clearly the final word on social disorganization theory's utility has not yet been written.

Ecology, Public Policy, and Criminal Justice Practices

If community disorganization causes crime and delinquency, perhaps communities should strengthen local social control mechanisms. In the 1930s Shaw initiated the Chicago Area Project (CAP) to encourage grassroots organizing against crime. Local community leaders provided recreational opportunities. CAP workers improved the area's physical appearance by removing trash and cleaning property, and they mediated among the courts, schools, and communities to reduce conflict and incarceration. They also promoted conventional behavior, particularly among young people.

As urban architects plan new areas of expanding cities, they may wish to apply defensible-space concepts. For example, increased mobility in and around modern cities has long been associated with increased crime (Walker 1983:13–14). Restricting vehicular traffic by limiting access to residential areas or controlling traffic flow in commercial areas could reduce the incidence of some forms of crime (Poyner 1983). Gated communities, in which guards allow only residents, guests, and service and delivery vehicles to enter, are also becoming increasingly common.

Creating defensible space is possible for existing neighborhoods as well. In the early 1990s planners in Dayton, Ohio, invited Newman to create defensible space for Five Oaks, a neighborhood in decline. Newman created a series of gated mini-neighborhoods, reasoning that smaller neighborhoods enhanced the sense of community and made anonymous crimes harder to commit. These changes decreased community traffic by 67 percent, and total crime declined by 26 percent, with violent crimes cut in half (Cose 1994:57).

Patricia and Paul Brantingham imported Crime Prevention through Environmental Design (CPTED) to Canada, where plans for new housing projects, businesses, and even schools in British Columbia conform to the principles of CPTED (Brantingham and Brantingham 1991, 1993). They recommended locating malls and schools far from each other to prevent school children from congregating during lunch hours and after school, high-prevalence times for vandalism and drug use. The popularity of the CPTED model has resulted in its application to a wide range of environmental settings, including event facilities, retail businesses, and playgrounds (Crowe 2000).

Law Enforcement Practices Observations about **community malaise** and **disorder** have reshaped the police role in the community. In challenging the police to regain control of the nation's cities, neighborhood by neighborhood, James Q. Wilson and George Kelling (1982) made two key observations. Community disorder—including public drunkenness, vagrancy, suspicious persons, and youth gangs—creates a climate of fear. Crime and disorder also "are usually inextricably linked, in a kind of developmental sequence" (Wilson and Kelling 1982:30). The key, they observed, is understanding the significance of the broken window: If one broken window in a building is left unrepaired, then soon all the windows will be broken; if a neighborhood is left unattended, then disorder will grow, and with it crime.[3]

The specific programs that followed this call to arms exhibited close kinship to ecological theories. For example, **community policing** is an approach to police work designed to bring officers and the community they serve into closer contact. Such programs have at least five goals: (1) Decrease fear of crime, (2) increase citizen satisfaction with the police, (3) develop programs that address the problems of a community's residents, (4) reduce social disorder at the neighborhood level by using the police as informal social control agents, and (5) reduce crime by addressing the first four goals (Riechers and Roberg 1990).

Community policing involves improvements in neighborhood ecology. The police help to broker services that improve the appearance of, and thus the pride residents have in, a community. This includes better trash collection, removal of abandoned vehicles, and the boarding up and destruction of abandoned structures. An emphasis on policing street disorder—in the form of aggressive panhandlers and streetwalkers, and disorderly or intimidating youths—encourages residents to spend more time on the streets, thus raising natural surveillance levels. If residents believe the streets to be safer, they will become safer as more people interact with their neighbors.

Does it work? Community policing programs include foot patrols, "storefront" police stations, and problem-oriented policing focusing police resources on a single community-level problem such as drugs or prostitution (Bowers and

Hirsch 1987; Eck and Spelman 1987; Esbensen 1987; Hayeslip 1989; Moore and Trojanowicz 1988; Spelman and Eck 1987; Trojanowicz 1987; Trojanowicz et al. 1982). These programs meet with generally positive results, particularly enhanced public perceptions of police.

Houston's community policing program is an interesting case in point. This program included community police substations, a victim recontact program, a community newsletter, a citizen contact patrol, and a community response team (Brown and Wycoff 1986; Skogan and Wycoff 1986). It had the most positive impact on those who already had favorable images of the police (i.e., whites, homeowners, and older people). One reason cited for the failure of the Houston experiment was that the city had an "almost nonexistent neighborhood life" (Skogan 1990). When the program failed to work as predicted, the researchers turned to social disorganization theory for an explanation.

Correctional Practices　The environmental lesson that we can design crime in or out is applicable to prisons and jails as well. Two primary facility designs keep inmates (and staff) safe and secure (Mays and Winfree 2002:130–31). **Linear-design** facilities arrange individual cells or dormitories along hallways. However, these facilities, owing to their sterile and impersonal environment, are major sources of both physical and psychological stress (Mueller 1983). The environment they create bears a striking resemblance to the criminogenic areas described by environmental criminologists.[4] **Podular-design** facilities feature more open, self-contained environments, in which inmates reside in "pods" or small, self-contained housing units. In addition, a constant staff presence provides direct supervision of all inmates in each pod. Podular facilities, particularly those with direct supervision, report lower victimization rates and lower rates of vandalism to the facility (National Institute of Corrections 1983; Nelson 1988; Sigurdson 1985, 1987; Zupan 1991). Just as importantly, both inmates and staff seem to respond positively to the far less rigid and alienated environment created by podular design and direction supervision (Zupan and Menke 1988; Zupan and Stohr-Gillmore 1987). We can view prisons as micro-ecological systems in which the environmental criminologists' social forces are at work.

CRIME AND SOCIAL STRUCTURE

- Did you ever wonder why, during your grade school days, you pledged allegiance to the flag? Why does every nation believe it necessary to have a flag and a national anthem?

- What society-wide condition may confront both the victors and the vanquished after a war? What might they share with a prosperous society or one in an economic downturn?

- Are you pursuing the "American Dream"? What is that dream? Is it all about material things, consumer goods, and the like?

In the late nineteenth century sociologists began a search that would eventually provide answers to these questions. They explored the structure and functions of different societal parts, and the accompanying culture. According to structural functionalists society consists of various institutions and groups that, owing to their constant contact with one another, shift, move, and alter their mutual influence. The result—after cooperation, competition, accommodation, and even conflict—is a unified social system. Thus, any given practice, tradition, or custom persists over time because it is functional—that is, it provides something beneficial to society. Conversely anything that threatens to destroy society is dysfunctional.

Structural Functionalism, Anomie, and Crime

Emile Durkheim (1961[1925]) considered structural elements to be central to any analysis of society and its ills. As a society moves from mechanical solidarity to organic solidarity, Durkheim claimed, unstable relationships evolve. **Mechanical solidarity** is a primitive stage of societal development in societies characterized by traditional family-based social relationships. They also exhibit a strong **collective conscience,** or consensual ways the group views the social and physical world. **Organic solidarity** is common in more advanced industrial societies, which are characterized by a high degree of differentiation and specialization. An inverse relationship exists between the collective conscience and individualism: As one increases, the other declines. Societies with high levels of organic solidarity experience greater difficulties in socializing members, in promoting a feeling of "us." Therefore, social cohesiveness requires an external mechanism, the state.

The Anomie Tradition and Deviant Behavior For Durkheim **unrestrained ambition**—individualism at its worst—caused deviance.[5] He saw the process by which ambition is set free in structural functionalist terms.[6] The collective conscience assists in governing a community's members. A societal disturbance or transition, even one that seems to be beneficial, changes the balance and alters or even diminishes the collective conscience's ability to control social behavior (Durkheim 1951[1897]:252). The problem centers on disturbances in the collective order or **social equilibrium.** The scale is upset; society cannot immediately improvise an acceptable new balance. It takes time for the public conscience to reclassify people and things, to create a new social equilibrium. Unbridled individualism becomes the norms, as old values and norms become irrelevant, and normal social restraints on behavior are lacking.

Such disturbances are problematic, whether they are negative (e.g., an economic depression or failure in war) or positive (e.g., economic prosperity or success in war). Durkheim called the resulting societal condition **anomie,** meaning a relative absence or confusion of norms and rules. Given society-wide stresses, nothing in humankind's experience sets limits on the quantity of comforts craved. Excited appetites become just as free of social constraints: "Appetites, not being controlled by public opinion become disoriented, no longer recognize the limits proper to them. . . . At the same time, the struggle grows more violent and painful, both from being less controlled and because competition is greater" (Durkheim 1951[1897]:253).

Durkheim saw in anomie an explanation for the deviance that results in times of war and rapid industrialization and urbanization. The breakdown in social controls throws many people's lives out of whack. Society is left in a condition best described as "normlessness," or anomie, a feeling of being adrift without customary social guideposts or constraints on behavior. The absence of social discipline results in unrestrained individual appetites. Readjustments eventually restore social controls and moderation, but until then a lag occurs, during which society can expect high levels of deviance, including crime.

Strain Theory: The Americanization of Anomie

Robert K. Merton, who in 1938 "Americanized" anomie, believed that "good" can cause "evil." He saw unrestrained ambition as a prime cause of crime in the United States. Merton argued that no other society comes so close to considering economic success as an absolute value. He believed that the pressure of achieving success may eliminate effective social constraints on the means employed to this end. The "end-justifies-the-means" doctrine becomes a guiding tenet for action when the cultural structure unduly exalts the end and the social organization unduly limits possible avenues to approved means.

Merton, who saw "American culture" as generally uniform throughout all classes, posited that a differential social structure is the source of the lower-class's high crime rates. Social structure determines access to **legitimate opportunities** (i.e., acceptable means to achieve economic success): they are most available in the higher social classes and absent in the lower social classes. According to Merton's **ends–means schema,** anomie results when people confront the contradiction between culturally defined goals and societally restricted means. Normlessness arises out of the disjuncture or *strain* between goals and means—hence the name **strain theory.**

How do individuals respond to this **anomic trap**? Most simply "grin and bear it"—that is, they make the best of the situation and suffer in silence. These **conformists** accept both the goals (ends) and the means, and they strive to achieve success within the rules even if this necessarily limits their goals. Others become **ritualists,** rigidly adhering to and accepting their station in life. Three adaptations to anomie, however, have implications for criminology:

1. **rebels** reject the goals and attempt to overthrow the existing social order and its cultural values.

2. **retreatists** abandon all attempts to reach conventional social goals in favor of a deviant adaptation (e.g., dropping out or abusing drugs).

3. **innovators** use illegitimate, and sometimes illegal, means to gain societally defined success goals, because their experiences limit access to legitimate means.

Thus, crime may be a utilitarian adaptation to the anomic trap, as expressed by the innovators' claim that "the ends justify the means." Rebels, especially those who seek change by force, are also a threat to formal social control mechanisms. Retreatists can create difficulty for control agencies, ranging from the police to social services. Dropping out of society may also place them at odds with various codes and laws. Consider, for example, the fate of homeless families who do not take their children to school. Similarly drug abusers who use their federal or state aid checks to support their misbehavior may have trouble with "the system."

Differential Opportunity Theory Richard Cloward and Lloyd Ohlin (1960) integrated Merton's strain theory with the Chicago School's ideas about the cultural transmission of criminality and Cohen's negativistic subculture thesis.[7] Cloward and Ohlin (1960: 106–7) stated that the dilemma of many lower-class people is that they are unable to find alternative avenues to success goals: "Delinquent subcultures, we believe, represent specialized modes of adaptation to this problem of adjustment." Criminal and conflict subcultures provide illegal avenues to success—the former through illicit income, the latter through violence. Meanwhile, the retreatist "anticipates defeat and now seeks to escape from the burden of the future" (Cloward and Ohlin 1960:107). Crime, then, is not an individual endeavor, but part of a collective adaptation.

Merton viewed lower-class youths as striving for monetary rewards, whereas Cohen saw them as striving for improvement in social class status. Cloward and Ohlin maintained that both money and status are important but that they operate independently of each other. Their classification scheme featured four distinct types of lower-class youths. The first two types, populated by boys who aspired to middle-class membership but placed different emphasis on monetary success (i.e., one was oriented toward improvement in economic position while the other was not), pose little real criminal threat to the community. Collectively the boys in these two groups exemplified what William Foote Whyte (1955) called "college boys." The members of a third group—described by Whyte (1955) as "corner boys"—aspired to neither middle-class membership nor economic success; critics called them socially "unmotivated," but corner boys were similarly unmotivated to serious offending. The final group expressed no orientation toward the middle class but sought to improve their economic position (e.g., more disposable income, "hot" clothes, "flashy" cars, and the like). Cloward and Ohlin (1960:96) saw such youths as the "principal constituents of delinquent subcultures," including those whose members engage in crime for profit, fight other gangs, and consume illicit drugs.

Cloward and Ohlin (1960:145) also pointed out that the illegitimate means of success, like the legitimate ones, are not equally distributed throughout society. Failing with legitimate opportunity structures, despondent youths cannot simply turn to a wellspring of **illegitimate opportunities.** For the average lower-class adolescent a career in professional or organized crime can be as difficult to attain as a lucrative career in society's legitimate spheres.

Cloward and Ohlin understood that both system injustice and system blaming occur when youths perceive no opportunity, when they see a discrepancy between formal ideology and unfair practices. The former may promise equality of access while the latter reflects the realities of prejudice and discrimination. Some youths in this situation regard this blockage as an injustice. For differential opportunity proponents (Cloward and Ohlin 1960; see also Simons and Gray 1989), lower-status persons, especially lower-class minorities, are far more likely to respond negatively to blocked opportunities, viewing them as part of a continuing pattern of exclusion. Higher-status individuals lack this particular justification.

Finally Cloward and Ohlin described the **double failure,** which refers to people who are unsuccessful in both legitimate and illegitimate contexts. Cloward and Ohlin (1960:184) suggested that such people are "more vulnerable than others" to engaging in retreatism, including joining hedonistic, drug-using subcultures. Retreatism may also manifest itself in other ways. Failed criminals may unconsciously retreat to prisons because of their inability to succeed using either means. Periodically they emerge, fail, and then return to prison. Cloward and

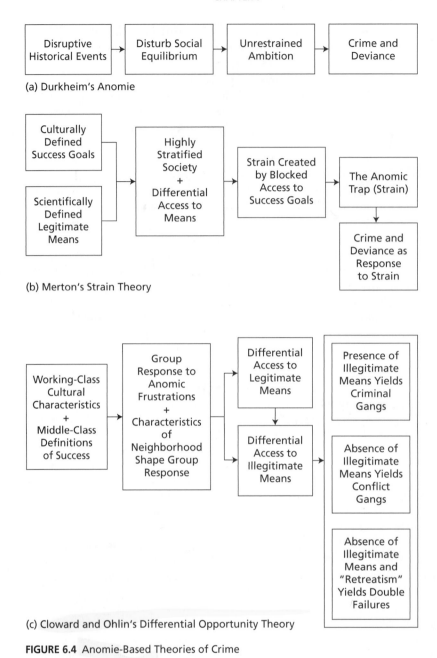

(a) Durkheim's Anomie

(b) Merton's Strain Theory

(c) Cloward and Ohlin's Differential Opportunity Theory

FIGURE 6.4 Anomie-Based Theories of Crime

Ohlin (1960:184) recognized that some double failures adopt conventional lower-class lifestyles. Figure 6.4 summarizes anomie-based theories of crime.

Anomie Theory Rediscovered

In the late 1980s and early 1990s, the view that anomie theory was passé came under reconsideration. Recent restatements have taken several approaches.

Redefining Strain There has been a call for a redefinition of the disjuncture between means and goals as measured by aspirations and expectations. That is, most strain researchers have assumed that strain exists when people's educational *or* occupational expectations fall short of their aspirations. For example, if someone wants to earn a medical degree (an aspiration) but does not anticipate graduating high school (expectation), then the strain is defined as high. Similarly, if someone aspires to a career as a corporate executive but expects to be a janitor, then the strain is defined as high. However, disjuncture between these forms of expectations and aspirations rarely provide insights into criminal conduct (Hirschi 1969; Johnson 1979; Kornhauser 1978; Liska 1971).

Margaret Farnworth and Michael Lieber (1989) proposed that disjunctures between economic goals *and* educational means define the real strains. If individuals have high economic goals but do not have the education necessary to achieve those goals, then they can fall into the anomic trap, and delinquency or crime is one solution. Indeed, Farnworth and Lieber (1989:271) reported that "the gap between economic goals and educational expectations was more effective in predicting the prevalence of serious utilitarian than serious nonutilitarian delinquency. . . . It was also a better predictor of both the prevalence and frequency of nonserious nonutilitarian than of nonserious utilitarian types." Farnworth and Lieber found little support for the criticism that strain theory is largely unable to predict types of delinquency other than those involving material payoffs.

General Strain Theory and Delinquency A second development was Robert Agnew's (1985, 1992) **general strain theory.** Agnew expanded the goals of American youths to include such short-term aspirations as popularity with the opposite (or same) sex, good school grades, and athletic achievements. This redefinition helps to explain conditions of strain experienced by middle-class youths because these goals are not necessarily class-linked. And for adults the failure to achieve expected goals causes strain that, in some persons, leads to anger, resentment, and rage—emotional states that can lead to criminal behavior (Agnew 1992). He suggested that social injustice or inequity might be at the root of strain; a sense of being dealt with unfairly—adversity is blamed on others—and not simply an inability to reach goals, results in strain.

The difference between traditional strain theory and general strain theory is crucial to understanding Agnew's insight into the process. Traditional strain theory is best viewed in terms of a person running *toward* something—in most cases societally defined success goals, such as money, fame, cars, and jewelry. General strain theory, in contrast, suggests that some people are running *away from* something—in this case undesired punishments or negative relationships with others. Thus, adolescents are *"pressured into delinquency by the negative affective states—most notably anger and related emotions—that often result from negative relationships"* (Agnew 1992:49; emphasis in original).

Agnew identified three major types of strain:

1. *Strain as the failure to achieve positively valued goals.* This form of failure includes a) strain as the disjunction between aspirations and expectations or actual achievements (rewards); b) strain as the disjunction between expectations and actual achievements; and c) strain as the disjunction between just or fair outcomes and actual outcomes.

2. *Strain as the removal of a positively valued stimuli from the individual.* This state occurs with the actual or anticipated loss of something valued (e.g., the loss of a close friend, death of a relative, or suspension from school, if school is valued.)

3. *Strain as the presentation of negative stimuli.* Delinquency may ensue when a youth attempts to avoid or escape negative stimuli, terminates or alleviates the source of the negative stimuli, or seeks revenge against the source.

In all cases actual and anticipated strains may create a *predisposition* for delinquency or function as a *situational event* that instigates a particular delinquent act.

As youths attempt to avoid the problems created by the strain, four factors predispose them to delinquency (Agnew 1992:61). First, their nondelinquent strategies for coping are likely to be stressed to their absolute limit. Second, chronic strain lowers the threshold for tolerance of adversity, meaning that the youths are unable to deal with increasing levels of discomfort. Third, repeated or chronic strain may lead to a hostile attitude. Finally chronic strain increases the likelihood that the youths will be high in negative effect/arousal at any given time—that is, prone to fits of anger that focus the blame for bad events on others. Figure 6.5 summarizes general strain theory.

The American Dream The connections between anomie and crime are central to Steven Messner and Richard Rosenfeld's (1994) restatement of anomie theory. They described the "social reorganization" of American society to reestablish the **American Dream.** This process would lead to a "mature society," one that maximizes the talents and capabilities of its citizens "on the basis of mutual support and collective obligations" (Messner and Rosenfeld 1994:111).

Messner and Rosenfeld proposed a two-step program for crime reduction through social reorganization. First, society must reform its social institutions. Crime reduction would be a logical consequence, claimed Messner and Rosenfeld (1994:103), of "policies and social changes that vitalize families, schools, and the political system, thereby enhancing the 'drawing power' of the distinctive goals associated with these institutions and strengthening their capacity to exercise social control." Second, they called for a redefinition of the American Dream to reduce the cultural pressures toward criminality and society's over-emphasis on materialism. Concurrently society must develop a greater sense of altruism so that other practices—parenting, teaching, and learning—become more highly valued and desired.

Messner and Rosenfeld urged that we must view the social role of parenting as an end unto itself. Pundits are quick to note that we require no license to have children and that children do not come with instructions. Perhaps, they suggested, public and private entities could fill this void, encouraging, placing greater value on, and rewarding quality parenting. But whose standards should apply? That is, who decides what skills and techniques are good or bad, positive or negative, constructive or destructive? In short, the enhancement of general parental management sounds intuitively appealing, but its accomplishment may be very difficult.

These recastings and revisions of anomie theory force us to go beyond the traditional views espoused by Durkheim, Merton, and Cloward and Ohlin. Farnworth and Lieber's suggestion affects only how we view the source of the

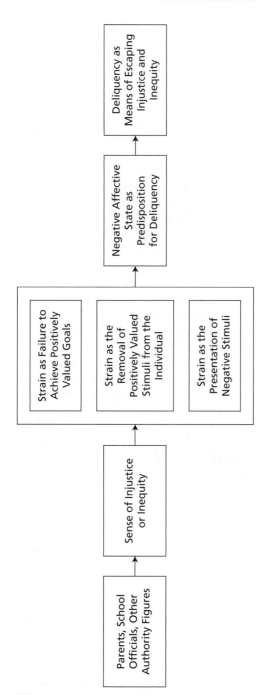

FIGURE 6.5 Agnew's General Strain Theory

strain—as a disjunction of occupational goals and educational means—in an approach that represents only a tinkering with the theory. Agnew's proposal, in contrast, represents a partial recasting of strain theory in the language of the social psychologist (i.e., reinforcements and punishments, aversive and rewarding conditions); here a new theory emerges. Finally Messner and Rosenfeld's mandate is for a restructuring of society's basic values and the adoption of a new orientation on many deeply held beliefs, resulting in a recasting of the classic American Dream.

Recent Anomie Studies Reconstituted anomie theory has given criminologists new insights into crime. Mitchell Chamlin and John Cochran (1995) explored Messner and Rosenfeld's idea that structural and cultural pressures to secure monetary rewards—amid weak controls from non-economic social institutions—promote high property crime levels. They studied the 1980 rates for property crime (i.e., robberies, burglaries, larcenies, and auto thefts) for each state. They merged these aggregated data with state-level measures of non-economic social institutions, including divorce rates, voting behavior, and religious membership, and then measured economic deprivation in terms of the percentage of families below the poverty level. They found tentative support for **institutional anomie theory:** "It appears that it is the interplay between economic and other social institutions that determines the level of anomie within a collectivity and, in turn, the level of crime" (Chamlin and Cochran 1995:423).

Two other recent studies relied on individual-level data to test the macro-level ideas underlying Merton's strain theory. Both addressed the quest for monetary status. Robert Agnew and his associates (1996) focused on dissatisfaction or frustration with achieved monetary success. Using a sample of adults living in a single city, they explored several possible strain determinants, including the importance of monetary success, social class position, expectations for future monetary success, and comparisons with the success of others. Ultimately the level of monetary dissatisfaction should predict self-reported, incoming-generating crime—and this is precisely what Agnew and associates reported. As the researchers observed, their study suggested a new direction for anomie studies: "Rather than focusing only on the determinants of strain, such as the disjunction between aspirations and expectations, one should measure the individual's level of anger/frustration or dissatisfaction" (Agnew, Cullen, Burton, Evans, and Dunaway 1996:699).

Steven Cernkovich and his associates (2000:135) surveyed a group of 12- to 19-year-old youths living in Ohio in 1982 and resurveyed them again in 1992. Part of the 1982 sample was housed in juvenile correctional facilities. The researchers explored both success goal orientation, as a measure of the American Dream, and economic satisfaction. Although blacks appeared to "buy into" the American Dream, their self-reported offending rates were not related to either materialism or career importance. Overall the strain measures revealed far more about white than black offending. Cernkovich and associates (2000) provided a series of possible explanations: the lack of candor by blacks, the high levels of frustration felt by whites at failure, the lower expectations of blacks, and a more well-developed repertoire of survival strategies for blacks. The relative power of strain theory to explain norm-violating behavior among whites but not blacks led the researchers to argue for more research into this disparity.

Assessing Strain Theory

Durkheim's theory is rarely tested. However, comparative criminologists have examined crime in developing nations, which experience social and normative changes. As a rule comparative studies are more speculative than definitive, focusing on official data pertaining to crime, industrial development, and urbanization. Louise Shelley (1981) reviewed many comparative studies of the crime-and-modernization hypothesis. She found that the patterns of crime first observed in western European countries were occurring in the emerging nations of Asia, Latin America, and Africa. Shelley (1981:142) reported that the research "suggests that only the changes accompanying the developmental process are great enough to explain the enormous changes that have occurred in international crime patterns in the last two centuries."

Most critics of strain theory (cf. Bernard 1984; Cernkovich and Giordano 1979; Clinard 1964; Clinard and Meier 1985; Cohen 1965; Kornhauser 1978; Simons, Miller, and Aigner 1980) focus on the following theoretical and empirical shortcomings:

- *Deviance is a relative concept.* Merton's emphasis on the importance of economic success is misplaced. Coming to Merton's defense, Messner and Rosenfeld (1994:60) contended that critics offered only a caricature of his work. But they overlooked Merton's own statement that it would be "fanciful to assert that accumulated wealth alone stands as a symbol of success" (Merton 1968:190). And it would also be wrong to discount the importance of economic success in relation to individual behavior in modern America. Or, as a street philosopher might assert, "Money is important only when you don't have enough."

- *Class-biased.* Anomie assumes that crime is disproportionately more common in the lower socioeconomic classes, where gaps between goals and means are greatest. Ruth Kornhauser (1978) reported that, although anomic theory predicts that delinquents will have higher aspirations than expectations, they often possess low expectations *and* low aspirations. Her assessment: Delinquents do not want or expect much, and so they do not experience the anomic trap. Still, Ron Simons and Phyllis Gray (1989:99) reported a relationship between *anticipated* occupational success and delinquency, but "only for lower-class youth, and particularly lower-class minority youth, as these are the individuals whose life expectations are apt to lead to system blaming."

- *Not a general theory of misbehavior.* Anomie may not explain crime by elites, including white-collar and corporate crime, or nonutilitarian crime, such as vandalism and violent offenses. Recent thinking about anomie, however, suggests that it exists even in corporate boardrooms (Passas 1990). What is price-fixing or other forms of corporate crime if not "organizational innovation"? Perhaps we need to ask, How much wealth is enough?

- *Too simplistic an answer to a complex problem.* The supposed linkage between retreatism and misconduct may represent an oversimplification of a complex process. For example, retreatism confuses cause and effect about drug use and abuse. Do drug users retreat *to* drugs, or do they retreat *because* of drugs? Elliott Currie (1993) noted an interconnection between drug abuse and anomie's breeding conditions, conditions exacerbated by the growing gap between the nation's wealthiest citizens and its poorest. Of course, anomie does not explain why people select one adaptation over another.

- *Untested.* Due to measurement problems the theory remains untested. Even with uniform measures, such as Srole's (1956) **anomia,** it is unclear whether individuals experience anomie or whether it is a social condition.

- *Few tests of adult samples.* Most anomie researchers study juveniles. Yet strain is more about adults than children, especially Merton's anomie (Agnew 1995).

- *Possibly racist, sexist, or both.* A key problem with traditional strain theory has been its focus on minority-male delinquency. More recent forms, such as the micro-sociological variants examined in the next chapter, move beyond class and race. However, its gender bias remains an issue because researchers have not addressed strain's failure to explain female delinquency. Are females immune to strain?

Social Structure, Public Policy, and Criminal Justice Practices

Public Policy Initiatives   The idea of extending opportunities to the disadvantaged fits with the liberal view of good government. For example, the work of Cloward and Ohlin (1960) led to significant public policy initiatives. Attorney General Robert Kennedy, after reading *Delinquency and Opportunity,* asked Ohlin to develop a program that addressed the nation's juvenile delinquency problem. The Juvenile Delinquency Prevention and Control Act of 1961 was a direct attempt to extend legitimate opportunities for success to lower-class youths. The act was, after the death of President John F. Kennedy, extended to all lower-class citizens through President Lyndon B. Johnson's **War on Poverty.**

A key goal was to empower local antipoverty groups to open up opportunities using rent strikes, demonstrations, voter registration, and political mobilization. However, Cloward and Ohlin's work may have inadvertently created an "us versus them" mentality on both sides. Federally funded community legal services sued local and state governments, and rent strikes and demonstrations sponsored by federally funded antipoverty groups generated considerable publicity. The nation's business and political sectors opposed these programs. Finally, although Washington funded no evaluations, President Richard Nixon declared the programs a failure and dismantled them.

These programs exhibited three fatal flaws. The first culprit, claimed Daniel Patrick Moynihan (1969), was a philosophical shift away from providing access to political and social empowerment. Program leaders assumed increasingly activist positions on behalf of the poor and disenfranchised. These changes brought them into conflict with local and federal politicians, a conflict they were destined to lose. As Lamar Empey (1982) observed, "Influential members of Congress made it clear that the mandate of the President's Commission was to reduce delinquency, not to reform society or try out sociological theories on American youth." Second, the opportunity-based programs' goals created obvious problems. Assuming that such programs increase the education and job skills of participants, only an expanding economy allows them to secure a level of economic success sufficient to negate the anomic trap. And failure to secure such employment, after investing considerable time and effort, may cause an escalation of the anomic condition. Finally Stephen Rose (1972) believed that the War on Poverty failed because the established and entrenched poverty-serving bureaucracies transformed it to serve their own interests.

Law Enforcement Practices The concept of strain provides insight into police corruption. Society's desire for law and order contrasts with its antipathy toward governmental authority. This often places police officers in an anomic trap, as they suffer from the strain of being pulled between competing goals: the arrest, indictment, and conviction of offenders on the one hand, and the rule of law on the other. Consequently they perjure themselves, engage in entrapment, falsify evidence and incriminating statements, and even plant evidence at crime scenes. Sometimes they administer "street justice"—for example, effectively executing street-level drug vendors. David Carter (1990) contrasted this form of corruption with far more self-serving (and illegal) acts, such as accepting bribes, drugs, and protection money from these same offenders. Officers also may suppress evidence or information that might lead to an arrest. In either case we can understand police deviance as resulting from strains created by an ambiguous social system.

CRIME AND SUBCULTURES

- Did you know people in school who did not seem to have the same values as most of the other students and who were always rebelling, going against the rules?

- Do members of the lower social classes have different values from those in the middle class? If so, what are their theoretical and policy implications?

- What happens when individuals are unable to achieve success by legitimate means? Is it possible that they form groups with similar likes and dislikes, and similar views of the American Dream?

- The media often portray certain persons or groups that use violence to resolve disputes. Do these images have a basis in fact?

Culture refers to the beliefs and moral values of a society. Not everyone in a modern pluralistic society supports them all. This is especially true of some **subcultures,** a term that refers to both a set of normative expectations and a group. James Short (1968:11) explained, "Subcultures are patterns of values, norms, and behavior which have become traditional among certain groups." As a group, Short noted (1968:11), subcultures "may be of many types, including occupational and ethnic groups, social classes, occupants of 'closed institutions' [e.g., prisons, mental hospitals] and various age grades. [They are] important frames of reference through which individuals and groups see the world and interpret it."

The term *subculture* has enjoyed widespread popularity in relation to studies of work and occupations, adolescence, social class, political organizations, and any number of other academic applications. In criminology the term has different roots and applications.

Delinquent Subcultures

One group of theorists focused on collective responses to conflicts between sub-cultural values and the dominant culture. They are heirs to Thorsten Sellin, who did groundbreaking work on culture conflict (see Chapter 8). That is, those in a subculture occupy an essentially subordinate position in the social structure. The subculture expresses values and norms that are, in the assessment of the dominant culture, wrong and sometimes criminal.

All **delinquent subculture theories** share the wholesale rejection of the dominant culture's values. Yet even within this theoretical perspective, criminologists often disagree about the origins of the conflicts or the manner of their resolution.

Reaction Formation Thesis Albert Cohen (1955:13) saw the delinquent sub-culture as "a way of life that has somehow become traditional among certain groups in American society. These groups are the boys' gangs that flourish most conspicuously in the 'delinquent neighborhoods' of our larger American cities." Gangs are primarily a male and lower-class phenomenon in which status is de-pendent upon a repudiation of the conventional norms of the wider mainstream culture. No attributes distinguish a gang boy from the youngster who joins the Boy Scouts. The only difference is the culture endorsed by each group.

Cohen suggested that the delinquent subculture takes the larger culture's norms, ones he described as middle-class values, and turns them upside down in a process psychoanalytic theory calls **reaction formation.** The anal stage's destructive urges remain unresolved, and conflict with internalized middle-class norms is the result. The subcultural delinquent's conduct is correct "by the standards of his subculture, precisely because it is wrong by the norms of the larger culture" (Cohen 1955:28). Delinquent activities are nonutilitarian, malicious, and negativistic, and delinquents have little regard for profit or personal gain (Cohen 1955:26). Rather, the goal is status. According to Cohen delinquents see the broader society's rules as not some-thing merely to evade. They must *flout* them, with elements of active spite, malice, contempt, ridicule, challenge, and defiance. Cohen (1955:13) also observed that, al-though gang boys eventually outgrow their delinquent ways, the tradition of delin-quency is "kept alive by the age-groups that succeed them."

Lower-Class Culture Thesis Walter Miller (1958) argued that street-corner adolescents in lower-class communities *do not flout* conventional middle-class norms. Instead, the delinquents are merely sticking to behavior defined as accept-able by their community. The delinquent subculture, according to Miller, did not rise in conflict with the larger, middle-class culture, nor is it geared to the delib-erate violation of middle-class norms. Rather, lower-class culture is simply *differ-ent,* the focal characteristics being (1) **trouble,** or law-violating behavior; (2) **toughness,** or physical prowess and daring; (3) **smartness,** or the ability to "con" and act shrewdly; (4) **excitement,** or a tendency to seek thrills, risk, and danger; (5) **fate,** the idea of being lucky or unlucky; and (6) **autonomy,** or the desire to be independent from external control.

Collectively these characteristics dictate behavioral norms. Trouble for men often involves fights, police encounters, or sexual promiscuity; trouble for women frequently means sexual activities with disadvantageous consequences, including rape and unwanted pregnancies. For both genders the consumption of large quantities of alcohol plays a facilitative or enabling role. Miller contended that members of the lower class rarely seek to avoid troublesome behavior based on a sense of commitment to social order norms or laws. Instead, they try to avoid the possible negative consequences of their actions. Altough trouble-producing behavior is a source of status, trouble avoidance is necessary to forestall legal complications. Individuals may, in an attempt to resolve this conflict legitimately, become part of highly disciplined organizations, such as the military or law enforcement.

Miller pointed out that lower-class attachment to peers and commitment to their norms prevent lower-class youths from moving into middle-class (i.e., conventional) society. The larger society stifles their upward mobility unless they can break free, and it also supports this stratification. Because the lower class does the dirty work of an industrial society, members are encouraged to indulge their whims in liquor, sex, and violence. Crime and delinquency are the costs of a smooth-running industrial machine. Figure 6.6 summarizes these theories of delinquent subculture.

Violent Subcultures In his study of homicides in Philadelphia, Marvin Wolfgang (1958) found that most criminal homicides—those not premeditated or caused by some serious mental disease or defect—occur predominantly among the members of certain social groups living in certain neighborhoods. These homicides followed relatively trivial events. Wolfgang speculated that the events took on greater significance due to the meanings attached to them by participants, mostly minority-group males. What was this special meaning? Many criminal homicides, Wolfgang (1958:188–89) believed, followed a predictable pattern:

> The significance of a jostle, a slight derogatory remark, or the appearance of a weapon in the hands of an adversary are stimuli differentially perceived and interpreted by Negroes and whites, males and females. Social expectations of response in particular types of social interactions result in differential "definitions of the situation." A male is usually expected to defend the name or honor of his mother, the virtue of womanhood. . . . When such a cultural norm response is elicited from an individual engaged in social interplay with others who harbor the same response mechanism, physical assaults, altercations, and violent domestic quarrels that result in homicide are likely to be common.

Working with Franco Ferracuti, Wolfgang developed a theory of homicide. Most perpetrators, they wrote, are young, nonwhite, lower-class males who share a value system, the conduct norms of a **subculture of violence** (Wolfgang and Ferracuti 1967:153). Echoing Sellin's culture conflict thesis, they viewed such individuals as in conflict with the values of members of the dominant culture. The latter value life; the former value pride, self-respect, dignity, and status in the community more highly than human life. In this subculture, when someone verbally or physically challenges another person, the conduct norms often require action. Only by this means can he or she counter the loss incurred by the actions of the challenger. If both participants are members of the subculture of violence, the event may quickly escalate into a deadly confrontation. Wolfgang and Ferracuti (1967:156) likened it to a wartime situation in which "it is either him or me."

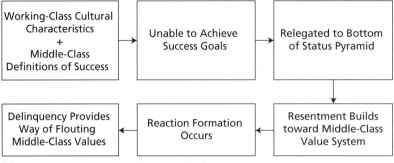

(a) Cohen's Reaction Formation Hypothesis

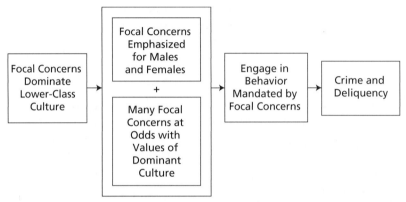

(b) Miller's Lower-Class Focal-Concerns Thesis

FIGURE 6.6 Delinquent Subculture Theories

What is the source of the subculture of violence's norms? Wolfgang and Ferracuti pointed to social origins. Group members pass them from one generation to the next, a process similar to cultural transmission. The difference is that Wolfgang and Ferracuti described this subculture of violence as having social class origins. They saw much of society's violence originating with lower-class, minority-group members. Many of Wolfgang and Ferracuti's adjectives and descriptions of lower-class values have direct ties to Miller's observations about the lower-class focal characteristics. They even used the phrase "Cohen-like negative reaction" to describe how these conduct norms become regularized and institutionalized (Wolfgang and Ferracuti 1967:162).

In sum, Wolfgang and Ferracuti observed that middle-class families and communities avoid routine corporal punishment, do not take exceptional umbrage at derogatory remarks or incidental slights, and view violence as unacceptable in dispute resolution. In lower-class families and communities, in contrast, attempts to end disputes by words rather than actions often meet with ridicule and derision. Wolfgang and Ferracuti (1967:163) did not know the origins of such values and norms. They simply acknowledged that these differences are endemic and that lower-class residents culturally transmit them to successive generations, especially males.

Criminologists have extended the subculture-of-violence thesis. For Lyn Curtis (1975a,b) an exaggerated definition of "manliness," in which verbal skills play a major role, largely defined the actions of African American males. The verbally adroit manipulate women for sexual favors and handle confrontations without resorting to physical force. The verbally maladroit must resort to violence to obtain sex and to resolve personal or group conflicts. In either case this exaggerated sense of manhood requires that black males address all challenges and enjoy almost routine sexual contacts with women. All too often, assaults and homicides result.

Curtis, unlike Wolfgang and Ferracuti, did not stop at describing the subculture of violence. He went on to suggest that a full understanding of it requires an appreciation for the general social conditions that underlie its creation. Curtis blamed repressive police violence directed at black ghettos and a general absence of legitimate opportunities for success. As Curtis argued, attempts to reduce the subculture of violence must do more than dilute its influence and give hope for assimilation. Policy makers must also address the root causes of the subculture in the first place.

Subcultural Delinquency

If Sellin was the progenitor of delinquent subculture theories, then Edwin Sutherland was the father of the **subcultural delinquency theories.** These two criminologists were contemporaries. Before joining the faculty at Chicago, Sutherland (1929) wrote on conflict and crime. After Sellin published his seminal work, *Culture Conflict and Crime,* Sutherland (1949) observed that **white–collar criminals,** a term he devised, espoused values with strong connections to the dominant culture. Yet they engaged in criminal conduct, violating federal and state law with impunity, and expressing little remorse when caught. After all, what was wrong with their acts of bribery, fee splitting, price-fixing, fraud, embezzlement, graft, and the like? They had, in the words of Sutherland's student Donald Cressey (1965), committed "respectable crimes."

Delinquent subculture theories limit their descriptions and explanations to the misbehavior of subordinate members of society. Subcultural delinquency theories provide insights into misbehavior by the social structure's subordinates and superordinates. According to this argument white-collar criminals were superordinates who took business norms and twisted them to suit their needs. It remained for David Matza, Gresham Sykes, and John Hagan to ground these ideas in youthful transgressions.

Subterranean Values and Delinquency Sykes and Matza (1957) shed light on the process whereby criminals of all sorts, superordinates and subordinates, violate the law largely without regard for the consequences of their actions. As they stated, "Values or norms appear as qualified guides for action, limited in their applicability in terms of time, place, persons, and social circumstances" (Sykes and Matza 1957:666). For example, some violent deaths are calculated homicides; others are lawful acts committed in self-defense; and still others are mandated by law, as with state executions or wartime casualties.

Sykes and Matza (1957) studied the mechanisms that permit delinquents to accept society's norms and, simultaneously, to violate them. Delinquents, they observed, used various **techniques of neutralization** to deny in moral terms that a crime or rule violation had taken place. According to Sykes and Matza delinquents are not necessarily committed to their misdeeds, nor do they necessarily see themselves as outside the law. Rather, they justify their misdeeds in a way that, although not valid for the larger society, is valid for them. Specific justifications include the following:

- *The denial of responsibility.* The offender may point to the absence of intent, suggesting that it was an accident or that the injured party "got in the way." At other times forces outside the youth's control are to blame, including uncaring or abusive parents, a failed educational system, and an indifferent community.

- *The denial of injury.* The perpetrator carefully suggests that, in fact, no one was hurt. This technique plays well for victimless crimes, such as drug abuse or underage consumption of alcohol and cigarettes. In the case of pranks or vandalism, the youth may point out that no real harm occurred: no harm, no foul.

- *The denial of a victim.* If no injury occurs, it follows that there can be no victim. Or, even if an injury occurred, the perpetrator may claim that it was a righteous act of retaliation, that the victim—although this term is avoided— "had it coming." Individuals earn this status by race, gender, sexual orientation, and even economic status. For the latter the youth defines an act of thievery as redistribution of the wealth. The key is to transform the victim into someone deserving of injury.

- *The condemnation of the condemners.* The delinquent shifts the blame to the persons doing the complaining, whomever that might be. This offender views the condemners as just as bad and, what is worse, hypocritical. If the condemner is a police officer, all police are brutal and corrupt; if a schoolteacher condemns them, all schoolteachers are lazy and incompetent. The intent is to shift attention from the delinquent's behavior.

- *The appeal to higher loyalties.* Friends, siblings, and youth gangs often provide the final technique's content. Faced with obeying either society's rules or those of a peer-based entity, the perpetrator often comes down on the latter's side. Society's norms are not so much rejected; rather, other norms take precedence.

Matza and Sykes (1961) expanded on subcultural delinquency theory by including subterranean values and their role in leisure-time activities. They noted that certain values set delinquents apart: "Juvenile delinquency appears to be permeated by a cluster of values that can be characterized as the search for kicks, the disdain for work and a desire for the big score, and the acceptance of aggressive toughness as proof of masculinity" (Matza and Sykes 1961:715). They argued that these values, often thought to be uniquely juvenile, have parallels in the dominant culture, particularly in leisure-time activities. For example, the search for kicks is a **subterranean value** that parallels middle-class thrill seeking. One set of values represents living on the edge; the other is far more centrist in the middle-class value system.

John Hagan (1997) viewed these values as providing a shield—albeit only a temporary one—from the anomic condition. He disputed the causal order espoused by most strain theorists, linking the defiant stance of the subcultural delinquent to an engulfing sense of despair provoked by educational and employment problems. As Hagan (1997) noted, the subculture of delinquency may serve to insulate members from socioeconomic stresses, delaying their impact until adulthood. It is only at this point, observed Hagan (1997:133), that they feel the full impact of subcultural involvement: "The same subculture that in adolescence is a source of confidence, or defiance, leads to a loss of confidence, or despair, in adulthood."

Considered together, the techniques of neutralization and subterranean values argue for a view of juvenile delinquents that avoids ideas like assimilation into an oppositional subculture (Yinger 1960). As Matza and Sykes (1961:719) concluded, "The explanation of delinquency may be clarified by exploring the delinquent's similarities to the society that produced him rather than his dissimilarity." This perspective fits well with Ruth Kornhauser's (1978) admonition that delinquent subcultures are nonexistent and James Short and Fred Strodtbeck's (1965) finding that even gang youths accept middle-class prescriptive norms. Delinquents simply take society's values to the normative edge and, in some cases, beyond.

Delinquency and Drift Do juvenile delinquents move on to become adult criminals, or do they mature into law-abiding citizens? Matza (1964) viewed delinquents as moving between criminal and conventional actions but behaving most of the time in a noncriminal mode, a process he called **drift.** Such youths often feel ambivalent about their episodic criminal conduct. Matza believed that juveniles experience less alienation than adults and are not yet committed to an oppositional culture. He was also highly critical of most delinquent subculture theories, which paint a picture of nonstop delinquent behavior, especially for gang youths. Most of the time, delinquents engage in law-abiding activities. How do these theories account for the fact that most delinquents seem to grow up and out of delinquency?

Although Matza did not entirely reject the idea of delinquent subcultures, he did not see it as a binding force on its members: "Loyalty is a basic issue in the subculture of delinquency partially because its adherents are so regularly disloyal. They regularly abandon their company at the age of remission for more conventional pursuits" (1964:157–58). Many if not most delinquents abandon their misbehaving peers in favor of adult prosocial or conventional behavior. As he observed earlier with Sykes, the youths' subterranean values reflect society's core values. As edge values, they are distortions of those values, but part of them nonetheless. The move to more traditional and less threatening centrist values is not a long or a difficult journey.

Hagan (1991) also found the concept of drift useful when applied to juvenile conduct. He contended that youths may drift in and out of different kinds of subcultures, some of which (e.g., party subculture), have net positive effects on youths. Other subcultures (e.g., delinquent subcultures), he admitted, have far more damaging effects. In Hagan's view a party subculture socializes non-working-class males to participate in social networks that are essential for success later in life. Intervention and prevention strategies that fail to take into account those differences may remove important socializing features from a youth's environment.

Assessing Subcultural Theories

Several basic assumptions underlying subcultural theories are suspect. First, some critics question whether a lower-class culture exists at all. On the contrary lower-class families apparently socialize their children in ways similar to middle-class families (Leacock 1971; Piven and Cloward 1971; but see also Hacker 1992; Wilson 1987). Members of the lower class often condemn rather than condone violence, perhaps to a greater extent than those in the upper strata of society (Erlanger 1974; Renzetti and Curran 1989). "Subcultural theories may be a better reflection of middle-class stereotypes about the poor than an empirically accurate depiction of a 'lower-class lifestyle'" (Curran and Renzetti 1994:158). Without a unique and distinct lower-class subculture, subculturalists have little to contribute to criminology. And we have reason to question the characterization of lower-class children as different from middle- and upper-class children.

Early in the twentieth century the Chicagoans, using official records, police reports, court statistics, and correctional summaries, observed an over-representation of lower-class children (Shaw and McKay 1942). In the 1950s social scientists began using self-report data to supplement official statistics. Lamar Empey (1967:31; emphasis in original), a self-report advocate, suggested that within-group comparisons might prove insightful: "The behavior of some middle-class groups suggests that we might discover as many differences *within* classes regarding delinquency as we now discover between them."

For self-reported delinquency class differences nearly disappear (Tittle and Villemez 1977). Charles Tittle and his associates' review of studies examining social class and delinquency included both official and self-reported involvement. They found the presence of *at best* a small negative relationship (i.e., lower-class youths are slightly more inclined to have higher levels of involvement). Tittle (1983; Tittle, Villemez, and Smith 1982) warned that those who insist that poverty causes crime may also view poverty as immoral and inferior, a biased view at best.

Crime involvement aside, do lower-class children experience greater status frustration? Does the delinquent subculture stand against middle-class standards, as suggested by Cohen, or is it part of a widespread deviant tradition? Are lower-class delinquent subcultures countercultures? Cohen and Short (1958) suggested that the progeny of the "parent male subculture" includes several criminal variants. But Empey (1967) questioned these characterizations, saying that there is more empirical support for the idea of an amorphous "parent" subculture than for the idea of highly focused delinquent subcultures. Albert Reiss and Lewis Rhodes (1963) also reported that most youths do not experience status deprivation. Even delinquents differ little from nondelinquents on this dimension. As a rule subcultural theorists tend to "blame" the poor and minorities for their troubles. However, they often ignore two key facts: (1) Structural factors contribute to both poverty and crime, and (2) the various social classes are highly heterogeneous in their beliefs, values, and norms (Curran and Renzetti 1994:158).

Recent Subcultural Studies The subculture-of-violence thesis has its critics, most of whom question its racial motivations; thus the theory is sometimes called the black subculture-of-violence thesis (Adler, Mueller, and Laufer 1994; Barlow 1996; Coser, Nook, Steffan, and Spain 1990; Siegel 1992; see also Messner 1983; Parker 1989). Liqun Cao and associates (1997) questioned whether blacks are more likely to express violent tendencies than whites. Using data from a national survey, and focusing on males under the age of 65, they found that white males are significantly more likely to express violent tendencies in defensive situations and that there were no racial differences in offensive situations. Although this study does not resolve the issue, "being black does not imply a greater probability of embracing a subculture of violence as measured by individual's beliefs and attitudes" (Cao, Adams, and Jensen 1997:376).

IN THEIR OWN WORDS:
Subculturalists on Structure, Culture, and Delinquency

Sociologists express many opinions about the culture supporting juvenile misconduct. The following excerpts from the two groups of "subculturalists" highlight these differences.

- *Shaw and McKay on the conflict of values:* "Conflicts of values necessarily arise when boys are brought in contact with so many forms of conduct not reconcilable with conventional morality as expressed in church and school. A boy may be found guilty of delinquency in the court, which represents the values of the larger society, for an act which has at least tacit approval in the community where he lives" (p. 166).

- *Miller on "focal concerns" and ties to the immediate culture:* "Focal concerns of male adolescent corner groups are those of the general cultural milieu in which it functions. As would be expected, the relative weight and importance of these concerns pattern somewhat differ-

ently for adolescents than for adults" (p. 15).

- *Matza and Sykes on the idea of an oppositional subculture:* "Rather than standing in opposition to conventional ideas of good conduct, the delinquent is likely to adhere to the dominant norms in belief but render them ineffective in practice by holding various attitudes and perceptions which serve to neutralize the norms as checks on behavior" (p. 712).

- *Hagan and associates on subterranean values:* "A recurring theme in American social theory is that core values in American society contain an undercurrent that can cause subcultural delinquent and criminal behavior. . . . The core of this theoretical tradition is the idea that subterranean versions of market-oriented values stimulate subcultural crime and delinquency" (p. 334).

Sources: Hagan et al. (1998); Matza and Sykes (1961); Miller (1958); Shaw and McKay (1942).

Hagan and his associates (1998) explored the cross-cultural utility of subterranean values. Employing school-based surveys conducted in the former East Germany and West Germany, they tested the subterranean influence of self-interest and anomic amorality. They found evidence that the former creates the latter. Moreover, anomic amorality leads to inequality acceptance and a repudiation of societal out-groups. In parts of Germany this has led to attacks on "marginalized groups," such as Turkish residents. Group delinquency is a likely final stage. The researchers concluded that "none of these forces alone is overwhelming, but they combine to form a subterranean causal web that is linked to the core values of market society, and the strands of this causal web can lead to subcultural delinquency" (Hagan, Hefler, Classen, Boehnke, and Merkeas 1998:335).

Subcultures, Public Policy, and Criminal Justice Practices

Subcultural theories provide logical, if overly simplistic, explanations for the concentration of crime among the nation's minorities and poor. Unfortunately, these explanations do not appear to bear much resemblance to the facts as we can discern them. Moreover, even if criminal subcultures exist, what are those who fight crime to do with this information? Remember that subcultures are based on conduct norms and values. The policy options for eliminating this problem are, given these parameters, limited.

One option would be to create local, state, and federal programs to provide alternative cultural messages, but this resembles the existing system of public education. Wolfgang, Ferracuti, Curtis, and others also warned that several potential policies have a dark side. For example, one possibility would be the forced removal of an entire generation from these subcultures, allowing the undesired and offensive norms and values to die out. The U.S. government tried this method to eradicate American Indian culture, using the Bureau of Indian Affairs' Indian Schools. Another possibility would be to isolate the entire subculture. These alternatives resemble the practices of totalitarian regimes, both in fact (Nazi Germany) and in fiction (*Brave New World, 1984*).

Elijah Anderson (1994) viewed the reduction of alienation among minority-group inner-city youths as a precursor to providing alternatives to a unique street code that promotes violence. He warned against the "get tough" approach: "Many feel not only that they have little to lose by going to prison but they have something to gain. The toughening-up experienced in prison can actually enhance one's reputation on the streets. Hence the system loses influence over the hard core who are without jobs with little perceptible stake in the system" (Anderson 1994:94).

Law Enforcement Practices Culture and social structure are important to the police. Many researchers have noted the existence of an insulated and isolated police subculture. For example, the violence of the police work world can spill over into officers' encounters with citizens. Just as represented in the subculture-of-violence thesis, small insults become large ones, and a lack of respectful tone takes on greater symbolic meaning for police officers. They may not only accept and respect the use of force by brother and sister officers but require such acts for full membership in the police subculture (Dorschner 1989; Hunt 1985).

Researchers have also described a police subculture that promotes a sexist and macho role perception (Martin 1980). Moreover, managing the stress of police work takes subcultural forms. Outsiders can easily interpret the ridiculing of suspects and the use of racial or sexual joking as callous or racist (Moyer 1986; Pogrebin and Poole 1988). Indeed, during the social unrest of the 1960s and at various times since, social activists have described the police as an occupying army for Caucasians (Boesel, Berk, Groves, Edison, and Rossi 1969). The police subculture does little to deflect this criticism. One response to these multifaceted problems is to increase police cultural awareness by means of multicultural education. Academy and in-service training programs attempt to accomplish this by educating police about the multiple meanings attached to various acts within lower-class and minority communities (Roberg and Kuykendall 1992:299–301).

Training addresses only part of the issue. The nation's police forces are overwhelmingly Caucasian (Sullivan 1989; Walker 1992). Minority recruitment may help sensitize officers to a wider range of subcultures, but this practice overlooks the issue of occupational socialization. Police work has evidenced an ability to shape those who wear the shield (cf. Bennett and Greenstein 1975; Rokeach, Miller, and Snyder 1977; Van Maanen 1973). Researchers also have shown that minority officers working with minority populations to be rougher and more assertive than white officers (Alex 1976; Kephart 1957; Sullivan 1989). This pattern, however, may be changing (Berg, True, and Gertz 1984). In short, subcultural norms and values are powerful instruments, including those found in the police subculture (Felkenes 1991).

Correctional Practices Like anomic persons in the free society, inmates must deal with unique strains. John Irwin (1980) described four lifestyle adaptations: (1) **Doing time** means that the inmates view prison as a temporary break in their criminal careers; (2) **gleaning** involves taking advantage of every opportunity to improve one's resources; (3) **jailing** resembles colonization, whereby inmates who have little commitment to conventional life adjust well to institutional life and live more comfortably than most inmates; and (4) **disorganized criminals** are inmates who, because of low intelligence, or physical or mental disabilities, develop no real adjustment pattern in prison and often are the prey of other inmates.

Contemporary prisons resemble inner cities. They contain many subcultures, ranging from the ethnic gangs (e.g., Crips, Bloods, Mexican Mafia, Latin Kings, and Black Guerrilla Family), to white supremacist groups (e.g., Aryan Brotherhood), to motorcycle gangs (Hell's Angel's, Gypsy Jokers), to religious groups (e.g., Black Muslims). This extreme heterogeneity not only makes inmate survival difficult (Austin and Irwin 2001; Irwin 1980), it also creates problems for correctional staff. Inmates often control the day-to-day functioning of the institution. Staff who fail to recognize the variability in inmate responses to incarceration are in for a hard time. They may bend to the pressures, or inmates may coopt them (Hawkins and Alpert 1989:337–39). Prison guards are clearly "the other prisoners" (Hawkins 1976).

The significance of cultural-based theories for corrections extends beyond prison walls. For example, probation or parole agreements, or participation in other community-based programs, may require participants to refrain from contacts with known criminals. Often a location, such as their "home turf," is off-limits. This requirement becomes hard to enforce when community programs meet with local resistance. The call often becomes "not in my back yard." In other words local residents may meet attempts to disperse correctional clients into low-crime areas, a goal consistent with subcultural theories, with considerable resistance. (See Table 6.1 for an overview of social organizational theories of crime.)

SUMMARY

Several themes emerged from this review of macro-level criminological theories. First, all three theories earned many well-deserved criticisms from peers. For example, the early social ecologists provided poor independent measures of social disorganization, social controls, and crime. In addition to proposing a theory that seemed to be a tautology, the Chicagoans may have committed the ecological fallacy. The anomie theorists wrestled with whether anomie was applicable only to large-scale societal problems or was a problem measurable within individuals. Assumptions about the relativistic nature of crime and deviance, and the universality of goals and means, merged with questions about the theory's class, race, and gender biases. For their part subculturalists engaged in a long-running debate about whether they should study delinquent subcultures or subcultural delinquency. The

Table 6.1 Social Organizational Theories of Crime

Theory	Major Figures	Central Assumptions	Causal Arguments (Key Terms)	Strengths	Weaknesses
Social disorganization theory (*SDT*)	Shaw, McKay	SDT and human ecology tell us that looking at relationships between humans and their environs yields the best understanding of human social life; cities are ecological spheres; people are not crime-prone but areas of the city are.	SDT sees the cause of crime as a poor sense of community and weak social controls; crime is greatest around *interstitial zones*.	*SDT:* Fits with what the Chicagoans observed in their living laboratory; causal arguments are logical; supported by research during the 1930s and 1940s.	*SDT:* Has two main flaws: (1) with no independent measures of social disorganization, theory may be a tautology; (2) the researchers may have committed the ecological fallacy.
Extended social disorganization theory (*ESDT*)	Bursik, Groves, Sampson		ESDT focuses on a community's capacity to regulate itself.	*ESDT:* Revitalized urban studies of crime; enjoys high theoretical relevance and reasonable empirical support from urban studies of crime and delinquency.	*ESDT:* Must remain vigilant to avoid the same mistakes made by early proponents of SDT.
Environmental criminology (*EC*)	Brantinghams, Jacobs, Jeffery, Newman	ESDT includes the idea that crime and a broader community-level frame of reference can explain other social ills. EC suggests that designing out crime's ecological factors may be possible.	EC views physical and social environs as creating opportunities conducive to crime and delinquency.	*EC:* Includes plans to reduce crime by promoting a watchful public and an involved criminal justice system.	*EC:* Needs further studies to support basic ideas about the impact of urban planning on crime control.
Anomie theory	Durkheim	Anomie theory sees society in terms of its structural parts and functions; society exists in a state of equilibrium that it prefers to others; society must address imbalances.	*Anomie theory:* Disruptive historical and social events yield disturbances in the social equilibrium, leading to unrestrained behavior and deviance.	*Durkheim's anomie:* As the precursor to social deviance seemed to fit with historical, anecdotal, and cross-cultural evidence.	Is difficult to define or measure society-wide anomie; the idea remains intuitively interesting, but empirically hard to prove.
Strain theory and American Dream	Cloward, Merton, Messner, Ohlin, Rosenfeld		*Strain theory:* Contradictions between go'ials and means can create the anomic trap; ways of responding to it may be deviant or criminal.	*Merton's strains:* Made sense during the depression and prohibition (hobos as retreatists and "rum runners" as innovators), and even in the 1950s with a new retreatist culture ("beat generation").	Is easier to measure strain; has not yielded definitive results.

Table 6.1 Social Organizational Theories of Crime (continued)

Theory	Major Figures	Central Assumptions	Causal Arguments (Key Terms)	Strengths	Weaknesses
Subcultural delinquency	Sutherland	Subcultures, consisting of subordinates or superordinates, engage in norm-violating behavior that reflects general social norms taken to the extreme.	Certain social norms become marginalized in the sense that certain elements of their content are taken to the edge of normalcy and beyond; at times these subterranean values promote deviance and neutralize offenders.	Removes the class and race biases common in structural theories; explains how those who violate some laws also obey others; shows a logical tie to other structural theories, especially anomie.	Remains an interesting if poorly refined theory, although Hagan's recent reformulations address this issue.
Subterranean values	Matza, Sykes, Hagan				
Drift	Matza, Hagan				
Delinquent subcultures	Sellin	*Reaction formation:* Children engage in group misbehavior for status; cannot measure up to a middle-class measuring rod.	*Reaction formation:* Delinquents take middle-class values and do the opposite; delinquency is okay because it is wrong; status is the goal.	Offer graphic images of youthful misconduct, whether it is delinquent gang-specific or class-specific behavior.	Is possible that delinquent gangs may merely discourage conventional values, not flout them; juveniles lack a singular loyalty to delinquent subcultures, appearing instead to drift between conventional and unconventional behavior; a lower-class culture may not exist; ultimately crime may be common to all levels of society, and not the unique domain of one; gangs based on retreatism, populated by double failures, may not exist, calling into question theory's basic premise.
Reaction formation	Cohen			*Cohen:* Provides integration of strain's intuitive appeal with Chicagoans' descriptive energy.	
Lower-class culture hypothesis	Miller	*Lower-class culture hypothesis:* The lower class has unique norms and rules different from those of the dominant culture.	*Lower-class culture hypothesis:* Class-based dictates (e.g., being *tough*) may put members on a collision course with the legal system.	*Miller:* Applies the eye of an urban anthropologist to crime problems; studies of violence also provide graphic and powerful subcultural, if race-based, images.	
Differential opportunity structures (DOS)	Cloward, Ohlin	*DOS:* Variable opportunities exist for both legitimate and illegitimate means; uses the ideas of Cohen, Merton and Chicagoans.	*DOS:* Gangs are responses to problems of adjustment created by limited access to legitimate and illegitimate means to achieve success goals.	*Cloward and Ohlin:* Has appealing logic: Increase legitimate opportunities and reduce crime.	
Subculture of violence	Curtis, Ferracuti, Wolfgang	*Subculture of violence:* Many violent acts, including murder, involve members of definable groups; those values that endorse violence to settle disputes and right wrong are found primarily in ethnic and racial minority groups and in the lower class.	*Subculture of violence:* Conduct norms demand violence in the face of certain derogatory remarks and other "assaults" on one's dignity.		

differences involve more than the proper ordering of words. Delinquent subculture theories imply that only subordinates are delinquent; subcultural delinquency extends to superordinates and subordinates.

Second, all three traditions experienced rediscovery and revitalization in the 1990s. Part of this process was methodological, as new data sources merged with powerful new statistical techniques. However, the most important elements were definitional in nature. Social disorganization theorists grounded their approach in the local community, providing important answers to the century-old question, What can we do about crime in the community? The anomie tradition received an infusion of new ideas, especially with respect to the American Dream and monetary acquisitiveness. Just as importantly, new versions of strain theory addressed gender issues.

Third, we found many connections between the theories. The traditional subculturalists obviously were influenced by the Chicago School tradition and anomie theory, and the subcultural delinquency theorists also used elements of the anomie theory and the American Dream. The strong interplay between theories, especially in the 1950s and 1960s, predates the current interest in integrated theories, a theme we explore in Chapter 10. Even the disagreements between theorists, from Sellin and Wolfgang to the contemporary subculturalists, resulted in contributions to the criminological enterprise, as theorists tried to clarify their respective positions.

Fourth, social organizational theories yield many policy implications but fewer insights into criminal justice practices. This "shortcoming" is not surprising. All these theories employ a macro-sociological approach to the study of crime and justice.

The future for macro-level criminological theories is bright. First proposed at the end of the nineteenth century, they remain vital at the start of the twenty-first century. This observation is even more remarkable given that, at various times, each theory was declared a theoretical or empirical dead end.

KEY TERMS

American Dream

anomia

anomic trap

anomie

autonomy

collective conscience

community malaise

community policing

concentric zone

conformists

cultural transmission theories

culture

defensible space

delinquent subculture theories

disorder

disorganized criminals

doing time

double failure

drift

ecological fallacy

ecology

ends–means schema

excitement

fate

general strain theory

gleaning

illegitimate opportunities

image

innovators

institutional anomie theory

interstitial zones

jailing

legitimate opportunities

linear design

macro-sociological

mechanical solidarity

milieu

natural surveillance

organic solidarity

podular design

reaction formation

rebels

retreatists

ritualists

smartness

social disorganization

social equilibrium

strain theory

subcultural delinquency theories

subculture of violence

subcultures

subterranean value

techniques of neutralization

territoriality

toughness

trouble

unrestrained ambition

War on Poverty

white-collar criminals

zone of transition

CRITICAL REVIEW QUESTIONS

1. What is the basic assumption embodied in the ecological approach to the study of crime? What are the major criticisms of this approach?

2. What did the Chicagoans see as the links between a city's physical and social development and its incidence of crime and other social ills?

3. Why was social disorganization theory largely discounted for nearly half a century? What remedies did new proponents of social disorganization theory propose?

4. How would you characterize ecological theories in general? Which ones seem to provide the greatest insights into contemporary urban crime problems?

5. How might some neighborhoods that sociologists characterize as disorganized actually be quite well organized?

6. How does Durkheim's theory of anomie explain criminal behavior?

7. What is the substance of Merton's "anomic trap"?

8. Explain how the following, individually or collectively, link culture, crime, and delinquency: Cohen, Ferracuti, Miller, Short, Matza, Reiss, Wolfgang, Cloward, and Ohlin.

9. For each of the following groups of theories, identify its most important policy implication or application: social ecology theory, social structural theory, and subcultural theory.

10. For each of the following groups of theories, identify the most important practical application: social ecology theory, social structural theory, and subcultural theory.

NOTES

1. The researchers were able to break down, or disaggregate, the arrest statistics for men and women; they then used gender as a variable.

2. They did note two differences, however. First, the model worked slightly better for

males. Second, it explained female homicide and robbery rates very well, and female aggravated assault, burglary, and larceny rates moderately well.

3. Skogan (1990) observed two main types of urban disorder. First, disorderly human

behaviors included public drinking, corner gangs, street harassment, and commercial sex. Second, physical decay referred to vandalism, dilapidation, and abandonment of dwellings and other buildings, and rubbish-filled streets and alleys. This description reverberates with the imagery of social disorganization and environmental theories.

4. Environmental criminology is also closed allied to routine activities/opportunity theory, a topic explored in Chapter 2.

5. Compare this unrestrained ambition with Bonger's idea of excessive egoism (see Chapter 9).

6. Durkheim used a sociological analysis of suicide to demonstrate the power of sociology.

7. Francis Cullen (1988) suggested that Cloward and Ohlin's theory owes more to the Chicago School than to Merton.

7

Social Process Theories

CHAPTER OVERVIEW

Learning Theories

Differential Association Theory

Social Learning Theory

Assessing Learning Theories

Learning Theories, Public Policy, and Criminal Justice Practices

Social Control Theories

Early Control Theories

Social Bond Theory

Assessing Social Control Theories

Social Control, Public Policy, and Criminal Justice Practices

Self-Control Theory

Defining Self-Control

Assessing Self-Control Theory

Self-Control, Public Policy, and Criminal Justice Practices

LEARNING OBJECTIVES

- Reveal how social processes create or work against crime problems in society.
- Provide insights into how crime propensities are learned, including the various mechanisms involved in the learning process.

- Explore society's control mechanisms that collectively and individually stand as a bulwark against crime propensities, ranging from individual to group controls.
- Investigate various expansions on the social control theme, including the effects of effective (and ineffective) parenting and too little self-control.

INTRODUCTION

A social process is any identifiable, repetitive pattern of interaction between humans in a group or social context. Each theory in this chapter views crime as the product of social processes. The theories tend to emphasize individuals and their responses to social interactions, although some acknowledge the role of larger social forces. In several cases the social process theorists are at odds with one another as they look at the same problems—crime and delinquency—and see very different forces at work. That is, some process theorists see elements within society as the chief culprits, producing crime by endorsing or failing to stop the learning processes by which criminals are taught. Others focus on breakdowns in the social fabric, social institutions, or failed attempts to control youthful misbehavior.

Social process theories are largely sociological; however, unlike the theories discussed in Chapter 6, which for the most part looked for answers in large-scale social forces (for an exception see general strain theory), these theories begin with the premise that to understand crime we must understand how people become criminals. What, they ask, are the forces behind these processes? Several are "informed" by psychological principles and ideas, and so are social psychological theories. This fact should not be too surprising given that criminology is the study of criminals and crimes. Social psychology is the branch of sociology that addresses individual behavior in terms of social factors and in a group context. Social psychologists often look for insights into individual behavior in terms of statuses and roles: how individual statuses and roles relate to the group or larger community. Indeed, social learning and self-control theories, although making different assumptions about criminals, all emphasize the social application of basic psychological principles.

The theories in this chapter are held together by their focus on the basic social processes underlying criminal conduct. We begin with learning theories of crime.

LEARNING THEORIES

- Babies aren't born criminal; rather, as children they must be taught evil ways, lessons that are best learned in close contact with those who endorse law-breaking. Can a theory tell us where, when, and in what context this learning is likely to take place?
- Adolf Hitler died a generation or more before today's neo-Nazis were born, yet many of them look to the Third Reich's führer as a spiritual leader. How is this possible?

- What, exactly, is the content of what is learned by those who commit crimes?

- If we are all exposed to ideas, information, definitions, and the like that support law violations, why do some of us commit crimes and others do not?

If criminals are not born, they must be made. Perhaps all social behavior, including criminality, comes about through a process of learning. While most of us are learning reading, writing, and arithmetic, some are learning the A-B-Cs of crime and delinquency. How is crime learned? Is one generation's criminality the legacy of previous generations? Edwin Sutherland addressed these questions early in the twentieth century.

Differential Association Theory

Edwin L. Sutherland (1883–1950) is remembered as the sociologist who proposed **differential association theory,** which represents a social psychological explanation for how criminal behavior is transmitted—but not how it originates. According to Sutherland criminal behavior is learned, and most learning occurs within intimate personal groups. He was unyielding in his belief that close contacts between "teachers" and "students" is essential for learning to occur. But these two terms were not part of Sutherland's vocabulary, in spite of the fact that he also believed that the same mechanisms that support any learning are at work in criminal learning. He did not think it possible to learn criminal behavior through the mass media; that is, motion pictures, newspapers, or, more recently, television and videos. Such mechanisms, he claimed, cannot provide the required social context in which learning occurs.

From this perspective all behavior has the same goal: securing economic and personal status. Differential association theory accounts for the difference between selecting criminal or noncriminal methods for achieving these goals. Criminal behavior ensues when the motives, drives, and rationalizations direct the individual to view the law unfavorably. Sutherland's (1947:7; emphasis added) Chicago roots—and contacts with Thorsten Sellin—were showing when he stated:

> In some societies an individual is surrounded by persons who invariably define the legal codes as rules to be observed, while in others he is surrounded by persons whose definitions are favorable to the violation of legal codes. In our American society these definitions are almost always mixed and consequently we have *culture conflict* in relation to the legal codes.

The Principle of Differential Association The excess of definitions favorable to law violations compared with unfavorable ones determines a person's criminality—according to what Sutherland called the **principle of differential association.** People turn to crime "because of contacts with criminal patterns and also because of isolation from anticriminal patterns" (Sutherland 1947:8). He also believed that there had to be normative content—questions and answers addressing issues of right and wrong—or else the learning was neutral and had little effect.

Sutherland observed that differential associations vary in terms of the degree of frequency, duration, priority, and intensity. The first two, **frequency** and **duration,** are "modalities of associations." How often one has these contacts and how long the contacts last are self-explanatory. What Sutherland meant by priority, and especially by intensity, however, has proved to be more problematic for those interested in testing the theory.

Sutherland believed that early childhood socialization was critical and that many of the most important definitions of "right" and "wrong" were learned then and held throughout life. Therefore, the associations someone has first in life—those with the highest **priority**—may be the most important ones. Sutherland (1947:7) further stated that **intensity** "is not precisely defined but it has to do with such things as the prestige of the source of a criminal or anticriminal pattern and with emotional reactions related to the associations."

According to the tenets of differential association theory, criminal behavior results from the strength (i.e., frequency, duration, priority, and intensity) of an individual's criminal associations—although choosing one's associates involves an indeterminate amount of "free will"—and is a cumulative learning process. A scale that starts out balanced provides insights into differential associations. On each side criminal and noncriminal associations accumulate over time. At some theoretical point criminal activity will ensue if there is an excess of procriminal definitions favoring law violations compared to definitions supporting these same laws. Figure 7.1 summarizes Sutherland's differential association theory.

Variations on a Theme: From Differential Identifications to Differential Reinforcements After Sutherland's death a number of sociologists and criminologists critiqued several of his basic assumptions. The result was a series of theories expressing the idea of differential learning. For example, Daniel Glaser (1956) questioned the necessity of intimate personal contacts in learning and further suggested that merely identifying with criminal roles may be sufficient. For example, during the 1990s members of the Serbian militia, who had never met Adolf Hitler but who seemed to admire him, emulated his philosophy and methods, especially with respect to "ethnic cleansing." Glaser (1965:335) used the phrase **differential identification** to describe the role-taking process in which "a person pursues criminal behavior to the extent that he identifies himself with real or imagined persons from whose perspective his criminal behavior seems acceptable."

Glaser later refined differential identification and renamed it **differential anticipation theory.** Expectations, wrote Glaser (1978), determine behavior and derive from several sources:

- Procriminal and anticriminal "social bonds," or punishments and rewards for law-violating behavior that conforms to the expectations of others
- Differential learning, by which one is exposed to the attitudes, orientations, and behavior associated with the gratifications of criminal and noncriminal activities
- The perceived opportunities for success or failure in criminal pursuits

Glaser (1978:237) stated that "a person will try to commit a crime wherever and whenever the expectations of gratification from it—as a result of social bonds, differential learning, and perceptions of opportunity—exceed the unfavorable anticipations from these sources." Thus, **differential expectations** replaced differential associations.

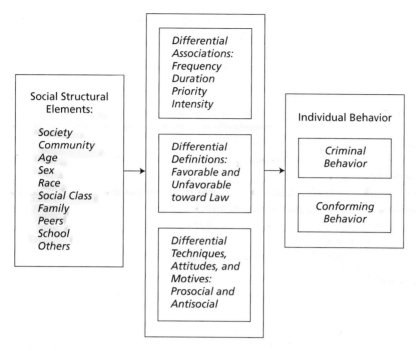

FIGURE 7.1 Sutherland's Differential Association Theory with a Little Help from Akers (1994)

C. Ray Jeffery's **differential reinforcement theory** ties psychological learning processes (i.e., behaviorism and operant conditioning) to differential association theory. He believed that "criminal behavior is operant behavior; that is, it is maintained by the changes it produces on the environment" (Jeffery 1965:295). Social *and* physical environmental changes are important; the latter include material gains. According to Jeffery (1965:296), "A criminal act occurs in an environment in which in the past the actor has been reinforced for behaving in this manner, and the aversive consequences attached to this behavior have been of such a nature that they do not control or prevent the response." For example, an armed robbery may produce not only the reward of money but also the aversive consequences of being shot, arrested, convicted, or imprisoned. An armed robber will stop only after associating the act with aversive consequences. Jeffery (1965:300) observed that "punishment decreases a response rate only if used in a consistent manner, and . . . applied near the time of the occurrence of the forbidden act."

Social Learning Theory

Sutherland's emphasis on crime as *learned* behavior led Robert Burgess and Ronald Akers (1966) to offer **differential association/differential reinforcement theory.** To social interactions they added nonsocial situations that are reinforcing or discriminative, the latter referring to certain individuals or circumstances, such as the presence of a parent or a peer, that may control a person's behavior. Burgess and Akers (1966:140) restated the principle of differential association using operant conditioning terms: "Criminal behavior is a function of norms which are discriminative for criminal behavior, the learning of which takes place when such behavior is more highly reinforced than noncriminal behavior."

The How, What, and Where of Social Learning In 1973 Akers called the emergent theory social learning. Social learning theory addresses the how, the what, and the where of learning. As for *how,* he found the answer in instrumental conditioning, a process identified as "Skinnerian, operant conditioning, reinforcement, or simply behavior theory" (Akers 1973:45). Human behavior takes two forms: (1) **operant behavior,** which is voluntary and mediated by the brain; and (2) **respondent behavior,** which is automatic and reflexive. Operant behavior depends largely on **instrumental conditioning,** meaning it is acquired (or conditioned) by the "effects, outcomes, or consequences it has on the person's environment" (Akers 1985:45). Instrumental conditioning is associated with two processes:

1. **Punishments,** including punishments received (e.g., when a law violator receives a prison sentence) and rewards lost (e.g., when a law violator has property confiscated). In each case the illicit behavior is likely to decrease.

2. **Reinforcements,** including rewards received or punishments avoided, to increase the behavior: For example, when a law violator scores "the big one" or avoids a conviction, criminal activity is likely to continue. Reinforcements are both social and nonsocial. The former are often symbolic and abstract, such as the attainment of ideological, religious, or political goals; the latter may be physiological, unconditioned, and intrinsically rewarding. Akers, however, emphasized the social over the nonsocial.

Social learning occurs in two ways. The first is by **imitation** or **modeling:** Observing what happens to others, people can be vicariously reinforced and may imitate the rewarded actions. They may also develop new behavior without other forces at work simply by modeling what others do. A second method is the **principle of differential reinforcement:** Given two or more forms of behavior, the most highly rewarded one is retained and repeated. As Akers (1985:47) observed, when two forms are similar, the learning is "most dramatic and effective when the alternatives are incompatible and one is rewarded while the other is unrewarded."

Akers' theory also addresses the content—the *what*—of learning. The importance of techniques is elementary. Unless one knows how to commit a crime, motivation and intent are meaningless. **Motivating definitions** form the basis of what Akers called **discriminative stimuli,** two forms of which define the reinforcement process. First, some definitions place the criminal conduct in a positive light, defining it as acceptable and permissible. Second, some stimuli resemble Sykes and Matza's (1957) techniques of neutralization (see Chapter 6) and serve to "*counter or neutralize definitions of the behavior as undesirable*" (Akers 1985:50; emphasis in original). Akers postulated that the latter probably originate through negative reinforcement, providing a means to escape the social disapproval of others and oneself.

Akers believed that learning takes place—the *where*—primarily among **differential associations.** This emphasis is behavioral (i.e., associating directly and indirectly with people who engage in various types of legal and illegal behavior) and attitudinal (i.e., coming to know the normative beliefs and orientations of these people). One's associations are the sources of reinforcements and punishments. Those that occur most often and in the greatest number, and that enjoy the greatest probability of reinforcement, tend to be the ones that guide behavior.

Social Learning Processes Social learning theory outlines a process in that it describes how people move from nonoffender status to offender status and back again (Akers 1998; see also Winfree, Sellers, and Clason 1993). The reinforcers and punishers assume more prominent roles once an initial act is committed, and imitation assumes a decreasingly important role. People's personal definitions change after repeated episodes, depending on the reinforcers and punishers. Whether an act is committed in a given situation "depends on the learning history of the individual and the set of reinforcement contingencies in that situation" (Akers 1994:99).

Feedback is also important. An obvious example of feedback is when one's definitions are influenced by one's behavior. Only the first, tentative criminal acts can be said to be free of feedback; afterwards both responses to the behavior and emerging personal definitions become cues for future behavior (Akers 1994:100). Causal ordering for deviant peers is also a problem. Initially, individuals have both deviant and nondeviant peer groups; however, once instrumental conditioning occurs, the balance may shift to one group over the other (Akers 1994:100).

Finally Akers (1998) acknowledged a role for social structure. Society, community, and even individual characteristics—race, gender, religion, and class—create the individual's learning context. Akers (1998:322) assumed that "social learning is the primary process linking social structure to individual behavior." Figure 7.2 summarizes Akers' reconfigured theory.

Assessing Learning Theories

Two forms of learning theory—differential association and social learning—have received the greatest attention from criminologists. Each has its share of supporters and detractors.

Differential Association Theory Given differential association theory's seniority, the large body of work both praising and condemning it is to be expected (Matsueda 1988). Initial objections were so strong that in 1944 Sutherland (1973) wrote a self-critical paper titled "The Swan Song of Differential Association," in which he sounded his own theory's death knell. Major criticisms of Sutherland's argument, many of which appeared in his lifetime, include the following:

- Sutherland's propositions are not testable as stated, mainly because important concepts were not operationalized by Sutherland (e.g., what does he mean by "definitions," and how much is "an excess of definitions"?).

- Differential association theory is a "general theory of criminal behavior" that does not explain all crimes (e.g., what about crimes of passion and most violent crimes?).

- The theory is based on an oversocialized view of human beings; it does not account for individual motives.

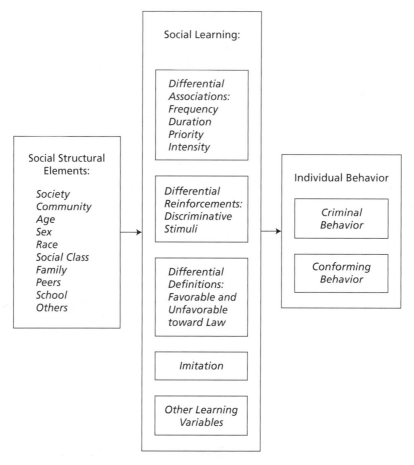

FIGURE 7.2 Akers' Social Structure/Social Learning Theory

Source: Akers (1994).

- The theory is tautological. Criminal-norm learning is central, but the behavior is viewed as evidence of those norms; there is no independent evidence.

The theory did not die with Sutherland. Over the past 50 or so years, researchers have tended to take one of two paths. The first consists of detailed examinations of the theory's implications (Cressey 1965; De Fleur and Quinney 1966; Glaser 1956; McKay 1960). For example, Melvin De Fleur and Richard Quinney (1966:20) claimed that the theory, far from being untestable, was capable of generating "more hypotheses than could be adequately tested in several lifetimes." Sheldon Glueck (1956) doubted if the essential ratio between definitions favorable and unfavorable to law-violating behavior could be measured; if the theory's main elements could not be tested, the theory was of little value (see also Gibbs 1987; Hirschi 1969). Even Sutherland (1947:7), who was interested in quantifying the theory and developing a "mathematical ratio," admitted that this formulation would be difficult. This sentiment is embodied in Cressey's observation that differential association should be regarded "as a general principle that organizes and makes sense of the data on crime rates" and, in this manner, helps organize our knowledge about crime correlates. What the critics and supporters often overlooked was the fact that "theories—being sets of interrelated propositions explaining a given phenomenon—are rarely tested as a whole. What are tested are specific hypotheses, propositions or empirical implications of a theory" (Matsueda 1988:285).

The second path consists of empirical studies. After Sutherland's death a flurry of such studies purported to test the "differential association hypothesis" or "differential association theory" (cf. Glaser 1960; Reiss and Rhodes 1964; Short 1957, 1958, 1960; Stanfield 1966; Voss 1964). As a rule these studies supported the principle of differential association. The researchers reported that juveniles with delinquent peers also tended to commit—or at least report—more delinquent acts than those who had no such contacts.

Differential association theory addresses more than merely contact with delinquent peers. Otherwise, the theory would be little more than a restatement of the observation by the Gluecks (1950:164) that "birds of a feather flock together." Indeed, several generations of researchers focused on the issue of favorable and unfavorable definitions. For example, Gresham Sykes and David Matza (1957) studied the mechanisms that permit delinquents to accept society's norms and, concurrently, to violate them. They observed that delinquents used various techniques of neutralization to deny (not in a *legal* but in a *moral* sense) *mens rea:* The victim was denied victim status because he or she deserved what happened, or the crime was not a crime but a prank. Sykes and Matza's techniques are Sutherland's rationalizations, drives, and attitudes, which form "a favorable disposition to criminal behavior." Sutherland told us how these dispositions were acquired; Sykes and Matza revealed what they were and how they worked.

The results of cross-sectional surveys support Sutherland's basic tenets (Griffin and Griffin 1978; Jensen 1972; Tittle, Burke, and Jackson 1986), as do longitudinal studies (Sellers and Winfree 1990) and even experimental evaluations of correctional treatment programs (Andrews 1980; Empey and Erickson 1972). Some criminologists have provided tests of competing theories, which differential association usually "wins" (Matsueda 1982; Matsueda and Heimer 1987), or integrated different theories to show that they are complementary (Elliott, Huizinga, and Ageton 1985; Marcos, Bahr, and Johnson 1986). For example, Ross Matsueda (1982) noted that Hirschi (1969) and Gary Jensen (1972) used the same data to test differential association theory, but neither supported it. Matsueda reanalyzed the data and found more support for differential association theory than for social bond theory. Anastasios Marcos and his associates (1986) developed an integrated bonding association model of adolescent drug use and found general support for it, although association with misbehaving friends was the best single predictor of adolescent drug use.

Social Learning Theory Of the theories generated by Sutherland's seminal ideas, Akers' has received the most empirical attention. Although Sutherland failed to specify exactly how the definitions become part of an individual's social-psychological makeup, Akers did: Those behaviors that receive more positive than negative *reinforcements* and fewer positive than negative *punishments* will be repeated. Critics of this application of operant conditioning to Sutherland's crime-learning process point out several major shortcomings:

- Reed Adams (1973) attacked early versions of social learning theory as misleading sociologists and criminologists about the principles of operant conditioning.

- William Chambliss (1988:244–45) observed that social learning theory fails to state what is rewarded and not rewarded, and what is considered rewarding and not rewarding. Akers (1985:43) concurred: "The theory is . . . incapable of accounting for why anyone or anything is socially defined as undesirable. . . . The theory does not say how or why the culture, structure, and social patterning of society sets up and implements certain sets and schedules of reactions to given behavior and characteristics."

- Social learning, like differential association theory, is tautological. Some learning theories attribute crime to deviant norms and proceed to take the forbidden behavior as evidence of those norms (Goode 1984:30).

- Most tests involve relatively minor forms of social deviance (e.g., youthful cigarette smoking); largely missing are tests that involve serious delinquency or crime (Curran and Renzetti 1994:196). A corollary of this criticism is that social learning, like differential association theory, is not a general theory, because few tests involve behaviors beyond minor forms of youthful rule breaking.

The limited range of dependent variables used in many of these tests has caused some skeptics to question social learning theory's viability. About half of nearly 120 tests of the theory published between 1966 and 1999 focused on self-reported drug use (Sellers, Pratt, Winfree, and Cullen 2000). Even Akers, in his first empirical test of social learning theory, surveyed adolescent drug- and alcohol-related activities (Akers, Krohn, Lanza-Kaduce, and Radosevich 1979). Akers and associates found a strong association between drug and alcohol *use* and social learning variables, but a somewhat weaker relationship when the dependent variables were drug and alcohol *abuse*. Nearly all of the remaining studies published between 1966 and 1999 examined self-reported delinquency, including many serious acts of law-violating behavior (Sellers et al. 2000; see also Boeringer, Shehan, and Akers 1991; Fagan and Wexler 1987; Morash 1983; Winfree, Mays, and Vigil-Backstrom 1994; Winfree, Vigil-Backstrom, and Mays 1994). The results do not differ significantly from study to study on the basis of offense alone; the more important feature tends to be which social learning variables are included in the analysis (Sellers et al. 2000). A **meta-analysis**—a quantitative synthesis of existing research studies that is capable of making sense of the topic under study—of nearly 120 tests of social learning theory provided considerable backing for Akers' contentions: Support for differential associations and differential definitions was high, and support for differential reinforcements and modeling was lower (Sellers et al. 2000).

The Search for Social Learning Given that social learning is a process, longitudinal tests are seen as essential. Marvin Krohn and his associates (1985) found that social learning variables predicted changes in the cigarette smoking exhibited by junior high and high school boys at two different times. L. Thomas Winfree and his associates also found support for social learning principles as predictors of adolescent drug use by successive cohorts (Winfree and Griffiths 1983) and panels (Sellers and Winfree 1990; Winfree 1985). Although both of these studies addressed longitudinal elements of social control, they looked at minor forms of youthful misconduct: the use of forbidden psychoactive substances.

Several researchers responded directly to the criticism that few tests of social learning theory (and differential association theory as well) have involved offending beyond status offenses and drug use, or the issue of the theory's generalizability (see also Alarid, Burton, and Cullen 2000). William Skinner and Anne Fream (1997) employed a social learning model to study computer crime among college students. They reported that measures of differential association, differential reinforcements, and punishments, as well as definitions and sources of imitation, performed well in predicting self-reported computer crime (e.g., engaging in software piracy, guessing passwords, inserting viruses, modifying computer files without permission, and accessing accounts or files without permission). Similar results have been reported in studies of cheating among college students (Lanza-Kaduce and Klug 1986), youth gang membership (Winfree, Mays, and Vigil-Backstrom 1994; Winfree, Vigil-Backstrom, and Mays 1994), and rape and sexual aggression (Boeringer, Shehan, and Akers 1991; Sellers, Cochran, and Winfree 2002), although Akers (1998:262) reported that the theory did better in predicting the proclivity to use nonphysical coercion than actual physical force in rape.

Social learning principles appear to cross cultural barriers. In a series of studies, Winfree and associates demonstrated the theory's ability to predict delinquency and drug use even when the groups studied included minority-group members. For example, social learning variables performed well in predicting drug use among junior high and high school students, irrespective of race or ethnicity (Sellers, Winfree, and Griffiths 1993; Winfree and Bernat 1998; Winfree and Griffiths 1983; Winfree, Griffiths, and Sellers 1989). Tests involving youth gang involvement and serious delinquency by high school students in cities with large Hispanic American populations yielded similar results. Gang involvement and self-reported delinquency are best understood in terms of social learning, regardless of the respondents' race or ethnicity (Sellers, Winfree, and Griffiths 1993; Winfree, Bernat, and Esbensen 2001; Winfree, Griffiths, and Sellers 1989; Winfree, Mays, and Vigil-Backstrom 1994). Learning variables performed best when the self-reported behavior was characterized as "group-context offending" (e.g., group fighting or drive-by shootings).

Learning Theories, Public Policy, and Criminal Justice Practices

The differential association/social learning tradition troubles some policy makers. On a commonsense level the "crime-as-learned-behavior" argument seems clear, but some policy makers miss key parts of the theory. Perhaps the best example involves the concept of "bad companions." This oversimplification of the social learning model is promoted in families, public schools, businesses, and other social institutions including the military. Often this concept operates in the following manner: When we are young, our parents encourage us to avoid bad companions. Early in school we learn to avoid contact with people identified by teachers and friends as troublemakers, people who often find themselves suspended or expelled from the school. Later, as we start our careers, we continue to encounter warnings against bad companions, especially slackers and others with poor work habits. We get promoted; they get fired.

This conceptualization overlooks the fact that social learning involves more than merely steering clear of bad companions. However, controlling the sources of definitions favorable to law-violating behavior is a far more difficult task than avoiding bad companions, although some zealots may attempt this task by censoring music, books, and movies. Sutherland, Akers, and other proponents of social learning might argue that such efforts will meet with limited success because social groups, and not the mass media, are a necessary ingredient.

Other elements of social learning find their way into the lexicon of our social and public institutions, including, once again, the family and schools. For example, operant conditioning, with its concomitant reinforcement and punishment processes, is used by parents, schoolteachers, social workers, correctional officers, and corporate leaders. Few of these individuals know the formal terms for the processes or their related elements, but they appreciate the method and understand the expected results. If this discussion sounds a little like deterrence theory, the similarities are intended. Indeed, Akers (1990) believed that all of the causal elements embodied in deterrence theory and rational choice theory are contained in social learning theory. In any event social learning principles of criminal conduct, given their ties to general learning principles, are an integral part of the nation's sociolegal fabric.

Law Enforcement Practices   In addition to *what* they do, *who* the police are and *how* they perceive their world may be related to the processes implicit in differential association and social learning theories. There is a longstanding debate as to whether police work attracts certain types of people or the job shapes the people. If certain types are attracted to police work, then society must rely on psychological screening devices to keep out the undesirable ones. If who police officers are is related to police work, then we need to study professional socialization. For example, police are often described as cynical although there is disagreement among researchers as to the implications of police cynicism (cf. Anson, Mann, and Sherman 1986; Langworthy 1987a,b; Niederhoffer 1969; Regoli 1976; Wilt and Brannon 1976). A cynical cop is one who views the public and other institutions, including the Supreme Court, with a measure of distrust and perhaps even hostility. But is this necessarily bad? Sam Walker (1992:333) suggested that cynicism might be a positive attribute protecting officers from certain aspects of their work that are unpleasant or difficult to deal with, including the victims of crime. Does this sound familiar? If not, we suggest that you review techniques of neutralization.

Process theories may help us to understand police corruption, or the misuse of authority by police officers for personal gain or the benefit of others. This behavior is most likely to occur in heterogeneous societies with a high level of conflict and dissensus (Walker 1992:268). Police corruption is often linked to pressures emanating from deviant peers and the need for group solidarity. Officers who refuse to "play along" may be ostracized or worse (Walker 1992:269-70; see also Stoddard 1968; Westley 1970). Thus, police deviance may be understood in terms of social learning theory: Rewarded behavior is repeated behavior.

Judicial Practices   Researchers suggest that differential association/social learning principles are at work throughout the judicial system. Attorneys must learn to work with the courtroom work group—all attorneys and other key players in the judicial system—or suffer potentially negative consequences (Clynch and Neubauer 1981; Eisenstein and Jacobs 1977); jurors, as novices to the process, must quickly learn both the practice and the philosophy of their fact-finding roles (Balch, Griffiths, Hall, and Winfree 1976); and, probation/parole officers must learn what judges expect in their presentence investigations (Abadinsky 1994:119; McShane and Krause 1993:369–74; see also Rosencrance 1987). Here we focus on the role of differential association/social learning theories in shaping attorney responses to the various roles they perform in the administration of justice.

Some legal scholars have suggested that lawyers are subject to the same social learning forces as criminals; only the direction traveled is different (except in the case of unethical conduct and corruption) (Pollock 1994:136–62; Wrightsman, Nietzel, and Fortune 1991:78–84). Central to this position is legal education. Thanks largely to the efforts of the American Bar Association, legal education in this country is extremely homogeneous. This uniformity is not necessarily a bad thing; it ensures that attorneys share a common understanding of the law and its application to meet the needs of a rational legal system. Lawyers can predict what a court will do; judges treat cases according to shared guidelines so as to earn the respect of the legal community. The courts' operations are made far more predictable by the homogeneous nature of legal education.

In law school would-be attorneys quickly learn what is acceptable and unacceptable from law professors, their most immediate role models. One survey of law students found that "the ability to think like a lawyer" was the skill on which they rated themselves highest (Gee and Jackson 1977). This skill translated to thinking unemotionally in the sense that the human element in complex issues can be put aside (Willging and Dunn 1982). Learning principles—ones associated with legal definitions, behavioral modeling, and differential social and nonsocial reinforcements such as partnerships and high salaries—play a central role in legal education.

Consider the links between learning theory and the role of prosecuting attorneys. Research on legal interns in prosecutors' offices suggests that as they immerse themselves in "real-life" legal situations would-be prosecutors quickly learn that, once a decision to prosecute has been made, there can be no turning back (Winfree, Kielich, and Clark 1984). Some legal scholars see this as "conviction psychology" (Felkenes 1975). That is, legal interns and new prosecutors alike must learn definitions that place prosecutorial work in a positive light; they are protected from the possible negative implications of prosecutorial work by other definitions (Hubka 1975; Winfree and Kielich 1979; Winfree, Kielich, and Clark 1984). Akers (1985) called such definitions discriminative stimuli. Moreover, few careers reflect a greater appreciation for the concept of differential associations than the law: Lawyers work together, socialize together, and often live in the same neighborhoods.

The significance of learning theory extends into the judge's chambers. Five stages of judicial professional socialization have been identified, most of which involve elements of learning theory (Alpert 1981). The first stage, general professional socialization, begins in law school. Elevation to the bench starts the second phase, initiation, the first of the four on-bench stages, wherein the judge–initiate learns the basics about being a judge. Next judges enter the resolution stage as they move from being advocates to being arbiters. In the fourth stage judges enter the establishment phase, when they settle into being judges. The final stage, commitment, is a time when judges really begin to enjoy the act of judging; it is also demarked by comradeship with other participants in the process (Alpert 1981). What they have learned along the way is more than merely how to be judges. Judgeships' less tangible expressive content—the unique values, ideologies, decorum, and coping strategies—must also be learned. The expressive aspects of being a judge are not taught in law school; they must be learned on the job (Holten and Lamar 1991:100–102).

Correctional Practices Learning theories provide insights into the lives of correctional clients. For example, "prisonization" is the process of embracing, to a greater or lesser extent, the prison's culture (Clemmer 1940; Thomas 1970). Prison researchers contend that negativistic prison and jail inmate societies (1) are caused by attitudes and orientations that inmates bring with them into the institution, (2) are created by the deprivations of institutional life, or (3) are a result of the actions of both forces (cf. Akers, Hayner, and Grunninger 1974; Thomas 1970). It seems highly likely that the ability of prison society to shape inmate responses to incarceration is a reflection of the principles of differential reinforcement and differential association: again rewarded behavior is repeated behavior, especially given omnipresent and omnipotent peer groups such as are found in the inmate society.

Social learning principles have also been tied to offender prosocial changes, particularly in therapeutic drug communities. These communities, which are located both in correctional facilities and outside prisons and jails, provide drug-using criminals with support, understanding, and affection from people who have had similar life experiences. They find a *community* with which they can identify and people toward whom they can express their best human emotions rather than their worst (Yablonsky 1989; see also Johnson 1988). Such programs are based on social learning theory. Treatment does not eliminate the negative behavior patterns and attitudinal orientations. Instead, it offers appropriate alternative approaches to resocializing individuals—teaching them behaviors and orientations that will promote prosocial adjustment, and offering a totally new lifestyle. This process includes reinforcers to continue acceptable behavior and punishers to extinguish the unacceptable. Program participants appear to have lower-than-typical recidivism (Lipton 1994; see also Andrews, Zinger, Hoge, Bonta, Gendreau, and Cullen 1990).

SOCIAL CONTROL THEORIES

Most criminologists acknowledge the roles played by informal control mechanisms, such as family members and neighbors, and formal control mechanisms, such as schools, police, and the courts. The weaker the former, the greater the reliance on the latter (Black, 1976). The strength of the formal control apparatus, especially the criminal justice system, is rarely sufficient to do more than react to crime, let alone prevent it. Social control theorists assume that, if left to their own devices, all people would violate norms. For them the key question is, Why don't more people commit crimes? This question has several answers.

Early Control Theories

In the 1950s and early 1960s, four criminologists examined the social control factors associated with delinquency. In looking to the individual offender for answers, they laid the groundwork for social control theories.

Personal Control Albert Reiss (1951) observed that youthful probation revocations are more likely when juveniles receive poor psychiatric evaluations. He attributed both poor psychiatric conditions and probation revocations to failures in **personal control.** Low-control youths meet their personal needs in a manner that conflicts with community rules. However, Reiss found little empirical support for this contention.

A Stake in Conformity Perhaps the problem is a weak **stake in conformity.** Jackson Toby (1957) believed that, although every youth is tempted to break the law, some—particularly those doing well in school—risk a great deal by giving in to temptation. Being caught means possible punishment and threatens the future career being contemplated. Poor school performers risk only punishment: Their futures are less bright, so their stake in conformity is lower. Toby speculated that there is more delinquency in urban areas than in suburban areas because low-stake urban youths are exposed to similarly disposed peers; in contrast, suburban low-stake youths, with fewer similarly disposed peers, are "merely unhappy" and not necessarily delinquent.

The Family and Social Control Reiss and Toby barely acknowledged the family as a source of social control. In contrast, F. Ivan Nye (1958) forged the links between family, social controls, and youthful misbehavior. According to Nye social control has four manifestations: (1) direct controls, such as family-level punishments and restrictions; (2) indirect controls, such as affectional identification with one's parents and noncriminals generally; (3) internal controls derived from one's conscience; and (4) the availability of the means necessary to gratify personal needs. Nye found impressive support for his theory: Misbehavior was greatest among those youths with poor family relationships and weak social controls. However, as critics, principally Toby (1959), have pointed out, Nye failed to study serious delinquency. Moreover, actively delinquent youths may have been more willing than others to report poor family relationships, thus creating a bias that resulted in high levels of support for Nye's theory.

Containment Theory Walter Reckless (1961) took the search for social controls to a new level with **containment theory.** He saw forces pulling people away from conventional society or pushing them toward misbehavior, including these:

- **Social pressures,** such as poor living conditions, minority-group status, poor lifestyle opportunities, and family conflicts
- **Social pulls** that keep the individual away from acceptable behavior, such as criminal and delinquent subcultures or bad companions
- **Biological** or **psychological pushes,** such as inner tensions, hostility, and aggressiveness

- **Rebellion against authority** that originates within the individual and leads to unacceptable norms of living

Given these forces, only outer and inner containment stands between any individual and a life of crime (Reckless 1961). Reckless observed that these restraining forces are sufficient to control most behavior. **Outer containment** comes from the family and other support groups in society; it involves, among other things, a consistent moral front, reasonable norms and expectations, effective supervision and discipline, and group cohesiveness. **Inner containment,** a psychological concept not unlike Reiss's personal controls, involves ego strength, the superego, a sense of responsibility, and goal orientation.

Social Bond Theory

Beginning in the late 1960s, the work of Travis Hirschi came to define social control theory. According to Hirschi (1972:83), "The bond of affection for conventional persons is a major deterrent to crime." The **social bond** is the sum total of the forces in a person's social and physical environment that connects him or her to society and its moral constraints. For example, a lack of attachment to others frees an individual from moral constraints, a concept that has direct ties to Durkheim's anomie but that is expressed in individual terms rather than at the societal level. Such people are free to deviate, to act without "moral" restraint.

According to Hirschi's social control theory, weak bonds do not predict deviance, but simply make it possible or probable. The question becomes, How is control, or a lack of it, to be measured or differentiated between persons in similar circumstances?

The Social Bond's Key Elements Hirschi described the social bond as curbing the natural human propensity for misbehavior. Youths bonded to various social institutions, including family and school, are less inclined to commit delinquent acts. Hirschi's bond consists of four elements, all of which are tied to conventional norms, rules, activities, and significant others:

1. **Attachment** is affection for and sensitivity to social group members. Without attachment there is no internalization of norms and values. This element is similar to the control mechanisms described by Nye and Reiss. The child who exhibits no affective, or emotional, bonds to others, particularly sensitivity to their feelings, may feel, in Hirschi's (1969:18) words, "free to deviate." Researchers measure attachment by the level of parental supervision or discipline, the quality of child–parent communications, or attitudes toward school and school authority.

2. **Commitment** refers to investment in conventional norms and rules; this concept recasts Toby's stake in conformity. Attachment and commitment reflect personal attitudes or orientations. Researchers measure commitment by two methods. First, children's engagement in adult activities, including smoking, drinking, and sex, indicates a lack of commitment. Second, educational or occupational aspirations and expectations—two strain concepts— also find their way into social control tests as measures of commitment to conventionality.

3. **Involvement** is behavioral and measures the level of conventional activity. Often presented as a modern version of the age-old dictum "idle hands are the devil's workshop," involvement represents an opportunity element (Curran and Renzetti 1994:200).

4. **Belief** contrasts with Sykes and Matza's neutralization techniques. For Sykes and Matza conventional moral beliefs are paramount, and to engage in misbehavior, youths must neutralize their moral force. According to Hirschi belief in the correctness of norms is variable; he questioned whether everyone feels bound to adhere to the dominant moral beliefs. He hypothesized that delinquency is more likely when a youth attaches less significance to conventional moral beliefs.

Delbert Elliott and his associates (1985) concluded that the strength of delinquent peer bonding is related to the actor's bonds to conventional groups. We would expect delinquent behavior when familial bonds are overcome by bonds to the peer group. The strength of the bond can be observed: If any of the social bond elements are weak, even if other strong ones are present, there is a heightened probability of misconduct. As Hirschi (1969:16) expressed it, "Delinquent acts result when an individual's bond to society is weak or broken." Figure 7.3 summarizes the social bond and its ties to conformity and misbehavior.

Parents, Peers, and Social Control Social control theory's treatment of parental and peer ties has been questioned since its inception. Early social control tests placed great emphasis on parental attachment and yielded considerable empirical support (Hepburn 1976; Hindelang 1981; Johnson 1979; Krohn and Massey 1980; Thomas and Hyman 1978; Wiatrowski, Griswold, and Roberts 1981). Social bond theory excludes two aspects of parental control. First, Hirschi dismissed direct parental controls, ranging from parental specification of rules and constraints to physical punishments, as inconsequential. The important question was "whether the parent is psychologically present when the temptation to commit a crime occurs" (Hirschi 1969:88). Other researchers have suggested that direct parental control plays a role in reducing proneness to delinquency, either in concert with strong parental bonding (Patterson 1982) or independently (Rankin and Wells 1990; Williams, Clinton, Winfree, and Clark 1992).

Second, social bonding theory ignores the effects of parental behavior in modeling youthful misconduct (Foshee and Bauman 1992). In Hirschi's (1969:73) words, "We honor those we admire not by imitation but by adherence to conventional standards." At least in the case of adolescent cigarette smoking, children honor those they admire by imitation: Strongly attached children of nonsmokers view nonsmoking as conventional and imitate their parents; strongly attached children of smokers view smoking as conventional and imitate their parents (Foshee and Bauman 1992; see also Jensen and Brownfield 1983).

In addition, social bond theory poorly describes links to peers. Attachment to peers does not necessarily guarantee conventional behavior unless the peers themselves are conventional. Attachment to deviant peers may, in fact, weaken the social bond to conventional society: Youths attached to delinquent friends are themselves more likely to be delinquent (Conger 1976; Elliott, Huizinga, and Ageton 1985). The inclusion of attachment to delinquent peers in any test of social bond theory

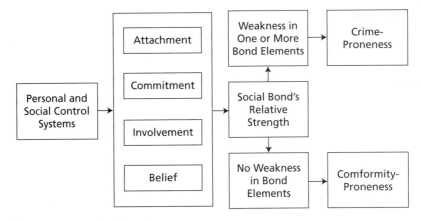

FIGURE 7.3 Social Control Theory: Hirschi's Social Bond

increases the model's overall predictive power; however, this inclusion makes the test virtually indistinguishable from one of differential association theory.

Assessing Social Control Theories

Social control theory has many variants. In this assessment we elected to include the most popular form, social bonding, and the most recent form, self-control theory. Since 1969 tests of control theory have largely been tests of Hirschi's social bond theory although a few studies have combined different control theories. For example, Anastasios Marcos and Stephen Bahr (1988) combined belief in conventional values and attachment to parents, religion, and school with Reckless's inner containment. The inclusion of inner containment resulted in a significant improvement in the ability to predict adolescent illicit drug use, but final results remained modest at best. Other criminologists, recognizing the natural links between control and strain theory, and their mutual impact on school performance, have incorporated elements of both in their tests (cf. Cernkovich and Giordano 1992; Elliott and Huizinga 1984; Elliott, Huizinga, and Ageton 1985; Rodriguez and Weisburd 1991). We will return to theory integration in Chapter 10.

Since the publication of Hirschi's *Causes of Delinquency* in 1969, researchers and theorists have expressed several general concerns about the social bond:

- *Conventional versus unconventional involvement.* Involvement has proved problematic since Hirschi's first test. Involvement in conventional activities, he reported, was directly related to delinquency: the greater the involvement in dating, reading, working, watching television, and playing games, the higher the reported frequency of delinquency. Perhaps the theory "overestimated the significance of involvement in conventional activities" (Hirschi, 1969:230-31). However, comparing youths involved in conventional activities (e.g., supervised social events and noncompetitive sports) with those involved in nonconventional and unsupervised peer-oriented activities revealed that the former group is less delinquent than the latter (Agnew and Peterson 1989).

- *Natural aggression assumption.* That humans possess innately aggressive or violent tendencies is a much debated assumption in the social and behavioral sciences (Vold and Bernard 1986:247).

- *Trivial versus real delinquency.* Most tests of social control theory employ "relatively trivial offenses committed by essentially nondelinquent youths" (Vold and Bernard 1986:245), a fact attested to by Hirschi (1969:41): "Delinquents are so obviously underrepresented among those completing the questionnaires that the results need not be taken seriously." In tests involving *both* minor delinquency (e.g., alcohol and marijuana use) and serious delinquency (e.g., property and violent offenses), social control theory did a far better job of explaining the former than the latter (Krohn and Massey 1980; Rosenbaum 1987; Rosenbaum and Lasley 1990).

- *Social control versus differential association.* Early empirical studies comparing the relative merits of differential association and social control tended to support the latter over the former. However, Ross Matsueda's (1982) reanalysis of Hirschi's data, along with reconceptualizations of key differential association elements, yielded the opposite results. Gerben Bruinsma (1992), employing a sample of Dutch youths, reported findings very similar to Matsueda's.

The Search for Social Bonds Criticisms aside, social bonding was one of the most influential criminological theories of the last third of the twentieth century. Studies that tested its main hypotheses have yielded a number of interesting, if somewhat troubling, results. First, although the empirical findings have been described as "moderate" or "good" (Minor 1977; Wiatrowski, Griswold, and Roberts 1981), most early studies employed cross-sectional data. Longitudinal research tends to reveal less support for social bonding. Parental attachment, commitment, and involvement are largely unrelated to future delinquency (Agnew 1991).

Second, social bonding is one of the few theories that addresses the differences in male and female misbehavior. For example, a breakdown in the social bond is a better predictor of drug use by females than males (Dull 1983). The same general trend holds for female delinquency when compared to the same behaviors for males (Hindelang 1973; Jensen and Eve 1976). Even more importantly, control theory appears to provide special insights into why females have lower delinquency rates than males (Box 1981). According to Jill Rosenbaum (1987:129) there are no real differences in the natural motivations to commit misbehavior among males and females; rather, males enjoy more freedom to engage in "occasional delinquency without jeopardizing their relationships with others or their chances of success." For a female to violate rules—and laws—her bonds must be weaker than a male's for the same level of offending to occur. The bonds may also function differently for males and females. Leanne Alarid and her associates (2000), in a study of incarcerated male and female felons, reported that parental attachments were a better predictor of violent offending among women than men (i.e., the higher the attachment, the lower the participation in violent offending).

Third, Hirschi (1969:79) stated that, "the official reaction hypothesis aside, there is no reason to believe that the causes of crime among blacks are different [from] those among whites." However, the research contradicts Hirschi's contention. Researchers report that the theory predicts better the self-reported delinquency of whites over African Americans, upper-class youths over those in the lower classes, and rural residents over urban dwellers (cf. Gardner and Shoemaker 1989; Rosenbaum 1987; Rosenbaum and Lasley 1990). The common explanation is that African Americans, urban dwellers, and lower-class youths all have lower expectations to conform; conformity is less instilled in them than in Caucasian, rural residents, and upper-class youths. These statements resemble those made earlier for anomie and opportunity theory. Collectively, these findings further cloud the issue: Is social control theory free of race and class biases, or does the theory work better to explain differential bonding present in some groups and not in others?

Social Control, Public Policy, and Criminal Justice Practices

According to Hirschi's social control theory, delinquent acts result when an individual's bond to society is weakened or broken. Attachment for conventional persons is, from this perspective, a major deterrent to crime, whereas lack of attachment frees others from moral constraints. In areas of poverty in urban America, increasing numbers of children live with neither a mother nor a father, creating what Jane Gross (1992) called America's "new orphans." Parents are institutionalized—in prisons, jails, or residential drug programs—or living marginal existences under the influence of heroin or other drugs. When they are present in the home, parents may be unwilling or ill-equipped to care for their offspring. These children are farmed out to relatives, friends, foster care, or institutions, and experience little stability and few, if any, lasting emotional ties.

A 1994 report prepared for the Carnegie Foundation (Chira 1994; McMahon [Carnegie Taskforce] 1994) painted a bleak portrait of the living conditions of millions of children, the offspring of parents overwhelmed by adolescent pregnancy and poverty. Disintegrating families characterized by child abuse and neglect are threatening the physical and emotional development of millions of infants. These problems are beyond the scope of the criminal justice system.

One policy response being considered is a modern version of the traditional orphanage. However, federal and state laws typically seek to keep children in the family, which for hundreds of thousands, and perhaps millions, is not a viable option. Funding institutional care, group homes, and residential treatment centers for such large numbers of children would prove quite expensive, at least in the short term; long-term, such efforts might benefit society's crime control efforts. In any event, given their lack of a stake in society, such children are freer to deviate, to act without "moral" constraint. The theory suggests that policy makers need to focus on strengthening social bonds to conventional groups, institutions, and activities. Indeed, this strong ideological appeal may help explain the longevity of social bond theory more than the empirical evidence marshaled in its support (Greenberg 1999).

Law Enforcement Practices Control-based explanations also define prosocial elements of police work. For example, the Police Athletic League (PAL) allows off-duty officers to interact with youths, especially troubled adolescents, so that the police and youths have positive contacts with each other. PAL emphasizes positive, supportive interactions rather than negative, confrontational ones. This perspective is rooted in social control theory, especially social bonding. Other programs involving uniformed police officers, including Drug Abuse Resistance Education (DARE) and Gang Resistance Education and Training (G.RE.A.T.), provide similar attachments to police and promote participation in conventional activities and development of prosocial beliefs. In the case of both DARE and G.R.E.A.T., youths are exposed to "hard lessons" of unconventional life from empathetic police officers. Consequently one could argue that such programs are intended to reinforce ideas associated with rational choice, which is a key component in self-control and several other theories.

Judicial Practices The family is at the center of most control theories. In some it was blamed; in others it was viewed as the key to preventing delinquency. Since their inception in 1899, juvenile courts have played an interesting role in this debate, with the preservation of the family, perhaps at any cost, a nearly universal mandate (Mays and Winfree 2002). Children are removed from the family only when the court believes that it serves the child's best interests (Krisberg and Austin 1993). What may be needed is a forced separation, and perhaps even an emancipation of the child. In short, the juvenile courts, by following a policy of family preservation, may be creating the very condition they are called on to prevent.

SELF-CONTROL THEORY

In the late twentieth century Michael Gottfredson, working with Hirschi, took on the criminal justice and criminological establishment by questioning the value of the career criminal concept. In so doing, they challenged many contemporary crime control policies and intervention strategies, including the policy of selective incapacitation and "three-strikes-and-you're-out" legislation. Hirschi and Gottfredson also challenged much of the developmental and life-course criminology discussed in Chapter 5, and questioned the ideas advanced by Blumstein, Farrington and Cohen about the role played by frequency of offending in criminological research (cf. Blumstein and Cohen 1987; Blumstein, Cohen, and Farrington 1988; Gottfredson and Hirschi 1986; Hirschi and Gottfredson 1986; see also Cohen and Vila 1995). In place of traditional social organizational and social process theories, Gottfredson and Hirschi (1990) proposed a "general theory of crime," one that they claimed comported well with the observed stability of crime propensity and versatility. This perspective has come to be called both **self-control theory** and **event-propensity theory** (Gottfredson and Hirschi 1989; Grasmick et al. 1993).

Hearkening back to classical rational theories, Gottfredson and Hirschi explained that self-interest motivates human behavior and further reflects a universal desire to secure pleasure and avoid pain. Sounding like conventional control theorists, they described criminality's origins in child rearing. These early beginnings, Gottfredson and Hirschi (1989:61) claimed, "suggest that criminality is more or less naturally present, that it requires socialization for its control."

For Gottfredson and Hirschi, all crime and what they described as analogous acts (e.g., drinking, smoking, drug use, illicit sex, and even accidents) collectively and individually offer short-term pleasures (e.g., money, altered states of consciousness, thrills, and excitement) for very little effort. Unrestrained individuals, or those with little commitment to conventionality and equally low concern for the long-term consequences of their behavior, are thus attracted to crime. They exhibit what Gottfredson and Hirschi have called low self-control.

IN THEIR OWN WORDS: Process Theories of Crime and Delinquency

The process theorists each had unique ways of viewing the attainment of criminal status. An important difference was that one group—the learning theorists—observed that humans must be exposed to intense and personal socialization forces before becoming criminal. Conversely the control theorists placed great stock in the role played by social institutions in maintaining control over otherwise hedonistic and mischievous humans. The following quotations by the key control theorists help to clarify these differences.

- *Sutherland on crime and opportunity:* "The tendencies and inhibitions at the moment of the criminal behavior are, to be sure, largely a product of the earlier history of the person, but the expression of these tendencies and inhibitions is a reaction to the immediate situation as defined by that person. The situation operates in many ways, of which perhaps the least important is the provision of an opportunity for a criminal act" (p. 327).
- *Burgess and Akers on criminal behavior:* "We know from the Law of Differential Reinforcement that that operant which produces the most reinforcement will become dominant if it results in reinforcement. Thus, if lawful behavior did not result in reinforcement, the strength

of the behavior would be weakened, and a state of deprivation would result, which would, in turn, increase the probability that other behaviors would be emitted which are reinforced, and such behavior would be strengthened" (p. 143).

- *Hirschi on control theory:* "Control theories assume that delinquent acts result when an individual's bond to society is weak or broken. Since these theories embrace two highly complex concepts, the *bond* of the individual to *society,* it is not surprising that they have at one time or another formed the basis of explanations of most forms of aberrant or unusual behavior" (p. 16; emphasis in original).
- *Hirschi and Gottfredson on the role of parents:* "First, the parents may not care for the child . . . ; second, the parents, even if they care, may not have the time or energy to monitor the child's behavior; third, the parents, even if they care and monitor, may not see anything wrong with the child's behavior; finally, even if everything else is in place, the parents may not have the inclination or the means to punish the child" (p. 98).

Sources: Burgess and Akers (1966); Gottfredson and Hirschi (1990); Hirschi (1969); Sutherland (1947).

Defining Self-Control

Self-control theory's key causal elements are straightforward: Parental management and inadequate child-rearing practices are central because self-control is established as early as age 8. Adequate parental management includes (1) the monitoring and recognition of deviant behavior in a child, (2) appropriate punishment in response to inappropriate behavior ("let the punishment fit the crime"), and (3) emotional investment in the child (Gottfredson and Hirschi 1990; see also Gibbs, Giever, and Martin 1998; Hay 2001a). They concluded that inadequate parental management results in low self-control, which influences an individual's choices when faced with an opportunity for immediate gain through little investment. In the end low-self-control persons exhibit a wide variety of behaviors, including crime, because such activities hold the promise of immediate pleasure for minimal effort.

Low-self-control individuals—the unrestrained—share six common characteristics:

1. *A need for immediate gratification.* They seek short-term, immediate rewards (pleasures); the concept of deferred gratification, whereby pleasures and rewards are postponed to a more appropriate time or even renounced entirely, is completely foreign to them.

2. *Simplicity.* They avoid complicated tasks and decisions, preferring to seek easy answers and easy work.

3. *Physicality.* They prefer to keep physically active.

4. *A need for risk taking.* They are supreme risk takers. They tend to be impetuous and impulsive; they enjoy taking their lives in their own hands; and they seek excitement and danger over sameness and safeness.

5. *Self-centeredness.* They tend to emphasize personal needs, wants, and desires while ignoring those of others, including significant others such as relatives and friends.

6. *Anger.* They have a low frustration tolerance and exhibit a tendency to resort to aggressive coping strategies when faced with frustrating situations or events.

Figure 7.4 summarizes Gottfredson and Hirschi's self-control theory.

Assessing Self-Control Theory

Self-control theory, with its opposition to traditional social processes, has drawn much scrutiny since its introduction. As T. David Evans and his associates (1997:495) observed, "The general theory is a controversial perspective that many criminologists may, for ideological reasons, prefer to be proven false." Opponents and supporters generally focus on one or more of the following issues:

- *The generalness of self-control.* As articulated by Gottfredson and Hirschi, self-control theory is a general theory that explains all criminal behavior. But critics have pointed out that much crime does not fit the theory. Gottfredson and Hirschi, claim some critics, carefully tailored their crime facts to fit their theory. For example, Ken Polk (1991) observed that there is no "typical" homicide, and whatever exists is far from the two forms described by Gottfredson and Hirschi (i.e., homicides as the result of a heated argument and pursuant to a burglary). Similarly criticisms abound of Gottfredson and Hirschi's claim that white-collar crime is uncommon and that its participants conform to the same age and race distributions of other criminals. White-collar and corporate crimes simply do not work well within a self-control model (Ermann and Lundman 1991; Polk 1991; Reed and Yeager 1996; Steffensmeier 1989; see also Hirschi and Gottfredson 1989). Organizational offending must take into account factors not acknowledged by Gottfredson and Hirschi, including the actions of political, economic, and bureaucratic systems (Reed and Yeager 1996:377).

- *Self-control versus criminal personality.* Larry Siegel (1992:237) noted that "saying someone 'lacks self-control' implies that they suffer from a personality defect that makes them impulsive and rash." How does this characterization

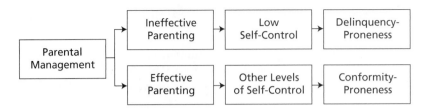

FIGURE 7.4 Gottfredson and Hirschi's Self-Control Theory

differ from the "criminal personality," a generalized description that is of little use to psychological clinicians or criminal justice practitioners?

- *Self-control is a tautology.* Akers (1994:122-23) saw self-control theory as a tautology. He observed that Gottfredson and Hirschi used terms like "low self-control" and "high self-control" when they referred to the "differential propensity to commit or refrain from crime." According to Akers, reduced to its basic causal elements, the theory posits that low self-control is caused by low self-control. The lack of separate definitions for low self-control, crime propensity, and crime measures makes the theory untestable.

- *Multidimensionality versus unidimensionality of self-control.* Virtually since its inception, criminologists have debated self-control theory's answers to several important measurement questions. Is self-control a single dimension, as suggested by Gottfredson and Hirschi, or are the various characteristics of low self-control equally important? Early evidence supported the unidimensionality position (Arneklev, Grasmick, and Bursik 1999; Grasmick, Tittle, Bursik, and Arneklev 1993); however, Peter Wood and his associates (1993) suggested that disaggregating self-control elements provides more insights into self-reported criminal conduct (see also Arneklev, Grasmick, and Bursik 1999; Longshore, Stein, and Turner 1998; Longshore, Turner, and Stein 1996). This debate is far from resolved, as even those who previously viewed self-control as a single dimension (Piquero and Rosay 1998) have adopted the opposite perspective (Piquero, MacIntosh, and Hickman 2000). This debate must move beyond semantics if criminologists hope to measure self-control and its consequences.

- *Immutability of self-control measures.* The claim that self-control levels, established early in one's youth, do not change—the immutability-of-self-control hypothesis—is one of the theory's more controversial elements. Preliminary analyses of self-control measures over time support the stability position, although the time frames employed are relatively short (Arneklev, Cochran, and Gainey 1998; Arneklev, Grasmick, and Bursik 1999).

The Search for Self-Control   Tests of self-control theory fit into several categories. First are those that address the theory's ability to yield insights into a variety of analogous behaviors. For example, Dana Lynskey and associates (2000) found an inverse relationship between self-control, as measured by an index of impulsivity, risk-seeking behavior and physicality, and self-reported youth gang involvement among a sample of eighth-grade students. The strongest single predictor of self-control was the level of parental monitoring: the greater the monitoring, the higher the self-control. Christine Sellers (1999) explored self-control in a study of intimate violence in a sample of college students; she reported significant ties between courtship aggression and low self-control, opportunity, and perception of immediate gratification. Other topics addressed in self-control tests include cheating by college students (Cochran, Wood, Sellers, Wilkerson, and Chamlin 1998; Gibbs and Giever 1995), youthful drug use (Winfree and Bernat 1998; Wood, Cochran, and Pfefferbaum 1995), drunk driving (Keane, Maxim, and Teevan 1993), and accidents (Tremblay, Boulerie, Arsenault, and Junger 1995). In general, tests of analogous behavior and self-control provide support for self-control theory (Pratt and Cullen 2000; but see also Britt 2000; Paternoster and Brame 1998, 2000).

A second type of test has provided indirect, inferential insights into self-control. Gottfredson and Hirschi predicted that low-self-control people will have higher rates of delinquency, regardless of any other characteristic. Terence P. Thornberry and his associates (1993), in a study of the role of youth gangs in facilitating delinquency, reported that gang members do not appear to be recruited based on their high propensity for delinquency. Gottfredson and Hirschi's theory recognizes that gang membership might provide the opportunity for any underlying delinquency propensity to be manifested more often and so accounts for the higher delinquency rates of active gang members. However, they have difficulty coming to grips with the fact that these gang members are *not* more delinquent than nongang members before or after they are active in the gang (Thornberry, Krohn, Lizotte, and Chard-Weischem 1993). Similarly David Evans and his associates (1997) reported higher misbehavior by low-self-control individuals, irrespective of other community or individual characteristics. The quality of their lives and their life outcomes were also negatively impacted, including reduced church involvement, lower educational and occupational attainment, and diminished interpersonal communications with friends and relatives.

International and comparative tests represent a third form. Teresa LaGrange and Robert Silverman (1999) supported self-control in a Canadian study of self-reported delinquency; they also reported variations by gender, a finding replicated in the United States (Longshore, Turner, and Stein 1996; Lynskey et al. 2000). That is, females may have lesser inclination and fewer opportunities, findings consistent with the theory. Bradley Wright and his associates (1999) explored the effects of social bonds and self-control on a sample of Dunedin, New Zealand, residents, following them from birth to age 21. Low self-control in childhood predicted disrupted social bonds and delinquency in adolescence; however, social bonds apparently mitigated (i.e., caused a temporary reduction in) these effects on adult criminality. In an ambitious cross-national test, Alexander Vazsonyi and his associates (2001) examined levels of self-control and deviance for mid- and late adolescents in Hungary, the Netherlands, Switzerland, and the United States. Their findings were consistent with the theory, supporting the culture-free nature of self-control concepts. However, the self-control measure revealed more about minor offending than serious delinquency.

During the 1990s dozens of studies explored the utility of self-control theory. Travis Pratt and Frances Cullen (2000) conducted a meta-analysis of 21 empirical studies of self-control theory, all published between 1993 and 1999. They reported that low self-control was an important predictor of crime and analogous behavior, irrespective of the sample employed. However, the constructs fare poorly in longitudinal research, and, when self-control theory is compared with social learning theory, the latter receives more empirical support than the former.

COMMENTS AND CRITICISMS:
Learning Theories as Social Deviance Theories

Each perspective—social learning and social control—makes rather different assumptions about human nature and social behavior. These assumptions have been at the heart of an ongoing discourse about each perspective, especially between Hirschi and Akers. Akers has questioned the validity and viability of self-control theory. Perhaps, he suggested, self-control is merely another element of the social bond. Akers also addressed the critics, but especially Ruth Kornhauser, who questioned the assumption upon which both differential association and social learning theories rest: "Man has no nature, socialization is perfectly successful, and cultural variability is unlimited"—a critique also advanced by Hirschi. Given this assump-

tion, both theories are limited to explaining only criminal or subcultural deviance and cannot explain individual offending. It is Akers' position that this critique is based on a misinterpretation of Sutherland and a nearly complete misreading of his own work. Neither Sutherland nor he, Akers claimed, made the "cultural deviance assumptions." Hirschi, in responding to these observations, remained firm in his original position. The title of his reply speaks volumes: "Theory without ideas: Reply to Akers." Essentially Hirschi dismissed Akers' challenge of the cultural deviance critique.

Sources: Akers (2000); Hirschi (1969, 1996); Kornhauser (1978:34); see also Costello (1997); Matsueda (1997).

Self-Control, Public Policy, and Criminal Justice Practices

Adding parental management, opportunity, and rational choice to the social control debate creates a new set of policy implications. The rational choice component of self-control theory portends many of the same policy implications found in rational choice theory (see Chapter 2). That is, rational choice supporters see merit in educating the public as to the consequences of certain acts and, when that fails, providing for the swift and certain imposition of those punishments on transgressors. For example, state legislatures are experimenting with policies that reduce the economic supports associated with large "dependent" families, and federal welfare reform may limit the total length of time recipients can receive funds under the Aid to Dependent Families program. Parents are being encouraged to take responsibility for their acts and their creations. As Gottfredson and Hirschi have pointed out, the processes of education and reinforcement begin with a solid foundation of parental management.

Steven Messner and Richard Rosenfeld (1994) suggested that parenting as a social role needs to be viewed as an end unto itself and as a meaningful alternative to material acquisitiveness. In this context we could reasonably state that self-control theory supports the acquisition of better parenting skills. Pundits are quick to note that no license is required to have children, and children do not come with instructions. Perhaps public and private entities could fill this void, placing greater value on, encouragement of, and rewards for quality parenting. The crucial question becomes, Whose standards are applied? That is, who decides what skills and techniques are good or bad, positive or negative, constructive or destructive? In short, the enhancement of general parental management sounds intuitively appealing, but

Table 7.1 Social Process Theories of Crime

Theory	Major Figures	Central Assumptions	Causal Arguments (Key Terms)	Strengths	Weaknesses
Differential association	Sutherland	Like all behavior, criminal behavior is learned, and by the same mechanisms.	Criminality is due to an excess of definitions favorable to law violations over definitions unfavorable to law violations (*principle of differential association*); *differential associations* vary by *frequency, duration, priority,* and *intensity.*	Is a commonsense answer to crime; provides propositional statements for the operation of differential associations and conceptual base for other criminological theories; is suggestive of what needs to be done to change the behavior of offenders; is not class-bound.	As stated by Sutherland, is not testable; may not prove useful for explaining certain types of crime (e.g., violent crimes or "irrational" crimes); does not include individual motives; may be tautological.
Social learning	Akers	Criminal behavior is learned through a process of operant conditioning in which some behavior is reinforced and other behavior is extinguished.	The probability that a person will commit crime is increased by the presence of normative statements, definitions, and verbalizations that, by the process of *differential reinforcements,* have acquired *discriminative value.*	Adds missing piece to differential association by including operant conditioning; has many applications, especially to situations intended to alter undesirable behavior; tests of theory tend to support social learning's causal process.	May be bad sociology and too psychological, or bad psychology and too sociological; fails to explain how some behavior is rewarded and others punished; may be tautological; lacks tests of serious misconduct.
General social control	Reiss, Toby, Nye	People, if left to their own devices, would engage in hedonistic, self-serving, and often law-violating behavior; culture provides the glue that holds society together	*Reiss's control theory: Personal control* problems create poor psychiatric conditions; low-control persons may meet personal needs in ways that conflict with community's rules. *Toby's stake in conformity:* Some youths have a lower *stake in conformity* than others as their futures are not as bright; they risk only punishment. *Nye's control theory:* The family's role in the establishment of *direct controls* (e.g., family-level punishments) and *indirect controls* (e.g., family affection) must be internalized as part of the conscience.	Provides logical answers to the crime problem for those persons who hold the basic assumption that people are prone to evil; appeals to those who hold the position that at the center of the crime problem is a dysfunctional family, given the emphasis on the family's contribution (see Nye and Reckless, next); the stake-in-conformity concept makes sense to those who have never seriously considered committing a crime; most control theories have policy implications: Increase social controls and ties to both family and community, and crime will decline; answers some questions about personal goals.	Has very little empirical support.

Table 7.1 Social Process Theories of Crime *(continued)*

Theory	Major Figures	Central Assumptions	Causal Arguments (Key Terms)	Strengths	Weaknesses
Containment	Reckless	See General social control.	Biological and social forces push and pull youths toward crime; only *outer containments* (e.g., the family, other support groups) and *inner containments* (e.g., a sense of responsibility, a conscience) keep them from crime.	See General social control; is appealing to supporters of psychological factors because the theory includes the influences inner containments.	See General social control.
Social bonding	Hirschi	See General social control.	The *social bond* curbs the natural propensity for misbehavior; it consists of *attachment, commitment, involvement,* and *belief;* when any element of the bond is weakened, misbehavior ensues.	See General social control; is one of the most frequently tested social process theories; is one of the few "traditional" criminological theories to explore differences between male and female delinquency rates, as well as differences in observed rates for various ethnic and racial groups.	Ignores parents as models, and barely addresses peers; involvement in conventionality may not insulate youths against the propensity to misbehave; "natural aggression" may be overstated and oversimplified; tests often examine trivial delinquency; when tested against other theories, receives less empirical support.
Self-control	Gottfredson, Hirschi	All human behavior is motivated by self-interest and reflects the universal desire to secure pleasure and avoid pain; those unrestrained by society's norms create its problems.	The unrestrained, or those with certain characteristics (e.g., a search for immediate gratification, simplicity in all tasks and decisions, and anger-proneness), are likely to engage in acts—including crimes—that offer short-term pleasures for little effort; the fact that they have little commitment to conventionality and little concern for long-term consequences of their acts makes crime all the more attractive; the origin of *low self-control* is found in poor *parental management* (e.g., inadequate monitoring or poor emotional ties to their children).	Represents a welcome addition to criminological thinking for persons seeking a new form of classification (i.e., a restatement of free-will concepts in the language of social psychology); also continues the popular "family values" theme by placing emphasis on parental management.	Are doubts the theory's generalness (i.e., its ability to explain all crime); leaves unanswered any critical differences between person with low self-control and those with a criminal personality; reflects major theoretical inconsistencies between Hirschi's social bond theory and self-control theory; may be a tautology as currently constructed (i.e., the terms *low self-control* and *high self-control* may be labels for the differential propensity to commit or refrain from crime); attempts to test theory have been mixed.

its implementation may be very difficult. (See Table 7.1 for an overview of social process theories of crime.)

SUMMARY

This chapter reviewed a wide range of social process theorists. Learning theorists emphasized the mechanisms and processes by which otherwise normative people become delinquent and criminal. How, they asked, are people socialized into law-violating behavior? Control theorists turned the crime causation question around: Why isn't everyone a criminal?

Each perspective's assumptions are central to the orienting questions. For example, answers to the first question review the processes by which definitions favorable to law violations are learned, as well as the role of interpersonal relationships. Sutherland's differential association theory provided a fertile base for other learning theories, including Akers' social learning theory, which integrated differential association propositions and operant conditioning. Although the evidence has tended to support differential association and social learning, criticisms of causal sequencing, conceptual fuzziness, and tautologies plague both theories. Nonetheless, learning theories have contributed much to criminal justice policies and practices.

Initial answers to the second question range from the presence of strong internal controls to strong familial support. Social bonding, the most popular social control theory, has been much studied; empirical support for its claims ranges from low to moderate, depending on whether the delinquency in question is minor (moderate support) or major (low support). Self-control theory, which some critics call a restatement of social bonding shrouded in rational choice theory (cf. Akers 1994; Curran and Renzetti 1994; Siegel 1992), has been alternately pilloried and praised for refocusing attention on parental management. Much remains unknown about this theory: its conceptual integrity and empirical verifiability, and its reliability and validity. As Akers (1991:201) has written, the theory cannot be discounted, due largely to the "power, scope and persuasiveness" of Gottfredson and Hirschi's arguments.

What this chapter reveals more than anything else is the following: An original idea, brilliant in its simplicity and design but vaguely stated and incompletely operationalized, can give rise to many different views of the same phenomenon. There seems to be little doubt that the lack of social control and social learning are *somehow* responsible for crime. But precisely how they function and whether they work in concert or at odds with one another remain to be seen.

KEY TERMS

attachment	containment theory	differential associations
belief	differential anticipation theory	differential association/differential reinforcement theory
biological pushes		
commitment	differential association theory	differential expectations

differential identification

differential reinforcement theory

discriminative stimuli

duration

event-propensity theory

frequency

imitation

inner containment

instrumental conditioning

intensity

involvement

meta-analysis

modeling

motivating definitions

operant behavior

outer containment

personal control

principle of differential association

principle of differential reinforcement

priority

psychological pushes

punishments/punishers

rebellion against authority

reinforcements/ reinforcers

respondent behavior

self-control theory

social bond

social pressures

social pulls

stake in conformity

CRITICAL REVIEW QUESTIONS

1. List and discuss the propositions inherent in differential association theory. How is this theory related to the Chicago School's cultural transmission theory?

2. How did Glaser alter differential association theory to produce differential identification/differential anticipation theory?

3. How does Jeffery's theory of differential reinforcement differ from Burgess and Akers' differential association/differential reinforcement theory?

4. According to social learning, when is someone most likely to commit a crime?

5. What are the key processes associated with instrumental conditioning?

6. Compare and contrast tests of the theories of differential association and social learning.

7. Describe how the various social control theorists might answer this

question: Why don't more people commit crimes?

8. With respect to control theory, how do internal and external restraints differ?

9. How does self-control theory differ from bonding theory?

10. Defend or attack the following statement: Many of the social control theories seem quite similar.

11. What are the basic elements of the social bond?

12. How does social bonding theory differ from social learning theory?

13. How does self-control theory differ from both social bonding and social learning theory?

14. Describe how each theory reviewed in this chapter conforms with the idea of social process theories. In what ways do one or more diverge from this central theme?

8

Labeling and
Conflict Theories

LEARNING OBJECTIVES

- Understand the role of power in defining crime and criminals, and the way society responds to both.

- Recognize that being called a criminal and viewing oneself as a criminal may be quite different.

- Learn that conflict is an important idea in defining crime and criminals, and the threats that both pose for the community.

- Appreciate that conflict is multilayered and highly contextual: An individual, group, value, idea, or relationship may create conflict; in response to the actual conflict or threat of conflict, more powerful groups may criminalize the "offending" party.

INTRODUCTION

In this chapter we examine two theoretical perspectives on the role of power in "creating" crime and delinquency. The first perspective has several names, including labeling theory and the societal reaction perspective, and is one of the most intuitively comprehensible theories on crime and delinquency. The key to understanding law-violating behavior, claim its proponents, lies in the ways social institutions—including the family, schools, and criminal justice system—respond to conduct viewed as outside the limits of acceptability.

Although it places great emphasis on how individuals come to view themselves and to be viewed by society as offenders, labeling theory provides few insights into the mind and motives of offenders. These theoriests leave unanswered, or even unasked, questions about the motivations of those exercising the power to label, beyond the goal of controlling undesired conduct. Proponents also give very little attention to the process of defining what is acceptable and unacceptable. Instead, the focus is on the processes and mechanisms by which those with power come to define persons or acts as unacceptable, and how those so labeled resist or accept their new status.

The second is the conflict perspective. As used in this context, conflict exists when two or more reasonably well defined social or cultural groups compete for the same physical space, power base, or social position in a community or a nation.[1] Crime results when one group defines another's unique values, beliefs, or behavior as illegal, contravening the legal authority. The goal of this process is to define the out-group or outsiders and their conduct as beyond the law's protection. Consequently the group with the power uses it to solidify and strengthen its position within the community or nation.

These two perspectives share a focus on power, but they are also different. In both perspectives power is an instrument used to control others. Labeling theory describes how social institutions define people and actions, and perhaps even beliefs and values, as meriting negative social reactions, including criminalization. Conflict theory specifies that different groups in society seek the same limited goals, and the competition for them often criminalizes members of the group with less power.

LABELING THEORY

- Did you ever wonder how you escaped adolescence without being called delinquent? (For those of you to whom this label was applied, you probably already know the answers to the remaining questions.) Is who does the name calling important? If your misdeeds escaped the notice of your family or the legal system, labeling theory provides insight into your conduct as well.

- Were you ever called names that were cruel and hurtful by friends, family members, teachers, or others in positions of authority? Did you internalize the labels, allowing them to define who you were? Or did you ignore both the labels and the labelers? If you were in the latter category, how did you accomplish this feat?

These are not entirely rhetorical questions. We are interested in your answers to each one, except that asking you to respond could violate your right to privacy.[2] Many of these questions are, after all, personal and invasive, and you may not wish to self-disclose, for reasons related to the topics addressed in this chapter. That is precisely the point. A complete understanding of power often requires that we examine questions and issues that are personal, sensitive, "hot button" issues. These issues may even define whom we are as human beings. A good starting point is the role of symbols in setting the parameters of labeling theory.

Symbolic Interactionism and Labeling Theory

Symbols are incredibly important in any culture. Simply put, a **symbol** is something that stands for something else. A symbol usually captures the essential meaning of a cluster of more abstract ideas, ideologies, beliefs, practices, concerns, and the like. For example, the "Stars and Stripes," the flag of the United States, stands for many things, such as freedom, democracy, imperialism, and capitalism. When it is worn, flown, or burned, people are making cultural and political statements, ranging from "I love my country" to "We hate your devil nation." Language contains the most basic symbols for any society. Language is at its core simply sound—utterances—with no intrinsic meaning. However, culture ascribes shared meaning to certain sounds or, with written language, shapes.

Symbols can galvanize groups to action. Consider the ironies embedded in the following:

- If someone sets fire to an unoccupied structure, it is arson. But if the building happens to be a church, mosque, or synagogue, it becomes a hate crime.

- We spend billions in the "War on Drugs," arresting and imprisoning thousands; however, alcohol and nicotine—two highly addictive and very dangerous drugs—are legal.

- Most people agree that the private sexual practices of consenting adults are beyond the scope of the criminal justice system. But what do we mean by "adult"? Is there universal agreement on what age a person becomes an adult? What happens if the parties are not married or are married to different persons? What if the two people are of the same sex?

- Illegal gambling is a curse to the poor and to compulsive gamblers, and a key part of the business of organized crime. At the same time, state-supported gambling (e.g., lotteries and casinos) is a popular recreational activity that stimulates the economy and painlessly adds dollars to public coffers.

- If a professional athlete speaks his or her mind on matters of race, ethnicity, and immigration, the media and any number of interest groups may vilify him or her. If a popular musician sings those same ideas, they may defend it as creative art, part of the rebelliousness of the current youth culture, and protected free speech.

To understand these apparently contradictory responses to similar situations and information, we must consider labeling theory's origins in **symbolic interactionism.** This perspective explores the ways in which individuals render the world meaningful. Symbolic interactionists "argue that individuals, in reaction to group rewards and sanctions, gradually internalize group expectations. These internalized social definitions allow people to evaluate their own behavior from the standpoint of the group and in doing so provide a lens through which to view oneself as a social object" (Quadragno and Antonio 1975:33). The focus for symbolic interactionists is not on the behavior of any social actor, but on how others, including society and the criminal justice system, view that behavior or actor. Thus, Kai T. Erickson (1966:6; emphasis in original) stated, "Deviance is not a property *inherent* in any particular kind of behavior; it is a property *conferred* upon that behavior by people who come into direct or indirect contact with it."

Symbols have the power to galvanize social action. For labeling theorists deviance—which is broader than but includes crime and delinquency—is important for its symbolic contribution to our interpretation of the social world. W. I. Thomas and Florian Znaniecki (1918) observed that reality is less important to our definition of the social situation than is our subjective belief in that situation. If we believe something to be true and act according to that belief, it does not matter if that belief is, in fact, "true." Symbolic interactionists are less interested in "facts" or "truth" than in the societal reaction to beliefs.

Societal Reaction: From Tagging to Labeling

Frank Tannenbaum (1938) was among the first to articulate the idea that social institutions can cause society to view some people as not only different but also criminal. His focus was on the social-psychological implications of being defined as delinquent, nonconformist, or criminal. The principal difficulties, observed Tannenbaum, are definitional ones. What a youth views as a lark or an adventure the community at large may define as a nuisance or evil. Divergent views such as these bring youths and the community into conflict. If neither side tries to resolve the definitional differences, a gradual shift occurs, from the deed-as-evil to the person-as-evil. Tannenbaum described this process as the **dramatization of evil.** He also suggested that the redefinition process occurs through the intervention of an institution created specifically for this task—the criminal justice system.

According to labeling theory the first dramatization ritual separating out some children for specialized treatment plays a central role in creating criminals. "It cannot be too often emphasized that for the child the whole situation has become different. He now lives in a different world. He has been tagged. A new and hitherto nonexistent environment has been precipitated out for him" (Tannenbaum 1938:20).

Successive generations of symbolic interactionists addressed society's power to redefine social situations. Erving Goffman described how people respond to so-called spoiled identities—both the community at large and those whose identities were spoiled—through the process of **stigmatization.** Goffman (1963:43–44)

IN THEIR OWN WORDS: Thomas on Defining the Situation

Social interpretation is subjective: What people believe to be true is indeed so if they organize their response or behavior according to that interpretation. This perspective has its roots in W. I. Thomas's observations about the definition of a situation:

> Very often it is the wide discrepancy between the situation as it seems to others and the situation as it seems to the individual that brings about the overt behavior difficulty. To take an extreme example, the warden of Dannemora Prison [for the criminally insane] recently refused to honor the order of the Court to send an inmate outside the prison walls for some specific purpose. He excused himself on the ground that the man was too dangerous. [The inmate] had killed several persons who had the unfortunate habit of talking to themselves on the street. From the movement of their lips [the inmate] imagined that they were calling him vile names and he behaved as if this were true. *If men define situations as real, they are real in their consequences.*

Source: Thomas and Thomas (1928:571–72; emphasis added)

---

distinguished **prestige symbols,** which convey "a special claim to prestige, honor or desirable class position," from **stigma symbols,** which draw "attention to a debasing identity," negatively altering how society views that person. Honor societies traditionally award pins or keys to their members as an indication of their special status. Members of the U.S. Congress receive special license plates and reserved parking spots in Washington to indicate their privileged status. Universities and colleges bestow honorary degrees upon persons they wish to designate as having led exemplary professional or personal lives. Conversely female collaborators in occupied Europe during World War II—women who engaged in social and sexual behavior with enemy soldiers—routinely had their heads shaved after the occupation ended. In the United States prior to desegregation, separate and unequal public facilities reinforced the second-class status of African Americans. As a result of a recent nationwide trend in state legislation, convicted and released sex offenders have their pictures, offense records, and current addresses posted on public Web sites. These prestige and stigma symbols send strong messages to society: *These people bear watching!*

Important, too, are the processes by which stigma symbols become the defining criteria for a person's identity. Harold Garfinkel (1956:421; emphasis in original) saw **status degradation ceremonies,** including trials and prison intake procedures, as providing ritualistic and public denunciations of individuals viewed as unworthy: "The paradigm of moral indignation is *public* denunciation. We publicly deliver the curse: 'I call upon all men to bear witness that he is not as he appears but is otherwise and *in essence* of a lower species.' "

Goffman and Garfinkel placed societal reactions in a symbolic interactionist framework. The work of three sociologists—Howard Becker, Edwin Schur, and Edwin Lemert—captures the essence of contemporary labeling theory. We begin with Becker, who expanded on Tannenbaum's dramatization of evil and tagging by describing deviance as a social status.

Deviance as Status

Howard Becker (1963:9; emphasis in original) believed that

> social groups *create deviance by making the rules whose infraction constitutes deviance,* and by applying those rules to particular people and labeling them as outsiders. From this point of view, deviance is *not* a quality of the act the person commits, but rather a consequence of the application by others of rules and sanctions to an "offender." The deviant is one to whom that label has successfully been applied; deviant behavior is behavior people so label.

According to this view negative societal reactions result in tarnished and even damaged self-images, deviant identities, and a host of negative social expectations. How does this happen? Think about how members of your community typically react to the terms *ex-con, parolee, child molester,* and *serial killer;* now think about your current social status. We all play many roles in our communities, including teacher or student, child or parent, and worker or boss. What if we traded one of the latter, positive statuses for one of the former, far more negative ones? Which one would define how others view us, or how we see ourselves?

This distinction embodies the idea of the **master status.** According to Becker the master status defines how others view us and how we see ourselves. The especially potent negative criminal label has *the potential* to become a master status, overriding all others (Becker 1963; see also Hughes 1945). Even though criminals rarely specialize in terms of a single type of crime, the public assumes that the publicized crime is the offender's specialty or crime of choice and so provides the definitive identity. As a consequence the offender may actually embrace the master status, especially if it is a high-status one (e.g., mob hit man or professional art thief), and not a low-status one (e.g., child molester or street drug dealer).

The impact of stigma symbols, labels, and degradation ceremonies on social status in general and on master status in particular can be devastating. Consider the fallout if the newspaper or morning news show revealed that the police had arrested your professor on child molestation charges. At that point all of the professor's education, college or university rank and status, and professional standing would cease to have meaning. Would factual innocence matter? The professor would be an accused pedophile, a particularly damning master status in our society, likely to elicit high levels of rejection no matter whether there was a trial, guilty verdict, or legal sanction. The policy of placing the names and addresses of convicted sex offenders in the newspapers or on the Internet raises important labeling issues. What if the information is inaccurate? What if it identifies the wrong person—someone with the same name or a similar one? What if the sex offense was a consensual act, between adolescents of similar ages?

Not all stigma symbols are of equal social significance, and in spite of powerful status degradation ceremonies, they may not have a negative impact on the person being labeled. Even a successful status degradation ceremony may not result in a new master status. For example, what if a faculty member at your college or university decides that not enough is being done to help the homeless in your community. Rather, it is widely believed that the local police target the homeless for arrest and removal from the community. Because of strongly held beliefs, your professor decides to join a picket line outside the city council meeting hall while inside the

---

IN THEIR OWN WORDS: Becker on Master Status

Becker was not, strictly speaking, writing about issues of crime and justice when he described the distinction between master and subordinate statuses; however, the implications are clear:

> Some statuses, in our society as in others, override all other statuses and have a certain priority. . . . The status of deviant (depending on the kind of deviance) is this kind of master status. One receives the status as a result of breaking a rule, and the identification proves to be more important than most others. One will be identified as a deviant first, before other identifications are made.

Source: Becker (1963:34).

---

city council meets to consider new, even tougher "antiloitering" ordinances. The police order the picketers to disperse when members of the city council feel threatened by several very vocal protesters. They take the protestors, including your professor, into custody; the charge is creating a public disturbance. At trial your professor enters a plea of no contest, pays a $10 fine, and serves 10 days of community service at the local homeless shelter. Rather than viewing the professor as an outcast and a criminal, colleagues and students praise the individual as a victim of conscience. The status of the much-arrested Dr. Martin Luther King was only enhanced by encounters with southern criminal "justice." Both examples teach us that we must also assess the relative weights of both the stigma symbols and the prestige symbols.

Not all people so labeled have earned their deviant status. Becker (1963) pointed out that society knows that some individuals are deviant, that they have earned the label of **true deviants.** Such individuals have few advocates, other than those who would see that they receive a just review of the charges and evidence, and, where appropriate, a just penalty. Society labels other individuals as deviants who have not, in fact, committed the undesired conduct; these are the **falsely accused.** In the minds of many critics of the criminal justice system, the presence of the falsely accused in the nation's prisons and jails justifies unrelenting vigilance. Society also sees some persons as innocent of any wrongdoing who have indeed committed no deviance; these are the **true innocents**—the angels among us. Finally, some members of society are **hidden deviants;** that is, they have committed an evil act, but society perceives them to be nondeviant, so they escape labeling.

Societal Reactions and Individual Responses

The damaged self-image and its meaning for the individual can result in a "self-fulfilling prophesy," or the idea that what people believe to be real becomes real in its consequences (see Merton 1957:421–24; see also Thomas and Thomas 1928). For example, an initial foray into a criminal activity, unless it involves an extremely serious crime, may be nothing more than what Edwin Lemert (1951) called **primary deviation,** a condition in which the individual has almost no commitment to a deviant career or vocation.

As Edwin Schur (1973:124) noted, "Once an individual has been branded as a wrongdoer, it becomes extremely difficult for him to shed that new identity."

After all, the accusations may appear on the front page of the newspaper, but the exonerations are relegated to the back page. Many ex-convicts find it difficult to secure employment, or at least meaningful and rewarding jobs, increasing crime's attraction and the likelihood of subsequent labeling. According to Lemert (1951:76) the labeled may reorganize their behavior according to society's reactions and respond to society in terms of that negative label. Lemert called this condition **secondary deviation.** The shift from primary to secondary deviation follows a pattern (Lemert 1951:77): (1) Primary deviations elicit social penalties, usually of a mild nature, which often stimulate, (2) further primary deviations, causing, in turn, (3) stronger penalties and rejections by a wide range of groups and individuals, causing (4) further deviations, possibly including hostilities and resentment toward those doing the penalizing, which creates a (5) crisis in the tolerance quotient, expressed in formal action by the stigmatizing body, meaning (6) harsher reactions to misdeeds, further strengthening the deviant conduct as a reaction to the stigmatization and penalization, and ultimately yielding (7) psychological acceptance of the deviant status and reorganization of one's social-psychological makeup around that deviant role, or secondary deviation.

Labeling theorists such as Becker and Schur emphasized the effects of societal reactions on the development of individuals' self-image and subsequent behavior. As Tannenbaum (1938) long ago contended, formal labeling creates the very behavior we intend to reduce or eliminate. Edwin Schur expanded labeling theory by specifying the various elements of successful labeling.

Labels and Their Consequences

Labeling: A Four-Step Process Schur (1971) believed that successful labeling requires four elements. First, **stereotyping** is essential in helping people make sense out of that which is new and unfamiliar. A stereotype is a simplistic and unchanging mental image or pattern resulting from the presence of certain cues, visual or auditory. Moreover, stereotypes are biased generalizations about a group or individuals that are often unfavorable or exaggerated. For example, an older couple, passing a group of adolescents and hearing loud music coming from a boom box, might denigrate them and their music as "trash." Schur's (1971:38) concern was with a far more damning form of stereotyping that begins with police observations of or encounters with youths and culminates in the use of prejudicial stereotypes at sentencing.

Second, labeling can continue after the fact and may require reinforcing. This is the case when the media describe an offender as "a former mental patient"—as if to say, "What can you expect?" Schur (1971:152) used the term **retrospective interpretation** to describe the process of looking to the past for hidden or overt causes of behaviors that occur in the present. The implication is that these causes should have alerted society to the possibility of a criminal's current aberrant behavior: What else could be expected from a person who had "done time" in a mental hospital or suffered from an undiagnosed brain tumor? Of course, few such persons actually commit crimes, but society rarely lets the facts get in the way of a good retrospective interpretation. Rather, this mechanism allows society to make sense of otherwise unfathomable behavior, such as why an honor student would kill her entire family or an Eagle Scout would engage in serial killings. If we discover that the accused had a brain tumor, recently suffered a mental breakdown, or had suffered abuse at the hands of a parent, the criminal actions become easier to explain—a deterministic view of human behavior.

The third element consists of **negotiations** between the labeled and the labelers (Schur 1971:56). Superficially the parties involved are negotiating the formal charge, the plea, and the eventual sentence, but actually they are negotiating the label. Stereotypes play a major role in the negotiation process, as does retrospective interpretation. The negotiation process includes how the police defined the youth upon detainment or arrest and what the probation officer can piece together about the youth's life prior to the offense. Occasionally the youth may promote a negative stereotype by acting belligerent and unresponsive to officials, an indication of role engulfment.

Role engulfment, the fourth element, is different from Lemert's secondary deviance. Secondary deviance includes *both* the impact of labeling on the individual's self-concept and "secondary expansion of deviance problems at the situational and societal levels" (Schur 1971:69). Role engulfment, a narrower facet of secondary deviation, relates to society's response to the individual now recognized as a deviant, criminal, or delinquent. That is, role engulfment is the social-psychological process by which the individual assumes the master status; it is the culmination and sum total of a process of stereotyping, retrospective interpretation, and negotiation. Because legitimate roles are no longer available to the individual, all that remains is to become engulfed in the deviant role, to the exclusion of all others. This step, Schur believed, is necessary to stabilize one's self-concept.

Schur (1971:151–71) viewed the delinquent label as so detrimental to future conduct that he argued for a policy of **radical nonintervention.** The focus, he believed, should be on keeping adolescents away from contact with the official agencies of social control. Symbolic interactionists are especially concerned with the process by which official control agents—particularly psychiatrists, police, and judges—label behavior. Do the police uniformly enforce the law when they encounter similar behavior, or do the persons or circumstances influence decisions about whether to intervene or arrest? Aaron Cicourel (1976:190) found that many juvenile activities "that might go unnoticed or [be] regarded as 'minor' pranks will not be so viewed by the juvenile officers . . . because [the juvenile may fit] their conception of the potential delinquent, and they will seek him out whenever there is reported 'trouble' in his neighborhood. Routine juvenile activities, therefore, can be turned into serious 'delinquent acts.' " Figure 8.1 graphically depicts labeling as a process.

Labeling: A Deviance Amplification System? Leslie Wilkins (1965) described a **deviance amplification** system by which deviance is amplified and made worse: Less tolerance leads to more acts being defined as crimes, which leads to more action against criminals, which leads to more alienation of deviant groups, which leads to more crime by deviant groups, which leads to less tolerance of deviants by conforming groups—and the cycle continues. In short, the actions of individuals that become defined as deviant and criminal limit those persons' options in many areas, including choice of companions. Those whom the system has condemned and excluded can hardly be expected to feel as if they are a part of it. The continued criminal acts of the "outliers" (outlaws) and the

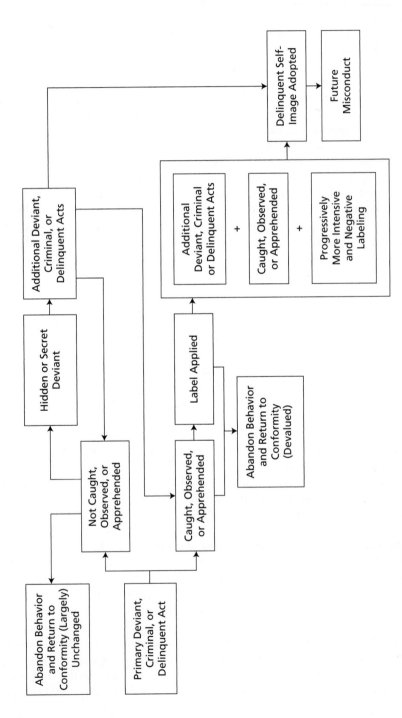

FIGURE 8.1 Labeling as a Process

amplifying effects of self-perception typically result in even harsher responses by conforming groups.

Employing a system similar to Wilkins', Jock Young (1971) proposed that, in the case of illegal drugs, police serve as deviance amplifiers. Because the police occupy a socially isolated position in the community, they are susceptible to stereotypes about a variety of social behaviors, including drug use. Given their position of power, police officers negotiate the evidence—the reality of drug-taking behavior—to fit preconceived stereotypes. Because of repeated "police action against the drug-taker changes occur within the drug-taking groups involving an intensification of their deviance and in certain important aspects a self-fulfillment of these stereotypes. That is, there will be an amplification of deviance, and a translation of stereotypes into actuality, of fantasy into reality" (Young 1971:28).

Long-Term Effects of Labeling For those who cannot avoid the "convict" label, the consequences can be serious and long-lasting, particularly in terms of trying to secure lawful employment. Richard Schwartz and Jerome Skolnick (1962), providing a rare look at the impact of criminal convictions, studied the effects of a criminal record on the employment opportunities of unskilled workers. Four employment folders, which were the same in all respects other than the criminal records of the applicants, were prepared as follows:

- Folder 1 showed that the applicant had been convicted of and sentenced for assault.
- Folder 2 stated that he had been tried for assault and acquitted.
- Folder 3 also indicated that he had been tried for assault and acquitted, but with a letter from the judge certifying the finding of not guilty.
- Folder 4 folder did not mention any criminal record.

The study involved 100 employers whom Schwartz and Skolnick divided into units of 25, with each group being shown a folder as that of a real job applicant. The results were startling:

- Of the employers shown the "no record" folder, 36 percent gave positive responses.
- Of the employers shown the "acquitted" folder with the judge's letter, 24 percent expressed an interest in the applicant.
- Of the employers shown the "acquitted" folder, 12 percent expressed an interest in the applicant.
- Of the employers shown the "convicted" folder, only 4 percent expressed an interest in the applicant.

To reduce the legal harm caused by a criminal record, some states have removed various statutory restrictions on gaining licenses necessary for employment. A few have even enacted "fair employment" laws for former offenders. New York, for example, prohibits the denial of employment or a license because of a conviction. There are, however, exceptions to this practice—such as if a direct relationship exists between the crime and the specific employment or license, or if it involves an unreasonable risk to persons or property. According to the direct-relationship requirement, the nature of the criminal conduct for which the person was convicted must have a direct bearing on his or her fitness or ability to carry out the job's duties or responsibilities (e.g., a drug offender working in a hospital pharmacy). The statute requires that a public or private employer provide, upon request, a written statement setting forth the reasons for denial of license or employment. The New York State Commission on Human Rights enforces the statute.

Assessing Labeling Theory

Attacks on labeling theory date from the 1970s, with most skeptics focusing on several themes:

- *Theoretical shortcomings.* Critics point to labeling theory's poor or missing conceptual definitions, to its tautological nature by which evidence of labeling is the presence of a label (i.e., crime is behavior so labeled, or the criminal is the person so labeled), and the lack of formal propositions as causal statements from which to derive testable hypotheses (Paternoster and Iovanni 1989; see also Gibbs 1968; Gove 1980; Wellford 1975).

- *Theory-generated research problems.* Theoretical shortcomings lead to substantial empirical problems. For example, Milton Mankoff (1976) was quite explicit about the links between one theoretical shortcoming—initial rule breaking and the application of the label. The significance of the initial rule breaking, and whatever caused it, ceases to be considered after it has occurred. At that point it is the societal reaction that becomes the focus of the theory (Mankoff 1976:247). Perhaps, observed Mankoff (1976:248), rule breakers continue their evil ways because of "positive attachment to rule-breaking." Crime may provide monetary rewards, immediate gratification, and excitement (see the discussion of operant conditioning principles in Chapter 5).

- *Poor research results.* Those who have tested "labeling hypotheses" and failed to find support for them often call for the theory's death (Hagan 1974; Wellford 1975). However, others have argued that "for the most part, empirical tests of labeling propositions have been conducted with grossly misrepresented hypotheses that are more caricature than characteristic of the theory" (Paternoster and Iovanni 1989:360).

- *Overstatement and misstatement of labeling's importance.* Akers (1968) observed that many youth gang members have well-formed deviant identities but have never been formally labeled. Mankoff (1976) noted that a criminal status may be achieved, and not ascribed, by individuals who aspire to a career of crime. For some of the most violent norm violators—terrorists and revolutionaries— an official label may mean that they have received recognition for their deeds. Gang jackets and other gang paraphernalia serve as reminders that for some persons deviant labels are valued. Consider, too, the antithesis of labeling— deterrence theory (Tittle 1975). Some children do "go straight" and never engage in subsequent misconduct after an encounter with the juvenile justice system (see the discussion of correctional uses of behaviorism in Chapter 5).

In spite of the fact that many criminologists declared labeling theory "dead" in the 1980s, new conceptualizations of the process account for its resurgence a decade later (Paternoster and Iovanni 1989). The first, the **status characteristics**

hypothesis, proposes that certain personal characteristics, such as race, sex, and social class, determine whom social control agencies label. Researchers using the status characteristics hypothesis studied "label applications" by different agencies within the criminal justice system, including police, prosecutors, and courts, in arrests, trials, and postadjudicatory dispositions. Their findings suggest that, given certain contexts and stages in the criminal justice process, a person's race, ethnicity, gender, or social class functions to ease the label's application. For example, a black male accused of harming a white female may stand in greater legal jeopardy than if his victim had been another black male (Baldus, Pulaski, and Woodworth 1983; Smith, Visher, and Davidson 1984; Vito and Keil 1988). Also, the importance of social class and race increases during the later stages of processing for juvenile suspects (McCarthy and Smith 1986).

Raymond Paternoster and Lee Ann Iovanni (1989) also proposed the **secondary-deviance hypothesis,** which focuses on the criminal label's stigmatizing and segregating *consequences.* This complex hypothesis infers that as official labeling occurs individuals may experience changes in personal identity and in levels of access to conventional persons and career/job opportunities. Ultimately greater involvement in crime and delinquency results (see the ideas of role engulfment, secondary deviance, and deviance amplification).

Jon Lofland (1969) believed that the probability of assuming a criminal identity (i.e., role engulfment and secondary deviance) and engaging in further criminal behavior increases when the individual has (1) a criminal self-identity, (2) low self-esteem, and (3) emotional ties to *both* normal and deviant others. To explore these contentions, Frances Palarma and her associates (1986) studied two groups of youths. One group had no police contacts at the start of the study; the other already had police contacts. By the study's end, not only did the officially labeled youths exhibit more delinquency, but their levels of psychological impairment were higher than those of the youths not previously labeled. This study highlights the problems of disentangling labeling theory's causal ordering. It is possible that those with police contacts were more delinquent or committed prior to the study.

Douglas Smith and Paternoster (1990) tested a "deviance amplification model" of formal court processing on juvenile suspects. They reported that appearance in court was related to recidivism, or future acts of delinquency, by higher-risk juveniles, the ones with more extensive youthful misconduct records. Apparently, through their interactions with juvenile suspects, officials sometimes *cause* future misbehavior. Schur (1973:30) warned that labeling can set in motion "a complex process of response and counter-response with an initial act of rule-violation and developing into elaborated delinquent self-conceptions and a full-fledged delinquent career."

However, tests of other specific labeling subelements have yielded contradictions. Specifically the notion that contact with the juvenile court is detrimental may be in error. For example, one study found that "the majority of those whose first referral was a status offense did not become more serious delinquents. If anything, they became something considerably less than serious delinquents" (Sheldon, Horvath, and Tracey 1989:214). Another study found that youngsters adjudicated delinquent in juvenile court on their first referral were less likely to have criminal records as adults than those whose referrals were delayed until further offenses (Brown, Miller, Jenkins, and Rhodes 1991), findings supportive of deterrence theory (Tittle 1975).

Social scientists have found the idea of a master status intriguing (Miethe and McCorkle 1997; Zatz 1985). The gang member label, in particular, fits Becker's original notion of a status that overwhelms and neutralizes all others. A comparison of gang and nongang felony prosecutions lends support to the idea of the importance of gang member as a master status (Miethe and McCorkle 1997). However, the direction of that impact was not expected: Although other offender and offense characteristics play less crucial roles in the dispositional decisions made about gang members, gang members received less harsh outcomes than nongang persons, particularly a higher dismissal rate and less severe sentencing decisions (Miethe and McCorkle 1997:420).

Faced with such anomalies, the researchers considered and rejected two explanations: (1) Pressures to clear cases meant that weaker ones were dismissed (i.e., the sentencing outcomes were also less severe), and (2) a benevolent criminal justice system rendered more lenient treatment to youths who were victims of economic inequality (i.e., elected judges, faced with a climate of "gang-banging" youths, would be unlikely to render "soft justice" to gang members). Instead, the researchers speculated that the judiciary viewed the offenses of gang members as wholesale crimes. Retail crimes are expensive and include crimes that outrage the public; wholesale crimes, in contrast, cost little and involve victims and perpetrators who have low status in the community. The latter characterization reflected the types of offenses resulting in the court appearances of gang members. When gang members prey on one another, it is wholesale crime and so receives different justice than if the offense is designated as a retail crime committed "outside their immediate socioeconomic environment" (Miethe and McCorkle 1997:423).

Key questions remain unanswered: Why has research into labeling theory shown so little support for the substance of its assertion that the reaction to deviance is the cause of continued deviance? Is the label powerful enough to ensure a deviant career? Do deviants have choices? Do some persons, including members of delinquent gangs, outlaw motorcycle clubs, and organized crime groups, actively seek out a deviant lifestyle? Do they seek this lifestyle not in spite of the label that goes with it, but because of the label? Labeling theory fails to provide adequate answers to these central questions. Nevertheless, as anyone who has worked with ex-offenders knows, the "criminal" label can have a devastating impact on individuals seeking legitimate employment. Currently we do not clearly understand labeling's symbolic effects, especially the mechanisms by which they take shape and form. Nonetheless, we easily recognize and understand the practical, pragmatic effects of being stigmatized as a criminal or ex-con.

Labeling, Public Policy, and Criminal Justice Practices

Policy Initiatives and Programs Public policy emerges out of a political process. By definition power-based theories have implications for the development of public policy, including those policies defining society's response to the "crime problem." In particular, proponents of public policy based on labeling theory seek to reduce the stigma that attaches to being labeled a delinquent or criminal. For example, **decriminalization** refers to a reduction in the number of outlawed behaviors (e.g., possession of small amounts of marijuana for personal or medical use). **Diversion** reflects an attempt to avoid unnecessarily stigmatizing persons who violate the law by providing alternatives to official criminal justice processing. The police or prosecutor's office can operate diversion programs for adults and juveniles. Instead of being arrested and prosecuted, offenders are referred to treatment, counseling, and employment training programs. However, many observers of the criminal justice system have criticized diversion for contributing to the larger problem of **net widening.** That is, the police would not have arrested these individuals, nor would the prosecutor's office have charged them in the first place, absent official diversion programs. In effect, diversion efforts may add to the number of people caught in the "criminal justice net" (Austin and Krisberg 1981:171; see also Blomberg 1980).

Labeling theorists are all too aware of the negative effects of incarceration. Given that incarceration may push offenders toward secondary deviation, **deinstitutionalization,** or the removal of inmates from prisons, jails, and juvenile detention centers, is deemed by many labeling supporters to be a productive counterresponse. In the wake of federal mandates, most states have deinstitutionalized **status offenders.**[3] Also, other federal legislation, principally the Juvenile Justice and Delinquency Prevention Act of 1974, has required states to remove juveniles from jails intended to house adult suspects and offenders although many states have been slow to act (Gilliard and Beck 1996; Schwartz 1991).

Currently most states are moving in the opposite direction, driven by rising fear of crime, especially fear of violent juvenile crime. That is, state legislatures are lowering the age at which juveniles can be tried as adults and institutionalized in prisons for adults (Mays and Winfree 2000:147–51). In labeling terms the increasingly harsh sanctioning of younger offenders—and their movement deeper into the criminal justice system, with its attendant possibilities for secondary deviance—is likely to increase the undesired behavior.

Labeling theorists also recognize the state's power over the individual. Consequently it is not surprising that during the 1960s and 1970s labeling supporters also championed the extension of **due process guarantees.** This effort met with notable successes (e.g., *Kent v. United States* 1966; *In re Gault* 1967; *Breed v. Jones* 1975) and failures (e.g., *In re Winship* 1971; *McKiever v. Pennsylvania* 1971; *Schall v. Martin* 1984). *Stanford v. Kentucky* (1989) was a mixed blessing: Youths who were less than 16 years of age at the time they committed a capital crime could not be executed, but the state could execute those age 16 or 17. Recent due process guarantees have been granted to juveniles because of *increased* criminalization. That is, as courts decide whether to try youthful offenders in an adult court, the accused enjoy many of the rights accorded adults. They may soon find themselves accorded *all* such rights as states try them as adults, with adult sanctions also possible.

Legislative and judicial responses to youth crime set up an ironic situation: When controlling for the severity of the offense, a lack of significant differences in sentencing outcomes for youngsters adjudicated in juvenile court and those tried in criminal court exists. For example,

the juvenile court may not be as lenient as its critics contend, and furthermore, in some jurisdictions minors are more likely to be looked upon as special persons by prosecutors, probation officers, and judges in criminal court. They are younger than the main population of defendants before the criminal court. Even jurors may view the young person in criminal court differently. In the cases examined, there were more findings of "not guilty" in the criminal court than in the juvenile court. The labeling process may be different in two courts. While a minor may be looked upon as a hardened criminal in juvenile court, (s)he may be viewed as a mere innocent youngster in criminal court. (Sagatun, McCollum, and Edwards 1985:87)

Real punishments await youthful offenders tried in adult courts under judicial waiver or prosecutorial discretion. For example, researchers in one jurisdiction found that conviction rates for juveniles were very similar to those for adults, with fines or probation imposed on half of those convicted. Juveniles convicted of serious violent offenses, however, were likely to receive jail or prison terms averaging nearly seven years (Hamparian et al. 1982). Differences exist in some jurisdictions by type of crime as well: "Property offenders with a long history of property offenses tend to receive a substantially lighter sentence in adult court than they would have received in juvenile court. Conversely, personal and aggravated personal offenders with few prior offenses received significantly more punitive treatment in adult court than did comparable offenders in juvenile court" (Barnes and Franz 1989:133).

Is there a way out of the labeling dilemma? Can labeling be undone? The philosopher and social psychologist George Herbert Mead (1863–1931) argued that the labeled will not be accepted back into society. Nearly 100 years ago, Mead (1918:591) stated that "hostility toward the lawbreaker inevitably brings with it the attitudes of retribution, repression and exclusion. These provide no principles for the eradication of crime, for returning the delinquent to normal social relations." Mead believed that, owing to the psychology of punitive justice, adjudged criminals can never regain society's trust.

Law Enforcement Practices Law enforcement officers are central figures in labeling's preliminary stages, especially the movement from primary to secondary deviance.[4] Commonly discretionary decisions made by patrol officers determine whether a person will enter the criminal justice system. Officers who opt for a warning or reprimand, particularly with juveniles and adults who engage in minor law-violating behavior, may prevent deviance amplification.

Labeling theory may also help us understand police responses to various identifiable groups in society, particularly ethnic and racial groups. Much police street work is based on stereotyping, a process not dissimilar to that described by Schur as the preliminary stage in labeling. In fact, this process has become an integral part of the police culture, because officers must make many immediate, reactionary-style decisions after processing very few cues. Offender types—**symbolic assailants**— elicit very different responses from the police than do normal citizens. From this perspective the Los Angeles officers' responses to Rodney King—as well as more recent cases in New York, Detroit, Philadelphia, and Los Angeles—are recognizable, if excessive, examples of stereotyping and labeling in action.

At the end of the twentieth century, DWB—"Driving While Black"—emerged in the lexicon of criminal justice literature (Gates 1995; Harris 1999): police targeting black drivers of certain types of vehicles for stops on the nation's roadways. Proponents of what is now referred to as profiling assert a need to confront the problem of guns and drugs moving from city to city (see, e.g., *Wilkins v. Maryland State Police* 1996). The only reason that individuals were subjected to roadside stops, claimed those opposed to the practice, was that they fit a racially motivated profile. The rates at which minority drivers were stopped and searched exceeded reasonable expectations (American Civil Liberties Union 1999). Based on research that revealed the racial bias for these police actions, many state and local police agencies were ordered to stop using such profiles (*State v. Soto-Fong* 1996).

Judicial Practices Throughout the trial process court actors—ranging from the judge or jury, to the attorneys, to witnesses, to the defendant—exercise some influence. Adjudication itself serves as "an interpretive process" in which legal authorities, especially judges and attorneys, "must assess the defendant and the offense for evidence that official sanction is warranted. Such evaluation and interpretation may be guided, in part, by popular stereotypes of criminality" (Swigert and Farrell 1976:90). It is the courts that are responsible for much institutionalization of criminal stereotypes (Swigert and Farrell 1976). Trial courts formalize and popularize criminal stereotypes through the trial process. Appellate courts, including the Supreme Court, may have less power in reversing this process even when they fail to certify a guilty finding. As critics have pointed out, the accused's factual guilt was attested to by the jury's decision; procedural mistakes (i.e., due process errors) committed by the state before or during the prosecution resulted in the reversal. That is, the accused is still a criminal by act, just not by law.

Besides the role trials play in the definitional process, many labeling theorists view them as public **shaming ceremonies** (Garfinkel 1956; see also Goffman 1963). The trial's purpose is to finish the criminalizing process begun with arrest, arraignment, and indictment. The "discreditable" become "discredited" through the symbolic interaction of the court (Goffman 1963). As for formal labeling, it is the court that has the power to change the adjective "accused" to "convicted," effectively altering the individual's master status as well. For example, accused murderers become convicted murderers and accused child molesters become convicted child molesters only through the intercession of the court. Harold Garfinkel's (1956) entire description of the "denunciation" process sounds like a trial. The "denouncer" (i.e., the prosecuting attorney) must identify him- or herself to the "witnesses" (i.e., the judge or jury members) as a public person speaking for the society. In the final stage—sentencing—they must show the denounced to be outside the legitimate order, to be opposed to it and not a part of it.

Another court-based program based on diversionary principles is deferred sentencing, which usually involves a plea of guilty followed by either restitution or some form of community service instead of incarceration. Satisfactory completion of the conditions of the deferred sentence results in the dropping of charges. Failure, in contrast, can result in immediate incarceration. Diversion programs, then, seem designed to limit individuals' contact with the criminal justice system although in practice they often have the opposite effect and more. A study of diversion in Sacramento County (California) included random assignment. The researchers reported that roughly 80 percent of the juveniles diverted into short-term treatment would have been released except for the existence of the program (Dunford, Osgood, and Weichselbaum 1981; Palmer, Bohnstedt, and Lewis 1978). Even when diversion programs work to prevent deeper penetration into the justice system, particularly the juvenile justice system, we may find class biases: "Diversion program clients tend to be drawn from groups that are predominantly middle-class. . . . As a result, many lower-class youth who might benefit from diversion's family services are being denied these services" (Blomberg 1980:10).

Finally labeling depends on negotiation, an idea critical to court proceedings. As Schur (1971:56) observed, it is not clear at the beginning of the process which labels attach. Robert Emerson (1969) detailed three statuses for juvenile defendants: (1) "normal" children, whose involvement with the law is ruled "accidental"; (2) "criminal-like" children, who consciously pursue criminal ends and evidence intense distrust of and dislike for society through their actions; and (3) "disturbed" children, whose actions seem senseless and irrational, thus requiring more of a psychological treatment approach than a criminal justice response. Emerson contended that the status awarded a child was not "proved" in the classic sense of the laws of evidence. Rather, the concerned parties, including the court, the public school, the reform school, the social services system, and other community agencies, negotiated it.

Correctional Practices Labeling theory also provides insights into two related aspects of corrections. First, labeling makes it easier to understand why convicted felons who spend time in an antisocial, violent environment such as contemporary prisons are unlikely to emerge as better persons or more productive members of society. About all that we can hope for, it seems, is that they have paid their debt to society. Negativistic social systems dominate prisons that punish rather than reward adherence to prosocial goals (Bartollas and Conrad 1992; Champion 1990; see also the discussion of culture and group conflict in the next section). A prison has few peers as a place in which to complete the process of secondary deviance and role engulfment.

Second, deinstitutionalization is a key juvenile justice policy outcome resulting from labeling. Failing to eliminate correctional institutions entirely, community corrections programs stand as alternatives. In fact, labeling theory was a major force in the development of community corrections: "The labeling theorists viewed formal processing through the criminal justice system and incarceration in prisons and jails as the most serious forms of excommunication. . . . Correctional programs that avoided stigmatizing offenders and enabled them to maintain ties to the larger community could be expected to encourage responsible, law-abiding behavior" (McCarthy and McCarthy 1992:7, 8).

Labeling clearly involves the use of power informally by groups and individuals and far more formally by the state. Without the ability to act upon or control the fate of others, one definition of power, labeling would be merely a largely ineffectual naming process, with no consequences attached to it. Given the involvement of the powerful criminal justice system, and its equally significant subordinate system of juvenile justice, the effects of formal labeling are far from inconsequential. This emphasis on power, and its exercise, leads to conflict theory. A key difference is that this latter perspective asks questions ignored by labeling theory, including this important one: Who wields the power to criminalize conduct, and why?

CONFLICT AND CRIME

- Are you a member of a racial or ethnic minority group? What does the term *minority* mean? Is it all about numbers, or is something else involved? If not numbers, then what is that something else?

- Did you or your family recently emigrate to the United States? Did members of your immediate family have trouble adjusting to American culture, preferring instead to keep to the "old ways"? If you are not a recent immigrant but still celebrate your culture of origin, do these actions pose problems?

- Besides race, ethnicity, or nationality issues, do you hold beliefs or engage in practices or rituals that some members of society might question or even condemn? Could they be a violation of the law—a crime—in this or any other country?

Conflict theorists address gaps in power relationships. Supporters of the "soft" conflict perspective take literally the meaning of conflict (see Chapter 9 for the "hard" version of conflict). They suggest that it occurs whenever and wherever two or more groups attempt to exercise control and dominion over a social situation (Vold and Bernard 1986:269; Williams and McShane 1988:98). As **conflict criminologists** they explain why one group has more power, particularly as measured by access to the creation of laws, than another, and so is more likely to obtain whatever is the object of conflict.

We present two variants of "soft" conflict, both emphasizing the legal use of power to subjugate others but each differing about conflict's source. The first theory identifies conflict's cultural roots and the creation of criminals; in the second, group interests are central.

Culture Conflict Theory

Societal conduct norms require that in a given situation certain people act in a specific way (Wirth 1931). Thorsten Sellin (1938) claimed that conduct norms express the group's cultural values. In a homogeneous society the conduct norms express group consensus: Few people disagree about what is right and wrong. The same is not true of more heterogeneous societies, in which considerable disagreements may exist about what is right and wrong, and about what is to be valued and what is to be demeaned.

Sociologists have long used the term *subcultures* to refer to subgroups within society that have divergent sets of values, although this term was not used by Sellin (see also the discussion of subculture and crime in Chapter 6). In a heterogeneous society laws represent the conduct norms of the dominant group. However, members of subcultures may be constrained by the conduct norms of both their subculture and the dominant group. If they "march to a different drummer," if subcultural values are at odds with the dominant culture's values as expressed in the criminal codes, then there is not only culture conflict but crime as well.

Sellin (1938) described two sources of culture conflict. **Primary cultural conflict** exists when one culture brings its legal norms to bear on people socialized in a different culture. Primary cultural conflict occurs in three different social situations. First, border areas between two cultures provide an opportunity for holders of different conduct norms to clash directly and openly. World events provide many examples. In the former Yugoslavia predominantly Roman Catholic Croats, Eastern Orthodox Serbs, and Bosnian Muslims variously clashed and cooperated with one another throughout the 1990s and into the new century, making that part of the world a focus of much international attention. India and Pakistan have a longstanding border dispute that periodically erupts into open warfare; their recent acquisition or development of nuclear weapons has done little to reduce tensions in the Indian subcontinent. Lastly the citizens of the United States and Mexico share a long, open border. Conflict along this border, with its roots in Anglo and Mexican cultures, existed even before the 1848 Treaty of Guadalupe Hildago that formalized the boundaries after the Mexican–American War, and has yet to end.

Colonization may also lead to a second form of primary cultural conflict, particularly when the colonizing power declares the indigenous culture to be inferior. We need not turn only to the colonial histories of European nations to understand this idea. The historical relationship between American Indian tribes and the U.S. government also highlights this form of conflict. This treatment resulted in physical genocide (e.g., General Philip Sheridan's infamous quote that the only good Indian was a dead Indian) and cultural genocide (e.g., the creation of Indian Schools to "assimilate" American Indian children into the American mainstream). Those individuals who resist either form of genocide—and who may be viewed by their supporters as freedom fighters or patriots—run the risk of being designated as criminals by the colonial power.

Whenever immigrants leave one culture for another, they also run the risk of encountering primary cultural conflict. Sellin described a Sicilian father who avenged his family's honor by killing the "despoiler" of his daughter. Sellin viewed the father's reactions as an example of primary cultural conflict. The father could not understand why the police viewed him as a criminal, and in the eyes of his cultural peers, he was exacting expected and demanded retribution (Sellin 1938). Recent immigrants from certain African nations that circumcise female children (i.e., remove all or part of the clitoris) at an early age, a practice also known as female genital mutilation (FGM), run the risk of primary culture conflict. A female child who has not had this operation would, in all likelihood, be unacceptable in marriage. This practice is seen as culturally acceptable in some parts of the world but is considered mutilation and child abuse in the United States and many other nations. As of 2000 sixteen states and the federal government had adopted legal measures targeting FGM. Among members of the Hmong people from Southeast Asia, traditional shamans are preferred over modern medical practitioners, even when reliance on the former may result in death. Failure to secure medical treatment for underage children is generally viewed as a crime in the United States, placing many Hmong immigrants to this country at odds with local authorities (Faderman 1998; Fadiman 1997; see also Armstrong 2000; Tsai 2001). Primary cultural conflict remains a viable concept in the twenty-first century.

Secondary cultural conflict occurs whenever a subculture emerges within a dominant culture and that subculture has significantly different values and conduct norms. According to Sellin such developments were normal and natural. They were simply outgrowths of social differentiation, creating many "social groupings, each with its own definitions of life situations, its own ignorance or misunderstanding of the social values of other groups" (Sellin 1938:105).

In Sellin's view culture conflict is a mental construct, "primarily the clash between antagonistic conduct norms incorporated in personality" (Sellin 1938:66). For this mental condition to exist, the individual must acknowledge the conflict. In much conflict—primary and secondary—the conflict is external, between cultural codes and norms. For the conflict to be mental, the individual must be a

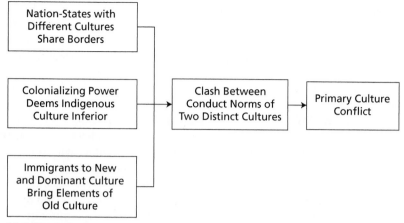

(a) Sellin's Primary Cultural Conflict

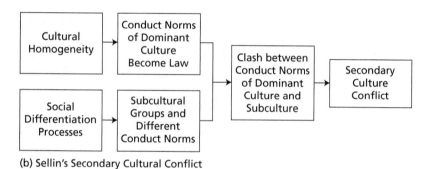

(b) Sellin's Secondary Cultural Conflict

FIGURE 8.2 Sellin's Primary and Secondary Cultural Conflict

cultural hybrid caught between two conflicting sets of conduct norms. Figure 8.2 summarizes Sellin's primary and secondary cultural conflict.

Group Conflict Theory

Georg Simmel's sociology of conflict emphasized the interests of the group. According to Simmel (1955) humans need groups to survive; he also made several key observations about the links between groups and their members:

- Members are both part of and products of the groups to which they belong.
- We best describe the behavior of group members as collective behavior.
- We can best understand the phenomenon of group creation as rooted in common interests and common needs.

Ultimately, as Simmel observed, consensus is an illusion that masks the underlying conflict.

Group actions are based on these operating principles, and sometimes the outcome is conflict. Simmel believed that, when individuals recognize that they have interests or needs in common with others, they form a group. The group then seeks, through collective behavior, to further its interests and fulfill its needs. Eventually they develop a sense of group loyalty and form emotional attachments. Those who seek to infringe on the interests and needs of the group become its enemies. From this perspective group members exhibit loyalty and identification with the group's interests or needs, and often the result is intergroup conflict.

Simmel's work influenced George Vold (1958:283–84), who focused on group interests and the problems they create. Whereas Sellin was describing crime as a conflict of cultures, Vold saw the group itself as a source of conflict. He noted that group conflict is not much different from a pitched battle between persons or groups seeking to attain the same limited goals. Groups conflict with one another when they seek to expand or protect their group's interests, and as they do so, in-group loyalties intensify. Conflict of this sort is healthy, inevitable, and continuous, as groups seek redress for wrongs, improvement of their status, and redistribution of power (Vold and Bernard 1986:272). "The result is a more or less continuous struggle to maintain, or to improve, the place of one's own group in the interaction of groups" (Vold and Bernard 1986:273).

How is group conflict related to criminality? According to Vold's **group conflict theory,** groups in positions of authority have their values woven into the law to protect that which they hold dear. Because the laws are based on their own values and interests, the likelihood of criminalizing their behavior is reduced even as it increases for those with conflicting values.[5]

Vold saw the legislative process, an arena of compromise and accommodations, as a key battleground. For example, one group wishes to criminalize that which threatens its interests and needs, and another may view these attempts as threats to its interests and needs. In the resulting conflict the group with the most power or votes wins—or there is compromise.

In the end the law intrudes on the interests of the losers. Group interests and differences in relative power help us understand why legislatures outlaw certain harmful substances such as marijuana while taxing freely available tobacco and alcohol (Abadinsky 2001). The poor, lacking the ability to influence lawmakers, often find behavior in which they habitually engage criminalized. For example, numbers betting, with its promise of quick riches from a small investment of time or money, contradicts the middle-class values of hard work and industry. A redefinition of this activity as a harmless amusement by powerful political interests enables cash-hungry state governments to sponsor lotteries.

Vold supported the view that crime is the behavior of **minority power groups.** These groups, by definition, lack sufficient influence to promote or defend their interests and needs. Groups that find themselves disconnected from the lawmaking process are more likely to violate existing laws, which may conflict with their own interests, needs, and purposes ("If it's not my law, why should I do as it says?"). For example, inner-city youth gangs, rather than being culturally different, may feel disenfranchised from the power structure represented by the dominant majority. They may engage in behavior that the law prohibits, such as underage drinking, and illicit drug use. At odds with the dominant majority, youth gangs conflict with the police who represent the interests of that majority. As in most conflicts, actions by the police against gangs only help to solidify the gangs and intensify their in-group loyalties (Vold and Bernard 1986).

Assessing Conflict Theory

Several general themes dominate critiques of conflict theory:

- *A lack of general empirical support.* Most conflict theorists employ historical and event analyses. For example, Isaac Balbus (1973), in his analysis of the 1960s riots in Watts (Los Angeles), Detroit, and Chicago, observed that they posed major challenges to the authority of law enforcement. The courts, in Balbus's opinion, sided with the "power elites" and viewed the reestablishment of order as their first priority. Critics allege that conflict theorists frequently select supporting evidence and ignore contradictory evidence (Friday 1977).

- *The law not the "cause" of behavior.* Without laws crime would not exist, but the presence of laws does not *create* crimes (Clinard and Meier 1985:91). Certain behaviors have always troubled society, and some more than others. Those that require a formal response because of the nature of the threat to social cohesion or the social order become crimes, but only with the passage of laws.

- *A lack of attention to individual motivations.* Although we learn a great deal about the creation of laws from conflict theory, we learn very little about *why* people commit crimes. Because these are group-level explanations, they more clearly articulate the motivation of social groups, government officials, and parents than those designated as offenders.

Anecdotal evidence does provide support for the conflict perspective on crime and violence. For example, Vold's theory gives us insights into the 1992 South Central Los Angeles riot that followed the jury's decision in the trial of police officers accused of beating Rodney King. King was the recipient of unlawful force at the hands of the arresting officers, a portrayal supported by police communications tapes and a videotape viewed by millions. Many black and Hispanic residents of South Central Los Angeles responded to the officers' acquittal with outrage and disbelief. In the resulting riot thousands of crimes were committed, including opportunistic crimes by individuals with lengthy criminal records. For many others this episode of urban violence was rooted in feelings of frustration; the local community's disenfranchised and powerless residents may have been expressing disdain for a system they believed did not represent their interests by the crimes they committed.

The rioters targeted Asian businesses with which the black and Hispanic residents of South Central Los Angeles were in conflict. The Asians were engaging in a process of ethnic succession, physically replacing the long-term black residents of the area who, threatened by these new groups, became concerned that they would also replace them in the economic system. Albert Bergesen and Max Herman (1998:52) suggested that the riots were a "defensive response to in-migration [as] part of the process of ethnic succession, particularly when succession occurs rapidly. Thus, hyper-ethnic succession can lead to collective violence." Analyses of other race riots have also found that competition for scarce resources, especially between racial and ethnic groups that are replacing one another in a geographic area, can precipitate violence (see, e.g., Myers 1997; Olzak and Shanahan 1996). As Susan Olzak and Suzanne Shanahan (1996:953) observed, "Our analyses suggest that one strategy for understanding race riots can be found by exploring the forces that elevate levels of racial competition."

Global politics, particularly revolutions, provide an example of group conflict creating criminals. "A successful revolution makes criminals out of the government officials previously in power, and an unsuccessful revolution makes its leaders into traitors subject to immediate execution" (Vold and Bernard 1986:275). Consider the following:

- Hours after the collapse of the communist regime in Romania, a military tribunal tried, convicted, and executed the former Marxist dictator Nicolae Ceauşescu.

- In the Republic of South Africa anti-apartheid groups acted out the process of political struggle, rebellion, and revolution. For decades their supporters were minority-power-group criminals, but ultimately they became the dominant and legitimate power group. This transformation did not occur before the previously "warring" parties drafted a plan for the distribution of power. In 1994 one of these former minority-power-group criminals, Nelson Mandela, became president of South Africa.

Closer to home, conflict criminology may yield unique insights into the nation's drug laws and drug control policy. During the 1980s, when the nation was believed to be in the midst of a crack cocaine epidemic, states enacted different sentencing guidelines for persons convicted of possessing crack cocaine versus powder cocaine. The drugs are chemically identical, but crack provided a different delivery system from powder cocaine. That is, it was cheaper, because changing cocaine into crack geometrically expanded the amount of "product" available for sale, and at a lower price than powder cocaine. Moreover, the delivery system—crack was smoked, as compared to snorting powder cocaine—was more efficient. The drug was especially popular among the nation's minority power groups. Creating laws that called for sentences far harsher than those for the possession of a chemically identical substance could be construed to be an example of culture conflict: It takes 100 times the weight in powder cocaine to trigger the same penalties as for crack (U.S. Sentencing Commission 1995). Those who made the laws—and their children—were far more likely to use powder cocaine than crack, although in reality the statistical probability of using either drug was probably rather low. For example, in the mid-1990s, among crack cocaine defendants, nearly 90 percent were black, but only 7 percent were Hispanic and 5 percent were white; for powder cocaine, 40 percent were black or Hispanic and 18 percent were white (U.S. Sentencing Commission 1995). Challenges of the sentencing laws as unfair and inequitable have consistently been ignored by appellate courts (*Edwards v. United States* 1997).

Conflict, Public Policy, and Criminal Justice Practices

Policies related to conflict theories necessarily emphasize power sharing, a difficult idea to sell to those who wield power. In modern, complex societies group conflicts, such as those described by Simmel and Vold, are endemic. Obviously an *interested* third party could step in to resolve issues in a coercive fashion. However, as proved on the international scene in Africa, the Middle East, and the Balkans, such measures often fail spectacularly or end up creating new conflicts. Steven Vago (1990:178–83) identified various methods of conflict resolution, several of which have implications for criminal justice:

- *Negotiation.* The parties attempt to resolve their differences without the intercession of a third party, normally through a process of compromise. This method is often used with prison uprisings (although sometimes mediation is employed) and military stalemates (e.g., the Korean conflict and the Vietnam War).

- *Mediation.* An impartial mediator acts as a facilitator and advisor to help the conflicting parties work out an agreement. For instance, neighborhood dispute resolution centers provide a local-level means for mediating everything from personal disputes to minor crimes. Judges, police, and prosecutors refer most of the participants (Abadinsky 1998; Vago 1990).[6]

- *Arbitration.* This process also uses an uninvolved and neutral third party; however, unlike in mediation, arbitration's results are binding on all parties. For example, if during a police strike officers and management cannot reach a settlement through negotiations or mediation, a court may order binding arbitration. In some jurisdictions disputing parties may employ retired judges as arbitrators (Goldberg, Green, and Sanders 1985).

- *Adjudication.* This represents a public and formal method of resolving disputes. Whether a judge or jury is present, civil law litigants place their fates in the hands of others. They become relatively passive participants in the proceedings, especially compared with other methods of peaceful conflict resolution. In criminal matters the state represents the interests of the injured party, effectively limiting that party's role in the proceedings. Also, adjudication is far more oriented than the other methods described toward "zero sum" outcomes in which neither party wins (Vago 1990:182).

Law Enforcement Practices Conflict theory helps us understand both disputes between officers and management and problematic interactions between police and citizens. First, when police officers disagree with management about any number of mutual concerns, ranging from salaries to fringe benefits to shift work, a classic interest-group conflict exists. On those rare occasions when the officers and management cannot reach an agreement, a strike may result. Management can criminalize the striking officers' behavior because in most jurisdictions the police cannot legally strike. In the face of a court order, normally an injunction against the illegal strike, officers have two choices: (1) Continue the strike and risk arrest, or (2) end the strike. Occasionally the officers have opted to continue the strike and suffer the legal consequences. Several such strikes have turned violent when the police believed that their peaceful efforts to resolve the dispute were failing. As Vold (1958) observed, they may feel disconnected from the lawmaking process and in conflict with the existing laws. And the disconnection can result in violence, as in the police strikes in Cincinnati (1918), Boston (1919), and San Francisco (1975) (Ayers 1977; Bopp, Chignell, and Maddox 1977).

Judicial Practices As described in the policy section on conflict theory, the role of the judiciary varies depending upon the type of explanation being considered. For example, courts play a central role in adjudicating competing or conflicting group interests only when one or more of the parties bring that issue to the attention of the court. A common example involves the abortion issue, in which both sides have attempted to use the courts, with varying results. In 1994, for example, courts in several states upheld laws restricting abortion and also awarded abortion clinics million-dollar judgments against anti-abortion groups. As Vold (1958) noted, the conflict view does not explain all crime, but it works best in relation to the distinctions between consensus and conflict crime (see also Hagan 1994:56–57).

Correctional Practices Prisons and jails are "total institutions" because they exercise control over virtually every aspect of inmates' life. By their nature community-based corrections and other alternatives to incarceration are less controlling. Nonetheless, the role of power in corrections is undisputed. For example, prison and jail communities are based on group interests. That is, guards have interests they wish to preserve, as do inmates, civilian employees, treatment staff, and administrators. From an administrative point of view, one set of interests, however, outweighs all others: the desire to maintain control over the inmates, or custody interests. All others are secondary, a fact that can generate conflict among different types of staff. For example, treatment staff may feel as if their work is seen as unimportant, exacerbating existing tensions between them and custodial staff (Clear and Cole 1990; Hawkins and Alpert 1989). Prison uprisings and riots are the ultimate form of correctional conflict, having, as they do, the potential to destroy a correctional facility.

As a case in point, consider prison gangs. Group and culture conflict theories do not explain why people join them; the explanations are perhaps best left to other theories (compare learning theories in Chapter 5 and subcultural theories in Chapter 6). These theories can, however, give insights into why gangs exist in prison and how they function. At one level nearly all prison inmates—members of the inmate subculture—have traditionally been described as solidly against both normative society and prison administrators, but especially correctional officers (Sykes and Messinger 1960). From a group conflict perspective this animosity is easily understood. Guards, as the ones with power, see inmate attempts to thwart their authority and undermine their position in the prison structure as threatening. Inmates are a classic minority power group, confronting an institutionally more powerful entity, the guards. Moreover, members of prison gangs with close ties to criminal street gangs may be even more threatening than other inmates. Correctional officers are more likely to criminalize the conduct of the inmate gangs that threaten the orderly operation of the correctional facility.

Culture conflict theory also helps explain prison life and inmate–staff conflicts. The majority of prison inmates are minority-group members (Mays and Winfree 2002). Many of the nation's prisons are located in rural counties, with the guards drawn from the local population, which means they are unlikely to have much in common either racially or culturally with the prisoners they are guarding. It is widely believed, for example, that the correctional officers at Attica State Prison, in rural, upstate New York little understood the minority inmates from downstate New York and that this cultural gulf helped exacerbate the traditional guard–inmate conflict and sparked the resulting 1971 prison riot (New York Special Commission on Attica 1972). In other words, culture conflict existed on top of group conflict.

This description may not be limited to the Attica of 30 years ago. Given the multicultural nature of contemporary prison gangs (e.g., the Mexican Mafia,

Black Guerrilla Family, and Aryan Brotherhood), it is possible that group *and* culture conflict combine to exacerbate historical differences between guards and inmates (Mays and Winfree 2002:198). This speculation was bolstered by the increase in reported assaults on staff during the 1990s (Stephan 1997). (See Table 8.1 for an overview of labeling and conflict theories of crime.)

SUMMARY

The theories in this chapter share several features. Power is the most obvious one, in that labeling theory and both culture conflict and group conflict theories purport to explore power's role in defining crime and criminals. Although the definitions differ slightly from theory to theory, power's role as a causal factor is unchanging. That is, some groups or individuals have power, use it to further their own interests, and are not above exploiting it to control (i.e., make deviant, criminalize, or otherwise discredit) the conduct of those perceived to be threats. Of equal importance is the fact that, to differing degrees, each theory is critical of the use of power. Labeling theorists question its use in criminalizing certain behavior, especially youthful misconduct, and suggest a reconsideration of any policies related to youth–police contacts. Conflict theorists similarly condemn the misuse of power by those seeking to maintain or improve their positions in society. They, too, argue for its measured and considered use. However, an implicit acknowledgment of the "right" of the powerful to exercise control over the less powerful may mute this criticism. In other words, even while pointing out the problems with power differentials created by labeling and conflicts, these theorists generally support the existing social order.

Second, the theories reviewed in this chapter are essentially deterministic in nature, blaming forces beyond the control of the individual for causing the criminal condition. Labeling theory focuses largely on society's responses. After all, crime is behavior so labeled; the criminal is the person so labeled. Conflict theory forces us to consider how the powerful may use laws to maintain their position in society. For some conflict theorists group interests guide the criminalizing process; for others the motives of the state are central.

Third, power's insertion into any discussion of crime results in confusion about what to call the resulting theories. Labeling theory is the labeling perspective to some, social reaction theory to others, and labeling theory to still others (Chambliss 1988:276; Davis and Stasz 1990:44; Vold and Bernard 1986:249). For some criminologists the term *conflict theory* evokes images of Marxism; for others, such as Sellin and Vold, the term is reserved for "soft" conflict (cf. Clinard and Meier 1985:87; Vold and Bernard 1986:269).

Fourth, at times conflict and labeling theories seem to overlap. That is, groups identified as problematic for society may be on the receiving end of negative labels that devalue the groups, their members, and their respective values. This may be the case for street gangs.

Lastly, except for Sellin's culture conflict theory, this chapter's theories rose to prominence during the 1960s and early 1970s, a turbulent time for the nation. Conflict and labeling theories gave liberals a means of attacking the excesses of governmental control without condemning the entire system. Labeling and conflict

Table 8.1 Labeling and Conflict Theories of Crime

Theory	Major Figures	Central Assumptions	Causal Arguments (Key Terms)	Strengths	Weaknesses
Labeling theory	Tannenbaum, Goffman, Becker, Lemert, Schur	Social interpretation is highly subjective: What we believe to be true becomes true if we organize our responses or behavior to that interpretation; power—especially as used in the control of misconduct—is neither good nor bad, but simply exists and is used to further some end.	If we observe the offender, initial acts of deviance (*primary deviance*) elicit social penalties; each successive time the actor commits the act and is caught, there is a tendency to "up the ante," increasing the sanctions and devaluing the actor's social worth; at some point the actor assumes the deviant's master status (*secondary deviance*).	Enjoys broad popular support among field practitioners (e.g., social workers, juvenile officers); the public intuitively understands its concepts and causal processes; provides direct policy implications, as in diversion, deinstitutionalization, and decriminalization; new versions have met with empirical successes.	Has major theoretical problems, including concern for tautological causal ordering; is a general lack of empirical support; includes a "value neutral" and questionable definition of power; focuses on the midrange agents of power; the need to justify policies seems to drive efforts to verify the theory.
Conflict theory Culture conflict Group conflict	Sellin, Vold	Conflict is inevitable because power is a scarce and valued resource; various groups will attempt to seize and use power in furtherance of their interests or, at a minimum, seek to protect their interests; access to laws and the mechanisms for their creation is essential to the consolidation and continuation of the group's power base.	*Culture conflict theory:* We say that crimes occur when individuals follow the cultural imperatives of their culture of origin and those imperatives are at odds with the dominant culture in which they live. *Group conflict theory:* Crime is the behavior of minority power groups; the powerless may feel disenfranchised from the law and free to violate it.	Includes a definition of power that is more "mature" than that found in labeling theory; seems to fit with historical and anecdotal accounts of conflict.	Lacks empirical support, especially for the more established versions; different analyses of events used to support theories often yield different conclusions about the value of the theories for explaining crime; not all laws protect the interests of the few; law does not cause behavior; the theories inform us about law formation but give few insights into individual motivations.

perspectives enjoyed a resurgence in the 1990s. The key difference is that when these power-based theories first emerged many criminologists lauded them for their intuitive and logical insights into crime. Simultaneously they condemned the theories for their reliance on rhetoric and disregard of empirical proof. The new variants place a far greater premium on the links between theory, methods, and practice.

KEY TERMS

conflict criminologists

decriminalization

deinstitutionalization

deviance amplification

diversion

dramatization of evil

due process guarantees

falsely accused

group conflict theory

hidden deviants

master status

minority power groups

negotiations

net widening

prestige symbols

primary cultural conflict

primary deviation

radical nonintervention

retrospective interpretation

role engulfment

secondary cultural conflict

secondary-deviance hypothesis

secondary deviation

shaming ceremonies

status characteristics hypothesis

status degradation ceremonies

status offenders

stereotyping

stigma symbols

stigmatization

symbolic assailants

symbolic interactionism

true deviants

true innocents

CRITICAL REVIEW QUESTIONS

1. With respect to crime, what is meant by the "definition of the situation"?

2. Compare and contrast Tannenbaum's dramatization of evil, Goffman's stigmatization, and Garfinkel's status degradation ceremonies.

3. What is the value of Becker's use of the term *master status* in the study of crime and delinquency? Do you agree with his ideas about the relationships between perceived and actual behavior? In either event explain why you feel the way you do.

4. Give an example and justification for a person moving immediately from the first act of misconduct to

secondary deviation and all that the notion infers.

5. In your opinion, which of Schur's four elements of labeling is the strongest? Which is the weakest? In both cases explain why you made that particular selection.

6. Compare and contrast Wilkins' deviance amplification and Schur's labeling process.

7. How do you feel about the idea that we should allow some convicted offenders to secure licenses or certain forms of employment?

8. What is, in your opinion, the greatest shortcoming of labeling theory? Explain your thinking. Do you

believe that the restatements of labeling may eventually overcome this or the other shortcomings?

9. Which single policy implication associated with labeling seems to pose the greatest threat to the fair administration of justice? Explain.

10. Labeling theory is important to the courts, police, and corrections. In which specific instance or practice do you believe that labeling theory best explains what is happening?

11. Sellin's statements about culture conflict include three sets of conditions. Which one seems to explain best certain types of crime in the United States? Explain your choice.

12. What do you see as the greatest shortcoming of conflict theory?

13. Which single policy implication associated with conflict theory seems to pose the greatest threat to the fair administration of justice? Explain.

14. Conflict theory is important to the courts, police, and corrections. In which specific instance or practice do you believe that conflict theory best explains what is happening?

NOTES

1. As the next chapter discusses, power is used in very different ways, by very different groups, to maintain their positions of influence. Chapter 9 explores Marxists' "blaming" of capitalism for crime, and the use of gender roles and Marxism by feminist theorists to explain male dominance and the subjugation of women. The conflict examined in this chapter could be considered "soft" conflict, and that explored in the next chapter as "radical" or "hard" conflict.

2. If you are not familiar with the Buckley Amendment, a right-to-privacy law that governs access to student records and other academic privacy issues, you may wish to research it.

3. Status offenders are juveniles who have committed law violations that would not be offenses at all were it not for the offenders' age.

4. One criticism of official labeling is that it does not account for those criminals who move from primary to secondary deviance without ever having been observed; that is, they are hidden secondary deviants who completed role engulfment.

5. Vold excluded impulsive, irrational criminal acts as beyond the scope of conflict theory. These acts are unrelated to any clash between groups with differing interests and goals.

6. A related concept has to do with the ombudsman, an official associated with a public agency who receives complaints against that agency and investigates them. For example, an ombudsman in the public prosecutor's office may be asked to investigate a citizen complaint about a particular case that was dropped or to resolve disputes between other officials in the office. A correctional system ombudsman may investigate complaints and charges made by inmates and staff alike. This process combines mediation and investigation.

9

Marxist and Feminist Theories

CHAPTER OVERVIEW

Marxism and Crime

Instrumental Marxism

Structural Marxism

Left Realism and Peacemaking Criminology

Assessing Marxist Theory

Marxism, Public Policy, and Criminal Justice Practices

Feminist Criminology

Liberal Feminism: The Liberation Hypothesis

Radical Feminism: Patriarchal Society, Oppressed Females, and Survival

Socialist Feminism: Power–Control Theory

Marxist Feminism: The Critique of Sexual Politics

Assessing Feminist Theory

Feminism, Public Policy, and Criminal Justice Practices

LEARNING OBJECTIVES

- Place Marxism in the proper social, political, economic, and historical context.

- Appreciate that not all Marxists are strict followers of Karl Marx; some have modified his nineteenth-century philosophy to fit today's multilayered society, a social system not predicted by Marx.

- Comprehend the breadth of feminist theories of criminality and women's positions of power in society compared with those of men.

- Understand the extent to which arguments couched in Marxist and feminist theories yield insights into the nature and extent of female criminality.

INTRODUCTION

Who wields power is as important as the idea of power itself. Two groups of criminological theorists, Marxists and feminists, share this view of power. For instance, Marxists know who and what to blame for society's misfortunes, including crime: Capitalism is the offending economic system, and capitalists are the enemy. Capitalism exploits those who provide the labor that turns the wheels of commerce. To maintain their dominant position, capitalists form alliances amongst themselves in an ongoing conspiracy against the interests of the working class. Does this sound like political rhetoric? It should. These ideas provided the philosophical underpinnings for international communism during most of the twentieth century.

Feminist theorists express similar views on the causes of crime and delinquency. They, too, look at the uses and abuses of power, particularly as wielded by men or employed by a male-dominated justice system. Some feminists have much in common with the conflict theorists reviewed in Chapter 8. The focus for these liberal feminists is on gender as the basis of group distinctions. Other feminists share many beliefs with Marxists and socialists. Thus, a good starting point is the general contributions of Marx to the study of crime.

MARXISM AND CRIME

- Do you know a student who feels compelled to major in a subject that, although not very interesting or exciting, promises great financial rewards? According to Marxists that person has fallen victim to capitalism's false consciousness.

- Have you looked at the nation's prisons and jails? Besides tending to share race and ethnicity, the inmates have similar class origins. Not many are capitalists although some may aspire to be capitalists.

- Have you ever felt betrayed by charges that your government violated the law by illegally spying on its citizens? What if government officials broke international laws, as in government-sponsored assassinations of heads of governments? Prior to the 1960s such charges rarely surfaced.

- Have you followed the troubles of the cigarette or handgun industries? Both have struggled with their public image, and neither enjoys the same level of respect—and power—it did a decade ago. One Marxist theory should help you better understand this phenomenon.

The common element in all these questions is the German political philosopher Karl Marx (1818–1883) and his sociopolitical philosophy, known as **Marxism.** During the nineteenth century Marx described industrialized nations as divided societies in which **capitalists** own the means of production, and workers, or the **proletariat,** provide the labor. For Marx power derived from ownership of property and control over the means of production. Capitalists use power to subjugate the workers, guaranteeing consolidation of wealth in their hands. Thus, society is characterized by a class struggle between capitalists and the proletariat. In this struggle or class war, capitalists mobilize the resources of government and religion to protect their positions of advantage. As capitalism advances, so does the gap between the capitalists and the workers, with the former gathering wealth at the expense of the latter.

Outside these two classes—owners and workers—is the **lumpenproletariat,** a parasitical group whose predations are based on selfish concerns and the need to survive. Their behavior is antithetical to the capitalist order. They and members of the working class defined by capitalists as dangerous or disposable stand the greatest probability of becoming criminals. Over time Marxists placed the **bourgeoisie,** or middle class, and the **petite bourgeoisie,** or shopkeepers and government officials, between the capitalist and worker classes.

A crucial idea to Marxists is **false consciousness.** This condition exists when workers, and even members of the middle class, believe that there is a societal consensus on critical social issues like crime and justice. A key part of false consciousness is the notion that capitalists care about interests other than their own. Thus, capitalists may promote positive-sounding doctrines such as freedom of the press. Marxists believe that an inevitable revolution will signal the end of capitalism and the beginning of communism. To achieve this end, Marxists must expose the false consciousness and, in so doing, the capitalist system's inequities.

Marxists express unique views on crime, distinguishing between three types. First, the crimes of the proletariat are usually directed at capitalists and so are revolutionary. Second, the crimes of the lumpenproletariat are typically directed against the working class and so, to the extent that we can define them as "political," are reactionary. Third, the crimes of the capitalists—the *real* crime—are acts of greed and avarice, and typically involve actions directed against the workers and harmful to the common good (e.g., industrial pollution).

Marxists view crime as capitalism's inevitable by-product. They condemn positivists for studying only minor forces in crime causation. Positivists, they argue, fail to see the larger social context of crime—the bigger picture in which capitalism leads to a class system of severely differentiated wealth. The resulting social system is one in which the behavior of the weak has a greater chance of being defined as criminal than do the actions of the powerful. Wealth and power inequities also cause **alienation** and **demoralization.** The alienated underclass reacts in ways defined by capitalists as deviant: Some abuse alcohol and other drugs, and others seek even more destructive escapes from the crushing power of capitalism. The resulting demoralization generates criminal behavior.

Two themes dominate Marxist criminology. First, **instrumental Marxism** emphasizes the role of law, law enforcers, and government in subjugating the working class. This perspective was popular during the late 1960s and early 1970s, when the government, along with other social and economic institutions, came under scrutiny and attack. Class war and revolution were espoused by radical antiwar groups such as the Weather Underground in the late 1960s and early 1970s. Radical civil rights spokespersons and groups—from prison inmates Eldridge Cleaver and George Jackson to Black Panthers Bobby Seale and Huey Newton—also understood revolutionary Marxist doctrines. Moreover, events such as the riot at the 1968 Democratic Convention in Chicago, confirmed what these Marxists already knew. In their view the police were the "running dogs" of capitalism, oppressing the working class at every turn. Oppression, conflict, and state control were common themes in the works of early instrumental Marxists (cf. Krisberg 1975; Quinney 1973; Taylor, Walton, and Young 1973).

A second theme emerged in response to criticisms of instrumental Marxism. In the late 1970s a group of emerging sociologists saw the role of law in defining society as causing structural or "built-in" inequality and, by extension, crime (Colvin and Pauly 1983:513; see also Appelbaum 1979). They often linked economic inequality to violence (Blau and Blau 1977, 1982; Wallace and Humphries 1981), homicide (Braithwaite 1984), rape (Messerschmidt 1986; Schwendinger and Schwendinger 1983), and prostitution (Miller 1986). Even youthful misbehavior has not escaped the attention of structural Marxists. They view children as totally left out of the capitalist cycle. Capitalists exclude children from the labor market but expect them to take on the values of that market. This condition produces unique strains that find individual and group expression in adolescent rebellion and delinquency (Colvin and Pauly 1983; Greenberg 1981; Schwendinger and Schwendinger 1985). The work of this group became known as **structural Marxism.**

Instrumental Marxism

The Dutch criminologist Willem Bonger (1969[1916]) saw capitalism as promoting greed and self-interest, what he called **excessive egoism.** Capitalists encourage citizens to seek ends that benefit themselves with little regard for others. But they criminalize only the greed of the poor, allowing the wealthy (i.e., themselves) to pursue their desires with impunity. Bonger viewed socialism as a solution to this problem. Socialism, he wrote, would promote the general welfare of all citizens and alleviate the legal bias enjoyed by the rich (Bonger 1969[1916]).

Contemporary Marxist criminologists, including Richard Quinney, William Chambliss, and Barry Krisberg, have expanded the instrumentalists' basic arguments.

Crime and Demystification We can best understand crime, Quinney (1973:vi) wrote, as "how the capitalist ruling class establishes its control over those it must oppress." He described **demystification,** a central idea in his critical philosophy, "as the removal of the myths—the false consciousness—created by the official reality. . . . The underside of official reality is thereby exposed" (Quinney 1973:11).

Quinney (1980) engaged in the demystification of crime by defining its many forms, tying each to Marxist class conflict. For Quinney crime takes two main forms: (1) crimes of the working class and (2) crimes of the elite. Working-class crimes include crimes of accommodation and crimes of resistance. **Crimes of accommodation** do not challenge the social order but take place within it. For

---

IN THEIR OWN WORDS: Kropotkin on Anarchy and Crime

Peter Kropotkin, a member of the Russian royal family, was a nineteenth-century anarchist. **Anarchism** dates from Ancient Greece. Basic to the philosophy and practice is the idea that people are intrinsically good and that social institutions corrupt them, which means the best way to achieve change is to abandon all social conventions. Anarchism is often associated with lawlessness. For example, after the assassination of President William McKinley by anarchist Leon Czolgosz in 1901, U.S. immigration officials forbade anarchists from entering the country. Following the overthrow of the czar in 1917, the Bolsheviks outlawed anarchists in the Soviet Union, effectively silencing them as a force in European communism.

- *On criminal sanctions:* "We are continually being told of the benefits conferred by law and the beneficial effects of penalties, but have the speakers ever attempted to strike a balance between the benefits attributed to laws and penalties, and the degrading effects of these penalties upon humanity?" (p. 216).

- *On the ties between prison and future crime:* "Another significant angle is that the offense for which a man returns to prison is always more serious than his first. If, before, it was petty thieving, he returns now for some daring burglary, if he was imprisoned for the first time for some act of violence, often he will return as a murderer" (p. 221).

- *On society's role in creating criminals and glorifying crime:* "Society itself daily creates these people incapable of a life of honest labor, and filled with anti-social desires. She glorifies them when their crimes are crowned with financial success. She sends them to prison when they have not 'succeeded' " (p. 233).

Source: Kropotkin (1970[1927]).

---

example, predatory crimes of accommodation mimic capitalism, in that offenders get property from their victims (e.g., robbery, theft, burglary, and auto theft). Violent crimes of accommodation—including homicide, rape, and assault—reflect capitalism's own use of institutionalized brutalization.

Crimes of resistance are working-class reactions to the ruling elite's exploitation. These crimes include both predatory and violent crimes, with both revolutionary and nonrevolutionary goals. For example, a revolutionary group—whose members are rarely from the working class—could engage in crimes of violence against the state, such as bombing court buildings or other governmental facilities. Revolutionaries also commit predatory crimes, such as bank robbery and kidnapping, to finance their cause and to hit capitalists where it hurts the most.

The class conflict aspects of some crimes of resistance are harder to comprehend, but the radicalization of prison inmates gives some insight. While incarcerated, some prison inmates, especially people of color, begin to view their crimes as directed against capitalism and so come to define themselves as **political prisoners** (cf. Cleaver 1968; Seale 1968). For example, the inmate leaders of New York's Attica State Prison uprising in 1971 used Marxist rhetoric (Abadinsky 2000; Winfree 1995).

The crimes of the elite take three forms. First, as elites capitalists commit **crimes of domination** and **crimes of repression** to protect their interests, property, and profits. They engage in crimes intended to create economic domination, such as bid rigging and price-fixing. Elites commit violent acts directly against the public, such as selling faulty or dangerous products even after they are aware of the dangers (Michalowski 1985; Pepinsky and Jesilow 1984). Corporate America also commits crimes directly against its own workers and the public, by failing to conform to worker safety standards (Michalowski 1985).

Crimes of control involve police, courts, and corrections, the ruling class's instruments of social control. Some control efforts are explicitly designed to crush the state's enemies, as often happened in nineteenth- and early twentieth-century union-inspired strikes. At other times social control agents serve capitalism in more implicit ways, through the lack of organizational controls, administrative oversight, or operating policies. In particular capitalists view the lumpenproletariat as "social dynamite" (Spitzer 1975). Arrest and detainment practices, sentencing patterns, and prison conditions protect them from this dangerous class.

Finally **crimes of government** are both complex and important. They include criminal acts in which governments violate constitutional guarantees and the civil rights of citizens (Balkan, Berger, and Schmidt 1980; Chambliss 1989a). Those who commit these crimes do so for the state. According to this view governments also launch illegal military operations and violate the sovereignty of other nations (Chambliss 1988; Clinard and Quinney 1967; Roebuck and Weeber 1978). For example, shortly after the U.S. invasion of Panama and the arrest of its ruler, Manuel Noriega, legal scholars questioned the legality of those actions (Lewis 1990).

According to Alfred McCoy (1991) the U.S. government, primarily using the Central Intelligence Agency, aided heroin traffickers during the Vietnam War (see also Balkan, Berger, and Schmidt 1980:196–98; Chambliss 1988). More recently, in Central America and the Middle East, drugs and weapons smuggling figured prominently in the Iran–Contra scandal. Critical criminologists linked governmental motives to ideological positions, although profit motives definitely played a role as well (Chambliss 1989a).

By redefining criminology's scope to include a critical orientation, instrumental criminologists have uncovered many previously unrecognized crime forms. Barry Krisberg, another instrumental criminologist, favored a far broader perspective in his critique of privilege.

Crime and Privilege The **New Criminology** provided an alternative way of viewing crime and criminals (see Taylor, Walton, and Young 1973). Krisberg's *Crime and Privilege,* published in 1975, was a clear testament of the New Criminology. Krisberg berated traditional (i.e., "old") criminology as serving the power elite's interests. He was particularly harsh toward liberal sociologists, whom he called "hip sociologists." They understood the nature of political struggles but, he claimed, succumbed to institutionalized cynicism and simply stopped "tilting at windmills." That is, they bemoaned the unfairness of a modern capitalist state but did nothing to change it.

We should frame crime studies, noted Krisberg (1975:20), within "the broader quest for social justice." **Social justice** is best viewed as a condition of equality, self-determination, and liberation that results in the elimination of all conditions of human suffering. **Privilege** is "the possession of that which is valued by a particular social group in a given historical period" (Krisberg 1975:20). As the early conflict theorists noted, some groups win and others lose, whether by force or by compromise. Krisberg (1975:20) viewed this conflict as an injustice. Class, power, and status are essential and interrelated aspects of various privilege systems. From initial police contacts to processing in the correctional system, privilege systems associated with race, class, and economic status determine one's fate. The poor, the lower-classes, and minorities do not commit more crime, but rather are simply more likely to suffer negative processing at the hands of the "(in)justice system" (Krisberg 1975).

This characterization includes women among the society's "disprivileged." Although women commit quantitatively less crime than men, they "are often subjected to harsher conditions than men," including disrespect and brutality at the hands of criminal justice officials (Krisberg 1975:25). When the privileged engage in rules violation, observed Krisberg, they rarely accord it the status of crime. And if they do criminalize it, the penalties are far lighter than those accorded the crimes of the disprivileged, when—*and if*—they are imposed. Figure 9.1 summarizes instrumental Marxist crime theory.

Structural Marxism

Academic Marxists have largely abandoned the instrumental perspective for an alternative structuralist view in which they describe a far more complex ruling class. Structuralist Marxists view the state as ensuring the long-term dominance of capitalism as a way of life (Chambliss and Seidman 1982:313). Consequently the state must balance the interests of many groups, at times even allowing the less powerful the appearance of victory. But it never loses sight of its ultimate goal: the survival of capitalism as the dominant system.

Crime and Law A key contribution to structural Marxism is found in the analysis of late medieval English property and vagrancy laws by Chambliss. As feudalism declined and was replaced by capitalism, formal laws concomitantly emerged, especially laws designed to protect the interests of emergent capitalists (Balkan, Berger, and Schmidt 1980:48–49). For example, Chambliss (1964, 1976) observed that English vagrancy laws reflected the interests of the economic elites. A compelling force in the creation of vagrancy laws was the bubonic plague, which decimated the labor force. The elites used the first English vagrancy law, passed in 1349, to force work from beggars, set low wages for their labor, and limit their movement through the countryside (Chambliss 1976:71).

The growth of commerce and trade intensified the need for the cheap labor previously supplied by feudalism's serfs. And these are not merely historical facts. Until recent court decisions eliminated broad and ill-defined vagrancy laws, law enforcement officials often enforced them during harvesttime in agribusiness states. Selective enforcement increased the transitoriness of migrant workers, as police moved them to other job sites, guaranteeing cheap labor (Spradley 1970).

Theft laws protect property, capitalism's cornerstone. Jerome Hall (1952) has noted that no systematic laws protecting private property existed in England prior to 1473. As feudalism gave way to commerce and trade, landowners lost control of the lawmaking process to the emerging economic elites. However, the new elites could not rely on existing laws because they were too unsophisticated and narrowly defined. In fact, they commonly prohibited only theft by servants (Chambliss

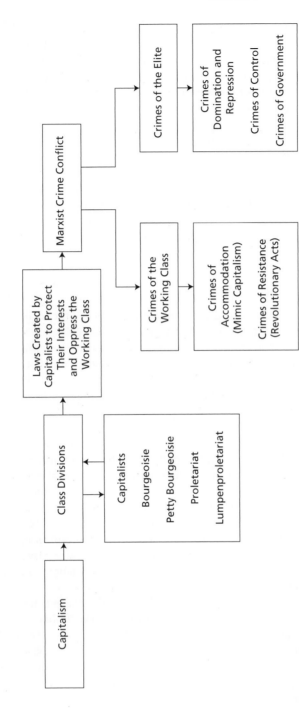

FIGURE 9.1 Instrumental Marxist Theories of Criminality

1976:85); the act of stealing by a so-called carrier transporting goods from one city to another was not a crime. In the carriers case of 1473, an English court found a carrier guilty and thereby created a law "which was central to the well-being of the emergent class of capitalist traders and industrialists" (Chambliss 1976:86).[1]

A parallel situation emerged in the United States, where, during the nineteenth and early twentieth centuries, the Supreme Court thwarted federal legislative efforts to aid children. For example, in 1918 and again in 1922, the Court ruled unconstitutional federal laws intended to restrict the use of child labor. In the first case a father fought for the right of his minor children, one under age 14 and the other between 14 and 16, to find employment in North Carolina's cotton mills (*Hammer v. Dagenhart et al.* 1918). In the second case a North Carolina furniture manufacturer successfully fought the imposition of federal taxes intended to restrict the use of child labor (*Bailey et al. v. Drexel Furniture Company* 1922a). In both cases the Court ruled that the federal government had no business restricting the rights of parents or the exercise of free trade (*Bailey et al. v. George et al.* 1922b).

Power, Authority, and Crime   John Hagan (1989a) saw power relations as central to crime. Hagan viewed power as relational; that is, power is meaningful only in terms of how it connects social actors to one another and ultimately to crime. He described two such relationships:

1. **Instrumental power relationships** occur when those with power manipulate it to achieve certain goals. Corporate criminals use their resources, such as disposable capital or local, state, national, and international political influence, to commit white-collar crime; similarly street-level criminals have power resources at their disposal, such as semiautomatic weapons or brute strength.

2. **Symbolic power relationships** are ones in which society comes to view certain individuals or groups as less vulnerable to control agents because they have comparatively more power. The corporate criminal may only appear to be more reputable and credible than the street-level criminal.

More importantly, these two forms of power relationships often occur simultaneously and complement each other. Consider the following hypothetical examples of both types of power relationships:

- Many in society view domestic marijuana growers as bloodsucking drug purveyors, living off human weaknesses. Local, state, and federal law enforcement agencies hunt these individuals, who face major sanctions as manufacturers, growers, and distributors of an illegal substance. They may have instrumental power, including vast financial resources and increasingly high-tech farming methods. However, their symbolic power relationships are typically low, owing to the negative aspects of their work.

- Tobacco growers and tobacco producers have immense instrumental power relationships, ranging from *Fortune* 500 status to federal farm subsidies. Historically, based on their symbolic power relationships, they were reputable and credible—simply agribusiness persons trying to earn a living. Yet little room for debate exists, outside the tobacco lobby, about the human costs of tobacco versus marijuana. Interestingly, as the tobacco giants started losing personal damage suits, they began to diversify, buying companies with public-friendly images, such as baby food producers, perhaps to rehabilitate their symbolic power relationships.

The distinction between social class as a status position and as a power relationship is important to understanding some crimes (Curran and Renzetti 1994:270–71). Hagan defined class in relation to ownership and authority. Some social actors, the owners of businesses and those in positions of occupational authority, have greater resources, including the resources to commit crimes that have great impact on society, such as white-collar and corporate crime. Those with little authority and no ownership commit unimportant crimes (Hagan 1989:4).

Left Realism and Peacemaking Criminology

In the final two decades of the twentieth century, criminologists offered several new but somehow familiar theories. One, originating in Great Britain, had its roots in the New Criminology of the 1970s. The New Criminology fit well with Britain's postwar **social democracy.** After World War II the British state assumed ever-increasing responsibility for providing everything from power and public transportation to health care, housing, and education. The New Criminology influenced this social democracy's justice policies through the admonition that official labeling contributes to the crime problem. For example, consider Young's work on the police role in deviance amplification for drug users (see Chapter 8). The police tendency to make a bad situation worse is central to the New Criminology's view of institutional power.

Britain's social and economic climate changed with the 1979 national elections, and widespread policy changes occurred throughout the 1980s. In particular, the elevation of Margaret Thatcher to prime minister signaled the New Right's emergence in Britain. Thatcher, who shared much ideological ground with Ronald Reagan, set about dismantling Britain's social democracy. Violent offenders, especially as related to street crime and drugs, became targets of what British criminologists called **right realism** (Matthews and Young 1992). Right realists view crime's origins as not within society but within the individual; people *choose* crime. Rehabilitation and the search for crime causes are, in their view, wasted efforts. Right realists argue strongly for conservative approaches to crime control, including more prisons, harsher penalties, longer prison terms, and the death penalty.

In response to right realism, a group of British criminologists, led by Jock Young, made a break with basic Marxist tenets. They dismissed instrumental Marxists as **left idealists** who (1) romanticize working-class criminals who, after all, prey mainly on their own class; (2) emphasize crime in corporate suites to the literal exclusion of predatory crime and its devastating impact on society; (3) ignore the impact of society's structure on crime, including such things as unemployment and poverty, and instead highlight crime control ideologies; and (4) provide no insights into what can be done within the existing capitalist system to facilitate law and order (Lea and Young 1984; see also DeKeseredy and Schwartz 1996:245–58).

Young and his colleagues proposed **left realism** as an alternative (Lea and Young 1984).[2] The perspective is leftist because it calls for increased governmental involvement in the lives of citizens. It is realistic because proponents view working-class crime as a real problem for the working class and recognize the need to work within the existing socioeconomic system.

Left realism also is rooted in what Young (1992) called the **square of crime.** Four elements—the four corners of the square—define crime; they include the victim, the offender, the state, and the society or community. As Young (1992:27) noted about the square of the crime, "It is the relationship between the police and the public which determines the efficacy of policing, the relationship between the victim and the offender which determines the impact of crime, the relationship between the state and the offender which is a major factor in recidivism."

Finally left realists emphasized relative deprivation's role in leading to crime. **Relative deprivation** is a sociological principle whereby, no matter how much material wealth someone possesses, someone else always has more. However, in order for relative deprivation to mean anything, people must first learn about how little they have and how much others possess. In this sense people's own reference groups—the constructed social entities in which they come to believe that they share membership with others based on education, occupation, or place of residence—assume great importance. It is through the perceived advantages of the reference group, or what the members believe they share in common with everyone else in the group, that individuals learn about their disadvantages. Left realists see relative deprivation as causing crime, then, in the following way: "Relative deprivation equals discontent; discontent plus lack of political solution equals crime" (Lea and Young 1984:88).

Peacemaking criminology emerged from the collaborative efforts of Quinney and Harold Pepinsky. Their coedited book, *Criminology as Peacemaking* (1991), clearly shows peacemaking's Marxist roots. Peacemaking criminology views crime as another form of violence perpetrated on humanity, much like war, racism, sexism, poverty, and human rights violations. Society should stop using the "war" metaphor to resolve social problems. There must be peace, claim proponents, between the criminal and the victim. Quinney (1991:11) wrote that crime is suffering and can be ended only through the establishment of peace. A state of peace and justice will occur—and crime be eliminated—only when we transform ourselves and our social, economic, and political structure (Quinney 1991:12).

Besides its critical and Marxist roots, peacemaking criminology has close ties to anarchism, humanism, Christian socialism, Eastern meditative thought, and feminism. Indeed, peacemaking typically takes one of two forms: sacred or secular. The sacred form emphasizes the spiritual and transcendental elements of nonviolence as a path to truth and righteousness. The secular form places great emphasis on such legalistic practices as mediation, reconciliation, conflict resolution, and reintegration of the offending parties.

As with left realism, peacemaking criminology is not so much a causal theory as a prescription for social change. Peacemakers reject the repressive and punitive policies of right realists, and at times they sound **utopian.** However, proponents endorse several unique and interesting practices intended to achieve peace between the victim, the offender, the criminal justice community, and the community at large.

Assessing Marxist Theory

Instrumental Marxists, being antiempirical, view traditional criminological research as supporting state interests (Gibbons 1984; Nettler 1984). Many instrumentalists adopt analytical techniques more common to muckraking and yellow journalism than social science (Friday 1977). And proponents generally ignore or overlook contradictory evidence. Critics argue that instrumental Marxism has become more of a crime ideology than a crime theory (Akers 1979, 1994; Inciardi 1980). Thus, instrumental Marxists recognize no source of conflict beyond social class and economic power, a position at odds with most conflict theories (Vold 1979). Moreover, should we expect the criminal justice system to secure the goals of social justice?

Structural Marxists' theories include responses to the instrumentalists' criticisms. Chambliss, for one, emphasized the complexity of laws in action, by acknowledging that people who occupy various social class positions—and not merely the powerful or rich—can respond to those who create and enforce laws. For example, even those people occupying positions of limited social or economic power have the ability to command the attention of the press, politicians, and others possessing far more power and greater resources with which to respond to the police, courts, and correctional systems. Hagan went beyond narrow definitions of class and economic struggles to include power relationships such as those reflected in gender, race, and ethnicity. Hagan's (1989a, 1994) research supports his thesis. Studies of the structural elements in punishment reveal relationships similar to those contained in Hagan's structural criminology (see also Bridges and Crutchfield 1988; Daly 1987b; Hagan and Parker 1985).

Structural Marxists sometimes share a shortcoming with their instrumental brethren: They ignore contradictory evidence. Jeffrey Adler (1989) contended that Chambliss's emphasis on economics as a motivating force behind the English vagrancy laws was misplaced. Forces other than economics, claimed Adler, were also at work. However, Chambliss (1964) did remind us that we must consider the social and historical context in which laws emerge.[3]

In general, then, structural Marxists respond to critics by substituting inequality, gender, race, urban density, and opportunity structures for Marxist rhetoric. However, the subsequent "new formulation" closely resembles traditional Marxist theory. Ronald Akers (1994:169) was far more blunt: "Except for the nuances of emphasis and terminology, [structural Marxism] becomes indistinguishable from other theories of crime."

The lack of empirical studies hampers the assessment of left-realist and peacemaking criminology. Most assessments look at its assumptions. For example, Schwartz (1991:119–20) noted that left realism's best contribution may be that it places a realistic assessment of crime squarely in the limelight. Victimization is not limited to criminals; the state also victimizes. However, left realism fails to address the concerns of feminists and other critical criminologists, but especially the excesses of state-sponsored right realism (DeKeseredy and Schwartz 1991). Left realists employ an oversimplified view of "the community" and fail to adequately define who is included and excluded in the definition of community. For example, it is conceivable that the community could be extremely heterogeneous, made up of groups that disagree on every major sociopolitical issue (DeKeseredy and Schwartz 1996:257). Finally left realists seem not to understand that they could become another tool of state oppression (Schwartz 1991).

Peacemaking criminology sets lofty, if not unattainable, goals, at least in the worldwide context. Peacemaking, with its ties to social justice, may add little to what we already know about crimes injustices (see also Akers 2000). The same criticism is true of left realism (Gibbons, 1994, 2000). Perhaps most critically, peacemaking criminology, like left realism, generates no testable hypotheses about crime. As Akers (2000:214) wrote about peacemaking criminology, "Explanations of crime and the criminal justice system might or might not be consistent with the religious and other precepts espoused by peacemaking criminologists, but these precepts do not themselves constitute a testable theory." Don Gibbons (2000:xxix) observed that replacing the pain and injustice of crime with a new sense of community through peacemaking is laudable; however, "there are serious doubts about the viability of the peacemaking project. At any rate, this version of the new criminology has relatively few subscribers."

Marxism, Public Policy, and Criminal Justice Practices

Policy Initiatives and Implications The chief Marxist policy implication is utopian—the replacement of a capitalist or imperfect communist economic system with a truly classless society. Because capitalists will not peacefully relinquish economic, political, and social control, Marxists must resort to violent revolution. Until then, radical criminologists must work with the leaders of oppressed groups in the quest for social justice. As Ian Taylor, Paul Walton, and Jock Young (1973:282) noted, "The task is to create a society in which the facts of human diversity, whether personal, organic, or social, are not subject to the power to criminalize."

Structural Marxists, while no less critical of capitalism, are far less idealistic and utopian than instrumentalists. The policies they propose seek to alter the causes of crime. For example, Stanley Cohen (1984, 1985) believed that the state must play a positive role in closing the income inequality gap, specifically targeting the lowest-income groups. Elliott Currie (1985) also argued that the government must provide for its neediest citizens, including children, single mothers, the disabled, the elderly, and the physically and mentally ill. The proponents of a "realistic critical policy" also targeted work conditions, the goal being to create a "more humane, just and workable alternative" to repressive capitalist control (Cohen 1986:23). All workers should "earn a substantial living wage with full benefits, including day care and household help for working mothers, health and welfare subsidies, [and] enriched education" (Davis and Stasz 1990:78).

Left-realist and peacemaking criminologists call for a new awareness of the "costs of crime," especially to the powerless and disenfranchised in society. Left realists support the use of both qualitative and quantitative information to support decision making by policy makers. Thus, they have conducted local surveys on a wide range of topics, including crime victimization and the fear of crime, abuse of women, and perceptions of law enforcement (DeKeseredy and Schwartz 1996:248; see also Crawford, Jones, Woodhouse, and Young 1990; Jones, MacLean, and Young 1986; Kinsey, Lea, and Young 1986; Mooney 1993). They used the results to provide a local base for policy responses, arguing that the community best knows its problems and likely solutions (DeKeseredy and Schwartz 1996:249; see also Lea and Young 1984).

Peacemaking criminology places crime in the larger context of world peace. Crime is but one form of violence; war, poverty, sexism, and racism are others. Reducing crime means working for peace. Societies should abandon the philosophy of declaring "war" on social problems, as in the "War on Crime," the "War on Drugs," or, even, the "War on Poverty." War dehumanizes the "enemy," an important idea if the enemy is one of us. In peacemaking, crime control has a community-based component, much as in left realism. Alternative sentencing options include "an apology, restitution (paying back the victim), volunteer work (paying back the community through free labor), a charitable donation, and victim–offender mediation" (DeKeseredy and Schwartz 1996:271).

Law Enforcement Practices Marxists view the police as primary offenders when it comes to crimes of control. As Raymond Michalowski (1985:196) observed about police work, " 'The policeman's lot is not a happy one'—so the saying goes. And indeed the policeman's lot in America is not enviable. This is primarily because police work is 'dirty work.' " The police find their work to be both socially stigmatizing and fraught with contradictions. They must enforce the laws against capitalism's "social junk," and, like the trash collector, stand between much of society and its less desirable elements. As a result we often view police with disdain; they tend to be shunned by much of society, which sees them and their work as distasteful.

The contradictions, noted Michalowski (1985:196), derive from the fact that the police often feel that they must violate the law to preserve the social order. For example, they may resort to illegal searches and seizures, excessive use of force, or illegally obtained confessions. Society condemns only *excessively* brutal or discriminatory abuses. In any case "state legitimacy rests on the ideology of fair and equal treatment under a legal system dispassionately enforced by professional police. When police behavior appears to contradict this image, the state must respond to protect its legitimacy" (Michalowski 1985:197). These contradictions are not lost on the police, who often feel abandoned when legal authorities question their behavior (Skolnick 1966).

Judicial Practices Marxists view courts with suspicion. Instrumentalists see them as reifying capitalistic values, and structuralists view judges as using power to respond to society's pluralistic demands. Mainly rich, old, white, and male, judges ultimately serve and preserve capitalism. At times the powerless appear to win, but this simply promotes acquiescence to a rule of law that serves as protection for capitalists (Chambliss and Seidman 1982).

Structural Marxists observe that being different makes a difference. Even when caught, criminals from the upper social classes avoid prosecution and imprisonment more frequently than their lower-class counterparts. For example, Clayton Mosher and Hagan (1994) studied sentencing patterns for narcotics offenders in Canada from 1908 to 1953. Early in the twentieth century judges handed down harsh sentences for working-class offenders. By the middle of the century, when increasing numbers of upper-class drug offenders were being arrested, they received disproportionately more lenient sentences than working-class offenders.

Peacemaking is well understood by the Indian peoples of North America (Dumont 1996; Hoyle 1995; Tso 1996). American Indian **peacemaker courts** offer a unique example of peacemaking in action (Yazzie and Zion 1995). Navajos view crime and violence as tears in the social fabric; crime and other social ills upset the community's balance (Yazzie and Zion 1995). Only through the timely intervention of a peacemaker—an elder skilled in listening and gentle persuasion—can that balance be restored. For example, the Navajos use peacemaker courts in cases of domestic violence and other family-based problems (Bluenose and Zion 1996). The peacemaker also uses the sacred **harmony ceremony** to reestablish balance both at the micro-level between the offended and offending parties, and at the macro-level within the Navajo Nation itself.

Correctional Practices From a Marxist perspective prisons and jails serve to control the dangerous class, the lumpenproletariat. Instrumental Marxists also believe that prisons warehouse surplus labor in times of economic downturns, which makes these inmates political prisoners. What they call the "struggles inside," in which prison inmates speak of the pain of imprisonment, are central themes for instrumental Marxists. These themes were popular in the 1960s and early 1970s. Today's prison inmates are more likely to be part of a prison gang, and not any group espousing radical or any other political views (Mays and Winfree 1998).

Structural Marxists point to the race, class, and power dimensions of punishment. The crimes of the less powerful—street crime—result in prison terms. Crime in the suites often results in only fines or forfeitures and, infrequently, in brief stays at minimum-security prisons. Race, too, plays a significant role in who goes to prison. As Michalowski (1985:238) pointed out, "The black proportion of prison inmates is just slightly less than double the black proportion of those arrested, indicating that once arrested blacks face a significantly greater likelihood of being incarcerated than their white counterparts." The structure of penal law may account for some racial disparities. Take, for example, laws controlling illicit drugs. Those convicted of possession or sale of crack cocaine receive far harsher mandatory sentences than those convicted of possession or sale of powder cocaine even though the substances are chemically indistinguishable from each other (see Chapter 8). Blacks disproportionately use crack, whereas whites prefer powder cocaine.[4]

FEMINIST CRIMINOLOGY

- Perhaps 1 in 10 prison inmates is a woman, roughly the same proportion as are arrested and tried in the overall population. Do these statistics mean that women make smarter criminals? Are women morally superior to men? Are other forces at work? A discussion of the first two questions could take the rest of the semester. We will provide answers to the third question in this chapter.

- Consider the following: If women would simply act more feminine and domestic, they wouldn't get into as much trouble as when they act like men's equal. What would you call a person who expressed such an opinion? (Some feminists view the justice system as using this perspective.)

- If you are female and have a brother, did your parents treat you the same when you were growing up, especially during your teenage years? Did you have the same rules, the same curfews, and the same behavioral expectations? (Males can tackle the obverse question.) Have you ever considered that gender-specific socialization might contribute to the gender differential in crime rates?

- Some feminists look at the economic system's role in criminalizing the conduct of women. How would you respond to the charge that the criminal justice system responds differently to women who are either economically disadvantaged or minority-group members? Is this political rhetoric or social reality?

The wide-ranging gender issues reflected in these questions have generated an equally wide array of feminist perspectives. Indeed, feminist criminologists defy easy categorization. Some feminists express liberal ideas on crime, challenging men's power; others are more radical, with ties to Marxism. Generally feminists explore why women, on the one hand, are exploited by men, and, on the other, have far lower criminality rates.

At the end of the nineteenth century, the classical school of criminology relegated women to the same legal category as children. These criminologists viewed both groups as incapable of making rational decisions and so excused them from criminal responsibility. The ascent of positivistic criminology in the nineteenth century did little to draw the attention of criminologists to female criminality. For one thing, crime committed by women was then, and remains, a rare phenomenon. And when Lombroso (see Chapter 3) and Freud (see Chapter 4) offered explanations of female criminality, they did so in a uniformly sexist fashion. Criminal women were too masculine or acquisitive, or were lacking in maternal instincts. Their crimes were limited largely to engaging in prostitution, shoplifting, and aiding and abetting their male counterparts.

The model of the overmasculinized and conniving criminal woman remained largely unchallenged until the 1970s. In the intervening years a few individuals, such as Otto Pollack (1950), addressed the nearly 10-to-1 difference in the arrest rates of men and women. Pollack claimed that three aspects of women's crime selection accounts for their underrepresentation in arrest statistics. First, their crimes (e.g., shoplifting, domestic theft, and theft by prostitutes) have a low likelihood of detection. Second, in the case of detection, it is unlikely that the victims will report such crimes to the police. Third, even when the crimes are detected and reported, owing to a double standard for men and women, police are less likely to arrest and prosecutors are less likely to seek convictions against female offenders. Even the male criminal, reported Pollack, adopts a "chivalrous" attitude toward his female counterpart, showing reluctance to implicate her.

Positivists' discounting of female offenders continued into the second half of the twentieth century. But this changed in 1975.

Liberal Feminism: The Liberation Hypothesis

The works of Freda Adler (1975) and Rita Simon (1975a) generated considerable public interest in gender-specific crime theories. Although criminologists often mention the two together, their positions are different. For example, Adler stressed a nearly epidemic-like involvement of women in almost every major crime category and forecasted a blurring of the traditional male–female gender-role distinctions. The women's liberation movement inadvertently opened up new crime opportunities as well.

After reviewing the women's liberation movement and alleged increases in female criminality, Adler described the events in the rhetoric of the movement. Simon (1975a), however, presented a different interpretation of the same crime statistics. She made these important points: (1) Female involvement in violent crime is decreasing (1975a:46); (2) female involvement in other serious crime is increasing (1975a:38–39); and (3) we cannot directly link increases in female crime to the women's movement; instead, they are a result of increased opportunities in

IN THEIR OWN WORDS: Adler on Female Criminality

Freda Adler's ideas shook a nation emerging from the Vietnam and Watergate eras. Many women marched in the streets for equal rights. The Equal Rights Amendment to the Constitution, passed by Congress in 1972, was languishing in several state legislatures, lacking the requisite support for formal adoption. Cigarette companies competed for the "women's market" with slogans like "You've come a long way, baby." Adler suggested that women had indeed come a long way.

- *On equality of opportunity in the crime world:* "Like her sisters in legitimate fields, the female criminal is fighting for her niche in the hierarchy, for, curiously enough, the barriers of male chauvinism in some areas of criminal activity are no less formidable than those which confront newcomers in the world of business" (p. 14).

- *On changes in offending rates:* "Although males continue to commit the greater absolute number of offenses, it is the women who are committing these same crimes at yearly rates of increase now running as high as six and seven times greater than those for males" (p. 15).

- *On female violent offenders:* "In some cases, she has had a taste of blood. Her appetite, however, appears to be only whetted" (p. 15).

- *On the future of the female offender:* "As women gain greater equality with men, the male dominated judicial process will likely treat them with less deference and impose more stringent sanctions; the condition of being a woman in a man's world will carry less protection" (p. 252).

Source: Adler (1975)

the labor market (1975a:19). Simon's analysis does not turn on the presence of liberated women. But the inference remains, because increased opportunity in the labor market is one victory claimed by the women's liberation movement.

Roy Austin (1982) explored what became known as the **liberation hypothesis** by looking at gender-role theory for conceptual support. First, he plotted the divorce rates and labor force participation rates for females. Increases in both rates, he observed, coincided with the founding of the National Organization for Women. Moreover, female contributions to crime rates followed the same patterns of growth along the same timeline. Austin (1982:421) believed that "the data satisfy the causal criteria of association and temporal order for [the liberation movement] proposition, and the proposition and findings have theoretical support."

Challenges to the concept of the "new female offender" soon appeared. Joseph Weis (1976) suggested that "the new female criminal is more a social invention than an empirical reality." His analysis of self-reported data led him to favor a sex-specific opportunity theory. That is, increased participation by women in the work world has given them more opportunities to commit crime. He noted the historical exclusion of women from certain means of success, both conventional and unconventional. Before women became CPAs or physicians in significant numbers, for example, they represented no real threat to embezzle funds or write phony prescriptions.

Many criminologists have expressed skepticism about the "new female offender" (Giordano and Cernkovich 1977; Jacobs 1975; Kramer and Kempinen

1978). In particular, Darrell Steffensmeier challenged statistics cited by Simon and Adler (Steffensmeier 1978, 1980, 1983a,b; Steffensmeier and Cobb 1981; Steffensmeier and Steffensmeier 1980). According to Steffensmeier, the increases in female arrest rates are (1) more artifacts than actual differences due to "flawed arrest rates"; (2) limited to certain nonviolent offense categories such as shoplifting, fraud, and larceny; and (3) the result of changes in reporting and policing behaviors. In any event Steffensmeier saw no conclusive evidence for a crime-rate convergence of the sexes.

Radical Feminism: Patriarchal Society, Oppressed Females, and Survival

In spite of questions about Adler's and Simon's interpretations, patriarchal (male-based) and chivalry arguments continue to inform criminologists. **Radical feminists** look at masculine power and privilege as the chief cause of all social relations and societal inequities (see Jaggar and Rothenberg 1984). For example, Meda Chesney-Lind (1973), an early proponent of the chivalry argument, observed that many youthful female crimes are "status offenses," or law violations related to the offender's age (e.g., incorrigibility, truancy, and running away). Criminologists, Chesney-Lind argued, often dismiss these offense types as inconsequential and unimportant. Therefore, positivistic theories do not address the types of offending most important to an understanding of female crime. Mainstream male-dominated and male-oriented criminal justice research also fails to tell us much about how the criminal justice system responds to female offenders, young or old (Chesney-Lind 1989:18–19).

Chesney-Lind also dismissed the liberation hypothesis as a flawed or discredited explanation. She argued instead for a feminist theory of delinquency. She defined young girls' crime—particularly running away and incorrigibility—as "survival strategies," or methods of dealing with dangerous or abusive environments.[5] They may make what is for them rational and logical, if extralegal, choices, such as engaging in minor criminality, to survive. In her theory young women are the victims of a **patriarchal authority** system that physically, sexually, and mentally abuses them. Laws intended to "protect" youths instead criminalize their survival strategies, especially those of young girls. And youth and family courts extend the patriarchal power of the fathers beyond the family. The patriarchal legal and judicial systems thus leave girls few options. As Chesney-Lind (1989:24) observed, "Young women in conflict with their parents (often for very legitimate reasons) may actually be forced by present laws into petty criminal activity, prostitution, and drug use."

The effects of this conflict, the girls' responses to it, and the influences of the criminal justice system last long after adolescence. Even serious adult delinquency may be tied to the implementation of earlier survival strategies. In particular, sexual victimization at home is often linked to prostitution and drug use as street survival techniques. These early behaviors continue in adulthood for these women because "they possess truncated educational backgrounds and virtually no marketable occupation skills" (Chesney-Lind 1989:23).

Chesney-Lind saw a feminist perspective on female delinquency as appropriate for two reasons. First, although both boys and girls are victims of violence and sexual abuse, girls' victimization, unlike that of boys', shapes their status as young women. Second, the victimizers of young women, who are, more often than not, adult males, can use formal control agencies to keep the young women at home. Girls' survival strategies provide not only their only hope but also the high potential for further criminalization.

Socialist Feminism: Power–Control Theory

A related form of feminism recognizes that class and gender are important, but neither assumes preeminence over the other. That is, **socialist feminists** see class and gender as reacting to and interacting with one another. Class is structured by gender and gender by class, and we cannot truly appreciate the one without the inclusion of the other. As James Messerschmidt (1986:42) observed about this relationship, "The interaction of gender and class creates positions of power and powerlessness in the gender/class hierarchy, resulting in different types and degrees of criminality and varying opportunities for engaging in them."

Beginning in the late 1970s, John Hagan (1990) and his colleagues (Hagan, Simpson, and Gillis 1979, 1985, 1987; Hagan, Gillis, and Simpson 1988, 1990) expressed the idea that we can best understand the relationship between gender and delinquency by focusing on intrafamilial power relations. Blending neo-Marxist and socialist-feminist perspectives, Hagan (1989a) saw family structure as incorporating patterns of power between spouses.[6] The relative positions of the husband and wife in the workplace and in the home determine spousal power. For example, in patriarchal families wives have little power compared with husbands, and daughters have little freedom compared with sons. These differences decrease in families with egalitarian structures, in which the spouses share power or in which the father is missing.

Hagan described a family dynamic. Patriarchal families generally produce daughters whose futures lie in domestic labor and consumption, and expect that sons will take part in economic production. In egalitarian families the two power–control models overlap. Two sets of forces act to produce these different family types (Hagan, Simpson, and Gillis 1979; see also Hagan 1989a). In patriarchal families the expectation is that fathers, as social control agents, will control daughters more than sons. In this way the control of children socially reproduces the power relationships of the parents. In contrast, parents in egalitarian families share control efforts, so that controls imposed on daughters are similar to those imposed on sons.

Besides differential control patterns, relationships between parents and daughters in patriarchal families promote a reduced preference for risk taking by daughters. Hagan (1989a) defined risk-taking behavior as the antithesis of the passivity inherent in the daughter's role in patriarchal families. Conversely sons in patriarchal families are encouraged to develop risk-taking tendencies. Patriarchal families see risk taking as a prerequisite for the development of entrepreneurial skills and other activities within the production and power spheres. In egalitarian families both daughters and sons are encouraged to develop risk-taking attitudes.

We can view delinquency as a risk-taking activity. Consequently power–control theory predicts larger gender-based differences in delinquency for patriarchal families than egalitarian families. The core assumption of the theory is that the presence of power and the absence of controls creates conditions conducive to common forms of delinquency (Hagan, Simpson, and Gillis 1985). Males will continue to exhibit a higher proclivity for crime and delinquency, but the gender ratio differences are less pronounced in egalitarian families. Figure 9.2, a and b, summarizes Chesney-Lind's and Hagan's feminist theories of crime.

Marxist Feminism: The Critique of Sexual Politics

Marxist feminists closely follow the writings of Friedrich Engels, Karl Marx's collaborator (Beirne and Messerschmidt 2000:205). According to Engels both class and gender divisions of labor account for the relative social class positions of men and women. The evolution of capitalism, say Marxist feminists, assured the dominant role of men. Male dominance clearly reflects the ideology of a society that is willing to subjugate women, first to capital and second to men. The labor of women, as homemakers, is often trivialized by capitalism. However, such labor is essential in that it profits the capitalist class. Interestingly Marxist feminists also point out that the crimes of women, including shoplifting and prostitution, are related to a twisted view of enforced domesticity. When they commit violent crimes, they prefer kitchen knives to guns (Balkan, Berger, and Schmidt 1980:211).

The analysis of rape by Julia and Herman Schwendinger (1983) provided a powerful illustration of a Marxist-feminist critique. Societies without "commodity production" exhibit high levels of egalitarianism, and violence against women is almost nonexistent. When these societies begin to produce items for exchange, however, men gain control of the emerging "industry," resulting in a division of labor with men at the top. The position of women in society declines, and rapes and other violence against women increase.

Assessing Feminist Theory

Three questions provide a guide for this assessment. First, what is the current state of research findings? The answer depends on what is included as a feminist-derived explanation. Feminists generally discount early liberation hypothesis studies (cf. Gora 1982; Steffensmeier 1980). Marxist feminists and radical feminists offer explanations that are, like earlier instrumental Marxist explanations, more ideologies than theories, making any tests difficult. Moreover, unless male domination and other aspects of patriarchal society are shown to vary, nearly any test will be impossible (Akers 1994:177). That is, a univariate independent variable "causes" all conditions of the dependent variable—crime and noncrime.

Tests of power–control explanations have yielded positive results for delinquency (cf. Hagan and Kay 1990; Singer and Levine 1988). As a rule, however, these studies find nearly identical gender difference between patriarchal and egalitarian families (Jensen and Thompson 1990; Morash and Chesney-Lind 1991; Sims 2000). Some critics question whether social class should be included in power–control theory at all (Jensen and Thompson 1990), although a restructured power–control theory (see below) gives it high prominence (McCarthy, Hagan, and Woodward 1999).

Other critics have expressed doubts about the variables used to test power–control theory. For example, Gary Jensen and Kevin Thompson (1990) raised questions about the dichotomization of families into (1) families with a male head of

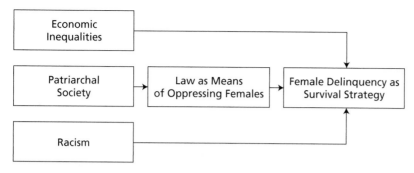

(a) Chesney-Lind's Patriarchal Society Thesis

FIGURE 9.2 Feminist Theories of Crime

household as patriarchal and (2) all others as egalitarian. Some female-dominated households may be that way because the father is absent and free to pursue his own economic goals. This situation is not egalitarian, representing instead the ultimate case of patriarchal dominance (Jensen and Thompson 1990).

Second, have the feminist theories responded to the critics? Consider, by way of example, criticisms of power–control theory. Hagan's original idea was to look at the reproduction of gender relations across generations of parents and children. The focus was on patriarchal family structures, which Hagan and his associates believed would perpetuate the higher delinquency rates of males. Extensions of this theory through the 1980s and 1990s addressed what might happen as women entered the job market: They predicted that the rates of delinquency among their daughters would increase (Hagan et al. 1990; Grasmick, Tittle, Bursik, and Arneklev 1993). Feminists attacked these extensions of power–control theory (Chesney-Lind and Shelden 1992; Messerschmidt 1993; Naffine 1987). Why, they asked, would daughters become more like their brothers as their mothers entered the workforce? Wasn't it possible, they speculated, that instead of daughters becoming like sons, sons might become *less* delinquent?

John McCarthy and his associates (1999) offered a feminist view of mothers' influence on sons in less patriarchal families. They noted that boys and girls are exposed to many "gender activity" schemas about what is and is not appropriate behavior, and that these schemas vary across family structures. McCarthy and associates (1999:784) found that, consistent with traditional power–control theory, in the more patriarchal families "males are more likely than females to support patriarchal schemas and offend." And consistent with the extended theory, "mothers in less patriarchal families appear to have made some inroads in challenging male resistance by altering their sons' support for conventional views" (McCarthy, Hagan, and Woodward 1999:785).

The original power–control theory overlooked the complex role of women in shaping the values and outlooks of their sons. Brenda Sims (2000) extended this thesis by suggesting that the role of fathers cannot be ignored either.[7] She reported findings that generally are consistent with previous power–control research. However, Sims included informal social controls, such as embarrassment and shame, and not just formal social controls, in her power–control model. Males raised in

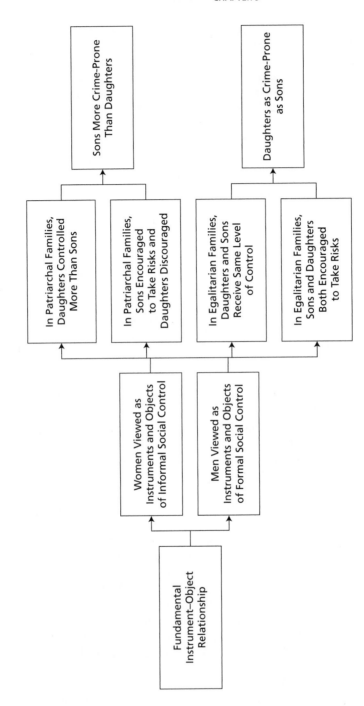

(b) Hagan's Power–Control Theory

FIGURE 9.2 Feminist Theories of Crime

less patriarchal families perceived greater threats of embarrassment than similarly situated females. Sims attributed this finding to the fact that in less patriarchal families fathers assume more child-rearing responsibilities. In these families sons, anxious to please their fathers, are more responsive to their use of informal social controls. The net result may be that such fathers have a significant impact on their children, but especially their male children.

Third, has feminist criminology influenced the study of crime and criminals? Feminist critiques of male-dominated "mainstream" criminology evolved into Marxist-feminist theoretical integrations. This body of work, including feminist examination of such traditionally all-male subjects as white-collar crime (Daly 1989), generally has yielded positive results.

Feminist critiques have had another major impact as well. Researchers rediscovered gender and used it to study, among other things, youth gangs (Esbensen and Deschenes 1998; Esbensen and Winfree 1998), street robberies (Miller 1998), homicide victimization rates (Marvell and Moody 1999), intimate killings (Gauthier and Bankston 1997), and urban crime rates (Steffensmeier and Haynie 2000). Gender's inclusion in tests of traditional criminological theories, once a rarity, is also on the rise (cf. Mazerolle 1998; Tibbetts and Piquero 1999). Increasingly criminologists have sought to understand the single best predictor of crime and delinquency: a person's biological sex.

Feminism, Public Policy, and Criminal Justice Practices

Feminists, like conflict and Marxist theorists, argue for power sharing. Due to the broad range of perspectives under the feminist umbrella, some calls to action resemble the policies of "conservative" conflict theorists, and other views are expressed in the militant tones of radical Marxists. For example, Daly and Chesney-Lind (1988) discussed several policies that would reduce the inequalities between women and men. They argued that men's violence toward women must be controlled, particularly sexual and physical abuse. Daly and Chesney-Lind (1988:521–24) questioned the role of the state in supporting, perpetuating, and encouraging the violence. As evidence they cited efforts to control pornography and prostitution. Police engage in these activities only reactively, in response to public pressures, and discontinue them when the spotlight moves to something new. Daly and Chesney-Lind also addressed the tacit acceptance of spousal violence and rape. They pointed to such policies as "presumptive arrest" of spouse abusers as a positive, if measured, attempt by the state to gain control; however, they doubt whether it will greatly reduce violence against women.

They further contended that equality with men is not the ultimate goal. Women generally have no interest in viewing the lives of men as a worthy behavioral norm. Under the doctrine of equality, "nearly all women's legal claims are construed as 'special treatment'" (Daly and Chesney-Lind 1988:524), Thus, the liberal feminist position of equal treatment is coming under increasing scrutiny and criticism. Invoking the imagery of racial discrimination, feminist legal scholars suggest that society may need to adopt new definitions of gender discrimination, ones that recognize "special needs." Some feminists are concerned that equal treatment of women in court, particularly at sentencing, "will prove unjust and may work ultimately against women," as in divorce and child custody laws (Daly and

Chesney-Lind 1988:525). Women may also suffer from correctional policies that call for equal treatment, ignoring women's unique health problems and problems with incarceration (Daly and Chesney-Lind 1988:526).

No unified feminist-derived crime control policies exist. Most feminists do agree that the evaluation of any public policies should include the "gender question." According to Daly and Chesney-Lind (1988:525), "A focus on gender and gender differences is not simply a focus on women or on what some scholars term 'women's issues' in a narrow sense. It is and should be a far more encompassing enterprise, raising questions about how gender organizes the discipline of criminology, the institutions that fall within its scope, and the behavior of men and women."

Given these observations, a complete discussion of the implications of these theories for criminal justice procedures is beyond the scope of this text. Instead, to stimulate discussion and debate, we present representative examples.

Law Enforcement Practices   Feminists look for discriminatory practices based on gender. Race appears to confound our understanding of female contacts with police, as reflected in the feminist/women-of-color perspective. Christy Visher (1983) observed that police chivalry exists only for white female offenders; black offenders were far more likely to be arrested. Similarly white female victims receive preferential treatment from the police, especially when compared to their black counterparts (Smith, Visher, and Davidson 1984). As Sally Simpson (1989:614) noted, "Although chivalry may be alive and well for white women, it appears to be dead (if it ever existed) for blacks." Largely absent from this debate is data on the treatment of other minority women, particularly Hispanics and American Indians.

Feminists emphasize the study of violence against females. In 1981 researchers led by Larry Sherman conducted the Minneapolis experiment on police resolution of domestic disputes. The findings supported the policy of arresting the abusive spouse and detaining him (or her) overnight in jail (Sherman and Berk 1984b). This experiment set three forces in motion. First, legal scholars, feminists included, praised the approach as promising to reduce male tyranny expressed in spousal battery (Daly and Chesney-Lind 1988; Ferraro 1989). Second, police departments across the nation adopted the policy. Third, criticisms of the Minneapolis experiment primarily focused on shortcomings in methods (Binder and Meeker 1989). Five replications failed to find the same results as reported in the Minneapolis experiment (Berk, Campbell, Klap, and Western 1992; Dunford, Huizinga, and Elliott 1986; Hirschel and Hutchinson 1992; Pate and Hamilton 1992; Sherman and Smith 1992). For example, following an experiment conducted in Omaha, Nebraska, researchers reported that such policies, by themselves, appeared to have no "impact on the likelihood of repeated violent acts" (Dunford, Huizinga, and Elliott 1986:391).[8] We return to this topic in Chapter 10.

Judicial Practices   Early in the evolution of feminist criminology, judicial decision making emerged as the point in the administration of justice at which the operation of sexist, paternalistic, or antifeminist attitudes could be observed (cf. Adler 1975:252; Simon 1975a:107). Court sentencing has been a traditional focus of feminist critiques of the criminal justice system. Evidence of the extent and nature of **gendered justice** (Simpson 1989:614) may depend upon the theoretical perspective that frames the research. For example, researchers using a liberal feminist argument reported that women receive lenient treatment early in the process, such as less restrictive and less expensive methods of release from jail before trial (Nagel 1983). At sentencing, however, the results were extremely variable. They ranged from more lenient sentences to no differences, once the researchers eliminated differences due to offense type and prior records (cf. Bernstein, Kick, Leung, and Schulz 1977; Farrington and Morris 1983; Wilbanks 1987). However, women who commit nontraditional female crimes or violate female sexual norms may face harsher sentences (cf. Bernstein et al. 1977; Chesney-Lind 1973).

Daly (1987a:154) observed other evidence of gendered justice decisions. Gendering occurs when the court formally recognizes that women are responsible for the care of others and that men must provide for their families' financial support. **Familied decisions** occur when the court perceives that removing either the man or the woman would cause hardship. Courts often view men or women without family responsibilities in nearly identical fashion: They receive harsher treatment than persons with family responsibilities. Women with families receive the most lenient treatment of all due to "the differing social costs arising from separating [women] from their families" (Daly 1987b:287). Thus, outright gender-based discrimination may not cause differential court treatment. Rather, the courts' behavior may best be understood as an attempt to protect nuclear families and the value systems associated with them (Daly 1989; Eaton 1986).

Critical feminists, including socialists and Marxists, look to social power and male control for explanations of justice gendering. From this perspective pretrial release and sentencing are best understood, after eliminating the confounding effects of criminal record and offense seriousness, in terms of the interaction between family and gender. Candace Kruttschnitt (1982) reported that women are more likely to receive probation if they are dependent upon fathers or husbands.

Correctional Practices Liberal feminists call women in prison "the forgotten offenders" (Pollock-Byrne 1990:59; Simon 1975b). This label may stem from the relative paucity of female prison inmates, accounting as they do for less than 10 percent of the adult prison population (U.S. Department of Justice 2002). Women's prisons are generally smaller than those for men, and there are far fewer such prisons (U.S. Department of Justice 2002; see also Simon 1975a). Finally, female inmates receive little attention from reformers because they, unlike their male counterparts, call little attention to themselves through such institutional behaviors as prison riots and uprisings (Bartollas and Conrad 1992:467).

The conditions of confinement for female inmates range from lenient to harsh (Simpson 1989:615). However, Clemens Bartollas and John Conrad (1992:474) reported, the place of confinement is typically uniform in appearance:

> Women's prisons, unlike men's, often resemble college campuses rather
> than fortress penitentiaries. There are no gun towers, armed guards, or stone
> walls. With few exceptions, there are no fences strung on top with concertina
> wire. . . . These institutions are frequently rural, pastoral settings that suggest
> tranquility and "easy time" for the inmate. Women's prisons may be more
> attractive than men's prisons, but this peaceful appearance is deceptive.

The "campus model," which emerged in the 1930s, was supposed to instill "traditional" feminine value systems and work habits (Clear and Cole 1997:300–301; Mays and Winfree 1998:158–59). Rehabilitation programs included cosmetology, parenting skills, and domestic training. These programs stressed moral and social improvement, goals borrowed from the early twentieth-century "reformatory era" (Champion 1990:448–50).

Feminist views of women's prisons vary widely (Simpson 1989:615–17). Radical feminists see prisons for women as institutionalized attempts to control female sexuality (Chesney-Lind 1973). For example, if diseased prostitutes were sent to prison or jail, their cure was a condition of release (Rasche 1974). For their part socialists often describe female prisoners in terms of their gender, race, and class. Custodial prisons were for evil and immoral women, where primarily black female felons were treated like men; reformatories were intended for white working-class misdemeanants, who were merely "fallen women" and so salvageable (Rafter 1985; Rasche 1974). For Marxist feminists women's prisons are places for the retooling of "deviant women for gender-appropriate roles in capitalist patriarchal societies. . . . Societal control of female deviance serves the needs of capitalism. When those needs change, so too will the mechanisms and directions of social control" (Simpson 1989:616–17).

As Nicole Rafter (1985:7) observed about New York's Western House of Refuge:

> Two groups of women—the working-class offenders and the middle-class reformers—met, so to speak, at the gates of the women's reformatory. The struggle between them was economically functional in some ways to the reformers: It helped maintain a pool of cheap domestic labor for women like themselves, and by keeping women in the surplus labor force, it undergirded the economic system to which they owed their privileged positions. . . . The struggle also involved the definition of gender. Reformers hoped to recast the offenders in their own images, to have them embrace the value (though not to assume social station) of the lady.

Clearly, in the women's prison of the early twentieth century, Marxism met feminism as correctional institutions pondered what to do with criminal women. Just as clearly, this dilemma exists in prisons today (Clear and Cole 1997:303; Mays and Winfree 1998:159). (See Table 9.1 for an overview of Marxist theories and feminist theories of crime.)

SUMMARY

The theories in this chapter share several features with those in the previous chapter. Power is the most obvious one. Marxist and feminist theories explore power's role in defining crime and criminals. Although the definitions differ slightly from theory to theory, power's role as a causal factor is relatively invariant: Some groups or individuals have power, use it to further their own interests, and are not above exploiting it to control (i.e., make deviant, criminalize, or otherwise discredit) the conduct of those perceived to be threats. Marxists and most feminists argue that power must be shared, even if it takes revolutionary acts to accomplish this goal.

Second, the theories are essentially deterministic in nature. Like conflict and labeling theories, they blame forces outside the control of individuals for causing the criminal condition. Critical or Marxist theorists typically adopt one of two

Table 9.1 Marxist Theories, Feminist Theories, and Crime

Theory	Major Figures	Central Assumptions	Causal Arguments (Key Terms)	Strengths	Weaknesses
Marxist criminology	Marx, Engels	A historical "class struggle" exists between capitalists and workers; a revolution will eventually occur that signals the end of capitalism and the beginning of communism.	*Marxism:* Workers (the *proletariat*) crimes against the wealthy (*capitalists*) are revolutionary; the crimes of the society's least desirable elements (the *lumpenproletariat*) are reactionary; the crimes of capitalists are the true crimes.	Provides a rather naive view of crime and justice issues.	*Instrumental Marxism:* Is a theology for true believers; is antiempirical.
Instrumental Marxist theory	Quinney, Spitzer, Chambliss, Krisberg		*Instrumental Marxism:* Emphasis is on the instrumental role of law and government in achieving subjugation of the working class; the crimes of the elite and government are key constructs.	*Structural Marxism:* Applies a more sophisticated view of the relationships between elites and power; provides unique and disturbing insights into the operation of the nation's government and corporate elites.	*Structural Marxism:* May ignore contradictory evidence; empirical results have been mixed.
Structural Marxist theory	Chambliss, Seidman, Hagan		*Structural Marxism:* Laws protect the ruling class's interests; power relationships are central to understanding crime.		Both perspectives suggest few policy implications of their own outside the revolutionary model; however, they do provide insights into criminal justice practices.

Table 9.1 Marxist Theories, Feminist Theories, and Crime (continued)

Theory	Major Figures	Central Assumptions	Causal Arguments (Key Terms)	Strengths	Weaknesses
Left realism and peacemaking criminology	Young, Matthews, Lea, Quinney, Pepinsky	*Left realism:* Violent crime has real consequences for the disenfranchised and the poor. *Peacemaking:* Crime is one form of worldwide violence.	*Left realism:* Working locally with the *square of crime* will reduce conditions causing crime. *Peacemaking:* Working for peace will eliminate crime.	*Left realism:* Brings local resources to bear on crimes that directly affect them. *Peacemaking:* Views peace as a solution to crime.	*Left realism:* Is a prescription, not a testable theory. *Peacemaking:* Rests on utopian principles.
Feminist theory Liberal feminism	Adler, Simon, Austin, Kruttschnitt	Society is patriarchal; women are viewed as second-class citizens, undeserving of the same form and nature of legal protections as men; in times past, women were legally defined as the chattel of their husband.	*Liberal feminism:* As women are treated as equal to men, their criminality will reach parity with that of men.	Helps us to understand the tremendous disparities in offending proclivities between men and women; points out basic gender-role socialization processes, especially those found in families; more radical forms offer arguments similar to various forms of Marxist criminology.	Yields research results, using traditional quantitative methods, that are mixed and inconclusive; however, legal analyses and qualitative methods yield far more support.
Radical feminism	Chesney-Lind, Daly		*Radical feminism:* Society criminalizes women for being "bad" (e.g., using drugs and prostitution), behaviors they use to escape society's oppression.		
Marxist feminism	Schwendingers		*Marxist feminism:* Females' place in the workplace is defined first by capitalism and second by men.		
Socialist feminism	Messerschmidt, Hagan (and associates)		*Socialist feminist:* Social life is best understood by blending class and gender.		

strategies in exploring the relationship between power and crime. They may hold capitalism at fault and look at the criminal justice system as the instrument of repression. Or they may critique society's structure as creating, endorsing, and maintaining basic social, racial, and economic inequities that benefit the interests of capitalists at the expense of workers. Feminist theorists propose that most criminologists have ignored gender both in theory and in research.

Third, power's insertion into any discussion of crime results in confusion about what to call the resulting theories. Marxist theory, besides its instrumental and structural forms, is known as radical conflict and critical theory. However, some criminologists see any theory that questions power's use as a critical theory (cf. Bohm 1982; Davis and Stasz 1990; Friedrichs 1982). For their part feminists are reluctant to endorse what other criminologists define as "feminist criminological theories." In spite of these definitional issues, the simultaneous consideration of power and gender clearly advances our knowledge of both male and female criminality.

Critical or Marxist theorists also advance the idea that crime is tied directly to economic exploitation of the workers by a repressive and oppressive capitalist system. Early feminists viewed male dominance of nearly all social institutions, including families, economic institutions, and the polity, as a crushing force against the liberation of women. When the winds of change blew across the nation in the 1960s, they influenced all disenfranchised minorities, including women. Even more interesting is the resurgence of interest in these perspectives in the late twentieth and early twenty-first centuries. The key difference is that when they first emerged these power-based theories were acclaimed for their intuitive and logical insights into crime but condemned for their reliance on rhetoric and disregard of empirical proof. New power theories place a far greater premium on the links between theory, methods, and practice.

A point not addressed in the previous chapter relates to the criminal justice system. The theories expressed in this chapter are as much about that system's operation and impact on society as they are about crime causation. They are theories of criminal justice and criminological outcomes (see, e.g., Akers 2000:165–235). The same could, of course, be said of labeling theory. This final observation relates directly to the first point made in this summary: Those with power can criminalize literally whatever conduct they wish, particularly if that conduct or those who engage in it threaten their interests.

Finally what distinguishes the theories in this chapter from other power-based theories is that they give faces to those abusing power for their own self-interests: They are capitalists, they are men, and they are Caucasians. Unless Marxist and feminist criminologists gain the attention of policy makers, as happened in Britain in the 1960s and 1970s, the chances of meaningful changes based on their theories seem slim. American Marxists tried frontal attacks throughout much of the 1970s but met with little success. This fact may account for the popularity among radical-liberal academics of left realism and peacemaking criminology. It is an open question whether this intellectual popularity will translate into policy and practices.

KEY TERMS

alienation

anarchism

bourgeoisie

capitalists

crimes of accommodation

crimes of control

crimes of domination

crimes of government

crimes of repression

crimes of resistance

demoralization

demystification

excessive egoism

false consciousness

familied decisions

gendered justice

harmony

instrumental Marxism/Marxists

instrumental power relationships

liberation hypothesis

left idealists

left realism

lumpenproletariat

Marxism

New Criminology

patriarchal authority

peacemaker courts

peacemaking criminology

petite bourgeoisie

privilege

political prisoners

proletariat

radical feminists

relative deprivation

right realism

social democracy

socialist feminists

social justice

square of crime

structural Marxism/Marxists

symbolic power relationships

utopian

CRITICAL REVIEW QUESTIONS

1. Compare and contrast instrumental Marxist and structural Marxist explanations of crime. Which approach makes the most sense? (Note: "None" is an unacceptable answer!)

2. Why are critical criminologists unapologetic in their disdain for positive crime theories?

3. What point made by Quinney do you believe is important even beyond its use by Marxist criminologists? Explain your selection.

4. Explain what instrumental Marxists meant by "social justice." Is this term used by people other than criminologists? In what context is it used?

5. Are there other instances, besides vagrancy and property laws, in which Chambliss's analysis of law in action makes sense?

6. In the opening section of this chapter, both the tobacco and handgun manufacturing industries were mentioned as fitting Hagan's structural criminology, although at that time you did not know the name of the theory. The handgun industry was not mentioned in the text. Explain how its power relationships fit within Hagan's model.

7. In which area of criminal justice policy or practice do Marxist-derived theories provide the best insights? Where is their application the weakest? (Note: See Question 1.)

8. Define *feminism*. Which "feminist theory" makes the most sense to you, and why? (Note: See Question 1.)

9. Suppose you are discussing the relatively recent advent of feminist criminology with a group of friends. One of them says, "Criminologists must be stupid. Of course

gender's an important variable in criminality." What do you say in defense of criminology?

10. Why do you think that many feminists do not like Hagan's power–control theory, with some even denying that it is truly a feminist theory?

11. In which area of criminal justice policy or practice do feminist theo-

ries provide the best insights? Where is their application the weakest? (Note: See Question 1.)

12. Why do you think feminist theories are not nearly as comprehensive or well developed as theories purporting to describe, explain, predict, and control the criminality of men?

NOTES

1. Law derived from court decisions is part of common law, or what we call case law.

2. DeKeseredy and Schwartz (1996:246) observed that left realists do not identify left idealists by name but attack their ideas in broad general terms.

3. Chambliss (1989b:231) saw Adler as the latest in a series of critics in whom "prejudice and ignorance combine to distort Marxist criminology." He recognized only two forms of criminology: Marxist and anti-Marxist (Chambliss 1989:237).

4. The Supreme Court has ruled that state interests may demand sentencing differentials, because crack appears to pose a far more serious threat to the nation. Marxists, of course, understand why the Court has consistently ruled in this fashion.

5. The use of the term *girls* is not meant to demean young women. It is used in the

spirit of recent discussions by feminists about restoring the status of girlhood as a transition between childhood and adulthood (Adler 1997; see also Esbensen and Winfree 1998).

6. Not all social feminists accept power–control theory as a reflection of their orientation toward crime and society. Indeed, not all feminists, as will be made clear later in this chapter, welcomed this theory as a true reflection of feminist thinking.

7. McCarthy, Hagan, and Woodward (1999:763) acknowledge that fathers in less patriarchal families might have a positive impact. However, they give much more attention to mothers' roles.

8. The debate moved beyond theoretical or research questions to personal attacks on those who support the policy and those who question it. See Binder and Meeker (1993) and Berk (1993) for this personalized debate.

10

The Future of Crime Theory

CHAPTER OVERVIEW

LEARNING OBJECTIVES

- Review briefly what we have learned about the search for theoretical insights into crime and criminals.

- Explore three questions (and related answers) about extending the search for insights into crime and criminals, and the implications of each for crime theory and crime control policy.

- Appreciate the crime-related challenges and opportunities that await criminologists—and the nation—in the twenty-first century.

INTRODUCTION

What is a crime? Who is the criminal? Answers to these two questions provided us with an initial set of definitions and guidelines. Later we added two more questions: Why is there crime? Why do people engage in law-violating behavior? The search for answers to these and other questions has taken us through the domains of many academic disciplines, including biology, chemistry, psychology, psychiatry, sociology, economics, political science, and philosophy. It has also covered hundreds of years, although much of the "real work" occurred in the twentieth century.

Several generalizations emerge from the crime theories, associated tests, policies, and practices reviewed in this text. First, much is known about why people commit crimes and why the level of crime is so high. Second, there is considerable variability in the levels of proof for the causal arguments, ranging from virtually none to consistently high levels. Third, supported or not, many theories exhibit interesting linkages to criminal justice policies and practices.

Given the overt and covert relationships between crime theories and criminal justice practices, the further separation of the chaff from the wheat becomes even more significant. Hence, the logically consistent and empirically verified theories should receive even closer scrutiny. We should also recognize that lack of support for a theory may tell us more about contemporary research designs and analytic capabilities than it does about the theory. As demonstrated on a number of occasions in this text, new ideas about old theories also hold much promise, as in new views on deterrence and rational choices, new conceptualizations of labeling, and new definitions of strain. In short, our efforts to test the various theories have been fragmented, incomplete, uncoordinated, and generally undersupported.

Answers to three general questions may assist criminological theory and research in gaining the empirical support necessary to inform more fully criminal justice policies and practices. Before exploring these questions, we issue a caveat: This material is meant to stimulate *your* thinking about crime. Nothing in the following pages should be construed as a mandate. Rather, the questions and answers represent divergent points of view that should spur you to speculate about both existing theories, research, policies, and practices, and those that will evolve over the course of the twenty-first century.

QUESTION 1:
SHOULD CRIMINOLOGISTS EMPHASIZE
SPECIFIC RESEARCH DESIGNS IN THE
SEARCH TO UNDERSTAND CRIME?

Much of what is known about crime and criminals comes from official statistics, victimization surveys, and self-report studies. Official statistics, such as the Uniform Crime Reports, provide data on crime and punishment trends and little else. Painting a complete picture of crime is beyond their scope; they merely reveal who and what is being processed by law enforcers. Victimization studies, like the National Crime Victimization Surveys, explore the nature and extent of offenses by studying households across the nation at regular intervals; however, the picture they provide is also incomplete. Self-report studies tend to focus on known offender populations and on youths. As Gresham Sykes and Francis Cullen (1992:88) observed, "No national study has been made of adult criminality, and knowledge of self-reported adult crime remains rudimentary." Precisely the information that is missing is the information that is needed. As observed separately by Robert Sampson (1993) and Ann Witte (1993), the use of longitudinal and experimental data will increase criminological knowledge, a position we advance as well, with a few caveats (see also Tittle, 2000).

Politicians and other policy makers understand the significance of longitudinal research. They could not make laws or engage in other public policy–related activities without knowing the trends or patterns over time of issues under consideration. This observation is true for crime control policies as well. In fact, Congress created the Bureau of Justice Statistics to provide it with just this kind of information about crime and justice issues.

The application of experimental designs to crime studies is a more difficult task. Many researchers consider the **classical experimental design,** with its control groups and treatment or experimental groups, to be the best way to explore cause-and-effect relationships (Babbie 1983; Hagan 1989b). In the classical experiment researchers maintain a high level of control over test and control subjects, something that is difficult in any human subjects research, let alone criminological studies. The classical design is best situated in a laboratory setting, which critics condemn as too artificial for studies of crime and justice (Babbie 1983; see also Chow and Hemple 1977). An alternative is the **natural experiment,** one that occurs in a real-world setting and is subject to some researcher manipulation and control. The findings generated by this design are limited by the extent to which nature or some other force exerts its influence over that of the scientist. Far more likely—and more easily "sold" to critics—is the **quasi-experimental design,** one that employs as much of the classical design as possible but lacks key elements, such as randomization, a control group, or researcher manipulation and control.

In addition to methodological problems with studies of crime and justice, there are ethical concerns. In any experiment only some of the subjects receive a treatment; the rest receive perhaps a placebo; that is, a false stimulus or treatment. In medical research this could mean that someone is cured while someone else dies. In crime-related experiments this could mean that someone is victimized while someone else is not, or that someone is "cured" of criminal proclivities while the control subject continues his or her criminal practices or is denied access to a potentially life-altering treatment.

Crime-based experiments have a high potential for being viewed as morally and ethically questionable. For example, in 1997 Lynette Feder sought to evaluate a program for men who had been convicted of misdemeanor domestic violence. She wanted to randomly assign men to either an experimental group that received probation and completed a mandatory 26-week batterer counseling program or a control group that received only probation (Short, Zahn, and Farrington 2000). Besides evaluating the program, Feder proposed to test competing domestic violence theories. The local prosecutor's office threatened to stop the study on legal grounds (i.e., the random assignment was a misuse of judicial discretion) and ethical grounds (i.e., the denial of treatment was based on chance). Feder requested a friend-of-the-court brief from the American Society of Criminology's Executive Board. Although the threat to curtail Feder's work never materialized, the Executive Board's position was clear: "The principle is that random assignment to treatment options is the best scientific method for determining the effectiveness of options such as those proposed in this case" (Short, Zahn, and Farrington 2000:296).

We review next two research projects. This review is by no means exhaustive or even representative. The projects were selected because they (1) included either a longitudinal or an experimental design (or both), (2) have had far-ranging and long-lasting impacts on criminal justice policy making, and (3) have implications for crime theories. In each case we summarize the research projects and their ties to the present topic, along with the current state of knowledge about each topic, and its ties to theory, policies, and practices.

Research Exemplar 1: The City Project

In the 1980s a group of social scientists proposed a major longitudinal study of crime-related issues in Chicago, a city known for its class, racial, and ethnic diversity, and in which no single group represented a majority of the population. The research project, formally titled the **Project on Human Development in Chicago Neighborhoods** and referred to hereafter as the City Project, called for dividing Chicago's commonly recognized community areas into neighborhood clusters, based on similar income, family structure, and racial and ethnic composition.[1] From these clusters the researchers identified 80 neighborhoods that showed enough variability to allow the detection of neighborhood effects.

Origins and Implementation The City Project has two distinct elements. First, Chicago's neighborhoods were surveyed in 1995 and 1996, including (1) a community survey of more than 8700 residents, (2) an observational study (called systematic social observation) that videotaped all interactions and physical evidence of disorder (e.g., garbage on the streets, litter, graffiti, abandoned cars, and needles and syringes) occurring on 23,000 blocks in 196 neighborhoods, 12 hours per day, seven days per week, during the summer of 1995, and (3) a survey of nearly 3000 randomly selected community leaders in education, religion, business, politics, law enforcement, and community organization. The second element in the City Project is an ongoing cohort study, employing an accelerated panel design, in 80 key neighborhoods. The City Project's subjects consist of seven age cohorts, each with roughly 500 males and 500 females: birth, 3, 6, 9, 12, 15, and 18. Their "life experiences" will be measured annually for eight years. Ultimately the researchers hoped to draw conclusions about aspects of human development for their subjects from birth through age 26. The first wave of interviews with about 6000 subjects—and their primary caregivers—began in 1997; the data collection will continue to 2004.

The City Project represents perhaps the most ambitious and expensive single study of crime ever conducted. As law professor Michael Tonry noted, "By a factor of 10 or maybe a factor of 20, it's the largest social science research project undertaken in this country concerning crime and delinquency" (Coughlin 1994:A8). The study examines the following interdisciplinary sources of influence: school, peers, family, and individual differences. The research questions are rooted in current biological, sociological, and psychological theories.

The Current State of the City Project   The City Project is ongoing, but certain parts of it are complete or have provided sufficient data to yield the following observations and conclusions:

- *Community survey results* (Sampson and Bartusch 1999). Chicago's black and Latino/a residents were significantly less tolerant of crime than whites, particularly when it came to perceptions of teenage fighting. Levels of **legal cynicism**—the idea that laws and societal rules are not binding on one's actions—was higher for blacks and Latinos/as than for whites; moreover, those with low socioeconomic status (SES) were twice as likely as those with high SES to report high levels of legal cynicism. The researchers reported that the neighborhood of residence affects attitudes. Minority-group members in neighborhoods characterized by poverty and instability were more cynical than whites; once the economic disadvantage found in a neighborhood was taken into account, the legal cynicism of whites and blacks converged. Blacks appeared to be more cynical only because they were more likely to live where disadvantage is concentrated.

- *Cohort study* (Earls 1998; Obeidallah and Earls 1999). Among 12- and 15-year-old white, African-American, and Latina girls, nearly 50 percent more of those who were mildly to moderately depressed compared to nondepressed girls engaged in property crime, and 100 percent more engaged in crimes against persons. The results for antisocial aggressive behavior were even more startling: Mildly and moderately depressed girls exhibited rates that were more than four times higher than those for the nondepressed. In the first-wave cohort of 9-, 12-, and 15-year-old youths, exposure to violence—hearing gunfire or witnessing a knife attack or a shooting—was strongly correlated with self-reported violent behavior. Because these results come from the first data collection wave, the findings are speculative, but they do suggest a neighborhood influence, as some neighborhoods clearly were safer than others.

- *Surveys and observational study* (Sampson and Raudenbush 2001). Kelling and Wilson's "broken window hypothesis" puts a community's crime squarely on its level of disorder (e.g., soliciting prostitutes, loitering, and committing other incivilities). Using systematic social observations (i.e., videotaping of neighborhood interactions and activities) as an objective and independent measure of disorder, City Project researchers linked it to several measures of crime, including residents' perceptions of crime and police records. They also created a subjective measure called **collective efficacy,** or the level of mutual trust between neighbors and a willingness to intervene on behalf of the common good. The researchers reported that, contrary to the broken windows hypothesis, disorder does not cause crime directly. Rather, collective efficacy and structural features proved far stronger influences. Once these factors were taken into account, but especially poverty and concentration of immigrants, the disorder–crime connection vanished in most instances. A major exception was robbery; the authors suggested that visual cues associated with social and physical disorder entice robbers to act.

Theory, Public Policy, and Criminal Justice Practices A City Project brochure (Project on Human Development in Chicago Neighborhoods n.d.:5; emphasis added) stated the following:

> Perhaps most important, the information generated by the study will help build a rational foundation for *urgently needed policy decisions.* The study's findings can help point the way to a more coordinated approach to social development and its failures—an approach that involves families, schools, communities, and public institutions working together. The findings can help *policy planners* make effective use of limited resources promoting social competence and designing new strategies for preventive intervention, treatment, rehabilitation and sanctions.

The City Project, even without the longitudinal data, is rich in policy implications and theoretical value. First, given the neighborhoods' influence, "policymakers and agents of the criminal justice system would do well to consider the role of community social norms" (Sampson and Bartusch 1999:2). Second, the preliminary findings support one of the oldest crime theories—social disorganization—and cast doubt on the broken windows hypothesis at the heart of aggressive policing intended to eradicate disorder in the nation's inner cities. According to Sampson and Bartusch (1999:5; emphasis in original), "The findings strongly suggest that policies intended to reduce crime by eradicating disorder solely through tough law enforcement tactics are misdirected. . . . Eradicating disorder *may* reduce crime indirectly by stabilizing neighborhoods."

Research Exemplar 2:
Domestic Violence and Arrest Policies

A confluence of forces in the mid-1980s led to a new awareness of the seriousness of domestic violence. Domestic violence traditionally had been accorded low status in police work; police saw it as more of an order maintenance or social work activity than real law enforcement (Zorza 1992; see also Chaney and Saltzstein 1998). The implementation of mandatory arrest policies, in which the aggressor—typically a male—is arrested at the crime scene by responding officers, owes much to lobbying by battered-women's advocates in the 1970s and 1980s (Frisch 1992; Zorza 1992). Litigation also played a role, as negligence and tort claims against police departments mounted (Zorza 1992). These pressures aside, what appears to have solidified support for mandatory arrest is the belief, based on empirical data, that such a policy actually deters future conduct (Jaffe, Wolf, Telford, and Austin 1986). The empirical data in question were provided by the **Minneapolis Domestic Violence Experiment.**

In 1981 the Police Foundation, an independent policy research institute, conducted a year-long evaluation in Minneapolis. A group of Minneapolis police officers was instructed to use one of three strategies when responding to simple (misdemeanor) domestic assaults: (1) Arrest the suspect, (2) send him from the scene of the assault for eight hours, or (3) give advice and mediate. A random lottery system predetermined each officer's response to a particular domestic violence assault call. At the experiment's conclusion Larry Sherman and Richard Berk had data on three randomly assigned responses to domestic violence cases, which they followed up on to see if there was further violence. Sherman and Berk (1984a:8) reported that "arrest was the most effective of three standard methods police use to reduce domestic violence. The other police methods—attempting to counsel both parties or sending assailants away from home for several hours—were found to be considerably less effective in deterring future violence in the cases examined."

In response to the research, Minneapolis changed its policy toward "wife beaters" from avoiding an arrest to arresting the assailant. Throughout the 1980s and 1990s, other state legislatures enacted either mandatory or presumptive arrest policies. In the former situation officers have to arrest either the aggressor or, if that person's identity cannot be determined, all parties involved; in the latter situation an arrest must be made "unless there are good, clear reasons why an arrest would be counterproductive" (Sherman and Berk 1984b:272; see also Ferraro 1989). The Minneapolis experiment became a policy maker's dream: It provided clear and unequivocal evidence that arresting the abuser deterred future offending. Or did it?

Challenges to the Minneapolis Experiment Findings Challenges to Sherman and Berk's conclusions came quickly. Five followup studies—part of the National Institute of Justice's **Spouse Assault Replication Program (SARP)**— failed to duplicate the original findings. In Omaha, Nebraska, arrest was no more effective than either mediation or separation as measured at six-month and one-year intervals (Dunford 1992). Researchers in Milwaukee, Wisconsin, reported variable effects: a short-term deterrent effect and lower violence for whites, married arrestees, and those who were employed, but higher violence levels for African Americans, the unemployed, the unmarried, and high school dropouts (Sherman et al. 1992). Employment status had a similar positive impact on arrest's deterrent effects in Colorado Springs, Colorado; the researchers also suggested that an arrest can make a bad situation even worse (Berk, Campbell, Klap, and Western 1992). A fourth study conducted in Charlotte, North Carolina, found that the batterer's previous criminal record may be the most efficacious indicator of whether arrest is the best policy (Hirschel and Hutchinson 1992). An experiment conducted in Metro-Dade County, Florida, found only marginal support for mandatory arrest, as recidivism dropped only slightly (Pate and Hamilton 1992).

Arnold Binder and James Meeker (1988) originally criticized the Minneapolis experiment for methodological weaknesses and problems with implementation. They questioned the wisdom of touting its findings as definitive when they were in fact weak and inconclusive. And when the SARP failed generally to replicate its findings, Binder and Meeker (1993:887) again assailed the Minneapolis experiment: "The consequence was a dramatic change in public policy with potentially substantial negative effects on many people and an unwarranted large expenditure of public monies." Jannell Schmidt and Lawrence Sherman (1993) added fuel to the debate when they questioned the efficacy of mandatory arrest policies; they further feared that mandatory arrest may do more harm than good (Schmidt and Sherman 1996). Elsewhere Sherman and associates (1992) suggested replacing mandatory arrest with a general list of mandatory actions. One option is mandatory prosecution, which removes the burden from the victim to prosecute the batterer and eliminates the victim's control over the decision whether to prosecute (Mills 1998:308).

Theory, Public Policy, and Criminal Justice Practices More than 20 years after the Minneapolis experiment, nearly 9 in 10 U.S. law enforcement agencies follow written policies on discretionary arrest and domestic disputes, affecting about 97 percent of all sworn officers (Hickman and Reaves 2001:19). The Office of Justice Programs, part of the Justice Department, annually requests proposals under the following title: "Grants to Encourage Arrest Policies and Enforcement of Protection Orders" (U.S. Office of Justice Programs 2001). Mandatory arrest seems a fixed part of the law enforcement policy lexicon.

Research into police responses to domestic violence continues and reveals that, although arrest policies appear to dominate police practices, bureaucratic discretion remains (Chaney and Saltzstein 1998). Moreover, restraining-order violations in domestic violence incidents appear to have the highest impact on arrest probability when risk of injury to the victim is low, and fall off as that risk increases (Kane 2000; Mignon and Holmes 1995). In a reanalysis of the SARP, Christopher Maxwell and his associates (2001) reported findings consistent with Sherman's original claims. The predicted relationship between the suspect's arrest and later aggression was observed, even controlling for differences across research sites. This relationship was described as "a consistent and direct, though modest deterrent effect of aggression by males against their female intimate partners" (Maxwell, Garner, and Fagan 2001:9). Their conclusion: "Our findings provide systematic evidence supporting the argument that arresting male batterers *may,* independent of other criminal justice sanctions and individual processes, reduce subsequent intimate partner violence" (Maxwell, Garner, and Fagan 2001:13; emphasis added).

Finally the domestic violence issue has received theoretical attention. Couching their arguments in terms of deterrence theory, labeling theory, and the "stake in conformity" hypothesis, Sherman and associates (1992) found that, contrary to deterrence theory, arrest did not reduce either official or victim-reported recidivism. Rather, consistent with labeling theory, offenders with a low stake in conformity actually increased their recidivism after arrest. It appears to have been this theory-based analysis that led to Sherman's recanting of his earlier position on mandatory arrest (Schmidt and Sherman 1993, 1996).

Problems and Pitfalls of Experimental
and Longitudinal Research Designs

Both experimental and longitudinal designs have long histories in criminology (see, e.g., Chapter 5). One of the oldest tests of a delinquency intervention strategy was the **Cambridge–Somerville Youth Study** (Powers and Witmer 1951). The experiment—in which randomly selected subjects were given intensive individual counseling and guidance denied to the control group—ran from 1937 to 1945; a follow-up assessment was conducted 30 years later (McCord 1978). Both studies failed to show positive effects. The **Provo Experiment,** which incorporated elements of differential association theory to create a prosocial treatment model, was aborted after a judge discontinued the random assignment of adjudicated youths; he wanted the "bad kids" in his court to get this new treatment (Empey and Erickson 1972). Rather than representing a new method, what the studies reviewed in this section have demonstrated is that, applied to unique and important topics, both approaches have the capability to shape (or reshape) both our understanding of crime and criminals and the policy responses of the justice system.

Although experiments and longitudinal studies are well suited for some criminological studies and crime theory tests, several caveats seem appropriate. First, as Michael Gottfredson and Travis Hirschi (1986) observed, longitudinal studies may add little—at great cost in money and time—to some types of crime studies. Cross-sectional studies may provide all the required insights. Consider, too, the lessons provided by the **National Evaluation of G.R.E.A.T.** As the social process theories (see Chapter 7) suggest, crime is but one stage in life, one that can be left behind or undone.

Second, as researchers embrace time-consuming, expensive, and (possibly) definitive experiments and longitudinal studies, they should not lose sight of the value of other methods, ones entirely unlike those described in this section. Specifically field research has, from the days of the Chicago School, added texture to the rather sparse findings provided by any quantitative crime study. The study of youth gangs has been enriched by such field research studies as John Hagedorn's (1998), which framed gangs as safety nets for the survival of economically depressed males, and Jody Miller's (2001), which offered unique insights into gang girls and the ways in which members resemble (or reject) stereotypical images. Crime as life and work is less mysterious due to Kenneth Tunnell's (1992) study of theft as a lifestyle, Darrell Steffensmeier's (1986) look behind the facade of the professional fence, and Neal Shover's (1985) research on the aging criminal. Even this cursory listing of recent qualitative works suggests a folk wisdom convergence: When it comes to crime research, don't put all your eggs in one basket.

QUESTION 2:

ARE NEW THEORIES NEEDED?

Many criminologists, concerned about the future of crime theory, have asked, Are new theories needed? For example, John Braithwaite (1990) observed that there is much criminological decay because more energy is spent criticizing the work of other scholars than building upon that work. As Braithwaite (1990:163–64) stated:

COMMENTS AND CRITICISMS: The National Evaluation of G.R.E.A.T.

In 1992, the Phoenix Police Department and the Bureau of Alcohol, Tobacco, and Firearms collaborated to offer Gang Resistance Education and Training, a classroom-based antigang program, on a national basis. Police officers entered middle-school classrooms, normally in the seventh grade, and gave a series of lectures about ways to avoid becoming involved in gangs. The National Institute of Justice awarded Finn Esbensen a grant to conduct the National Evaluation of G.R.E.A.T., a project that gathered data for five years, from 1995 to 1999.

The evaluation consisted of several parts, two of which were a cross-sectional study of 11 research sites in which roughly half of the students received G.R.E.A.T. and half did not (with no control over who did and did not receive it) and a panel (longitudinal) study of six sites with 153 classrooms, where the classrooms were randomly assigned to be a G.R.E.A.T. location. In the cross-sectional study the students were sur-veyed in the eighth grade, one year after roughly half of them had partici-pated in the G.R.E.A.T. program. These data revealed that the G.R.E.A.T. partici-pants reported more prosocial behavior and attitudes—ones derived from theo-ries such as social learning, bonding, op-portunity, and self-control—than their peers who did not finish the program or who failed to participate. An analysis of two years' worth of longitudinal data failed to yield the same prosocial differ-ences as observed in the cross-sectional study. However, after the full five years, "beneficial program effects" were ob-served, in that the G.R.E.A.T. students had more prosocial changes than the non-G.R.E.A.T. students. Esbensen at-tributed the differences between the two-year and five-year results to a lagged (or delayed) effect. Using the two-year data would not have revealed these effects.

Sources: Esbensen and Osgood (1997); Esbensen, Osgood, Taylor, Peterson, and Freng (2001).

Criminology as a science has failed to put us in a position to say sensible, empirically informed things about protecting the community from crime. . . . When a science fails us so utterly in this way, we must look to its fundamentals—its theory. The policy failure is a failure of explanation; we cannot solve it by retreating from the need to explain. The fruits of the atheoretical policy-oriented criminology of recent decades are not on the trees waiting to be plucked. The quick policy fixes are just not out there waiting to be discovered. . . . The mission of criminology as a science should be to build theories of as general a scope as we can manage. Then, one would hope that policymakers would work through these theories as alternative frameworks for thinking about particular policy interventions.

Besides the pronouncement that contemporary criminological theories must contribute explanations that are policy relevant (see McCord 1989; Wilson and Herrnstein 1985), other far more specific recommendations have been made by eminent criminologists concerned about the future of criminological theories. For example, Don Gottfredson (1989:1) wrote that most criminological theories are "unclear and lacking in justifiable generality." Nor do they, as Braithwaite and others have observed, offer practical guidance that "does not require heroic leaps of conjecture." As a consequence Gottfredson (1989:15) suggested that theorists should provide as much detail as possible—including any assumptions about crime,

---

IN THEIR OWN WORDS:
Qualitative Criminologists' Informants Speak for Themselves

Jody Miller interviewed 94 midwestern girls, about half of whom were in gangs and all of whom lived in areas with gang activity, and captured their attitudes about women in gangs:

> In describing themselves as "one of the guys," young women highlighted what they perceived to be the importance of being tough and physically aggressive and of not being preoccupied with "feminine" concerns. As Veronica noted earlier, girls who "get scared" or "don't wanna break their nails and stuff like that" don't belong in gangs. Tonya complained about girls who "don't fight, ones that think they too cute to fight, ones that be scared to sell drugs, just scared. . . . You can't be scared and be a gang member."

Kenneth Tunnell interviewed 60 male, chronic property offenders who had committed nearly 50,000 crimes. From one he learned the following lesson about legal sources of money:

I went to the bank four different times. I went to four or five different loan companies, you know the ones that say, "Come on in and borrow money on your word" and all this. That a crock of shit. They ain't anybody going to lend you nothing. I mean it's there for the taking, but it ain't there for the lending.

Neal Shover studied 50 convicted ordinary property offenders, 40 years of age or older. Many intended to quit the life, but not all, including one who observed about his return to crime:

> Well, at this stage in my life I think that's the only thing left open to me, that I can really profit from. I'm not going to be successful working. . . . I don't want that day-to-day grind and I don't want that regimentation that goes along with working a job.

Sources: Miller (2001:182); Shover (1985:45); Tunnell (1992:64–65).

---

criminals, and society; the measurement of key concepts and other abstract information; and any limits on the generalizability of the theory—to allow those who come after them the means to determine the adequacy of the theory. Moreover, the theory should be "reexamined in light of the evidence and revised if necessary."

Old Wine in New Casks or New Wine in Old Casks?

New theories provide but one means to alter the current state of criminological theorizing observed by Braithwaite, Gottfredson, and others (cf. Bernard 1990; Gibbons 1992; Hagan 1989; McCord 1989). Indeed, we reviewed few truly new and original theories proposed after 1970, outside of perhaps Cornish and Clarke's rational choice theory (see Chapter 2), Cohen and Felson's routine activities theory (see Chapter 2), Gottfredson and Hirschi's self-control theory (see Chapter 7), and Hagan's power–control theory (see Chapter 9). Some observers might argue that, with few exceptions, even these theories are examples of "old wine in new casks"—that is, old ideas masquerading as new theories on crime or criminality.

There is nothing inherently wrong with this approach to theory, so long as the ideas are recognized for what they are: Both the new and old varieties make the same or very similar assumptions about crime, criminals, and society. Researchers are guided to essentially the same places for answers, and they employ nearly identical concepts and variables in both the original and the "new wine" variety. Thus, rational choice theory enjoys close ties to cost–benefit analysis and classical deterrence theory; the IQ–crime connection is connected to classical conditioning and elements of deterrence; self-control theory, too, is a restatement of classical deterrence and rational choice principles within a bonding theory framework.

If there is new wine in old bottles, what about old wine in new bottles? To answer this question we need only refer to the resurgence of theoretical and research interest in social disorganization theory (see Chapter 6), especially given new measurement and analysis techniques. Researchers have proposed new methods for testing differential opportunity theory, as well as the redefinition of strain, all of which could be considered old wine in new bottles, especially given that their ties to the original theories are clear and well stated.

Integrated Theories

Criminologists have long used either theory falsification or theoretical competition as a means of reducing the number of theories. **Theory falsification** involves discarding those theories whose predictions are inconsistent with empirical observations (Bernard and Snipes 1996). In **theoretical competition** two or more theories that make contradictory predictions are tested together, and those whose predictions are inconsistent with the data are discarded (Liska, Krohn, and Messner 1989). Another approach is **theoretical integration.** *Integration* is a common term in theoretical discussions, as all theory " 'integrates,' or unifies, empirical findings" (Liska, Krohn, and Messner 1989:2). The phrase *theoretical integration* is usually reserved for "an activity that involves the formulation of linkages between different theoretical arguments. Theoretical integration is best viewed as one means of theorizing—i.e., as one strategy for developing more cogent explanations and for explaining theoretical growth" (Liska, Krohn, and Messner 1989:2). Another definition provides a more prescriptive set of instructions: "Theoretical integration can be defined as *the act of combining two or more sets of logically interrelated propositions into one larger set of interrelated propositions, in order to provide a more comprehensive explanation of a particular phenomenon*" (Thornberry 1989:52; emphasis in original).

Many previously considered crime theories are integrated theories. The terms *integrate, integration, combined,* and *synthesized* figured prominently in discussions of the similarities between differential association and social learning theories, social control and self-control theories, and classical deterrence and constitutional-learning theories. These theories and others reviewed in this book result from one of the following forms of theoretical development suggested by Allen Liska and his associates (1989:15–17):

- **Theoretical elaboration.** This strategy, which involves the full development of existing theories, is based on the following idea: "Extant theories of deviance and crime are so underdeveloped that we might better spend our time and energies on developing them rather than on integrating them" (Liska, Krohn, and Messner 1989:16). The preceding section ("Old Wine in New Casks or New Wine in Old Casks?") described this approach, and so elaboration of the intentional (new wine in old casks) and unintentional (old wine in new casks) forms of theoretical elaboration is unnecessary.

- **Conceptual integration.** Many theories may have similar or nearly identical core concepts. If we can reduce the conceptual information to common elements and consistent definitions, then the next step, propositional integration, is simplified (see Thornberry's definition of *integration*). For example, Ronald Akers (1990, 1994) has argued that the concepts contained in numerous theories (e.g., classical deterrence, rational choice, social control, strain) can be "subsumed" under existing social learning concepts. Belief, a central part of social control theory, is similar to social learning theory's definitions; strain theory's blocked opportunities is similar to social learning theory's differential reinforcements; the peer influences and moral judgments found in rational choice theory are, in Akers' (1990:655) words, "derived" from social learning theory.

- **Propositional integration.** Existing theories are part of even more general theories, and the goal is to "borrow ideas (concepts and propositions) from different theories and explore how they fit" (Liska, Krohn, and Messner 1989:17). For example, the differential opportunity structures found in Cloward and Ohlin (i.e., the ability to learn illegitimate means) are part of Sutherland's differential association theory and are not at all incompatible with Merton's strain theory. This approach is the highest form of theoretical integration.

Irrespective of the approach employed, the end product should meet two criteria (Liska, Krohn, and Messner 1989). First, the "new theory" should be logically coherent; that is, the synthesis of concepts or propositions should make sense, and not simply increase the predictability of the new "model." Second, "theories serve not only to organize the accumulated body of knowledge and to allow for predictions about empirical phenomena. They are also general 'intellectual puzzles' for scientists to work on" (Liska, Krohn, and Messner 1989:18). Theoretical integration should provide for the "emergence of theoretical statements that will open up new research agendas" (Liska, Krohn, and Messner 1989:18).

In the next section we examine control balance, a relatively new integrated theory. As with the other exemplars in this chapter, this one represents a type and should not be viewed as being better (or worse) than any other integrated theory. Control balance was selected because it (1) is a logically coherent, unique, and broad-ranging theory; (2) represents propositional integration, the most complex form of theory integration; (3) provides in its orienting concept—balance—a challenge to traditional criminological thinking; and (4) yields several policy implications.

Theoretical Exemplar 1: Control Balance Theory

In 1995 Charles Tittle offered a revision of control theory in his book *Control Balance: A General Theory of Deviance*. Tittle's work did not represent a break with traditional control theory. Indeed, he accepted that control is essential to conformity. However, Tittle extended this idea, noting that it is not the absolute presence or absence of control that is important, itself a break with the linear thinking that dominates crime theories (i.e., crime is related in linear fashion to more or less of something). Rather, he addressed the balance between the control one can exert and that to which one is subjected. Tittle expressed this relationship as a ratio, placing the former in the denominator and the latter in the numerator. Unless both forms are the same, an imbalance exists, and the *probability* of deviance increases.

Control Deficits and Surpluses Tittle described two types of control imbalance. The first is **control deficit,** which occurs when the amount of control to which one is subjected exceeds the control one has over others. For example, a child may have control over some aspects of the behavior of his or her younger siblings but may experience a deficit when it comes to parental control. Persons with control deficits engage in **repressive deviance,** of which there are three forms. The goal of each form is to escape the control deficit and reestablish control balance. First, **predation** is physical violence committed with the intent to harm others (e.g., sexual assault and robbery). These offenders "prey" on other humans due to marginal control deficit imbalance. Second, **defiance,** a result of medium control-deficit imbalance, consists of acts that challenge the dominant rules, especially those that are creating the deficit but that do not harm another person. Therefore, these individuals are *rarely* criminal or delinquent, with the exception of vandals and truants. Other forms of defiant behavior may, depending on the age of the "offender," violate laws or ordinances (e.g., drug usage and sexual activity). Third, **submission** means that persons no longer exercise control over their lives, responding instead with "passive, unthinking and slavish obedience" to what they think others want (Tittle 1995:139). Submission, resulting from extreme control-deficit imbalance, includes turning on those seen as less powerful to gain acceptance from those perceived to be more powerful (e.g., an act of aggression against a suspected gay person to gain the attention and respect of like-minded but higher-status homophobes). Submissives also allow themselves to be humiliated and degraded by others.

In those cases in which people's control over others exceeds that imposed on them, Tittle saw **control surplus,** a condition associated with **autonomous deviance,** which also takes three forms. First, **exploitation** resembles predation with a key difference, one related to minimal control surplus. Autonomous deviants have the ability to control others, so they hire, coopt, coerce, or otherwise secure the assistance of inidividuals who commit the actual miscreant acts. A powerful person who wishes to unseat a rival could, for example, hire a professional killer to do the deed. Second, **plunder,** a concept related to the idea of the "spoils of war," results from medium control-surplus imbalance. For example, a conqueror may feel so powerful that he (or she) takes what is desired from the vanquished, (e.g., rape or genocide). Third, **decadence,** involves irrational, spontaneous acts committed without much forethought. Plunderers do it because they can, and no one is powerful enough to stop them. This form of autonomous deviance is due to maximum control-surplus imbalance.

A seeming contradiction in the theory is that those with the least control deficits engage in the most serious forms of crime—predation. Tittle explained it in this way: When deficits are small, people will usually be deterred, but when they commit violations, the acts are far more serious in nature; when deficits are large, people are "less able to imagine that such behavior will escape controlling responses from others" and so engage in less serious forms (Tittle 1995:187). Surpluses function differently. Those with control surpluses commit acts that are proportionately as serious as the level of control surplus they perceive.

Control imbalances increase the probability for deviance, but they do not guarantee deviance. To explain individual responses, Tittle borrowed heavily from such theories as Sutherland's differential association, Merton's anomic trap, Marxist conflict, labeling, deterrence, and routine activities, and, of course, Hirschi's control theory. For example, following the logic of routine activities theory (see Chapter 2), Tittle contended that what determines whether an imbalance in control—too much or too little—produces deviance is largely determined by an individual's predispositional motivations, situational motivations, constraints, and, opportunities. **Predispositional motivations** are themselves a product of innate physical and psychological needs and desires; for example, in Tittle's view we all need food or desire autonomy. **Situational motivations** (or provocations) are more immediate and relate to an individual's perception of a power imbalance—for example, the person who is rejected by a supposed friend or, conversely, who perceives that another is easily intimidated or threatened by a word or look. Motivations alone will not produce deviance; rather, they must interact with **constraints,** which are "the actual probability that potentially controlling reactions will be forthcoming" (Tittle 1995:167). Thus, a person who becomes aware of an imbalance is naturally drawn to act upon that condition—either escape a deficit or extend a surplus— and in the absence of sufficient constraints (deterrent effects) has a heightened probability of engaging in those deviant acts that will offset the imbalance. The final element, **opportunity,** is nearly always present. It is the convergence of high motivations, low constraints, and high opportunity, in the presence of a perceived control imbalance, that increases the probability of deviance.

Assessing Control Balance Theory Critics were quick to point out problems with the theory, including the following:

- *The search for a general theory.* David Curry (1998) questioned whether such a general theory of deviance could exist. He noted that physicists have searched fruitlessly for a unified theory of matter in the universe. Moreover, even if he believed such a search would be profitable, Curry would not take Tittle's path.

- *Logical inconsistencies, definitional difficulties, and other lapses.* Joachim Savelsberg (1996, 1999) and Gary Jensen (1999) assailed Tittle's assumptions about the human condition; the vagueness of his definitions of deviance, power, and control; and the theory's general conceptual ambiguities. In striving to present a general theory, claimed the critics, Tittle provided too little concreteness.

- *Expressions of control imbalance.* The idea of an imbalance resembles Sutherland's differential association principle, and the same question is relevant here: How much of an imbalance, asked Braithwaite (1997) is required? Tittle described small, medium, and large imbalances but did not reveal the differences.

Braithwaite (1997) suggested four refinements to control balance theory. First, he proposed simplifying the major assumption: People always want more control, no matter how much they currently possess. Second, given conceptual imprecision between categories of autonomous deviance, they should be collapsed into one form. Third, he saw Tittle's work as a theory of predation, because the various forms of defiance are merely different techniques for engaging in self-benefit by taking advantage of someone or something. Finally Braithwaite would have Tittle treat submissiveness as a separate, nondeviant response.

Tittle (1997) responded that the distinction between maintaining a deficit and extending a surplus was essential to his challenge of the linear model "that has dominated theory and research about crime and deviance" (Tittle 1997:101). As for the qualitative distinctions, Tittle acknowledged that they were imprecise and agreed that they should be abandoned; however, he further noted that Braithwaite's proposed simplification jeopardized a central component of the theory. In similar fashion he rejected Braithwaite's suggestion that control balance was a theory of predation: "To reduce it to a strict theory of predation would not really achieve anything and it would sacrifice a lot" (Tittle 1997:104). Finally, although acknowledging problems with submission, Tittle remained unconvinced that it should be excluded, preferring instead to allow researchers to confirm or deny the correctness of its inclusion.

Alex Piquero, Matthew Hickman, and various associates have provided several tests of control balance's basic theses.[2] For example, Piquero and Hickman (1999) wrote that self-reported rates of predation and defiance acts among college students were, as predicted, high among those with control deficits; however, the rates were also high for those with control surpluses. In an examination of gender differences, Hickman and Piquero (2001) again obtained mixed results. Contrary to Tittle's theory, both forms of imbalance predicted both repressive and autonomous deviance with gender variations. That is, control imbalance works well to explain repressive deviance for female college students but not males, and it explains autonomous deviance for males but not females. Adding rational choice elements, Piquero and Hickman (2001) observed that the ability of imbalances to predict the intent to commit predatory offenses was greatest under conditions of high pleasure and low risk. Perhaps Braithwaite's suggestion was correct.

Piquero and his associates (2001) extended the theory to the study of victims. They reported that persons with both forms of control imbalance were more likely to be victimized by theft than were balanced persons. Hickman and associates (2001) applied the theory to police deviance. Using a survey of randomly selected patrol officers, they found support for Tittle's theory, albeit for a minor form of police deviance. Specifically, officers with control deficits were more likely to violate the police code of silence by reporting fellow officers' involvement in illicit behavior; however, the same was not true for control surpluses. Apparently Tittle's request is being answered: Control balance theory is being tested and refined by researchers.

Control Balance and Public Policy Braithwaite (1997:89–93) saw a number of policy implications in control balance theory. In particular Braithwaite (1997:89) reported that predation, exploitation, and plunder threaten **republican freedom,** or "freedom as non-domination, liberty that is assured by legal, social, and economic guarantees that those with greater power will have their ability to dominate us checked." From the standpoint of replication freedom, then, control balance theory has several implications, including these:

1. *Greater equality of control.* This idea entails redistributing control from those with surpluses to those with deficits. One way to achieve this is by redistributing wealth from the rich to the poor.

2. *Republication virtue in the exercise of control.* Control is essential, and so is commitment to a rule of law in which no one feels above the law even in the exercise of control. However, the favored republication way to exercise control is through dialogue, whereby the objects of control give their consent.

3. *Greater acceptance of control.* A key goal in any community must be to help those who resist being controlled to understand the necessity of it. According to Braithwaite (1997:92), "We should support those controls that in their ultimate effects increase freedom as non-domination, [and] resist controls that reduce republication freedoms."

4. *Stronger social bonds, social support, and communities.* Extreme inequalities wilt in the face of strong social bonds, social support, and communities. "When social bonds are strong in a society, shaming of domination, pride in non-domination and respectfulness are more likely to prevail. So is shaming of the predation that arises from the control imbalances that remain" (Braithwaite 1997:93).

These policy implications are broad and abstract, as is the theory itself. Similar observations were made about other crime theories when they first emerged. As control balance is further tested and refined, the policy statements may also become more focused and concrete.

Theoretical Exemplar 2:
Life-Course Criminology

Jane, a 16-year-old antisocial girl, has difficulty adjusting to a new school, her fourth in five years. She has failed the eighth grade for the third time, has no friends, and is beginning to move from drug experimentation to regular use of various controlled substances, punctuated by binge-drinking bouts. Each new form of antisocial behavior seems grafted onto an existing core of misconduct and rejection. Jane is an African American living in a socially disadvantaged neighborhood. What forces are moving Jane along a pathway of deviance and crime?

A relatively new criminological theory may yield insights into Jane's fate.[3] This theory has its roots in a 1930s study by Sheldon and Eleanor Glueck (see Chapter 3), who collected a wealth of information on two samples of youths, one delinquent and the other nondelinquent, who were matched in terms of general intelligence, ethnicity, and residence in underprivileged areas. Robert Sampson and John Laub (1993) reanalyzed the Gluecks' qualitative and quantitative data, employing an integrated theory that drew heavily upon social control and labeling theories, with a strong appreciation for large-scale structural forces such as poverty. Sampson and Laub's theory has social control as its organizing principle; however, they explored social bonding over the life course and included both institutions of formal *and* informal social control.

They proposed that different forces operated on individuals according to their age-graded status: (1) becoming juvenile delinquents, (2) making the behavioral transitions that accompany the transition from juvenile status to adulthood, and

(3) becoming an adult offender. To this end they employed two concepts: (1) trajectories, or long-term developmental pathways over the life course, and (2) transitions, or short-term specific life events that are part of trajectories and may mark movement from one status to another.

Sampson and Laub identified family context factors to explain juvenile delinquency. The family context included lack of supervision, erratic or harsh discipline, and parental rejection. Structural background factors, including family SES, residential mobility, and household crowding, combined with individual differences, including early conduct disorders and difficult temperament, to influence the social bonding associated with family and school.

They also acknowledged the relative stability of deviance over the life course, given that the best predictor of future delinquency is past involvement in delinquency or similar misconduct. However, change is an important feature of life-course development. For example, social capital emerged as a crucial force for change; those adults with strong ties to friends, family, and job have an investment in conformity even if they were seriously involved in delinquency as late adolescents and young adults. The key issue for Sampson and Laub was how many doors the past misconduct had closed for the individual (see labeling theory), something they called **cumulative continuity,** leading to a type of forced stability. **Transitory events,** then, *may* lead to **turning points,** or changes in life-course trajectories (Laub, Sampson, and Allen 2001:100).

Assessing Life-Course Criminology Sampson and Laub found that the Gluecks' 1930s data comported well with a life-course analysis. Bonds to school, family, and peers were among the strongest features, with the operation of the latter two forces leading one criminologist to wonder about the theory's ties to differential association and social learning theories (Akers 2000:251). Some tests have centered on central themes. For example, marriage is a key turning point. Using the Glueck data, John Laub and his associates (1998) found that marriage leads to a reduction in crime and delinquency, although this process of desistance appears to be gradual and cumulative. Mark Warr (1998) also found that marriage has an ameliorative impact on offending. However, marriage may not be the turning point, but a transition to other forces. That is, marriage reduces the time spent with delinquent friends and provides alternative peer associations, adding credibility to the notion that social learning forces may be at work as well. Critics note that to date researchers have emphasized change and desistance from criminal conduct, largely ignoring other key parts of the theory (Mazerolle 2000).

The life-course perspective provides additional grist for criminological discussions about the following important theoretical and practical issues:

- *An early childhood focus for sociological criminology.* James Wilson and Richard Herrnstein (1985) lambasted sociological criminology for largely ignoring childhood forces in shaping future criminals. Psychologists, including behavioral psychologists and developmental criminologists (see Chapter 5), study these forces in great detail, but sociologists do not. Recall, too, that sociologists—including Sutherland—were critical of the role given to biology by the Gluecks. Sampson and Laub's theory, by integrating several sociological crime theories into a life-course perspective, counters many sociological objections to psychologically oriented developmental criminology. Life-course criminology also answers antisociological critics like Wilson and Herrnstein.

- *A basis for sociological criminologists to disagree with Gottfredson and Hirschi about the unitary nature of crime causation.* Crime causation is static, according to the crime-propensity argument. Early attacks on this argument came from developmental psychologists (see Chapter 5). Sampson and Laub provided a far more sociological explanation, one that included large-scale structural and social-psychological forces.

- *A level of interdisciplinary cooperation rarely achieved in criminology.* As Sampson (2001:vi) observed on the subject of the various explanations for the processual nature of crime and delinquency, "In this regard I do not wish to claim that life-course criminology is of a uniform mind, or to claim a hegemonic status for particular theories. For example, while I personally happen to hold a more sociological view of the life course, I am fascinated by the possibilities of biological, psychological, and economic perspectives." This was not Sutherland's position or one endorsed by all contemporary sociologists. However, Sampson, as a key member of the City Project team, raised the stakes for those who oppose interdisciplinary studies.

Life-Course Criminology, Public Policy, and Criminal Justice Practices
Life-course criminologists believe that their theory points to important policy changes for American criminal justice. The showcase feature of the nation's current crime control policy is imprisonment. Between 1980 and 2000 the prison incarceration rate grew from 139 per 100,000 to nearly 478; during this same period the number of inmates rose from 315,974 to more than 1,287,172 (U.S. Bureau of Justice Statistics 2002a,b). James Austin and John Irwin (2001), Sam Walker (1998), and Richard Wright (1996) have argued against three-strikes practices, mandatory sentencing, and selective incapacitation as part of a failed penal harm movement. As Wright (1996:135) noted, "By promoting prison crowding and its related evils, the penal harm movement has clearly extended degradation, provocation, and deprivation well beyond the act of imprisonment to the daily conditions of confinement." Sampson and Laub (1993) added a future orientation to the debate. Lengthy incarceration of young persons, they claimed, cuts them off from the types of social bonds, transitory events, and turning points that increase crime desistance. Incarceration delays the inevitable and exacerbates existing crime-proneness. Especially troubling, noted Laub and his associates (2001), is the very high rate of incarceration among black males. This group accounts for nearly half of all state prison inmates (U.S. Bureau of Justice Statistics 2000) and more than 4 in 10 jail inmates (Maguire and Pastore 2000).

Laub and his associates (2001) suggested that a crime policy with a focus on prevention should replace the current one. They recommended that the nation adopt "a more complex and long-term perspective that recognizes the linkages among crime policies, employment, family cohesion, and social organization of inner-city communities" (2001:107). They included as examples the types of parent-training programs described in Chapter 5; job-training programs, such as Job Corps; and modification of current incarceration strategies for those who must be imprisoned, to include updated educational and occupational programs and greater reliance on alternative sanctions, including community-based corrections (Laub, Sampson, and Allen 2001:109).

QUESTION 3: ARE NEW QUESTIONS OR NEW PARADIGMS NEEDED?

Developing new questions may prove to be the broadest and most difficult strategy to implement. As a strategy it suggests that the questions currently informing criminologists either are inadequate to the task or have yielded all possible insights into crime and criminals. Ironically, before we can even begin to frame new questions, a number of historical and entrenched barriers to thinking about new questions must be broached.

Overcoming Disciplinary and Political Barriers

Our quest for knowledge is often delimited by those who have preceded us in that search or, more often, those who educated us. Existing knowledge, complete with ideological, philosophical, academic disciplinary, and political components, helps to define the issues and questions, which is good because it provides structure. However, structure is also confining, meaning that where we can look for possible answers is often defined for us by these same ideologies, philosophies, academic disciplines, and politics.

One person's theory is another person's ideology, and what is ideology for some may be theology for others. As was made clear in Chapter 1, a crime theory may represent more than simply one person's best insights into crime. It is possible that what we are seeing is something that has taken on a life of its own, to use a Latin (and structural-functionalist) term, *sui generis*. Challenging a particular theory or its underlying assumptions may assume the status of heresy. Similar problems exist for criminologists who suggest that the nature–nurture dichotomy inhibits thinking about crime. Life, they observe, is rarely a matter of either nature or nurture. Attempts to divine which is the more important force in human behavior may be the modern equivalent of the Gordian knot, an insoluble problem with a simple solution: Appreciate the differences but treat both forces as essential and interrelated.

Disciplinary Barriers In a similar fashion existing disciplinary barriers inhibit the creation of new questions. For example, such theorists as the biogeneticist Lee Ellis and the psychologist Hans Eysenck have suggested that we must look beyond parochial academic disciplines, such as biology, chemistry, psychology, sociology, or economics, as the source of answers to all questions of crime and criminality. Rather, crime is a complex problem requiring complex and multidisciplinary answers (see Jeffery 1978). Indeed, Ray Jeffery (1978:149–50) described how in the late 1940s three "giants" in the behavioral sciences—the legal philosopher Jerome Hall, the sociologist Edwin Sutherland, and the behavioral psychologist B. F. Skinner—worked within a hundred yards of each other on the Indiana University campus but had no significant mutual interaction. Such is the strength of disciplinary boundaries, ones criminologists such as Jeffery suggest have outlived their usefulness in the study of crime. Indeed, as his Indiana University example illustrates, they constitute barriers to the free exchange of ideas.

A number of sociologists have argued that criminology should be a social science in its own right. In Marvin Wolfgang's (1963) opinion criminology has amassed its own information and theories. Individuals who devote all or most of their scholarly time and resources to the study of crime and its control should be designated as criminologists. For his part Daniel Glaser (1965:773) has written that criminology should be regarded as a "synthesizing discipline." Don Gibbons (1979:4) observed that much criticism has focused on the fact that mainstream criminology is ignorant of criminal law and criminal procedure, two important elements in criminal justice. Moreover, "other commentators on the criminological enterprise have taken note of its ahistorical character, its silence on the question of psychological forces in criminality, and other signs of *academic provincialism*" (Gibbons 1979:4; emphasis added).

Some sociologists are less than sanguine about the prospect of nonsociological criminology. For example, Ronald Akers (1992) maintained that sociology remains "very much the intellectual 'center of gravity' in criminology, and criminology remains an important part of sociology." He defined criminology not as a separate discipline, but rather as an area of study in sociology. Akers drew upon the basic definition of criminology offered by Sutherland (1947): Criminology is the study of the making of law, the breaking of law, and the social reaction to laws. There is nothing in this definition that designates a particular approach or perspective; rather, all that is mentioned is the object of study. To be a discipline, argued Akers, there must be some sort of perspective—such as a sociological, economic, biological, or psychological perspective—that defines how crime is studied. Indeed, even Akers (1992:9) admitted that "too much is involved in the study of crime and criminal justice that is not sociological for it to be contained wholly within sociology, and there is much more substantial interest in and contributions to criminology from other disciplines than ever before. Sociology does not dominate criminology as much as it once did."

Political Barriers Science, scientists tell us, must be autonomous, that is, free from external restrictions and constraints (Kaplan 1963; see also Walsh and Ellis 1999). This does not mean that science need be free from criticisms or comments. Peer review—a process by which fellow researchers or other scientists review scientific findings to determine if they are devoid of bias or mistakes—is intended to keep scientists honest. Moreover, as we learned in the section on experimental designs, replications keep scientists honest. It is particularly distressing for scientists, therefore, when their work is subject to political pressures.

For example, in the early 1990s a conference at the University of Maryland titled "Genetic Factors in Crime: Findings, Uses, and Implications" was canceled because of political pressures in Washington (Wheeler 1992a; see also Jeffery 1993). First, the National Institute of Health (NIH) froze all funding for the project, citing "unanticipated sensitivity and validity issues" in spite of the fact that the NIH peer review board had previously reported that the organizers had "done a 'superb job of assessing the underlying scientific, legal, ethical, and public policy issues and organizing them in a thoughtful fashion'" (Wheeler 1992b:A6). Not everyone shared this glowing estimation of the conference, however. Considerable political pressure was brought to bear on the NIH to cancel the conference after concerns were expressed about issues of racism. Indeed, the underlying concern was that the findings discussed at the conference might promote racist attitudes. As one critic expressed it, "[The conference] is clear racism. It is an effort to use public money for a genocidal effort against African Americans" (Wheeler 1992b:A8). Another critic was equally direct: "The conference was simply the most visible and obviously atrocious example of an attempt to blame crime on the brains or the genes of little black children instead of addressing racism and poverty in America" (Wheeler 1992b:A8). A year later the NIH canceled the grant, citing as a primary reason that an objective discussion of the issues could no longer be achieved (Wheeler 1993b:A6). A representative of the NIH wrote in his letter of notification to the conference organizers, "The university prepared and distributed a brochure whose language appeared to discount the environmental factors in crime and gave the distinct impression that there is a genetic basis for criminal behavior, a theory that has never been scientifically validated" (Wheeler 1993b:A6). Interestingly the conference was supported by the Human Genome Mapping Project (Wheeler 1992b).

At one time it was believed that all researchers had to do was claim they were value neutral. This position, first advanced for sociology by Max Weber in 1918, was viewed as meaning that "sociology, like other sciences, needed to be unencumbered by personal values if it is to make a special contribution to society" (Babbie 1983:465). Research methods textbooks for criminology and criminal justice also stress that "the *role of the researcher* requires that one be objective and value free in approaching and reporting on the subject matter" (Hagan 1989a:346; emphasis in original). As the organizers of the "Genetic Factors in Crime" conference learned, adopting a value-neutral stance on a politically charged topic is no defense. Bridging the political barrier, then, may prove to be one of the most difficult tasks confronting criminologists in the twenty-first century.

The Case for the Paradigm Shifts
in the Study of Crime and Criminals

Thomas Kuhn (1970), physicist and philosopher, coined the term **scientific revolutions** to explain how quantum leaps in knowledge, or paradigm shifts, occur in the sciences. A *paradigm* is, according to Kuhn (1970), a fundamental model or scheme that organizes our view of something; it is "a set of recurrent and quasi-standard illustrations of various theories in their conceptual, observational, and instrumental applications." A paradigm may not give us the answers to our questions, but it tells us where to look by governing "not a subject matter but rather a group of practitioners" (Kuhn 1970:180).

After a period of growth in which scientific knowledge evolves, many sciences are characterized by periods of paradigm validation, followed by normal, incremental growth and, perhaps, intellectual stagnation. The old truths (and old paradigms) become the only truths. Any challenges to those truths are heresy and universally condemned by "true scientists." Indeed, Kuhn argued that the big breakthroughs in science—paradigm shifts that result in scientific revolutions—occur when new thinkers enter the arena and challenge the status quo. Eventually the clarity of their arguments and the level of their proof carries the day, and the science moves forward, often undergoing a radical transformation in the process and thus creating a scientific revolution. As evidence of this process, Kuhn cited examples from chemistry and physics, such as the replacement of Newtonian physics by Einstein's relativity. Kuhn suggested that scientific revolutions were not limited to the physical sciences, a suggestion taken to heart by more than a few social scientists.

Two paradigms have dominated the study of crime and criminals: the classical position and the positivistic position. Within positivism the nature–nurture controversy created a second-layer paradigm.[4] These paradigms have been challenged by Marxist and feminist paradigms, each suggesting different questions and different solutions. In the twenty-first century it is possible that new insights into crime will come from an emerging perspective: postmodernism.

Postmodernism: A New Paradigm for the Study of Crime and Criminals?

The 1960s were a decade of change in American society and culture. To some social critics the 1960s were ripe with secular humanism, a philosophy directed toward the attainment of a wide range of human interests but generally at the expense of traditional religious doctrines and practices. These critics called the 1960s "the Fall" (Woodiwiss 1993)—for some of them, the beginning of the end of the **modern era.** The beginning of the modern era is variously attributed to the 1930s New Deal era and the post–World War II era of American preeminence; it ended, according to most critics, in the late 1980s (Woodiwiss 1993:13). The modern era was notable for its emphasis on unchecked economic growth both as an end in itself and as a precursor to other positive changes (Cobb 1993). Dissatisfaction with the modern era, grounded as it was in laissez-faire capitalism, led to both antimodern sentiments and a belief that society must go beyond the modern to some new level. The worldview that evolved from seventeenth-century science—and the collective works of Galileo, Descartes, Bacon, and Newton—was rejected, a view that defined the **postmodern era.**

Postmodernism "refers to a diffuse sentiment rather than to any common set of doctrines—the sentiment that humanity can and must go beyond the modern" (Griffin and Falk 1993:xii). The fact of the postmodern era is taken as a given; what to do about it is open to debate. Postmodernists contend that there are two ways of achieving this goal (Griffin and Falk 1993; Rosenau 1992). **Deconstructive postmodernists** wish to completely abandon the past, the modern era. They adopt an antiworldview, that calls for the elimination of all the ingredients necessary to create a worldview, including "God, self, purpose, meaning, a real world, and truth as correspondence" (Griffin and Falk 1993:xii), a position some might label nihilistic (i.e., a total rejection of laws and institutions, morality, and judgments). **Constructive postmodernists** call not for the total dissolution of the modern era, but rather for a revision of those premises and traditional concepts that are a part of modernism. In short, constructive postmodernists separate and save the wheat of the modernist era while disposing of its chaff.

Postmodern Society and Culture Postmodernism has several implications for society at large. According to one view a generation of youths is being socialized into a mass-media-generated culture (Mead 1970), with an accompanying loss of historical consciousness in the youth-oriented media's "cut and paste" temporal orientation (MTV's "Rock the Vote" campaign in 1992) and an embracement of "just do it" youthful pragmatism. This postmodern culture reflects a loss of stable social-identity references and a sense of community. For example, Robert Bellah and his associates (1985) noted the loss of community ties in the United States and an increasing emphasis on **instrumentalism** (i.e., making money) and **expressive individualism** (i.e., exploring oneself). The theme of instrumental individualism, especially as related to the cultural trend of "by any means necessary," is a central component of Steven Messner and Richard Rosenfeld's (1994) call for a return to the American Dream (see Chapter 6). In this postmodern world competing images and symbols not only appear in contemporary life but are viewed as commodities and marketed worldwide by media and informational technologies in what has become an important structural feature of current capitalist society. One has only to consider the public interest in and merchandising of O. J. Simpson's trial for double homicide or the popularity of movies like *Silence of the Lambs* to understand the blurring of the distinction between fiction and reality in the postmodern era.

Media dominance in shaping culture is a popular theme in postmodernist literature (see Baudrillard 1988). Norman Denzin (1991), for example, noted that the sociological metaphor of the "dramaturgical" society has become interactional reality (see also Goffman's contributions to the dramaturgical approach in Chapter 8). Postmodernism emphasizes the idea that culture has become more fluid and relative, appropriated by the individual actor to meet situational needs. Because culture is itself a fusion of competing images, each individual has the more complex task of interpreting both behavior and the rapidly shifting cultural environment. The "self" becomes crafted by conflicting media symbols and images—images that are less cohesive and more "schizophrenic" (Deleuze and Guattani 1983; Jameson 1984). As a result people have trouble making sense of their environment or their place in space and time (Harvey 1989).

Losers and Winners in the Postmodern Era Shifts in power, loss of individual and community identity, culture in flux—postmodernism would seem, on the surface, to provide new grist for the social science mill through the incorporation of cultural themes as variables in existing empirical and theoretical work. However, as Pauline Marie Rosenau (1992) noted, the extremes of postmodernist thought, particularly "skeptical" or "deconstructionist" postmodernists, have created a serious challenge for social scientists. Skeptical postmodernists question the existence of a body of knowledge that can be regarded as "social scientific," that is, positivistic. They argue that no criteria of evidence can be used to empower one claim of truth over another, and they doubt whether any social science can adequately describe or "represent" the experiences of another person or group (Baudrillard 1988). The skeptics tend to follow the lead of the German philosopher Friedrich Nietzsche, "taking . . . 'perspectivist' and 'relativist' positions that theories, at best, provide partial perspectives on their objects, and that all cognitive representations of the world are historically and linguistically mediated" (Best and Kellner 1991:4).

Besides challenging positivism, many postmodernists also call into question Marxist images. In particular they criticize Marxists' analyses of capitalism for relying on historical and linguistic interpretations that are, for postmodernists, highly suspect (Woodiwiss 1993). However, neo-Marxist postmodernists (see, e.g., Harvey 1989; Jameson 1991) also theorize that postmodernism is a historical phase of capitalism. They argue that "the present consumer or post-industrial phase of capitalist development, far from contradicting Marx's earlier analysis, in fact represents a purer, more developed, and more realized form of capitalism" (Best and Kellner 1991:185). Depending on whom you read, Marxism is either refuted or supported by postmodern theory (Best and Kellner 1991; Giddens 1990; Habermas 1981; Woodiwiss 1993). A paradigm shift to postmodernism could mean new life for criminological theories based on the relative concept of power—especially, it would appear, power over the media.

Clear winners in the postmodern era include qualitative methodologies, such as symbolic interactionism, social phenomenology, and ethnomethodology. The relativism of postmodern theory seems comparable to the symbolic interactionist position that social reality is fluid, constantly re-created and reproduced in new situations. Denzin (1991), for one, was concerned with control over popular culture, definitions of the American Dream, happiness, gender, class, and the like, which are developed by the new power elite of journalists, politicians, and advertisers. As Denzin (1991:24) further noted, the postmodern tradition follows the methodological tradition "that society in the here-and-now, society-at-hand, is best understood as an interactional accomplishment . . . mediated by localized, interactional practices." Critical analysis also receives support from revisionist postmodernists: Although emphasizing critical theoretical positions that are largely antipositivistic, they provide new images of reform and revitalization for the social sciences (Rosenau 1992; see also Kvale 1992).

Postmodernism and the Study of Crime Postmodernism has several implications for the study of crime. Linguistic postmodernist criminologists would have us reject most, if not all, of criminology as another oppressive offshoot of the failed Enlightenment (Henry and Milovanovic 1991). However, the media's role in creating a pliable image of American culture is far more difficult to dismiss; some argue that criminologists should counter with a **newsmaking criminology** that provides an alternative reality (Barak 1988). It is becoming increasingly difficult to tell reality from fiction, truth from lie. The questions asked are similar to those discussed in Chapters 8 and 9: Who is in control of creating these images? Whose interests do they serve? Stuart Henry and Dragan Milovanovic (1994:110) offered answers to these questions in **constitutive criminology:**

> Constitutive criminology is concerned with identifying the way in which the interrelationships between human agents and their social world constitute crime, victims, and control as realities. It is oriented to how we may deconstruct these realities and to how we may reconstruct less harmful alternatives. Simultaneously, it is concerned with how emergent socially constructed realities themselves constitute human agents with the implication that, if crime is to be replaced, this necessarily must involve a deconstruction and reconstruction of the human subject.

A strength of the postmodern perspective is the fact that it emphasizes critical assessment, particularly radical neo-Marxist postmodernist theories. Such a post-

---

COMMENTS AND CRITICISMS:
Postmodernism, Chaos Theory, and Mainstream Criminology

Chaos theory sees change as nonlinear and fractal. T. R. Young (1991a) posited that small changes in the social fabric can produce large, untrackable changes in crime dynamics. Fractal geometry provides the second element. Rather than involving a binary world (present *or* absent, good *or* evil), fractal geometry allows two contradictions to exist simultaneously, as two objects can occupy the identical time–space region. According to Young (1996:19), "Criminological theory must deal with nonlinear *and* shifting fractals of criminal behavior—as must social policy."

Glenn Walters (1999) explored crime's chaotic parameters. Much about crime prediction, he noted, is fractal, as in the case of the juvenile who has multiple high-risk factors but no misbehavior and the low-risk youth who is delinquent. Positivism's over-reliance on linearity explains its failure to achieve absolute prediction. Reciprocity is more likely, in that deviant behavior (or crime) interacts with other conditions,

becoming both a cause and an effect, an idea rejected by most positivists as circular reasoning. Walters also noted that the process of measuring something inevitably affects the thing being measured, sometimes in unpredictable ways—a basic tenet of chaos theory.

Walters (1999:143) saw the positions of polar opposites—for example, the classicalism–positivism and consensus–conflict controversies—as reconcilable ideas that may advance crime studies "through the chaotic principle of growth achieved via the interaction and integration of polar opposites." He does not wish to abandon traditional theories; rather, he calls for a reassessment of how they operate in light of chaos theory. Walters (1999:150) also endorsed longitudinal designs to provide, in his words, "the collection of hundreds, if not thousands, of repeated data points." This reliance on empiricism may not sit well with other, more critical postmodernists.

Sources: Walters (1999); Young (1991).

---

modernist criminology would likely be concerned with deconstructing the texts of "law producers," in line with the work of Chambliss and Seidman (see Chapter 9). Given postmodernists' overriding cultural concerns, a critical question for postmodern criminology would be the following: Is criminal behavior simply another human response to the overwhelming aspects of contemporary postmodern society? As with any paradigm shift, then, not only are the truth claims of the old paradigm challenged, but new questions are asked as well. (See Table 10.1 for a review of key questions—and answers.)

Implications for Crime Theory

Theorists and researchers alike have questioned the wisdom of viewing the various paradigms as mutually exclusive. New theoretical perspectives have been merged with old ones, creating exciting and highly promising ways of viewing the "crime problem." The old reasons for rejecting various unappealing explanations for current crime problems no longer seem to hold currency. Existing historical, ideological-philosophical, disciplinary, and political barriers seem anachronistic in the first decade of the twenty-first century. The question is, Are we approaching a scientific revolution involving studies of crime and criminals?

Table 10.1 Summary of Key Questions (and Answers)

Questions	Basic Idea(s)	Strengths	Weaknesses	Overall Assessment
Focus on specific methods?	Two research methods—experimental and longitudinal designs—have the potential to answer the difficult causal questions buried within most crime theories.	Provides structured, highly scientific procedures to follow; yields high-quality information about any phenomenon for which time is a variable.	Is expensive and time-consuming; may lead to an over-reliance on quantitative methods at the expense of far richer and contextualized qualitative ones.	Proceed cautiously. Experiments and longitudinal studies are expensive and often time-consuming; they may not yield definitive answers.
Create new theories?	Criminology has reached a creative dead end; new theories are needed to jump-start the search for crime explanations.	Allows new ideas to enter criminology and old ones to be revisited, possibly merging the two.	May divert attention from highly fruitful existing theories, ones that only need better data, better analysis, or better conceptualizing.	This can yield important theoretical and empirical leads; however, researchers should proceed with caution and avoid conflicting assumptions.
Ask new questions/employ new paradigms?	We have exhausted the creative energy of "modern" ideas and theories, and are entering a new era with new theories, opportunities, and directions.	Provides something new that is attractive for what it represents: the potential to reveal truths hidden within that which is untried.	See strengths; offers new questions/paradigms that may require new methods and analytic procedures, along with new ways to test and build theories.	Some criminologists will explore new directions, but most energy will be expended in pursuit of existing paradigms.

SUMMARY

The three questions addressed in this chapter reflect the merger of theory, research, policy, and practices explored in Chapter 1 and throughout the text. First, experiments and longitudinal studies hold much promise for criminological theory testing, but not without costs. Longitudinal studies are often expensive and may not be appropriate for some causal questions. Experiments, especially ones involving random assignment, are likely to generate controversy, even though policies, procedures, and in some instances laws allow for their use (Boruch, Victor, and Cecil 2000; Krisberg and Schuman 2000). Another motivation is the availability of funds for social science research. For example, the National Institute of Justice, a major source of funding for criminal justice–related research, has a stated preference for randomized experiments (Garner and Visher 1988). Given sufficient safeguards, randomized experiments may answer seminal questions about program efficacy and causal sequencing (Dunford 2000; Feder and Boruch 2000). Whatever other reasons underlie their application, social scientists employing experiments should recall the experiences of medical researchers: "Progress toward more sustained use of experimental research in social settings is also likely to be driven by the lesson that social interventions, just like medical ones, may do more harm than good" (Oakley 2000:326). The qualified answer to the first question, then, is yes—that is, employ both longitudinal and experimental designs where appropriate, but not to the exclusion of other methods.

Second, the quest for new theories, like the increased use of experiments and longitudinal studies, is equally laudable and equally fraught with difficulties. The path to new crime explanations—even integrated theories—is not one to be taken lightly by criminologists. Their work, as Braithwaite pointed out and as exemplified by Tittle's control balance theory, often comes under unusually critical scrutiny, especially when they offer general theories. Theoretical elaborations continue, as evidenced by the body of work reviewed in this text. Perhaps we have not exhausted the ability of existing theories to yield meaningful insights into crimes and criminals, as some criminologists suggest (cf. Bernard 1990; Braithwaite 1989; Erickson and Carriere 1994; Tittle 1985; Williams 1984). In answer to the second question, then, criminologists most likely will continue on multiple paths. Some will pursue theoretical elaboration; others will integrate existing concepts, propositions, and theories; and a few will offer genuinely new and unique insights into crime and criminals.

Finally the movement toward new questions and especially new paradigms is far more difficult to predict. In the final decade of the twentieth century, postmodernist criminologists added their voices to those questioning the dominant paradigms. Little contemporary mainstream criminology survives in a postmodernist criminology. It seems unlikely that all knowledge about crime as we know it will be abandoned. However, as Kuhn noted (1970), a mature science is one with a single paradigm. By this measure criminology is far from a mature science.

As Shakespeare wrote in *The Winter's Tale,* "What's past is prologue." We offer this work as a prologue to crime theory in the twenty-first century. The study of crime and society's response to it have come a long way since the days of Lombroso. Feeble, ill-defined, and poorly articulated theories have given way to stronger ones; new methods of theory testing have replaced armchair conjecture and anecdotal evidence. Much work remains to be done, and part of that work must include the development of a spirit of cooperation that transcends the limitations we noted in this chapter. As Braithwaite (1990:165) wrote about creating a theoretical renaissance in criminology:

> What we must do is some fundamental thinking about theoretical methods in criminology. We must abandon the theoretical nihilism that unites us against anyone who scans the horizon beyond their entrenched niches of expertise, nurture bold and general theory, and work cooperatively to build upon it rather than kill it in the womb.

Perhaps the strategies outlined in this chapter will help move criminology in the direction suggested by Braithwaite and others (Gottfredson 1989; McCord 1989). Criminologists must, in the words of Bernard (1990), seek the falsification of theories (negative learning) simultaneously with the verification of knowledge (positive learning); that is, they must separate the good theories from the bad. Only then can science—in this case the study of crime, criminals, and society's reactions to both—assume a set of "findings and move beyond them to add to the depth and breadth of knowledge in the context of that theory," or what Kuhn called "normal science" (Bernard 1990:326). Problematically, Thomas Bernard (1990:329) saw "nothing in criminology that researchers can simply assume and move beyond when they organize new research," the first step in defining "scientific progress."

Little will happen to change Bernard's characterization until and unless the extant theories are critically examined, tested, and either accepted or rejected, for both their empirical soundness and their practical utility. As the psychologist Kurt Lewin (1951:169) is quoted as saying, "Nothing is as practical as a good theory." A generation before, Lewis Madison Terman (1906:72), the psychologist responsible for instituting the IQ test in America, wrote, "Theory that does not some way affect life has no value."

We also contend that American criminologists must increasingly connect with their global brethren and work to build and test theories cross-nationally. Recall that the goal of a given theory is to work at any time and in any place. Indeed, we presented numerous examples of crime theories that have been tested internationally or that have their origins partially or entirely in other nations. Criminology in the United States remains extremely parochial (Barberet 2001). Perhaps it is no coincidence that the same could be said of crime control policies in the United States (see, e.g., Tonry 1999). In 1997, largely in response to transnational crime, the National Institute of Justice created the International Center, with the goal of stimulating, facilitating, evaluating, and disseminating both national and international criminal justice research and information (Anonymous 2000). Unless criminologists can demonstrate the policy relevance of their work, this entity may not facilitate the development of cross-national studies in crime and criminals grounded in theory.

In conclusion we issue a couple of caveats. First, we have throughout this text sought to provide explanations of theory for the "theoretically challenged." Therefore, at times we have lowered the level of conceptual abstraction and, perhaps for theoretical purists, thereby altered slightly the original theory. We hope that this has not occurred with any regularity. Second, in this final chapter we made some marginally outrageous statements and suggestions about crime theories and the future. There is nothing in these strategies that should be viewed as a blueprint for success. We sought only to challenge you to think critically about crime theory. We hope we have succeeded.

KEY TERMS

autonomous deviance

Cambridge–Somerville Youth Study

classical experimental design

collective efficacy

conceptual integration

constitutive criminology

constraints

constructive postmodernists

control deficit

control surplus

cumulative continuity

decadence

deconstructive postmodernists

defiance

exploitation

expressive individualism

instrumentalism

legal cynicism

Minneapolis Domestic Violence Experiment

modern era

National Evaluation of G.R.E.A.T.

natural experiment

newsmaking criminology

opportunity

plunder

postmodern era

postmodernism

predation

predispositional motivations

Project on Human Development in Chicago Neighborhoods (City Project)

propositional integration

Provo Experiment

quasi-experimental design

repressive deviance

republican freedom

scientific revolutions

situational motivations

Spouse Assault Replication Program (SARP)

submission

theoretical competition

theoretical elaboration

theoretical integration

theory falsification

transitory events

turning points

CRITICAL REVIEW QUESTIONS

1. Are there any other generalizations we could make about the crime theories explored in the previous chapters?

2. How would you go about convincing a state or federal legislator to sponsor a longitudinal or experimental study? What logical arguments would you bring to bear in support of your position? You might want to reread "Problems and Pitfalls of Experimental and Longitudinal Research Designs" (p. 290) before formulating your answer.

3. Using the researchers' names or the City Project's formal name, search the Web or your library for more recent findings from this study. What did you find?

4. What is the official policy of your local law enforcement agency on

the issue of arresting persons at the scene of a domestic violence call? Why do they have this policy or, if they lack one, why not?

5. Can you think of any theories reviewed in this book that might provide a conceptual base for mandatory or presumptive arrests in misdemeanor domestic violence cases?

6. What do you consider to be the most important lesson about the problems and pitfalls of criminological research employing experimental or longitudinal designs?

7. What do you think will advance criminological theory more—theoretical elaboration or some form of theoretical integration? What is the basis of your answer?

8. If you had to place control balance theory in one of the previous chap-

ters in this book, which one would it be, and why?

9. Do the policy implications Braithwaite saw in control balance theory sound familiar? Where have you seen them before?

10. Which barrier do you think is most counterproductive—a disciplinary barrier or a political barrier? What is the basis of your answer?

11. Compare and contrast postmodernism and the theories contained in this text. Are there any that might exist in a postmodernist-dominated criminology?

12. Is the public's perspective on crime and criminals already in the postmodernist era, and criminology simply has not caught up to that fact? What evidence supports this claim?

NOTES

1. Much of the following is from Sampson and Raudenbush (2001).

2. Piquero has played a prominent role in the testing of self-control theory, particularly in the resolution of key self-control measurement issues (see Chapter 7), a role he duplicated in operationalizing and measuring balance control (Piquero, MacIntosh, and Hickman 2001).

3. Many different theories could be brought to bear on Jane's story. Developmental criminologists' answers might focus on neuropsychological risks as a child. J. David Hawkins and Joseph Weis (1985; see also Catalano and Hawkins 1996) proposed a social development model (SDM) of human behavior with two possible outcomes, one prosocial and the other antisocial. They drew heavily on social learning, social control, and differential association

theories, identifying the mirror images of each set of forces—one for good and one for bad—that shape one's social development. We selected Sampson and Laub's theory largely because it stands as a bridge between the more sociological developmental theories like the SDM and the far more psychological developmental criminology discussed in Chapter 5.

4. Babbie (1983:38) contended that three paradigms dominate the social sciences: conflict, interactionism, and functionalism. All three are important to crime theories. However, the more general paradigms that students of crime seem to acknowledge as guiding our search for answers tend to follow the classicalism–positivism and nature–nurture dichotomies, with secondary consideration paid to interactionism, functionalism, and conflict.

References

Abadinsky, Howard. (1994). *Probation and Parole: Theory and Practice,* 5th ed. Englewood Cliffs, NJ: Prentice-Hall.

———. (1998). *Law and Justice: An Introduction to the American Legal System,* 4th ed. Belmont, CA: Wadsworth.

———. (2000). *Organized Crime,* 6th ed. Belmont, CA: Wadsworth.

———. (2001). *Drug Abuse: An Introduction,* 4th ed. Belmont, CA: Wadsworth.

———. (2002). *Probation and Parole: Theory and Practice,* 7th ed. Upper Saddle River, NJ: Prentice-Hall.

Abadinsky, Howard, and L. Thomas Winfree, Jr. (1992). *Crime and Justice: An Introduction.* Chicago: Nelson-Hall.

Abraham, Henry J. (1975). *The Judicial Process: An Introductory Analysis of the Courts of the United States, England, and France.* New York: Oxford University Press.

Adams, Reed. (1973). "Differential association and learning principles revisited." *Social Problems.* 20:458–70.

———. (1974). "The adequacy of differential association theory." *Journal of Research in Crime and Deliquency* 11:1–18.

Addiction Research Unit/SUNY at Buffalo. (1998).

Adler, Alfred. (1963). *The Individual Psychology of Alfred Adler.* New York: Basic Books.

———. (1968)[c.1928]. *Understanding Human Nature.* Trans. Walter Beran Wolfe. London: G. Allen and Unwin.

Adler, Freda. (1975). *Sisters in Crime: The Rise of the New Female Criminal.* New York: McGraw-Hill.

———. (1986). "Jails as a repository of former mental patients." *International Journal of Offender Therapy and Comparative Criminology* 30:225–36.

Adler, Freda, Gerhard O. W. Mueller, and William S. Laufer. (1994). *Criminal Justice.* New York: McGraw-Hill.

Adler, Jeffrey S. (1989). "A historical analysis of the law of vagrancy." *Criminology* 27:209–29.

Adorno, Theodore, E. Frenkel-Brunswick, D. L. Levinson, and R. N. Sanford. (1985). *The Authoritarian Personality.* New York: Harper and Row.

Agnew, Robert. (1985). "A revised strain theory of delinquency." *Social Forces* 64:151–67.

———. (1991). "A longitudinal test of social control and delinquency." *Journal of Research in Crime and Delinquency* 28:126–56.

———. (1992). "Foundation for a general strain theory of crime and delinquency." *Criminology* 30:47–87.

———. (1995). "Strain and subcultural theories of criminality." In *Criminology: A Contemporary Handbook,* ed. Joseph F. Sheley. Belmont, CA: Wadsworth.

Agnew, Robert, and David Peterson. (1989). "Leisure and delinquency." *Social Problems* 36:332–48.

Agnew, Robert, Francis T. Cullen, Velmer S. Burton, Jr., T. David Evans, and R. Gregory Dunaway. (1996). "A new test of classic strain theory." *Justice Quarterly* 13:681–704.

Aichhorn, August. (1973)[1935]. *Wayward Youth.* New York: Viking Press.

Akers, Ronald. (1968). "Problems in the sociology of deviance: Social definitions and behavior." *Social Forces* 46:455–65.

———. (1973). *Deviant Behavior: A Social Learning Approach.* Belmont, CA: Wadsworth.

———. (1979). "Theory and ideology in Marxist criminology." *Criminology* 16:527–44.

———. (1985). *Deviant Behavior: A Social Learning Approach,* 3d ed. Belmont, CA: Wadsworth.

———. (1990). "Rational choice, deterrence, and social learning theory in criminology: The path not taken." *Journal of Criminal Law and Criminology* 81:653–76.

———. (1991). "Self control as a general theory of crime." *Journal of Quantitative Criminology* 7:201–11.

———. (1994). *Criminological Theories: Introduction and Evaluation.* Los Angeles: Roxbury.

———. (1996). "Is differential association/ social learning theory cultural deviance theory?" *Criminology* 34:229–47.

———. (1998). *Social Learning and Social Structure: A General Theory of Crime and Deviance.* Boston: Northeastern University Press.

———. (2000). *Criminological Theories: Introduction and Evaluation,* 3d ed. Los Angeles: Roxbury.

Akers, Ronald L., Norman S. Hayner, and Werner Grunninger. (1974). "Homosexual and drug behavior in prison: A test of the functional and importation models of the inmate system." *Social Problems* 21:410–20.

Akers, Ronald L., Marvin D. Krohn, Lonn Lanza-Kaduce, and Marcia Radosevich. (1979). "Social learning and deviant behavior: A specific test of a general theory." *American Sociological Review* 44:448–62.

Alarid, Leanne Fiftal, Velmer S. Burton, Jr., and Francis T. Cullen. (2000). "Gender and crime among felony offenders: Assessing the generality of social control and differential association theory." *Journal of Research in Crime and Delinquency* 37:171–99.

Alex, Nicholas. (1976). *New York Cops Talk Back.* New York: Wiley.

Alexander, Franz, and William Healy. (1935). *Roots of Crime.* New York: Knopf.

Alexander, Franz, and Hugo Staub. (1956). *The Criminal, the Judge and the Public.* Glencoe, IL: Free Press.

Allman, William F. (1994). "Why IQ isn't destiny: A new book's focus on IQ misses many of the mind's wondrous talents." *U.S. News & World Report,* 24 October:73–80.

Alpert, Geoffrey P. (1993). "The role of psychological testing in law enforcement." In *Critical Issues in Policing,* ed. R. G. Dunham and G. P. Alpert. Prospect Heights, IL: Waveland.

Alpert, Leonore. (1981). "Learning about trial judging: Socialization of state trial judges." In *Courts and Judges,* ed. J. A. Cramer. Beverly Hills, CA: Sage.

Alvarado, Rose, and Karol Kumpfer. (2000). "Strengthening America's families." *Juvenile Justice* 7(3):8–18.

American Civil Liberties Union. (1999). "Should 'driving while black' be a crime?" http://www.aclu.org/features/ nytimesad100698.html

Anderson, Elijah. (1994). "The code of the streets." *Atlantic Monthly,* May:80–94.

Anderson, Tammy L., and Richard R. Bennett. (1996). "Development, gender, and crime: The scope of the routine activities approach." *Justice Quarterly* 13:31–56.

Andreski, Stanislav, ed. (1971). *Herbert Spencer: Structure, Function, and Evolution.* New York: Scribner.

Andrews, D. A. (1980). "Some experimental investigations of the principles of differential association through deliberate manipulation of the structure of service systems." *American Sociological Review* 44:448–62.

Andrews, D. A. and James Bonta. (1994). *The Psychology of Criminal Conduct.* Cincinnati: Anderson.

Andrews, D. A., Ivan Zinger, Robert D. Hoge, James Bonta, Paul Gendreau, and Francis T. Cullen. (1990). "Does correctional treatment work? A clinically relevant and psychologically informed meta-analysis." *Criminology* 28:369–404.

Angier, Natalie. (2000). "Do races differ? Not really, genes show." *New York Times,* 22 August: F1.

Anonymous. (2000). "About the International Center." http://www.ojp.usdoj.gov/nij/international/about_text.htm

Anson, Richard, J. Dale Mann, and Dale Sherman. (1986). "Niederhoffer's cynicism scale: Reliability and beyond." *Journal of Criminal Justice* 14:295–305.

Appelbaum, R. (1979). "Born-again functionalism? A reconsideration of Althusser's stucturalism." *Insurgent Sociologist* 9:18–33.

Armstrong, Edward G. (2000). "Constructions of cultural conflict and crime." *Sociological Imagination* 37:114–26.

Arneklev, Bruce J., John K. Cochran, and Randy R. Gainey. (1998). "Testing Gottfredson and Hirschi's 'low self-control' stability hypothesis." *American Journal of Criminal Justice* 23:107–27.

Arneklev, Bruce J., Harold G. Grasmick, and Robert J. Bursik, Jr. (1999). "Evaluating the dimensionality and invariance of 'low self-control.'" *Journal of Quantitative Criminology* 15:307–31.

Atkins v. Virginia (00-8452), 260 Va. 375, 534 S.E. 2d 312 (2002).

Aubert, Vilhelm. (1983). *In Search of Law: Sociological Approach to Law.* Totowa, NJ: Barnes and Noble.

Austin, James, and John Irwin. (2001). *It's about Time: America's Imprisonment Binge,* 3d ed. Belmont, CA: Wadsworth.

Austin, James, and Barry Krisberg. (1981). "Wider, strong, and different nets: The dialectics of criminal justice reform." *Journal of Research in Crime and Delinquency* 18:165–96.

Austin, Roy L. (1982). "Women's liberation and increases in minor, major and occupational offenses." *Criminology* 20:407–30.

Ayers, Richard M. (1977). "Case studies of police strikes in two cities—Albuquerque and Oklahoma City." *Journal of Police Science and Administration* 5:19–31.

Babbie, Earl. (1975). *The Practice of Social Research.* Belmont, CA: Wadsworth.

———. (1983). *The Practice of Social Research,* 3d ed. Belmont, CA: Wadsworth.

Bachman, Ronet, Raymond Paternoster, and Sally Ward. (1992). "The rationality of sexual offending: Testing a deterrence/rational choice conception of sexual assault." *Law and Society Review* 26:343–72.

Bailey et al. v. Drexel Furniture Company, 259 U.S. 20, 42 S.Ct. 449, L.Ed. 817 (1922a).

Bailey et al. v. George et al., 259 U.S. 16, 42 S.Ct. 419, 66 L.Ed. 816 (1922b).

Bailey, William C. (1998). "Deterrence, brutalization, and the death penalty: Another examination of Oklahoma's return to capital punishment." *Criminology* 36:711–33.

Bailey, William C., and Ruth D. Peterson. (1989). "Murder and capital punishment in the evolving context of the post-Furman era." *Social Forces* 66:774–807.

Balbus, Isaac. (1973). *The Dialectics of Legal Repression.* New York: Russell Sage Foundation.

Balch, Robert W., Curt T. Griffiths, Edwin L. Hall, and L. Thomas Winfree, Jr. (1976). "The socialization of jurors: The voir dire as a rite of passage." *Journal of Criminal Justice* 4:271–83.

Baldus, David C., Charles Pulaski, and George Woodworth. (1983). "Comparative review of death sentences: An empirical review of the Georgia experience." *Journal of Criminal Law and Criminology* 74:661–753.

Balkan, Shelia, Ronald J. Berger, and Janet Schmidt. (1980). *Crime and Deviance in America: A Critical Approach.* Belmont, CA: Wadsworth.

Ball, Richard A., C. Ronald Huff, and J. Robert Lilly. (1988). *House Arrest and Correctional Policy: Doing Time at Home.* Beverly Hills, CA: Sage.

Bandura, Albert. (1974). "Behavioral theory and the models of man." *American Psychologist* 28:859–69.

———. (1977). *Social Learning Theory.* Englewood Cliffs, NJ: Prentice-Hall.

———. (1989). "Human agency in social cognitive theory." *American Psychologist* 44:1175–84.

Bandura, Albert, and Aletha Huston. (1961). "Identification as a process of incidental learning." *Journal of Abnormal and Social Psychology* 63:311–18.

Bandura, Albert, Dorothea Ross, and Sheila Ross. (1963). "Vicarious reinforcement and imitative learning." *Journal of Abnormal and Social Psychology* 67:601–07.

Barak, Gregg. (1988). "Newsmaking criminology: Reflections on the media, intellectuals, and crime." *Justice Quarterly* 5:565–87

Barberet, Rosemary. (2001). "Global competence and American criminology—An expatriate's view." *Criminologist* 26:1, 3–5.

Barlow, Hugh D. (1996). *Criminology.* New York: HarperCollins.

Barlow, Hugh D. (1997). *Criminology.* Reading, MA: Addison-Wesley.

Barnes, Carole Wolff, and Randal S. Franz. (1989). "Questionably adult: Determinants and effects of the juvenile waiver decision." *Justice Quarterly* 6:117–35.

Bartol, Curt R., and H. A. Holanchock. (1979). "A test of Eysenck's theory of criminality on an American prisoner population." *Criminal Justice and Behavior* v6:245–49.

Bartol, Curt R. (1991). *Criminal Behavior: A Psychological Approach,* 3d ed. Englewood Cliffs, NJ: Prentice-Hall.

———. (1999). *Criminal Behavior: A Psychosocial Approach,* 5th ed. Upper Saddle River, NJ: Prentice-Hall.

Bartollas, Clemens, and John Conrad. (1992). *Introduction to Corrections,* 2d ed. New York: HarperCollins.

Bartollas, Clemens, and Simon Dinitz. (1989). *Introduction to Criminology: Order and Disorder.* New York: Harper and Row.

Baudrillard, Jean. (1988). *America.* London: Verso.

Bavolek, Stephen J. (2000). "The nurturing parenting program." *OJJDP Juvenile Justice Bulletin,* November.

Bazemore, Gordon, and Mark Umbreit. (2001). "A comparison of four restorative conferencing models." *Juvenile Justice Bulletin,* February. Washington, DC: Office of Juvenile Justice and Delinquency Prevention.

Beccaria, Cesare. (1963)[1764]. *On Crimes and Punishments.* Trans. Henry Paolucci. Indianapolis, IN: Bobbs-Merrill.

Beck, Allen J., and Jennifer C. Karberg. (2001). "Prison and jail inmates at midyear 2000." Washington, DC: U.S. Bureau of Justice Statistics.

Beck, Allen J., and Laura M. Maruschak. (2001). "Mental health treatment in state prisons, 2000." Washington, DC: U.S. Bureau of Justice Statistics.

Becker, Gary S. (1968). "Crime and punishment: An economic approach." *Journal of Political Economy* 76:169–217.

Becker, Howard S. (1963). *Outsiders: Studies in the Sociology of Deviance.* New York: Free Press.

———. (1973). *Outsiders: Studies in the Sociology of Deviance,* rev ed. New York: Free Press.

Beirne, Piers, and James Messerschmidt. (2000). *Criminology,* 3d ed. Boulder, CO: Westview Press.

Bellah, Robert N., and associates. (1985). *Habits of the Heart.* New York: Perennial.

Bellair, Paul E. (1997). "Social interaction and community crime: Examining the importance of neighbor networks." *Criminology* 35:677–703.

Benekos, Peter, and Alida Merlo. (1995). "Three strikes and you're out! The political sentencing game." *Federal Probation* 59:3–9.

Benner, A. W. (1986). "Psychological screening of police applicants." In *Psychological*

Services in Law Enforcement, ed. J. T. Reese and H. A. Goldstein. Washington, DC: U.S. Government Printing Office.

Bennett, Richard R. (1991). "Routine activities: A cross-national assessment of a criminological perspective." *Social Forces* 70:147–63.

Bennett, Richard R., and Theodore Greenstein. (1975). "The police personality: A test of the predisposition model." *Journal of Police Science and Administration* 3:439–45.

Bentham, Jeremy. (1948)[1789]. *An Introduction to the Principles of Morals and Legislation.* New York: Kegan Paul.

Berg, Bruce, Edmond True, and Marc Gertz. (1984). "Police, riots, and alienation." *Journal of Police Science and Administration* 12:186–90.

Bergesen, Albert, and Max Herman. (1998). "Immigration, race, and riot: The 1992 Los Angeles uprising." *American Sociological Review* 63:39–54.

Berk, Richard A. (1993). "Policy corrections in the ASR." *American Sociological Review* 58:889–90.

Berk, Richard A., Alec Campbell, Ruth Klap, and Bruce Western. (1992). "A Bayesian analysis of the Colorado Springs spouse abuse experiment." *Journal of Criminal Law and Criminology* 83:170–200.

———. (1992). "The deterrent effect of arrest in incidents of domestic violence: A Bayesian analysis of four field experiments." *American Sociological Review* 57:698–708.

Berman, Harold J., and William R. Greiner. (1980). *The Nature and Functions of Law,* 4th ed. Mineola, NY: Foundation Press.

Berman, Louis. (1938). *The Glands Regulating Personality.* New York: Macmillan.

Bernard, Thomas J. (1984). "Control criticisms of strain theories: An assessment of theoretical and empirical adequacy." *Journal of Research in Crime and Delinquency* 21:353–72.

———. (1990). "Twenty years of testing theories: What have we learned and why?" *Journal of Research in Crime and Delinquency* 27:325–47.

Bernard, Thomas J., and Jeffery B. Snipes. (1996). "Theoretical integration in criminology." Pp. 301–348 in *Crime and Justice: A Review of Research,* ed. Michael Tonry. Chicago: University of Chicago Press.

Bernstein, Ilene Nagel, Edward Kick, Jan Leung, and Barbara Schulz. (1977). "Charge reduction: An intermediary stage in the process of labeling criminal defendants." *Social Forces* 56:362–84.

Berry, Brian, and John D. Kasarda. (1977). *Contemporary Urban Ecology.* New York: Macmillan.

Bersani, Carl A. (1989). "Reality therapy: Issues and a review of research." In *Correctional Counseling and Treatment,* 2d ed., ed. P. C. Kratcoski. Prospect Heights, IL: Waveland Press.

Best, Steven, and Douglas Kellner. (1991). *Postmodern Theory: Critical Interrogation.* New York: Guilford Press.

Bevis, C., and J. B. Nuttler. (1977). "Changing street layouts to reduce residential burglary." Paper presented to the American Society of Criminology, Atlanta, GA.

Binder, Arnold, and James W. Meeker. (1989). "Experiments as reforms." *Journal of Criminal Justice* 16:347–58.

———. (1993). "Implications of the failure to replicate the Minneapolis experimental findings." *American Sociological Review* 58:886–88.

Black, Donald. (1976). *The Behavior of Law.* Orlando, FL: Academic Press.

Blackstone, William. (1962)[1760]. *Commentaries on the Laws of England.* Boston: Beacon Press.

Blau, Judith R., and Peter M. Blau. (1977). *Inequality and Heterogeneity: A Primitive Theory of Social Structure.* New York: Free Press.

———. (1982). "The cost of inequality: Metropolitan structure and violent crime." *American Sociological Review* 47:114–29.

Blomberg, Thomas G. (1980). "Widening the net: An anomaly in the evaluation of diversion programs." In *Handbook of Criminal Justice Evaluation,* ed. M. Klein and K. Teilmann. Beverly Hills, CA: Sage.

Bluenose, Philmer, and James Zion. (1996). "Hozhooji Naat' Aanii: The Navajo justice and harmony ceremony." In *Native Americans, Crime and Justice,* ed.

M. A. Nielsen and R. A. Silverman. Boulder, CO: Westview Press.

Blumstein, Alfred, and Jacqueline Cohen. (1987). "Characterizing criminal careers." *Science* 237:985–91.

Blumstein, Alfred, Jacqueline Cohen, and David Farrington. (1988). "Criminal career research: Its value for criminology." *Criminology* 26:1035.

Blumstein, Alfred, Jacqueline Cohen, and Daniel Nagin, eds. (1978). *Deterrence and Incapacitation: Estimating the Effects of Criminal Sanctions on Crime Rates.* Washington, DC: National Academy of Sciences.

Blumstein, Alfred, Jacqueline Cohen, Jeffery Roth, and Christy Visher, eds. (1986). *Criminal Careers and "Career Criminals."* 2 vols. Washington, DC: National Academy Press.

Boeringer, Scot, Constance L. Shehan, and Ronald L. Akers. (1991). "Social contexts and social learning in sexual coercion and aggression: Assessing the contribution of fraternity membership." *Family Relations* 40:558–64.

Boesel, David, Richard Berk, W. Eugene Groves, Bettye Edison, and Peter H. Rossi. (1969). "White institutions and black rage." *Trans-Action* 6:24–31.

Bohm, Robert. (1982). "Radical criminology: An explication." *Criminology* 19:565–89.

Bonger, Willem. (1969)[1916]. *Criminality and Economic Conditions.* Bloomington: Indiana University Press.

Bonnie, Richard J. (1990). "The competence of criminal defendants with mental retardation to participate in their own defense." *Journal of Criminal Law and Criminology* 81:419–46.

Booth, Alan, and D. Wayne Osgood. (1993). "The influence of testosterone on deviance in adulthood: Assessing and explaining the relationship." *Criminology* 31:93–117.

Bopp, William J., Paul Chignell, and Charles Maddox. (1977). "The San Francisco police strike of 1975: A case study." *Journal of Police Science and Administration.* 5:32–42.

Boruch, Robert F., Timothy Victor, and Joe S. Cecil. (2000). "Resolving ethical and legal problems in randomized experiments." *Crime and Delinquency* 46:330–53.

Borum, Randy, and Harley V. Stock. (1993). "Detection of deception in law enforcement practices." *Law and Human Behavior* 17:157–60.

Bowers, William J., and J. H. Hirsch. (1987). "The impact of foot patrol staffing on crime and disorder in Boston: An unmet promise." *American Journal of Police* 6:17–44.

Box, Steven. (1981). *Deviance, Reality and Society.* London: Holt, Rinehart and Winston.

Braithwaite, John. (1984). *Corporate Crime in the Pharmaceutical Industry.* London: Routledge and Kegan Paul.

———. (1989). "The state of criminology: Theoretical decay or renaissance?" *Australian and New Zealand Journal of Criminology* 22:129–35.

———. (1990). "The state of criminology: Theoretical decay or renaissance?" In *Advances in Criminological Theory,* vol. 2, ed. W. S. Laufer and F. Adler. New Brunswick, NJ: Transaction.

———. (1997). "Charles Tittle's control balance and criminological theory." *Theoretical Criminology* 1:77–97.

———. (1999). "Restorative justice: Assessing optimistic and pessimistic accounts." In *Crime and Justice: A Review of Research,* ed. M. Tonry. Chicago: University of Chicago Press.

———. (2000). "Shame and criminal justice." *Canadian Journal of Criminology* 42:281–99.

Braithwaite, John, and P. Pettit. (1990). *Not Just Deserts: A Republican Theory of Criminal Justice.* Oxford, UK: Oxford University Press.

Brantingham, Paul, and Patricia Brantingham. (1991). "How public transportation feeds private crime: Note on Vancouver 'Skytrain' experience." *Security Journal* 2:91–95.

———. (1993). "Environment, routine situation, and situation: Toward a pattern theory of crime." In *Advances in Criminal Theory,* ed. R. V. Clarke and M. Felson. New Brunswick, NJ: Transaction.

Breckenridge, James, L. Thomas Winfree, Jr., James W. Maupin, and Dennis L.

Clason. (2000). "Drunk drivers, DWI 'drug court' treatment, and recidivism: Who fails?" *Justice Research and Policy* 2(1):87–105.

Breed v. Jones, 421 U.S. 519 (1975).

Brennan, P. A., Sarnoff Mednick, and J. Volavka. (1995). "Biomedical factors in crime." In *Crime,* ed. James Q. Wilson and Joan Petersilia. San Francisco: Institute for Contemporary Studies.

Bridges, George, and Robert Crutchfield. (1988). "Law, social standing, and racial disparities in imprisonment." *Social Forces* 99:699–724.

Britt, Chester L. (2000). "Comment on Paternoster and Brame." *Criminology* 38:965–70.

Broberg, Gunnar, and Nils Roll-Hansen, eds. (1996). *Eugenics and the Welfare State: Sterilization Policy in Denmark, Sweden, Norway, and Finland.* Lansing: Michigan State University Press.

Brounstein, Henry H., and Paul J. Goldstein. (1990). "A typology of drug-related homicides." In *Drugs, Crime and the Criminal Justice System,* ed. R. Weisheit. Cincinnati, OH: Anderson.

Brounstein, Paul J., P. Hatry, David Altschuler, and Louis H. Blair. (1990). *Substance Use and Delinquency among Inner City Adolescent Males.* Washington, DC: Urban Institute.

Brown, Janelle. (2001). "The Taliban's bravest opponents." Salon.com Life. http://www.salon.com/mwt/feature/2001/10/02/fatima/

Brown, Lee P., and Mary Ann Wycoff. (1986). "Policing Houston: Reducing fear and improving service." *Crime and Delinquency* 33:71–89.

Bruinsma, Gerben. (1992). "Differential association theory reconsidered: An extension and its empirical test." *Journal of Quantitative Criminology* 8:29–42.

Brunner, H. G., M. Nelson, X. D. Breakefield, H. H. Ropes, and A. van Oost. (1994). "Abnormal behavior associated with a point mutation in the structural gene for monamine oxidase A." *Science* 262:578–80.

Bryant, Kevin M., and J. Mitchell Miller. (1997). "Routine activity and labor market segmentation: An empirical test

of a revised approach." *American Journal of Criminal Justice* 22:71–100.

Buck v. Bell, 274 U.S.C. 200 (1927).

Buikhuisen, Wouter. (1987). "Cerebral dysfunction and persistent juvenile delinquency." In *The Causes of Crime: New Biological Approaches,* ed. S. A. Mednick, T. E. Moffitt, and S. A. Stack. New York: Cambridge University Press.

Burgess, Robert, and Ronald L. Akers. (1966). "A differential-association-reinforcement theory of criminal behavior." *Social Problems* 14:128–47.

Bursik, Robert J. (1986). "Ecological stability and the dynamics of delinquency." In *Communities and Crime,* ed. A. J. Reiss, Jr., and M. Tonry. Chicago: University of Chicago Press.

———. (1988). "Social disorganization and theories of crime and delinquency: Problems and prospects." *Criminology* 26:519–51.

Cadoret, R. J., E. Troughton, and T. W. O'Gorman. (1987). "Adoption studies: Historical and environmental factors in adoptee antisocial personality." *European Archives of Psychiatry and Neurological Science* 239:231–40.

Cao, Liqun, Anthony Adams, and Vickie J. Jensen. (1997). "A test of the black subculture of violence thesis: A research note." *Criminology* 35:367–79.

Cardozo, Benjamin. (1924). *The Growth of the Law.* New Haven, CT: Yale University Press.

Carey, Gregory. (1992). "Twin imitation for antisocial behavior: Implications for genetic and family environment research." *Journal of Abnormal Psychology* 101:18–25.

Carnegie Taskforce. (1994). "Starting points: Meeting the needs of our youngest children." Waldorf, MD: Carnegie Corporation of New York.

Carter, David. (1990). "Drug-related corruption of police officers: A contemporary typology." *Journal of Criminal Justice* 18:85–98.

Cason, Hulsey. (1943). "The psychopath and the psychopathic." *Journal of Criminal Psychopathology* 4:522–27.

———. (1946). "The symptoms of the psychopath." *Public Health Reports* 61:1833–68.

Cason, Hulsey, and M. J. Pescor. (1946). "A statistical study of 500 psychopathic prisoners." *Public Health Reports* 61:557–74.

Catalano, Richard F., and J. David Hawkins. (1986). "The social development model: A theory of antisocial behavior." Pp. 149–192 in *Delinquency and Crime: Current Theories,* ed. J. David Hawkins. New York: Cambridge University Press.

Cavalli-Sforza, Luigi Luca. (2000). *Genes, People, and Languages*. New York: Farrar, Straus and Giroux North Point.

Cernkovich, Stephen A., and Peggy C. Giordano. (1979). "Delinquency, opportunity, and gender." *Journal of Criminal Law and Criminology* 70:145–51.

———. (1992). "School bonding, race, and delinquency." *Criminology* 30:261–90.

Cernkovich, Stephen A., Peggy C. Giordano, and Jennifer L. Rudolph. (2000). "Race, crime and the American Dream." *Journal of Research in Crime and Delinquency* 37:131–70.

Chabris, Christopher E. (1998). "IQ since *The Bell Curve.*" *Commentary* 106:33–40.

Chambliss, William J. (1964). "A sociological analysis of the law and vagrancy." *Social Problem* 12:67–77.

———. (1976). "The state and criminal law." In *Whose Law, What Order? A Conflict Approach to Criminology,* ed. W. J. Chambliss and M. Mankoff. New York: Wiley.

———. (1988). *Exploring Criminology.* New York: Macmillan.

———. (1989a). "State-organized crime." *Criminology* 27:188–90.

———. (1989b). "On trashing Marxist criminology." *Criminology* 27:231–38.

Chambliss, William J., and Robert Seidman. (1982). *Law, Order and Power.* Reading, MA: Addison-Wesley.

Chamlin, Mitchell, and John K. Cochran. (1995). "Assessing Messner and Rosenfeld's institutional anomie theory: A partial test." *Criminology* 33:411–29.

———. (1997). "Social altruism and crime." *Criminology* 35:203–27.

Champion, Dean J. (1990). *Corrections in the United States: A Contemporary Perspective.* Englewood Cliffs, NJ: Prentice-Hall.

Chaney, Carole Kennedy, and Grace Hall Saltzstein. (1998). "Democratic control and bureaucratic responsiveness: The police and domestic violence." *American Journal of Political Science* 42:745–68.

Chermak, Stephen T., and Stuart P. Taylor. (1995). "Alcohol and human physical aggression: Pharmacological versus expectancy effects." *Journal of Studies on Alcohol* 56:449–56.

Chesney-Lind, Meda. (1973). "Judicial enforcement of the female sex role." *Issues in Criminology* 8:51–69.

———. (1989). "Girls' crime and woman's place: Toward a feminist model of female delinquency." *Crime and Delinquency* 35:5–29.

Chesney-Lind, Meda, and R. C. Shelden. (1992). *Girls' Delinquency and Juvenile Justice.* Pacific Grove, CA: Brooks/Cole.

Chesno, Frank A., and Peter R. Kilmann. (1975). "Effects of stimulation intensity on sociopathic avoidance learning." *Journal of Abnormal Psychology* 84:144–50.

Chira, Susan. (1994). "Study confirms worst fear on U.S. children." *New York Times,* 12 April:1,11.

Chow, Esther Ngan-Ling, and William E. Hemple. (1977). "Laboratory organizational experiments for corrections: An alternative method." *Criminology* 14:513–26.

Christiansen, Karl O. (1977). "A review of studies of criminality among twins." In *Biosocial Bases of Criminal Behavior,* ed. S. Mednick and K. O. Christiansen. New York: Gardner.

Cicourel, Aaron. (1976). *The Social Organization of Juvenile Justice.* New York: Wiley.

Clark, G. R., M. A. Telfer, D. Baker, and M. Rosen. (1970). "Sex chromosomes, crime and psychosis." *American Journal of Psychiatry* 126:1569.

Clear, Todd, and George F. Cole. (1986). *American Corrections.* Pacific Grove, CA: Brooks/Cole.

———. (1990). *American Corrections,* 2d ed. Pacific Grove, CA: Brooks/Cole.

———. (1997). *American Corrections,* 4th ed. Belmont, CA: Wadsworth.

Cleaver, Eldridge. (1968). *Soul on Ice.* New York: McGraw-Hill.

Cleckley, Hervey. (1976). *The Mask of Sanity.* St. Louis, MO: Mosby.

Clemmer, Donald. (1940). *The Prison Community.* Boston: Christopher.

Clinard, Marshall B. (1964). *Anomie and Deviant Behavior: A Discussion and Critique.* New York: Free Press.

Clinard, Marshall B., and Robert F. Meier. (1985). *Sociology of Deviant Behavior,* 6th ed. New York: Holt, Rinehart and Winston.

Clinard, Marshall B., and Richard Quinney. (1967). *Criminal Behavior Systems: A Typology.* New York: Holt, Rinehart and Winston.

Clinard, Marshall B., Peter C. Yeager, Jeanette Brissette, David Petrashek, and Elizabeth Harries. (1979). *Illegal Corporate Behavior.* Washington, DC: U.S. Government Printing Office.

Cloninger, Susan. (1993). *Theories of Personality: Understanding Persons.* Englewood Cliffs, NJ: Prentice-Hall.

Cloward, Richard, and Lloyd Ohlin. (1960). *Delinquency and Opportunity: A Theory of Delinquent Gangs.* Glencoe, IL: Free Press.

Clynch, Edward, and David W. Neubauer. (1981). "Trial courts as organizations: A critique and synthesis." *Law and Policy Quarterly* 3:69–94.

Coates, R., and John Gehm. (1989). "An empirical assessment." In Mediation and Criminal Justice, ed. M. Wright and B. Galaway. London: Sage.

Cobb, John B. (1993). "A presidential address on the economy." In *Postmodern for a Planet in Crisis,* ed. D. R. Griffin and R. Falk. Albany: SUNY Press.

Cochran, John, Mitchell B. Chamlin, and M. Seth. (1994). "Deterrence or brutalization? An impact assessment of Oklahoma's return to capital punishment." *Criminology* 32:107–34.

Cochran, John K., Peter B. Wood, Christine S. Sellers, Wendy Wilkerson, and Mitchell Chamlin. (1998). "Academic dishonesty and low self-control: An empirical test of a general theory of crime." *Deviant Behavior* 19:227–55.

Cohen, Albert K. (1955). *Delinquent Boys: The Culture of the Gang.* New York: Free Press.

———. (1965). "The sociology of the deviant act: Anomie theory and beyond." *American Sociological Review* 30:5–14.

Cohen, Albert K., and James F. Short, Jr. (1958). "Research in delinquent subcultures." *Journal of Social Issues* 14:20–37.

Cohen, Lawrence E., and Marcus Felson. (1979). "Social change and crime rate trends: A routine activity approach." *American Sociological Review* 44:588–608.

Cohen, Lawrence E., James R. Kluehel, and Kenneth C. Land. (1981). "Social inequality and predatory criminal victimizations: An exposition and test of a formal theory." *American Sociological Review* 46:505–24.

Cohen, Lawrence E., and Bryan J. Vila. (1995). "Self-control and social control: An exposition of the Gottfredson–Hirschi/Sampson–Laub debate." *Studies on Crime and Prevention.* 5:125–50.

Cohen, Stanley. (1984). "The deeper structure of the law or 'beware the rulers bearing justice.'" *Contemporary Crises* 8:83–93.

———. (1985). *Vision of Social Control.* Cambridge, England: Polity.

———. (1986). "Taking decentralization seriously: Values, visions, and policies." In *The Decentralization of Social Control,* ed. J. Lowman, R. J. Menzies, and T. Palys. London: Gower.

Colvin, Mark, and John Pauly. (1983). "A critique of criminology: Toward an integrated structural-Marxist theory of delinquency production." *American Journal of Sociobiology* 89:513–51.

Comings, D. E. (1995). "The role of genetic factors in conduct disorder based on studies of Tourette syndrome and attention-deficit hyperactivity disorder probands and their relatives." *Developmental and Behavioral Pediatrics* 16:142–57.

Conger, Rand. (1976). "Social control and social learning models of delinquency: A synthesis." *Criminology* 14:17–40.

Connors, Edward, Thomas Lundregan, Neal Miller, and Tom McEwen. (1996). "Convicted by juries, exonerated by science: Case studies in the use of DNA evidence to establish innocence after trial." Washington, DC: U.S. Department of Justice.

Cook, L. Foster, and Beth A. Weinman. (1988). "Treatment alternatives to street crime." In *Compulsory Treatment of Drug Abuse Research and Clinical Practice,* ed. C. G. Leukefeld and F. M. Tims. Rockville, MD: National Institute of Drug Abuse.

Coolbaugh, Kathleen, and Cynthia J. Hansel. (2000). "The comprehensive strategy: Lessons learned from the pilot sites." *OJJDP Juvenile Justice Bulletin,* March.

Cooley, Charles Horton. (1922). *Human Nature and the Social Order.* New York: Scribner.

Cornish, Derek, and Ronald Clarke. (1986). *The Reasoning Criminal: Rational Choice Perspectives on Offending.* New York: Springer-Verlag.

Cose, Ellis. (1994). "Color-coordinated truths: When blacks internalize the white stereotype of inferiority." *Newsweek,* 24 October:62.

Coser, Lewis A., Steven L. Nock, Patricia A. Steffan, and Daphne Spain. (1990). *Introduction to Sociology.* San Diego, CA: Harcourt Brace Jovanovich.

Costello, Barbara. (1997). "On the logical adequacy of cultural deviance theory." *Theoretical Criminology* 1:403–28.

Coughlin, Ellen K. (1994). "Pathways to crime: $32-million study will try to determine what leads some people into delinquency." *Chronicle of Higher Education,* 27 April:A8–9.

———. (1995). "Recollections of childhood abuse: Contending research traditions face-off in the debate of 'recovered memory.'" *Chronicle of Higher Education,* 27 January:A8, A9, A16.

Crawford, A., T. Jones, T. Woodhouse, and Jock Young. (1990). *Second Islington Crime Survey.* London: Middlesex Polytechnic Centre for Criminology.

Crawford, Colin. (2000). Criminal penalties for creating a toxic environment: *Mens rea,* environmental criminal liability standards, and the neurotoxicity hypothesis." *Boston College Environmental Affairs Law Review* 27:341–90.

Cressey, Donald R. (1965). "Changing criminals: The application of the theory of differential association." *American Journal of Sociology* 61:116–20.

"Criticized Freud show is revised and on." (1998). *New York Times,* 8 July:E1.

Crowe, Timothy D. (2000). *Crime Prevention through Environmental Design,* 2d ed. Woburn, MA: Butterworth-Heineman.

Cullen, Francis T. (1988). "Were Cloward and Ohlin strain theorists? Delinquency and opportunity revisited." *Journal of Research in Crime and Delinquency* 25:214–41.

Cullen, Francis T., Paul Gendreau, G. Roger Jarjoura, and John Paul Wright. (1997). "Crime and the bell curve: Lessons from intelligent criminology." *Crime and Delinquency* 43:387–411.

Cullen, Francis T., and Karen E. Gilbert. (1982). *Reaffirming Rehabilitation.* Cincinnati: Anderson.

Curran, Daniel, and Claire M. Renzetti. (1989). *Social Problems.* Boston, MA: Allyn and Bacon.

Curran, Daniel J., and Claire M. Renzetti. (1994). *Theories of Crime.* Boston: Allyn and Bacon.

Currie, Elliot P. (1968). "Crime without criminals: Witchcraft and its control in Renaissance Europe." *Law and Society Review* 3:7–32.

———. (1985). *Confronting Crime: An American Challenge.* New York: Pantheon.

———. (1993). *Reckoning: Drugs, the Cities, and the American Future.* New York: Hill and Wang.

Curry, G. David (1998). "Book review: *Control Balance: Toward a General Theory of Deviance. Social Forces* 76:1147–49.

Curtis, Lynn. (1975a). *Criminal Violence: National Patterns and Behavior.* Lexington, MA: Heath.

———. (1975b). *Violence, Race, and Culture.* Lexington, MA: Heath.

Dabbs, James, Robert Frady, Timothy Carr, and Norma Beach. (1986). "Saliva, testosterone and criminal violence in young adult prison inmates." *Psychosomatic Medicine* 48:73–81.

D'Alessio, Stewart, and Lisa Stolzenberg. (1998). "Crime, arrests, and pretrial jail incarceration: An examination of the deterrence thesis." *Criminology* 36:313–31.

Dalton, Katherine. (1961). "Menstruation and crime." *British Medical Journal* 2:1752–53.

———. (1964). *The Premenstrual Syndrome.* Springfield, IL: Thomas.

Daly, Kathleen. (1987a). "Discrimination in the criminal courts: Family, gender, and the problem of equal treatment." *Social Forces* 66:152–75.

———. (1987b). "Structure and practice of familial-based justice in a criminal court." *Law and Society Review* 21:267–90.

———. (1989). "Gender and varieties of white-collar crime." *Criminology* 27:769–93.

Daly, Kathleen, and Meda Chesney-Lind. (1988). "Feminism and criminology." *Justice Quarterly* 5:497–538.

Darwin, Charles. (1872). *The Expression of Emotion in Men and Animals*. London: Murray.

———. (1981)[1871]. *Descent of Man, and Selection in Relation to Sex*. Princeton, NJ: Princeton University Press.

Davidson, R. N. (1981). *Crime and Environment*. New York: St. Martin's.

Davis, Leigh Ann. (2000). "People with mental retardation in the criminal justice system." Silver Springs, MD: The Arc. http://www.open.org/~people1/articles/article_criminal_justice.htm

Davis, Nanette J., and Clarice Stasz. (1990). *Social Control of Deviance: A Critical Perspective*. New York: McGraw-Hill.

"Decoding the human body." (2000). *Newsweek,* 10 April:52.

De Fleur, Melvin, and Richard Quinney. (1966). "A reformulation of Sutherland's differential association theory and a strategy of empirical verification." *Journal of Research in Crime and Delinquency* 3:1–22.

DeFrances, Carol J., and Greg W. Steadman. (1998). "Prosecutors in state courts, 1996." Washington, DC: U.S. Bureau of Justice Statistics.

Degler, Carl N. (1991). *In Search of Human Nature: The Decline and Revival of Darwinism in American Thought*. New York: Oxford University Press.

DeKeseredy, Walter S., and Martin D. Schwartz. (1991). "British and U.S. left realism: A critical comparison." *International Journal of Offender Therapy and Comparative Criminology* 35:248–62.

———. (1996). *Contemporary Criminology*. Belmont, CA: Wadsworth.

Del Carmen, Rolando V., and Jeffrey T. Walker. (1991). *Briefs in 100 Leading Cases in Law Enforcement*. Cincinnati, OH: Anderson.

Deleuze, Gilless, and Felix Guattari. (1983). *Anti-Oedipus*. Minneapolis: University of Minnesota Press.

Denno, Deborah. (1985). "Sociological and human development explanations of crime: Conflict or consensus?" *Criminology* 23:711–41.

———. (1993). "Considering lead poisoning as a criminal defense." *Fordham Urban Law Journal* 20:377–85.

Denzin, Norman K. (1991). *Images of Postmodern Society*. London: Sage.

Devlin, Bernie, Michael Daniels, and Kathryn Roeder. (1997). "The heritability of IQ." *Nature* 388:468–71.

Dodson, Angus J. (2000). "DNA 'line-ups' based on reasonable suspicion standard." *University of Colorado Law Review* 71:221–54.

Dorschner, John. (1989). "The dark side of force." In *Critical Issues in Policing: Contemporary Readings,* ed. R. G. Dunham and G. P. Alpert. Prospect Heights, IL: Waveland Press.

Driver, Edwin, D. (1972). "Charles Buckman Goring." In *Pioneers in Criminology,* ed. Hermann Mannheim. Montclair, NJ: Patterson Smith.

Dull, Thomas. (1983). "Friend's drug use and adult drug and drinking behavior: A further test of differential association theory." *Journal of Criminal Law and Criminology* 4:608–19.

Dumont, James. (1996). "Justice and native peoples." In *Native Americans, Crime and Justice,* ed. M. A. Nielsen and R. A. Silverman. Boulder, CO: Westview Press.

Dunford, Frank. (1992). "The measurement of recidivism in cases of spousal assault." *Journal of Criminal Law and Criminology* 83:122–30.

———(2000). "Determining program success: The importance of employing experimental research designs." *Crime and Delinquency* 46:425–34.

Dunford, Franklyn, David Huizinga, and Delbert S. Elliott. (1986). "The role of arrest in domestic assaults: The Omaha police experiment." *Criminology* 28:183–207.

Dunford, Franklyn, D. Wayne Osgood, and Hart F. Weichselbaum. (1981). *National*

Evaluation of Juvenile Diversion Projects. Washington, DC: National Institute of Juvenile Justice and Delinquency Prevention.

Durham v. United States, 214 F. 2d 862, D.C. Cir. (1954).

Durkheim, Emile. (1951)[1897]. *Suicide.* Trans. J. A. Spaulding and G. Simpson. New York: Free Press.

———. (1961)[1925]. *Moral Education.* Glencoe, IL: Free Press.

———. (1966)[1895]. *Rules of the Sociological Method.* Trans. W. D. Halls. Chicago: University of Chicago Press.

Duyme, M. (1990). "Antisocial behaviour and postnatal environment: A French adoption study." *Journal of Child Psychology and Psychiatry* 31:699–710.

Earls, Felton. (1998). "Linking community factors and individual development." *Research Preview.* Washington, DC: National Institute of Justice, September.

Eaton, Mary. (1986). *Justice for Women? Family, Court, and Social Control.* Philadelphia: Open University Press.

Eck, John E., and William Spelman. (1987). "Who ya gonna call? The police as problem-busters." *Crime and Delinquency* 33:31–52.

Edwards v. United States, U.S. S.Ct. 96-1492, 61 CrL3015 (1997).

Egger, Steven A. (1990). *Serial Murder: An Elusive Phenomenon.* New York: Praeger.

Ehrlich, Isaac. (1975). "The deterrent effect of capital punishment: A question of life and death." *American Economic Review* 65:397–417.

Einstadter, Werner, and Stuart Henry. (1995). *Criminological Theory: An Analysis of Its Underlying Assumptions.* Fort Worth, TX: Harcourt Brace.

Eisenstein, James, and Herbert Jacobs. (1977). *Felony Justice: An Organizational Analysis of Criminal Courts.* Boston: Little, Brown.

Elliott, Delbert S., David Huizinga, and Suzanne S. Ageton. (1985). *Explaining Delinquency and Drug Use.* Beverly Hills, CA: Sage.

Elliott, Mabel A. (1967). "Social disorganization." In *Dictionary of Sociology and Related Sciences,* ed. H. Pratt. Totowa, NJ: Littlefield, Adams.

Ellis, Lee. (1990). "Conceptualizing criminal and related behavior from a biosocial perspective." In *Crime in Biological, Social, and Moral Contexts,* ed. L. Ellis and H. Hoffman. Westport, CT: Praeger.

———. (1991). "Monoamine oxidase and criminality: Identifying an apparent biological marker for antisocial behavior." *Journal of Research in Crime and Delinquency* 28:227–51.

Ellis, Lee, and Anthony Walsh. (2000). *Criminology: A Global Perspective.* Boston: Allyn and Bacon.

Emerson, Robert M. (1969). *Judging Children.* Chicago: Aldine.

Empey, LaMar. (1967). "Delinquency theory and recent." *Journal of Research in Crime and Delinquency* 4:28–42.

———. (1982). *American Delinquency.* Homewood, IL: Dorsey.

Empey, LaMar, and Maynard L. Erickson. (1972). *The Provo Experiment: Evaluating Community Control of Delinquency.* Lexington, MA: Heath.

"Environment beats heredity in determining IQ, study finds." (1997). (Las Cruces) *Sun-News,* 31 July:A7.

Erickson, Kai T. (1966). *Wayward Puritans.* New York: Wiley.

Erickson, Nels. (2001). "Healthy Families America." *OJJDP Fact Sheet.* Washington, DC: National Institute of Justice, June.

Erickson, Richard, and Kevin Carriere. (1994). "The fragmentation of criminology." In *The Futures of Criminology,* ed. David Nelken. London: Sage.

Erlanger, Howard S. (1974). "The empirical status of the subculture of violence thesis." *Social Problem* 22:280–92.

Ermann, M. David, and Richard Lundman. (1992). *Corporate and Governmental Deviance: Problems of Organizational Behavior in Contemporary Society.* New York: Oxford University Press.

Esbensen, Finn-Aage. (1987). "Foot patrol: Of what value?" *American Journal of Police* 6:45–65.

Esbensen, Finn-Aage, and Elizabeth Piper Deschenes. (1998). "A multisite examination of youth gang membership:

Does gender matter?" *Criminology* 36:799–827.

Esbensen, Finn-Aage, and David Huizinga. (1990). "Community structure and drug use from a social disorganization perspective: A research note." *Justice Quarterly* 7:691–709.

Esbensen, Finn-Aage, and D. Wayne Osgood. (1997). "National Evaluation of G.R.E.A.T." *Research in Brief.* Washington, DC: National Institute of Justice, November.

Esbensen, Finn-Aage, D. Wayne Osgood, Terrance J. Taylor, Dana Peterson, and Adrienne Freng (2001). "How great is G.R.E.A.T.? Results from a longitudinal quasi-experimental design." *Criminology & Public Policy* 1:87–118.

Esbensen, Finn-Aage, and L. Thomas Winfree, Jr. (1998). "Race and gender differences between gang and non-gang youths: Results of a multi-site survey." *Justice Quarterly* 15(3):505–26.

Evans, T. David, Francis T. Cullen, Velmer S. Burton, Jr., R. Gregory Dunaway, and Michael L. Benson. (1997). "The social consequences of self-control: Testing the general theory of crime." *Criminology* 35:475–504.

Eysenck, Hans J. (1973). *The Inequality of Man.* San Diego, CA: Edits.

———. (1977). *Crime and Personality,* 2d ed. London: Routledge and Kegan Paul.

Eysenck, Hans J., and Isli H. Gudjonsson. (1989). *The Causes and Cures of Criminality.* New York: Plenum.

Eysenck, Hans J., and Leon Kamin. (1981). *The Intelligence Controversy.* New York: Wiley.

Faderman, Lillian. (1998). *I Begin My Life All Over: The Hmong and the American Immigrant Experience.* Boston: Beacon Press.

Fadiman, Anne. (1997). *The Spirit Catches You and You Fall Down: A Hmong Child, Her American Doctors, and the Collision of Two Cultures.* New York: Farrar, Straus and Giroux.

Fagan, Jeffrey. (1989). "The social organization of drug use dealing among urban gangs." *Criminology* 27:633–67.

Fagan, Jeffrey, and Ko-Lin Chin. (1991). "Social processes of initiation into crack." *Journal of Drug Issues* 21:313–43.

Fagan, Jeffrey, Elizabeth Piper, and Melinda Moore. (1986). "Violent delinquents and urban youth," *Criminology* 24:439–71.

Fagan, Jeffrey, and Sandra Wexler. (1987). "Family origins of violent delinquents." *Criminology* 25:643–69.

Falk, Gerhard. (1966). "The psychoanalytic theories of crime causation." *Criminologica* 4.

Farabee, David. (2002). "Examining Martinson's critique: A cautionary note for evaluators." *Crime and Delinquency* 48:189–202.

Farnworth, Margaret, and Michael Lieber. (1989). "Strain theory revisited: Economic goals, educational means, and delinquency." *American Sociological Review* 54:263–74.

Farrington, David P., L. Biron, and M. LeBlanc. (1982). "Personality and delinquency in London and Montreal." In *Abnormal Offenders, Delinquency, and the Criminal Justice System,* ed. J. Gunn and D. P. Farrington. Chichester, England: Wiley.

Farrington, David P., and Allison Morris. (1983). "Sex, sentencing, and reconviction." *British Journal of Criminology* 23:229–48.

Farrington, David P., and Roger Tarling. (1985). *Prediction in Criminology.* Albany: SUNY Press.

Feder, Lynette, and Robert F. Boruch. (2000). "The need for experiments in criminal justice settings." *Crime and Delinquency* 46:291–94.

Felkenes, George T. (1975). "The prosecutor: A look at reality." *Southwestern University Law Review* 7:98–103.

———. (1991). "Affirmative action in the Los Angeles Police Department." *Criminal Justice Research Bulletin* 6:1–9.

Felson, Marcus. (1987). "Routine activities and crime prevention in the developing metropolis." *Criminology* 25:911–31.

———. (1993). "Review of *Choosing Crime* by K. Tunnell." *American Journal of Sociology* 98:1497–99.

———. (1994) *Crime and Everyday Life.* Thousand Oaks, CA: Pine Forge.

———.(1998). *Crime and Everyday Life,* 2d ed. Thousand Oaks, CA: Pine Forge.

————. (2000). "The routine activities approach as a general crime theory." Pp. 205–16 in *Of Crime and Criminality,* ed. Sally S. Simpson. Thousand Oaks, CA: Pine Forge.

————. (2001). "The routine activities approach: A very versatile theory of crime." Pp. 43–46 in *Explaining Criminals and Crime,* ed. Raymond Paternoster and Ronet Bachman. Los Angeles: Roxbury.

Felson, Marcus, and Lawrence E. Cohen. (1980). "Human ecology and crime: A routine activity approach." *Human Ecology* 8:389–406.

Ferraro, Kathleen. (1989). "The legal response to battery in the United States." In *Women, Policing, and Male Violence,* ed. J. Hanmer, J. Radford, and E. Stanka. London: Tavistock.

Feshbach, Seymour, and Robert D. Singer. (1971). *Television and Aggression.* San Francisco: Jossey-Bass.

Finckenauer, James O. (1982). *Scared Straight and the Panacea Phenomenon.* Englewood Cliffs, NJ: Prentice-Hall.

Fishbein, Diana H. (1990). "Biological perspectives in criminology." *Criminology* 28:27–72.

————. (1992). "The psychobiology of female aggression." *Criminal Justice and Behavior* 12:99–126.

Flynn, Leonard E. (1986). "House arrest: Florida's alternative eases crowding and tight budgets." *Corrections Today* 48:64–68.

Fogel, David. (1975). ". . . We are the living proof . . ." In *The Justice Model for Corrections.* Cincinnati: Anderson.

Forst, Brian E. (1983). "Capital punishment and deterrence: Conflicting evidence?" *Journal of Criminal Law and Criminology* 74:927–42.

Foshee, Vangie, and Karl E. Bauman. (1992). "Parental and peer characteristics as modifiers of the bond–behavior relationship: An elaboration of control theory." *Journal of Health and Social Behavior* 33:66–76.

Fraser, Steven. (1995). *The Bell Curve Wars: Race, Intelligence, and the Future of America.* New York: Basic Books.

Freedman, Jonathan L. (1984). "Effects of television violence on aggressiveness." *Psychological Bulletin* 96:227–46.

————. (1986). "Television violence and aggression: A rejoinder." *Psychological Bulletin* 100:372–78.

Freidrich-Cofer, Lynette, and Alethe C. Huston. (1986). "Television violence and aggression: A rejoinder." *Psychological Bulletin* 100:364–71.

Freud, Sigmund. (1933). *New Introductory Lectures on Psychoanalysis.* New York: Norton.

Friday, Paul C. (1977). "Changing theory and research in criminology." *International Journal of Criminology and Penology* 5:159–70.

Friedrichs, David O. (1982). "Crime, deviance, and criminal justice: In search of a radical humanistic perspective." *Humanity and Society* 6:200–226.

Friend, Tim. (2000). "Genetic map is hailed as 'new power.' Fruits of historic achievement could be seen in 5 years." *USA Today,* 27 June:1a.

Frisch, Lisa A. (1992). "Research that succeeds, policy that fails." *Journal of Criminal Law and Criminology* 83:209–16.

Fuchs, Joseph. (1965). *Natural Law: A Theoretical Investigation.* New York: Sheed and Ward.

Gallagher, Paul. (1998). "The man who told the secret: It took a non-Swede to get the full story of a government sterilization program." *Columbia Journalism Review,* January-February. http://www.cjr.org/year/98/1/Sweden/asp

Gardner, Howard. (1983). *Frames of Mind: The Theory of Multiple Intelligence.* New York: Basic Books.

Gardner, LeGrande, and Donald J. Shoemaker. (1989). "Social bonding and delinquency: A comparative analysis." *Sociological Quarterly* 30:481–500.

Garfinkel, Harold. (1956). "Conditions of successful degradation ceremonies." *American Journal of Sociology* 61:420–24.

Garner, Joel, and Christy A. Visher. (1988). *Policy Experiments Coming of Age.* NIJ Reports. Washington, DC: National Institute of Justice.

Gartner, Alan, Collin Greer, and Frank Reissman. (1974). *The New Assault on Equality: IQ and Social Stratification,* New York: Harper and Row.

Gates, Henry Louis. (1995). "Thirteen ways of looking at a black man." *New Yorker,* October:59.

Gauthier, DeAnn, and William B. Bankston. (1997). "Gender equality and sex ratio of intimate killing." *Criminology* 45:577–700.

Gay, William G., Theodore H. Schell, and Stephen Schack. (1977). *Routine Patrol: Improving Police Productivity.* Washington, DC: U.S. Government Printing Office.

Gee, E. Gordon, and D. Jackson. (1977). "Hand in hand or fist in glove?" In *Learning and the Law* 34.

Geerken, Michael R., and Walter R. Gove. (1975). "Deterrence: Some theoretical considerations." *Law and Society Review* 9:497–513.

Gendreau, P., M. Irvine, and S. Knight. (1973). "Evaluating response styles on the MMPI with prisoners: Faking good adjustment and maladjustment." *Canadian Journal of Behavioral Sciences* 5:183–94.

Gerbner, G., and L. Gross. (1976). "Living with television: the violence profile." *Journal of Communication* 26(2):173–99.

———. (1980). "The violent face of television and its lessons." Pp. 149–62 in *Children and the Faces of Television: Teaching, Violence, Selling,* ed. E. L. Palmer and A. Dorr. New York: Academic.

Gibbons, Don C. (1977). *Society, Crime, and Criminal Careers,* 3d ed. Englewood Cliffs, NJ: Prentice-Hall.

———. (1979). *The Criminological Enterprise: Theories and Perspectives.* Englewood Cliffs, NJ: Prentice-Hall.

———. (1984). "Forcible rape and sexual violence." *Journal of Research in Crime and Delinquency* 21:251–69.

———. (1992). *Society, Crime, and Criminal Behavior,* 6th ed.. Englewood Cliffs, NJ: Prentice-Hall.

———. (1994). *Talking about Crime and Criminals.* Englewood Cliffs, NJ: Prentice-Hall.

———. (2000). "Introductory chapter: Criminology, criminologists, and criminological theory." In *Crime and Criminality,* ed. Sally S. Simpson. Thousand Oaks, CA: Pine Forge.

Gibbs, Jack. (1968). "Crime, punishment and deterrence." *Southwest Social Science Quarterly.* 48:515–30.

———. (1972). *Sociological Theory Construction.* Hinsdale, IL: Dryden.

———. (1975). *Crime, Punishment, and Deterrence.* New York: Elsevier.

———. (1985). "The methodology of theory construction in criminology." In *Theoretical Methods in Criminology,* ed. Robert F. Meier. Beverly Hills, CA: Sage.

———. (1987). "The state of criminological theory." *Criminology* 25:821–40.

Gibbs, John J., and Dennis Giever. (1995). "Self control and its manifestations among university students: An empirical test of Gottfredson and Hirschi's general theory." *Justice Quarterly* 12:231–55.

Gibbs, John J., Dennis Giever, and Jamie S. Martin. (1998). "Parental management and self-control: An empirical test of Gottfredson and Hirschi's general theory." *Journal of Research in Crime and Delinquency* 35:40–75.

Giddens, Anthony. (1990). *Consequences of Modernity.* Stanford, CA: Stanford University Press.

Giordano, Peggy, and Stephen A. Cernkovich. (1977). "Male theories and female crimes: Understanding the impact of social change." Paper presented at the annual meeting of the Midwest Sociological Society, Minneapolis, MN.

Glaser, Daniel. (1956). "Criminality theories and behavioral images." *American Journal of Sociology* 61:433–44.

———. (1960). "Differential association and criminological prediction." *Social Problems* 8:6–14.

———. (1965). "Criminology." *Encyclopedia Britannica,* vol. 6. Chicago: Gilmore.

———. (1978). *Crime in Our Changing Society.* New York: Holt, Rinehart and Winston.

Glasser, William. (1975). *Reality Therapy.* New York: Harper and Row.

———. (1980). "Reality therapy: An explanation of the steps in reality therapy." In *Therapy,* ed. W. Glasser. New York: Harper and Row.

Glueck, Sheldon. (1956). "Theory and fact in criminology." *British Journal of Delinquency* 7:92–109.

Glueck, Sheldon, and Eleanor Glueck. (1950). *Unraveling Juvenile Delinquency.* New York: The Commonwealth Fund.

———. (1956). *Physique and Delinquency.* Cambridge, MA: Harvard University Press.

Goddard, Herbert H. (1914). *Feeblemindedness: Its Causes and Consequences.* New York: Macmillan.

———. (1921). "Feeblemindedness and delinquency." *Journal of Psycho-Asthenics* 25:168–76.

Goenner, Tanja. (2000). "Conflict, crime, communication, cooperation—Restorative justice as a new way of dealing with the consequences of criminal acts." Unpublished paper. Tuebingen, Germany: University of Tuebingen.

Goffman, Erving. (1963). *Stigma.* Englewood Cliffs, NJ: Prentice-Hall.

Gold, Mark S., Arnold M. Washton, and Charles A. Dackis. (1985). "Cocaine abuse: Neurochemistry, phenomenology, and treatment." In *Cocaine Use in America: Epidemiology and Clinical Perspective,* ed. N. J. Kozel and E. H. Adams. Rockville, MD: National Institute on Drug Abuse.

Gold, Steven. (1980). "The CAP control theory of drug abuse." In *Theories of Drug Abuse: Selected Contemporary Perspectives,* ed. D. J. Lettieri, M. Sayers, and H. W. Pearson. Rockville, MD: National Institute on Drug Abuse.

Goldberg, Stephen B., Eric D. Green, and Frank E. A. Sanders. (1985). *Dispute Resolution.* Boston: Little, Brown.

Goleman, Daniel. (1990). "Scientists pinpoint brain irregularities in drug addicts." *New York Times,* 26 June:B5.

Goode, Eric. (1984). *Drugs in American Society,* 2d ed. New York: Knopf.

Gora, Joann Gennaro. (1982). *The New Female Criminal: Empirical Reality or Social Myth?* New York: Praeger.

Gordon Robert. (1976). "Prevalence: The rare datum in delinquency measurement and its implications for the theory of delinquency." In *The Juvenile Justice System,* ed. Malcolm W. Klein. Beverly Hills, CA: Sage.

———. (1987). "SES versus IQ in the race–IQ–delinquency model." *International Journal of Sociology and Social Policy* 7:42–62.

Gottfredson, Don M. (1989). "Criminological theories: The truth as told by Mark Twain." In *Advances in Criminological Theory,* vol. 1, ed. W. S. Laufer and F. Adler. New Brunswick, NJ: Transaction.

Gottfredson, Michael R., and Don M. Gottfredson. (1988). *Decision Making in Criminal Justice: Toward the Rational Exercise of Discretion,* 2d ed. New York: Plenum.

Gottfredson, Michael R., and Travis Hirschi. (1986). "The true value of lambda would appear to be zero: An essay on career criminals, criminal careers, selective incapacitation, cohort studies, and related topics." *Criminology* 24:213–34.

———. (1987). "The methodological adequacy of longitudinal research on crime." *Criminology* 25:581–614.

———. (1989). "A propensity-event theory of crime." Pp. 57–67 in *Advances in Criminological Theory,* vol. 1, ed. William S. Laufer and Freda Adler. New Brunswick, NJ: Transaction.

———. (1990). *A General Theory of Crime.* Stanford, CA: Stanford University Press.

Gough, Harrison G. (1965). "The F minus K Dissimulation index for the MMPI." *Journal of Consulting Psychology* 14:408–13.

Gould, Larry. (1999). "The impact of working in two worlds and its effect on Navajo police officers." *Journal of Legal Pluralism* 44:53–71.

Gould, Stephen Jay. (1981). *The Mismeasure of Man.* New York: Norton.

———. (1995). "Curveball." In *The Bell Curve Wars: Race, Intelligence and the Future of America,* ed. S. Fraser. New York: Basic Books.

Gove, Walter R. (1980). *The Labeling of Deviance: Evaluation of a Perspective.* Beverly Hills, CA: Sage.

Gove, Walter R., and Charles Wilmoth. (1990). "Risk, crime, and neurophysiologic highs: A consideration of brain processes that may reinforce delinquent and criminal behavior." In *Crime in Biological, Social, and Moral Contexts,* ed. L. Ellis and H. Hoffman. Westport, CT: Praeger.

Grasmick, Harold G., and Robert J. Bursik. (1990). "Conscience, significant others, and rational choice: Extending the deterrence model." *Law and Society Review* 24:837–61.

Grasmick, Harold G., Charles R. Tittle, Robert J. Bursik, and Bruce J. Arneklev. (1993). "Testing the core empirical implications of Gottfredson and Hirschi's general theory of crime." *Journal of Research in Crime and Delinquency* 30:5–29.

Greenberg, David F. (1981). *Crime and Capitalism: Readings in a Marxist Criminology.* Palo Alto, CA: Mayfield.

———. (1999). "The weak strength of social control theory." *Crime and Delinquency* 45:61–81.

Greenberg, Stephanie, and Williams M. Rohe. (1984). "Neighborhood design and crime: A test of two perspectives." *Journal of the American Planning Association* 50:48–61.

Greenberg, Stephanie, Williams M. Rohe, and Jay R. Williams. (1982). *Safe and Secure Neighborhoods: Physical Characteristics and Informal Territorial Control in High and Low Crime Neighborhoods.* Washington, DC: National Institute of Justice.

Greenfield, L. A. (1998). *Alcohol and Crime.* Washington, DC: U.S. Department of Justice, Bureau of Justice Statistics.

Greenwood, Peter W., Karyn E. Model, C. Peter Rydell, and James Chiesa. (1996). *Diverting Children from a Life of Crime.* Santa Monica, CA: Rand.

Griffin, Brenda S., and Charles T. Griffin. (1978). "Drug use and differential association." *Drug Forum* 7:1–8.

Griffin, David R., and Richard A. Falk. (1993). *Postmodern Politics for a Planet in Crisis: Policy, Process and Presidential Vision.* Albany: SUNY Press.

Gross, Jane. (1992). "Collapse of inner-city families creates America's new orphans: Death, drugs, and jail leave voids in childhood." *New York Times,* 28 March:A1.

Grossman, Linda, T. W. Haywood, E. Ostrov, O. Wasyliw, and James L. Cavanaugh. (1990). "Sensitivity: MMPI validity scales." *Journal of Personality Assessment* 54:220–35.

Guy, E., J. J. Platt, I. S. Zwelling, and S. Bullock. (1985). "Mental health status of prisoners in an urban jail." *Criminal Justice and Behavior* 12:29–33.

Guze, Samuel B. (1976). *Criminality and Psychiatric Disorders.* New York: Oxford University Press.

Habermas, Jurgen. (1981). "Modernity versus postmodernity." *The German Critique* 22:3–14.

Hacker, Andrew. (1992). *Two Nations: Black and White, Separate, Hostile, Unequal.* New York: Scribner.

Hagan, Frank. (1989). *Research Methods in Criminal Justice and Criminology,* 5th ed. Boston: Allyn and Bacon.

Hagan, John. (1974). "Extra-legal attributes and criminal sentencing: An assessment of a sociological viewpoint." *Law and Society Review* 8:357–83.

———. (1989a). *Structural Criminology.* New Brunswick, NJ: Rutgers University Press.

———. (1989b). "Why is there so little criminal justice theory? Neglected macro- and micro-level links between organization and power." *Journal of Crime and Delinquency* 26:116–35.

———. (1990). "The structuration of gender and deviance: A power control theory of vulnerability to crime and the search for deviant role exits." *Canadian Review of Sociology and Anthropology* 27:137–56.

———. (1991). "Destiny and drift: Subcultural preferences, status attainment, and the risk and rewards of youth." *American Sociological Review* 56:567–82.

———. (1994). *Crime and Disrepute.* Thousand Oaks, CA: Pine Forge.

———. (1995). "Rethinking crime theory and policy: The new sociology of crime and disrepute." Pp. 29–42 in *Crime and Public Policy: Putting Theory to Work,* ed. Hugh Barlow. Boulder, CO: Westview Press.

———. (1997). "Defiance and despair: Subcultural and structural linkages between delinquency and despair in the life course." *Social Forces* 76:119–34.

Hagan, John, A. R. Gillis, and John H. Simpson. (1988). "Feminist scholarship, relational and instrumental control and a power-control theory of gender and delinquency." *British Journal of Sociology* 39:301–36.

———. (1990). "Clarifying and extending power control theory." *American Journal of Sociology* 95:1024–37.

Hagan, John, Gerd Hefler, Gabriele Classen, Klaus Boehnke, and Hans Merkens. (1998). "Subterranean sources of subcultural delinquency beyond the American dream." *Criminology* 36:309–41.

Hagan, John, and Fiona Kay. (1990). "Gender and delinquency in white-collar families: A power-control perspective." *Crime and Delinquency* 36:391–407.

Hagan, John, and Patricia Parker. (1985). "White collar crime and punishment: The class structure and legal sanctioning of securities violations." *American Sociological Review* 50:802–20.

Hagan, John, John H. Simpson, and A. R. Gillis. (1979). "The sexual stratification of social control: A gender-based perspective on crime and delinquency." *British Journal of Sociology* 30:28–38.

———. (1985). "The class structure of gender and delinquency: Toward a power-control theory of common delinquent behavior." *American Journal of Sociology* 90:1151–78.

———. (1987). "Class in the household: A power-control theory of gender and delinquency." *American Journal of Sociology* 92:788–816.

Hagedorn, John M. (1998). *People and Folks: Gangs, Crime and the Underclass in a Rustbelt City.* Chicago: Lake View Press.

Hall, Jerome. (1952). *Theft, Law, and Society,* rev. ed. Indianapolis, IN: Bobbs-Merrill.

Hall, Robert W. (1989). "A study of mass murder: Evidence underlying cadmium and lead poisoning and brain involving immunoreactivity." *International Journal of Biosocial and Medical Research* 11(2):144–52.

Hammer v. Dagenhart et al., 247 U.S. 251, 38 S.Ct. 529, L.Ed. 1101 (1918).

Hammond, Holly A., and C. Thomas Caskey. (1997). "Automated DNA typing: Method of the future." *NIJ Research Preview,* February. Washington, DC: U.S. Department of Justice.

Hamparian, Donna M., Linda K. Estep, Susan M. Muntean, Ramon R. Prestino, Robert G. Swisher, Paul L. Wallace, and Joseph L. White. (1982). *Youth in Adult Courts: Between Two Worlds.* Columbus, OH: Academy of Contemporary Problems.

Hancock, Lynell. (1994). "In defiance of Darwin: How a public school in the Bronx turns dropouts into scholars." *Newsweek,* 24 October:61.

Hare, Robert D. (1996). "Psychopathology: A clinical construct whose time has come." *Criminal Justice and Behavior* 23:25–54.

Harris, David A. (1999). *Driving While Black: Racial Profiling on Our Nation's Highways.* New York: American Civil Liberties Union.

Harry, Joseph, and W. William Minor. (1985). "Intelligence and delinquency reconsidered: A comment on Menard and Morse." *American Journal of Sociology* 91:956–62.

Harvey, David. (1989). *The Condition of Postmodernity.* Cambridge, England: Blackwell.

Hathaway, R. S., and E. D. Monachesi. (1953). *Analyzing and Predicting Juvenile Delinquency with the MMPI.* Minneapolis: University of Minneapolis Press.

Hawkins, Gordon. (1976). *The Prison.* Chicago: University of Chicago Press.

Hawkins, Gordon, and Geoffrey P. Alpert. (1989). *American Prison System: Punishment and Justice.* Englewood Cliffs, NJ: Prentice-Hall.

Hawkins, J. David, and Joseph Weis. (1985). "The social development model: An integrated approach to delinquency prevention." *Journal of Primary Prevention* 6:73–97.

Hay, Carter. (1998). "Parental sanctions and delinquent behavior: Toward clarification of Braithwaite's theory of reintegrative shaming." *Theoretical Criminology* 2:419–43.

———. (2001a). "Parenting, self-control, and delinquency: A test of self-control theory." *Criminology* 39:707–36.

———. (2001b). "An exploratory test of Braithwaite's reintegrative shaming theory." *Journal of Research in Crime and Delinquency* 38:132–53.

Hayeslip, David W. (1989). *Local-Level Drug Enforcement: New Strategies*. National Institute of Justice Research in Action. Washington, DC: U.S. Government Printing Office.

Healy, William, and Augusta F. Bronner. (1936). *New Light on Delinquency and Its Treatment*. New Haven, CT: Yale University Press.

Healy, William, Augusta F. Bronner, and Anna Mae Bowers. (1930). *The Structure and Meaning of Psychoanalysis*. New York: Knopf.

Heineke, John H. (1988). "Crime, deterrence, and choice: Testing the rational behavior hypothesis." *American Sociological Review* 54:303–05.

Henry, Stuart, and Dragan Milovanovic. (1991). "Constitutive criminology: The maturation of critical theory." *Criminology* 29:293–315.

Hepburn, John R. (1976). "Testing alternative models of delinquency causation." *Journal of Criminal Law and Criminology* 67:450–60.

Herrnstein, Richard J. (1971). "I.Q." *Atlantic Monthly* 228:43–64.

Herrnstein, Richard J., and Charles Murray. (1994). *The Bell Curve: Intelligence and Class Structure in American Life*. New York: Free Press.

Herronkohl, Todd I., Bu Huang, Rick Kosterman, J. David Hawkins, Richard F. Catalano, and Brian H. Smith. (2001). "A comparison of social development processes leading to violent behavior in late adolescence for childhood initiators and adolescent initiators of violence." *Journal of Research in Crime and Delinquency* 38:45–63.

Hickman, Matthew J., and Alex R. Piquero. (2001). "Exploring relationships between gender, control balance, and deviance." *Deviant Behavior* 22:323–51.

Hickman, Matthew J., Alex R. Piquero, Brian P. Lawton, and Jack R. Greene. (2001). "Applying Tittle's control balance theory and police deviance." *Policing* 24:497–519.

Hickman, Matthew J., and Brian A. Reaves. (2001). *Local Police Departments 1999*. Washington, DC: U.S. Department of Justice.

Hindelang, Michael J. (1972). "The relationship of self-reported delinquency to scales of CPI and MMPI." *Journal of Criminal Law, Criminology, and Police Science* 63:75–81.

———. (1973). "Causes of delinquency: A partial replication and extension." *Social Problems* 20:471–87.

———. (1981). "Variations in sex-race-age-specific incidence rates of offending. *American Sociological Review* 46:461–74.

Hippchen, Leonard. (1978). *Ecologic-Biochemical Approaches to the Treatment of Delinquents and Criminals*. New York: Van Nostrand Reinhold.

———. (1982). *Holistic Approaches to Offender Rehabilitation*. Springfield, IL: Thomas.

Hirschel, J. David, and Ira W. Hutchinson. (1992). "Female spouse abuse and the police response: The Charlotte, North Carolina, experiment." *Journal of Criminal Law and Criminology* 83:73–119.

Hirschi, Travis. (1969). *Causes of Delinquency*. Berkeley: University of California Press.

———. (1972). *Causes of Delinquency*. Berkeley: University of California Press.

———. (1996). "Theory without ideas: Reply to Akers." *Criminology* 34:249–56.

Hirschi, Travis, and Michael Gottfredson. (1986). "The distinction between crime and criminality." Pp. 55–69 in *Critique and Explanation*, ed. Timothy Hartnagel and Robert Silverman. New Brunswick, NJ: Transaction.

Hirschi, Travis, and Michael J. Hindelang. (1977). "Intelligence and delinquency: A revisionist review." *American Sociological Review* 42:571–86.

Hobbes, Thomas. (1957)[1651]. *Leviathan*. Oxford, England: Basil Blackwell.

Hoffer, Peter Charles. (1997). *The Salem Witchcraft Trials: A Legal History*. Lawrence: University Press of Kansas.

Hoffman, B. F. (1977). "Two new cases of XYY chromosome complement." *Canadian Psychiatric Association Journal* 22:447–55.

Hollin, Clive R. (1989). *Psychology and Crime: An Introduction to Criminological Psychology*. London: Routledge.

Holmes, Ronald M. (1990). *Profiling Violent Crimes*. Newbury Park, CA: Sage.

Holten, N. Gary, and Lawson. L. Lamar. (1991). *The Criminal Courts: Structures, Personnel, and Processes*. New York: McGraw-Hill.

Holzman, H. (1979). "Learning disabilities and juvenile delinquency: Biological and sociological theories." In *Biology and Crime,* ed. C. R. Jeffery. Beverly Hills, CA: Sage.

Hooton, Ernest. (1939). *The American Criminal: An Anthropological Study*. Cambridge, MA: Harvard University Press.

Horgan, J. (1993). "Eugenics revisited." *Scientific American* 254:122–31.

Horney, Julie. (1978). "Menstrual cycles and criminal responsibility." *Law and Human Behavior* 2(190):25–36.

Horney, Julie, and Ineke H. Marshall. (1992). "Risk perceptions among serious offenders: The role of crime and punishment." *Criminology* 30:575–92.

Horowitz, Irving Louis. (1967). *The Rise and Fall of Project Camelot: Studies in the Relationship between Social Science and Practical Politics*. Cambridge, MA: MIT Press.

Houston, James. (1995). *Correctional Management: Functions, Skills and Systems*. Chicago: Nelson-Hall.

Hoyle, Marcia L. (1995). "'A fitting remedy': Aboriginal justice as a community healing strategy." In *Popular Justice and Community Regeneration,* ed. K. M. Haslehurst. Westport, CT: Praeger.

Hubka, Vernon Edward. (1975). *The Fate of Idealism in Lawyers*. Ph.D. dissertation, University of California, Berkeley. University Microfilms International BMJ76-15069.

Hughes, Everett C. (1945). "Dilemmas and contradictions of status." *American Journal of Sociology* 50:353–59.

Huizinga, David, Rolf Loeber, and Terrence P. Thornberry. (1995). *Urban Delinquency and Substance Abuse: Recent Findings from the Program of Research on the Causes and Correlates of Delinquency*. Washington, DC: U.S. Department of Justice, Office of Justice Programs, Office of Juvenile Justice and Delinquency Prevention.

Hunt, Jennifer. (1985). "Police accounts of normal force." *Urban Life* 13:315–41.

Hunter, H. (1966). "YY chromosomes and Klinefelter's syndrome." *Lancet* 1:984.

———. (1977). "XYY males." *British Journal of Psychiatry* 121:468–77.

Hurwitz, S., and K. O. Christiansen. (1983). *Criminology*. London: Allen and Unwin.

Hutchings, Barry, and Sarnoff A. Mednick. (1977). "Criminality in adoptees and their biological parents: A pilot study." In *Biosocial Bases of Criminal Behavior,* ed. S. A. and K. O. Christiansen. New York: Gardner.

Inciardi, James A., ed. (1980). *Radical Criminology: The Coming Crises*. Beverly Hills, CA: Sage.

———. (1992). *The War on Drugs II: The Continuing Epic of Heroin, Cocaine, Crack, Crime, AIDS, and Public Policy*. Mountain View, CA: Mayfield.

In re Gault, 387 U.S. 1; 18 L.Ed. 2d 527, 87 S.Ct. 1428 (1967).

In re Winship, 397 U.S. 358 (1970); 397 U.S. 358 (1971).

Irwin, John. (1980). *Prisons in Turmoil*. Boston: Little, Brown.

Jackson, Patricia. (1984). "Opportunity and crime: A function of city size." *Sociology and Social Research* 68:172–93.

Jacobs, Carole. (1975). "The criminality of women." Unpublished paper presented to the Western Social Science Association, Denver, CO.

Jacobs, Jane. (1961). *The Death and Life of Great American Cities*. New York: Vintage Books.

Jacobs, P. A., M. Bruton, M. Melville, R. P. Brittain, and W. F. McClemont. (1965). "Aggressive behavior, mental sub-normality and the XYY male." *Nature* 208:1351–52.

Jaffe, Peter, David A. Wolf, Anne Telford, and Gary Austin. (1986). "The impact of police charges in incidents of wife abuse." *Journal of Family Violence* 1:37–49.

Jaggar, Alison M., and Paula Rothenberg. (1984). *Feminist Frameworks*. New York: McGraw-Hill.

Jameson, Frederic. (1984). "The politics of theory: Ideological positions in the postmodernism debate." *New German Critique* 33:53–65.

———. (1991). *Postmodernism, or the Cultural Logic of Late Capitalism*. Durham, NC: Duke University Press.

Jeffery, C. Ray. (1965). "Criminal behavior and learning theory." *Journal of Criminal Law, Criminology, and Police Science* 56:294–300.

———. (1971). *Crime Prevention through Environmental Design*. Beverly Hills, CA: Sage.

———. (1978). "Criminology as an interdisciplinary science." *Criminology* 16:149–67.

———. (1985). *Criminology: An Interdisciplinary Approach*. Englewood Cliffs, NJ: Prentice-Hall.

———. (1993). "Genetics, crime, and the canceled conference." *Criminologist* 18:1, 6–8.

Jeffery, C. Ray, Laura B. Myers, and Laurin A. Wollan. (1991). "Crime justice, and their systems: Resolving the tension." *Criminologist* 16:1, 3–6.

Jensen, Arthur R. (1969). "How much can we boost I.Q. and scholastic achievement?" *Harvard Educational Review* 39:1–123.

Jensen, Gary F. (1972). "Parents, peers, and delinquent action: A test of the differential association perspective." *American Journal of Sociology* 78:63–72.

———. (1999). "A critique of control balance theory." *Theoretical Criminology* 3:339–43.

Jensen, Gary F., and David Brownfield. (1983). "Parents and drugs." *Criminology* 21:543–54.

Jensen, Gary F., and Raymond Eve. (1976). "Sex differences in delinquency." *Criminology* 13:427–48.

Jensen, Gary F., and Dean G. Rojek. (1998). *Delinquency and Youth Crime*, 3d ed. Prospect Heights, IL: Waveland Press.

Johnson, Richard E. (1979). "Are adolescent theft, vandalism, and assault due to the same causal processes?" *International Journal of Comparative and Applied Criminal Justice* 3:59–69.

Johnson, Valerie. (1988). "Adolescent alcohol and marijuana use: A longitudinal assessment of a social learning perspective." *American Journal of Drug and Alcohol Abuse* 14:319–39.

Jones, T., MacLean, B., and Young, T. (1986). *The Islington Crime Survey*. Aldershot, England: Gower.

Jung, Carl Gustav. (1921). *Psychological Types*. Zurich: Verlag.

———. (1961)[1933]. *Modern Man in Search of a Soul*. New York: Harcourt, Brace and World.

Kanarek, Robin B. (1994). "Nutrition and violent behavior." In *Understanding and Preventing Violence,* vol. 2, ed. Albert Reiss, Klaus Miczek, and Jeffrey Roth. Washington, DC: National Academy Press.

Kane, Robert J. (2000). "Police responses to restraining orders in domestic violence incidents: Identifying the custody-threshold thesis." *Criminal Justice and Behavior* 27:561–80.

Kaplan, Abraham. (1963). *The Conduct of Inquiry*. Scranton, PA: Chandler.

Kappeler, Victor E., and Rolando V. Del Carmen. (1990). "Civil liability for failure to arrest intoxicate drivers." *Journal of Criminal Justice* 18:117–31.

Katz, Janet, and William J. Chambliss. (1991). "Biological paradigms." In *Exploring Criminology,* ed. W. Chambliss. New York: Macmillan.

Keane, Carl, Paul S. Maxim, and James J. Teevan. (1993). "Drinking and driving, self-control, and gender: Testing a general theory of crime." *Journal of Research in Crime and Delinquency* 30:30–46.

Kelley, Barbara Tatem, Terence P. Thornberry, and Carolyn A. Smith. (1997). "In the wake of child maltreatment." *Juvenile Justice Bulletin,* August. Washington, DC: Office of Juvenile Justice and Delinquency Prevention.

Kelling, George, Tony Pate, Duane Dieckman, and Charles Brown. (1974). *The Kansas City Preventive Patrol Experiment: A Summary Report*. Washington, DC: Police Foundation.

Kennedy, Leslie W., and Stephen W. Baron. (1993). "Routine activities and a subculture of violence: A study of violence on the streets." *Journal of Research in Crime and Delinquency.* 30:88–112.

Kent v. United States, 383 U.S.C. 541 (1966).

Kephart, Williams M. (1957). *Racial Factors and Urban Law Enforcement.* Philadelphia: University of Pennsylvania.

Kessler, S., and Rudolf H. Moos. (1970). "The XYY karyotype and criminality: A review." *Journal of Psychiatric Research* 7:164.

Khantzian, Edward J. (1985). "The self-medication hypothesis of addictive disorders: Focus on heroin and cocaine dependence." *American Journal of Psychiatry* 142:1259–64.

Kinsey, Richard, John Lea, and Jock Young. (1986). *Losing the Fight against Crime.* Oxford, UK: Basil Blackwell.

Klein, Lawrence R., Brian Forst, and Victor Filatov. (1978). "The deterrent effect of capital punishment: An assessment of the estimates." In *Deterrence and Incapacitation: Estimating the Effects of Criminal Sanctions on Crime Rates,* ed. A. Blumstein, J. Cohen, and D. Nagin. Washington, DC: National Academy of Sciences.

Kornhauser, Ruth. (1978). *Social Sources of Delinquency.* Chicago: University of Chicago Press.

Kramer, John H., and Cynthia Kempinen. (1978). "Erosion of chivalry? Changes in the handling of male and female defendants from 1970 to 1975." Paper presented at the annual meeting of the Society for the Study of Social Problems, San Francisco.

Kreuz, Leo, and Robert Rose. (1972). "Assessment of aggressive behavior and plasma testosterone in a young criminal population." *Psychosomatic Medicine* 34:321–32.

Krisberg, Barry. (1975). *Crime and Privilege: Toward a New Criminology.* Englewood Cliffs, NJ: Prentice-Hall.

Krisberg, Barry, and James F. Austin. (1993). *Reinventing Juvenile Justice.* Newbury Park, CA: Sage.

Krisberg, Barry, and Karl F. Schumann. (2000). "Introduction." *Crime and Delinquency* 46:147–55.

Krohn, Marvin D., and James Massey. (1980). "Social control and delinquent behavior: An examination of the elements of social bond." *Sociological Quarterly* 21:529–44.

Krohn, Marvin D., Williams F. Skinner, James L. Massey, and Ronald L. Akers. (1985). "Social learning theory and adolescent cigarette smoking: A longitudinal study." *Social Problems* 2:4455–71.

Kropotkin, Peter. (1970)[1927]. *Kropotkin's Revolutionary Pamphlets: A Collection of Writings by Peter Kropotkin,* ed. Roger N. Baldwin. New York: Dover.

Kruttschnitt, Candace. (1982). "Women, crime, and dependency." *Criminology* 19:495–513.

Kuhn, Thomas S. (1970). *The Structure of Scientific Revolutions,* 2d ed. Chicago: University of Chicago Press.

Kumpfer, Karol, and Connie M. Tait. (2000). "Family skills training for parents and children." *OJJDP Juvenile Justice Bulletin,* April. NCJ180140.

Kurki, Leena. (1999). "Incorporating restorative and community justice into American sentencing and corrections." *Sentencing & Corrections: Issues for the 21st Century,* no. 3. Washington, DC: U.S. Office of Justice Programs.

Kvale, Steiner. (1992). *Psychology and Postmodernism.* London: Sage.

LaGrange, Teresa C., and Robert A. Silverman. (1999). "Low self-control and opportunity: Testing the general theory of crime as an explanation for gender differences in delinquency." *Criminology* 37:41–69.

Langworthy, Robert H. (1987a). "Comment—Have we measured the concept(s) of police cynicism using Niederhoffer's cynicism index." *Justice Quarterly* 4:277–80.

———. (1987b). "Police cynicism: What we know from the Niederhoffer scale." *Journal of Criminal Justice* 15:17–35.

Lanza-Kaduce, Lonn, and Mary Klug. (1986). "Learning to cheat: The interaction of moral-development and social learning theories." *Deviant Behavior* 7:243–59.

Laub, John H. (1983). "Urbanism, race, and crime." *Journal of Research in Crime and Delinquency* 20:183–98.

Laub, John H., Daniel S. Nagin, and Robert J. Sampson. (1998). "Trajectories of change in criminal offending." *American Sociological Review* 63:225–38.

Laub, John H., and Robert Sampson. (1991). "The Sutherland–Glueck debate: On the sociology of criminological knowledge." *American Journal of Sociology* 96:1402–40.

Laub, John H., Robert J. Sampson, and Leana C. Allen. (2001). "Explaining crime over the life course: Toward a theory of age-graded informal social control." Pp. 97–112 in *Explaining Criminals and Crime,* ed. Raymond Paternoster and Ronet Bachman. Los Angeles: Roxbury.

Lea J., and Jock Young. (1984). *What Is to Be Done about Law and Order?* New York: Penguin Books.

Leacock, Eleanor Burke. (1971). *Culture of Poverty: A Critique.* New York: Simon and Schuster.

Leavitt, Glen. (1999). "Criminological theory as an art form: Implications for criminal justice policy." *Crime and Delinquency* 45:389–99.

Lederberg, Joshua. (1969). "The meaning of Dr. Jensen's study of IQ disparities." *Washington Post,* 29 March.

Lemert, Edwin. (1951). *Social Pathology.* New York: McGraw-Hill.

Leudtke, Gerald, and E. Lystad. (1970). *Crime in the Physical City. Final Report.* LEAA Grant 169-078. Washington, DC: U.S. Government Printing Office.

Leverant, Sharon, Francis T. Cullen, Betsey Fulton, and John F. Wozniak. (1999). "Reconsidering restorative justice: The corruption of benevolence revisited?" *Crime and Delinquency* 45:3–27.

Levinthal, Charles F. (1988). *Messengers of Paradise: Opiates and the Brain.* Garden City, NY: Doubleday.

Lewin, K. (1951). *Field Theory in Social Science: Selected Theoretical Papers,* ed. Dorwin Cartwright. New York: Harper and Row.

Lewis, Neil A. (1990). "Scholars say arrest of Noriega has little justification in law." *New York Times,* 10 January:A12.

Lindner, Robert. (1944). *Rebel without a Cause.* New York: Grove.

Lipset, Seymour M. (1969). "Why cops hate liberals—and vice versa." *Atlantic Monthly* 223:76–83.

Lipton, Douglas. (1994). "The correctional opportunity: Pathways to drug treatment for offenders." *Journal of Drug Issues* 24:331–48.

Lipton, Douglas, Robert Martinson, and Judith Wilks. (1975). *The Effectiveness of Correctional Treatment: A Survey of Treatment Evaluation Studies.* New York: Praeger.

Liska, Allan E. (1971). "Aspirations, expectations, and delinquency: Stress and additive models." *Sociological Quarterly* 12:99–107.

Liska, Allan E., Marvin D. Krohn, and Steven F. Messner. (1989). "Strategies and requisites for theoretical integration in the study of crime and deviance." In *Theoretical Integration in the Study of Deviance and Crime: Problems and Prospects,* ed. S. F. Messner, M. D. Krohn, and A. E. Liska. Albany: SUNY Press.

Liska, Allen E., and Steven F. Messner. (1999). *Perspectives on Crime and Deviance,* 3d ed. Upper Saddle River, NJ: Prentice-Hall.

Locurto, Charles. (1991). *Sense and Nonsense about IQ: The Case of Uniqueness.* New York: Praeger.

Loeber, Rolf, and D. F. Hay. (1994). "Developmental approaches to aggression and conduct problems." In *Development through Life: A Handbook for Clinicians,* ed. M. L. Rutter and D. F. Hay. Oxford, UK: Blackwell.

Loeber, Rolf, and Mark LeBlanc. (1990). "Toward a developmental criminology." Pp. 375–473 in *Crime and Justice,* ed. Norval Morris and Michael Tonry. Chicago: University of Chicago Press.

Loeber, Rolf, and Magda Stouthamer-Loeber. (1996). "The development of offending." *Criminal Justice and Behavior* 23:12–24.

———. (1998). "Development of juvenile aggression and violence: Some common misconceptions and controversies." *American Psychologist* 53:242–59.

Loeber, Rolf, Kate Kennan, and Quanwu Zhang (1997). "Boys' experimentation and persistence in developmental pathways toward serious delinquency." *Journal of Child and Family Studies* 6:321–57.

Lofland, John. (1969). *Deviance and Identity*. Englewood Cliffs, NJ: Prentice-Hall.

Loftus, E. F., and K. Ketcham. (1994). *The Myth of Repressed Memory*. New York: St. Martin's.

Loh, Wallace D. (1984). *Social Research in the Judicial Process: Cases, Readings and Text*. New York: Russell Sage Foundation.

Lombroso, Cesare. (1876). *L'uomo Delinquente* [The Criminal Man]. Milan: Hoepli.

———. (1968)[1911]. *Crime: Its Causes and Remedies*. Montclair, NJ: Patterson-Smith.

Lombroso-Ferrero, Gina. (1979)[1911]. *Criminal Man, According to the Classification of Cesare Lombroso*. New York: Putnam.

Longshore, Douglas, Judith A. Stein, and Susan Turner. (1998). "Reliability and validity of a self-control measure: A rejoinder." *Criminology* 36:175–82.

Longshore, Douglas, Susan Turner, and Judith A. Stein. (1996). "Self-control in a criminal sample: An examination of construct validity." *Criminology* 34:209–28.

Louscher, Kent, Ray E. Hossford, and C. Scott Moss. (1983). "Predicting dangerous behavior in a penitentiary using Megargee typology." *Criminal Justice and Behavior* 10:269–84.

Lynskey, Dana Peterson, L. Thomas Winfree, Jr., Finn-Aage Esbensen, and Dennis L. Clason. (2000). "Linking gender, minority group status and family matters to self-control theory: A multivariate analysis of key self-control concepts in a youth-gang context." *Juvenile and Family Court Journal* 51:1–19.

MacKenzie, Doris Layton. (1993). "Shock incarceration as an alternative for drug offenders." In *Drugs and the Criminal Justice System: Evaluating Public Policy Initiatives*, ed. D. L. MacKenzie and C. Unchida. Newbury Park, CA: Sage.

MacKenzie, Doris Layton, Angela R. Gover, Gaylene Styve Armstrong, and Ojmarrh Mitchell. (2001). "A national study comparing the environments of boot camps with traditional facilities for juvenile offenders." *Research in Brief*. Washington, DC: National Institute of Justice, August.

MacKenzie, Doris Layton, James W. Shaw, and Voncile B. Gowdy. (1993). *An Evaluation of Shock Incarceration in Louisiana*. Washington, DC: National Institute of Justice.

Maguire, Kathleen, and Ann L. Pastore. (2000). *Sourcebook 1999*. Washington, DC: U.S. Department of Justice.

Makkai, Toni, and John Braithwaite. (1994). "Reintegrative shaming and compliance with regulatory standards." *Criminology* 32:361–83.

Mankoff, Milton. (1976). "Societal reaction and career deviance: A critical analysis." In *Whose Law, What Order? A Conflict Approach to Criminology*, ed. W. J. Chambliss and M. Mankoff. New York: Wiley.

Marcos, Anastasios C., and Stephen J. Bahr. (1988). "Control theory and adolescent drug use." *Youth and Society* 19:395–425.

Marcos, Anastasios C., Stephen J. Bahr, and Richard E. Johnson. (1986). "Test of bonding/association theory of adolescent drug use." *Social Forces* 65:135–61.

Martin, Randy, Robert J. Mutchnick, and W. Timothy Austin. (1990). *Criminological Thought: Pioneers Past and Present*. New York: Macmillan.

Martin, Susan O. (1980). *Breaking and Entering: Policewomen on Patrol*. Berkeley: University of California Press.

Martinson, Robert. (1974). "What works?—Questions and answers about prison reform." *Public Interest* 35:22–54.

Marvell, Thomas B., and Carlisle E. Moody. (1999). "Female and male homicide victimization rates: Comparing trends and regressors." *Criminology* 37:879–902.

Marx, Karl. (1956). *Selected Writings in Sociology and Social Philosophy*. Trans. T. B. Bottomore. New York: McGraw-Hill.

Masters, Roger D. (1997). "Brain chemistry and social status: The neurotoxicity hypothesis. In *Intelligence, Political Inequality, and Public Policy*, ed. Elliott White. Westport, CT: Praeger.

Masters, Roger D., Brian Hone, and April Doshi. (1998). "Environmental pollution, neurotoxicity, and criminal violence," In *Environmental Toxicology: Current Developments*, ed. J. Rose. New York: Taylor and Francis.

Matsueda, Ross L. (1982). "Testing control theory and differential association: A causal modeling approach." *American Sociological Review* 47:489–504.

———. (1988). "The current state of differential association theory." *Crime and Delinquency* 34:277–306.

———. (1997). "'Cultural deviance theory': The remarkable persistence of a flawed term." *Theoretical Criminology* 1:429–52.

Matsueda, Ross L., and Karen Heimer. (1987). "Race, family structure and delinquency: A test of differential association and social control theories." *American Sociological Review* 52:826–40.

Matthews, Roger, and Jock Young. (1992). *Issues in Realist Criminology.* London: Sage.

Matza, David. (1964). *Delinquency and Drift.* New York: Wiley.

Matza, David, and Gresham Sykes. (1961). "Juvenile delinquency and subterranean values." *American Sociological Review* 26:712–19.

Maxwell, Christopher D., Joel H. Garner, and Jeffery A. Fagan. (2001). "The effects of arrest on intimate partner violence: New evidence from the spouse assault replication program." *Research in Brief.* Washington, DC: National Institute of Justice, July.

Mays, G. Larry, Charles Fields, and Joel A. Thompson. (1994). "Preincarceration patterns of drug and alcohol abuse." *Criminal Justice Policy Review* 5:40–52.

———. (2000). *Juvenile Justice.* New York: McGraw-Hill.

Mays, G. Larry, and L. Thomas Winfree, Jr. (1998). *Contemporary Corrections.* Belmont, CA: Wadsworth.

———. (2002). *Contemporary Corrections,* 2d ed. Belmont, CA: Wadsworth.

Mazerolle, Paul. (1998). "Gender, general strain, and delinquency: An empirical examination." *Justice Quarterly* 15:65–91.

———. (2000). "Understanding illicit drug use: Lessons from developmental theory." Pp. 179–204 in *Of Crime and Criminality: The Use of Theory in Everyday Life,* ed. Sally S. Simpson, Boston: Pine Forge.

McBride, Duane C., and James A. Swartz. (1990). "Drugs and violence in the age of crack cocaine." In *Drugs, Crime and the Criminal Justice System,* ed. R. Weisheit. Cincinnati, OH: Anderson.

McCarthy, Belinda, and Bernard J. McCarthy, Jr. (1991). *Community-Based Corrections,* 2d ed. Pacific Grove, CA: Brooks/Cole.

McCarthy, Belinda R., and Brent L. Smith. (1986). "The conceptualization of discrimination in the juvenile justice process: The impact of administrative factors and screening decisions on juvenile court dispositions." *Criminology* 24:41–64.

McCarthy, John D., John Hagan, and Todd S. Woodward. (1999). "In the company of women: Structure and agency in a revised power-control theory of gender and delinquency." *Criminology* 37:761–88.

McCold, Paul, and B. Wachtel. (1998). *Restorative Policing Experiment: The Bethlehem, Pennsylvania, Police Family Group Conferencing Project.* Pipersville, PA: Community Service Foundation.

McCord, Joan. (1978). "A thirty-year follow-up of treatment effects." *American Psychologist* 33:384–89.

———. (1989). "Theory, pseudohistory, and metatheory." In *Advances in Criminological Theory,* vol. 1, ed. W. S. Laufer and F. Adler. New Brunswick, NJ: Transaction.

McCord, Williams, and Jose Sanchez. (1983). "The treatment of deviant children: A twenty-five-year follow-up study." *Crime and Delinquency* 29:238–53.

McCoy, Alfred W. (1991). *The Politics of Heroin: CIA Complicity in the Global Drug Trade.* Brooklyn, NY: Lawrence Hill Books.

McDougall, William. (1908). *An Introduction to Social Psychology.* London: Methuen.

McInerney, Joseph D. (1999). "Genes and behavior: A complex relationship." *Judicature* 83:112–15.

McKay, Henry D. (1960). "Differential association and crime prevention: Problems of utilization." *Social Problems* 8:25–37.

McKiever v. Pennsylvania, 403 U.S. 528, 91 S.Ct. 1976, 29 L.Ed. 2d 6 (1971).

McShane, Marilyn D., and Wesley Krause. (1993). *Community Corrections.* New York: Macmillan.

Mead, George Herbert. (1918). "The psychology of punitive justice." *American Journal of Sociology* 23:586–92.

Mead, Margaret. (1970). *Culture and Commitment: A Study of the Generation Gap.* Garden City, NY: Natural Press/Doubleday.

Mednick, Sarnoff, Patricia Brennan, and Elizabeth Kandel. (1988). "Predispositions to violence." Special edition of *Current Theoretical Perspectives on Aggressive and Antisocial Behavior* 14:25–33.

Mednick, Sarnoff A., William Gabrielli, and Barry Hutchings. (1984). "Genetic influences in criminal convictions: Evidence from an adoption cohort." *Science* 224:891–94.

Mednick, Sarnoff A., Terrie E. Moffitt, and Susan A. Stacks, eds. (1987). *The Causes of Crime: New Biological Approaches.* Cambridge, England: Cambridge University Press.

Megargee, E. I. (1972). *The California Psychological Inventory Handbook.* San Francisco: Jossey-Bass.

———. (1977). "The need for a new classification system." *Criminal Justice and Behavior* 20:355–60.

Megargee, E. I., and Joyce L., Carbonell. (1985). "Predicting prison adjustment with MMPI correctional scale." *Journal of Consulting and Clinical Psychology* 53:874–83.

Meier, Robert F. (1977). "Introduction." In *Theory in Criminology: Contemporary Views,* ed. R. F. Meier. Beverly Hills, CA: Sage.

———. (1989). *Crime and Society.* Boston: Allyn and Bacon.

Meier, Robert F., and Weldon T. Johnson. (1977). "Deterrence as social control: The legal and extralegal production of conformity." *American Sociological Review* 42:292–304.

Menard, Scott, and Delbert Elliott. (1990). "Longitudinal and cross-sectional data collection and analysis in the study of crime and delinquency." *Justice Quarterly* 7:11–55.

Menard, Scott, and Barbara J. Morse. (1984). "A structuralist critique of the IQ–delinquency hypothesis: Theory and evidence." *American Journal of Sociology* 89:1347–78.

———. (1985). "IQ and delinquency: A response to Harry and Minor." *American Journal of Sociology* 91:962–68.

Mercer, Joan. (1994). "A fascination with genetics: Pioneer Fund is at center of debate over research on race and intelligence." *Chronicle of Higher Education,* 7 December:A28–A29.

Merton, Robert K. (1938). "Social structure and anomie." *American Sociological Review* 3:672–82.

———. (1957). *Social Theory and Social Structure.* New York: Free Press.

———. (1968). *Social Theory and Social Structure,* 2d ed. New York: Free Press.

Messerschmidt, James. (1986). *Capitalism, Patriarchy, and Crime: Toward a Socialist Feminist Criminology.* New York: Rowman and Allenheld.

———. (1993). *Masculinities and Crime.* Lanham, MD: Rowman and Allenheld.

Messner, Steven F. (1983). "Regional and racial effects on the urban homicide rate: The subculture of violence revisited." *American Journal of Sociology* 88:997–1007.

Messner, Steven F., and Richard Rosenfeld. (1994). *Crime and the American Dream.* Belmont, CA: Wadsworth.

Michalowski, Raymond L. (1977). "Perspective and paradigm: Structuring criminological thought." In *Theory in Criminology: Contemporary Views,* ed. R. F. Meier. Beverly Hills, CA: Sage.

———. (1985). *Order, Law and Crime: An Introduction to Criminology.* New York: Random House.

Miethe, Terance D., Hong Lu, and Erin Reese. (2000). "Reintegrative shaming and recidivism risks in drug court: Explanations for some unexpected findings." *Crime and Delinquency* 46:522–41.

Miethe, Terance D., and Richard C. McCorkle. (1997). "Gang membership and criminal processing: A test of the 'master status' concept." *Justice Quarterly* 14:407–27.

Miethe, Terance D., Mark C. Stafford, and J. Scott Long. (1987). "Social differentiation in criminal victimization: A test of routine activities/lifestyle theories." *American Sociological Review* 27:243–66.

Mignon, Sylvia I., and William M. Holmes. (1995). "Police responses to mandatory arrest laws." *Crime & Delinquency* 41:430–44.

Miller, Eleanor. (1986). *Street Women.* Philadelphia: Temple University Press.

Miller, Jody. (1998). "Up it up: Gender and the accomplishment of street robbery." *Criminology* 36:37–66.

———. (2001). *One of the Guys: Girls, Gangs and Gender.* New York: Oxford University Press.

Miller, Joshua, and Donald Lyman. (2001). "Structural models of personality and their relations to antisocial behavior: A meta-analytic review." *Criminology* 39:765–98.

Miller, Walter B. (1958). "Lower class culture as a generating milieu of gang delinquency." *Journal of Social Issues* 14:5–19.

Mills, John A. (1998). *Control: A History of Behavioral Psychology.* New York: NYU Press.

Minor, William W. (1977). "A deterrence-control theory of crime." In *Theory in Criminology: Contemporary Views,* ed. R. F. Meier. Beverly Hills, CA: Sage.

Mischel, Walter. (1976). *Introduction to Personality,* 2d ed. New York: Holt, Rinehart and Winston.

Moffitt, Terrie. (1993a). "Adolescence-limited and life-course-persistent anti-social behavior: A developmental taxonomy." *Psychological Review* 100:674–701.

———. (1993b). "The neuropsychology of conduct disorder." *Development and Psychopathology* 5:135–51.

Moffitt, Terrie, Donald Lynam, and Phil Silva. (1994). "Neuropsychological tests predicting persistent male delinquency." *Criminology* 32:277–300.

Moffitt, Terrie E., William F. Gabrielli, Sarnoff A. Mednick, and Fini Schulsinger. (1981). "Socioeconomic status, IQ, and delinquency." *Journal of Abnormal Psychology* 90:152–56.

Moffitt, Terrie E., and Phil Silva. (1988). "IQ and delinquency: A direct test of the differential detection hypothesis." *Journal of Abnormal Behavior* 97:330–33.

Moltich, Matthew. (1937). "Endocrine disturbance in behavior problems." *American Journal of Psychiatry,* March:1179.

Monachesi, Elio (1973). Cesare Beccaria. In Herman Mannheim (ed.), *Pioneers in Criminology,* 2ed, Montclair, NJ: Patterson Smith.

Monaghan, Peter. (1992). "Professor of psychology stokes a controversy on the reliability and repression of memory." *Chronicle of Higher Education,* 23 September:A9–A10.

Mooney, Jayne. (1993). *The Hidden Figure: Domestic Violence in North London.* Enfield, UK: Middlesex University, Centre for Criminology.

Moore, Mark H., and Robert Trojanowicz. (1988). *Policing and the Fear of Crime.* Washington, DC: U.S. Government Printing Office.

Morash, Merry. (1983). "Gangs, groups, and delinquency." *British Journal of Criminology* 23:309–31.

Morash, Merry, and Meda Chesney-Lind. (1991). "A reformulation and partial test of the power control theory of delinquency." *Justice Quarterly* 8:347–78.

Morganthau, Tom. (1994). "IQ: Is it destiny? An angry book ignites a new debate over race, intelligence and class." *Newsweek,* 24 October:53–60.

Moriarty, Laura J., and James E. Williams. (1996). "Examining the relationship between routine activities theory and social disorganization: An analysis of property crime victimization." *American Journal of Criminal Justice* 21:43–59.

Morse, Minna. (1997). "Facing a bumpy history." *Smithsonian* 28(24).

Mos, Leendert P. (1999). "Behaviorism: An ideology of science without vision." *Canadian Journal of History* 34:417–21.

Mosher, Clayton, and John Hagan. (1994). "Constituting class and crime in upper Canada: The sentencing of narcotics offenders, circa 1908–1953." *Social Forces* 72:613–41.

Moyer, Imogene. (1986). "An exploratory study of role distance as a police response to stress." *Journal of Criminal Justice* 14:363–73.

Moynihan, Daniel P. (1969). *Maximum Feasible Misunderstanding: Community*

Action in the War on Poverty. New York: Free Press.

Mueller, C. W. (1983). "Environmental stressors and aggressive behavior." In *Aggression,* vol. 2, ed. R. G. Green and E. I. Donnerstein. New York: Academic Press.

Mueller, Ingo. (1991). *Hitler's Justice: The Courts of the Third Reich.* Cambridge, MA: Harvard University Press.

Murray, C. A. (1976). *The Link between Learning Disabilities and Juvenile Delinquency.* Washington, DC: U.S. Government Printing Office.

Mustaine, Elizabeth Ehrhardt. (1997). "Victimization risks and routine activities: A theoretical examination using a gender-specific and domain-specific model." *American Journal of Criminal Justice* 22:41–70.

Mustaine, Elizabeth Ehrhardt, and Richard Tweksburg. (1998). "Predicting risks of larceny theft victimization: A routine activities analysis using refined lifestyle measures." *Criminology* 36:829–57.

Myers, Daniel J. (1997). "Racial rioting in the 1960s: An event history analysis of local conditions." *American Sociological Review* 62:94–112.

Naffine, N. (1987). *Female Crime: The Construction of Women in Criminology.* Sydney, Australia: Allen and Unwin.

Nagel, Illene. (1983). "The legal/extra-legal controversy: Judicial decision in pretrial release." *Law and Society Review* 17:481–515.

Nagin, Daniel S. (1978). "General deterrence: A review of the empirical evidence." Pp. 95–139 in *Deterrence and Incapacitation: Estimating the Effects of Criminal Sanctions on Crime Rates,* ed. Alfred Blumstein, Jacqueline Cohen, and Daniel S. Nagin. Washington, DC: National Academy Press.

Nagin, Daniel S., and Kenneth Land. (1993). "Age, criminal careers, and population heterogeneity: Specification and estimation of a nonparametric mixed Poisson model." *Criminology* 31:163–89.

National Advisor Commission on Criminal Justice Standards and Goals. (1973). *Corrections.* Washington, DC: U.S. Government Printing Office.

National Institute of Corrections. (1983). *New Generation Jails.* Boulder, CO: Library Information Specialists.

National Institute of Drug Abuse. (1998). "Genetics of drug addiction vulnerability." Washington, DC: National Institute of Drug Abuse.

National Research Council. (1996). *The Evaluation of Forensic DNA Evidence.* Washington, DC: National Institute of Justice.

Nelson, W. Raymond. (1988). "Cost saving in new generation jails: The direct supervision approach." *National Institute of Justice Construction Bulletin.* Washington, DC: U.S. Government Printing Office.

Nettler, Gwynn. (1984). *Explaining Crime,* 3d ed. New York: McGraw-Hill.

Newman, Graeme. (1978). *The Punishment Response.* New York: Pantheon.

Newman, Oscar. (1972). *Defensible Space.* New York: Macmillan.

New York Special Commission on Attica. (1972). *Attica.* New York: Praeger.

Niederhoffer, Arthur. (1969). *Behind the Shield: The Police in Urban Society.* Garden City, NY: Anchor.

Nye, F. Ivan. (1958). *Family Relationships and Delinquent Behavior.* New York: Wiley.

Oakley, Ann. (2000). "A historical perspective on the use of randomized trials in social science settings." *Crime and Delinquency* 46:315–29.

Obeidallah, Dawn A., and Felton Earls. (1999). "Adolescent girls: The role of depression in the development of delinquency." *Research Preview.* Washington, DC: National Institute of Justice, July.

Olds, David, Charles R. Henderson, Jr., Robert Cole, John Eckenrode, Harriet Kitzman, Dennis Luckey, Lisa Pettit, Kimberly Sidora, Pamela Morris, and Jane Powers. (1998). "Long-term effects of nursing home visitation on children's criminal and antisocial behavior: 15-year follow-up of a randomized controlled trial." *Journal of the American Medical Association* 280:1238–44.

Olweus, Dan, Ake Mattson, Daisy Schalling, and Hans Low. (1980). "Testosterone, aggression, physical and personality dimensions in normal adolescent males." *Psychosomatic Medecine* 42:253–69.

Omer, Harm, and Perry London. (1988). "Metamorphosis in psychotherapy: End of the systems era." *Psychotherapy* 25:171–80.

Osgood, D. Wayne, Janet K. Wilson, Patrick M. O'Malley, Jerald G. Bachman, and Lloyd D. Johnston. (1996). "Routine activities and individual deviant behavior." *American Sociological Review* 61:635–55.

Pagani, Linda, Richard E. Tremblay, Frank Vitaro, and Sophie Parent. (1998). "Does preschool help prevent delinquency in boys with a history of perinatal complications?" *Criminology* 36:245–68.

Palarma, Frances, Francis T. Cullen, and Joanne C. Gertsen. (1986). "The effects of police and mental health intervention on juvenile deviance: Specifying contingencies in the impact of formal reaction." *Journal of Health and Social Behavior* 27:90–105.

Palmer, Ted B., Marvin Bohnstedt, and Roy Lewis. (1978). *The Evaluation of Juvenile Diversion Projects: Final Projects.* Sacramento: Division of Research, California Youth Authority.

Parker, Robert Nash. (1989). "Poverty, subculture of violence and type of homicide." *Social Forces* 67:983–1007.

Passas, Nikos. (1990). "Anomie and corporate deviance." *Contemporary Crises* 14:157–78.

Passingham, R. E. (1972). "Crime and personality: A review of Eysenck's theory." In *Biological Bases of Individual Behavior,* ed. V. D. Nebylitsyn and J. A. Gray. New York: Academic.

Pate, Antony M., and Edwin E. Hamilton. (1992). "Formal and informal deterrents to domestic violence: The Dade County spouse assault experiment." *American Sociological Review* 57:691–97.

Paternoster, Raymond. (1987). "The deterrent effect of perceived severity of punishment: A review of the evidence and issues." *Justice Quarterly* 4:173–217.

———. (1989a). "Absolute and restrictive deterrence in a panel of youth: Explaining the onset, persistence/desistance,

and frequent offending." *Social Problems* 36:289–309.

———. (1989b). "Decision to participate in and desist from four types of common delinquency: Deterrence and the rational choice perspective." *Law and Society Review* 23:7–40.

Paternoster, Raymond, and Ronet Bachman. (2001). *Explaining Criminals and Crime: Essays in Contemporary Criminological Theory.* Los Angeles: Roxbury.

Paternoster, Raymond, and Robert Brame. (1998). "The structural similarity of processes for generating criminal and analogous behaviors." *Criminology* 36:633–69.

———. (2000). "On the associations between self-control, crime, and analogous behavior." *Criminology* 38:971–82.

Paternoster, Raymond, and LeeAnn Iovanni. (1989). "The labeling perspective and delinquency: An elaboration of the theory and an assessment of the evidence." *Justice Quarterly* 6:359–94.

Patterson, Gerald. (1982). *Coercive Family Process: A Social Learning Approach,* vol. 3. Eugene, OR: Castalia.

Patterson, Gerald, John B. Reid, Richard R. Jones, and Robert E. Conger. (1975). *A Social Learning Approach to Family Intervention,* vol. 1: *Families with Aggressive Children.* Eugene, OR: Castalia.

Pearl, David, Lorraine Bouthilet, and Joyce B. Lazar, eds. (1982). *Television and Behavior: Ten Years of Scientific Progress and Implications for the Eighties,* vols. 1 and 2. Washington, DC: U.S. Government Printing Office.

Penry v. Lynaugh, 109 S.Ct. 2934 (1989).

Peers, William R. (1979). *My Lai Inquiry.* New York: Norton.

Pepinsky, Harold, and Paul Jesilow. (1984). *Myths That Cause Crime.* Cabin John, MD: Seven Locks.

Peters, Michael, David Thomas, and Christopher Zanberlan. (1997). *Boot Camps for Juvenile Offenders.* Washington, DC: Office of Juvenile Justice and Delinquency Prevention.

Peterson, Ruth D., Lauren J. Krivo, and Mark A. Harris. (2000). "Disadvantage and neighborhood violent crime: Do local institutions matter?" *Journal of Research in Crime and Delinquency* 37:31–63.

Pickens, Roy W., and Dace S. Svikis. (1988). "Genetic vulnerability to drug use." In *Biological Vulnerability to Drug Use,* ed. R. W. Pickens and D. S. Svikis. Rockville, MD: National Institute of Drug Abuse.

Piliavin, Irving, Rosemary Gartner, Craig Thornton, and Ross L. Matsueda. (1986). "Crime, deterrence, and rational choice." *American Sociological Review* 51:101–19.

Piquero, Alex R., and Matthew W. Hickman. (1999). "An empirical test of Tittle's control balance theory." *Criminology* 37:319–41.

———. (2001). "The rational choice implications of control balance theory." Pp. 85–108 in *Rational Choice and Criminal Behavior,* ed. Alex R. Piquero and Stephen Tibbetts. New York: Garland.

Piquero, Alex R., Randall MacIntosh, and Matthew Hickman. (2000). "Does self-control affect survey response? Applying exploratory, confirmatory, and item response theory analysis to Grasmick et al.'s self-control scale." *Criminology* 38:897–928.

———. (2001). "Applying Rasch modeling to the validity of a control balance scale." *Journal of Criminal Justice* 29:493–505.

Piquero, Alex R., and Andre B. Rosay. (1998). "The reliability and validity of Grasmick, et al.'s self-control scale: A comment on Longshore, et al." *Criminology* 36:157–73.

Piven, Frances Fox, and Richard A. Cloward. (1971). *Regulating the Poor: The Functions of Public Welfare.* New York: Vintage.

Plomin, R. (1989). "Environment and genes: Determinants of behavior." *American Psychologist* 44:105–11.

Pogrebin, Mark, and Eric D. Poole. (1988). "Humor in the briefing room: A study of the strategic uses of humor among police." *Journal of Contemporary Ethnography* 17:183–210.

Polk, Kenneth. (1991). "Book review—*A General Theory of Crime.*" *Crime and Delinquency* 37:575–79.

Pollack, Otto. (1950). *The Criminality of Women.* Philadelphia: University of Pennsylvania Press.

Pollock, Joycelyn M. (1994). *Ethics in Crime and Justice: Dilemmas and Decisions,* 2d ed. Belmont, CA: Wadsworth.

Pollock-Byrne, Joycelyn M. (1990). *Women, Prison and Crime.* Pacific Grove, CA: Brooks/Cole.

Powers, Edwin, and Helen Witmer. (1951). *An Experiment in the Prevention of Juvenile Delinquency: The Cambridge–Somerville Youth Study.* New York: Columbia University Press.

Poyner, Barry. (1983). *Design against Crime: Beyond Defensible Space.* London: Butterworth.

Pranis, Kay. (1997). "Peacemaking circles." *Corrections Today,* December:72, 74, 76, 122.

Pratt, Travis C., and Francis T. Cullen. (2000). "The empirical status of Gottfredson and Hirschi's general theory of crime: A meta-analysis." *Criminology* 38:931–64.

Presidential Commission on Law Enforcement and Administration of Justice. (1967). *The Challenge of Crime in a Free Society.* Washington, DC: U.S. Government Printing Office.

Price, W. H., J. A. Strong, P. B. Whatmore, and W. R. McClemont. (1966). "Criminal patients with XYY sex-chromosome complement." *Lancet* 1:565–66.

Project on Human Development in Chicago Neighborhoods. (n.d.). Chicago: Project on Human Development.

Purcell, Noreen, L. Thomas Winfree, Jr., and G. Larry Mays. (1994). "DNA (deoxyribonucleic acid) evidence and criminal trials: An exploratory survey of factors associated with the use of 'genetic fingerprinting' in felony prosecutions." *Journal of Criminal Justice* 22:145–57.

Quadragno, Jill S., and Robert J. Antonio. (1975). "Labeling theory as an over-socialized conception of man: The case of mental illness." *Sociology and Social Research* 60:33–45.

Quinney, Richard. (1973). *Critique of Legal Order: Crime Control in Capitalist Society.* Boston: Little, Brown.

———. (1980). *Class, State and Crime,* 2d ed. New York: Longman.

———. (1991). "The way of peace: On crime, suffering, and service." In *Criminology as Peacemaking,* ed. Harold Pepinsky and Richard Quinney. Bloomington: Indiana University Press.

Rafter, Nicole Hahn. (1985). *Partial Justice: Women in State Prisons: 1800–1935.* Boston: Northeastern University Press.

———. (1992). "Criminal anthropology in the United States." *Criminology* 30:525–45.

Raine, A. (1993). "The psychopathology of crime: Criminal behavior as a clinical disorder." San Diego, CA: Academic Press.

Raine, A., P. Brennan, and S. A. Mednick. (1997). "Interaction between birth complications and early maternal rejection in predisposing individuals to adult violence: Specificity to serious, early-onset violence." *American Journal of Psychiatry* 154:1265–71

Raine, A., M. O'Brien, N. Smiley, A. S. Scerbo, and C. J. Chan (1990). "Reduced lateralization in verbal dichotic listening in adolescent psychopaths." *Journal of Abnormal Psychiatry* 99:272–77.

Raine, A., P. H. Venables, and M. Williams. (1990). "Relationship between central and autonomic measures of arousal at age 15 years and criminality at age 25 years." *Archives of General Psychiatry* 47:1003–07.

Raine, Adrian, Todd Lencz, Susan Bihrle, Lori LaCasse, and Patrick Colletti. (2000). "Reduced prefrontal gray matter volume and reduced autonomic activity in antisocial personality disorder." *Archives of General Psychiatry* 57:119–27.

Rainwater, Lee. (1966). "Fear and the home-as-haven in the lower class." *Journal of the American Institute of Planners* 11:35–47.

Rankin, Joseph H., and L. Edward Wells. (1990). "The effects of parental attachments and direct control on delinquency." *Journal of Research in Crime and Delinquency* 27:140–65.

Rasche, Christine. (1974). "The female offender as an object of criminological research." *Criminal Justice and Behavior* 1:301–20.

Reckless, Walter C. (1961). "A new theory of delinquency and crime." *Federal Probation* 25:4–46.

Reed, Gary E., and Peter Cleary Yeager. (1996). "Organizational offending and neoclassical criminology: Challenging the reach of a general theory of crime." *Criminology* 34:357–82.

Regoli, Robert M. (1976). "An empirical assessment of Niederhoffer's scale." *Journal of Criminal Justice* 4:231–41.

Reiff, Philip, ed. (1963). *Freud, Therapy and Techniques.* New York: Crowell-Collier.

Reilly, Philip R. (1991). *Surgical Solution: A History of Involuntary Sterilization in the United States.* Baltimore, MD: Johns Hopkins University Press.

Reiman, Jeffrey. (2001). *The Rich Get Richer and the Poor Get Prison.* Boston: Allyn and Bacon.

Reiss, Albert J. (1951). "Delinquency and the failure of personal and social controls." *American Sociological Review* 16:196–207.

Reiss, Albert J., and A. Lewis Rhodes. (1964). "An empirical test of differential association theory." *Journal of Research in Crime and Delinquency* 1:5–18.

Reiss, Albert J., and J. Roth. (1993). *Understanding and Preventing Violence.* Washington, DC: National Academy Press.

Reno, Janet. (1999). "Message from the Attorney General." In *Postconviction DNA Testing: Recommendations for Handling Requests.* Washington, DC: National Institute of Justice.

Ressler, Robert K., Ann W. Burgess, and John E. Douglas. (1988). *Sexual Homicide: Patterns and Motives.* Lexington, MA: Lexington-Heath.

Riechers, Lisa, and Roy R. Roberg. (1990). "Community policing: A critical review of underlying assumptions." *Journal of Police Science and Administration* 17:105–14.

Rilling, Mark. (2000). "How the challenge of explaining learning influenced the origins and development of John B. Watson's behaviorism." *American Journal of Psychology* 113:275–301.

Robbins, Michael S., and José Szapocnik. (2000). "Brief strategic family therapy." *OJJDP Juvenile Justice Bulletin,* April. NCJ 179285.

Roberg, Roy R., and Jack Kuykendall. (1993). *Police and Society*. Belmont, CA: Wadsworth.

Robins, Lee N. (1966). *Deviant Children Grow Up: A Sociological and Psychiatric Study of Sociopathic Personality*. Baltimore: Williams and Wilkins.

Robison, Sophia M. (1936). *Can Delinquency Be Measured?* New York: Columbia University Press.

Rodriguez, Orlando, and David Weisburd. (1991). "The integrated social control model and ethnicity: The case of Puerto Rican-American delinquency." *Criminal Justice and Behavior* 18:464–79.

Roebuck, Julian, and Stanley C. Weeber. (1978). *Political Crime in the United States: Analyzing Crime by and against Government*. New York: Praeger.

Rokeach, Milton. (1956). "Political and religious dogmatism: An alternate of the authoritarian personality." *Psychological Monographs* 70:1–43.

Rokeach, Milton, Martin G. Miller, and John A. Snyder. (1977). "A value gap between the police and the policed." *Journal of Social Issues* 27:155–71.

Roncek, Dennis W. (1991). "Dangerous places: Crime and residential environment." *Social Forces* 60:74–96.

Roncek, Dennis, and Ralph Bell. (1981). "Bars, blocks, and crimes." *Journal of Environmental Systems* 11:35–47.

Roncek, Dennis, and Pamela Maier. (1992). "Bars, blocks, and crimes revisited: Linking the theory of routine activities to the empiricism of 'hot spots.'" *Criminology* 29:725–50.

Roncek, Dennis, and Mitchell A. Pravatiner. (1989). "Additional evidence that taverns enhance nearby crime." *Sociology and Social Research* 73:185–88.

Rose, Stephen. (1972). *The Betrayal of the Poor: The Transformation of Community Action*. Cambridge, MA: Schenkman.

Rosenau, Pauline Marie. (1992). *Postmodernism and the Social Sciences*. Princeton, NJ: Princeton University Press.

Rosenbaum, Jill L. (1987). "Social control, gender, and delinquency: An analysis of drug, property, and violent offenders." *Justice Quarterly* 4:117–32.

Rosenbaum, Jill L., and James R. Lasley. (1990). "School, community context, and delinquency: Rethinking the gender gap." *Justice Quarterly* 7:493–513.

Rosencrance, John. (1987). "A typology of presentence probation officers." *International Journal of Offender Therapy and Contemporary Criminology* 31:163–77.

Roshier, Bob. (1989). *Controlling Crime: The Classical Perspective in Criminology*. Chicago: Lyceum.

Ross, H. Lawrence. (1982). *Deterring the Drinking Driver: Legal Policy and Social Control*. Lexington, MA: Lexington Books.

Roth, Jerome A., Xandra O. Breakefield, and Carmela M. Castiglione. (1976). "Monoamine oxidase and catechol-o-methyltransferase activities in cultured human skin fiboblast." *Life Sciences* 19:1705–10.

Rousseau, Jean-Jacques. (1954)[1762]. *The Social Contract*. Chicago: Regenery.

Rowe, David C. (1983). "Biomedical genetic models of self-reported delinquent behavior: A twin study." *Behavior Genetics* 13:473–89.

———. (1990). "Inherited dispositions toward learning delinquent and criminal behavior: New evidence." In *Crime in Biological, Social, and Moral Contexts*, ed. L. Ellis and H. Hoffman. Westport, CT: Praeger.

Rowe, David C., and B. L. Gulley. (1992). "Sibling effects on substance use and delinquency." *Criminology* 30:217–23.

Rowe, David C., and D. Wayne Osgood. (1984). "Heredity and sociological theories of delinquency: A reconsideration." *American Sociological Review* 49:526–40.

Rubin, R. T. (1987). "The neuroendocrinology and neurochemistry of antisocial behavior. In *The Causes of Crime: New Biological Approaches*, ed. S. A. Mednick, T. E. Moffitt, and S. A. Slack. New York: Cambridge University Press.

Rushton, J. P. (1996). "Self-report delinquency and violence in adult twins." *Psychiatric Genetics* 6:87–89.

Sagatun, Inger, Loretta McCollum, and Leonard P. Edwards. (1985). "The effect of transfers from juvenile to criminal court: A loglinear analysis." *Journal of Crime and Justice* 8:65–92.

Sampson, Robert J. (1993). "Linking time and place: Dynamic contextualism in the future of criminological inquiry." *Journal of Research in Crime and Delinquency* 30:426–44.

———. (2001). "Foreward." In *Life-Course Criminology: Contemporary and Classic Readings,* ed. Alex Piquero and Paul Mazerolle. Belmont, CA: Wadsworth.

Sampson, Robert J., and Dawn Jeglum Bartusch. (1999). "Attitudes toward crime, police, and the law: Individual and neighborhood differences." *National Institute of Justice Research Preview.* Washington, DC: U.S. Department of Justice.

Sampson, Robert J., and W. Byron Groves. (1989). "Community structure and crime: Testing social disorganization theory." *American Journal of Sociology* 94:774–802.

Sampson, Robert J., and John Laub. (1993). *Crime in the Making: Pathways and Turning Points through Life.* Cambridge, MA: Harvard University Press.

Sampson, Robert J., and Stephen W. Raudenbush. (2001). "Disorder in urban neighborhoods—Does it lead to crime?" *Research in Brief.* Washington, DC: National Institute of Justice, February.

Sarbin, Theodore R., and Jeffrey E. Miller. (1970). "Demonism revisited: The XYY chromosome anomaly." *Issues of Criminology* 5:195–207.

Sarri, R. C. (1986). "Gender and race differences in criminal justice processing." *Women's Studies International Forum* 9:89–99.

Savelsberg, Joachim. J. (1996). "Review: *Control Balance: Toward a General Theory of Deviance.*" *American Journal of Sociology* 26:620–22.

———. (1999). "Human nature and social control in complex society: A critique of Charles Tittle's *Control Balance.*" *Theoretical Criminology* 3:331–38.

Schafer, Stephen. (1969). *Theories in Criminology: Past and Present Philosophies of the Crime Problem.* New York: Random House.

Schall v. Martin, 467 U.S. 253 (1984).

Scheff, Thomas J. (1988). "Shame and conformity: The deference–emotion system." *American Sociological Review* 53:395–406.

Schmidt, Jannell, and Lawrence Sherman. (1993). "Does arrest deter domestic violence?" *American Behavioral Scientist* 36:601–10.

———. (1996). "Does arrest deter domestic violence?" In *Do Arrests and Restraining Orders Work?* ed. Eve Buzawa and Carl Buzawa. Thousand Oaks, CA: Sage.

Schur, Edwin. (1968). *Law and Society: A Sociological View.* New York: Random House.

———. (1971). *Labeling Deviant Behavior: Its Sociological Implications.* New York: Harper and Row.

———. (1973). *Radical Non-Intervention: Rethinking the Delinquency Problem.* Englewood Cliffs, NJ: Prentice-Hall.

Schwartz, David D., and Jerome Skolnick. (1962). "Two studies of legal stigma." *Social Problems* 10:133–42.

Schwartz, Ira. (1991). "Removing juveniles from adult jails: The unfinished agenda." Pp. 216–26 in *American Jails: Public Policy Issues,* ed. Joel A. Thompson and G. Larry Mays. Chicago: Nelson-Hall.

Schwartz, M. D. (1991). "The future of critical criminology." In *New Directions in Critical Criminology,* ed. B. MacLean and D. Milovanovic. Vancouver, BC: Collective Press.

Schwendinger, Julia, and Herman Schwendinger. (1983). *Rape and Inequality.* New York: Praeger.

Scott, J. P. (1987). "Review essay: On genetics and criminal behavior." *Social Biology* 34:256–65.

Seale, Bobby. (1968). *Seize the Time.* New York: Random House/Vintage.

Sellers, Christine S. (1999). "Self-control and intimate violence: An examination of the scope and specification of the general theory of crime." *Criminology* 37:375–404.

Sellers, Christine S., John Cochran, and L. Thomas Winfree, Jr. (Forthcoming). "A social learning theory of courtship violence: An empirical test." In *Advances in Criminological Theory: Social Learning Theory,* ed. Ronald L. Akers and Gary Jensen. Chicago: University of Chicago Press.

Sellers, Christine S., Travis C. Pratt, L. Thomas Winfree, Jr., and Francis T. Cullen. (2000). "The empirical status of social learning theory: A meta-analysis." Paper presented at the annual meeting of the American Society of Criminology, San Francisco.

Sellers, Christine S., and L. Thomas Winfree, Jr. (1990). "Differential associations and definitions: A panel study of youthful drinking behavior." *International Journal of the Addictions* 25:755–71.

Sellers, Christine S., L. Thomas Winfree, Jr., and Curt T. Griffiths. (1993). "Legal attitudes, permissive norm qualities, and substance use: A comparison of American Indians and non-Indian youth." *Journal of Drug Issues* 23:493–513.

Sellin, Thorsten. (1938). *Culture Conflict and Crime.* New York: Social Science Research Council.

Shah, Saleem A., and Loren H. Roth. (1974). "Biological and psychophysiological factors in criminality." In *Handbook of Criminology,* ed. D. Glaser. Chicago: Rand McNally.

Sharpe, James. (1997). *Instruments of Darkness, Witchcraft in England 1550–1750.* Oxford, UK: Oxford University Press.

Shaw, Clifford R. (1930). *The Jack-Roller: A Delinquent Boy's Own Story.* Philadelphia: Saifer.

———. (1938). *Brothers in Crime.* Philadelphia: Saifer.

Shaw, Clifford R., and Henry D. McKay. (1942). *Juvenile Delinquency and Urban Areas: A Study of Rates of Delinquency in Relation to Different Characteristics of Local Communities in American Cities.* Chicago: University of Chicago Press.

———. (1972). *Juvenile Delinquency and Urban Areas: A Study of Rates of Delinquency in Relation to Different Characteristics of Local Communities in American Cities,* rev. ed. Chicago: University of Chicago Press.

Sheldon, Randall G., John A. Horvath, and Sharon Tracey. (1989). "Do status offenders get worse? Some clarification on the question of escalation." *Crime and Delinquency* 32:202–16.

Sheldon, William. (1949). *Varieties of Delinquent Youth.* New York: Harper and Row.

Shelley, Louise. (1981). *Crime and Modernization: The Impact of Industrialization and Urbanization on Crime.* Carbondale: Southern Illinois University Press.

Sherman, Lawrence W. (1993). "Defiance, deterrence, and irrelevance: A theory of the criminal sanction." *Journal of Research in Crime and Delinquency* 30:445–73.

Sherman, Lawrence W., and Richard Berk. (1984a). The Minneapolis Domestic Violence Experiment." *Police Foundation Reports* 1:10–18.

———. (1984b). "The specific deterrent effects of arrest for domestic assault." *American Sociological Review* 49:261–72.

Sherman, Lawrence W., Patrick R. Gartin, and Michael E. Bueger. (1989). "Hot spots of predatory crime." *Criminology* 27:27–55.

Sherman, Lawrence W., Janell D. Schmidt, Douglas Smith, Patrick Gartin, Elizabeth G. Cohen, D. J. Collins, and A. R. Bacich. (1992). "The variable effects of arrest on criminal careers: The Milwaukee domestic violence experiment." *Journal of Criminal Law and Criminology* 83:137–69.

Sherman, Lawrence W., and Douglas Smith, with Jannell D. Schmidt and Dennis P. Rogan. (1992). "Crime, punishment, and stake in conformity: Legal and informal control of domestic violence." *American Sociological Review* 57:680–90.

Sherman, Lawrence W., Heather Strang, G. C. Barnes, et al. (1998). "Experiments in restorative policing: A progress report to the National Police Research Unit." Canberra: Australian National University.

Shockley, W. (1967). "A 'try the simplest cases' approach to the heredity–poverty–crime problem." *Proceedings of the National Academy of Sciences* 57:1767–74.

Short, James F., Jr. (1957). "Differential association and delinquency." *Social Problems* 4:233–39.

———. (1958). "Differential association with delinquent friends and delinquent behavior." *Pacific Sociological Review* 1:20–25.

———. (1960). "Differential association as a hypothesis: Problems of empirical testing." *Social Problems* 8:14–25.

Short, James F., Jr., and Fred L. Strodtbeck. (1965). *Group Processes and Gang Delin-*

quency. Chicago: University of Chicago Press.

Short, James F., Jr., Margaret Z. Zahn, and David P. Farrington. (2000). "Experimental research in criminal justice settings: Is there a role for scholarly scientists?" *Crime and Delinquency* 46:295–98.

Shover, Neal. (1985). *Aging Criminal.* Beverly Hills, CA: Sage.

Siegel, Larry. (1992) *Criminology,* 4th ed. St. Paul, MN: West.

Sigurdson, Herbert R. (1985). *The Manhattan House of Detention: A Study of Podular Direct Supervision.* Washington, DC: National Institute of Corrections.

Silberman, Matthew. (1976). "Toward a theory of criminal deterrence." *American Sociological Review* 41:442–61.

Simmel, Georg. (1955). *Conflict.* Trans. K. H. Wolff. Glencoe, IL: Free Press.

Simon, Julian L. (1969). *Basic Research Methods in Social Science: The Art of Empirical Investigation.* New York: Random House.

Simon, Rita James. (1967). *The Jury and the Defense of Insanity.* Boston: Little, Brown.

———. (1975a). *Women and Crime.* Lexington, MA: Heath.

———. (1975b). *The Contemporary Woman and Crime.* Washington, DC: National Institute of Mental Health.

Simons, Ronald L., and Phyllis A. Gray. (1989). "Perceived blocked opportunity as an explanation of delinquency among lower-class black males: A research note." *Journal of Research in Crime and Delinquency* 26:90–101.

Simons, Ronald L., Christine Johnson, Rand D. Conger, and Glen Elder, Jr. (1998). "A test of latent trait versus life-course perspectives on the stability of adolescent antisocial behavior." *Criminology* 36:217–44.

Simons, Ronald L., Martin G. Miller, and Stephen M. Aigner. (1980). "Contemporary theories of deviance and female delinquency: An empirical test." *Journal of Research in Crime and Delinquency* 17:42–57.

Simpson, Sally. (1989). "Feminist theory, crime and justice." *Criminology* 27:605–27.

Singer, Simon I., and Murray Levine. (1988). "Power-control theory, gender, and delinquency: A partial replication with additional evidence on the effects of peers." *Criminology* 26:627–48.

Skinner, B. F. (1974). *About Behaviorism.* New York: Knopf.

Skinner, William F., and Anne M. Fream. (1997). "A social learning theory analysis of computer crime among college students." *Journal of Research in Crime and Delinquency.* 34:495–518.

Skogan, Wesley. (1990). *Disorder and Decline: Crime and the Spiral of Decay in American Neighborhoods.* New York: Free Press.

Skogan, Wesley, and Mary Ann Wycoff. (1986). "Storefront police offices: The Houston field test." In *Community Crime Prevention: Does It Work?* ed. D. Rosenbaum. Beverly Hills, CA: Sage.

Skolnick, Jerome. (1966). *Justice without Trial: Law Enforcement in a Democratic Society.* New York: Wiley.

Smart, Francis. (1970). *Neurosis and Crime.* New York: Barnes and Noble.

Smith, Douglas, and Raymond Paternoster. (1990). "Formal processing and future delinquency: Deviance amplification as selection artifact." *Law and Society Review* 24:1109–31.

Smith, Douglas, Christy A. Visher, and Laura Davidson. (1984). "Equity and discretionary justice: The influences of race on police arrest decisions." *Journal of Criminal Law and Criminology* 75:234–49.

Smith, John L. (2001). "The legacy of behaviorism: Historical appraisal versus contemporary critique." *American Journal of Psychology,* Winter:654–58.

Smith, Michael E. (2001). "What future for 'public safety' and 'restorative justice' in community corrections?" *Sentencing & Corrections: Issues for the 21st Century,* no. 11. Washington, DC: U.S. Office of Justice Programs.

Smith, Richard A. (1961a). "The incredible electrical conspiracy." *Fortune,* April:132-37, 170, 175–76, 179–80.

———. (1961b). "The incredible electrical conspiracy." *Fortune,* May:161–64, 210, 212, 217–18, 221–24.

Snarr, Richard W., and Bruce I. Wolford. (1985). *Introduction to Corrections.* Dubuque, IA: Brown.

Sofair, A. N., and L. C. Kaldjian. (2000). "Eugenic sterilization and a qualified Nazi analogy: The United States and Germany, 1930–1945." *Annals of Internal Medicine* 132:312–19.

Solzhenitsyn, Alexander. (1974). *The Gulag Archipelago, 1918–1956.* New York: Harper and Row.

Spencer, Herbert. (1961)[1864]. *The Study of Sociology.* Ann Arbor: University of Michigan Press.

Spradley, James P. (1970). *You Owe Yourself a Drink.* Boston: Little, Brown.

Srole, Leo. (1956). "Social integration and certain corollaries: An exploratory study." *American Sociological Review* 52:709–16.

Stack, Steven. (1987). "The effect of temporary residences on burglary: A test of criminal opportunity theory." *American Journal of Criminal Justice* 19:197–214.

Stafford, Mark C., and Mark Warr. (1993). "A reconceptualization of general and specific deterrence." *Journal of Crime and Delinquency* 30:123–35.

Stanfield, Robert E. (1966). "The interaction of family variables and gang variables in the aetiology of delinquency." *Social Problems* 13:311–417.

Stanford v. Kentucky, 429. U.S. 361 (1989).

Stark, Rodney. (1987). "Deviant places: A theory of the ecology of crime." *Criminology* 25:841–62.

State v. Soto-Fong, 187 Ariz. 186, 928 P.2d 610 (1996).

Steadman, Henry J. (1972). "The psychiatrist as a conservative agent of social control." *Social Problems* 20:263–71.

Steadman, Henry J. (2000). "Survey of DNA crime laboratories, 1998." U.S. Bureau of Justice Statistics Special Report. NCJ 179104.

———. (2002). "Survey of DNA crime laboratories, 2000." U.S. Bureau of Justice Statistics Special Report. NCJ 191191.

Steffensmeier, Darrell. (1978). "Crime and contemporary women: An analysis of changing levels of female property crime, 1960–1975." *Social Forces* 57:566–84.

———. (1980). "Sex differences in patterns of adult crime, 1965–1977." *Social Forces* 58:1080–90.

———. (1983a). "Organizational properties and sex integration in the underworld: Building a sociological theory of sex differences in crime." *Social Forces* 61:1010–32.

———. (1983b). "Flawed arrest 'rates' and overlooked reliability problems in UCR arrest statistics: A thought on Wilson's 'The masculinity of violent crime—Some second thoughts.'" *Journal of Criminal Justice* 11:167–71.

———. (1986). *The Fence: In the Shadow of Two Worlds.* Totowa, NJ: Rowman and Littlefield.

———. (1989). "On the causes of white collar crime: An assessment of Hirschi and Gottfredson's claims." *Criminology* 27:345–50.

Steffensmeier, Darrell, and M. J. Cobb. (1981). "Sex differences in urban arrest patterns, 1934–1979." *Social Problems* 29:37–50.

Steffensmeier, Darrell, and Dana Haynie. (2000). "Gender, structural disadvantage, and urban crime: A test and elaboration of power-control theory." *Criminology* 38:403–38.

Steffensmeier, Darrell, and Renee N. Steffensmeier. (1980). "Trends in female delinquency: An examination of arrest, juvenile court, self-report, and field data." *Criminology* 18:62–85.

Sternberg, Robert J. (1985). *Beyond IQ: A Triarchic Theory.* New York: Cambridge University Press.

Stevenson, J., and P. Graham. (1988). "Behavioral deviance in 13-year-old twins: kAn item analysis." *Journal of American Academy of Child and Adolescent Psychiatry* 27:791–97.

Stoddard, Ellwyn R. (1968). "The informal 'code' of police deviancy: A group approach to 'blue-coat crime.'" *Journal of Criminal Law, Criminology, and Police Science* 59:201–13.

Strawbridge, Peter, and Deidre Strawbridge. (1990). *A Networking Guide to Recruitment, Selection and Probationary Training of Police Officers in Major Police Depart-*

ments of the United States of America. London: New Scotland Yard.

Sullivan, Peggy S. (1989). "Minority officers: Current issues." In *Critical Issues in Policing: Contemporary Issues,* ed. R. G. Dunham and G. P. Alpert. Prospect Heights, IL: Waveland Press.

Sullivan, Richard F. (1973). "The political economics of crime: An introduction to the literature." *Crime and Delinquency* 19:138–49.

Sumner, William Graham. (1906). *Folkways: A Sudy of the Sociological Importance of Usages, Manners, Customs, Mores, and Morals.* Boston: Ginn.

Sutherland, Edwin H. (1929). "Crime and conflict process." *Journal of Juvenile Research* 13:38–48.

———. (1947). *Principles of Criminology.* Philadelphia: Lippincott.

———. (1949). *White Collar Crime.* New York: Holt, Rinehart and Winston.

———. (1951). "Mental deficiency and crime." Pp. 357–375 in *Social Attitudes,* ed. Kimball Young. New York: Holt.

———. (1973). *On Analyzing Crime,* ed. K. Schuessler. Chicago: University of Chicago Press.

Sutherland, Edwin H., and Donald R. Cressey. (1974). *Criminology,* 9th ed. Philadelphia: Lippincott.

Suttles, Gerald. (1968). *The Social Order of the Slum: Ethnicity and Territory.* Chicago: University of Chicago Press.

Swanson, C., L. Territo, and R. W. Taylor. (1998). *Police Administration: Structure, Processes, and Behavior.* Upper Saddle River, NJ: Prentice-Hall.

Swigert, Victoria Lynn, and Ronald A. Farrell. (1976). *Murder, Inequality, and the Law.* Lexington, MA: Lexington Books/Heath.

Sykes, Gresham, and Francis T. Cullen. (1992). *Criminology,* 2d ed. New York: Harcourt Brace Jovanovich.

Sykes, Gresham, and David Matza. (1957). "Techniques of neutralization: A theory of delinquency." *American Journal of Sociology* 22:664–70.

Sykes, Gresham, and Sheldon L. Messinger. (1960). "The inmate social system." In *Theoretical Studies in the Social Organization of the Prison,* ed. G. N. Grosser, R.

McCleary, L. E. Ohlin, and S. L. Messinger. New York: Social Science Research Council.

Tannenbaum, Frank (1938). *Crime and the Community.* New York: Ginn.

Tappan, Paul. (1960). *Crime, Justice and Correction.* New York: McGraw-Hill.

Taxman, Faye S., and Alex Piquero. (1998). "On preventing drunk driving recidivism: An examination of rehabilitation and punishment approaches." *Journal of Criminal Justice* 26:129–43.

Taylor, Ian, Paul Walton, and Jock Young. (1973). *The New Criminology: For a Social Theory of Deviance.* New York: Harper and Row.

Taylor, Ralph B., and Jeanette Covington. (1988). "Neighborhood changes in ecology and violence." *Criminology* 26:553–89.

Taylor, Ralph B., and Stephen D. Gottfredson. (1986). "Environmental design, crime, and prevention: An examination of community dynamics." In *Communities and Crime,* ed. A. J. Reiss and M. Tonry. Chicago: University of Chicago Press.

Taylor, Ralph B., Stephen D. Gottfredson, and Sidney Brower. (1984). "Block crime and fear: Defensive space, local ties, and territorial functioning." *Journal of Research in Crime and Delinquency* 21:303–31.

Tennenbaum, David J. (1977). "Personality and criminality: A summary and implications of the literature." *Journal of Criminal Justice* 5:225–35.

Terman, Lewis M. (1906). "Genius and stupidity: A study of some of the intellectual process of seven 'bright' and seven 'stupid' boys." *Pedagogical Seminary* 13:307–72.

Thomas, Charles W. (1970). "Toward a more inclusive model of the inmate contraculture." *Criminology* 8:251–62.

Thomas, Charles W., and Jeffrey M. Hyman. (1978). "Compliance theory, control theory, and juvenile delinquency." In *Crime, Law and Sanctions: Theoretical Perspectives,* ed. M. D. Krohn and R. L. Akers. Beverly Hills, CA: Sage.

Thomas, W. I., and Florian Znaniecki. (1918). *The Polish Peasant in Europe and*

America, vol. 1. Chicago: University of Chicago Press.

Thomas, W. I., and Dorothy S. Thomas. (1928). *The Child in America.* New York: Knopf.

Thornberry, Terence P. (1989). "Reflections on the advantages and disadvantages of theoretical integration: In *Theoretical Integration in the Study of Deviance and Crime: Problems and Prospects,* ed. S. F. Messner, M. D. Krohn, and A. E. Liska. Albany: SUNY Press.

Thornberry, Terence P., Marvin D. Krohn, Alan J. Lizotte, and Deborah Chard-Weischem. (1993). "The role of juvenile gangs in facilitating delinquent behavior." *Journal of Research in Crime and Delinquency* 30:55–87.

Tibbetts, Stephen G., and Alex R. Piquero. (1999). "The influence of gender, low birth weight, and disadvantaged environment in predicting early onset of offending: A test of Moffitt's interactional hypothesis." *Criminology* 37(4):843–78.

Tittle, Charles R. (1969). "Crime rates and legal sanctions." *Social Problems* 23:3–18.

———. (1975). "Labeling or deterrence?" *Social Forces* 53:399–410.

———. (1983). "Social class and criminal behavior: A critique of the theoretical foundation." *Social Forces* 65:405–32.

———. (1985). "The assumption that general theories are not possible." In *Theoretical Methods in Criminology,* ed. R. F. Meier. Beverly Hills, CA: Sage.

———. (1995). *Control Balance: Toward a General Theory of Deviance.* Boulder, CO: Westview Press.

———. (2000). "Theoretical developments in criminology." Pp. 51–101 in *The Nature of Crime: Continuity and Change,* ed. Gary LaTree. Washington, DC: U.S. Government Printing Office.

Tittle, Charles R., Mary Jean Burke, and Elton F. Jackson. (1986). "Modeling Sutherland's theory of differential association: Toward an empirical clarification." *Social Forces* 65:405–32.

Tittle, Charles R., and Alan R. Rowe. (1974). "Certainty of arrest and crime rates: A further test of the deterrence hypothesis." *Social Forces* 52:455–62.

Tittle, Charles R., and Wayne J. Villemez. (1977). "Social class and criminality." *Social Forces* 56:474–502.

Toby, Jackson. (1957). "The differential impact of family disorganization." *American Sociological Review* 22:505–12.

———. (1959). "Review of *Family Relationships and Delinquent Behavior* by F. Ivan Nye." *American Sociological Review* 24:282–83.

———. (2000). "Are the police the enemy?" *Society* 37:38–42.

Tonry, Michael. (1999). "Parochialism in U.S. sentencing policy." *Crime and Delinquency* 45:48–65.

Tremblay, Richard E., Bernard Boulerie, Louise Arsenault, and Marianne Junger. (1995). "Does low self-control during childhood explain the association between delinquency and accidents in early adolescence?" *Criminal Behaviour and Mental Health* 5:439–51.

Tremblay, Ricard E., Frank Vitaro, Lucie Bertrand, Marc LeBlanc, Hélène Beauchesne, Hélène Boileau, and Lucille David. (1992). "Parent and child training to prevent early onset of delinquency: The Montréal longitudinal-experimental study." Pp. 117–138 in *Preventing Antisocial Behavior: Interventions from Birth through Adolescence,* ed. Joan McCord and Richard Tremblay. New York: Guilford.

Tricarico, Donald. (1984). *The Italians of Greenwich Village.* Staten Island, NY: Center for Migration Studies of New York.

Trojanowicz, Robert. (1987). "Community policing: Attacking crime at its roots." *Police Chief,* August:16.

Trojanowicz, Robert, Robert Baldwin, Dennis Banas, David Dugger, Donna Hale, Hazel Harden, Philip Marcus, Stephen McGuire, John McNamara, Francisco Medrano, Catherine Smith, Paul Smyth, and Jesse Thompson. (1982). *An Evaluation of the Neighborhood Foot Patrol Program in Flint, Michigan.* Lansing: Michigan State University.

Tsai, Jeanne L. (2001). "Cultural orientation of Hmong young adults." *Journal of Human Behavior in the Social Environment* 3:99–104.

Tso, Chief Justice Tom. (1996). "The process of decision making in tribal courts." In *Native Americans, Crime and Justice,* ed. M. A. Nielsen and R. A. Silverman. Boulder, CO: Westview Press.

Tunnell, Kenneth D. (1990). *Choosing Crime: The Criminal Calculus of Property Offenders.* Chicago: Nelson-Hall.

Udry, Richard M. (1990). "Biosocial models of adolescent problem behaviors." *Social Biology* 37:1–10.

Umbreit, Gordon. (1994). *Victim Meets Offender: The Impact of Restorative Justice in Mediation.* Monsey, NY: Criminal Justice Press.

U.S. Bureau of Justice Statistics. (2000). *Correctional Populations in the United States, 1997.* Washington, DC: U.S. Department of Justice.

———. (2002a). "Key facts at a glance: Correctional populations." http://www.ojp.usdoj.gov/bjs/glance/tables/corr2tab.htm

———. (2002b). "Key facts at a glance: Incarceration rate, 1980–2001." http://www.ojp.usdoj.gov/bjs/glance/tables/inrttab.htm

U.S. Department of Justice. (1992).*Census of State and Federal Correctional Facilities, 1990.* Washington, DC: U.S. Government Printing Office.

———. (1994). *Census of State and Federal Correctional Facilities, 1992.* Washington, DC: U.S. Government Printing Office.

———. (1999). *Census of State and Federal Correctional Facilities, 1997.* Washington, DC: U.S. Government Printing Office.

———. (2000). *Census of State and Federal Correctional Facilities, 1998.* Washington, DC: U.S. Government Printing Office.

———. (2002). *Census of State and Federal Correctional Facilities, 2000.* Washington, DC: U.S. Government Printing Office.

U.S. Government Accounting Office. (1980). *Jail Inmates' Mental Health Care Neglected: State and Federal Attention Needed.* Washington, DC: U.S. Government Printing Office.

U.S. Office of Justice Programs. (2001). *Grants to Encourage Arrest Policies and Enforcement of Protection Orders Program. Fiscal Year 2001 Application and Program Guidelines.* Washington, DC: U.S. Government Printing Office.

U.S. Sentencing Commission. (1995). *Cocaine and Federal Sentencing Policy.* Washington, DC: U.S. Government Printing Office.

Vago, Steven. (1990). *Law and Society,* 3d ed. Englewood Cliffs, NJ: Prentice-Hall.

Van den Haag, Ernest. (1975). *Punishing Criminals: Concerning a Very Old and Painful Question.* New York: Basic Books.

Van Dusen, K. T., S. A. Mednick, W. F. Gabrielli, and B. Hutchings. (1983). "Social class and crime in an adoption cohort." *Journal of Criminal Law and Criminology* 74:249–54.

Van Maanen, John. (1973). "Observations on the making of policemen." *Human Organization* 32:407–18.

Vazsonyi, Alexander T., Lloyd E. Pickering, Marianne Junger, and Dick Hessing. (2001). "An empirical test of a general theory of crime: A four-nation comparative test of self-control and the prediction of deviance." *Journal of Research in Crime and Delinquency* 38:91–131.

Veysey, Bonita, and Steven F. Messner. (1999). "Further testing of social disorganization theory: An elaboration of Sampson and Grove's 'community structure and crime.'" *Journal of Research in Crime and Delinquency* 36:156–74.

Visher, Christy. (1983). "Gender, police arrest decisions, and notions of chivalry." *Criminology* 21:5–28.

———. (1994). "Op/Ed." American Sociological Association, *Crime, Law and Deviance Newsletter,* Fall/Winter:1, 5–7.

Vito, Gennaro F., and Thomas J. Keil. (1988). "Capital sentencing in Kentucky: An analysis of the factors influencing decision making in the post-Gregg period." *Journal of Criminal Law and Criminology* 79:483–503.

Vold, George B. (1958). *Theoretical Criminology.* New York: Oxford University Press.

———. (1979). *Theoretical Criminology,* 2nd ed. New York: Oxford University Press.

Vold, George B., and Thomas J. Bernard. (1986). *Theoretical Criminology,* 3d ed. New York: Oxford University Press.

Volkow, N. D., Gene-Jack Wang, Joanna S. Fowler, Jean Logan, Samuel J.

Gatley, Andrew Gifford, Robert Hitzemann, Yu-Shin Ding, and Naomi Pappas. (1999). "Prediction of reinforcing responses to psychostimulants in humans by brain dopamine D2 receptor levels." *American Journal of Psychiatry* 156:1440–43.

von Hirsch, Andrew. (1976). *Doing Justice.* New York: Hill and Wang.

Voss, Harwin L. (1964). "Differential association and reported delinquency behavior: A replication." *Social Problems* 12:78–85.

Votey, Harold L. (1984). "The deterioration of deterrence effects of driving legislation: Have we been giving the wrong signals to policy makers?" *Journal of Criminal Justice* 12:115–30.

Waldo, Gordon, and Theodore Chiricos. (1972). "Perceived penal sanctions and self-reported criminality: A neglected approach to deterrence research." *Social Problems* 19:522–40.

Waldo, Gordon, and Simon Dinitz. (1967). "Personality attributes of the criminal: An analysis of research studies." *Journal of Research in Crime and Delinquency* 4:185–202.

Walker, Samuel. (1983). *The Police in America: An Introduction.* New York: McGraw-Hill.

———. (1992). *The Police in America: An Introduction.* New York: McGraw-Hill.

———. (1994). *Sense and Nonsense about Crime and Drugs: A Policy Guide,* 3d ed. Belmont, CA: Wadsworth.

———. (1998). *Popular Justice: A History of American Criminal Justice,* 2d ed. New York: Oxford University Press.

Wallace, Don, and Drew Humphries. (1981). "Urban crime and capital accumulation: 1950–1971." In *Crime and Capitalism,* ed. D. Greenberg. Palo Alto, CA: Mayfield.

Wallace, Walter L. (1971). *The Logic of Science in Sociology.* Chicago: Aldine.

Walsh, Anthony, and Lee Ellis. (1999). "Political ideology and American criminologists' explanations for criminal behavior." *Criminologist* 24:1, 14.

Walters, Glenn D. (1999). "Crime and chaos: Applying nonlinear dynamic principles to problems in criminology." *International Journal of Offender Therapy and Comparative Criminology* 43:134–53.

Warr, Mark. (1998). "Life-course transitions and desistance from crime." *Criminology* 36:183–216.

Wasyliw, O. E., L. S. Grossman, T. W. Haywood, and J. Cavanaugh. (1988). "The detection of malingering in criminal forensic groups: MMPI validity scales." *Journal of Personality Assessment.* 52:321–33.

Watson, James D. (1990). "The human genome project: Past, present and future." *Science.* April:44–49.

Watson, John B. (1913). "Psychology as the behaviorist views it." *Psychological Review* 20:158–77.

———. (1914). *Behavior: An Introduction to Comparative Psychology.* New York: Holt.

———. (1930). *Behaviorism,* rev. ed. New York: Norton.

Weber, Max. (1947)[1918]. *The Theory of Social and Economic Organizations.* Trans. A. M. Henderson and Talcott Parsons. New York: Free Press.

———. (1967)[1925]. "On Law." In *Economy and Society,* ed. M. Rheinstein and E. Shils. New York: Simon and Schuster.

Weis, Joseph. (1976). "Liberation and crime: The invention of the new female criminal." *Social Justice* 1:17–27.

Wellford, Charles. (1975). "Labeling theory and criminology: An assessment." *Social Problems* 22:332–45.

Welsh, Wayne N., Patricia H. Jenkins, and Philip W. Harris. (1999). "Reducing minority overrepresentation in juvenile justice: Results of community-based delinquency prevention in Harrisburg." *Journal of Research in Crime and Delinquency.* 36:87–110.

Welsh, Wayne N., Robert Stokes, and Jack R. Green. (2000). "A macro-level model of school disorder." *Journal of Research in Crime and Delinquency* 37:243–83.

Westley, William (1970). *Violence and the Police: A Sociological Study of Law, Custom and Morality.* Cambridge, MA: MIT Press.

Wexler, David B. (1975) "Behavior modification and other behavior change procedures: The emerging law and proposed

Florida guidelines." *Criminal Law Bulletin* 11:600–16.

Wheeler, David L. (1992a). "U. of Md. Conference that critics charge might foster racism loses NIH support." *Chronicle of Higher Education,* 2 September:A6–7.

———. (1992b). "Meeting on possible links between genes and crime cancelled after bitter exchange." *Chronicle of Higher Education,* 16 September:A7–8.

———. (1995). "A growing number of scientists reject the concept of race." *Chronicle of Higher Education,* 17 February:A8, A9, A15.

Whyte, William Foote. (1955). *Street Corner Society.* Chicago: University of Chicago Press.

Wiatrowski, Michael D., David B. Griswold, and Mary R. Roberts. (1981). "Social control and delinquency." *American Sociological Review* 46:525–41.

Widom, Kathy Spatz. (1989). "Child abuse, neglect, and violent criminal behavior." *Criminology* 27:251–71.

Wilbanks, Willam. (1987). *The Myth of a Racist Criminal Justice System.* Monterey, CA: Brooks/Cole.

Wilkins v. Maryland State Police, No. CCB-93–468 (1996).

Wilkins, Leslie. (1965). *Social Deviance: Social Policy, Action and Research.* Englewood Cliffs, NJ: Prentice-Hall.

Willging, Thomas E. and T. G. Dunn. (1982). "The moral development of law students: Theory and data on legal education." *Journal of Legal Education* 31:306–58.

Williams, III, Frank P. (1984). "The demise of the criminological imagination: A critique of recent criminology." *Justice Quarterly* 1:91–106.

Williams, III, Frank P., and Marilyn McShane. (1988). *Criminological Theory.* Englewood Cliffs, NJ: Prentice-Hall.

Williams, Kirk, and Richard Hawkins. (1986). "Perceptual research on general deterrence: A critical overview." *Law and Society Review* 20:545–72.

Williams, L. E., L. Clinton, L. T. Winfree, and R. E. Clark. (1992). "Family ties, parental discipline, and delinquency: A study of youthful misbehavior by parochial high school students." *Sociological Spectrum* 12:381–401.

Wilson, James Q., and Richard J. Herrnstein. (1985). *Crime and Human Nature.* New York: Simon and Schuster.

Wilson, James Q., and George Kelling. (1982). "Broken windows: The police and neighborhood safety." *Atlantic Monthly,* March:29–38.

Wilson, William Julius. (1987). *The Truly Disadvantaged: The Inner City, the Underclass, and Public Policy.* Chicago: University of Chicago Press.

Wilt, G. Marie, and James D. Brannon. (1976). "Cynicism or realism: A criticism of Niederhoffer's research into police attitudes." *Journal of Police Science and Administration* 4:38–45.

Winfree, Jr., L. Thomas. (1985). "Peers, parents and adolescent drug use in a rural school district: A two-wave panel study." *Journal of Youth and Adolescence* 14:499–512.

———. (1995). "Attica." In *Encyclopedia of American Prisons,* ed. Marilyn D. McShane and Franklyn P. Williams III. New York: Garland.

———.(2002). "Peacemaking and community harmony: Lessons (and admonitions) from the Navajo peacemaking courts." In *Restorative Justice: Theoretical Foundations,* ed. Elmar Weitekamp and Hans-Juergen. Devon, UK: Willan.

Winfree, Jr., L. Thomas, and Frances Bernat. (1998). "Social learning, self-control, and substance abuse by eighth grade students: A tale of two cities." *Journal of Drug Issues* 28:539–58.

Winfree, Jr., L. Thomas, Frances Bernat, and Finn-Aage Esbensen. (2001). "Hispanic and anglo gang membership in two southwestern cities." *Social Science Journal* 38:105–17.

Winfree, Jr., L. Thomas, and Curt T. Griffiths. (1983). "Youth at risk: marijuana use among native American and Caucasian youth." *International Journal of the Addictions* 18:53–70.

Winfree, Jr., L. Thomas, Curt T. Griffiths, and Christine S. Sellers. (1989). "Social learning theory, drug use, and American Indian youth: A cross-cultural test." *Justice Quarterly* 6:501–23.

Winfree, Jr., L. Thomas, and Larry Kielich. (1979). "Criminal prosecution and the labeling process: An analysis of the application of official sanctions." In *Legality, Morality and Ethics in Criminal Justice,* ed. Nicholas Kittrie and Jackwell Susman. New York: Praeger.

Winfree, Jr., L. Thomas, Lawrence Kielich, and Robert Clark. (1984). "On becoming a prosecutor: Observations on the organizational socialization of law interns." *Work and Occupations: An International Sociological Journal* 11:207–26.

Winfree, Jr., L. Thomas, G. Larry Mays, and Teresa Vigil-Backstrom. (1994). "Youth gangs and incarcerated delinquents: Exploring the ties between gang membership, delinquency, and social learning theory." *Justice Quarterly* 11:229–55.

Winfree, Jr., L. Thomas, Christine S. Sellers, and Dennis Clason. (1993). "Social learning and adolescent deviance abstention: Toward understanding reasons for initiating, quitting and avoiding drugs." *Journal of Quantitative Criminology* 9:101–25.

Winfree, Jr., L. Thomas, Teresa Vigil-Backstrom, and G. Larry Mays. (1994). "Social learning theory, self-reported delinquency, and youth gangs: A new twist on a general theory of crime and delinquency." *Youth and Society* 26:147–77.

Wirth, Louis. (1931). "Culture conflict and misconduct." *Social Forces* 9:484–92.

Witkin, H. A., Sarnoff, A. Mednick, F. Schulsinger, E. Bakkestrom, K. O. Christiansen, D. R. Goodenough, K. Hirschhorn, C. Lundstean, D. R. Owen, J. Philip, D. R. Rubin, and M. Stocking. (1977). "Criminality, aggression, and intelligence among XYY and XXY men." In *Biosocial Bases of Criminal Behavior,* ed. S. A. Mednoff and K. O. Christiansen. New York: Gardner Press.

Witte, Ann Dryden. (1993). "Some thoughts on the future of research in crime and delinquency." *Journal of Research in Crime and Delinquency* 30:513–25.

Wolfgang, Marvin E. (1958). *Patterns of Criminal Homicide.* Philadelphia: University of Pennsylvania.

———. (1963). "Criminology and criminologists." *Journal of Criminal Law, Criminology and Police Science* 54:155–62.

Wolfgang, Marvin E., and Franco Ferracuti. (1967). *The Subculture of Violence.* London: Tavistock.

Wolfgang, M. E., R. M. Figlio, and T. Sellin. (1972). *Delinquency in a Birth Cohort.* Chicago: University of Chicago Press.

Wood, Elizabeth. (1961). *Housing Designs: A Social Theory.* New York: Citizens' Housing and Planning Counsel of New York.

Wood, Peter B., John K. Cochran, Betty Pfefferbaum, and Bruce J. Arneklev. (1995). "Sensation-seeking and delinquent substance use: An extension of learning theory." *Journal of Drug Issues* 25:173-93.

Wood, Peter B., Betty Pfefferbaum, and Bruce J. Arneklev. (1993). "Risk taking and self-control: Social psychological correlates of delinquency." *Journal of Criminal Justice* 16:111–30.

Woodiwiss, Anthony. (1993). *Postmodernity USA: The Crisis of Social Modernism in Postwar America.* London: Sage.

Worthman, Carol M., and Elizabeth Loftus. (1992). *Psychology.* New York: McGraw-Hill.

Wright, Bradley R. Entner, Avshalom Caspi, Terrie E. Moffit, and Phil A. Silva. (1999). "Low self-control, social bonds, and crime: Social causation, social selection or both." *Criminology* 37:479–513.

Wright, Richard. (1996). "Afterward." In *Life without Parole: Living in Prison Today,* by Victor Hassine. Los Angeles: Roxbury.

Wrightsman, Lawrence S., Michael T. Nietzel, and William H. Fortune. (1994). *Psychology and the Legal System,* 3d ed. Pacific Grove, CA: Brooks/Cole.

Yablonsky. Lewis. (1989). *The Therapeutic Community.* New York: Gardner Press.

Yazzie, Robert, and James W. Zion. (1995). "'Slay the monsters': Peacemaker court and violence control plans for the Navajo nation." In *Popular Justice and Community Regeneration: Pathways of Indigenous Reform.* Westport, CT: Praeger.

Yeudall, L. T. (1977). "Neuropsychological assessment of forensic disorders." *Canadian Mental Health* 25:7–15.

Yinger, Milton J. (1960). "Contraculture and subculture." *American Sociological Review* 25:625–35.

Yochelson, Samuel, and Stanton E. Samenow. (1976). *The Criminal Personality*, vol. 1. New York: Aronson.

Young, Jock. (1971). "The role of the police as amplifiers of deviancy, negotiators of reality, and translators of fantasy: Some consequences of our present system of drug control as seen in Natting Hill." In *Images of Deviance,* ed. S. Cohen. Middlesex, England: Penguin.

———. (1992). "Ten points of realism." In *Rethinking Criminology: The Realist Debate,* ed. Jock Young and R. Matthews. London: Sage.

Young, T. R. (1991). "Crime and chaos." *Critical Criminologist* 3(2):17–21.

Zatz, M. (1985). "Los Cholo: Legal processing of Chicano gang members." *Social Problems* 33:13–30.

Zickler, P. (1999). "NIDA studies clarify developmental effects of prenatal cocaine exposure." http://165.112.78.61/NIDA_Notes/NNVol143/Prenatal.html

Zimring, Frank E., and Gordon J. Hawkins. (1973). *Deterrence: The Legal Threat in Crime Control.* Chicago: University of Chicago Press.

Zingraff, Matthew T., Jeffrey Leiter, Kristen A. Myers, and Matthew C. Johnsen. (1993). "Child maltreatment and youthful problem behavior. *Criminology* 31:173–202.

Zingraff, Matthew T., William R. Smith, and Donald Tomaskovic-Devey. (2000). "North Carolina Highway Traffic and Patrol Study: 'Driving While Black.'" *Criminologist* 25:1, 3–4.

Zorza, Joan. (1992). "The criminal law of misdemeanor domestic violence, 1970-1990." *Journal of Criminal Law and Criminology* 83:46–72.

Zupan, Linda. (1991). *Jails: Reform and the New Generation Philosophy.* Cincinnati, OH: Anderson.

Zupan, Linda, and Ben Menke. (1988). "Implementing organizational change: From traditional to new generation jail operations." *Policy Studies Review* 7:615–25.

Zupan, Linda, and Mary K. Stohr-Gillmore. (1987). "Doing time in the new generation jail: Inmate perceptions of gains and losses." *Policy Studies Review* 7:626–40.

Author Index

Subject Index